THE BIGGER PICTURE

Essays in History and Politics

Guy Blythman

Second Edition

ISBN: 978-1-80031-576-1

www.newgeneration-publishing.com

 New Generation Publishing

ABOUT THE AUTHOR

Guy Blythman was educated at Millfield School, Somerset, and Southampton University and is currently based in the southwest London/northwest Surrey area. His interests include philosophy, theology, current affairs, classical music and creative writing. He goes on long country walks in order to be alone, but isn't averse to meeting people for a drink and a chat from time to time. He has variously been a political activist, a civil servant, president of his school and college debating societies and secretary of diverse committees.

He is a member of Walton-on-Thames Wordsmiths, a local workshop group which aims to provide help and support to aspiring authors by offering constructive criticism and advice and suggesting possible markets. He has written for the *Doctor Who* fanzines *Mandria, Time-Space Visualiser* and *The Doctor's Recorder*.

Visit his website at www.guyblythman.com.

Also by Guy Blythman

Philosophy: A View From The Edge
Rediscovering God: A Defence Of Christian Belief In The Twenty-first
Century
Tapestry: Collected Essays And Short Stories

Fiction:

Eye Of The Sun God
The Argus Memorandum
The Ishtar Stratagem
Piper One
The Greatorex Imperative (Parts 1 and 2)
The Ragnarok Dossier (Parts 1 and 2)
Polymer
The Kambatan Assignment
Cryptids

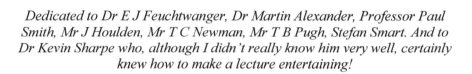

Dedicated to Dr E J Feuchtwanger, Dr Martin Alexander, Professor Paul Smith, Mr J Houlden, Mr T C Newman, Mr T B Pugh, Stefan Smart. And to Dr Kevin Sharpe who, although I didn't really know him very well, certainly knew how to make a lecture entertaining!

With acknowledgements to all the above, and to the British Museum

Contents

Introduction

If I was trained as anything, it was as a historian. I studied history at A Level and at university (Southampton), though I didn't in a professional capacity get that much chance to put the knowledge to practical use, not in a paid job anyhow. But I thought I ought to make all my efforts worthwhile by translating my observations on the subject into print.

In the past I have been as interested in politics, in fact the original intention with this book was to present it as a *political* study of the subjects it covered. Which it effectively is, but I later realised that chapters four and five were essentially histories; political histories maybe, but it cannot be said that they belong only within the pages of a politics textbook. History is more than just kings and battles, dictators and revolutions, but they obviously form an important part of it and are by definition political subjects. (The old saying that war is a continuation of politics by other means is of course true up to a point; there may in the past have been rulers who were determined to be militarily aggressive whatever happened, in order to increase their power and prestige and add to the territories under their control, but sometimes the problem was that the politics had failed, and in addition war *creates* political issues by the legacies it leaves behind and the hopes for a better world which arise as a response to it.) But history, unless it is simply the recording of previous events whether or not they had/have any significance (and therefore including someone scratching their nose or having a particular foodstuff for dinner on a particular day), is essentially a study of politics – of how the interaction between human beings, who may disagree with each other intellectually or emotionally, affects important activities whether they be government, art, science, technological development, religion, culture, sex, or the exploration and exploitation of a particular geographical area or areas. The interaction means that virtually all human affairs could be described as political; as well as politics in the sense in which the term is normally understood there is church politics, family politics, office politics, the politics of organisations from governments and large multinational businesses down to the Lower Muggleton Amateur Dramatic Society. While political events which occurred in the past, and which we are studying because it helps to improve our understanding of politics in general, are by definition history. The two subjects are therefore, to some extent, interchangeable.

As indicated, history as an academic discipline has various different branches; besides "political" history there are social history, the history of art, intellectual history, the history of science and technology, and arguably other "histories" too. It is something people have become increasingly aware of in the past hundred years, and I have tried to reflect it in chapter five.

There are two ways of writing history, both of them equally valid. It should be borne in mind that each chapter in this book is intended to be a literary essay on the topic in question – as well as, in the case of chapter two, partly a polemic

– rather than the product of detailed research as opposed to philosophical reflection plus personal knowledge gained from academic study. Although I have nonetheless benefited from the latter, since leaving university I have for the most part embarked on it only with respect to esoteric, or relatively so, local history topics (traditional windmills, lunatic asylums). I still hope to write a "proper" history book based on such research someday, once other demands on my time have been met and if a suitable subject matter comes along.

I've always preferred to be an all-rounder where history (or knowledge in general) is concerned, not confining my interest to a particular topic or period; waging academic wars with someone else over the question of how effective was Charles I's personal rule is not for me[1]. This may mean that my in-depth knowledge of any one historical era is not as great as certain other people's. And inevitably what I write will bear the stamp of my own particular interests. I must confess there are also points where I indulge in some (justified) axe-grinding. Finally, literary essays, of which this book is essentially a collection, have to be punchy, even florid, at times and thus there is a risk at least of bypassing the strict truth without really meaning to. I can only hope I have managed to avoid that pitfall.

Of course, in the case of current events the observations made may well be out of date by the time the book is published. This raises the whole question of attempting to write "contemporary" history the same way one would write about the Romans, the Aztecs, the French Revolution or the Cold War. I suppose there might seem to be a danger that it will politicise history, but it is really no more than an extension of what happens anyway; people comment on an important, in national or international terms, political event and discuss how and why it happened. It could be regarded as a different matter if we are trying to predict the future, based on what has happened in the recent (or less recent) past; is that really a historian's business? But perhaps it is inevitable we should do so if we have, as we should have, a group concern for the destiny and also for the wellbeing of our species, an interest in its affairs and in properly understanding it. We would feel divorced from such a crucial thing if we were only allowed to comment on events (and what can for the common good be learned from them) some time after they happened (the cut-off point perhaps being difficult to identify). And an interest in the future could be purely academic as much as ideological. For the real peril in studying contemporary history is that our judgements may be biased in favour of our own political affiliations, whether left-wing or right-wing; we may end up saying what *should* be done, and according to our own subjective views, rather than attempting to analyse what has already been done and cannot be changed. But the latter is itself a business that requires some objectivity, the lack of such being dangerous. All we can ask is that we try to keep our historical scholarship free of that bias for or against a particular ideology; there will still be scope for differing opinions, not everyone being the same. I find both reading and writing history much more satisfactory when the bias is eliminated. The most deplorable example of blatant prejudice is found in A J P Taylor's comment on the undoubtedly reactionary nineteenth-century Austrian Chancellor Metternich that "his thoughts were banal, like those of most conservatives". If Taylor can make sweeping and unfair statements about conservatives, he can make them about anyone or anything else, so his judgement is altogether called into question.

The tone of my first two essays might nonetheless be considered right-wing, that is ideologically biased, by some. I should stress that the point of chapter one is not to agree with Enoch Powell but rather to argue that the more vehement denunciations of him as a man may have been based on a flawed perception as to what exactly he was. If to vilify him as racist in the generally understood sense of the term is a left-wing trait (it is, but the division between detractors and defenders is not necessarily on party ideological lines) then in opposing it we will inevitably to some extent be moving to the right. The same occurs when, while not maintaining that it is all bad or that it is somehow preferable to be a racial bigot, we denounce the more extreme aspects of political correctness. Regarding chapter two, since anti-Semitism is a disease it can be left-wing people who suffer from it as much as right-wing ones. But I refute the charge of racism, which some would level at me because of the article, in any case and there are passages in it which ought to demonstrate that that charge is unjust. Partly for reasons of intellectual pleasure and partly from fairness, I find I can't resist telling a story from both sides.

I have already to some extent set out my views on how history should be presented (and where the value of learning it lies) in my book *Philosophy: A View From The Edge*. Suffice to say here that there are certain recent developments in this field which give cause for concern. I'm not ashamed to say that I walked out of the cinema in protest over the scene in the film *Darkest Hour* where Winston Churchill, who has recently become British Prime Minister, makes an unscheduled solo journey on the London Underground to talk to ordinary people and establish whether they want the war against Hitler to continue. It is said that you can't prove a negative; this is not always the case. You can prove it by what would happen or have happened if it was true, and if those consequences are absent it follows by deduction that it isn't. If the episode had occurred in real life it would have entered popular mythology. People would have remembered it, talked of it and been interviewed about it on documentaries. It is clear they did not and were not − because it didn't happen! It is totally fictitious and by the example it sets, which will presumably be imitated if the taking of liberties which it represents is considered acceptable, risks turning study of the past into an exercise in alternative history, something that although it may be useful at times ought not to be confused with objective reality. Like any fiction book, a novel about Hitler winning the Second World War (for example) never pretends to be actual truth. Even if there had been a "health warning" making it clear that the film would include scenes that were not historically accurate, if the scenes are not historically accurate they have no place in it, full stop, because they belong to a different genre. What makes it so damaging is that if the *vox populi* encounter on the Tube is instrumental in bolstering Churchill's determination to carry on the fight, then not only the plot of the film but, apparently, the actual course of historical events hinges on something which never took place!

Obviously, whenever those historical events are dramatised there will have to be a certain degree of embellishment, because drama whether on TV, film or radio or in printed works must follow its own rules to be what it is. But there is a common-sense limit. As with much else that puts "spicing things up" before accuracy, or is too politically correct, the infringement of a vital principle is defended according to a spurious half-logic. The producer of *Darkest Hour* justified the Tube scene on the grounds that it was the sort of thing Churchill might have done. Perhaps he might. But that does not mean that he *did* do it, and if he didn't then to suggest he did is distorting history. There is a difference between "did" and "might have". History is by definition the analysis of events that actually took place in the past, or of how likely it was that they happened, where there is any uncertainty, and not of what *could* have happened in the sense merely that it was possible.

As is acknowledged, accuracy is harder to achieve with classical and mediaeval than with modern (in which field there is less excuse for misrepresentation) history because we are so much dependent on the writings of chroniclers who may well have been biased in their outlook. People did not in those days generally write their memoirs and there were no newspapers, TVs or radios. In producing histories of the Hundred Years War or biographies of Henry V or Charlemagne we can only seek to achieve the best interpretation of events and personalities, of the motives of the major players, according to what we *do* know, building a picture of someone's character from their actions. It is not our fault if we can do no more than that. But we should be wary of saying things like "As he watched the enemy forces gathering to attack King X's thoughts were a mixture of such-and-such" because the book then begins to seem more like a (historical) novel than an attempt, at least, at an authoritative factual study. We cannot be sure that those were the King's exact feelings at that moment, even if it seems likely, and as well as being irritating the tendency runs the risk of encouraging bad habits. Historical novels in themselves are fine of course, but they do not claim to be accurate, beyond what is generally established as having been true, any more than do *Star Wars* or *Lord of the Rings*, or indeed any work of fiction whatever the genre. They *may* be accurate, to a greater or lesser extent (though I don't know about *Star Wars* etc.!), but that is not the point.

An issue discussed in *Philosophy: A View From The Edge*, as well as to some extent in chapter five of this book, is that of the precise reason why events happen, something which will obviously be of interest to historians. Sometimes a particular cause would be bound to have a particular effect if there was no factor operating to prevent it doing so and without any other *causal* agency. But consider the following case, if you will forgive me quoting my own work:

"Let's suppose that I'm involved in a serious car accident. It cannot really be due to "chance" – or, therefore, to "accident", the two words meaning much the same thing as in both cases what happens is unintended and unforeseen. Why, though, does it happen? I decide to take a certain route rather than another when out for a drive one day. A stray dog runs out into the middle of the road whereupon I swerve to avoid it, crash and am gravely injured, only just escaping with my life. The decision to go by that route, without which the "accident" might not have occurred, was mine alone. The dog certainly did not have free will, being a creature of pure instinct, so its decision to run out in front of me was due to some fact of animal psychology (i.e. the tendency, which I don't know whether animal psychologists could explain, for cats and dogs to sometimes behave in ways which in humans would be termed irresponsible). It's part of the way the world is (if you believe that animals do have free will and the dog could have been more considerate if it had tried, imagine instead that the accident was caused by a tree suddenly falling onto the road – the tree would have even less choice in the matter). And I certainly did not know that the tree was going to fall or I would have chosen a different route. So there are three essential factors explaining what happened – my free will, certain facts of nature, and the limitations to my knowledge. In some situations only two might be involved; there might be only one way to get to where I wanted to go, unless I was prepared to take an impractically long walk. But most complex situations are a development of this three-way scenario, in one form or another, or, alternatively, one of the elements producing the same outcome occurs in a number of cases."

What happens might be due to an interplay, sometimes complex, of different factors: the way the universe is, our decisions to say or do certain things, and the degree of knowledge we have. In war, the reason why one side or the other fails to win either an individual battle or a wider conflict can reflect this. There are some cases where defeat is inevitable, despite what the protagonist thinks, because you have too many forces ranged against you, unless you can come up with a trump card in the form of a really devastating weapon which your enemies do not possess; this was Hitler's gamble during the Second World War, and it failed. Otherwise, within reason a numerically inferior force can defeat a numerically superior one if it is better organised and deployed, even if it has poorer quality weapons. The exceptions to this rule, among modern armies, are due to fuel shortages and inadequate air support though even these may only matter beyond a certain point. Where no single factor, or a combination of factors, is sufficient to tip the balance the outcome is down to chance, or rather to that complex interplay of things referred to above: in this case human error, the total number of enemy troops you happen to kill, and vehicles destroy, during the course of the conflict, plus technical faults which mean that vital radio messages are not received in time.

Another aspect of the discipline of history covered in the philosophy book was its potential role in our collective psyche of helping us to judge people and respond to situations fairly and sensibly by highlighting issues, through placing them in a historical context and thereby throwing them into starker relief. We can identify what should have been done in a particular scenario, whether or not it *was* done (and if it was it serves as a case study to imitate). Protector Somerset's response to Ket's rebellion of 1549, recently the subject of one of C J Sansom's Matthew Shardlake novels, should have been to march to Norwich at the head of an army, in order to show the rebels who was boss, but tell it to hold off while he dealt with them fairly, setting up a commission – with teeth – to investigate the legality and the effects of enclosure and meeting just grievances. The commission's remit should not have extended as far back as 1485 if that made its job more complicated and thus harder to accomplish. The demand that the rebels, most of whom were from the "lower classes", be given a share in government was too radical for the period and should have been withdrawn. I expect that at the time there were many who would have considered this fair. What happened, of course, was that the rebels were defeated, suppressed and punished. Though the severity of the punishment, in terms of its extent, was mitigated by the consideration that if it continued there would be no peasantry left, one regrets that there was not a better outcome.

We can perhaps also profit, in the same way, from considering how we might have acted if history had followed a different course from the one it actually did. Suppose that Hitler had been assassinated by a group of non-Nazi German army officers, who had then assumed power, at any time after the battle of Stalingrad, which marked the turning-point of Axis fortunes in the Second World War. What sort of overtures should they have made to the Allies when seeking a peace settlement, if they did not want to continue the war, and how should the Allies have responded? Germany could probably not have continued the war in any case, because the coalition of powers ranged against her was bound to prove victorious in the end. And since the war had been wholly unjust she was not in a position to make demands as opposed to proposals, even if it could be argued that she was only clearing up the mess which one crazed individual and his henchmen had created. The proposals should have been that Germany withdraw to at least her pre-1939 borders, that she make reparations, with these being carefully phased as to minimise damage to the European economy, that she accept an international inquiry into war crimes and that in the future she be allowed to maintain armed forces which were in strength roughly equal to, but not greater than, Britain's or France's individually. All this ought reasonably to have been accepted by the Allies, and one can conceive of Churchill or Roosevelt agreeing to it; whether the vengeful Soviets would have done so is another matter. (Concerning the

Anschluss, the union between Germany and Austria, there is a case for saying it should have been permitted if both countries were in favour of it, as otherwise we would actually be going against national self-determination. The Sudetenland is a more controversial matter; if we abide by the principle that the rights of national minorities should not be put before the interests of the majority, annexation of the territory by Germany should have been ruled out because it deprived Czechoslovakia of much of its industry and so compromised its viability as a state.)

Of course the actual situations represented by the above two examples, or something similar to them, are unlikely to recur. For one thing, WMD mean that there will never again be a war like the Second World War, i.e. one which uses conventional weapons but affects at least a continent. We might ask what the point is in merely engaging in intellectual games. But as argued, those exercises do help us to consider questions of right and wrong in ethical matters. Otherwise, apart from being interested in the business in a purely academic sense one can only dismiss it with the rueful conclusion "It was all done a long time ago, and badly!".

Which leads into the question of whether we are ever correct to look at the past through "rose-tinted spectacles". History is vital in putting things in an overall perspective and thus discouraging illusions whose shattering can be psychologically unwelcome. The fortunes of human beings wax and wane, and some states of affairs have undoubtedly been better, or worse, in absolute terms than others, though not it must be appreciated for everyone. Cultures have gone through periods when even the less well-off (with exceptions) are fairly prosperous and happy, and the state seems free both from domestic conflict, which is always to be regretted even where grievances are just, and external aggression. But this idyllic view can be qualified, at least. A sliding scale is in operation, due to the strange human need to have something to be afraid of (and sometimes the fear is valid). If what would have been the most serious threat in those absolute terms is absent, we worry about the next worst thing. And according to a sort of logic, anything which seemed like a real threat to the security and prosperity of the British Empire, for example, would have been as galling to those who sensed it as the actual loss of the Empire, and of Britain's position as a major world power, was to some in the post-World War Two period. The fear of something, if it is taken seriously enough, can be as enervating (and as important in deciding the course of events) as its actuality.

Is it ever acceptable to romanticise history? Not if it leads to true, if unpalatable or humdrum, facts being obscured. But can one still do it nonetheless? Sometimes of course reality does imitate fantasy; people really have been larger-than-life and done colourful and extraordinary things. If it was the simple truth that they did then that truth ought to be acknowledged. Otherwise; well I think it would be impossible to approach the study of history in a way that was entirely cerebral, and I'm not sure anyone really does. There must be something about it that emotionally appeals, or historians would not find it possible to do their job, and therefore since that job is an essential one the romanticism is important. There must be some notion of gallant deeds being performed by brave warriors against a background of rugged, mist-wreathed moorland or other stirring scenery; of bewigged or wing-collared Dickensian lawyers scribbling with quill pens among dusty documents in oak-panelled rooms. (We forget, of course, that the atmosphere and patina of old buildings is acquired only with time, and they would not have had that same appealing feel to them when first built; while any archive or library, then as now probably, which allowed its documents to be "dusty" would not be meeting proper professional standards!) On a certain level I think historians do feel this kind of attraction to the past even if they are not fully aware of it. It does not, of itself, prevent them being objective and realistic. Though it may remain as a driving influence at the back of the mind, it's a means to an end, that end being historical analysis, rather than an end in itself. The historian may still be prone to bias or, sometimes, impulsiveness in making judgements but that is a different matter. For reasons given below history will succeed in being interesting even if "romantic" is not a term which can always be applied to it.

It is of course possible to teach or write history in a stale and boring fashion, to present true facts in a way which does not make the learning process pleasurable and so instill a liking for the subject. There will always be good and bad (here meaning dull) teachers, though the dull ones may in other respects be entirely competent; historians whose style one finds unreadable. Certainly, to write a history book in the thoroughly dry fashion – scholarly, as anything with an academic purpose must be, but entirely unengaging – that until recently was often encountered would be impossible today, and that is not wrong even if the book would intellectually still be of value. The popular historians of the modern era, who meet the need of publishers and television companies to make history interesting, are doing no harm provided what they say is accurate, and by and large it is, always taking into account the impossibility in a great many cases of first-hand evidence (that is, having been alive at the time of the Norman Conquest or whatever and directly witnessing those events or their consequences). As long as academic integrity isn't compromised we can see them as merely a symbol of changing times. Of course, many older texts are not dull; they often have a wonderful turn of phrase and should continue to be appreciated. A classic study of the Reformation ought still to be on the syllabus along with newer works, provided that where its conclusions have been proved wrong by later research this is pointed out (I would suggest course notes describe it as "dated but still relevant"). This has the merit of permitting students to see how opinions on a historical subject, and styles of historical writing, have changed over time.

The value of teaching history in the first place has sometimes been questioned by students of other disciplines, because it may seem like simply a narrative of things that have happened in the past. It is more than that, for reasons stated. But the objections do raise what may seem a valid point, which ought to be addressed. History, if written well, can be exciting in a similar way to a fiction book. But is that all it is – an interesting story? Take the example of a mediaeval monarch who has to endure a difficult wife (someone like Eleanor of Aquitaine, say), plus rebellious sons or nobles who threaten trouble if they don't get what they consider their rightful inheritance, and also becomes embroiled in a war with France over territories he holds there. His attempts to resolve his problems may be complicated by his falling ill and being out of the running for a while, or by a papal interdict, or whatever. He will also make mistakes and alienate potential supporters, or for that matter do something bold and clever which enables him to get what he wants. Now all this is highly absorbing, but what does it tell us? That disputes over inheritance, conflicts between monarchs and powerful aristocrats, differences with the Pope and foreign entanglements were recurring features of mediaeval politics (as any student of the period will come to realise before long whatever they or anybody else wishes to make of the knowledge). Well and good. But why not simply say, if we are concerned about the past at all, "Disputes over inheritance, conflicts between monarchs and powerful aristocrats, differences with the Pope and foreign entanglements were recurring features of mediaeval politics"? If we then wanted to take things further, on a personal and private level, by studying the events in question in more detail and maybe writing a book on them there would be nothing to stop us. Each to their own. But should teaching history be an organised activity which the government goes to all the bother of providing financial and other resources for at schools and institutes of higher education?

Well, to appreciate why it should let's imagine the whole school-attending population (you could not really do it with adults) being told by their teachers in class, "Disputes over inheritance, conflicts between monarchs and powerful aristocrats, differences with the Pope and foreign entanglements were recurring features of mediaeval politics", or words to that effect (it would be phrased in such a way that the pupil could understand it), along with a few other basic facts of history, and given a sheet of paper or two on which the information was printed, perhaps in more elaborate form with examples cited, before the subject then turned to geography or French or chemistry. Although, otherwise, history would only be mentioned incidentally the pupils would be expected to refer to the information sheets from time to time so that they didn't forget the message, and would be questioned every now and then to make sure they hadn't. Apart from the fact that this itself implies some sort of recognition that history ought to be in our collective selfconsciousness it is also quite inadequate. We know instinctively that learning history should be much more than this, however far each individual chooses to take it.

When we discover that human nature has always been the same, and human affairs, regardless of how the issues change over time, always a matter of politics (often seen as a shady business) if not necessarily in a party sense, we become more understanding, more tolerant, of ourselves and each other. If that is what we have always been like, it is clearly a part of our nature and thus can't be helped, however much greed or cruelty or foolishness may make it needlessly worse. Appreciating this ought to make violence less likely, and so has a civilising effect on society. Of course it doesn't always work; for one thing many of those who gratuitously commit violent acts are people with no interest in or knowledge of history (except for events in the recent past which had a particular impact and which they may feel strongly about because it affects them negatively), or, as part of the same sad package, any other aspect of higher culture. But there have always been such types. And morality demands that we make the effort. Simply understanding the period we live in now, without reference to what has gone before, isn't enough to make us worldly wise. Learning about history is also a sign of respect to past generations – and thus morally and culturally necessary – because where they did something that was good, in ethical, practical or artistic terms, we ought to remember and appreciate it, and where they did something bad we should heed the warning this amounts to.

I believe this beneficial effect of being taught history works on a certain level, and in a way which perhaps is not always easy to detect. It operates even if one does not become a professional historian or take any other interest in the subject that is more than casual. But it can only work through repetition. I do not mean in the sense of mindlessly learning something by rote. Just as cats remain embedded in our consciousness because we see them on a fairly regular basis, through necessary repetition the *particular* whatever it may be helps to emphasise the universal. The same themes – foreign wars, "evil counsellors", troublesome nobles – tend to recur in mediaeval history in a way which can sometimes render it boring except when kings are horribly and colourfully butchering their enemies. But the more examples of them we absorb the more we get the message not only about what the Middle Ages could be like but about the human condition in general. Even the troublesome wife serves to remind us that women in the Middle Ages were not always quiescent and subservient creatures. And even if one deems it unlikely in any case that they were, so we are therefore dealing with a fact about human nature, we still need to be acquainted with that fact through exposure to it. Generally the behaviour of past people, whether we are interested in it on account of any moral lessons we may draw or for academic reasons only, amounts to a story, and a story needs a setting, needs props if we compare it to a play; the policies and actions of popes, monarchs and their consorts, rebel leaders, military commanders, dictators and political activists are those props since they provide the reason why, the occasion for, a historical figure acting as they did. History cannot make sense without them.

While if, otherwise, Eleanor of Aquitaine merely serves to add colour, interest and amusement to the proceedings there is in truth nothing "mere" about that. No-one has ever said that history shouldn't be fun. I remember a teacher at school who was led to make this point when we found it amusing that the wife of the Sultan of Turkey was called the Sultana, putting us in mind of a type of fruit. It is of course possible for a fact about the Middle Ages, about how the church or the civil service or the armed forces were organised in those days or what people believed in religion and politics, to be intellectually interesting regardless of its overall significance. There is no reason why we should not seek intellectual gratification any more than we should not seek emotional gratification if the latter is supposed to be a different quantity (if something is intellectually interesting, it is perhaps not emotionally so in the sense of being exciting or funny). Learning is meant to be a pleasure anyway, and if it wasn't I doubt if any of us – any of us, and not just the student who is lazy or finds a particular lecturer dull – would be able to participate in it.

The above things explains why so much effort is put into the detailed study, on a regular basis, of events that happened hundreds or more years ago. It is not always the same story; we may study the French Revolution, the Wars of the Roses, or the Renaissance. But it can be gripping. The way different factors interact with one another in human or natural affairs means that the exact course of events is never the same in each case. This is one reason why history can legitimately be likened to a fictional book, the main difference being that the author of the latter is deliberately manufacturing its narrative in the knowledge that those who read it will not mind this as long as they enjoy reading it. Those who participated in actual historical events obviously did not experience them in the same way. But history can be equally entertaining; provided that we at least draw instruction from those things which nobody would have enjoyed happening to them or, if one is in one's right mind, to others.

While my abovementioned history teacher saw nothing wrong in seeing a funny side to his subject he nonetheless thought it should be taken seriously. For this reason he at one point gave up teaching O Level history, seeing it as a simple presentation of facts with nothing much to recommend it. I think he was wrong, because it is important children at all educational levels have some knowledge and hopefully appreciation of the past. The process has to begin from a relatively early age, especially as it may have to cease later when one starts at the A Level stage to specialise and might choose to concentrate on other subjects. I personally found the crucial change, in terms of intellectual challenge, to be that from O to A Level rather than from A Level to university-taught history. There was not much difference between the two; both essentially involved using one's thinking abilities to make a decision (as to how far Bismarck's foreign policy was premeditated, for example) in a way one might not quite have had to do before. It was still possible to look down on history as a subject because unless you happened to come across a previously undiscovered document which threw a revolutionary new light on someone's aims or the things which motivated them you were essentially cobbling a thesis together from what others had written, with no scope it seemed for being original. After all, you were not yourself personally responsible for Magna Carta or the unification of Germany, nor would you have had much opportunity yet to do your own research. What you were essentially doing, because at that stage in your career it was all you could do, was to identify the most common thread running through all the books on the relevant historical subject, the point or points on which most historians seemed to agree, and use that as the basis for your essay. Still derivative and unoriginal, many would say. But it was still a useful intellectual exercise, which assisted the development of your reasoning skills. And what you read might inspire original ideas of your own.

On balance, and whatever stage you are at professionally and intellectually, the most common interpretation of a historical phenomenon (meaning political movement, social trend or the policies of a prominent individual) may reasonably be thought likely to be correct. All those historians can't be wrong if by and large they are good at their job, as one supposes most people are. This is fine as long as you appreciate it may not *always* be the case. Sometimes the radical, maverick interpretation may be the correct one. The ability to come up with our own ideas – my history teacher was always telling us to risk them, which sooner or later, in any walk of life, you will have to do – and thus, potentially, with the radical interpretation increases as we continue to intellectually mature. The maverick view at least deserves to be heard, if we are not to become narrow-minded (because intolerant) and stagnant in our thinking. A related question is that of what to do if you are a history tutor who comes up against an interpretation with which they fundamentally, even viscerally, disagree. Needless to say, the behaviour of Howard Kirk in Malcolm Bradbury's book *The History Man*, who downmarks an essay by a Tory student because he dislikes his politics, is reprehensible. But what do I do if I am a right-wing tutor who is presented with an essay written from a Communist perspective? The crux of the matter is that student A is entitled to be a Communist if he wishes, and his beliefs will inevitably influence his thinking. What matters, in the writing of all history and in whatever phase of one's life, is that is student A makes some sort of coherent case for his conclusions, irrespective of whether it is to the tutor's personal liking. The tutor can still indicate that he or she does not agree with it, but ideally do no more than that.

Ethnic and national affiliations will, I suspect, always influence our conclusions or at least the emphasis we give to things, however much we try to avoid it. And objective historical truth is perhaps hard to arrive at as long as there can be any scope for more than one interpretation of matters. The only form of historical research which can produce it, or anything like it, is archaeological (history and archaeology are obviously related subjects), because the evidence is more in the realm of hard, undisputed physical fact even allowing for the decay of buried matter over the centuries. Ashes and calcined artefacts may prove that an ancient Greek city was sacked at this or that approximate point in time. But they will not show *why* it was sacked; they can give no clue as to how the intangible, meaning the minds of prominent figures of the age, was functioning, especially given that humans have free will and may have to choose between more than one course of action or have more than one motive for doing a particular thing. To arrive at the truth is a lot easier in the modern age because of the greater abundance of records (restrictions on "classified" documents notwithstanding) in various forms and media concentration on events and personalities (which despite the tendency to bias does make it easier to form an opinion of a leading politician's character). But it is still difficult as long as people have different opinions and none can be regarded as absolute truth without seeming to adopt the somehow disturbing principle that opinions are logically quantifiable as facts.

This leads us to ask how *many* interpretations there can be of history. What if there is a limit to them, and historians eventually exhaust all the options so that all we are left with are the frivolous ones, or those dictated by partisan politics however credible they aren't? I very much hope this has not already happened. We don't want to end up either regurgitating the same material over again or making things up – perhaps unconsciously – just for the sake of doing something different. It's a very postmodern dilemma, and all one can say is that one hopes the crunch can be avoided for as long as possible. While we are in this world, we have a commitment to tell its story without malice or bias.

As well as preserve objectivity, the historian must also stick to their subject. But inevitably, in order to reach conclusions, they must venture into other disciplines on occasions. To decide whether a historical personality, or a society, was at fault in allowing such-and-such a thing to happen and could have acted otherwise they need to be a moral philosopher (most obviously so, perhaps, when discussing the crimes of the Nazis and other totalitarian regimes). Is such behaviour reprehensible or was there simply no alternative; in other words, *why* did it happen, which is what the historian is asking. But this is only for the sake of history itself. That is, history is serving a moral purpose for society in general by providing a background, a relief, against which ethical questions can be discussed, through the actions (or non-actions) of historical figures, but only as itself, for otherwise it risks clouding its own objective judgement and thus cannot fulfil the role it, for society's own benefit, must perform. It must stand apart from the whole, and from other parts of the whole, just as a hoe is not the garden nor should be confused with a rake or watering-can.

Finally, although this is strictly a semantic rather than a historical issue, the teaching of history is like other things prone to the potentially damaging effect of tinkering with language. In the study of wars and how support for them is maintained, there has been some attempt to replace the term "propaganda" with "war culture". This seems to me very strange. It is quite correct in itself to talk of "war culture", of which propaganda is obviously a part, but to speak of the former *instead of* the latter is like mentioning the body but never the heart or the lungs or the teeth. By being too general it does not create the frame of mind in which "propaganda" can be fully considered.

Whether it comes under the category of political correctness (a pejorative term often applied too widely) is debatable since its purpose is not political so much as semantic. But the politicisation of history, merely because some people understandably feel strongly about certain issues and/or a particular point of view happens to have become influential in key areas, is another thing we need to watch. The issue is seen in the alleged (for all I know actual) victimisation of a university don who said that the British Empire was neither all good nor all bad. The teaching of history must not be an agent for inculcating a particular opinion, because that is to reject objectivity and so is almost by definition the antithesis of things like "study" and "analysis".

On what has become a related subject, it needs to be reiterated that approaches to history can't be dictated simply by strong emotions, any more than they can by ideological affiliation (sometimes the two may amount to the same thing). If we are to objectively understand and draw lessons from it, those emotions cannot determine how we interpret it or, and this is just as harmful if not more so, airbrush it out of the common consciousness. Since no human ethnic group or culture is beyond reproach the history of a society will be inextricably tied up with its harmful features as well as its positive ones. Hence, to obliterate all kinds of memorial to people who had some sort of connection to the slave trade, because of anger at this past injustice risks generally distorting historical perspective. Because Gladstone's father made his living out of the slave trade, and he himself delivered a few speeches in favour of slavery in his youth, his name was removed from a university hall of residence (we are not talking here about just the hotheaded element within the black British community, which is what makes the affair so worrying). If the idea is to excise any official recognition of such people then the logical development of the university authorities' action would be to cut Gladstone out of history altogether (there would be no point in it if it was not taken to its ultimate conclusion). So important is Gladstone, along with Disraeli, for an understanding of the nineteenth-century British political system and its development that this is simply not possible. You would have to rewrite the whole story, in other words replace it with a fictional version in which Gladstone's role was assigned to a made-up character or ascribed to some other politician of the period; and *that* is hardly the proper study of history! Alternatively, we could I suppose ensure that every time Gladstone comes up in a publication or lecture on the Victorian age, or other historical subject, he is referred to not by name but as "the figure who as well as being instrumental in mid-late nineteenth century British politics was also a supporter of the slave trade and who therefore we do not advertise any more than we need to". The impracticality of this is so obvious that it is barely worth commenting upon. And a truly objective study of the history of cities like Bristol and Liverpool would emphasise not only that they owed their development in the eighteenth and early nineteenth centuries to slavery, but also that many of their buildings are genuinely and strikingly beautiful; in other words that good can come out of evil, if one thinks of the slavery as the latter. Banish significant chunks of history from the group consciousness except as objects of condemnation and you destroy that consciousness, while at the same time envenoming the business if passions are high enough – at the risk of seeming slightly vulgar, it is a double bummer – unless of course you are going to teach only black history (with the whites as villains, because of the slavery) in a predominantly white country with a predominantly white past. The proper representation of history is essential for the sense of identity, and thus cultural and psychological wellbeing, of particular societies as well as of humanity in general.

July 2020

NOTE: I ought to stress that when I state that something or other happened in the "1800s", for example, I generally mean the decade 1800-1810, or whatever. The practice that has recently become common of using "1800s", "1500s", "1900s" etc. to denote the nineteenth century, sixteenth century, twentieth century and so on, rather than particular decades within them is in my view confusing and, since the old way of doing things worked perfectly well, unnecessary. I'm not so much against language change in itself as saying "If it ain't broke, don't fix it."

(1) Here it may be commented that Kevin Sharpe's enormous tome seeking to prove it *was* effective succeeds admirably in its purpose, but at the cost of going into overkill.

1

Understanding Enoch

I never met Enoch Powell personally, though I corresponded with him a couple of times, in 1981 and 1994. I also saw him twice in the House of Commons. On the first occasion, in April 1981, the great man was speaking on the fascinating subject of electricity supplies in Northern Ireland, and so perhaps one did not get the opportunity to appreciate his full brilliance, though it showed his devotion to the more mundane but nonetheless important aspects of constituency affairs, and thus to the welfare of the constituents. I thought his habit of tucking his thumbs into his lapels when going to sleep (as he did at one point, the day's business not being, as I say, of a particularly exciting nature) rather absurd and excessively old-fashioned; he is the only person I have ever seen do it in real life and was probably one of the last to.

The second occasion was in November 1985, when the House was debating the Anglo-Irish agreement over which the Ulster Unionist MPs, Powell included, had pledged to resign their seats in order to fight by-elections which would demonstrate to the Thatcher government the extent of Ulster's disapproval of the measure. Powell had at first seemed reluctant to take this step, which caused some friction between him and the other Unionists. But his hesitation was forgiveable. As he had a slender majority there was every possibility he would lose, ending for him a life to which he had become deeply attached, perhaps the only one he knew; because Enoch Powell was undoubtedly a devoted parliamentarian.

I was one of a group from the Southampton University Conservative Association who had been invited to tea at the Commons by the parliamentary party; whether that date had been chosen because of the subject being debated I don't know, but a few of us, myself included, were able to spend some time in the Chamber listening to the speeches. Unfortunately we were not present when Enoch did his bit; earlier though I could see him sitting with his fellow Unionists, with whom his relations as noted had been a little strained over his apparent unwillingness to stand down. Clearly visible even from the opposite side of the Chamber was that prominent scar-like jowl which ran down one side of his face, a face which seemed to wear a grimly disgruntled, baleful expression. He didn't look very happy. Yet after a while he turned to his neighbour with a friendly smile and began speaking to him in what was obviously a warm and amicable conversation. Another of our party confirmed that Powell had seemed generally to be getting on well with his colleagues. Altogether, it was a sign that he was not always the cold, aloof figure his enemies portrayed him as. I felt it showed a very different side to his personality.

In many ways I regret that I never met him properly, although what would have happened if I had is difficult to say. Powell could sometimes snub those who showed interest in him, though much depended on how the approach was made. The American academic Douglas E Schoen, author of *Enoch Powell and the Powellites*, describes his own experience thus:

"I approached Mr Powell in October 1975 with a request to interview him for this study. Mr Powell replied that he could not grant me an interview as this would imply collaboration between the two of us. Nevertheless he agreed to provide (and subsequently did provide) copies of speeches he had delivered in Ulster since 1973 plus additional requested materials. Unfortunately Mr Powell took exception to my interviewing other MPs about him and made his feelings known to my supervisor. Both my supervisor...and I indicated to Mr Powell that I was doing serious academic research and was not, as he maintained, engaging in "political gossip". Mr Powell did not respond to Mr Johnson {Schoen's supervisor}'s or my letter except by directing his secretary to send me a bill for £1 for duplicating the speeches he had earlier provided."

Powell could cold-shoulder even the faithful. In 1977 the *Daily Express'* gossip column reported how he had stonewalled a supporter who had attempted effusively to talk to him about something or other on an Underground train. One wonders how those members of the public who admired him, met with such a rebuff, would react; it would be very disillusioning. Would they have retained their admiration if subjected at first hand to his notorious frostiness?

These incidents arose because Powell was a very private person, and with this went, as it often does, a dislike of obsequious flattery (though Schoen had not been guilty of that). The man on the Tube seems to have been over-familiar and annoying. Powell's left-wing detractors regard the right-wing praise that has so often been showered on him as "flatulent"; privately at any rate he would probably have agreed with them. Where it did not impose on him directly and irritatingly his attitude was that if they wanted to be like that he could do nothing about it; it was their choice.

My own contact with Powell was as follows. I once wrote to him asking for his autograph and for any advice he might give to someone with political ambitions (at that time I very much wanted to be an MP). I suppose I was a bit naive in expecting a fulsome reply with detailed advice on this and that. I duly received the autograph – along with a list of books that Powell had written, and of his speeches, plus an order form. I felt rather as if I had been short-changed, though his signature remains a treasured possession (along with those of Harold Wilson, Barbara Castle and several other political illuminaries of the 1960s and 70s). Much later, in 1994, I sent him for his perusal an article (in the end unpublished) which I had written on immigration and race in modern Britain for the Conservative Political Centre. Powell stated that he had only one comment to make, which he did not wish to be published, thereby rendering it completely worthless from the point of view of posterity.

It was regrettable given that Enoch Powell was the sort of person with whom I ought to have had a lot in common. We were both intensely patriotic. We were both regarded as child prodigies, and as being for much of the time in worlds of our own. We spent a lot of time buried in books rather than communicating with other people. We both had frustrated careers; in my case, work prospects were fatally damaged by an inability to find anything other than casual employment, to escape from the benefit trap, or, because of the enormous obstacles faced nowadays by non-established authors, to make a name for myself through writing. We could be irascible when we felt people had failed to understand us.

There is no doubt Powell could be a cold fish, as my father, in many ways an admirer of him – Enoch was always highly regarded in our family – admitted. In 1974 it was not the fact that he did what he did in defecting from the Tories and telling his supporters to vote Labour, who among other things were less favourably disposed towards the Common Market, in the February election which was bad, if he did it from conscience, but rather the curt way he treated his constituency organisation in Wolverhampton over the matter, after an association of twenty-four years (later he did write personally to thank them for their efforts).

Even Simon Heffer, high priest of the cult of Powell, admits that he sometimes seemed not to care what the effect might be on people's feelings of things he said and/or did. He made hurtful remarks which would have alienated many of those who supported him, had they heard them. At one point towards the end of his life he stated that he held any man or woman who went to the European Court to redress a grievance to be a "scoundrel." And yet many ordinary people of the kind who revered him because they felt he spoke for them on immigration would take, and in some cases have taken, that route when they felt the existing UK law discriminated against them, or otherwise failed to serve them well, on some important matter. Had that not been the case they would not have done so. Beyond a certain point it is unreasonable to expect people to put up with too much in the name of patriotism, even though it's noble if they do.

Was it fair, though, that Powell should have been so reviled by some? And was it right his career should have been such a failure?

There have been many biographies of Powell in recent years, far more than of those politicians who achieved the Premiership or one of the other major offices of state. The obsession, one might say infatuation, there has been with him requires some explanation. It is simply that he was the most *interesting* of post-war politicians, regardless of whether you agreed with him. The reason for this is that Powell, with the possible exception of Margaret Thatcher, had the greatest stature. He is certainly more interesting than Attlee, Major or Home, or the dependable (up to a point) but stolid James Callaghan, and seems more a man of principle than Harold Wilson even if the latter was not quite the shady character he has so often been represented as. Churchill was past his best by his peacetime ministry. Heath had an intellect, and was certainly not immoral, but was let down by his U-turns, which made him appear inconstant, and a tendency to bully in order to get his way. David Cameron had the brains but was something of a "dour Scot" – as, though psychologically an intriguing case nonetheless, was Gordon Brown – as well as being too much in hock to political correctness and Thatcherite free enterprise, the two ideologies which, by the way they are practised rather than because they are entirely bad in themselves, have done so much damage to British national life in recent years. If Tony Blair had an intellect, as opposed to "intelligence" which is a different thing altogether, it was of a very strange kind. Not all the above were/are bad people, by any means. But they somehow don't compare with Enoch Powell.

This essay is not intended to be another biography of Powell; there is something of a surfeit of Powell biographies. The definitive is of course the substantial volume by Heffer. I felt that a study was needed which was more concise and less unwieldy than his 900-plus-page tome. And more critical; given that Powell's speeches on immigration are said to have incited racist attacks on Asian children, which may well be true, greater sensitivity is required than is shown by those who too often praise him loudly and without qualification. If the allegations *are* true, no admirer of Powell can fail to be disturbed by that.

Mr Heffer also has the tendency to excessively denigrate anyone who ever opposed or criticised Powell's policies. One eminent figure is treated to an account of his subsequent career which is not intended to be particularly flattering and ends with the words "later he joined the SDP." The intention here is to establish the idea in people's heads that the SDP were ineffective and a refuge for nonentities and has-beens. Even though they may have been a little naïve, there is nothing wrong with decent – and in many cases highly intelligent – people getting understandably sick of the childish and unhelpful squabbling between left and right which characterised British politics in the 1980s and attempting to make a difference by founding a third party (which as part of the Alliance did win by-elections). Heffer's reference to the death of Stephen Milligan as a result of a kinky sex session gone wrong is gratuitous, especially when Milligan's election as an MP, and his death, took place over 24 years after the incident where he protested against Powell's views on immigration, even if it is only stated that Milligan died "in unfortunate circumstances." With certain exceptions, anyone who isn't a right-wing free marketeer is regarded as self-righteous and possibly morally dubious. Heffer's objectivity is under question. Writers and journalists who are irascible and opinionated are praised because they render things more interesting. But if this is so, then we can't complain when someone says something unfair about *them*. Heffer's snideness towards Powell's enemies is no less distasteful than Jeremy Paxman's completely wrong, and in fact utterly deplorable, assertion in *The English* that what Powell objected to in the matter of immigration was simply the entry into this country of lots of people with a different-coloured skin. Given that the issue is much more complex than that suggests, it is a dangerously unhelpful way of looking at things. But of course we find Paxo makes it all so much more exciting, don't we? In any event, I feel that neither Heffer's book nor *Enoch At 100*, a 2012 anthology of essays published to commemorate Powell's centenary, really answers the question of what Powell *was* and why he said and did the things which made him so controversial.

He aroused strong emotions. The *Daily Telegraph* was embarrassingly excessive in its coverage of his death, a whole page being devoted to his obituary (when apparently its then editor, Charles Moore, had once insisted that only two people, Mrs Thatcher and the Pope, merited such treatment). If this was a sign of the paper's adulation of Powell the *Guardian* and the *Independent* positioned themselves at the other end of the scale. Into the 1980s Powell was held in high regard by many on the left, despite everything. The *Guardian* would publish letters and articles by him. Michael Foot, a man of principle who for that reason recognised in Powell a kindred spirit, had always admired and spoken kindly of him, although interestingly he made no comment when asked on Powell's death for his opinion on the man's career. There was a civilised magnanimity about things. But by the time Powell died all that had changed; a very nasty spirit had crept in. The left-wing or "middle-of-the-road" papers had so little regard for him they indulged in a distasteful kind of character assassination. To accompany their obituaries they chose photographs of Powell which might have been designed to show him in an unflattering light. That used by the *Independent* makes him appear cruel and satanic while the *Guardian*'s choice, in which the signs of Parkinson's Disease are evident, suggests a brooding mental trauma with its fixed, hostile stare, and its caption describes Powell as a "tense, unsmiling man". Norman Shrapnel's assertion that Powell "had always been slightly deranged" is not likely to satisfy its readers, or future historians, that the writer is being objective. It is cheap as well as unscientific; Powell's problem, if one views it as that, was not insanity as will be made clear later on. This scathing treatment was probably due to the influence of the late Paul Foot.

As for the black newspapers, the *Voice* devoted a surprisingly small section to the matter, perhaps showing their contempt by not giving Powell the publicity they didn't feel he deserved. A similar publication had "Burn in Hell, Enoch", and "Enoch Powell was a... " (readers were invited to tick whatever one out of a list of possible descriptions of Powell, none of them very complimentary, they thought appropriate).

Look up Powell on Google and you will find among the various websites on which he is mentioned one where Paul Foot sums up his career by saying in essence "Enoch Powell was a filthy racist, whatever anyone thinks." Apart from the basic injustice of this, how the adjective "filthy", in a moral sense, can be applied to someone who was in many ways excessively honourable, with a very strong awareness of what was proper and improper, takes some explaining. Powell could be standoffish and high-handed, but that isn't quite the same thing. Without wishing to do a Simon Heffer, Paul Foot was not himself always admirable. He stood up for many good causes, exposed the people who needed to be exposed. He was right about the Lockerbie disaster, among other matters. But apart from his unfairness towards Powell, he deserves censure for his comment in a *Private Eye* special publication on the (farcical) Lockerbie trial that the lawyers for the prosecution had held "triumphalist" meetings with relatives of the dead, which makes it seem as if he is criticising the latter too, in a way which is highly inappropriate even though, to his credit, he admits in thanking those who helped him in his research – including a few of the bereaved – that they are unlikely to agree with the style of his piece. Foot wrote a whole book, *The Rise Of Enoch Powell*, which presents a coherent argument for Powell having been misguided (though to some extent he was), if not fraudulent and repellently bigoted, in what he thought about immigration in 1968. But because a particular kind of mind (Foot's), not by any means stupid or wicked, thinks in a particular way it will consistently interpret facts and events according to that pattern, without necessarily being in the right. An entire volume can be devoted to an argument which although structured, and apparently convincing, is also entirely wrong.

Admittedly, we are not bound to exonerate Powell purely because he was an intelligent and cultured man. There have been plenty of intelligent and cultured people who have used their learning and eloquence as a smokescreen and launch pad for base prejudices. But again, what *was* he exactly?

Before we attempt to answer that question, a summary of Powell's career is called for. He was a University Professor at twenty-five and a brigadier (the British Army's youngest) in the Second World War, when he was in his early thirties. He was elected to parliament in 1950. He became a junior minister but left the government over economic policies he considered too interventionist. He was appointed Minister of Health in 1960 but resigned in 1963 over Harold Macmillan's sidelining of R A Butler in recommending a successor to the Queen on his standing down as Prime Minister, which Powell considered unethical (he had a history of resigning on matters of principle, one reason why he would not have lasted long as Prime Minister and was perhaps never meant to occupy that position if Fate is seen as having any hand in human affairs). He had by now made his name within the Conservative party as a strong supporter of monetarist economics, becoming in effect a prototype Thatcherite. He was sacked from the Shadow Cabinet, in which he sat as defence spokesman, in 1968 over his controversial speech against Commonwealth immigration. Although from then on he was confined to the backbenches Powell remained an important political figure because of his considerable popular following, which in the end was the basis of his influence rather than any support he enjoyed within the Conservative establishment itself. Though this is difficult to prove, it was probably his support for the

Tories which put them in power in 1970 and his rejection of them which turfed Heath out of it in 1974 (supporters of Powell claim that it was, detractors that it wasn't). There is a parallel here with Joseph Chamberlain, another West Midlands political tribune; with the difference that Powell acted from principle more than personal ambition he, like Chamberlain, could wreck parties. However, his leaving the Conservatives over the election of 1974, which he regarded as fraudulent since it had been called by Heath in a fit of pique over the miners' strike – though his motive was as much annoyance at Heath's having brought Britain into the EU – to return in October as an MP for a minor party marked the end of his ability to influence events in any significant way, with the arguable 1979 exception of his role in the negotiations between James Callaghan and the Ulster Unionists which were intended to prop up the former's minority government and save it from possible defeat in the forthcoming general election (Powell didn't play ball). I suspect, as do many, that he subsequently regretted the decision, wondering – despite speeches to the contrary – whether it might not have been a serious mistake. Some, like Sir Gerald Nabarro, thought his influence had already begun to wane by '74. Certainly, the fact that he was a controversial, fairly caricaturable, and therefore much reported personality made him seem more important in the scheme of things than, relatively speaking, he was. After all, Nabarro himself with his handlebar moustache, fleet of Rolls Royces and outrageous right-wing views was frequently caricatured and there was never any suggestion of *him* ever becoming Prime Minister or being in any way a major player in the political game. Gradually after 1974 Powell came to be put on the back burner by the media, as it consciously or subconsciously sank in how much his defection to Ulster had relegated him there. That did not mean he ceased to be reported, because he remained an active politician with a tendency to controversy. Of course, fuss continued to be made by the Left whenever he made anti-immigration comments because of their particular concern over such things. Nowadays, given the political and cultural changes which have taken place, it is unlikely Powell would have been accorded as much coverage as he got in the first instance; he would simply have been regarded as a crazed extremist who merely happened to have previously occupied positions in the government.

During the most important phases of Powell's career, I either had not yet been born or was too young to really know what was going on. However, he continued to be that controversial figure. In 1984, following a Christmas message which seemed to him to focus unduly on ethnic minorities and on the inhabitants of the Commonwealth at large rather than mainstream Britain, he caused a storm by suggesting that the Queen was failing to speak for the majority of her people (Powell had no time for the Commonwealth, regarding it as a fiction with no real purpose and a waste of time and money). To many on the Left, inside and outside parliament, he remained anathema, mainly because of his views on immigration which never seemed to change. During the 1980s certain left-wing elements among the population of British universities − aided and abetted, it was strongly suspected, by student union officials − followed a policy of disrupting meetings with eminent visiting speakers who were considered to be racists or fascists, even if they were not actually speaking on anything to do with race or immigration. On several occasions, notably at Bristol in the autumn of 1986, meetings at which Powell spoke were broken up. This was one reason why he was forced to cut down on speaking engagements as he grew older; for a man in his seventies, such incidents were likely to prove increasingly stressful.

He seemed to be back in the public eye in the spring of 1985, when he put forward a private members' bill to outlaw the use of human embryos for scientific research, something he considered an affront to human dignity. It is quite likely that some of the opposition to the measure was based on spite towards Powell, a feeling that he was being hypocritical in taking the moral high ground when (they believed) he was guilty of racial prejudice. A speaker against the bill at a Union meeting at Southampton University complained, "Enoch Powell couldn't give a --- about black people, now he's all concerned about embryos." Nonetheless, though in the end the bill failed to become law, his stance on the issue might have been seen as a sign of moral sensitivity on his part. Some correspondents in the letters pages of national newspapers certainly thought so, but the perception could well have been more widespread than that. Sadly, however, his speech after the Broadwater Farm riots in October destroyed any goodwill the embryo bill might have fostered on the part of those who were not generally disposed to like him; and perhaps of others too. His reiteration of the views he had first expressed in 1968 met with anger and derision from the right and centre of the political establishment, who felt he had learnt nothing. Roy Hattersley called him "the Alf Garnett of British politics" (unfortunately perhaps for Powell *Till Death Us Do Part,* renamed *In Sickness And In Health*, was at this time enjoying a revival on TV). Shortly after his re-election to parliament the following January he made remarks which appeared to condone violence by Ulster loyalists against the Anglo-Irish agreement; the heated and unfriendly TV interview in which he defended them was a low point in his career. A few months later there occurred the incident at Bristol.

The embryo bill, even if it failed, was a *high* point for Powell; over Broadwater Farm he had only been repeating views which he had always held, just as there had always been those who barracked him. Nonetheless it could be concluded that he was now past his best; he had become too eccentric, too crotchety, too inclined to get bees in his bonnet. A fellow member of the Conservative Association at Southampton told me he thought Powell was getting "a bit funny in the head." How much it was due to age and how much to things which had always been a part of his character is difficult to say, but the former factor probably did not improve matters. It was in many ways sad when his political career finally ended with the loss of his seat at the 1987

General Election; because of his old-fashioned ways and support for traditional values, he could be seen as a reassuring link with the past, part of the national furniture. The *Daily Telegraph* commented after he only narrowly succeeded in winning South Down in 1983 that the Commons would not be the same without him sitting in his usual place glowering at everyone, and indeed it wasn't. But his defeat in 1987 was also, to be frank, a blessing.

It happened at the same time that the first black and Asian MPs, out of the politically significant influx of nonwhites from the 1940s onwards, entered parliament. Some would have viewed this as appropriate but it didn't seem to be commented on that much, a measure of how far Powell was by now regarded as "old hat".

Electorally Powell had been a victim of the turbulent and seemingly absurd Ulster politics which had seen him scrape home by barely the skin of his teeth in 1983 yet be returned with an increased majority at the 1986 by-election, and was now casting him out once and for all into the wilderness. As it happened his last speech in the Commons was about Ulster and the need for it to be retained as an integral part of the United Kingdom. He was unable to continue to speak on this or other issues from a parliamentary platform as he rejected the offer of a life peerage, seeing such things as a nonsense.

As he grew older Powell became more and more convinced that the truth of what he said on any issue was self-evident and little elaboration was needed. By 1990 his answers to questions on TV political discussion programmes, such as the BBC's *Question Time*, consisted of about four short, succinct sentences which to him summed up the matter quite adequately. But he certainly continued to speak and write on current affairs and other matters, and to be, as always, a cause of contention. Until the early 1990s, due partly to the tendency for men to become better-looking in middle and later life, he was still an impressive presence, despite not being particularly tall (and thus maybe less intimidating than his reputation, if you weren't sure you liked him, might suggest). There then occurred a sudden and shocking change, brought about by the onset of Parkinson's Disease. In April 1994 he appeared on an edition of *Timewatch* which discussed immigration and its consequences for the subsequent shape of Britain. Many people commented how ill he looked, "like someone about to have a stroke and die," in the words of one of my work colleagues who also saw the programme. According to Heffer, many already thought Powell was dead – at the risk of seeming cruel, they could be forgiven for thinking they hadn't been far wrong – and were surprised to find this was not the case.

All in all, it was another not particularly uplifting occasion. But Powell did live on for another four years and for the first part of that period, at least, still had his marbles. He did a TV interview with Michael Cockerell which was broadcast in the autumn of 1995. He also wrote *The Evolution of the Gospel,* a book which is worth reading as part of a study of the nature of belief, of what must be regarded as crucial to a theological system and what can be discarded, but whose conclusions most Christians regarded as suspect. Powell had interpreted the Hebrew scriptures in such a way as to be convinced Christ was stoned to death and not crucified as we are told in the Bible. It's true that the four Gospels don't always agree with one another in their record of events; for one thing there seems some confusion as to who exactly was present at Jesus' tomb when the stone was rolled away. Though the Bible is an account of God's intervention in human affairs it was written down by humans themselves, who are fallible. But the setting of a story, the props as it were, is crucial to the whole performance (to use the analogy of a theatre) and it is not possible to be mistaken about such an important detail as the manner of Jesus' death, even if that detail is nonetheless an essentially factual point and makes no difference to the spiritual reality of the sacrifice and resurrection and their role in atoning for sin. It was further confirmation that the author's brilliant mind, under the onset of old age, was taking divergent paths from those which most would have followed on this matter, or indeed many others.

It was unfortunate for Powell that the issue with which he became most identified was a particularly sensitive one (and also that the day he made the so-called "rivers of blood" speech, 20th April, was Hitler's birthday, although the timing was pure coincidence and mercifully it is not often commented upon). Powell's entire reputation rests on his motives for taking the stand he did on immigration. The objection to any *more* immigrants entering the country was quite reasonable, in view of the culture shock to the indigenes and the possible strain on resources. If Powell had confined himself to demanding a limit to the scale of *future* immigration, he might have avoided a good deal of opprobrium, but he had to go further and call for repatriation, for which there was much less of a case.

Certainly he wasn't motivated by anything so crude as dislike of the colour of a person's skin. He was courteous towards individual blacks or Asians; the issue was not, in his opinion, a question of individuals anyway. A black person once told me that it was a characteristic of Black culture and psychology to like the person who hated you (I have never understood quite why), but that he made an exception in Powell's case. In fact, Powell was the one least deserving of such revilement, because although in his day he probably did more actual damage to the cause of racial integration than any single individual he did *not* hate blacks as such. The irony was that he became the model for the archetype of the racist politician playing on people's fears and prejudices because they either shared those sentiments or were exploiting them for personal gain, when in fact he was less racist, according to what ought to be the accepted definition of racism, and more honourable than other right-wing anti-immigration ideologues. We need to emphasise that it was the continuing increase in the non-white population that concerned Powell, not the fact that it was here at all. He certainly did not believe that people were undesirable simply because they happened to be a bit different from other people. In itself, that difference was not the problem. Rather, I believe his argument was that as the non-white population grew the white would have to change its perception of itself in a way that would be difficult and thus psychologically damaging for it. In order to avoid this, it would try to drive out the other races by force. The other races would naturally resist since by then they would have become accustomed to living in Britain, regarding it as home – as they do, which is why they can be forgiven for taking an adverse view of Powell and his opinions. Put this way one can understand Powell's views even if not ultimately endorsing them.

I think he accepted, despite the what left-wing people of whatever race may claim, that the ethnic minorities would in time come to consider themselves British and that they belonged here. In a sense that was part of the problem; it might result in irresistible force being pitted against immovable object. The minorities were not going to leave but at the same time the demographic shift had cultural implications for the whites that the latter would find unacceptable and seek to resist.

In a speech to the Rotary Club of London in November 1968 Powell talked of the "slow mercy of the years" absorbing "that unparalleled invasion of our body politic." He was referring to a relatively small immigrant/ethnic minority community rather than the large and constantly growing population which is a feature of Britain today. But he would probably have conceded that *eventually*, the most serious conflicts caused by demographic change would end, and somehow or other things would be sorted out. All being equal, time would heal the damage. However, if someone pointed out to him all the long and bloody conflicts of the past which had ultimately been got over he would have replied that neither he nor anyone else would want to go through such trauma in order to resolve matters. If the conflicts could had been avoided at the time they occurred, or before, they would have been. It was right for the Saxons to have resisted the Norman Conquest even though, 900 or so years later, the descendants of both Saxons and Normans would be living peacefully together and subscribing to a common British identity. He was following, perhaps rather brutally, a certain logic.

If the multicultural experiment worked, well and good, but if it didn't we would be in trouble. It was that trouble he was trying to save us from. He didn't think we should take the risk. To embark on the experiment when, if it failed, it could have the most appalling consequences in terms of social unrest, and not to draw attention to that danger, was in his view irresponsible.

Powell never properly explained precisely *why* he found the growth of the non-white population to be so dangerous, with the result that people either vilified him as a racist or supported him for the wrong reasons, not really understanding what he said in his speeches (since intellectually he was undoubtedly head and shoulders above so many others) but glad that he was on their side in wanting the blacks and Asians out, the spirit that motivated them often being one of hatred. If he had explained himself properly the discerning element within the nation would at least have had a better idea of what he was getting at, even if they still did not agree with him in the end, and to some extent the situation would have been detoxified, while still leaving the issues over which he was speaking out unresolved. He forgot that ordinary mortals did not occupy the same intellectual pedestal as himself and expected the meaning of what he said to be self-evident when it was not (though he did once confess, rather engagingly, to being arrogant in this respect, in an interview for BBC Radio in 1986). Like Gladstone, he had the measure of Man but not always of men. He would say things, things that might be misinterpreted, and expect people to understand them. A statement like "What's wrong with racism? We are all racist" in the 1995 Cockerell interview would by many people, and particularly on the Left, only be construed one way. What Powell really meant, of course, was that all of us are aware of race, are proud of our ethnic identity, and therefore consider it a factor of importance in politics. But even though the difference between this and actual hatred for those of other ethnicity has been explained both by Powell himself, in his famous David Frost interview, and his biographer Robert Shepherd such a way of putting things is bound to give the wrong impression, even if we make allowances for people being what they are, and so is best avoided. Like many very clever people, (a) Powell's intellect worked faster than the rest of him and (b) he failed to appreciate that those less clever might not get the point, or misconstrue him. The misunderstanding was particularly dangerous on a sensitive issue like immigration. At the same time, his tendency sometimes to be irritable and standoffish in his behaviour, and adopt what seemed a balefully brooding manner, damaged his anti-racist credentials by making it seem less likely to those unhappy at his views that he was basically benign in his intentions. Frequently, Powell was his own worst enemy.

"In theory, Powell's support for equality was unexceptional. He did object, he said, to a black person being refused service in a pub. But there were limits to his sense of equality. In some circumstances, he said, an individual should not be prevented from advertising a job or a home with the caveat "No coloured person may apply". Powell placed the right of the individual against the rights of the minority." (Tom Bower, in *Enoch At 100*, ed. Lord Howard of Rising, 2012, p154–5). What Powell meant was that within certain limits, and rightly or wrongly, he must retain the freedom to be a racist if he wanted because virtue, including tolerance towards those different in one way or another from oneself, could not be forced on people and it was indecent, and impractical, to try. It was the mindset of someone very aware of how important conscience was to himself and ought to be to others. Again, however, he failed to see how his statements would be interpreted by those to whom he had not sufficiently explained his thinking. People were free to disagree with him in any case, and many probably would; but it was not what he said but the way he said it which inflamed the situation unnecessarily. Misunderstanding was caused by his taking his principles too far, which he often did and which was the product of an admittedly exceptional, some might say peculiar, mindset (it

27

led some people to suspect he was actually mentally deranged). His objecting to the Race Relations Act on grounds of freedom of conscience is one example. I see no reason whatsoever why one should not have laws against racial abuse and discrimination, since potentially they are *particular* sources of injustice, along with other things such as sexism; we cannot simply pass a single law against "doing something wrong" and if the Act ought not to have been passed because it was too prescriptive we should also have to throw a lot of other legislation off the statute book. To be fair, Powell's objections may have been in large measure because the Act was seen as unfair to whites in certain respects. But it was amended in 1976; and for him to oppose black and Asian immigration into the country *and* a law intended to combat racial prejudice looked highly suspicious. It is understandable if anti-racists thought they were putting two and two together. In all this, the fact that Powell was an intelligent and erudite man undoubtedly did encourage those who responded positively to him for racist reasons in thinking themselves justified, regardless of whether this had been his intention (it wasn't).

That Powell inflamed the situation unnecessarily, making it hard for many years to discuss questions of immigration and race objectively and reasonably – a problem which endures today and can credibly be attributed, in part, to Powell even though it is twenty-two years since he died and over forty since he ceased to be politically influential – is undisputed. Tom Bower is quite correct to say so in his contribution to *Enoch At 100*. Powell caused the trouble by not fully explaining his thinking on why immigration was harmful and by using language which could be called extreme. "Rivers of blood" is the phrase so often associated with the 1968 Birmingham speech; what Powell actually said was "Like the Roman, I see the River Tiber foaming with much blood". Even if allowance be made for media hype, there is semantically not that much difference between the two. Both imply that a certain red bodily substance will be evident in large quantities, and the cause is identified as tension over race, immigration and demography, which will lead to violence. Even if Powell's predictions *had* come true, in which case there would indeed have been a lot of blood, it does not excuse his error of judgement in saying what would ratchet up feelings (even if he did not intend to do so, in the sense of deliberately stirring up hatred for political ends) at a relatively early stage in the history of the issue and make it harder to resolve it sensibly, possibly resulting in the very thing he wanted to avoid. Powell was a combination of the passionate and emotional with the cool and logical; a potentially deadly mixture which Asperger Syndrome (see below) helped ignite.

One might have put it to Powell that while he had never argued for anything other than voluntary repatriation, there was little point in such a policy, if it was designed to reverse the demographic changes being brought about by Commonwealth immigration, since if given the choice the vast majority of blacks and Asians would not go. (As was recognised even by people of similar political affinities to Powell, who thought his position untenable, something reflected in *Daily Telegraph* leader columns. They admired his courage in saying what he thought but did not agree with him, which is the standard "fair" view of the man). They could only be *forced* out, provoking just the kind of civil strife that Powell claimed he sought to prevent and which would be potentially more awful the more the ethnic minority population had increased. A man of logic should have understood this. So what was the point in his continuing to talk as if desiring repatriation, in one form or another? He was laying himself open to the charge that in bringing up the issue so determinedly, however he proposed it should be solved, he was trying to sow racial discontent by talking about the black and Asian presence in this country as something that might not be desirable. It (his behaviour on the issue) undoubtedly did have that effect (of sowing racial discontent), in the short and possibly the long run.

The answer must be that despite his high intellect and moral standards he was nonetheless a politician, and politicians have to calculate what the effect will be on the public of any position they take on a given issue, or a shift in that position, and how it will influence the success or otherwise of their policies. Had Powell changed from advocating repatriation to not advocating it he would have seemed to lack integrity and honesty, and apart from not wishing to give that impression, his moral reputation meaning so much to him, would have lost the confidence of that constituency – in his view the majority of the nation – he felt himself to be the much-needed spokesman for. At best it would have confused people. This ability to calculate politically (for reasons other than purely personal gain) makes no difference to his essential integrity. There was an intellectual calculation too, though it tied in with moral ones. He was so convinced of the ultimately disastrous consequences of a major change in the racial composition of the country that if, in some way, his advocating even voluntary repatriation helped to prevent it then he should do so. If he felt strongly enough about the danger he thought the country was in, and forcible repatriation was distasteful to him, then he logically had to speak out in the only way which remained, even if it ultimately proved pointless. A philosophical evaluation was being made, involving careful weighing of both the desirability and the utility of a particular position. He believed demographic change had to be reversed but shrank ethically from advocating involuntary repatriation or personally organising, directly or through henchmen, acts of violence or intimidation against ethnic minority people (it was wrongly claimed by some blacks that he did so). His attitude was an attempt to find some sort of compromise between opposed imperatives and to his mind, confining himself to talking about the inevitability of the racial situation producing disaster, which might *perhaps* persuade ethnic minorities themselves that it was better to return whence they had come from, emerged as a logical consequence of this; for in Powell's mindset logic was paramount and had to be obeyed even if it meant being quixotic (the ethnic minorities not wanting to return from whence they had come from).

In a photograph taken of him electioneering in 1970 and published in a recent edition of the BBC *History* magazine, Powell appears to cold-shoulder two Asian children who have approached him curiously. It ought to be borne in mind that he cold-shouldered other people too. But additionally, a friendlier attitude would have given the impression that he accepted, and therefore must see no harm in, what he had claimed would be ultimately disastrous. The trouble with Powell is that he was such a complex man that any explanation of his thinking and behaviour will look like an elaborate excuse of the sort so often contrived to justify what is *not* excusable. To put it another way, he cannot be placed in any clearly defined category such as "racist" or "fascist"; he was simply, as one commentator observed, Enoch Powell.

Another serious charge which is justly laid at his door is his failure to condemn violence against immigrants by those who were genuinely racist. But Powell believed that if the prevailing situation continued it was going to happen anyway, whether or not his own statements helped to incite it, and thus there was little point in condemning it (there is a contradiction in criticising what you think is inevitable as it implies it can be stopped). Even if there is a difference between what is unavoidable and what comes from hatred, the two might have become confused in the public mind and condemning one therefore seem to be condemning both, with the result that Powell would have appeared hypocritical or at any rate self-contradictory. For the same reason he could not castigate himself for any harm, by being racially divisive, which his own statements might cause. To understand his stance on various matters it is essential to see him as someone formulating their opinions on issues by balancing the pros and cons carefully in their mind and always analysing the possible consequences of an action or statement before making it. It is impossible to comprehend him except as a philosopher attempting to apply philosophical principles to his chosen career of politics (to some degree, Gladstone did the same thing with religion); even if he was also, and perhaps inevitably, having to be "political" in the sense of taking into account the effect of his statements and actions on the public and thus on the success of his policies. He was a combination of ambitious politician and man of conviction, the expression of whose beliefs was affected by the individualistic and extraordinary nature of his mind, in part the product of Asperger Syndrome. Both principle and pragmatism motivated him, though never to the detriment of the former.

But it could be said that he was standing excessively on his own dignity, as he did in other matters (such as the Schoen business). He felt that since his motives were very different and far more honourable than those of racist thugs there was no special onus on him to condemn their violence; to suggest there was would be to link him to them in a way he found insulting. He did not appreciate that condemnation would still have been the considerate, and sensible, thing and have also boosted his standing in the eyes of those inclined to get the wrong idea about him. He was incorrect in thinking it would have made much difference to his argument, though it was an intellectual flaw of which he was guilty and not a moral one.

His belief that people in a certain situation were bound to react, sooner or later, with aggression also explains his refusal in 1986 to condemn the violence by Unionists against the Anglo-Irish agreement. Partly because he was for most of his life a Christian, if not always of an orthodox kind (a highly individualistic person is likely to follow a highly individualistic form of Christianity), he had no illusions about the sinfulness, at any rate the imperfection, of human nature. This was coupled with an appreciation that partly because of the flaws in the Earthly world large populations, or at any rate distinct communities, of human beings (who to some extent were still animals) would always follow blind socioeconomic and political forces relating to identity and territory, leading in some scenarios to conflict. It was what he meant by "we are all racist". He may to some extent have been right (note I say "to some extent"). It had nothing to do with the (all-important) question of the moral and spiritual worth of *individuals*, which explained his Christianity and his high personal standards of integrity, both of which he held to while also espousing views that seemed contrary to the principle of racial integration and harmony.

But was he *right* in what he said in 1968? One senses that Powell today is becoming increasingly forgotten – he was always of more interest to the older than the younger generation after his loss of political prominence – or, maybe, the more sensitive the racial situation in Britain becomes the more inflammatory it seems to mention his name. Nonetheless his predictions serve as a litmus test for the success of the multicultural society. The trouble is that this whole thing tends to get put through a politically correct filter in that whereas there may be a case for expressing concern at the effects of more recent immigration, much of which is for one thing illegal (though even there, the parrot-cry of "racist" is heard) it is a different matter altogether when speaking of people whose families have now been living in this country for forty, fifty, sixty, even seventy years. To identify them as part of the problem is certainly regarded as unacceptable and indeed feels uncomfortable. It seems that some "multi-racial" societies work while others do not. Maybe further research is needed; I have not myself made a special study of these matters. In some cases the different races get on alright most of the time but periodically conflict flares up, which in itself highlights the complexity, and also perhaps the downside, of the whole business even if we are talking about a problem which is intermittent rather than chronic.

The proliferation at one time of TV programmes in which the question of national identity, and how to define it, was examined does tend to suggest an uneasy soul-searching, an underlying *angst*, rather than a nation confident that it knows which way it is going and that that direction is the right one. We would rather do without this. Then there is the "white flight", something which no less a personage than Trevor Phillips, former head of the Commission for Racial Equality, alluded to in a statement where he warned that Britain was sleep-walking towards segregation. The reason some areas of London and the other big cities have such a large ethnic minority (given how long some of it has been here for, it is vulgar and inaccurate to call it "immigrant") population is that the whites have voted with their feet. And although I am not convinced Powell was right when he appeared to think blacks and Asians would never integrate, would never be "British", it is possible for the conflict to be over race rather than nationality. After all, gender issues, another crucial topic within modern society, might be said to have caused social unrest, leading to violence, in early twentieth-century Britain when the suffragettes campaigned for the vote and met opposition; as we know there were demonstrations that turned ugly, hunger strikes, and what might be called terrorism (if in a relatively mild form) involving destruction of property. Things might have got a lot worse if the First World War had not intervened, resolving matters by creating an environment where all sections of society contributed to the war effort so that women afterwards had to be rewarded by being given what they wanted. The fact that both parties in the dispute, the suffragettes and those who would deny their sex the right to political participation, would have regarded themselves as "British" made no difference.

Meanwhile, there is often an over-promotion, much criticised, of ethnic minorities in advertising and the media, while attempts to celebrate specifically *white* culture, perhaps with the aim of highlighting the fact that whites are themselves an ethnic group with their own valid fears and aspirations, would almost certainly be regarded dubiously by political correctionists. And anti-white racism receives less attention from the establishment than the opposite – as in the decision by a judge that the killing of a white person by two Asians was not racist even though one of them had been heard to say "that'll teach a white man to poke his nose into our business". Such things prove that in one sense at least, if not in others, the black (or brown) man does have the whip-hand over the white, as Powell predicted he would. In racial matters as in his career as a whole it is possible to say that some of his forecasts have been borne out by events but others have not. There exists in fact a ludicrous situation in which the minorities are given too much attention at a relatively low level but not enough of them are appointed to senior positions; in other words, the political establishment has only succeeded in annoying whites while not giving nonwhites what they really want.

There is one respect in which the "multicultural society" has undoubtedly backfired disastrously. It can no longer be seriously denied that the white majority (along with ethnic minority citizens too) is at physical risk from certain elements within the Asian-descended population of Britain. I mean of course terrorism by radicalised Muslims, as seen in the 2005 London bombings plus the recent mass shooting in Manchester and the incident on Westminster Bridge. Particular groups within the white population are also vulnerable, as the grooming of young girls for sex by Asian men in certain parts of northern England, as a result of complex cultural issues which I won't go into in detail here, makes clear. When these things are reported one can almost physically sense Powell's presence in the room as he says "I told you so". And it is almost certain that if people in the 1940s, 50s and 60s had known they were going to happen, they would have frozen immigration immediately once it had served the purpose of filling the demographic and economic gap left by those killed in the Second World War. We did not see them coming, or recognise that they were a possibility in certain circumstances, and as a result have painted ourselves into a corner. It is not in any way racist to suggest that if people go to one country from another which has a history of political violence and instability (such as hasn't happened to anything like the same extent in most of the West most of the time, during the last couple of centuries) they will bring their faults with them; after all, white people exported their own to the territories they conquered during the imperial era, with shattering consequences for the indigenes. Admittedly, the terrorists in this case are usually relatively recent immigrants, as well as lone individuals with a tenuous connection to the mainstream Muslim community and a poor understanding of true Islam. But multiculturalism was undoubtedly a factor in their being here at all.

One must be fair, though. There is considerable and widespread discontent among young Muslims on account of the marginalisation and deprivation that exists within society and which no government, of whatever party, has really addressed. The feeling is shared by many young whites as well. It is akin to that engendered by the poverty and alienation of the early 1980s, when it was attempted to implement harsh Thatcherite economic policies during a recession. The latter issue led to the riots in Brixton and Liverpool in 1981, which likewise were not entirely a nonwhite v. white affair. Lord Scarman was entirely wrong in recommending "positive discrimination" as a means of solving the problem, but correct in identifying economic decline and social exclusion as the main cause of the violence (as it is now a cause of terrorism). Basically, a lot of what has gone wrong in the past has been the fault of the (predominantly white) political establishment, which among other things failed to see how different issues could link up.

And concerning the terrorism, most whites seem to take the view that we should not respond to anger with anger, hatred with hatred, violence with violence, and stereotype Asians/Muslims in a way which could lead to the breakdown of social harmony. If this is the case there is little point in objecting to it, if white concerns are considered to be the key factor, though to some extent, it is hard to say how great, people are probably inhibited from saying what they think because of the anticipated liberal reaction. Certainly, to attempt to "repatriate" the bulk of the nonwhite population against its wishes, or to try to force it to leave by sidelining it, would now result in as much of a bloodbath as a situation where the white and nonwhite elements were demographically balanced and one felt the other's presence to be an obstacle to its interests, resulting in civil war. Despite the danger of embarking on experiments where the stakes are high, there is a case for saying that only if we first try seriously to make the multicultural society work can we condemn it if it fails. On the sex grooming issue, when it was reported on the BBC recently one Muslim community leader did exactly the right thing in arguing that the feeling among some Asians that white girls were somehow worthless, which meant they could be used without scruple as sex toys, was a form of racism (which it was). That a member of an ethnic minority should say this ought to help towards reassuring whites that someone appreciates they may be vulnerable in a situation where they no longer form the majority of the population.

In extremis, perhaps, there is a view that the problems human society is currently facing, including potential racial conflict, are a sign of the End Of Days, during which law and order along with everything else breaks down and all kind of fears and hatreds rise to the surface, to be followed by the return of Christ and the Last Judgement. If this does occur then the "Rivers Of Blood" scenario may happen, though not for the exact reasons Powell thought they would. Nor in the same way; it may be a case not of all or most of the white population turning on the rest because they are considered a threat to it in one way or another, so much as of conflict between those who are prepared to subject society to political correctness on the minorities' behalf to avoid the evils of racism and those who think that is a step too far. And if the catastrophe does happen, whatever the form it takes and the precise explanation for it, that does not mean it would have happened in any case.

Meanwhile, most people don't seem inclined to rock the boat whether or not, by such forebearance, they are preventing the catastrophe or merely delaying it. Like most white British people Powell was a mixture to some extent of Celtic (his ancestors in fact came from Wales) and Germanic (through the Saxons) or Scandinavian genes. There is a case for arguing that in the British temperament the Nordic characteristics are dominant, resulting in a stoicism, even apathy, which prefers to let things take their course and eventually adapt to them. Though the contradictory sides of his personality – the passionate and excitable, versus the ruthlessly rational – were as much due to the different aspects of what could be called a medical condition, Germanic influences on Powell might help to explain his rigid devotion to logic (he was fascinated by the German philosophers), Celtic ones his volatility and the dark, melancholy aspect he took on while apparently contemplating some future Armageddon. When Enoch predicted that ordinary Britons would rise against multiculturalism I think his Celtic side failed to appreciate the power of Anglo-Saxon stolidity and sobriety. Those qualities can be dangerous in that they cause people to ignore problems until they can only be solved by doing something nasty, or beneficial in that they help change to take place peacefully, depending on your point of view.

The failure for the prophesied bloodbath to materialise is held up as proof that Powell was at best deranged and at worst just trying to stir up trouble out of hate. However the important thing to remember is that he was not concerned with the situation in the 1960s, 70s or 80s so much as the situation in the 1990s, 2000s, 2010s, 2020s and after. So perhaps, his supporters argue, the fact that the race war he predicted hasn't happened doesn't mean it won't. It merely hasn't happened *yet*. We could simply be talking about a time bomb, or a stick of dynamite with a long fuse. And whites have never been in a situation where they have gone from being the majority in a certain country to being the minority (which demographic projections imply they might eventually do in Britain), as opposed to the other way round (the USA, as it is now); in South Africa, Kenya etc. they were essentially a small ruling elite, however much they might have been resented as such.

Yet disaster is still not a foregone conclusion; for one thing Powell overlooked the possibility that younger whites, being more accustomed to a society less racially homogenous than it once was, will find the demographic changes easier to adjust to. On the understanding of course that one must be careful to avoid generalisations, there is much the young can be legitimately criticised for: their refusal to get involved in institutions, as opposed to communicating via the internet, their lack of interest in anything that is not "modern", their stereotyping of older people as racist because of the Brexit among other matters, and their unwillingness to do certain vital jobs which immigrants have to be brought in to fill, adding to population pressures. On the other hand no reasonable person can object if they simply have a different outlook on things, because they have grown up in what is in so many ways a different environment from their parents and grandparents; after all, it makes future racial tension much less likely. Being an academic, a scholar, an intellectual, Powell if he had read the passage in question – whether he ever did I have no idea – would not have minded, I suspect, Schoen's comparing him in his political behaviour to a philosopher formulating ideas, establishing that they are the incontrovertible truth and then basing his conduct around them. Now a philosophical thesis is flawed if it leaves out certain crucial factors or is based on assumptions that may be unwarranted. Here it might be added that although the increase in the size of the non-white population must inevitably change the character of the nation to some extent, it is the case that while the process is going on the minorities are living in what is still an overwhelmingly white society, which must necessarily change *them*, so that in many ways they are being absorbed into the majority community rather than the other way round. There may always be a difference between black and white, and in an imperfect world that difference can cause problems, but that does not mean the black has not "integrated", which is a different matter. Powell seemed to think that the ethnic minorities would *not* integrate, and yet I don't altogether get the sense that he was right. Certainly in the case of nonwhites who settled here from *Empire Windrush* up to, say, the 1980s. One might argue that it is rather the more recent immigration (some of it illegal, and/or from outside the Commonwealth) that has been encouraged not to assimilate under political correctness, which in its well-meaning attempts to recognise "diversity" stresses the differences rather than the similarities between people, and has tended in some cases to espouse militant anti-Western Islam, which does not integrate. We do not want to confuse two separate historical trends one of which might not happen if people were more prudent.

To take an overview of the situation during the first few postwar decades, Commonwealth immigrants were initially invited in to do the often dirty jobs that could not be performed by those who had been killed in the war. However the fact that they continued to come at a fairly fast rate into the 1960s and early 70s, and for cultural and economic reasons had large families, transformed society in a way that had not been expected. The white majority had not been prepared for the scale of the immigration and the impact it would have upon national life. But was that the immigrants' fault? In response to those who complained about their presence in the country they could have said perfectly reasonably, "If you don't want us here why did you let us in in the first place?" For their own part, they had expected prosperity and to be treated fairly and were frequently disappointed on both counts.

Where apparent statements of fact were concerned, Powell in the claims he made in 1968 was sometimes too ready to take things on trust, which didn't help his case; it appears the old white lady in an area affected by large-scale immigration who, it was alleged, had been frequently terrorised by young black thugs didn't actually exist. While if he really did make that remark about "wide-grinning piccaninnies", it was a rather poor show; all one can say there is that Powell, being human, was as potentially likely to be guilty at some point of actual racial offensiveness, however one regards his conduct the rest of the time, as anyone else.

But we can regard him as having indicated that at least the *possibility* of future racial warfare was inherent in the transformation immigration was bringing about. Originally I thought he was simply misguided on the issue; then I could at least understand what he meant, disassociating it correctly from mere prejudice, and can picture him looking down from Heaven, if that's where he is, with an expression of sardonic amusement at my *volte face*. But as stated above I do not necessarily agree that his fears were valid, as I might have done once; it was a *volte face* X2. It has been said of Powell that he got some things spectacularly right (i.e., his prediction that the Common Market/European Community/European Union would try to turn itself from a purely commercial affair to a political entity overriding the constitutions of its member states, and so provoking opposition to it) and others spectacularly wrong. The things he got spectacularly wrong are regarded as including his predictions on race/immigration. And he undoubtedly was mistaken on certain vital points, as has been indicated.

In his view the nation state is the primary unit of political organisation. It must therefore be protected from internal strife as well as hostile foreign powers. Since its character derives from that of the race which makes up most of its population, changes in the demographics can therefore have a dysfunctional and divisive effect on national identity and unity, creating the kind of internal conflict which has to be avoided. Powell was right in thinking that the desirability or otherwise of immigration was really a matter of numbers, since only large ones risked having the consequences he sought to avert. He was too rational, too cerebral a person to object to someone simply because they had a different skin colour or culture; nor was he opposed to the principle of interracial marriage, as we will see.

But the question is not whether one considers oneself to be *British*, because it is clear many ethnic minority people do (even if there are significant elements, such as the Islamic extremists, who do not or who attach a label to themselves merely because it is convenient to do so). The quarrel is more over racial identity – always a factor whatever happens – than national, more over how Britishness should be defined than whether such a quality exists, the implication seeming to be that it does.

We can qualify our reaction to Powell's views by recognising not that the "rivers of blood" scenario is inevitable, but rather that it is a possibility, at any rate, *if people are not sensible.* There is a failure, from an excessive guilt complex about a racist and imperialist past, to address legitimate white fears, to acknowledge issues such as cross-racial sexual abuse, and to accept that the overconcentration on white racism may merely make whites more vulnerable to revenge attacks when they themselves become an ethnic minority – as current predictions make clear will at some point happen. As long as these matters are not confronted racial tension will always be there and we cannot assume it will never explode catastrophically, maybe despite differences of outlook between generations.

To be brutally frank, the claim that the failure for there to be, with the exception of certain districts at certain times, "rivers of blood" proves Powell was wrong is questioned if, as seems possible, it is due to the "white flight" from areas of the big cities which are predominantly black and/or Asian; a phenomenon which in the long run will not resolve the issue and only succeeds in dividing the nation dangerously. But if the catastrophe does occur it will be down to the flaws in an imperfect world – or to people foolishly ignoring valid white concerns over certain matters – rather than to anyone being inferior or superior. Powell was too logical and rational to believe in the latter notion. If he had not been, he would have joined the National Front or the BNP, yet it is conspicuous that he didn't.

In fairness to him and his supporters, it is probably not a good thing to have a non-white town dominating a still predominantly white countryside, as clearly it will if the demography continues to change. Not least because the city is where all the action is going on. There are cultural implications; apparently schoolchildren at a village in rural Dorset were upset at being given storybooks in which a high proportion of the characters were black, reflecting urban realities, because they were expected to identify with a situation that was alien to them. Black children in apartheid South Africa often drew themselves as whites because there were no images of their own race in publications issued under a white government; though its historical causes would not have been quite the same, could we not get the same thing happening here in Britain, in reverse? Solving the problem by federating the nation would not meet with Powell's approval as that would go against its essential unity, a principle he always adhered to. He anticipated this kind of dilemma, just as he anticipated that ethnic minorities would be frozen out to some extent, exacerbating racial tension, as a response to what in some ways was their growing power. I don't know what the solution to it is, although I will not say that it can't be a peaceful one.

Another serious issue which we need to confront represents an exception to the integration of ethnic minorities with mainstream society; it is arguably the only, but also a particularly serious, one as it is so much to do with national identity, which is bound up with history and the latter's role in the cultural selfconsciousness of a nation or race. I will mention again, in a later chapter, the apparent lack of interest by ethnic minorities in white history unless it is with the aim of focusing attention on past racism. The failure to identify with it because of slavery has implications for future white cultural identity. How is a predominantly white history to be taught in what will eventually be a predominantly nonwhite country? If it is not, whites will find that vital cultural identity compromised, and despite the different philosophies of the older and younger generations (something which itself emphasises the tendency for outlooks to change as people age) it is hard to see how this can cause anything other than rootlessness and restlessness, alienation, unless one takes the view that you can simply present history how you like (a view encouraged, if perhaps unintentionally, by the liberties taken in the film *Darkest Hour*), which would merely be to foster an equally harmful phenomenon. Whether Powell during his lifetime was conscious of this potential issue is not clear but it would not be surprising if he was. Probably he took the ruthlessly realistic (and thus typical of him) view that human beings were not so nice or rational as to either refrain from enslaving people or, in the long run, react to the slavery in a sensible way.

It may not be the case that Powell always held the views he did without reservation. In 1988, when asked by broadcaster Nick Ross what he thought about ethnic intermarriage, he suggested it might be a good thing because the blending of races would mean there was less likely to be antagonism between them. It promoted the integration which in the past he had suggested would *not* happen. Apart from the fact that this is not the kind of thing you would expect from someone who was racist in the generally understood sense, it suggests, given that intermarriage was by then on the increase, and known to be on the increase including presumably by Powell himself, that he was prepared to consider the possibility his essential thinking back in 1968 might after all have been mistaken. It is not something his detractors generally seem aware of and one suspects they would not give him credit for it if they were, although I may be wrong.

One last word on the question of Powell and immigration. In early 1969 Powell was interviewed on TV by David Frost in what became a heated and therefore highly entertaining discussion on the subject. Twenty-five years later, in 1993, Frost commented on the occasion thus in a documentary on his career: "We tried to expose Enoch Powell as a racist…we didn't succeed." This is an interesting statement because it suggests one can, indeed, express the views Powell did without being guilty of racism, which makes the vehement condemnation of him for it by the Left look unfair and unwarranted. One thing they overlook is that not all ethnic minority citizens saw Powell as they did; on his death Tara Mukherjee, President of the Confederation of Indian Organisations UK, opined along with Denis Healey that he was not a racist but rather an extreme nationalist. Nor did all left-wing politicians, in fact. Michael Foot has already been mentioned; on a personal level Healey's relations with Powell seem to have been friendly, despite the two strongly disagreeing on political matters; and then there is Tony Benn, perhaps most significant at all given that he was the ideological opposite of Powell and one of the people you'd have thought most likely to be hostile to him. The two were on good terms throughout most of Powell's life; and commenting on the "rivers of blood" speech, Benn stated that it had given succour to various unsavoury and bigoted characters "of whom he {Powell} was not one." At the time of the speech Benn had declared that the same flag which flew over the Nazi concentration camps was now flying over Wolverhampton. But it has to be accepted that for many the game of politics is a business of nailing your colours to a chosen mast, appealing to a certain constituency, in order to gain attention, build a power base and so further both your own prospects and your chances of putting your policies into practice through achieving office. The issues on which one chooses to do this can be reflected on with objectivity and humanity in the autumn of one's career, when these considerations no longer apply.

In any case it would be wrong to let our estimate of Powell be coloured, so to speak, by this one issue even if we were justified in thinking the worst of him because of his opinions on it. Powell suffered along with Neville Chamberlain, though not quite in the same way, from becoming closely identified with a controversial approach to a particular matter, in Chamberlain's case foreign policy. It should be remembered that he, Powell, had strong views on a wide range of matters. As well as immigration he was concerned with Britain's place in the modern world and in particular her relationship with the rest of Europe. He seems to have felt that she should pursue an independent course in world affairs, rather than play second fiddle to Washington (he was never happy with what he saw as Margaret Thatcher's kow-towing to Ronald Reagan) or Brussels. He believed that membership of the EEC, with laws enacted in Brussels taking precedence over those passed at Westminster, would compromise Britain's independence, and thus her freedom – it amounted basically to the same thing – as well as any focus for patriotism because there would no longer be a state in its own right which one could feel loyalty towards. Whether he was correct to argue for total withdrawal from the EU is a matter of opinion, but his fears would seem substantiated by increasing evidence of, and public concern over, the growing power of Brussels and the implications of absurd laws – affecting the proper punishment of wrongdoers among other things – which had a damaging effect upon British identity and liberties yet which the government in London seemed powerless to prevent until the Brexit. Powell realised, correctly, that the nation was the only sensible unit of government in the earthly world. Anything else would be too large to run efficiently or democratically, nor could it keep the loyalty of its citizens. The nation state therefore needed to be preserved. A comparatively recent (nineteenth century) creation, it has not yet had its day and in fact will always be essential as a counter to unitary tendencies which may be harmful to liberty even if well-intentioned. For these reasons it is necessary to ensure its independence and its cohesion as a social and political organism.

In economic affairs Powell's support for monetarism and the free market – for what, in Britain, later became Thatcherism – against state intervention and corporatism was perhaps inevitable in a man of a strongly individual temperament. And who was perhaps cold and ruthless – though not in any wicked sense – enough to reject the idea of the state as a benevolent guardian protecting the ordinary citizen from potential hardship, if such was not seen as a guarantor of efficiency. I think the best comment on Thatcherism would be that it was a good idea done badly. It has now had its day, become more a liability than an asset. Its chief defect, of course, was the assumption that left to its own devices the private sector would behave sensibly, acting in the interests of the consumer as well as itself, without any need for regulation. The recession caused by the banking crisis, controversial bonuses, a situation where employees and unions are often left without any power at all, and the widening gap between rich and poor prove this to be false.

Powell was wrong about the Commonwealth and about life peers. It is nice to think that the Empire lives on in a more acceptable form, even if it is more of a (hopefully) friendly club than an institution with real clout on the international scene. As for the Lords, a body which, let's face it, is fundamentally undemocratic yet intended to have some influence over policy, even if it can only delay legislation, would be entirely impossible to defend if it did not make some concession, at least, to merit; a man or woman cannot be considered competent to play a part in the constitutional process just because of who their parents happen to be. On the subject of embryo research, the ability to get what one wants from stem cells is perhaps a way of making the practice more acceptable, and therefore less controversial.

There were, of course, many other issues on which Powell commented eloquently and with passion, but there is not the space to go into them all here.

*

I may have said this already, but the more one learns about Enoch Powell, the less likely it seems he could ever have become Prime Minister. Not only does his history of resigning on matters of conscience suggest he would fairly soon have stepped down for some principled reason, but a man who never quite accepted the twentieth century could not have functioned effectively in such a capacity. At Westminster he didn't have a proper office, working instead from the House of Commons library by the light of a pair of Victorian brass candlesticks. He took eccentricity and love of tradition to absurd lengths. The pinstripe suit and homburg he often wore seemed to belong to an earlier era. On a colloquial level he probably did not understand the modern world and this was an obstacle to his gelling and communicating with people beyond his immediate social, professional and academic circle. His frequent prickliness, too, would have made him difficult if not impossible to work with (being Prime Minister requires very different skills from those involved in simply holding ministerial office, even at a senior level). The kind of relationship between the person at the top, and their subordinates in whatever capacity, which is essential in such a situation (a different one from giving orders as an army officer, which of course Powell had done during the war, and having them obeyed without question) would have been impossible for him. Moreover, evasiveness and double-dealing have always characterised politics to some extent and the greater the power one wields, and the higher the stakes, the more such tactics are likely to be employed if they seem the best, perhaps the only, way of doing what is desired or needed. A man of Powell's integrity would have found the ethical compromises forced on him by the office impossible to make. Altogether, the idea of Powell as PM just doesn't ring true. But assuming he ever had a chance of reaching the top in the first place, and the fact that he stood for the Tory leadership in 1965 suggests he would have liked to, what lessons can those wishing to challenge the political establishment on crucial issues learn from his failure to get there? There are several. We have already mentioned the need to explain your beliefs properly. Secondly you must be prepared to organise support for yourself. Powell never tried to create an official political party, or an organised party within a party, to back him up; had he done so the course of his career and of British politics might have been very different. But he felt that kind of thing was beneath him. His very individualism, and his excessively high standards, stood in the way of his success. Whether this was ultimately a good or a bad thing, he did as we have noted take standing on principle to excessive lengths. At any rate, though he acted as a focus for a particular strand of opinion – anti-immigration, anti-

Europe, defensive of traditional institutions and customs – within the country he never translated that into formal political structures geared to attaining power, though arguably it had a significant effect in purely *electoral* terms.

It is worth noting that the results of Schoen's research into the basis and extent of Powell's support in the country and in parliament suggest more people admired him than were prepared to campaign actively in his favour, whether within or outside the official Tory Party machine. As is the case in such situations, an actual "Enoch Powell Party" would probably have consisted of the kind of people whose support Powell would not actually have wanted, that is an eccentric/extremist minority. Furthermore, it is not going too far to suggest that by failing to organise his supporters in the same way that maverick right- or left-wing politicians on the Continent have sometimes done (which the British character balks at in any case), Powell might well have saved his life. With a coherent and distinct party machine ("Powellight" was not that but rather a series of publications of his speeches) behind him he would have seemed more of an effective threat to racial harmony and might well have been assassinated, either by black militants or by MI5 seeking to eliminate a danger to peaceful community relations and thus the stability of the realm.

What, then, was Enoch Powell's contribution? What did he achieve? The answer to this is not immediately apparent, which has enabled his critics to mock him, as did *Private Eye* (probably because of Paul Foot, a leading contributor to it) in the edition which came out just after his death, where he is mentioned as the man who ran the Footpaths Committee in the parish of St Albions in 1958. But he accomplished rather more than is apparent at first sight. He was, for a time, a political force to be reckoned with despite not being a party leader or holding ministerial office, because of the support he commanded within the country. He could boast that he had turned Labour out in 1970 and put them back in in 1974. He has been called the original Thatcherite, his monetarist economic policies anticipating those which later were actually implemented by the Conservatives, although it is probably true to say the Thatcherite revolution would have happened regardless of what Powell had believed in the 1950s, 60s and 70s; there is no causal, if interrupted, link between the two. He was a good Minister of Health, although one biographer of Iain Macleod, whose subject served in the same post for a time, remarks that Powell came over as an efficient inspector, Macleod as a man who cared. He was responsible by his badgering for a considerable reduction in the scale of immigration (gaining on this issue roughly half of what he had wanted). And, viewed from any angle, his career is of importance precisely because he *did* fail to attain the dizzy heights of Number Ten, or anything approaching it. It shows the strength, for better or for worse, of the existing mainstream political system.

Otherwise, whether the achievement has survived is more doubtful. Any benefits to be gained from cutting immigration have been offset in recent years by the general increase in those entering the country both from within the

European Union, between whose members there now operates an "open door" policy, and outside it, the latter category including what are called "asylum seekers", along with the continuing growth of the ethnic minority population already here (supposing one regards it as a problem). Until recently most of the other causes for which Powell fought seemed hopelessly lost, too. The general assault on traditional British identities from political correctness, and the increasing intrusion, often in absurd ways, of the ever-more powerful EU into national life would have saddened and sickened him. As would devolution for Scotland and Wales, perhaps a prelude to the breakup of a United Kingdom he always strove to keep intact, and in particular the "West Lothian" question; the haemorrhaging of power from his beloved parliament to presidential-style Prime Ministers; and the debasement of public life by spin doctors and by the premiership of Tony Blair, side-by-side with a general decline in the morality and integrity of politicians. What would have offended him most about political correctness would have been its apparent belief that you could legislate to make people virtuous, something which went against his whole approach to public affairs and to life.

It was fortunate that Powell never lived to see the worst of all this. The "West Lothian" issue would particularly have excited, and angered, him because England was unable any more to legislate for Scotland on important issues but Scottish and Welsh MPs could still vote at Westminster on matters affecting England. As he saw it, for communities to be part of the same national unit was only possible if they governed each other equally. He would have seen the form devolution took in 1999 as political chicanery of the worst kind, designed to strengthen New Labour's position north of the border (and it hasn't always served *that* purpose in any case!).

Posthumously, he would seem to have secured at least one major triumph, though how far, in 2016 when he had been dead for some time and faded from the public consciousness to some extent, it was due to his influence is debatable. The Brexit would presumably have delighted him – I am constantly imagining Edward Heath's ghost fuming, and Powell's rejoicing, over it – though one can conceive of him expressing reservations as to whether it would amount to as much as he wished.

Globally, the relative decline in Britain's status would appear to be irreversible. It stems from a historical process which neither Powell nor anyone else could have arrested. Its native mineral resources having become exhausted, Britain no longer has the economic strength to be a world power in other than those relative terms; accordingly she is subject to decisions made in the US, Germany, Japan, China and India. She does not have the means to pursue an independent course in world affairs and must choose between Europe (which means submerging her identity in an emerging federal superstate that is becoming increasingly autocratic) and America (potentially unfortunate given the results of Tony Blair's entanglement with George W Bush, which one can hear Powell's shade bemoaning for he was always against military involvement where no actual threat to the security of the United Kingdom was evident, and the behaviour of Donald Trump). She does at least retain her nuclear deterrent, although how far she could use it without US permission is debatable (probably not very far actually). Powell was always dubious about the value of having a weapon which, unless you were mad, you would probably never deploy anyway; however, no-one could ever be 100% *sure* you wouldn't, and it is that uncertainty, however slight, that allows the deterrent to work, preventing both nuclear wars and conventional ones which could be just as devastating or, depending on their extent, even more so. This was another area where Powell, rigidly logical, failed to understand the *illogical* (perhaps) thinking of other people.

It is difficult to say what Powell would have thought of power-sharing and the other political changes made in Northern Ireland since the Good Friday agreement; but essentially, what has happened in Ulster, and has made real progress towards peace possible, is an effective separation of the civil rights issue from that of whether there should be a "united Ireland". This ought to have pleased Powell, whether or not it would have done, since preserving Ulster's status as part of the United Kingdom was one of his main concerns.

*

Enoch Powell was a person of contrasts; a man who could be very warm and friendly one moment and very cold and unfriendly at another. One could put it down to having been an only child, which is known to sometimes, though by no means always, have that effect (witness Arthur Scargill). His apparent rudeness was a result of a shyness, an insecurity, which persisted all through his adult life. Even when a distinguished parliamentarian of many years standing, he still confessed to an attack of nerves before getting up to make a speech.

There could have been something else, too (and others have realised that, as a trawling of the internet will show). In Powell one can recognise some, at least, of the symptoms of Asperger Syndrome, a medical condition not fully diagnosed until 1994. There need be nothing offensive about such a suggestion. Many sufferers are, like Powell, highly intelligent. They are child prodigies of enormous talent and ability who can sometimes find it difficult to emotionally relate to other people. They are single-minded to the point of being obsessive. They may dislike change and identify very closely, sometimes excessively, with the historic ethnic/national community into which they were born and its traditions (Powell failed to see that many of the policies he recommended were simply not practical in modern conditions). They may experience frustration and failure later on, through the effect of their own personalities and/or the failure of others to understand them, and be marginalised in a way which prevents society from making full use of their talents. They can stubbornly cling to beliefs even when they are erroneous.

They can find it hard to relax. They can be highly emotional and their behaviour at times eccentric. They can sometimes stare fixedly. They can be insensitive and unnecessarily abrupt. They are less likely to care what others think of them, though they may in the first place have chosen whatever course of action they did with methodical precision, which can also be a symptom of the condition.

Asperger's is far more common than is usually understood; one current theory is that as many as 5-7% of the population suffer from it in some form. Mozart, Isaac Newton and Einstein are among historical figures thought to have had it. It can be severe or relatively mild in its effects. It also takes a variety of forms, which is why one hears talk of the "autism spectrum". There is a horizontal as well as a vertical differentiation. Some sufferers are barely articulate, cannot communicate, find contact of any sort with others repellent and are prone to embarrassing behaviour in public (though the worst of this is often overcome as the sufferer progresses from child- to adulthood). Others speak beautiful English (as Powell did), run their own companies, can form friendships and be happily married with two children (as Powell was). Some can be unfeeling, a part of the time at least, and others deeply compassionate.

The characteristics that Powell and I both had in common could possibly have been explained by Asperger's, and the more I came to realise I had the condition the more I became interested in him. His insensitive side (which I like to think I lack) might have been due to it, as also might a particularly strong attachment to his own culture and nationality. It must also explain, by a similar token, his being old-fashioned to the point of potential absurdity, which is a not uncommon feature of the condition; the pinstripe suit, along with other of his habits, endured into the 1980s at least.

It would be degrading to Enoch Powell, as to anyone else with the condition, to suggest that everything he did and said and thought was down to it. That people, not necessarily bad people, make that sort of assumption is a common problem faced by Asperger's sufferers. And it is often the tendency of one's opponents to consciously or subconsciously portray as the product of illness (if that is the right way to describe the condition) a belief with which they don't happen to be comfortable as a way of discrediting it, whatever they think of the "sufferer" morally. There are many human faults which are not a preserve of those who happen to have Asperger Syndrome. Powell could conceivably have held the views he did whether he had had the condition or not; he was just more likely to be forthright in the way he expressed them, and regardless of whether some would find them offensive. Depending on the severity of the condition, it does *not* mean that one is not responsible for one's actions. That can hardly be true of a man who deliberated for some time before making up his mind on important issues – and who waited so long before speaking out the way he did on immigration, another thing held against him by those who accuse him of hypocrisy, precisely because of the unpleasantness he knew it would cause. The failure to see the need to properly explain his "racist" beliefs *was* a product of the Asperger's, and one which caused a lot of trouble for himself and others.

On many political issues he was a pragmatist, rather than a wicked man. He felt that when practicalities necessitated a particular policy morality didn't come into it anyway, though the disastrous results of abandoning a common sense approach meant that it could be seen as immoral to do so, if our aim should be to strive for the (inevitably imperfect) best. He felt that because time had made them irreversible the consequences of the English occupation of Ulster in the sixteenth and seventeenth centuries should be accepted *whether or not that action had been justified;* he was not denying that the British could wrong the Irish, that Unionists could mistreat Nationalists. On race his view would have been that if, in Heaven, there were no nation states and anyone could live wherever they liked without damaging others' sense of identity, that would be fine. But the earthly world was not a perfect one and while it endured you had to play the game according to its rules, which meant being realistic – in Powell's case, because of the flaws in his character, brutally and coldly so.

The game, where it involved politics, could be harsh. He recognised that and it was humility which caused him to apply his own dictum that "all political lives end in failure" (though he was not quite expressing an absolute truth there) to himself. He did admit to being intellectually arrogant at times, but knew he should make no special claim to power or be bitter and offended (as opposed to merely regretful) when he failed to achieve it or saw his policies rejected. The same kind of integrity entailed, I believe, that if he could be shown any of his cherished convictions to have been wrong in the long run he would have admitted it. Had he been transported fifty or a hundred years forward in time and found a world where full racial integration had been achieved in Britain, the whites even accepting the loss of their traditional status and not in any way suffering from it, he would have acknowledged his error quite happily.

I suspect the less attractive aspects of his personality were things he couldn't easily help; we know the reason for them. Much else stemmed from conviction, rather than perversity. From a Christian point of view, if he still believed, albeit in his own peculiar way, in the necessity of redemption through faith in Jesus Christ and His sacrifice then perhaps he has earned a place in Heaven. I would certainly like to think so. You certainly can't get there without being motivated by conscience in what you do, as opposed to prejudice or any other unworthy motive. On that score Enoch Powell is up there among the angels, however unlikely it might seem to some. Certainly, we need to be objective about him. I realise that sometimes this may not be possible, but where it is we ought to make the effort. Because political correctness is so dominant, and the nonwhite population in the big cities growing and thus increasingly powerful in many ways, Powell cannot, sadly, be honoured in his native Birmingham and Wolverhampton (the city where he was born, and that which he served dutifully as an MP for nearly twenty-five years, respectively).

Such is inevitable. But in addition, it will eventually become very difficult to publish a balanced account of Powell's life, career and beliefs; the winning side writes the history. And yet this is a trend which must be resisted. For without objectivity history is simply propaganda, or passion, however understandable, that is not tempered by reason and may therefore result in a skewed to a greater or lesser extent view of things. A necessary part of avoiding this is to appreciate the factors which motivated a historical personality in their words and deeds rather than demonise them, even where they were wrong. If you don't mind me putting it this way, the matter can't be seen only in black and white.

2

Israel, the Jews and the Holocaust

You may remember the controversy over the War Crimes Bill back in the 1990s. I suspect the fervent desire that suspected Nazi war criminals resident in Britain be prosecuted arose partly from fear that since they were all now quite elderly, they might die before they could be brought to justice. Another reason for it, which may to some extent have been a cover for vengefulness but was not in itself altogether invalid, was that by bringing the whole issue of the Holocaust to the public mind it would ensure people did not forget it and would therefore, among other things, make it less likely it would be repeated. Whatever the exact motivation behind the lobbying for the Bill its supporters were undoubtedly passionate and determined, and sufficiently dismayed by the House of Lords' initial rejection of it for Greville Janner MP to describe their decision as a "misjudgement".

Despite its undemocratic nature the Lords – which contains, as well as hereditary peers and political nominees, a significant number of people who have been elevated to it because of excellence in their chosen fields (in other words are experts, and from the point of view of intelligence and competence probably more qualified to run the country than our elected representatives) – has often been perceived as wiser than the Commons, and its power to delay legislation in order to allow time for a rethink as not necessarily a bad thing. The danger of the War Crimes Bill, as it saw it, was twofold. Firstly, due to the time which had elapsed since the atrocities mistakes might occur and an innocent person be wrongly convicted. In fact, I suspect this wasn't that likely; if someone had treated me as Jews and other victims of the Nazis were treated in the concentration camps, I'd probably recognise them even 60 or 70 years later. But maybe one can't be entirely sure, and in any case it would not be a principle that could be admitted by the law, which must necessarily operate in an entirely different way. The other principal objection to the Bill is even more pertinent and possibly the one which really motivated the Lords in throwing it out. To spend a lot of time hunting down, prosecuting and imprisoning men who may not be in jail for very long before illness demands their release on compassionate grounds, or they die of natural causes, somehow seems mean, even grotesque and farcical. The case of a suspect who died before he could be tried (he was very feeble, as a news clip of him being helped to a car showed) highlights the point. How do we know that (a) he wasn't innocent, unlikely as it seems, and that (b) the stress of the matter didn't contribute to his death? The argument that prosecution of the accused was necessary because it reminded society of the crime which was being punished could be met with the objection that it was liable to have exactly the opposite effect to that intended; it reminded people in entirely the wrong way. It came over as vengeful and vindictive, and in some respects inhumane; making *us* seem to be the oppressors, rather than the Nazis. Apart from being questionable in itself it was as much likely to fuel anti-Semitism as to combat it. I fail to see how acting from both sensible and humanitarian motives, as I believe the Lords did, can be called a "misjudgement".

Clearly it won't do to be heavy-handed; Greville Janner's attitude was understandable, given that he lost half his family to the Nazis. In his position, I might well have adopted the same stance. But what we understand, we do not have to condone. We might well have felt and acted as he did, had we been in his shoes. Nonetheless, we must at least try to be objective. In the end, of course, the Lords did not get their way; the Commons passed the Bill. There were, so far as I am aware, no tragic miscarriages of justice as a result of it, though that does not mean Greville Janner was right. I suspect any surviving Nazis who have not yet been tried are too old now to prosecute. If the measure ever was likely to be harmful in any way I suspect that harm has already been done. It was altogether a messy business and emphasises how unfortunate it was that for one reason or other many war criminals were not brought to justice decades earlier when they were a lot younger. But the purpose of this article, none of whose content is intended lightly, is to argue that responses to anti-Semitism can themselves be unjust, and therefore counter-productive.

A lot of the pressure to punish those who perpetrated the Holocaust, whatever the arguments against doing so where there is a query, and to emphasise its horrific nature has stemmed from a belief that somehow it was uniquely awful, worse than any other atrocity committed by human beings during the bloody history of our species. If we pose the question of whether this view is correct it is not just because of the War Crimes Bill but because the whole subject is controversial and emotionally highly charged; with the potential, for that very reason, to perhaps lead to injustice and discrimination.

Those who make the claim imply that the Holocaust was worse in terms of (a) scale, (b) nature or (c) both. On all three counts their assertions may be questioned.

Scale. The argument falls flat here because Stalin is reckoned to have killed more people than Hitler (Genghis Khan is said to have run up an even more impressive death toll, some forty million Chinese peasants over a certain period, which speaks for itself). The exact figure cannot be known, because such things are always impossible to establish, but by the same token the figure of six million Jews murdered by the Nazis can only be an arbitrary one, David Irving notwithstanding. According to a sort of sliding scale, if one figure can be inaccurate then so can the other, and the former may still in proportion be greater. Even if the number of Jews (and that is leaving out those of his victims who were *not* Jews) Hitler slaughtered *was* greater than the number of people murdered by Stalin for whatever reason he thought fit, there are no grounds for supposing that other atrocities could not have wiped out even more lives, given the difficulty of arriving at accurate totals, along with the known tendency of some humans to carry out massacres on whatever scale opportunity allows. This is the crucial point; if it is *possible* to kill more people (of whatever kind and for whatever motive) than the Nazis did then the Holocaust cannot, in principle, be considered unique. We'd end up conducting the argument on the basis of chance – on whether or not the person intending to carry out the crime actually managed to do so. It may be added that weapons of mass destruction, whether bacteriological, chemical or nuclear, now enable us to destroy far more of our fellow creatures than Hitler and Stalin combined.

In one sense, of course, scale does make one atrocity more serious than another. If lives have individual value then they will have cumulative value, and therefore a crime is obviously more terrible the more people die in it, whatever the exact numerical difference involved. But by this yardstick the Holocaust would have to be considered a *lesser* crime than some. We should be careful, in any case, of making scale the principal issue. It matters on both a practical and a moral level because the ethical thing to do is preserve as many lives as possible. But if, say, we choose saving six million Jews over saving five million Gentiles – or the converse – from some unspecified tragedy, whether natural or man-made, it must be because of the numbers involved rather than who the people are. When someone pointed out that the Nazis had murdered X (a greater) number of Jews as opposed to Y (a lesser) number of gypsies, the writer Christopher Isherwood replied "Oh, are you in real estate?". It can seem like we are simply playing about with statistics when contrasted with the awful reality of mass murder, irrespective of who is being murdered. In one sense Isherwood was wrong to object, as I've made clear. But if the speaker was implying that once it's established that it exists the numerical difference, however great, is a serious matter because of the category of people who are being killed, this view is only permissible if we regard the murder of a Jew as more serious than that of a gypsy or a homosexual (and we can't, even if we are among those who still think that homosexuality is a sin).

Nature. Another reason the Holocaust is considered unique is the character of the crime itself. As with anything emotionally and morally repugnant the full horror of it is hard to describe in words, but one reason why it is thought *particularly* horrible is the chillingly efficient way it was carried out – the transformation of people into numbers, statistics, by Nazi bureaucrats, and the way that efficiency seemed to justify it in the minds of its perpetrators. Undoubtedly, this *was* horrible. But surely the abduction, rape and murder of young children (Milly Dowler, Holly Wells and Jessica Chapman, and the victims of the Moors Murderers), in the latter case at least involving sexual torture, can't be any less so. Serial killers, whether or not their motive is sexual, usually don't manage to despatch thousands or millions of people unless they're very lucky (it would help if they could get their hands on weapons of mass destruction), and some for whatever reason may only kill once (whether Ian Huntley would have gone on to commit other murders if not jailed for those of Holly and Jessica we don't know). But the actions of these people show that it takes the same amount of evil to kill one person as it does to kill six million. It's not the awfulness but rather the motive – the latter does not make a difference to the extent of the former – that is different. The killing of the six million is usually political, in that it stems from a debased ideology, and it requires membership of some kind of an organisation which can become the government, as the Nazis did in Germany, and thus be in a better position to arrange mass genocide if it wants to. This is ruled out for many (perhaps not all) serial killers by their being dysfunctional loners, even if sometimes their crimes are an attempt to make a kind of statement (and may be motivated by hatred of a particular group within society). The nature of the crimes is *different*, in many ways, from those of the Nazis but that doesn't make them any less appalling. I suspect we all have our favourite atrocity, meaning that which we find affects us the most. Personally, the most distressing thing that comes to my mind where human evil is concerned, after watching a TV programme on the Moors Murders, is Lesley Ann Downey's mother knowing that her daughter, being abused by Brady and Hindley, had been crying for her and that she had been unable to help. Which does one regard as worse: the crimes of Hindley and Brady, the Holocaust because of the chillingly bureaucratic way it was carried out, 9/11 because it was the first and has so far been the only time aircraft carrying live passengers were used as bombs – always the most disturbing aspect of that particular business – or the 2004 Beslan school siege in Russia because of the way the terrorists specifically targeted children? Apart from the suggestion that one atrocity can be more atrocious than another seeming rather like my once describing Doctor Who's TARDIS as semi-indestructible, or Eccles in the Goon Show trying to prove his immortality ("I'm living forever as fast as I can!"), attempting to distinguish between the two in terms of seriousness would be at best a minefield and at worst invidious. I don't know – perhaps I can never know – what it must have been like for the trainloads of people who were to pass through the gas chambers, whether they guessed what was going to happen to them, although the gassing itself was not, I understand, a pleasant death. But imagine a panel of experts sitting down to decide, by quantifying the degree of mental and physical suffering involved (is that even possible?), whether it is worse for a little girl to be abducted, stripped naked, sexually abused and then murdered, or arrested, packed onto a train, stripped and then sent to a gas chamber because someone does not like her ethnicity, and you can see what I'm trying to get at. The only thing which might make the Moors Murders less serious than the Holocaust would be the number of people involved – obviously a lot less – but even then, most would balk at being forced to say which was worse. All we *can* say is that it would be permissible for us to let scale be the deciding factor, but forgiveable if we didn't.

The Holocaust produces revulsion because of the clinical, mechanical fashion in which its victims were disposed of. It was an operation carried out with ruthless technical efficiency, which one might regard as typically

Germanic. A comparison, always interesting, between Stalin and Hitler, the two great mass murderers of the twentieth century, reveals contrasts in the way they did things. If Hitler employed the bureaucratic skills of the German middle classes, their ability to organise, to execute his victims the way Stalin operated was characterised more by a coarse peasant brutality – his social origins were after all different. With him it was more a case of "Ah, throw another Cossack on the fire." This is no less appalling (and no less excusable because life may have seemed cheap in a country with a vast population, hardened by a cold climate, and a history of treating people harshly). It's more the *way* in which it's appalling that differs. Stalin killed anyone he had a grudge against or who he sensed did not altogether agree with his policies, which is surely no more legitimate than doing it on grounds of race. He escaped, and still escapes, condemnation as severe as that meted out to Hitler because he was our ally, not our enemy, in the Second World War. Because the Cold War never escalated into a hot one in which his troops might have committed atrocities in occupied territories. Because although the inhabitants of the Eastern European nations were not well treated when absorbed against their will into the Soviet Bloc after 1945, most of Stalin's victims during the whole period of his ascendancy, as opposed to Hitler's in his, were domestic – as if that makes it any better (the treatment of German civilians by the Red Army is perhaps more forgiveable, if still wrong, on account of what the Germans themselves had done earlier on). And because Stalin had not at the time of his death begun to persecute the Jews – although the indications are that he was planning to. Above all else, it should not matter if someone is gassed according to a certain plan or crudely bludgeoned to death (the Nazis did that sort of thing too). The result is the same; a life which may be innocent has been wrongly taken. Morally, that need be the only thing which concerns us.

Except from the academic point of view there is nothing to be gained by drawing a distinction between the Holocaust and the more uncoordinated kind of killing which went on under Stalin, as Laurence Rees does on p211-212 of *War of the Century* (BBC 1999), his book on the Soviet-German conflict during World War Two. Certain facts may, on top of purely scholarly interest, be useful in predicting what *sort* of atrocities are likely to happen, how and where, and therefore in preventing them. But it does not prove that one atrocity really is more atrocious than another. There is a danger we may simply end up debating the aesthetics of evil, if I may put it like that. Alan Bullock ends his *Hitler and Stalin: Parallel Lives* by concluding that the nature of the Holocaust demonstrates Hitler was, in fact, the more evil of the two men. On the back cover of my edition of the book a reviewer comments that its conclusions are "sane and balanced"; if this is meant to apply to an argument which is in fact not logically sustainable, and also discriminatory, I beg to differ with it; that is, while Bullock was clearly not insane when he wrote the book it implies that asserting, out of humanity, one unjust killing to be as wrong as another is somehow a sign of extremism or mental disturbance, while discrimination in the matter is eminently sensible and just. The European Union's decision in 2007 to criminalise Holocaust denial if it was likely to incite violence or racial hatred (which it would be anyway), but not the atrocities of Stalin or the massacre of Armenians by Ottoman Turks during the First World War was either simply *un*just, or due to legalistic factors (the ruling excluded cases that had not been dealt with by the International Criminal Court at The Hague) in which case the law should be changed. Criminalising denial of atrocities is a policy which has its dangers, but if the principle is to be applied at all it should be applied evenly.

Finally we may add that if the technical means of bringing about the Holocaust, which enabled the death toll to be so huge, had been available to previous persecutors of the Jews (or anyone else wishing to commit genocide) they would have used them, and over as large an area as Hitler conquered had that been possible. Often, the person who is able to kill a few million people is merely luckier than the person who has killed a few hundred or less.

Another telling point is this. We may say that the Holocaust was more serious than anything Stalin did. But I suspect that in practice, if Stalin had been brought to trial for the murders he ordered or at least permitted we would nonetheless have sought the ultimate punishment: execution or at any rate life imprisonment. Even Jews would have said, if asked, that this was the correct course of action, whatever their views as to the relative evil of one atrocity compared to another. So what is the point in arguing that one atrocity *can* be worse than another when in practice we would not actually endorse that principle, going by how we punish it (which must be the yardstick)? There is little purpose in adhering to principles unless we are prepared to put them into effect, and only capital punishment or a life sentence for those who violate this particular one can show we are serious about it.

Opponents of the relativist case might point out that Stalin was not generally vilified by Russians; however this was because the German invasion of 1941 made him seem the lesser evil, as the Soviet people rallied round him as the focus of opposition to Hitler and the Nazis. Had the invasion never taken place things might have been different.

The identity of the victims. A third reason why the Holocaust is presented as a uniquely serious matter is the extent of the suffering inflicted on the Jews, who were numerically its principal victims; coming as it did on top of thousands of years of pogroms etc. Obviously both the Holocaust itself and the anti-Semitism which preceded it add up to something which is shameful to say the least, and at worst indescribably appalling. But if you go too far down that particular line of argument you would seem to be maintaining that Jewish suffering is a more ghastly business than other people's, which could be viewed as racially discriminatory. It is a line that places too much stress on races as opposed to individuals. In the last resort it is as the latter that suffer, even if our ethnicity was the specific reason why someone wanted to kill or otherwise mistreat us. Suppose you were a Jew in the modern (but pre-1945) era who because they lived in a country like Britain or the US most likely never experienced persecution on the scale or of the kind inflicted on fellow Jews whose ancestors happened to have settled in Germany or Russia instead? Your lot would have been better than that of Gentiles living in countries like Iraq, Iran, Cambodia, the old Soviet Union or South Africa in the apartheid period who suffered directly from the policies of Saddam Hussein, Ayatollah Khomeini, Stalin, Pol Pot etc.

In any case, if we are inclined to see the significance of the Holocaust largely in terms of the Jewish death toll it is because Hitler didn't get around to slaughtering the Slavs, and perhaps all the other non-Aryan races, on the same scale (as there is every reason to suppose, given his view of them, he would have done). Fortunately it so happened that he was defeated before he could do such a thing. Had events turned out otherwise, our attitudes to the Holocaust might in some ways be different. If, therefore, any of us do see its importance as lying purely in its *Jewish* dimension it is not because such a view is moral and justified but because of chance – the same as with scale being supposedly the crucial issue. There are those who out of hatred or revenge for past injustice would have killed all the black people in the world, or all the white people, or any ethnic group other than their own that one might care to mention, if they had had the chance and we cannot say whether they will attempt to do so in the future, or what degree of success they will have.

It is quite permissible to say that a particular atrocity has a particular significance *in some respects*. It is acceptable to argue that the importance of the Holocaust in history is that it demonstrates the evils anti-Semitism if unchecked can lead to, for such is indisputably true. It is when people say it is worse in an *absolute* sense that I have to disagree with them. You could go further and say that it doesn't even have a relative significance, except in terms of scale, because Jews had been persecuted before, to the extent of being burnt alive in riots in York and Nuremberg in the Middle Ages (to give one example). (It does of course have a historical significance because of its political consequences, which included the creation of the state of Israel, and the effect on the world of the often subjective but extremely powerful feelings it gives rise to). But no difference is made to what it *was* – an infinitely horrible event – by saying that other things were/are infinitely horrible too, and so no offence need be taken (though it probably will) if we seek to relativise it (I use the term as an alternative to "normalise" because I would prefer to think that mass murder, or indeed unlawful killing in any form, doesn't happen everywhere every day, though where some parts of the world are concerned this might I fear be overoptimistic). Though there cannot, in kind, be anything *worse* than the Holocaust there may be things *as bad*. But logically, to compare is not necessarily to diminish, as Brian Sewell (whatever his faults) once pointed out. It isn't anti-Semitic or in other ways unacceptable to suggest that the Holocaust was not more of a tragedy than the crimes of Stalin – or, strange as this may seem, that it is as serious a matter for someone to have a genuine dislike of blondes or redheads (say), whether or not you went so far as to kill them, if any wicked thought is an incalculable evil. But it would surely be a sign of irrationality to suggest it was *less* serious than either. In fact, relativising the Holocaust, if that is what I am doing, can provide a useful counter to those who seek to pretend it never occurred. It is precisely because so much else has happened, before and after it in human history, that has been brutal and horrifying that we can believe the Holocaust did. This is where those who seek to stress its supposed uniqueness in order to emphasise the need not to let it recur shoot themselves in the foot.

I say again that if the Holocaust was awful in terms of the nature of the crime perpetrated, then the rape and murder of young children can't be any less so. Their families would certainly take that view and would be very upset if you implied they shouldn't. I suspect that the response of some of them, assuming they did not actually physically attack you, would probably be two short words, of which the first begins with "f" while the second would most likely be "off". Those Gentiles who out of solidarity with Jews share the view many of the latter hold that the Holocaust *was* unique among atrocities would not stick to it if their loved ones became victims of unlawful killing.

Taking the "exceptionalist" position may be down to social and psychological factors as much as moral outrage. The Holocaust seemed a defining moment because it was the first time anything quite like it had occurred in modern history, or so people thought. It was naively believed Man had advanced so far that he was above such things (once again it is the nature of the act and not its scale which distinguishes civilisation from barbarism). This view has subsequently been disproved by the actions of some of the dictators I mentioned above, along with Slobodan Milosevic and Radovan Karavic among others. However, even in 1945 there ought to have been enough evidence to contradict it; for example, the massacre of Armenians by Turks in 1915 and the behaviour of Japan in China only a few years before the Second World War broke out. The idea seems to have been that such things were only to be expected from non-Western peoples, but in a Western nation itself were unforgiveable since we were supposed to be beyond all that. Insistence on the Holocaust being morally exceptional, at the time such a belief first developed in the Western world, can therefore to some extent be viewed as racist in character. It probably also stemmed from a dislike of the Germans on account of their having started two World Wars (at least it was the popular perception that they started the first), during which many citizens of other Western countries were killed. The Holocaust provided an ideal stick to beat them with.

Another contributory factor, obviously, was sympathy for the Jews, because the Holocaust was seen as the culmination of thousands of years of anti-Semitism, even if people had not been so solicitous towards them before the death camps had the effect of pricking consciences. As for the Jews themselves, what happened to them – even where they only heard about the atrocities and were not directly affected by them – was so traumatic, so horrible a shock that they needed to go into overkill in stressing its awfulness, and in trying to make sure it didn't recur, for fear that otherwise people might not give sufficient attention to the matter. (Of course, it is not quite true that all of them reacted to the Holocaust in the same way. Some thought it was a just divine punishment for their sins, to the point of being ashamed of what they were and downplaying it. Others, perhaps, were inclined to trumpet their Jewishness; it may have been the case that they had not considered themselves to be particularly Jewish, in terms of what they identified with, previously. To the Nazis at any rate they were Jews – and should be exterminated accordingly. It occurs to me that one consequence of being victimised for something you don't actually consider to be an important part of yourself is a feeling of bewilderment, distress and hurt; and one way of responding to it, to cope with the psychological shock and disruption it causes, is to embrace the thing in question whereas beforehand you might not have done: "All right then, in that case I'm a Jew. See how you like it.")

Not all Jews take the view that the Holocaust was uniquely awful. But there are many for whom even to relativise the business runs the risk of trivialising and thus forgetting it. They cannot cope with it otherwise. Their feelings are understandable, but dangerous; they are making it more likely it *will* be forgotten. As time goes by and the events of the Hitler era recede further into the past, fading from living memory, and more and more evidence emerges, from either historical research or philosophical reflection on the matter, for the *general* wickedness of Mankind (if I may so describe it) it will become less and less possible to insist the Holocaust was exceptional, unless perhaps a further such atrocity occurs which of course we don't want. Persistently trying to remind people of it, because of that supposed exceptionalness, both provokes a hostile reaction from those who correctly perceive this as unjust and also results in a certain fatigue on the part of society, which is either desensitised towards anti-Semitism or may even become guilty of it, because of anger at Jews seemingly arguing that their sufferings have been worse than others'.

None of this excuses anti-Semitism itself, one aspect of which is the belief the Holocaust didn't happen. There are those who attempt to present it as a myth; their claims are of course total rubbish. If it didn't happen, then six million plus people just vanished into thin air – abducted by aliens perhaps? Besides which, it is unlikely that so much obvious grief and horror, which among other things led to the establishment of the state of Israel and thus to a major upheaval in international affairs, could have been without a cause. The figures could be out by two million, I suppose. But how significant is that, really? We know the Holocaust took place because of the trace it has left, just as scientists can show the Big Bang occurred because of the background radiation from it. And even if the exact total − always a matter for dispute − *was* out by a million or two we would still be talking about an infinitely ghastly tragedy.

But are we not sometimes overprotective, and do we not sometimes draw attention to, punish, or try to prevent anti-Semitic prejudice by entirely the wrong means? It seems inappropriate that we should be seeking to educate our children about the evils of the Holocaust, and instilling in them awareness of the need for a non-racist society and for avoiding any repetition of past atrocities, laudable as those aims are, whilst our regard for the principle that all wrongs should be punished regardless of motive is in question and there remains the suspicion that they (our children) would not secure justice if they were to be the victims of crimes carried out in revenge for, or as an indirect consequence of, the Holocaust. How likely the latter scenario is to occur nowadays I am not sure, but it *has* occurred and the moral issues are worth exploring.

It is possible of course to be ennobled by suffering, and with some Jews that does seem to be what has happened, although of course they may well have been noble before. Although I still disagree with him about a number of things Simon Wiesenthal was an example, as his insistence on bringing war criminals to justice through legal means, of limiting vengeance to Nazis themselves rather than their relatives, his acknowledgment that other groups besides Jews were victimised and/or exterminated and on presenting the Holocaust as a debasement of Mankind in general rather than as just a quarrel, however nasty, between Nazis and Jews, all demonstrated. But not everyone, sadly, has been affected by the business in the same way.

What is chilling and disturbing is that some people openly and unrepentantly assert that taking an eye for an eye, even where it is innocents who suffer or die, is not as serious as the original crime. They do not actually have to *approve* of it for their attitude to be morally unacceptable. Commenting on the affair of Solomon Morel, a Polish Jew who lost members of his family to Hitler and when employed as a prison guard by the Soviets after the war took the opportunity to work off his anger by mistreating innocent Polish civilians who had been locked up by them, with the result that some died, Efraim Zaroff, director of the Simon Wiesenthal centre in Jerusalem, criticised those who tried to make out that there was a symmetry, one he regarded as "false", between such events and the Holocaust. I think there is enough of a symmetry for Mr Zaroff's remarks to be inappropriate. It is not an *exact* one; in a complex world, symmetries rarely are exact. One could say Morel was provoked, whereas the Nazis were not; a justified grievance over the way Germany was treated after the First World War is one thing, a lunatic desire to commit genocide quite another. It all depends on how far we believe one wrong excuses another.

We are committed to maintaining that it doesn't purely because of the dangerous trend which would be set otherwise; all kinds of people would be committing murder or other crimes and defending themselves on grounds of the mental and/or physical suffering the victim had caused them. Even if the motive for punishing Morel would here be sociopolitical convenience rather than ethics it would still be justified, if only on practical grounds. Unless perhaps it can be shown that the killer was so crazed by grief and rage that he was not responsible for his actions − an excuse only valid if the act was committed within a fairly short time of the atrocity it was designed to avenge − and/or was only killing those who were undeniably guilty, for which he had a far better excuse, he must be regarded as criminally culpable because what he did was still wrong, sufficiently so to justify execution or a life sentence. Neither of the right conditions are met in the Morel case. At least indirectly he killed the innocent as well as the guilty, and without any conscience. As for the "diminished responsibility" argument, it only holds if the mental damage can be proved to be permanent. When tackled on the matter by a survivor of the camp − without any particular Nazi connections − who said, "I know you had a hard life, but you murdered people. Why? If you do as the Fascists do, you're as bad as the Fascists", Morel snapped back, "No, you are the Fascist. It's people like you who killed my mother and father." Another of his victims stated that all she wanted him to do was say sorry, and if I had been in her position and he had done so, citing the effect the horrors he had been through had had on him as his explanation for his actions, I think I would have let the matter rest there. But he didn't say sorry. This is not just a case of understandable rage and grief leading to terrible things which one might not do in later years when the wounds had healed to some extent. Over fifty years after the event, Morel was still warped by hatred, was still blaming innocent people for what had happened and deeming it appropriate to have victimised them. However horrendous the trauma that damaged him in this way, it appears to be what he preferred to think, rather than what mental illness made him think − unless he *was* mad and the mental damage *was* permanent, in which case one ought to give him some quarter. This is something a trial could have established. But if Morel was not mad and his actions are not punished then the sanctity of human life − the same principle that was so obviously violated in the Holocaust − of *all* human life, unless we are to discriminate between Jew and Gentile, is not endorsed, because if taking a life is not considered to merit the maximum penalty then its preservation could not have been very important.

It does seem offensive to the fair-minded that the request from the Poles to extradite Morel from Israel was regarded there as some sort of sick joke, which implied that the deaths of his victims, though presumably regrettable nonetheless, were not morally a very serious matter at all. To the director of the international department of Israel's Ministry of Justice it came as a surprise, particularly when Israel had never tried to extradite many of the Poles who had been responsible for murders of Jews. There is no reason why the latter should not have been brought to account, although since the murders were committed in Poland they should have been punished there (extraditing the guilty to Israel, because she was the country set up as a result of the Holocaust and in defiance of the hatred which led to it, would contravene a vital legal principle and imply that she has the right to do so where others would not be permitted that exemption, as well as that her original creation as opposed to toleration of her existence today was justified, which is a sensitive area one might prefer to avoid if possible). For both Morel and the Polish war criminals to face justice would seem to have been the fairest approach. For whatever happens, justice should not be one-sided. As Israel did not concede that the charges against Morel amounted to genocide (though that was not what the Poles alleged), he was protected by their statute of limitations. Since just one murder, whether the victim is killed outright or dies as the effective result of ill-treatment, is bad enough, one tends not to see any valid reason for the restrictions on extradition. It is not a matter of whether "genocide" was committed (bearing in mind the frequent debates over what constitutes it and what doesn't). In fact there was another, and far better, reason why Morel wasn't extradited, namely that anti-Semitism remained widespread in Poland and the Israelis understandably feared he would not get a fair trial (to which he was of course entitled). In which case, the Poles themselves are partly to blame for the failure to secure justice for his victims. They should have used the affair as an opportunity for some soul-searching and to confront unpleasant aspects of their past; the best course to take would have been for this to be combined with an apology from Morel, with there not being necessarily any question of further action. Matters like these require a measure of humility all round. As it is, it still seems galling that Morel, who died in 2007, got away with it; just as Israel has killed innocent people in order to protect its interests while still expecting the West to support it, and has never properly been brought to account for that.

There appear to have been other cases where the avengers got their wish; to exact retribution and ensure that they were not punished for it. In *Fat Man In Argentina*, (Michael Joseph 1990), journalist and writer Tom Vernon's account of his travels in that country, the following incident is reported: "In one town {it was near the village of La Cumbra-Cita} there had been a tragic fire not long before in which a whole family had died, including the children. Local people had known that the head of that family had been an SS man and a war criminal; they had also noticed − for it was a small town − that a small squad of strangers arrived just before the incident and departed immediately afterwards." We are dealing here with a relatively recent incident. It is quite likely the children inherited or absorbed the prejudices of their parents, but that may not necessarily have been so, and no-one ought in any case to regard that as a good reason for killing them. And they, like those killed in the Holocaust, would have had wives/husbands, boyfriends/girlfriends, brothers and sisters. Yet there is no indication that the perpetrators of the atrocity (let us call it that) were ever brought to justice. On the other hand, enormous fuss was made over the punishment of octogenarian and nonagenarian Nazi war criminals, despite the dangers involved, with the necessary legislation being pushed through the

House of Lords in a manner which I at any rate did not care for, the peers' ruling when they initially threw it out being described as a "misjudgement". There's got to be something wrong there somewhere.

In 1981 Michael Elkins, at one time a BBC correspondent in Jerusalem, wrote a book called *Forged In Fury*, about the Jewish brigade formed within the British army during the Second World War and, in addition to their officially recognised wartime service, the murders they carried out of Nazis and also, far more controversially, the attempted murder of millions of Germans by poisoning water supplies. Nowhere in the book is there any condemnation of the killings they committed or planned, or even a statement to the effect that they were not right but could be forgiven, which would have been more acceptable. Alarmingly, Elkins took the view that it had not been his brief to write a balanced account of things. Nor, evidently, did his publisher question this approach. Yet normally, if one wrote a book that was one-sided and intemperate in this way one would be pilloried for it. And in a matter like the Holocaust, which obviously arouses strong emotions on all sides, an even-handed approach is particularly important.

The genocide attempted in Germany did not succeed; nor is it easy to say what the reaction would have been if it had. But reason should have told those who contemplated it, as it should have told Solomon Morel, that an entire people could not be depraved criminals who deserved the maximum penalty, and also that the world is hardly made a better place after something like the Holocaust by destroying millions more innocents. On the contrary, the plotters knew they would be killing people who had opposed Hitler (would those people have felt like doing the same again if, say, their loved ones had been among those who died?) but did not let that deter them. Perhaps they were so crazed by their experiences that the balance of their minds was disturbed; it would not be humane to discount that possibility even if it might be too easily used as a convenient blanket excuse. If you are going to pardon something like revenge genocide – though hopefully you would try to prevent it, whatever happened – let it be for the right reasons.

We should also mention the law adopted in Switzerland, for example, that denying the Holocaust is an offence. Perhaps politically it is inevitable in countries which have a dubious past where Nazism, or compliance with the latter's wishes, is concerned and which may also be facing a rise in right-wing extremism; they need to demonstrate their anti-racist credentials and reassure the world that there is not going to be a repeat of what happened under Hitler. But it *is* political; the moral reasons for it are a little suspect. If denying the Holocaust is a crime because it is morally offensive, one would have to make the denial of *any* such atrocity an offence, yet it seems it is not. In fact it doesn't stop there; where would one draw the line? It is precisely because of this that the treatment of Mr David Irving, dubious though he is, is counterproductive. To me, suggesting the Holocaust was worse than other incidences of mass murder – or indeed any case of unlawful killing – because you punish the denial of it but not the denial of those other atrocities is itself offensive. There are all kinds of remarks uttered every day, on all sorts of matters, which are ill-considered and unjust. The trouble with imprisoning Holocaust deniers, whatever the principle behind it, is that it risks merely making them into martyrs.

It is worth looking at some examples of how the question of punishing the Holocaust is treated in fiction. The heavy-handed approach can be seen in Ian Rankin's 1998 John Rebus novel *The Hanging Garden*. On page 98 Inspector Rebus is told by Holocaust investigator David Levy that British Intelligence are protecting a number of big name Nazi war criminals, "maybe their children." Rebus tells Levy to make sure he and his colleagues "keep digging." That is the end of the conversation. The wording is unfortunate, and not excused by the need for dialogue in a work of fiction to be punchy. Why are the children as much of a concern as their parents, as they seem to be here? They are obviously not to blame in the same way, unless we believe in the concept of hereditary guilt, and although it may be wrong for them to hide the truth (assuming they know it) from the authorities it is also forgiveable, and not just for reasons of family loyalty; since people aren't always fair-minded and reasonable, they may be afraid of acquiring a stigma they do not deserve. To some extent we should expect heavy-handedness from a character like Rebus, who, though as a Scot his feelings are maybe understandable, is for example unreasonably prejudiced against the English, partly to cover up his own dysfunctionality (as I think we are meant to infer). That doesn't make it any less distasteful.

One of the best-known novels to have Holocaust vengeance as its theme is P D James' *Original Sin* (1994; television adaptation broadcast 1997). Here Gabriel Dauntsey, whose Jewish wife and children were betrayed to the Nazis in occupied France by resistance leader Jean-Philippe Etienne, takes his revenge by killing Etienne's own children, Gerard and Claudia, in the same way that the Nazis did his. Gerard is trapped in a room into which lethal gas is pumped, Claudia garotted and then (on TV) exposed to carbon monoxide fumes from a car engine. The fact that they are, as we later learn, only his adopted children obviously does not make the crime any less serious (it was as a direct result of Dauntsey's blind pursuit of revenge that they died). Nor does the fact that none of the people Dauntsey kills in the story (one of whose themes, I think, is the way the general nastiness of society reinforces the conviction of individual wrongdoers that their actions are justified) are particularly nice. Dauntsey is eventually found out and arrested, but one of DCI Adam Dalgliesh's team, Daniel Aaron, is a Jew who feels some sympathy with the prisoner because of what he lost in the war and allows him (reluctantly, it should be noted) to escape so that he can commit suicide.

One reviewer commented that basing the plot around the Holocaust and its legacy "drew praise in some quarters but unbalances the book and gives it a worthiness which it cannot carry." If the implication is that the subject matter is so awful it requires greater literary skills than even those of a P D James to portray – and thus that with atrocities there is somehow a scale of dreadfulness – then you can guess what I think of it. But essentially, my gripe is this. *Original Sin* has been called "admirable" for the way it dares to tackle the Holocaust as its subject. Baroness James was a very moral writer and no injustice was ever intended by her. She does not condone Dauntsey's actions; indeed one cannot help thinking that had Gerard and Etienne been much nicer people, he could not have killed them. Nonetheless, one wonders if the novel is the sort of thing a Jew should be grateful for. In one respect it certainly was a misguided project. The murderer's targeting of the innocent, about which there is nothing worthy, does not portray Holocaust victims in a good light. It is a chilling kind of victimisation which Jews do not want to be associated with and which I found actually left me somehow feeling more sympathy for Gerard and Claudia than for Dauntsey, which I doubt was the idea. Moreover, what looks like Jewish solidarity has allowed the crime to go unpunished. (It is never in fact explicitly stated that Dauntsey is Jewish – we are left to decide whether the fact that his wife and children were means that he must be too – but, significantly perhaps, it is not explicitly stated that he isn't, either. And he seems to be in the TV version). *Original Sin*, though wonderfully terrifying, is also as the reverse side of that token unpleasantly disturbing. If something like its plot were to happen in real life, the consequence might well be an increase in anti-Semitism. Though I have to say that my adverse reaction to it produces a certain guilt feeling, a fear of being too critical of it on account of the Jews' past sufferings; altogether it's an emotional roller coaster I'd rather not go through. *Original Sin* is all the more distressing if there really have been real life incidents where the philosophy of "an eye for an eye" was put into practice. But it's all compounded, if anything, by doubts as to whether the plot is in any case plausible. It has been commented on elsewhere that P D James' murderers seem to wait an inordinately long time before punishing the wrongdoings which give them their motives. It takes Dauntsey some fifty years to find out why his loved ones ended up in the gas chambers. Despite the incident at La Cumbre-Cita – if what happened was what it is implied happened – and the scars the Holocaust can inflict, which we know run very deep, it does somehow seem far-fetched to suggest that Jews would be determined upon killing the child of a war criminal, rather than the war criminal themselves, six decades after the event. There may be no need for the emotional roller coaster in the first place. Though it is no less terrible, of course, if they *would* have done it. And you can't help thinking, given the repugnance many naturally feel towards the Holocaust, that if Dauntsey had gone to trial he might have been let off lightly.

Equally disturbing, though written as was *Original Sin* by an author who does not approve of their chief villain's actions, is Robert Wilson's *A Small Death in Lisbon*. Here, a girl (admittedly of a dissolute sort) is murdered as a result of a chain of events deliberately set in motion by someone (a Gentile) who is, among other things, trying to reclaim money stolen during the Second World War from the Jewish community in neutral Portugal. He ultimately escapes justice for what he has done. His scheme involves getting someone to sodomise and then shoot the girl, to whom they are actually related. The linking of Holocaust retribution with such a crime, through it being one of the villain's motives or at least one of the reasons why he feels satisfaction at the success of his scheme, is unfortunate at most. The book was published in 1999, five years after *Original Sin,* along with which it creates a soul-crushing impression of the twentieth century ending with the punishing of one injustice by another, a sign that Man has learned nothing. Even the blurb on the back refers to the "wheel of vengeance rolling on to the century's end." There is of course no such thing as a "small" death. Any life is of value, potentially at any rate, and its loss therefore an incalculable tragedy. Merely because we are ourselves and not anyone else, and our thoughts, including the very awareness of being alive, are our own and not another's even where they are of the same things, it is true to say as a Muslim scholar once did that if you kill one person it is as if you have killed the whole universe.

*

This chapter must inevitably encompass the question of Israel because that country was born out of the Holocaust, in that its creation was seen as a means of protecting Jews from further such horrors. Hence, whether one agrees with its existence, and with what is regarded as necessary to defend that existence, is seen as a test of whether or not one is anti-Semitic. Concur with that or no, the issue can engender attitudes with which we may take issue.

Following the atrocities of the Nazis, which surpassed any persecution they had previously experienced both in scale and awfulness, there was an understandable desire on the part of European Jews to be safe. This feeling led to Zionist Jews and their supporters completely disregarding the wishes of the Arabs, at that time a majority in Palestine. The consequences of this have been terrorism, both in the region itself and internationally, and on occasions localised war (which in 1973 is believed to have come close to nuclear conflict between the superpowers, potentially threatening a much larger number of people than makes up the population of Israel), with the aim of preserving or overturning the status quo created in 1948. The West, and especially the United States, has tended to support Israel against her Arab enemies, partly as compensation for the way Jews were persecuted in the past and partly as a result of pressure from influential Jewish organisations. No lasting peaceful solution to the conflict has been achieved and thousands have died as a result.

Stephen Brook in *Winner Takes All: A Season In Israel* (Hamish Hamilton 1990) attacks those who believe the establishment of Israel was wrong, saying that such arguments come from the same sort of people who persecuted Jews under Hitler. It is the only sour note in a book whose tone is otherwise reasonable. Although he might not see it that way he is being, probably unintentionally, rather offensive to quite a few. An anti-Semite would of course be the most likely person to object to Israel. But given that there were sensible reasons as well as racist ones for opposing its creation, the labelling of all those who do so as Nazis is extremely unfair and it is for that reason that I raise the issue. It is a different matter from agreeing with those who think that Israel should *now* be dismantled (I am not one of them). But to have believed, at the time it was being sought, that her establishment was wrong and ought to be prevented if possible, and to wish to avoid similar cases in the future, does not in itself constitute anti-Semitism (even if one believes it to be wrong *now* one might still believe that Israel's existence should be accepted in the present day, and for moral as well as practical reasons). There are important lessons to be learned from the business. Stephen Brook was arguing that the creation of the Israeli state was right in absolute terms and definitely should *not* have been prevented, with the implication that we should do or at least allow the same again if necessary; there is more than one reason why we may disagree with him.

In 1946-8 an Arab majority in the region of Palestine was replaced by a Jewish majority not by natural increase of the Jewish population (which would have caused problems enough) but by the immigration of Jews from outside the region. The worrying implications of this are that a majority can be created artificially, against the wishes of the existing one and from people who have lived outside the area in question for thousands of years, whatever their ancestral connection with it. Anyone could say they had the right to do such a thing because of a situation which had existed millennia before. The principle is established across time as well as space, and therefore appears to be given greater legitimacy. Unless we take the racist view that Jewish sensibilities are of more importance than other people's, then if the normal conditions which should apply to these matters can be waived for their benefit it can be waived for others' too (it is conceivable that other similar cases *could* arise, since Jews are not the only people who suffer). It becomes a destabilising factor because majorities could all too easily be displaced, anywhere. The whole principles of democracy and of sovereignty (because the people who were going to constitute the new majority would not have been citizens of the region, and would be coming into it from without; they would effectively be foreigners) would both be undermined simultaneously.

It is important to appreciate that Jews and Arabs were coexisting quite happily in Palestine until large-scale Jewish immigration began after the First World War and started to change the character of the region in ways that were not acceptable to the majority. There was obviously even greater scope for conflict after 1948. And the consequences for the world in general of the creation of Israel may be said to have been negative in many respects. The West by coming down on Israel's side has incurred the wrath of Arab states, manifested in acts of terrorism towards its citizens and armed forces, against itself. Israel has been of vital assistance in the fight against that terrorism, using the expertise she has gained from being in the frontline, but this may be countered by the point that a lot of it would not be happening if she did not exist. She may have saved many Western lives; but it could be argued that had she not been set up in the first place, and subsequently defended so consistently by the West (and Jewish communities there), she would not have needed to, nor would we have lost those Westerners who have died as a direct or indirect result of the conflict. (It is not only the West who gets caught in the crossfire or is targeted as guilty by association. I would like to mention here the anguished cry of a (Kenyan) girl injured in an attack on Israeli tourists in Kenya that she had never even heard of Israel before the tragedy happened).

Apart from the violence within Palestine itself, and the atrocities committed against Jewish or Western interests outside it there is the dangerous exacerbation of the tension between the superpowers in 1973, already mentioned. On the subject of nuclear weapons, if Israel is ever sufficiently vulnerable in her estimation to use hers (everyone knows she has them even though she has never been particularly open about their existence) – and if she is not prepared to do so in the last resort there is no point in them – she will have inflicted the ultimate disaster upon the world. Her creation introduced a new factor into the global political equation, one which made that equation more complicated, and the planet a more dangerous place for you and I to live on.

In attempting to protect itself from its enemies Israel has in the past been quite prepared to risk the lives of citizens of those countries who support, or are expected to support, her. In Beirut in January 1979 a bomb detonated by a Mossad (Israeli secret service) agent killed PLO activist Ali Hassan Salameh. It also killed a number of passers-by including a British secretary. As Israel did not admit liability for the incident at the time, and there was no evidence which could be upheld in an international court of law, the chances of compensation were virtually nil. A private protest at the death of an innocent British citizen was made to the Israeli government, but no proper reply was received. Salameh was thought − wrongly, some believe − to have been involved in the killing of Israeli athletes at the 1972 Olympic Games. The other motive for his assassination was that he was a liaison man between PLO chairman Yasser Arafat and the US Embassy in Beirut, and represented the Palestinians' viewpoint to the Americans. In other words he constituted a political threat to the survival of Israel, but not a direct one, and thus there was insufficient justification for jeapordising blameless lives. On the one hand Israel was seeking America's support; on the other, it was effectively trying to dictate to it what it should and should not listen to (by killing those who espoused the pro-Arab line), and in a way which led to innocent casualties. The fact that most of world Jewry − some 60% of it, at least − does not live within its borders makes the damage done, the lives sacrificed, in the cause of

65

its preservation a lot harder to accept.

It may also be questioned whether the events of 1948 were a good thing from the Jewish point of view. The establishment of Israel could be viewed as in some respects a miscalculation, because in the long run it has only made the Jews more unpopular and by its various consequences increased the likelihood of anti-Semitism, while not always benefiting the rest of the world either. Had those in the West who encouraged the setting up of the new state known what it would lead to, is it a foregone conclusion they would still have acted as they did? A motion in the United Nations equating Zionism with racism was defeated. This was done out of pragmatism as much as anything else, since to have accepted it would effectively have undermined the whole policy, whether motivated by principle or political expediency, of preserving the state of Israel – something the world has in the end no real option but to support, as I will argue below. Nonetheless there are lessons to be learned, as I said.

After 1945 it might have been better to have capitalised on the widespread, though sadly not universal, sympathy which existed for Jews following the Holocaust to ensure better treatment for them in the nations of Europe. You would perhaps have had political correctness forty years before you in fact did, and with a different object, but the overall consequences may well have been less damaging for the world. Instead, there appeared what in some ways could be called a racist state – for the same reasons why it was created, you were and are infinitely more likely to become a citizen of it if Jewish. It was a state which in order to survive in an environment where its foundation had (understandably) aroused the hostility of neighbours it had to elect leaders, some of them former terrorists – Begin, Shamir, Sharon, Netanyahu – who were racialist in that they were virtually indifferent to the sufferings of non-Jews, whether Arabs or Westerners who died because of their countries' support for Israel, because that kind of person (ruthless and bloody-minded) is often, unfortunately, the one most effective at defending the nation from its enemies. The nicer ones, like Shimon Peres, have not been so successful. And a dangerous new factor was introduced into world affairs. The refugees from Hitler might perhaps have gone to Britain instead; there was undoubtedly anti-Semitism there, but this wasn't helped by the activities of Jewish terrorists fighting for the creation of Israel (such as hanging British soldiers attempting to enforce the UN mandate and then booby-trapping the bodies). There was a strong element of hypocrisy involved in the foundation of Israel and her subsequent attitudes towards the world community, from whom she wanted financial, military, and economic aid, protesting indignantly if she didn't get it. What she was effectively saying was, we don't want to be part of you because you're potentially racist and might persecute us but we do, by the way, expect you to help us OK? There is something deeply insulting about it.

It has been said that the Palestinians have no-one to blame but themselves for the situation they now find themselves in because they should have accepted the partition of Palestine when it was proposed. This however is not a reasonable line to take. Just ask British people, for example, how they would feel if what was effectively a foreign people (in the Palestinian case they were diaspora Jews, albeit in alliance with native-born Israelis) decided to annex half of Britain, and when they naturally objected to this the result was a war leading to their losing the whole of the country, and when they protested about that they were told they should have given up the half when they had the chance. They would not have been happy, which is why those of them who criticise perceived Arab intransigence in 1946-8 are hypocritical. Land also has a position of crucial importance in Arab thinking, in accordance with the logic of having changed from being a nomadic people to being a settled one, and the Arabs, no more than Jews or Anglo-Saxons or blacks, cannot help being a distinct people with their own particular way of looking at the world.

It is claimed by some that there is a religious justification for the founding of the modern state of Israel – the return of the Jewish people to their national home – and thus by extension for keeping it in being, because it is foretold in the Bible and therefore is in line with God's purposes. But of course the Bible, some of the time at least, is open to more than one interpretation – especially when it conflicts with common sense – and I suspect that although there must be those who honestly believe the passages in question to have the meaning they ascribe to them, they are nonetheless used by people who are not really religious or follow a distorted form of Christianity to justify the political aim of preserving Israel.

The fact that most of world Jewry doesn't live in Israel rather knocks the argument on the head. Moreover, as all Christians appreciate, God's purpose in Biblical times was to work initially through a particular people (who therefore, logically, had to be protected from aggression and so permitted something akin to nationhood if it helped them to defend themselves), in a particular part of the world for the ultimate moral and spiritual redemption, through Jesus Christ, who as an extension of God's previous modus operandi was in his earthly form a Jew, of *all* people. The focus shifted from that particular race when Christian missionaries – at first Jews by birth, but then anyone who responded to the call – began carrying the Gospel all over the world. There is therefore no reason why God should now be more concerned with the survival of the *political* entity of Israel than he should that of the Federated States of Micronesia, or Guatemala, or Poland, or Great Britain, unless the idea is that the wishes of Jews are more important, at any time in history, than those of other people; the latter would essentially be a racist belief, which I don't think God is guilty of somehow. Israel has already achieved its *special* purpose in history, from the Christian point of view, by being that out of which Christianity, which has now spread to the ends of the earth, grew. Whether those who refuse to take it up continue to do so can only be their business, however serious the affair may be spiritually if they don't. But politics isn't really God's concern. Even the Roman occupation of Jewry, which many people at the time justly resented was nowhere near as important

67

to him as the spiritual redemption of humanity, as Jesus' exhortation "Render to Caesar…" makes plain. Obviously injustices can be committed in the area of politics, as elsewhere, and I'm not aware of God saying at any time that human beings, Christians included, should not take political sides if their moral principles direct them to do so. It just had to be a question of individual conscience. Politics matters, but it matters to other people besides Jews. Its importance only serves to make the discrimination a more serious business. And since other things are as vital in the earthly context as politics – economic wellbeing, and protection from natural disaster or disease – discrimination would have to be extended to those areas too, even if it would only take the form of what God *sought* to do (the consideration of free will preventing him from making life perfect for anyone). It would then become even more unacceptable. Except in the sense that a larger number of people would be affected in one way or another, because her population is bigger, the preservation of Israel is no more, or less, important than that of Andorra, and it is no insult to either country to say so. Neither morals nor reason suggests an especial need to restore, and hereafter to protect, Israel among states, especially given (a) that this perceived special need was an integral part of a US foreign policy which proved very dangerous under the second President Bush, and (b) the disastrous consequences, which we have seen only too clearly, in many walks of life of displacing populations because of what may have been the case thousands of years ago.

As in other matters, where the Bible appears to conflict with reason we must conclude that we have read it wrongly. And from the Christian point of view most Jews (along with many Gentiles, of course) are currently falling down on a count which has to be more important than any political consideration. They are either Jewish in the religious sense, or secular in their outlook (in Israel itself the latter is more commonly the case), though adopting the outward forms of religion on special occasions, rather than Christians. With the exception (generally negative in its influence where it has any) of the orthodox religious parties Israel's struggle to preserve herself is a tribal and political one which invokes religion in its support when it needs to do so. The idea, if it is true that non-Christians are condemned to everlasting suffering in Hell at the Day of Judgement, that Jews should be exempt from this punishment is discrimination of the most horrible kind imagineable. Finally, since the principal cause of Israel's establishment was the Nazi Holocaust, to take the fundamentalist religious view of the matter we would have to regard Hitler's atrocities as divinely ordained, which apart from implying a very strange or cruel kind of God would suggest that Hitler was merely carrying out His will and could not be blamed for his actions – something Jews and indeed any person with moral sensibilities would never accept!

We should not oppose the existence of Israel, but we should make sure we support her for the right reasons. She must be defended because we have to allow the majority within a certain territory, once it *is* the majority (even if we do not like the means by which that situation was brought about), to determine its political status (as well as be pragmatic – in the last resort Israel would fight, causing all manner of devastation and suffering in the process). For both moral and practical reasons she must be regarded as a *fait accompli*. We must not support her because we think she is the product of divine will, or that her original (1948) creation was justified for any other reason, and we should try to ensure no similar situation is allowed to occur anywhere else in the world. The events of 1948 set what is potentially a bad precedent; giving a particular people the right to settle wherever they like, regardless of anyone else's wishes and the possible geopolitical consequences, is both unjust and dangerous. The problem is that to emphasise this point one would have to cite the example of Israel – which would be letting off a political firework. It is a frustrating position to be in; we will just have to be very, very careful. It would of course set an equally bad precedent to dissolve Israel, because it could overturn the principle of democracy just as 1948 did; even if the argument that the latter point doesn't count where the majority is of relatively recent creation was valid, at what stage, what number of years ago, would you draw the line? Certainly, most of Israel's population was probably born after '48, and knows no other home, no other nationhood. The angry remark by an Israeli woman during one heated discussion on the matter that to deny her country's right to exist would mean asking her to apologise for being born was not far wrong, because to seek to reverse the demographic status quo within Palestine would be effectively to do same. I think many people in the West who are hostile to Israel because of her consequences and the more questionable of her actions simply fail to comprehend that point, as a result of not having thought the matter through properly, rather than harbour a nasty mentality.

We ought not to feel hatred, as opposed to anger, towards Israel on account of her behaviour. To this end, it would be healthy if we were able to blame a lot of it on the influence of the far right orthodox religious parties in the Israeli parliament, who the more extreme statements and actions of some Israeli prime ministers may be designed to appease. Commentators suggest, however, that this influence is not as great as has often been supposed; which in a way is a pity as one does not like to feel tempted to *want* to denigrate Israel, and therefore anything which makes her conduct more forgiveable is welcome. The real reason for her belligerent and uncompromising stand is fear, a dread that any concessions will be exploited to bring about her destruction.

In defending Israel one might I suppose choose to particularly stress the Palestinians' being now the *minority* within the region, even if they became so because of what some at least consider unjust. It is why an attitude that has more sympathy for them than for the Israelis, and would force a major change in Israeli policy on their account, is anathema to Zionists. I believe this is a major factor in the characteristic bitterness of the issue. It raises the whole question of democracy and how far concern for the feelings of a minority should be allowed to influence events. The problem of course is that the

Palestinians are a fairly large minority and thus cannot realistically, *politically*, be ignored, because of international concern over the question and its capacity to cause trouble if the Palestinians are oppressed and disadvantaged to a sufficient extent. The international dimension exists among other reasons because of the way the issue fuels Islamic terrorism. Practically, if the whole world − a far greater number of people than the total Arab and Jewish population of Israel − is threatened, albeit indirectly, by it then it is right to force change on Israeli Jews for the sake of solving that problem, because that would actually be a case of putting the majority before the minority!

We certainly cannot begrudge the Palestinians their resentment at their status. They have lost political control over their own lives, to a greater or lesser extent, enjoy a far poorer standard of living than do most Israelis, and suffer grievously as a result of actions by the Israeli Defence Force. When a Palestinian woman was interviewed by a BBC reporter about the whole situation and reminded of the things done to the Jews under Hitler, in an attempt to present the Israeli point of view to her, her response was not so much that the Holocaust didn't happen or was not a dreadful thing as that she didn't see why she should have to suffer for it. The reason why the film *Schindler's List* isn't shown in Lebanon (at least that was the case not long ago, I don't know if it still is) is not an insistence on denying the historical reality of the events it portrays, or their horror, but rather fear that by focusing on the Holocaust it will distract attention from the sufferings of the Palestinians and by the same token appear to justify what has caused them.

There is undoubtedly a lot of nonsense talked about the Israeli-Palestinian conflict, as always when controversial issues raise the blood pressure. I have referred to the need equally to accept the existence of Israel and to do so for the proper reasons. On either side the situation is made worse by extremism and unnecessary brutality. There is no doubt that Israelis have in the past acted callously towards both Palestinians and the Western peace activists who defend them. When I brought up the subject of the murder − as I saw it − of peace activist Rachel Corrie with one British MP he said she was in a foreign country and should have obeyed the rules. This is rubbish, because if the Israelis had found her activities a nuisance there were other ways they could have dealt with her, such as arrest or deportation. Maybe her behaviour was foolish, but morally speaking it is better to be foolish than to commit what must be regarded as manslaughter at least. In a civilised country, you don't punish wrongdoers by driving bulldozers over them.

The Palestinians are wrong in blaming the West for the basic policy of supporting Israel even where it is not expressed in the skewed thinking and crass behaviour of a George Bush or a Tony Blair. Had the West chosen not to recognise her once she had become a reality it might have established the principle that the sovereignty of the majority can be disregarded, if it became so in a given state only recently, and this as I have pointed out could have a domino effect. Jews might also, if the West had somehow prevented her foundation, have carried out acts of terrorism in both Palestine and the West until their wishes were granted. In the long run, had the West chosen to recognise Israel it would have had precisely the effect that it has done. Had it chosen *not* to support her it might have caused just as many problems if not more, and set what could have been a dangerous precedent. A decision had to be made and the West should not be criticised for turning one way rather than the other. By logic, once Israel's existence was accepted she then had to be supported, with economic and other aid, in line with that policy. The Arabs have been hot-headed and unreasonable in refusing to understand these things. Their spiteful action in 1973 in cutting off the West's oil because of its siding with Israel in the Yom Kippur War – though it is another demonstration of how much trouble her creation has caused – was not only spiteful but unwarranted. They also fail to appreciate that the West's rallying behind Israel is probably due as much to a pragmatic fear of what might happen if she felt her back was to the wall as to a guilt complex over past anti-Semitism or even the considerable electoral influence of the Jewish community in the USA. Remember, Israel has nuclear weapons and if denied support in terms of conventional military equipment there is no telling what she might do if she felt herself to be vulnerable enough. America's reasons for buttressing her – the electoral factors and the fear of her nuclear capability – are understandable but cannot be admitted to because to do so would cause just as much trouble as not admitting to them. It is politically impossible. It would be a public acknowledgement that the US is afraid or in hock to a certain lobby and not its own master (that such is widely perceived, correctly or otherwise, to be actually the case makes no difference; it is the psychological effect of stating it openly which does). This would diminish its authority and prestige and make it difficult to deal effectively with foreign countries in other matters. It often happens in life, and not just in politics, that policies and actions which cause offence and create serious discontent cannot be explained because to do so would have consequences that would be just as bad if not worse. This is another thing the Arabs fail to appreciate.

We need to make clear what we mean by "Zionism", something much vilified by Israel's enemies or those who are simply unhappy about her behaviour. I for my own part would take it to mean a policy of supporting Israel right or wrong, rather than that of merely upholding the right of the state to exist. There are of course various other reasons for the conflict between the West and the Islamic/Arab world, which resolution of the Arab-Israeli dispute wouldn't necessarily make any difference to. It would be unfair to blame the problem entirely on Israel. But her conduct, and the West's tacit or otherwise tolerance of same, is *a* reason for it. I am not suggesting we should change our policies simply out of fear of terrorism; I just resent the West being targeted because of something which is unjust anyway. It would be tempting, though sad of course, if the West could turn its back on the issue, to disengage from it; we would at least be reducing the total death toll from the conflict by removing the threat to ourselves. But this policy is rejected by Israel and its supporters because they desire the West to be the former's protector. If they demand that the West continue to function in that capacity, while preventing a resolution of the conflict by discouraging the putting of pressure on Israel to soften her attitudes, they are effectively insisting that we trap ourselves in a situation which is dangerous to our population – civilian and military, public and politicians. They attempt to justify this through a distortion of the truth, as do many people who are unwilling to abandon a certain policy whatever the moral and political objections to it. They present the situation as being one where Israelis and Westerners stand bravely side by side in dealing with a problem which is entirely of a third party's perverse making. In fact it is Israel's attitude to the Palestinians which perpetuates the problem in the first place. It seems we are all supposed to gallantly sacrifice, or at least risk, our lives and those of our loved ones for the sake of Israel and that it is somehow indecent for us to object to that!

Israel and those in the Jewish diaspora who champion her need the help of the powerful West in defending her interests. Any attempt to suggest that the favour shown her by it is damaging to its citizens because it helps to attract Arab/Islamic terrorism is roundly attacked by Zionists because if such a view became accepted it might render the West's aid less likely; for them an unwelcome prospect. Their protectiveness towards fellow Jews, understandable in the light of historical events, and crystallised in a love of the state of Israel, leads them by a process of logic to criticise any attempt by the West to protest at the risks which accompany Zionism.

So what is to be done to resolve matters? Whatever the difficulties in the way of a two-state solution, in which an independent Palestine existed alongside an independent Israel, it is the only course with the remotest chance, that I can see, of bringing about an improvement in the situation, and to reject it is to give the Palestinians nothing. In a vox pop interview for British television on the peace process some years ago, an Israeli (though with a Home Counties English accent) woman expressed some scepticism as to whether the Palestinians would keep their side of the bargain, asking "What have they ever given us?". An odd choice of words because the Palestinians are not in a position to "give" Israel anything. They simply have not the wealth or the power. They are the underdogs. I gave up on the *Daily Mail*, which generally seemed to be taking a strikingly and excessively Zionist viewpoint, when it described the two-state policy as "lunatic." Well, it is the approach which most sensible and well-intentioned people favour. Perhaps most important of all, it gives those who are angry at the Palestinians' situation but seek an accommodation with Israel and try not to feel or encourage hatred towards her something to hang onto. Without it, the issue is more likely to become embittered.

Realistically the Palestinians must give up the right of return as part of the package. Practically, there is simply no way Israel will accept what would result in the swamping of its Jewish population, its ceasing to be a Jewish state. We must be brutally concerned with what is right, and also the best way to achieve a lasting settlement; not with what is easy. That remains true whether the person asking for the sacrifice to be made has it easy themselves or not (a Palestinian might well retort if I asked them to make concessions on the right of return that it was all right for me because I lived in a country whose political status was not in question). I say to Muslims who cannot accept this: the creation of Israel and the displacement or subjugation of the Palestinians was to them unjust, but at the risk of seeming blasé about it the world is a very unjust place. If they have faith in God, in Allah, they will surely believe that ultimately He will triumph (His purposes may take a long time to work themselves out, but He has infinite patience). In the next life, which is more important than this one, all injustices will be swept away. You will have your free Palestine, or maybe something will happen which will do away with the need for nations altogether while still meeting everyone's requirement for an identity and for security from aggression. If it is necessary for the Israelis to be punished for anything they have done, then punished they will be. In the meantime it isn't worth messing up this life over the matter by killing or otherwise harming people, whether they be Israelis, Diaspora Jews, other Arabs/Muslims, or innocent Westerners and Africans who have been "caught in the crossfire". If it is simply pragmatism to give up the right of return, God/Allah will not blame us for doing so. Talking of pragmatism, perhaps the best solution of the issue, from the point of view of political calculation, is to make things sufficiently attractive for expatriate Palestinians in the lands where they have settled that they will not *want* to return.

We must continue to grope our way towards that two-state solution. Meanwhile an end to all new Jewish settlement, in return for guarantees of Israel's security and renunciation of the right to return, seems a reasonable quid pro quo, a fair price to pay for an end to the conflict; an area where progress might constructively be made. To put a stop to the settlement process would not be the same thing as dismantling Israel or leaving her open to hostile attack either from within or without. I suspect the settlement is seen as an essential bulwark against a growing and discontented Palestinian population. But all it means is that a growing and discontented Palestinian population will be further straining against what it sees as encroachment onto its territory. You cannot solve the problem through genocide or by simply expelling the Palestinians; world opinion would not tolerate either. It serves to highlight the need for the two-state solution (with, again, proper safeguards respecting Israel's territorial integrity). Meanwhile, the constant backtracking on the settlement issue is one of those things which does more than anything else to sabotage the peace process and invite the justified anger of the world towards the Israeli state. The Palestinians lost enough of their land in 1948 and are now losing even more of it. What sickens me is the mercenary way Israel resumed building new settlements almost the moment Donald Trump, who they knew to be more sympathetic to them, replaced Barack Obama as US President. It epitomises the cynical and insensitive attitude of the Israelis and their contempt for the sensibilities of the world, though as hinted above there are perhaps limits which even they cannot go beyond. The effective halting of settlement was one reason why Obama's Presidency, which in many ways sadly failed to meet expectations, can be considered not to have been entirely wasted. The business also serves to demonstrate, blatantly, the connection between what goes on in America and what goes on in Israel.

In all this we must recognise that Jews and Israel are not necessarily the same thing; many of the Diaspora are disgusted by Israel's behaviour and feel it is giving the Jewish people a bad name. After all, there are Jews and Jews, and always have been. When I appear to criticise "the Israelis" I am really talking about the Israeli state and armed forces rather than the people as a whole. There do seem to be many decent Israelis, and one should feel sympathy towards those who are killed, injured or bereaved in HAMAS rocket attacks (retaliation against which is justified, even if the response may be heavy handed) or who feel they have got a raw deal when the terrorists who killed their loved ones are released as part of peace moves (the latter may be politically necessary, if only as part of the stalling tactics at which Israel is an expert). It is worth noting, however, that becoming a state has in some ways not benefited the people who opted to be citizens of that state (or the Jews who were already living in the region) any more than it has those who were dispossessed by it or suffer from its creation in any other respect. As a state Israel has to do all the things which states – such as Britain, France, the US, Germany etc. – have to in order to protect themselves, including practise *Realpolitik* and have armies and intelligence services who may find it necessary in the course of their work to be ruthless and employ dirty tricks. Organisations and industries, necessarily linked in with the global village if they are to function, develop whose activities are clearly not ethical; organised drug dealers and white slave traders are to be found in the Promised Land as anywhere else. It is difficult to avoid. We can't blame Israel simply for having the same faults that other countries do. However, although we can't say how the Jewish people would have fared had there never been a Holocaust (and thus an Israel), just as we can't say what the consequences for them as a whole would be if Israel were to be overcome by her enemies and disappear – anti-Semites would obviously rejoice, but I like to think that it would not act as the trigger for a worldwide outbreak of persecution – it is hard to entirely avoid the feeling that they, or a sizeable portion of them at any rate, lost their self-respect to some extent on becoming a state. If suffering as is claimed has ennobled Jews (as it can ennoble others), attaining statehood was not necessarily part of that process. Indeed, one gets the impression that Israelis are seen as the yobs of the Semitic world by other Jews (the Palestinians are regarded in a similar vein by Arabs).

There is, in fact, much to admire in the state of Israel. Apart from having a sneaking respect for it on account of the way it has stood up for itself, there is the whole way it has been built up since its creation into an efficiently organised unit whose citizens (apart from the Palestinians) enjoy a high standard of living, of education and culture. It gives the lie to Hitler's belief that Jews were incapable of building their own state and could only flourish off the achievements of others; that they were so long stateless was due to factors beyond their control. What Israelis obviously cannot do, of course, is recognise that the creation of their country was in any way controversial. They cannot say "Yes, we know it was unfair on the Palestinians and set a dangerous precedent but we couldn't help it and now it's been around for nearly seventy years there's no option but to accept it as an accomplished fact". That is no basis for patriotism! Patriotism, not an evil in itself, requires something more robust, and without that something there is not the psychological energy which is necessary to keep the state in being.

*

Israel or no Israel there is, as I have said before, no justification for what is purely anti-Semitism. As events have shown it is more trouble than it is worth, and there seems something very cheap about perpetuating a historically common tendency to animosity and prejudice towards a group who have already suffered far more than their fair share of oppression purely because one is jealous of their cleverness or doesn't like the fact that they are a bit different from oneself. (One can be different because of a medical condition, or simply because of the normal operation of genes. As a person with Asperger Syndrome, I know what it is like to be "different".) Jews are not to be demonised. Amongst some of them at least a certain offhandedness, a lack of concern or interest in the affairs and needs of non-Jews, has been detected in the past. But someone can't be disinterested in someone else's affairs and actively bothered about dominating or mistreating them at the same time, which is why the Protocols of the Elders of Zion (a Tsarist forgery) and the propaganda of the Nazis, which would have us believe the Jews want to take over the world and oppress all the other peoples who inhabit it, are so much nonsense. In both mediaeval and modern Europe (though less so in the latter, beyond certain elements) the notion was entertained that Jews had this sinister plan to achieve world mastery. The Diaspora, which saw them spread to a variety of different countries once expelled from their Palestinian homelands rather than congregate in just one part of the globe, might have seemed damning evidence. But if there was this widespread and concerted conspiracy I would have thought there'd have been more proof of it unless, in concealing that proof, Jews were being fiendishly clever beyond what was humanly possible. They *are* clever, a good people to associate with if you want an intelligent conversation, but not *that* clever. They had settled in a great many countries but in no way were they trying to take them over.

There are many reasons why Jews have been mistreated, but none of them are valid. It could be people simply didn't like the way they looked, and their tight-knit exclusiveness, which one might have more reason to object to, relatively speaking, was used by anti-Semites as a cover for less understandable sentiments. All I can say to this is that if someone for example saves your life, you aren't going to be bothered by what they look like, or you shouldn't. If we are opposing a Jew to someone who is fair-haired, blue-eyed and what we would call Aryan in appearance we should recognise that because of intermarriage with Gentiles in Germany, Britain, Scandinavia and elsewhere, or some other reason, there are in fact quite a few blond, Aryan-looking Jews, more in fact than there are in the Arab world (so my so often taking the side of the Palestinians is in no way due to any physical preference). A vital point which should be made here concerns a certain actress whose father is Danish and whose mother is Jewish. She takes after her dad and is fair-haired and blue-eyed. Her mother might of course be the same, I don't know. The point is this. I suppose, though I am made to feel guilty about it, that it is her "Aryan" side which I find attractive. But I wouldn't be able to enjoy it if her Jewish mother hadn't got together with her Danish father, because then she wouldn't have existed in the first place.

We need to understand that in past centuries Jews' distancing of themselves from mainstream society was to some extent due to persecution or fear of it, though of course it made matters worse by making them seem even more remote and alien, and rendering it easier for absurd myths and fancies to grow up about them (confining themselves to commerce, as Christian nonconformists in a not dissimilar situation did until the nineteenth century, helped of course to establish the idea that they were obsessed with wealth and its acquisition). That Jews arguably band together so closely in their own interest, something which Gentiles have often complained about, is likewise the result of persecution. It may merely add to anti-Semitism, but cause and effect are so hopelessly bound up with one another that either both sides, or neither, are responsible for the problem. I think these days Jews are much less exclusive, perhaps because of greater intermarriage with Gentiles (though that went on in the past a lot more than we assume). A survey a few years ago revealed that 50% of Diaspora Jews married non-Jews. Where they did not, in the past, it was from the natural fear of a minority of losing its identity if it becomes too absorbed into mainstream society. The idea of Jews as being stingy is another misconception which, if it ever was true (and at best it would (a) still be a generalisation, only valid to a certain extent, and (b) merely prove that Jews had their faults like other races) doesn't somehow resonate any more. There may once have been, perhaps still is, a Jewish *type* who is parsimonious or domineering; after all, some blondes *are* gold-diggers, or bitchy, or scatty. We just shouldn't, in both cases, ascribe the faults in question to the whole of the species (so to speak). To some degree, though, it may be that in identifying these negative types among an ethnic or other group to which we do not belong we are unconsciously being influenced by a primitive tendency to find fault in what is different; after all, it could be a question of *individuals* being flawed rather than a race or a sub-type within it, and wicked or annoying people are to be found everywhere. It may not matter what the explanation is, as long as we don't generalise.

Perhaps Jews are disliked because of their intelligence. But if they are just naturally clever, then one simply has to accept that. If, as some have said (though it seems insulting to suggest this), their cleverness is the result of the persecution they have suffered rather than any natural factor, hardship producing original thought, then it is their oppressors and not they who are to blame for what is being resented. At any rate, persecuting them for it merely looks like sour grapes and is entirely the wrong attitude to take. It would help if we all of us, Jews and Gentiles, were to reflect that it is not intelligence by which the worth of a human being is ultimately measured but their virtue, so no-one need have a complex about being less clever than somebody else, whether for racial or personal reasons.

The Nazis were jealous of the Jews, and disliked their having any kind of high profile in Germany because if they did their extra-national sense of identity would compromise the sense of nationhood they (the Nazis) thought a people should have. When this was combined with the Jews' undoubted success in the arts and sciences, they may have felt that German identity and achievement was being hijacked, and diluted, by something different from itself, Jewishness being in the past very distinct from other ethnic and national narratives. At the time Hitler came to power only 0.76% of Germans were Jewish, and they were for the most part assimilated, but the Nazis may have felt that as Jewish genes were further distributed throughout the general population people would be even more likely to say that the German achievement was in part at least actually a Jewish one. This is understandable, but they should have stopped to think that putting people in gas chambers is not a very good way of demonstrating your moral and cultural equality/ superiority over someone. The damage to the self-respect and dignity of the Aryan race – if you believe there is such a thing (the Aryan race), which in itself need not be a problem – outweighed any benefits from dealing with the supposed threat to its identity, apart from being wrong in the first place, although it had a degrading effect on its perpetrators *because* it was wrong.

As a people the Jews never really did much harm in the West, one reason why I said above that anti-Semitism was more trouble than it was worth. Apart from generally screwing up the world, in ways that have been or will be described, it gave Jews the ability to take the moral high ground even when they were not necessarily entitled to do so. Because of their sufferings the idea has developed that they are beyond criticism, which is not a good thing. But historically, where they have involved themselves in the affairs of the wider world the effect – their cultural, scientific and financial contribution to Western if not global society – has on the whole been benign, in fact enormously valuable. The only harmful aspects, even if they are potentially very harmful indeed, are oversensitivity regarding the Holocaust and the pro-Israeli lobby. There is not the slightest evidence that Jews have, for example, plotted to kidnap and murder Gentile children in obscene blood rituals. Jews in that sense are not a malicious people. As a race, rather than as individuals, where inflicting suffering wilfully and without provocation is concerned they have a very poor record. If there is anything approaching a Jewish conspiracy it exists primarily not to make life difficult for Gentiles, but rather to protect Jews from anything which might threaten their lives or wellbeing. And if the Jews find it hard to be objective, one should be sensitive when criticising them for that, in view of their past experiences, even if two wrongs don't make a right. Our anger should be tempered by understanding. In the matter of Israel, we ought to recognise that that state would probably not exist, and the elements which support it not be a problem, if it wasn't for anti-Semitism. It was a reaction to an infinitely horrendous atrocity, the culmination of thousands of years of persecution, which convinced many European Jews they would not be safe unless they had the protection of statehood. What Gentiles so dislike, an excessive and often harmful influence of Jews in geopolitical matters, only became a reality because of their own misconception that it was one when it wasn't, and what that misconception led to.

But when on those matters Jews do band together in what they perceive to be their own interest, there's no doubt those of Gentiles can suffer; and it appears to give credence to the racist allegations of a Jewish conspiracy. It's debatable whether there can be said, racism apart, to be one; people are often attacked for appearing to suggest there is, even if that wasn't quite their intention. There is undoubtedly a Jewish (for the most part) *lobby* which is influential, in a way that's disturbing and often damaging, in certain quarters in the West, particularly and most dangerously in the United States (though under George Bush's Presidency, the problem there was just as much due to right-wing neocon WASP Christians).

The criticism that Jews are not objective, in the sense that they do not put the good of the world community as a whole before that of their own kind, has tended in the past to be met by accusations of anti-Semitism. But, with the reservation that such criticisms are inevitably always generalisations, there is an uncomfortable degree of truth in them. (They may also be an attempt at being understanding, where the causes of that lack of objectivity, which lie in past persecution, are recognised, and so don't deserve to be labelled racist.) That there are so many Jews in important, and thus influential, positions in Western society is a tribute to the hard work and intelligence of the race. But it is one thing to seek to understand the reasons for that influence and quite another to condone its being exercised in questionable ways.

There is undoubtedly an element in society and politics which sees a particular importance in Jewish issues and is keen to promote them in ways others would not. In Britain in 1993 the Hendon South Conservative

Association submitted to the Party Conference the motion that the government "end its one-sided embargo on arms exports to Israel." Relatively speaking, this is a specialised issue and its being raised here in this way is striking. There is no reason for it that one can see other than the high Jewish population of the part of North London in question, here being reflected proportionately in the composition of its Conservative Association. In most other places there would be different priorities. The matter is, I feel, highly illustrative. It is too obviously and uncomfortably one of a sectional interest attempting to promote itself; the issue over which it is concerned affects a foreign country, with which the proposers happened to identify because of a common ethnicity and a solidarity explained by certain sad facts of history.

Whether the motion ever got to debate, and whether it was passed, I don't know but there is certainly a strong pro-Jewish, pro-Zionist element in the Party whose influence is not always positive. If the arms embargo were ended it could have resulted, in a situation where the Israelis and Palestinians had failed to come to a proper understanding, in British-made weapons being used to kill Palestinian children, to no avail whatsoever if the aim is to bring about peace in the Middle East. Far better to nudge Israel in the direction of the negotiating table by not encouraging her to think she can get what she wants and doesn't have to make any concessions. Once, Tory leader and Prime Minister David Cameron praised Israel for the work it did towards defending "innocent people". By this I don't think he meant the Palestinians, among whom his words would ring hollow, being met at best with sardonic laughter. He meant innocent Jews, not innocent Arabs. It is obvious which constituency he was courting. His reasons were arguably excusable. Now here I have to choose my words very carefully, because I know what I will be labelled if I don't, or even if I do. The Jewish people are skilled at finance – in saying so I am trying to be complimentary – and so they will be fairly well represented among the membership of the Conservative Party, which is the party of business. Given that Zionism, although by no means universal within the Jewish community, is not uncommon there either a reasonable proportion of those Jewish Conservatives may also be Zionists. There is a certain overlapping, as with a Venn diagram. Like any capitalist party, or indeed any political party whatever its philosophy, the Tories are opportunistic, seeking always to maximise support by adding to it or consolidating it where it already exists. Hence they don't want to antagonise their Zionist Jewish element by being too critical of Israel. This sounds like the kind of accusation made against Jewish bankers and politicians in the late nineteenth and early twentieth century, from what was undoubtedly racial prejudice. But it is rather a reflection of the complexities of politics and of the latter's calculating nature.

As controversial as the Hendon motion, and altogether far more serious, was the suspension of Mayor of London Ken Livingstone over a supposedly anti-Semitic remark made to reporter Oliver Feingold. Feingold was being too demanding in attempting to secure an interview with Livingstone, who was on his way home from a party. Neither side acquitted themselves very well: Livingstone called Feingold a "scumbag", which is not the kind of language someone occupying public office should be using. But when he accused him of acting like a Nazi concentration camp guard Feingold took offence, and said that he objected to the comment because he was Jewish. This is to imply that Jews cannot act in a rude and bullying fashion (as you will see later on, my experience suggests they can) or are somehow exonerated from blame for it, because of the past, when they do. Yet to say that someone is acting "like a little Hitler", for example, is a figure of speech and there is no reason why it should not be used in respect of Jews as of anyone else, since we cannot regard one branch of the human family as being necessarily more saintly than the others. The most troubling aspect of the matter was that the remark, not in itself racist, caused Livingstone to be suspended from his post for a time by the London Assembly while it debated the affair. Because of the sensibilities, or what were thought to be the sensibilities, of a minority of the population a democratically elected leader, a leader voted for by the majority, was prevented from exercising his functions. Even if this was only done for the sake of form, the signals it sent out are disturbing. It makes it look as if Nazis are right and Jews have an inordinate influence over the rest of society. The one thing you *don't* do is lend Nazi propaganda a disturbing element of truth (in some respects if certainly not in others). I say that for the sake of the Jews as well as that of general fairness and justice. (From the point of view of manners, it should be stressed that Feingold continued to demand answers to his questions from Livingstone after effectively accusing him of anti-Semitism, which would still have been rude (though more forgiveable) if the accusation had been just and was *particularly* rude because on this occasion it wasn't). None of these points are invalidated by Livingstone's later making remarks about Jews and Israel which were not quite so defensible as the "concentration camp guard" one; although the fact that he did is another sad example of how people on either side of a sensitive issue are prone to exacerbate it.

There is without doubt a lobby which on Jewish issues the Establishment feels should be appeased, whether or not they share its opinions and sentiments; though sometimes the Establishment may be imagining its existence, or that it would take offence over something which has been or is intended to be said/done, in the paranoid and overcompensatory manner of political correctness (despite the kind of people out of whom political correctness arose being, on the issue of Israel, more inclined to take the side of the Palestinians). I have sensed the lobby's existence whenever an article or short story I have written which is critical of Israel has been rejected for being "too political." It made itself felt when a Liberal Democrat MP was sacked from her post as a party spokesperson (therefore suffering a setback to her career) for saying it was understandable the Palestinians committed acts of terrorism against Israel considering the conditions in which they had to live –

a statement which showed humanity, and was not the same thing as condoning violence for its own sake − by Lib Dem leader Charles Kennedy. We should emphasise here that this overindulgence towards the lobby's wishes is a fault of Gentiles as much as of Jews.

You will have gathered that I am using the term "lobby" instead of "conspiracy" because the former is the less controversial and inflammatory term. You might approve, or you might think me too lily-livered. Why don't I come out and say what I really think, whether or not my motives are racist? Well, it's true that I don't want to raise the temperature any more than is necessary, and it should be sufficient for the purpose of argument just to call it a lobby and say why you criticise its actions. That is despite there being good reasons, mere hatred apart, for using the dreaded c-word. If our "lobby" knows what it's about, is at all serious concerning what it does − and given the effect of those thousands of years of persecution, I believe it is − it will meet to plan what it needs to do to achieve its aims and concert action among its members and sympathisers, and for reasons I have already given we cannot be sure it will be objective in its approach or rule out the use of underhand methods, practised away from the eyes of the general public or if necessary their leaders. It is, after all, affiliated to people whose attitude is "Israel first, last and always."

In general terms are we not, whatever our own ethnic origins, overprotective towards Jews, going rather too far in trying to highlight the evils of anti-Semitism? It can lead to a kind of attitude which seems worryingly dismissive of others. Going back in time somewhat, George Eliot's novel *Daniel Deronda* concerns equally the upheavals of Gwendolen Harleth's love life and the conflict between the title character's Jewish ancestry, something he has only recently discovered, and the pull of the Gentile environment in which he has been raised, with any link between the two seeming to lie in Gwendolen's not being entirely unattracted by the thought of marrying Daniel. Criticisms of the Jewish scenes, especially those made in the immediate aftermath of the Second World War, have been called anti-Semitic. How much truth there is in the charge I don't know, but it does seem to me − and I am arguing here from a literary point of view as much as anything else − that the two strands of the story never quite merge and ultimately seem inconsequential to one another. It would have made more sense if Gwendolen and Daniel *had* married in the end, something to which one could not object − their different cultural inheritances could in some way be allowed to enrich their relationship, whether or not either of them would have had to change their religion − but they do not. It is similar with *Charlotte Gray*, the third novel in Sebastian Faulks' *Birdsong* trilogy, where in fact the divergence is almost total, although this is made up for by the Holocaust scenes being the most powerful and moving likely to come from any writer's pen.

What I object to most regarding *Daniel Deronda* is that one commentator on the novel, discussing the two plot strands and the relationship between them, made the rather chilling, in my view, remark that Gwendolen's affairs are insignificant compared to the question of the destiny, the hopes and fears of an entire people (the Jews). Though from the purely democratic point of view it is impeccably just, there seems something ruthless and disturbing about this, the adding up of lives to outnumber the interests of one. It is an unnecessarily harsh way to put things. It has its origins in revulsion at anti-Semitism and a tendency to laud the Jews because of their cultural achievement and role in, among other things, the history of religion (the latter being an important cultural and historical factor). It is strangely and uncomfortably reminiscent of the statement in the Balfour Declaration that the wishes of the Palestinians are of little importance compared to the aspirations and historical destiny of an ancient people (the Jews). I cannot help linking it with the desire to present the Holocaust as uniquely horrendous, along with that to grant the state of Israel's wishes in all matters despite the way such a policy affects the rest of the world; because all three things have a common origin, a desire to compensate for the past and present troubles of the Jewish people even if it means putting their interests first.

Another manifestation of overcompensation for the past – though I really don't like to have to bring it up in this way – is the case of Leon Klinghoffer, a Jewish American passenger on the liner *Achille Lauro* who was thrown overboard to drown when the vessel was hijacked by pro-Palestinian terrorists in 1985. The murder of an elderly man in a wheelchair, simply because he was a Jew, is of course an appallingly wicked act – the kind with which the Palestinians shoot themselves in the foot, as they so often do – and one made worse, according to writer and investigative journalist David Yallop, by a particularly offensive remark from a Palestinian militant Yallop was interviewing about the incident, namely that maybe Klinghoffer did not drown but went for a swim and his wheelchair weighed him down (Yallop walked out, and I'd probably have done the same). Even so, it is *because* Klinghoffer was an old man in a wheelchair that to write and perform a whole opera about him seems, without in any way wishing to cause offence, absurdly and even grotesquely excessive; bathetic is perhaps the word. You might as well do one about anybody who has been unjustly and brutally murdered, whoever they were and whatever the circumstances, unless a man's murder is especially grievous *because* he is a Jew and not because he has been murdered, which is which isn't the way we should be looking at it. A memorial service, a TV film which among other things emphasises the unwarranted cruelty of the terrorists' actions – yes. But an opera...going to such lengths is a bad thing because I then need out of fairness to complain about it which tarnishes the memory of the deceased, something I have no wish to do.

On page 49 of *Praying The Psalms* (Cascade Books 2007, second edition), Walter Brueggemann writes: "When we have prayed for Jews, by turning to Jewish shapes of reality, then in our use of the Psalms we may perchance pray with the Jews. Our prayer life is always sorely tempted to individualism or at least to parochialism. We are urged by God's spirit to pray alongside and so to be genuinely ecumenical. As we use the Psalms it is appropriate to ask which Jews have used these same Psalms with passion and at risk. And a parade of victims comes to our imagination. Or, with more immediacy, which Jews now pray these Psalms, from the frightened victims of anti-Semitism to the fated soldiers in the Israeli army, to the Jews in our culture who are forever displaced and always at the brink of rejection and despisement." And a few years ago the writer of an article in a leading British newspaper on the rise of anti-Semitism in the West commented, "It's hard being a Jew in the world today." Something about the latter statement, anyway, makes me seethe. Even though anti-Semitism is unfortunately on the increase, there is still no way the global situation of Jews in 2020 compares with that before 1945. Jews may be killed, or otherwise suffer, in Israel because of Palestinian terrorism, the reasons for which we are well acquainted with, or terrorist/anti-Semitic acts elsewhere in the world, as individuals or in groups. But overall the situation of the Palestinians is far more grievous than that of the Jews. Most in the West would see it that way – would quite rightly feel more sympathy for the Palestinians than for the Israelis, even if they still saw the latter's point of view. It should be remembered that although Israelis can suffer as individuals, when they are blown up by suicide bombers etc., the Palestinians suffer more *as a people* because their standard of living is generally poorer and their national aspirations remain unsatisfied whereas Israel's do not in that she *is* a state even if under threat to a greater or lesser extent from her neighbours.

Whether or not because of the existence of the safe haven of Israel, nowhere are Jews persecuted in the institutionalised, and sometimes systematic and state-sponsored, way they used to be. There is still the fear, not invalid, of a revival of anti-Semitism on a large scale, which prompted the above-mentioned article in the first place, but what anti-Semitism is encountered in the world today is often due to real injustices against non-Jews (the treatment of the Palestinians plus certain views concerning the Holocaust). The Israeli soldiers Walter Brueggemann mentions may have been traumatised because of what they had been expected to do to Palestinian civilians, though to be fair to him this might have been what he was alluding to. At this point it seems appropriate to mention those who to their credit have actually refused to serve on the West Bank.

There is a tendency to excuse wrongs by Jews, or at any rate to deny society the opportunity to punish them, on account of the things which led to the wrongs being committed. The idea, advanced by some, that they have been purified by their suffering is dangerous, even morally offensive. It presumably means they should be immune from criticism, because the hardships and horrors they have experienced somehow make them right where others are not, or at least that they are exonerated from censure since censure would be indecent after everything they have gone through (but what about those who as individuals have not experienced the Holocaust or any other kind of persecution?). The notion can be used to excuse in the wrong fashion actions by Jews in the Bible which seem unacceptable, and in particular the massacre of the indigenous peoples of Canaan, man woman and child, by the Israelites so they could settle the land. This whole uncomfortable business has caused both theologians and Semitophiles all kinds of problems. There is sometimes a tendency, more psychological than intellectual, when puzzled or distressed by such things and unable to explain or defend them convincingly to try to solve the problem by an aggressive "in-your-face" response – the massacres *were* justified, and the victims in some way had only themselves to blame for their fate. This leads one American commentator on the Old Testament to excuse the Israelites' actions by arguing that the slaughtered peoples were morally inferior to the Jews, and therefore deserved to be exterminated. The moral inferiority was the very cause of the potential aggression against which the Israelites needed to protect themselves, by genocide if necessary.

Apart from the fact that even given the nastier practices some of them had it is difficult to see how whole peoples, without exception, could have been morally bad (and the Jews themselves are not always portrayed in a favourable light in the Bible) the writer sounds as if he is legitimising genocide by the same argument that Hitler used – that there are superior races who are justified in destroying their inferiors. The Canaanite children, the writer argues, had to be massacred too, partly because if they weren't they would grow up into Canaanite adults who would be immoral and anti-Semitic. We don't know this, even if the reservation only applies to individuals, and the whole principle is rather ugly. We need to remember here, of course, that what happened may not have been the Jews' fault anyway; it was *God* who told them to give the Canaanites no quarter and slaughter them indiscriminately. It isn't this book's brief to go into what this says about His morality, for theology is not its concern, but it is worth considering that actions such as those in question, or Cromwell's in Ireland, have a certain military justification (they are still horrible, of course) in that they may be the only way to safeguard oneself against hostile elements within the local population; in which case God was only being protective of a people he needed at that time in history to work through. The point is rather that events should not be explained and justified in a way that causes offence to general fairness and ethics and will, by association, probably lead to anti-Semitism. Since not all the people in each of the societies whom the Israelites were told to put to the sword could possibly have been wicked we need to adopt some other approach to the matter, and to ask if we have not perhaps misunderstood the language the Bible uses.

But generally the idea seems to be that those who are oppressed cannot be oppressors themselves. This is nonsense and would be nonsense whether we were talking about Jews or any other ethnic group. It is a sad but well-known fact that suffering does *not* always ennoble humanity. This is proven by the affair of Solomon Morel and, all too clearly, the behaviour of Israel towards the Palestinians. Those who have suffered are arguably *more* likely to commit wrongs than others because their minds have been poisoned by their sufferings and they have lost their objectivity. That counts as despoliation rather than purification. If Jews are regarded as having been purified by the Holocaust they will have a licence to do wrong and no-one could object (the same will apply to any other group which is being treated with sufficient indulgence out of sympathy for its tribulations). The danger of not being criticised by anyone except oneself is that being naturally biased, one will too often acquit oneself. One may not be the most objective judge. Dangerous attitudes will go unchecked. Connected with this is the idea that it is only acceptable to tell a joke about a Jew or Jews if you are a Jew yourself (though I am not sure how far the principle is insisted on in practice). This too is dangerous, because provided it is not malicious, making something the subject of humour is a way of liking it. Bringing what is different from oneself down to size makes it less likely you will hate and fear it. I have always suspected that all those jokes about Jews being obsessed with making money disguise a certain affection, part of which is a sneaking admiration for their business skills (the idea that they are stingy, which isn't necessarily the same thing, may not be entirely malicious either, or at any rate not reflect *hatred*, but as indicated above has less justification, many Jewish businesspeople having in fact been excessively generous with their favours in the past).

Holocaust or no Holocaust, Jews ought not to think – though nor ought anyone else – that you should be allowed to get away with your moral defects, whether personal or racial. When inviting the young Duke of Portland to Hughenden to thank him for his father's patronage during the statesman's earlier career, Disraeli told him "I belong to a race that never forgives an insult and never forgets a favour" (recounted in "*The Last Edwardian at Number Ten: An Impression of Harold Macmillan*", George Hutchinson 1979, p12-13). Disraeli's gratitude is admirable, but acknowledging a favour does not excuse refusal to forgive an insult. How would Disraeli have treated a presumably blameless Portland if his father had been an enemy? He was generalising in any case, since it is doubtful whether all Jews are so unreasonable, but not only is it altogether deplorable to have a diehard policy of not forgiving insults (presumably, it is abandoned where the insult is repented; it certainly ought to be) but Disraeli though Jewish by ancestry was a member of the Church of England, a Christian denomination, and thus of a religion where forgiveness is paramount. He was talking as if the refusal to forgive could be a fundamental – meaning there isn't much point in trying to change it – and even excusable part of a person's thinking. This is not a very Christian principle; that faith rather tends to take the view that if you do not forgive you will not yourself be forgiven. Conversion to Christianity is intended to purge sin or at least keep it in abeyance, whether it is the sin of an individual or of a people. Disraeli's Christianity is generally regarded as having been a bit of a sham, part of his attempts to ingratiate himself with the establishment, and it certainly appears so here; but whether it was or not makes no difference to the unfairness of his attitude.

One Norman Solomon, in an introductory book on Judaism I once read, tells his readers that if they find anything about Judaism strange or unjust they (he actually uses the second person, which only makes him seem more accusatory and judgemental) are only being impeded by the baggage, as he calls it, they have inherited from Christianity. Apart from the generally sanctimonious and high-handed tone in which he addresses Gentile Christian readers (at whom the book seems at this point to be aimed), his choice of language is deeply offensive to their beliefs. I do not consider my faith to be "baggage"; it is a comfort and a strength beyond the power of words to express. If Solomon was simply pointing out that Christians have in the past been guilty of anti-Semitic prejudice in one form or another, he should have been more careful to draw a distinction between this and Christianity *per se*, as well as to recognise that the Christian church these days is not what it was in the past. He compounds the offence by appearing to claim elsewhere in the book that Jews although of course they can still have their faults are morally superior, on average, to other people. Oh, of course we're not perfect but we're still better than you OK?

Were a Christian to be so disparaging about Judaism, it is doubtful they could escape censure in the way Solomon, as far as I know, did. Those Jews who are at fault in any way in their attitudes to race, religion or politics can too easily insulate themselves from criticism, and not just because of the Holocaust etcetera. One reason why Jews might (in some cases) be excessively vengeful is that they are still theologically in the Old Testament, where God seems rather vindictive and authorises the taking of "an eye for an eye". To suggest this has itself been attacked as racist, which when the suggestion may sometimes be valid is unhelpful. Some years ago I saw a television documentary on the Israeli-Palestinian issue in which an Israeli Jew who did not forgive killings of Israelis by Palestinians and wanted to hit the latter hard in revenge justified his stand by saying that forgiveness was "a Christian, not a Jewish principle". Ironically, we are dealing with a relatively small minority of extremists who are in fact distorting the actual spirit of the Bible, practising that vengeful Old Testament morality when God may not actually subscribe to it; analysis of language and textual criticism indicates, to Jewish and non-Jewish readers alike, that it is very easy to misunderstand the meaning of passages in Scripture.

Having been bullied mercilessly at school, surely I should sympathise with a people who have themselves suffered so acutely from persecution? Well I do, but I don't find that my experiences evoke in me any *particular* feeling of solidarity with the Jews as opposed to other distinct groups. Perhaps it was because one of my tormentors – the worst of them, in fact – was a Jew. I was bullied by a Jew and shown kindness, in that situation, by an Arab...I could easily have become biased with regard to certain issues, but chose not to be. For one thing it would be an insult to the Jewish people as a whole to become prejudiced towards them because of just one particularly disagreeable (though he may have had a behavioural problem) person. For another, whatever the trauma it does somehow seem cheap, because of its irrationality – one is not making the effort to be objective despite everything, as one should – and because it is predictable given human nature. And of course people would say, "you are only saying all these things because you were wronged by a Jew". They are probably thinking this anyway and I have no wish to appear to confirm them in being judgemental. I have no desire either to be guilty of anti-Semitism or to encourage people to think I am. (May I add that my last contact with the individual in question was friendly.)

Being bullied *does* make it impossible not to sympathise with the Jews to a greater or lesser degree, given all they've had to put up with. But awareness they could also be oppressors left me unenthused by any suggestion that we were excused in being one-sided in the matter because of history.

Then there is the tendency of some Jews to proclaim Semitic virtues and talents to the denigration, in effect, of other peoples. A Jewish entrepreneur and patron of the turf once said of a famous horse race that it was the only race greater than the Jews. This of course implies that the Jews are greater than other (human) races. Oh, thanks! If this remark were made by a white Anglo-Saxon about his own lot, you can imagine the outrage which would follow.

Gentiles sometimes seem to encourage such attitudes, attempting to assuage guilt feelings about anti-Semitism by belittling themselves in comparison to Jews. The suggestion, made in a letter to the *Metro* newspaper not so long ago, that most of the people who in the past contributed to Germany's cultural and technological success were Jewish is not only deeply offensive to Gentile Germans, who form the majority of Germans, as well as improbable but is liable to give them and others just the kind of racial inferiority complex which led to Hitler and the Holocaust. Two wrongs do not a right maketh, of course, but out of pragmatism if nothing else we shouldn't wish to encourage either of them. Ironically, this inverted racism arises from sour grapes (on the part of either Gentiles or Jews) at the Holocaust itself. When faced with bigotry towards a particular person or kind of person it is a common response to point out some way in which the object of the bigotry is actually more worthy than their perpetrators, because it highlights how ridiculous and unjustified the prejudice is. Don't we always say, when one human being treats another to verbal or physical nastiness, something like "You're just jealous, that's all", "You haven't exactly got a lot to shout about yourself", or make some remark prefaced by the words "just because you..."

It may not be unreasonable to do so; when we are dealing with entire races, however, it acquires a rather distasteful political aspect. I have no wish to unduly bash Benjamin Disraeli; he was a colourful and witty table companion, he was essential for the growth of the democratic parliamentary system in Britain, and where he was undoubtedly on the receiving end of anti-Semitism we should obviously feel for him. But he could be cutting. Responding in the

House of Commons to what he considered an anti-Semitic remark, he declared: "Yes, I am a Jew, and when the ancestors of the Right Honourable Gentleman were savages in an unknown land mine were priests in the temple of Solomon." This begs a discussion of what constitutes a civilisation; at worst that discussion risks becoming a silly point-scoring squabble, which speaks for itself, and at best it proves that the distinction between a civilisation and what is merely a society is invalid. We may be more inclined to call a society a civilisation if it has libraries, great public buildings, central heating and sewers. But those things merely fit the image better, just as a "gentleman" has traditionally been supposed to be a member of the middle or upper classes, with a refined accent and fastidious habits, whereas it is quite possible for a "working-class" person to be charming and courteous (and thus be in essence what "gentleman" really means in modern language). All societies go through periods of moral decline, but generally they are governed by laws and codes of conduct which prevent someone from seeking to acquire money or women or status simply by force. That is what constitutes civilised behaviour. In the ancient world it was possible to find barbarians who were virtuous, if perhaps in a rough and ready sort of way, and Romans who were corrupt and sexually perverted. Nor should technology be the defining mark of "civilisation"; it has after all been used, by Romans and by later peoples, in a most barbaric fashion to slaughter millions of innocent human beings. The word "savage" implies an uncontrolled, unthinking violence more suggestive perhaps of animals than people; of something barely above the level of a brute. No human person, however flawed, is really like that. Disraeli's retort was no less racist than the original insult. It certainly would be by the standards of political correctness, assuming that philosophy were being applied fairly. One can imagine the (justified) reaction of the PC lobby if someone were to gloat publicly about the fact of the West's having been at a pinnacle of cultural and technological achievement when the inhabitants of Africa were primitive tribes living in mud huts. The kind of people who are staunch politically correct liberals are probably not quite so defensive towards Jews, since they evolved from the Left of the 1980s who on Middle Eastern affairs were usually pro-Palestinian, but it need not be them at whom the criticism is directed.

Victor Serebriakoff in a book of puzzles written for MENSA (Treasure Press 1991 (omnibus edition)) sets the following problem. A little boy comes home crying because the ice cream man will not sell to him, though he will to all the boy's schoolfriends. "Why not?" his father asks. "He says he won't sell me ice cream because I am a Jewish boy." The father angrily confronts the ice cream man, who is Jewish himself which makes the implications of the whole thing more serious. The ice cream man declares "No Jewish child shall eat my ice cream!" He explains why he adopts this policy and the father's attitude completely changes: "So you see, my son, it seems quite reasonable after all that he wouldn't want to sell his ice cream to a Jewish boy." "I quite understand, Daddy, I think he was right to discriminate," says the son.

The Answers (If We Need Them) (yes, it really does say that) section tells us the reason was that the ice cream tasted horrible. It seems Gentiles can be served horrible ice cream but a Jewish boy shouldn't; another assertion of Jewish superiority. I think, and certainly hope, that Serebriakoff was attempting, probably uneasily, a rather bad joke, or testing his readers' reaction in some way. He was still being extremely unwise, because this is one of those cases where many people, whether intelligent or not so intelligent, would understandably take offence even if offence was not meant.

One might also consider the novels of George Eliot. What clearly annoys her is that Victorian England idealised fair-haired Aryan-looking people, as is evident from a lot of its artwork, yet while setting so much store on the Christian religion (which as an atheist, she didn't have much time for anyway) forgot that it owed so much to the Jews, a people the Victorians despised because they were in the main pale, dark-haired and (some of them at any rate, and probably all in the popular imagination) hook-nosed, and in particular to one Jew – its founder, Christ Himself. As a reaction against this, she sticks up for the Jews in her books, particularly *Daniel Deronda*, while making all the blond(e) people, those who in physical terms most exemplify the ideal of Aryan perfection, stupid or untrustworthy (consciously or otherwise making use of the fact that they often seem that way to others). She seems to praise the Jew and mock the blond(e), more Aryan type of Gentile, in what seems almost a sort of reverse discrimination and perhaps is. Read her, if you think my accusation is far-fetched. One sees her point, but in getting her own back for what she doesn't like she herself comes across as unkind, superior and smug, and rather puts a dent in her claim that by renouncing religion she was not compromising fairness and justice, just as she does when in *Deronda* she describes choral singing as "religious howlings". In the latter case the juxtaposition of the words is as offensive as "blonde bitch" or "black bastard", since it implies that's what religious people do – howl, rather than sing properly. You shouldn't have to be a Christian yourself to find it unacceptable. Her being in effect rather disparaging towards blondes may seem to be a small matter compared with putting people in gas chambers, but it is still disagreeable. In one of her books a character stresses that if it was the blonde girl who was the victim of injustice they would seek to highlight *that*, which is either an admission that she (Eliot) has gone too far or a way of teasing people who object to her approach, the way she liked to bait Christians, because she never does redress the balance in any of her novels. (Incidentally, viewed purely from a literary perspective Eliot is a great writer but not in my view as good as the Bronte sisters; I don't say this because I don't like the accent she gives to her politics.)

Niall Ferguson in the course of his book *Civilisation* makes several comments which amount to something enormously offensive and ill-considered. He both suggests that Jews have a genetic advantage over other races in the intelligence stakes, because of the number of them who have achieved distinction in all walks of life – it almost seems to be arguing for some sort of inherent racial superiority – and that the atrocities committed by the Japanese in World War Two, whether the victims were Europeans or Asians, "pale into insignificance" besides the Holocaust. The latter argument we have already roundly sent packing. But taken together it all comes over like a massive slap in the face.

It is very doubtful whether every great achievement in science, the arts, politics or economics has been the work of the Jews. They couldn't have done all that, or even most of it, on their own, one reason for this being that there simply aren't enough of them and wouldn't be regardless of pogroms and Holocausts and the like. One could point to any number of intelligent and influential people in history who were not Jewish. Let's take science. Of what we might call the "big four" who were responsible for the most important developments of recent centuries – the psychologist Freud, the physicists Einstein and Newton, and the biologist Darwin, two (Einstein and Freud) were Jewish, the other two were not. (When all these men are considered as makers of the modern world some would add Marx (a Jew) to their number, but they are either Communists and therefore biased or are simply stating that Marx's beliefs had a major influence on the course of historical events, not that he necessarily achieved anything beneficial). Einstein's work built to a great extent on the research of people like James Clerk Maxwell. Nor did he supersede, rather than add to, Newton whose laws still remain basically valid besides having the advantage of being easier to understand; for the latter reason they were used successfully in planning the Apollo missions, where one would have thought the consequences of going wrong would be disastrous. None of this is to belittle Einstein who, though I disagree with his Zionist politics, was apart from anything else a far more likeable man than the vindictive Newton. Winning the battle with Leibniz over which of the two of them should be given the credit for inventing calculus, Newton remarked that he took great satisfaction in breaking his adversary's heart.

Besides, as I pointed out earlier our worth as human beings does not depend on how clever we are; what counts most is virtue. By that standard either a Jew or a Gentile could fall or be vindicated. We must not be tempted to take sides in the Israeli-Palestinian dispute just because the Jews/Israelis so often seem cleverer. And being smart in one sense does not necessarily mean being smart in the other, does not preclude foolish *attitudes*; Jews who argue the uniqueness of the Holocaust when it is dangerously inflammatory to do so are not being very smart at all.

We ought to be aware that a feeling of inferiority in comparison with the splendid culture and achievements of Greece and Rome, and with the Jews because of the latter's role in the founding of Christianity as well as their producing so many clever and talented individuals, was one of the factors explaining the belief system of the Nazis and their theory of Aryan "superiority." Those with an inferiority complex often tend to act aggressively, and in the case of the Nazis we all know what that tendency led to. It is quite obvious from their writings that they did suffer from such a complex, and a massive one at that. How far all this is having a damaging effect today is not clear; what I'm saying, I suppose, is that I don't know whether the Nazis, who of course have spawned plenty of modern imitators, ever read George Eliot. But the dangers are there. It is no service to either Jews or Gentiles to suggest that the former are somehow superlative. It might mean that when they got things wrong there would have to be some sinister reason for it. Hitler's mother died under the care of a Jewish doctor, because Jews can no more work miracles than other people and like them are often unable to fight the sheer force of Nature. The tendency to celebrate the Jews as being particularly clever, talented etc. arose partly as a reaction to the Holocaust, but we cannot rule out the possibility that Hitler (while being on good terms with the doctor in question) was subconsciously influenced by feelings such as I have described.

Family history research has suggested I may have a few drops of Jewish blood myself. Should I feel proud of that; or, like Charlie Chaplin, say that I'm not a Jew but wish I was, out of solidarity with and admiration for a skilled and industrious, yet in the past much maligned, people? I have resisted any temptation to do either. To wish that one should be a member of a particular race as opposed to another inevitably belittles the latter, since its corollary must be that they are less prestigious or exciting to belong to. Jews responded to the enormous shock that was the Holocaust in different ways. Some believed the *Shoah* was divine punishment for the sins of their race, when in fact Jewish people were no more sinful, if at the same time no more saintly, than anyone else. It was no less irrational for other Jews to go so far as to downplay or even deny their Jewishness, to be afraid of making it too obvious because it was the reason why they had suffered so much; no-one should apologise just for being what they are, i.e. a branch of the diverse human family, and to do so only encourages those who would persecute others for it. But nor should a third category have decided to trumpet it stridently, even aggressively, to the point sometimes of ignoring the needs and sensibilities of the world at large. I don't know, in any case, at what point someone becomes a Jew; there is a difference between having, say, 5-10% Jewish genes in you and being Jewish. If you *are* Jewish, by any reckoning, then you should never be uncomfortable about it any more than one should regret being anything else. It's pointless and silly to be ashamed of a genetic heritage you did not choose in the first place and can do nothing about; without it you wouldn't be here! It's not the only thing which defines you, anyhow, even if it may nonetheless do so to some extent and inevitably. But for someone like me, the only thing which would cause me to feel dismayed on learning I had Jewish ancestors would be the possibility others would attribute any talents I possessed to that; that it made me special in any other way than that in which an individual or a distinct (roughly speaking) race always is, purely through being themselves. (By the way, I don't think Jews as a rule are any more racially egoistic than anybody else.)

We perhaps ought to bring religion into the discussion somewhere, since the fact the Jews (along with the Romans, of course) murdered Christ explains a lot of Christian anti-Semitism, perhaps by serving as an excuse for what people were inclined to do anyway. However I won't enter into a discussion on such matters here as I believe they are adequately explored in my book *Rediscovering God: A Defence Of Christian Belief In The Twenty-first Century* (2017). All I would say – apart from that the prejudice in question was obviously deplorable – is that the tendency of (some) Jews to insist Christians should be grateful to their race for its part in the birth of that faith, while refusing to take it up themselves, is a bit cavalier, especially if it is theologically correct that one needs to be a Christian, barring extenuating circumstances, to avoid damnation after death, in which case the attitude in question is also dangerous. That of course is a complex, and also highly sensitive issue. (I hasten to add that the "extenuating circumstances" might well apply to our own time and Western social context, where hostility/apathy towards religion has become endemic, and to some degree institutionalised, so that the spread of the Gospel beyond the walls of a church is inhibited and individuals may not therefore be to blame for atheism, agnosticism or subscribing to a different belief system.)

There is no need for us to hate the Jews or to see them as a threat; like a lot of races nowadays, they are if anything probably going through an identity crisis because of cultural changes one aspect of which is greater intermarriage with other races. Nonetheless anti-Semitism is regrettably still a problem. We need to look at what, in the modern world, are its causes and deal with them. The trouble is, this itself means confronting some uncomfortable home truths. The reason for modern anti-Semitism may, as in a lot of historical prejudices, be a case of ignorant and/or ill-disposed people simply not liking what is a bit different, and you just have to try to counter that through better education and the right laws. Otherwise it is two-fold; the behaviour of the state of Israel and the insistence that the Holocaust should be seen as worse than other atrocities. Both have their origin in things which were thought to be necessary to *protect* Jews, but in fact are having the opposite effect. The Holocaust is seen as such a terrible thing that to prevent it recurring it is necessary to go into overkill. Israel's existence is a symbol of resistance to anti-Semitism and therefore she must be defended, right or wrong. Somehow or other, we must retreat from these positions without going back to the other end of the scale.

Several months ago there was outrage on the part of Jewish and anti-Fascist groups over a T-shirt advertising "Hitler's European Tour", as if the Nazis between 1933 and 1945 had been a rock band. I well remember the offending item from my student days in the 1980s; in other words it's been around a long time, so why are we getting so uptight about it now? I think it was intended as much as anything else as a satire on Hitler's lunacy in invading so many countries against their wishes, and how it ultimately led to his downfall (his last stop was "The Berlin Bunker, 1945"). I might also mention, though it now seems embarrassing to do so, my performance as Hitler in an informal House photograph at school in 1981. I wore a pair of shorts and an ordinary shirt. I attached a pair of crudely made Nazi armbands with swastikas to my wrists, and drew a toothbrush moustache under my nose in black felt tip. I wasn't a member of the royal family (I have in mind, of course, a certain incident involving Prince Harry), nor would my costume have been seen for more than a few minutes (as opposed to a few hours), diminishing any harmful effect it might have had. There was no intention to be offensive, it was simply larking about. Of the two Jewish boys in the House, one was away on exceat at the time, the other didn't bat an eyelid. But if I were to do that kind of thing now, whatever the circumstances, something tells me I wouldn't get away with it quite so easily.

Actually I'm not sure I'd *want* to do it now, and not just because of the onset of middle-aged gravitas. It's hard to say why exactly. But the example does highlight how we seem if anything to be getting *more* sensitive about the Holocaust, etcetera, as time goes on, which is not necessarily a good thing. I remember one Jewish writer to a leading national newspaper saying he feared a rise in anti-Semitism because Gentiles were so afraid to say anything which might offend Jews. I know what he means; the very fact of being expected to be oversolicitous towards Jews, when it becomes sufficiently irksome, means people will be anti-Semitic simply as a way of rebelling against that. It will be the same with other ethnic groups who in the past have been discriminated against in one way or another and who we are now expected to go to sometimes excessive lengths not to upset. The purpose of this essay was to highlight the respects in which our reaction to the wrongs of the past may actually be questionable from a moral and intellectual point of view. It was also to sound a warning.

POSTSCRIPT

I argued at the beginning of this chapter that ageing Nazi war criminals should not stand trial. In 2014 Lord Janner, who I criticised for the position he took on the issue, was charged and put in the dock for alleged child sex abuse, despite having begun to suffer from dementia. If one thinks of the "misjudgement" remark as unfair there might seem to be a terrible justice in this, especially considering that Janner had also, and unwisely as it turned out, suggested at one point that if the media were making a big enough fuss about something (an allegation of wrongdoing on someone or other's part) it must be true, on the principle of "no smoke without fire". But although dementia can be only partial, and inconsistent in its effects, as someone who opposed the War Crimes Bill I feel constrained to say out of fairness that what applies to Nazis should clearly also apply to Lord Janner (even if he did commit crimes of the sort he was accused of and which of course I deplore). And not least because some of those gloating over the matter, which would be the wrong thing to do in any case, are probably doing so for particularly unhealthy reasons. You can guess what they are.

That there is taking place a resurgence of anti-Semitism is undoubted; nasty internet posts prove it. For a fan of the rock star Bryan Ferry, his statement a few years ago that he admired the architecture of concentration camps, because of the order and efficiency it represented, is particularly regrettable. In Freudian terms the remark is interesting, representing an amalgam of sentiments not necessarily wicked with those that are deplorable; admiration at Hitler's success in putting his will into practice, which I suppose is understandable in itself though not in the context of concentration camps, and an underlying anti-Semitism.

My fear is that if the revival of anti-Semitism goes far enough even moderate Jews will feel they are forced to take up extreme positions. But I don't retract the assertions I have been making about the attitudes which if anything make it more likely that there will be another Holocaust, or something equally nasty, in the future, though obviously we trust not. Recently one ninetysomething-year-old man came forward of his own volition to confess to having been a concentration camp warder, which I suppose was the right thing to do. He went on trial. We do not adopt the principle that people should be spared punishment for a crime merely because they have owned up to it; for one thing it prevents justice from having a deterrent effect by encouraging criminals to insincerely repent in order to be let off. But when at the same time his age was taken into account it seemed extremely mean; like a punishment for being virtuous, and indicative of just that relentless, indeed almost hysterical, vengefulness, the keen edge of which appears sharpened rather than blunted by the years, whose dangers I have been seeking to point out.

The time factor is important in other respects, too, when discussing reactions to the Holocaust. There is a Holocaust Museum in New York where visitors are given a card with details of a concentration camp inmate at the outset of their visit and find out at its end whether he or she survived or died. This could be seen as encouraging empathy (which was probably its purpose) but also as a tasteless, in the circumstances, advertising gimmick. There seem to me to be parallels with the event recently held at a preserved steam railway in Britain which involved the re-enactment of scenes from the Second World War, including vicious SS soldiers forcing Jews onto the train which was to take them to a concentration camp. It could have been that the organisers were merely showing it as it was, with the aim partly of getting people to think about the awfulness of such things. But a Jewish family were upset and complained. Whether people were warned beforehand about what they might see, but not everyone could get the message in time, I don't know. But the increasing lapse of time since the Holocaust, which means that outside the Jewish community it will cease to have quite the psychological effect it does, will make it easier to slip over the sometimes thin line between what is acceptable and what is not. We can only ask that people use their judgement. I don't think either of the two cases I mentioned are symptomatic of genuine anti-Semitism. By themselves they needn't do much harm. The crucial factor is that in the future we will not feel so automatically obliged to make a point of avoiding what may cause offence to Jews, whether it is fair comment or foul. This will be liberating but also carry with it a certain responsibility. We might by degrees find ourselves going to the other end of the scale or at least creating the environment where that could happen. A particular worry is that if Jews felt sufficiently threatened, physically and in other ways, by a resurgence of anti-Semitism even those who don't like Israel would go there in order to be safe from it, which would be natural enough. They could not be accommodated without expelling the remaining Palestinians, and that would set the region ablaze. Equally, what the Jews would do if there *was* a second Holocaust, to make absolutely sure there could never be a third, I do not like to contemplate. It would be wrong and need to be stopped, but somehow it seems unfair not to try to understand those who might commit it. So although it comes across as trite to say this, we must take great care to ensure there is *not* a second Holocaust, for the sake both of its victims and of those who might suffer from their revenge, whether or not the suffering was deserved.

On that score, I do not know how likely it was that the tendencies recently evident in the British Labour Party could have contributed to such a tragedy; but it was a factor in the defeat of Jeremy Corbyn in the 2019 general election, and we may regard it as comforting that the people can be said to have given a verdict against extremism and prejudice, or at any rate the failure to deal with them properly.

Appendix: The World Wars and the Holocaust – the question of German guilt

It would seem fitting in all this to discuss the way in which blame for the Holocaust tends to be apportioned. The tendency to criticise ordinary Germans, and with particular harshness, on account of Hitler is one manifestation of it. It is certainly unfortunate for them that it should have happened in their country; although we may be misunderstanding the German character there is a streak in it which sometimes makes it seem insensitive, and thus uncaring about such matters. But although it is understandable that the part of the body at which an infection enters it should receive particular attention from those trying to cure the illness or prevent a recurrence of it, that is not to suggest it could not have happened in some other part. If the circumstances are right, it could happen anywhere. All it takes is for economic conditions to be so poor, national pride so dented, moral decay so advanced, and the existing government so ineffectual, that a small group of extremists, if they seem the only people with sufficient drive and ability to get things back on their feet, will be able to lever themselves into power and afterwards keep hold of it. As in the First World War, the Germans are being made a scapegoat for the sins, real or potential, of humanity in general. But were they nonetheless culpable, and can we say that anyone else would have been in their situation?

I feel a need to defend the Germans, or at least see that they are treated fairly over issues like this, on account of perceiving a racial and cultural kinship with them; as I think many English people, even some who fought in the Second World War, traditionally have done. This doesn't necessarily mean that one subscribes to Hitler race theories or is unconscious of a wider world in which ultimate loyalty should be to the human race in general. In fact, one reason why I began, at the age of about sixteen, to experience a sense of belonging with the Germans in a "Teutonic" identity, apart from needing I suppose to find a place in the scheme of things as a member of a particular race or family of races/cultures, could without any inclination to moral conceit be called humanitarian. Previously, Germans had seemed an aggressive and also treacherous people, constantly scheming to dominate you in one way or another. There were the two world wars of course. In the boys' comics I had read as a child, there were frequently strips set in World War Two where villainous Germans, uttering dialogue such as "Britischer pigdog {schweinhund}!" were trounced by heroic British soldiers like "Captain Hurricane" who would exclaim "Take that, Fritz!" or words to that effect and call them "Hamburg hogwashers" or "Dresden ditch-diggers" while dishing out the just desserts. Even now they were still potentially the foe, to be regarded with suspicion, seen as not altogether trustworthy. On a family holiday on the continent in 1972 my brother poked his tongue out at a German woman. Then I read that the Anglo-Saxons, who colonised Britain in large numbers after the Roman legions withdrew, had originally come from Germany. The people who had been so much reviled as a national enemy (who we fought in *two* world wars, remember), of a particularly disagreeable sort, were also those from whom, I then believed, most of the English – probably including myself, on statistical grounds – were descended. Later of course I learned that the Saxons had only been one of several north European tribes to have made the crossing, also that the "Germanic" element in our ancestry was much less than had been supposed. But I found this to make no difference, true as it was, nor am I convinced it should have done.

You may be wondering whether I have ever taken a DNA test to establish my own provenance with (supposed) certainty. The fact is I haven't. The results from my mother's stated that a certain, relatively small percentage of her genes came from Scandinavia (the Vikings, if one applies the term to all Norse and Danish "immigrants" between the eighth and eleventh centuries), another from Eastern Europe (the Celts) and a third element, intriguingly, from Finland. So far, fine. The rest (82%) was simply "Great Britain". We know of course that humans did not evolve separately in the British Isles from anywhere else; they had to have migrated from somewhere. "Great Britain" tells us nothing. It was not part of the tests' brief to go as far back as Africa, so they were seeking to identify where one's ancestors came from in *Europe*. Given that a large part of our genetic inheritance does comes from the Saxons, that they are known to have settled here on a not inconsiderable scale, "Great Britain" ought to have been "Germany". Why it was not, why the Saxons were missed out when the other principal migrant groups who contributed to our DNA were taken into account, is difficult to say. I would add that myself, my brother and mother are among those English people who look very like Germans (my father and paternal grandfather did too, although the former had darker hair and a darker complexion, maybe indicating some other influence), although there are obviously other strains in our genetic make-up, too.

The only explanation I can think of for the omission is a political one, namely that someone does not want to encourage the idea that the British are part with the Germans of a Teutonic (Aryan) race, as that was what Hitler believed and what far-Right racists in modern Britain still do. This might seem far-fetched, too much of a conspiracy theory, but no other answer comes to mind. In my view it can't be ruled out owing to the increasingly peculiar, and invasive, character of political correctness. But whatever the explanation *is*, the omission doesn't make sense and certainly is of no help to people who really do want to know where they came from. I don't see why I should pay money for a test whose result might not be sufficiently informative.

However. If one feels a sort of family kinship with someone, one does not like to see them disgrace themselves by doing what ought not to be done, or not doing what ought to be done. How then should we view the failure of the ordinary German population between 1939 and 1945 to prevent the Holocaust?

From their disappearance, plus rumours too widespread to be without some degree of truth, the general public plus many in the armed forces and government must have guessed that *something*, probably bad, had happened to the Jews, but not necessarily what it was (the Nazis seem not to have been in a hurry to tell them). Perhaps we ought to ask not how much they knew but what they could have done. In the 1930s and in the early part of the war there were actually quite a few cases of soldiers obtaining transfers from postings where they had to obey orders they knew to be immoral and inhuman. But this was less easy in the latter half of the war, when Germany was pressed for resources whether human or material and everyone was needed where they were. And the transfers merely meant that posts were filled by those who *were* prepared to carry out the atrocities in question without remorse. So what we are suggesting is that people should have gone further and actively opposed the regime as long as it was intending to commit genocide.

When some deliberate act involving terrible loss of life is committed, whether it is a terrorist bombing or the systematic extermination of millions of people over a period of years, one tends to shout "Why didn't someone do something to stop it? Why didn't someone speak out?". That is only natural, especially if we belong to the group which has been victimised and/or has relatives among the dead. But those who complain about the refusal of German soldiers, bureaucrats and civilians to do more to stop Nazi atrocities never ask themselves what they would have done in the same position. Are they honestly saying that if they had been, they would have refused without hesitation to comply with the authorities, regardless of the consequences? Can any of us claim we would have had such courage? As Brian Sewell wrote in the *Evening Standard*, "The consequence would, of course, have been death − and who among us now, with the choice of living with a troubled conscience or immediately dying with one clear, would refuse to obey a dishonourable order, knowing that one's own death would not, in any case, save the life of another man or woman, Jew, gipsy, Slav or homosexual; that one's own corpse would tumble with a hundred others into the fresh-dug pit or end as just one more smudge of grease on the oven floor? The man with his hand on the instrument of death had no bargaining power with the man who gave the orders." This is of course quite right; if it is not moral to demand that someone makes such a sacrifice, when we might not do it ourselves, it is even less so if the sacrifice would achieve nothing other than make a further contribution to the whole human tragedy of the business. In the case of soldiers, we are maybe inclined to ask why those who risked death anyway on the battlefield did not risk it by disobeying their superiors' orders. There is a difference between physical and moral courage, but I think the essential answer is that on the battlefield a soldier has at least a chance of survival, whereas here death would more or less have been certain.

Jewish revenge squads active in Germany in the aftermath of the Holocaust who made it a principle to kill only those directly involved in the murder of Jews, if by this they meant the man who pulled the trigger, may actually have been killing those who *least* deserved to die, though to be fair they did honestly believe they were attempting to be just (it really depends on whether someone committed the act on their own initiative or what chance they had of concealing disobedience from higher authority, or those who would report it to same). The UN took the view that punishment for Nazi war crimes should be restricted to those who initiated (presumably on their own account) atrocities by giving the order for them, rather than those who were simply obeying those orders. I think this was the correct approach. As we've effectively already said, it is entirely possible, given the sort of people the Nazis were, that those who refused to carry them out might themselves have come to a sticky end (as would anyone who opposed the regime in any way; consider the fates of Hans and Sophie Scholl, Bonhoeffer, and the July 1944 bomb plot). Much would depend, in any trial, upon how far a person could be said to be aware of the dangers of refusal. It may not be easy to distinguish, either, between those who killed because they were ordered to, but may not have relished the task, and those who *enjoyed* doing so (and thus would probably have carried out the atrocity anyway if given the chance), supposing that to be the incriminating factor where the guilt of subordinates is concerned. Altogether, we would be venturing into a moral and legal minefield and thus complicating the process of securing justice. The main disadvantage would be that we might be letting people who deserved, if the sin of something lies in its spirit, to be executed or imprisoned for life go free, but it would be compensated for by the sparing of many who arguably did not merit that punishment.

A linked question to this one is that of the collective guilt of the German people, something we have already discussed to some extent. Reason suggests that it is simply not possible for one race or nation to be significantly worse, in moral terms, than any other. How then do we explain what was allowed to happen in Germany between 1933 and 1945? Why did more people not actively resist the Nazi regime? Undoubtedly racial and national temperament – the tendency of the German to be obedient to authority – had a certain amount to do with it; in a more individualistic and rebellious culture, Hitler might not have got away with so much. But that was only one of the factors involved. You have to look at how the psychology of the totalitarian state operates. If you actively resist it, there is the possibility that you and/or your family might be killed/imprisoned (and you/they don't matter any less than the people already in the concentration camps). There is no doubt that all the apparatus of the terror state was in place in Nazi Germany – as Alan Bullock among others makes clear – and constantly looking out for those whose behaviour did not show sufficient dedication to the regime. There were spies in the crowd watching for people who seemed unenthusiastic about giving the Hitler salute, fanatical Nazis serving as informers in the *Wehrmacht* (the ordinary German army), and average citizens who would be quite happy to betray neighbours, work colleagues, even family members in order to curry favour with their rulers. I once came across in my local museum a British newspaper from 1939 which contained an item reporting how a man had found himself under arrest for showing compassion to a Polish prisoner-of-war. One might object that if *everyone* pulled together and opposed the regime, it would be brought down at relatively little cost and all the above prevented. But unless you can be absolutely sure what everyone else is going to do – in other words, be telepathic – you can't be certain of having that safety which lies in numbers and so you won't take the risk. And secondly, it is likely there would be *some* loss of life (for one thing, a soldier faced with a crowd of people converging on a government building he is guarding may panic and start shooting, particularly if he is trigger-happy or young and inexperienced). And you might be among the people killed. The Nazis knew all this and turned it to their advantage, like all autocrats. How do you think the tiny island of Great Britain was able to hold down the whole of the Indian subcontinent, in fact rule altogether a third of the Earth's surface? The method used was the same in both cases, even though it would be base to compare the Raj with the Reich in every respect. With someone like Hitler, to resist the evil would be saintly; not to resist it, forgiveable. And again, in totalitarian regimes the families of dissidents or potential dissidents are often threatened. It may be noble of me to risk my own life if I choose, but is it not morally wrong – a bit like playing God – to insist that a third party be involved in the sacrifice, is expendable in a dispute between two others; certainly if its own consent is not forthcoming? Well actually it isn't, because you should not put your own relatives before the common good. But it is still distasteful, and the kind of sacrifice which it would be indecent to expect either the person making it, or the victim, to contemplate lightly. It is notable that Pastor Dietrich Bonhoeffer sent his family out of the country before he embarked on his campaign of resistance against the Nazis. Those who did not have the opportunity of taking this precaution might not have made the sacrifice. No doubt these excuses are often used to cover failure to protest at or prevent atrocities, but they are valid nonetheless.

The German people, then, have no more reason to be condemned for allowing the Nazis to kill Jews than have the Iraqi people for Saddam Hussein's atrocities against the Kurds (against which the ordinary population did not protest *en masse*, the world community failing to condemn them for this as it had condemned Germans in 1945). It makes the plot by the Jewish revenge squad to poison German water supplies all the more disturbing, even if we cannot lightly condemn those whose minds have been twisted by appalling loss and suffering. Where Germans on trial for war crimes too often went wrong was in not citing understandable human weakness as the cause of their inaction; it might have gone down a lot better. Instead, by saying "I was only obeying orders" they gave the impression they did not care either way.

I have heard people say that because the Holocaust was a particularly distressing event, any merciful distinction between the giver and the executor of orders should be suspended. But we have examined the idea that it was worse than other atrocities and found such arguments wanting. How exactly do we distinguish between those actions complicity in which merit the maximum penalty, execution or a life sentence, and those which do not? At which point does one draw the line, and does it depend on the number of those killed, who was killed, or how they were killed? From an ethical point of view all such qualifications are unfair, since the unlawful death of just one person, by whatever means and regardless of their race, creed etc., should be distressing enough. Reject these considerations and we become discriminatory in a way which is unjust or, at best, results in a highly invidious argument over whose sufferings were the worst. Unless we abandon altogether the principle that the servant is as guilty as the master, even when he will die if he refuses to obey him. I don't think we can; and if we apply it at all, it must be applied across the board.

It is worth mentioning here that there were some Germans who although unable to prevent atrocities being committed at least tried to make sure, out of personal honour, that it was not they who literally or metaphorically pulled the trigger. One concentration camp guard applied for a transfer to a different post because he knew he was being debased by having to join in the laughter as Jews in the camps were beaten up or humiliated in one way or another. It is important to recognise that as with the war crimes of the Japanese, it would have indicated disapproval of what was going on, and thus jeopardised his own safety, if he had not done so. His request was refused, but it had been made nonetheless. What difference there would have been to the general course of the Holocaust if it had been granted is hard to say; probably very little. But he had at least tried to do the right thing, in the only way he could, and it would be unduly harsh of us not to regard this as morally commendable.

There is little doubt that with the exception of diehard Nazis, the experience of 1933-45 was traumatic for ordinary Germans, in the way that being forced to assist in someone else's murder inevitably is. In one sense they too were oppressed, by being forced to participate or at least permit, on pain of torture, imprisonment or death, in atrocities which they must have inwardly found distressing, feeling guilty about, and which earned them the hostility, often enmity, of the international community and of Jewish groups (the latter with potentially terrible consequences). What was nightmarish and morally brutalising for them they obviously abandoned with alacrity (though never showing their emotions as much as others might, which is a very German thing) once they no longer had to do it; it was as understandable that they should do so as it was that they had obeyed the Hitler regime beforehand. If someone makes you help them unjustly kill someone you find it a hideous situation to be in and are obviously going to be well-disposed towards whoever has rescued you from it, and thus happy to co-operate with them. Plus the national German tendency to obedience applied whoever was in control, the Nazis or the Allies. The eagerness of German civilians to help the controlling Allied authorities in their task after the war was therefore not a sign that their race was two-faced and craven, that Germans were either at your throat or, once vanquished, your feet. As pointed out people could not, during the war, show any unease at what was going on as this would be interpreted as disloyalty. You went through a stage of unquestioning submission to one set of rulers to an attitude of helpfulness to another. What the Germans could not do was talk about the matter that much, and that is why they appeared insensitive. They are a reticent people in any case. But, ashamed by everything yet naturally unwilling to accept blame for what was not entirely their fault, if acquiescence in it was down to human weakness, they were also unable to articulate their feelings openly.

The implausibility of any single ethnic group or national community being made up of demons means that if they do seem to be particularly cruel or indifferent it must be due to things they cannot easily help. So we are not justified in regarding the Germans as any worse than other peoples because of Hitler. If they were, then there would have to be a reason for that. It would be a bit strange, a bit arbitrary, if this particular nastiness was confined to the Germans and not found anywhere else. It would require to be explained. Logically an action, or the failure to commit it, can only be either the result of conscious choice or of something that cannot be avoided. Since the initial tendency towards a particular kind of behaviour must be genetic, because in the first instance we do not choose the desires, the impulses, that we find ourselves prone to the explanation for it must be to do with the nature of the universe and of human beings. It is something fundamental, even if it may sometimes be spiritually bad, and we cannot blame Germans in particular for it. If on the other hand the translation of a desire into an action, which if harmful is in one sense a more serious matter than the desire itself, is a matter of choice it is a bit odd, despite the world wars and the Holocaust, that Germans should have *consistently* opted to do harm while others did not. Such a dichotomy between their conduct and that of the rest of Mankind would have to be accounted for. It is either the result of chance, to a degree which is improbable, or something which the Germans for some reason could not avoid and therefore *not* a conscious choice for which they could be blamed. But either they did choose to do wrong, consistently or otherwise, in which case they are also capable of choosing to do good and it is better to encourage them to do so rather than vilifying, ostracising or even exterminating them; or they were incapable of acting otherwise, in which case we can't blame them for what they did even though we should still have tried to stop them.

When the Israeli ambassador to Britain visited Stuttgart in 1992 for the trial of Nazi war criminal Josef Schwammberger, "{He} took the opportunity to remind the German people of their collective responsibility for the past. He told the German press that one could not separate the cultural heritage of Goethe, Schiller, Bach and Beethoven from the terror of the Nazi regime." (Ian Buruma, *Wages of Guilt*, Jonathan Cape 1994, p137). One is minded to respond:

a) What about Germans born since 1945, or who were still children when the war ended?

b) This is like saying Shakespeare was a member of the English Defence League, or would be if he was alive today, and that the British people should collectively feel shame on that account. Being a playwright, composer or a poet evidently gives someone racist tendencies, so we'd better all avoid such activities from now on.

c) The rise of Hitler was a product of a complex combination of different factors of which the character of German society and culture was only one. Had they not all happened to come together, the Third Reich might never have occurred and we would never have regarded the Germans with such hostility. They were to some extent the fault of the Allies, as we will see below.

This example shows that it *is* possible, in spite of what some people have argued, to victimise Germany over the Holocaust (though this has not, mostly, happened in the same way that the Nazis victimised the Jews). If someone is *excessively* blamed for a wrong or – and this is the real crux of the matter – if the question of how far they could have done something about it is not properly addressed, with insufficient distinction drawn between the rulers and the ruled, then that could be called victimisation. Again, it is understandable that if an infection has broken out in a particular part of the body and in a particularly big way, people should afterwards treat it with some wariness. If I were to sum up what Germans' own attitude to the Holocaust should be, I would say that Germany has no reason to feel particularly ashamed compared to other countries, but she should not *forget.*

The Germans are, of course, particularly guilty in some people's eyes because as well as the Holocaust they were responsible for two (*two*, note) World Wars. What started the First World War was their invasion of Belgium. I am not going to condone that particular act, and certainly by modern standards it was wrong. However there's something we need to bear in mind. Undoubtedly all nations at that time in European history were being imperialistic in one way or another; it may be unfair to put the blame for the consequences of that on Germany alone or apportion her the largest share of it. It is perhaps a controversial, and sensitive, issue. But Germany was only doing in Belgium – if the invasion is seen as unacceptable colonialism – what other western countries had been doing in what we now call the Third World, that is annexing territory and drawing it into one's political and economic orbit. She was making up in Europe for what she had not been able to do elsewhere; her colonial possessions in Africa and the Pacific were much fewer than those of Britain and France, since she had joined the imperialist party far later. Is colonialism supposed to be a worse evil when the colonised are a Western people than when they are a non-Western one? To suggest it is quite rightly meets with accusations of racism.

Returning to events during the second war, and the period leading up to it, a particular element within German society whose conduct deserves scrutiny is the army. It was the one organisation which could have overthrown Hitler without a bloodbath, and yet it did not (the unsuccessful bomb plot of July 1944, which took place relatively late in the day, excepted). The only possible explanation for this failure is that as German patriots they initially supported Hitler (to whom, it must be remembered, they had taken a personal oath of loyalty) as someone who had turned the country round and then, as soldiers, were dazzled by the string of military victories he was able to pull off in 1939-41. The attitude of ordinary troops mirrored this. In the later stages of the war the Allies complained that the Germans were contrite while they were losing, recognising the futility of their sacrifice and the lunacy of the regime which was demanding it of them, yet they seemed to buck up and become more militant whenever there was a temporary improvement in their fortunes, as in the Ardennes offensive of 1944-5. But this was a natural tendency which one might have encountered in any army. Concerning war crimes, rather than the suffering both civilians and combatants will inevitably experience during military conflict, the ordinary German army, the *Wehrmacht*, as opposed to the SS kept its hands relatively clean throughout. The one exception was on the Russian front where it undoubtedly became brutalised (as was the enemy), because it had been sent into harsh weather conditions, having failed due to Hitler's blunderings to achieve its task before they set in, and against a foe which was as ruthless and determined as the Nazis, the more so since it was engaged in a struggle for survival and had little choice but to fight back in a spirit of hatred (which only began to soften after the German defeat and occupation of Berlin, when the Russians discovered that "German children cried the same way ours did"). The very commitment to prosecuting a war meant that the Germans resented this.

Hitler's aim was to essentially destroy or subjugate the Slav peoples, though the campaign had to be sold to the German people and army as defence against the menace of Communism (a relatively more plausible justification) since he was not quite sure how far they actually approved of brute genocide. He had little to worry about in the end because fear and tyranny achieved their objectives, but nonetheless didn't want to take any chances. There is a story about a non-Jewish German family, a mother and her two children, mistakenly boarding a train which was carrying Jews to a death camp and then, once the SS realised what had happened, being gassed and cremated along with everyone else so that they could not tell what they had seen. I do not know if this is apocryphal, but it strikes me as the sort of thing the Nazis would have done. In pursuit of a fantasy they were even prepared to kill their own people, the "Aryans", who were the ones meant to be benefiting from it. However Russia might have presented Hitler with certain problems. He was callous in dealing with the conquered peoples of western Europe but his attitude to them was nonetheless different from that he entertained towards the Slavs. This would have become apparent in the long run had he succeeded in defeating Russia, and it is interesting to speculate how far the German occupying forces would have found their loyalty to the Reich tested. Making a minority disappear is perhaps another matter.

We need to explain the general support given willingly, and not just because there seemed no other option, by Germans who were not necessarily fanatical Party ideologues to the Hitler regime regardless of either its persecution/destruction of "undesirable" peoples or its unjustified annexation of foreign territories, which led to most of Europe suffering the horrors of a terrible war. Here you have to remember that their only experience of democracy had not been a happy one. The Weimar Republic did quite well in the period of economic prosperity in the mid- and late 1920s, but ultimately it failed, proving unable to withstand the shock of the Great Depression. The breakdown of law and order, with everything seeming to be collapsing around oneself, meant that the country seemed ungovernable, and in that situation one has no time to spare for high moral questions; nor do you think of particular elements within society, such as Jews, but rather what is best for the common good. In Germans' collective consciousness there was no alternative, workable model of a political system to which they could give their allegiance. Hitler's restoration of order (however harshly) and his solving of the unemployment problem, part of a general restructuring of the economy in a way which though itself flawed was undoubtedly an improvement on the previous chaos, and with it constituting the one thing which he got right and maybe deserves (qualified) praise for, helped to convince them that their preference for the regime was justified.

Albert Speer

Speer, Hitler's architect and also armaments minister during the war, when he ended up controlling much of German industry and so becoming one of the most powerful men in the Third Reich, was sentenced to twenty years' imprisonment at Nuremberg on account of having used slave labour in military construction projects. He later appeared to apologise for his part in the regime's crimes, being thought of as "the Nazi who said sorry". But many felt his punishment ought to have been far more severe. His case raises interesting issues, and undoubtedly is also tragic. Though he did run a successful architect's practice for some years, like the film-maker Leni Riefenstahl this talented man was inevitably tarnished by his association with the Nazis, and regarded with some suspicion as a result, so that he was unable, and this is a great pity, to make his full contribution to building up the post-war world. But how much sympathy does he really merit, in the end? In the first edition of this book I took the view that Speer like many others in Nazi Germany went on serving the regime through fear alone, but his awareness of its vileness as seen in the Holocaust among other things nonetheless engendered in him a feeling of guilt which made him uneasy and thus unconvincing as a penitent. Having read Gitta Sereny's *Albert Speer: His Battle With Truth*, I feel I should revise this assessment somewhat. What is striking regarding all Sereny's books about the Nazis and their crimes is her fair-mindedness; perhaps, as a former nurse, she is unable to think of even the worst people as anything other than patients who need to be cured (rather than demons), and in the case of these criminal psychopaths can be if they only face up to certain uncomfortable truths about themselves. Nor however does she pull any punches. Speer emerges as far less admirable than he had previously seemed. Most telling is Sereny's assessment that he could, being highly placed, have arranged for himself and his family to get out of Germany safely, so that he would no longer be instrumental in making it possible for the Nazi regime to do such harm to humanity. Sereny does not elaborate on how exactly he could have accomplished this, but if she is right the "innocence through fear" argument does not apply.

The key to understanding Speer is to appreciate that although he was highly intelligent there was also an emotional immaturity to him. This was true of other Nazi leaders, including arguably Hitler himself, though in Speer it was not manifested in quite the same way. Starved of affection by his parents as a child, he needed an alternative father figure as an adult in order to compensate for that, and found it in the Fuhrer.

Speer was a career architect, an ambitious professional who obviously wanted to succeed in his chosen vocation. You can only do that by working through the authorities of the day, and it would have been a reasonable assumption in the mid-1930s when he was first coming to prominence that the Hitler regime, which by then had firmly established itself in power, was going to last for some considerable time. In addition Speer like many others had fallen under the spell of a man who apart from anything else seemed to have lifted Germany out of a morass of political instability, lawlessness and economic depression. Psychologically dependent on that man, he remained loyal to him almost until the end. Afterwards, being naïve (which often goes along with emotional immaturity), he fancied that the victorious Allies would retain him in a position of importance in the German government because his skills were essential in rebuilding the country, though he may also have cleverly calculated that if he stayed to argue his case before a court rather than flee like a rat to South America along with the Mengeles and Eichmanns, which would only have made him look more guilty, it would go better for him. He undoubtedly played the system, and you always had the impression that he was far more involved in the regime's atrocities than he was letting on. There is indeed a sense in his interviews of unease and nervousness lurking just beneath the surface, because of things not admitted to, though this may partly be due to hesitant English. Speer's ministry provided equipment that was used in the Holocaust, even if he did not volunteer the assistance. He was at a meeting where Himmler, assuming chillingly that everyone present would endorse his actions or, equally chillingly, taking blatant advantage of the probability they would do nothing whatever their true feelings, more or less declared the SS's intention of exterminating the remaining Jews of Europe and Russia.

Of course the desire for self-preservation, whether one is good or bad, guilty or innocent, is understandable. But there is little doubt that Speer should have been hung at Nuremberg. The air of almost childlike naivety and immaturity, which he may or may not have consciously exaggerated, clearly had an effect on the British and American judges if not on the rather harder Soviets. It was unfair he should have been spared while his subordinate Fritz Sauckel, who had the job of directly procuring the slave labour, was not. Speer's plea of "not guilty" while accepting, as part of the Nazi regime, "collective responsibility" makes no sense. A government or other organisation is made up of individuals, who as long as they have free choice whether to be part of it are therefore personally responsible for its actions. If on the other hand the collective entity is something mindless, motivated by blind forces, then it cannot be held culpable. Speer after 1946, before and after he was released from prison, was always, like Nixon brought to account for Watergate, trying to find a formula for confession which suited him. Many years later, he unlike Nixon admitted to the truth, which was that he was "guilty by looking away". But he waited until there was no point in hanging him before he did so.

Speer was certainly not a "monster", as one recent book on his case unhelpfully describes him; the reality is more complex than that. He does not come over as repellent in quite the same way as, say, Hitler or Goebbels or Himmler, and even they need to be viewed as seriously damaged human beings if one is to understand why they did what they did. There is no doubt however that his conduct was deplorable. We must be grateful, however, that he was not executed as it permitted him to start himself on a path to becoming a "better man". This obviously could not have happened if he had been hung. His giving money to Jewish organisations and becoming friendly with a rabbi who was working towards Christian-Jewish reconciliation shows that he at least wrestled with his conscience over the matter, entailing that he had one in the first place. Many of his colleagues did not, or at least didn't allow themselves to be unduly troubled by it.

As a final observation, the general public would not have been aware in detail of the reasons why one defendant at Nuremberg might be executed and another let off. It is doubtful whether Goering, who had been one of what might be regarded as the "Big Four" Nazis, would have been acquitted in any case. But it is also doubtful whether the imprisonment of Speer for twenty years, instead of hanging him, served as a major boost for Nazism in the post-war period. I have to disagree with the plot of a recent novel in which the monitoring of neo-Nazi activity is a priority for Western intelligence services in those years. It is always best to keep an eye on the Far Right, but Nazism had simply been too comprehensively crushed for it to experience a major revival, even if it was nonetheless seeking to creep back in. If an organised Nazi network did still exist it was mainly concerned with protecting war criminals. No power which adopted Nazism as a system of government would have been strong enough to oppose Russia or the United States, especially when only they and China possessed weapons of mass destruction. The West would have concentrated on countering what seemed the new, and more serious, threat of its former ally the Soviet Union, along with, later, terrorism in its various forms and would not have had the financial and administrative resources to deal with anything else in addition to those objectives, not on a significant scale. If in the early twenty-first century far-right racism and fascism have been making a certain comeback, domestically at any rate, this is because of the issues, involving both understandable fears and simple prejudice, which the end of the Cold War has brought to the fore.

Asking why the Holocaust was allowed to happen is to some extent the same thing as asking why the Second World War was, because the former would probably not have occurred, at least on the scale it did, without the latter. The Jews of Germany would still have suffered, or had to leave the country, but the vast majority of Hitler's Jewish victims were of course from the occupied territories. And the war created a "no-holds-barred" situation, especially given Hitler's fatalistic view of things; the Nazis felt they had passed the point of no return and therefore that it didn't matter much what they did.

The reasons why the Second World War broke out are discussed in chapter five. Nonetheless, the cut-off point for doing something about the Holocaust was long before the existence of the death camps was first established beyond doubt. Had the liberation of the camps been accorded a priority, at the cost of compromising other vital war aims and risking the lives of Allied soldiers who might otherwise not have been in any more jeopardy than one usually is in battle, it would have seemed to give credence to Nazi propaganda claims that the Allies were fighting a Jewish war. Western leaders must accept a certain degree of blame for what happened to the Jews, undoubtedly. But one could argue that the cut-off point, after which not much could have been done to avert the tragedy, came some time earlier, in the mid-1930s at the latest; the time when German rearmament reached such a stage that it was impossible to stop Hitler without a fight. It is probably impossible to identify an exact date. But had the Allies not treated Germany unduly harshly after the First World War, creating resentment which was exploited by Hitler and partly explains his rise, and then when under him she became too aggressive being too soft on her, instead of rearming earlier than they did – even if this was for reasons that were at least understandable – the Nazis could not have achieved so much in the way of bloodshed and genocide.

Much attention has been focused on the refusal of Britain to admit more German Jewish refugees in the late 1930s, something which was remembered after the war when Holocaust survivors and displaced persons flocked to Israel, as she was to become, rather than Britain despite the latter having been actively involved in defeating those who wanted to exterminate them (in what can seem an act of ingratitude). It may have contributed to the death toll. But here again there were "extenuating circumstances". Understandably unable to be objective, these people would have formed a numerous and persistent group pressurising the government into taking a stronger stand against Hitler when it was not sure, for pragmatic among other reasons, that it wanted to go to war with him (if we had done so and lost, it would not have helped the Jews much). There was enough concern about the anti-appeasement attitudes of Jews already living in Britain, though it did not justify Oswald Mosley in demanding their expulsion from the country (if they were in some way undesirable then we would also have had to expel obnoxious (for whatever reason) native-born Gentiles, but we didn't, at best putting them in prison instead; it was alienness, that is not belonging to the majority community, which was the crucial factor and this more than anything else identifies Mosley as an anti-Semite). Altogether it was a harsh policy; yet had the reaction of the western powers to

Hitler been different from what it was, the situation would not have arisen. There would have been German Jewish refugees, but war would not have been the issue which served to keep many of them out of Britain. Other factors might, though; the *spirit* behind the exclusion was genuinely anti-Semitic. Later, Britain in the person of Ernest Bevin tried to prevent refugees entering Israel, sensing the trouble it would cause with the Arabs but also recognising that Jews were not the only people who had suffered in the war and feeling that they should not be allowed to jump to the front of the queue. Perhaps he was right; but apart from the fact that they were constitutionally incapable, after Hitler, of seeing his point of view his characteristic bluntness and insensitivity, which in these particular circumstances was unforgiveable even if his ruthlessness was not, made matters far worse (and earned him death threats, which it was unsuccessfully attempted to put into practice).

I often wonder what it would have been like if all the Jews who migrated to Israel had ended up going to Britain, a country with a fairly good reputation for tolerance (compared to some) even if not blameless, instead, rather than the Asians, Africans and West Indians who arrived here in increasingly large numbers from around the same time that Israel was established. Geopolitically a lot of trouble would have been avoided. Certainly the face of this one nation would have been very different. But those who now live in Israel are grateful that they do, just as our Asians and blacks are glad to be, in one way or another, "British". And there, I suspect, we will have to leave it.

3

Maggie And Her Works

My feelings towards Margaret Thatcher have fluctuated over the years; the experience, it seems, is not uncommon. I thought it was great when she first got in in May 1979. The country was suffering from economic stagnation and abuse of trade union power. Generally the Labour ministers seemed an incompetent lot who were lowering Britain's standing and making it a laughing stock. David Owen's performance as foreign secretary was uninspiring – he did not then have the relative stature of his later career – and one also thinks of Defence Secretary Fred Mulley falling asleep next to various heads of state at official engagements. Thatcher seemed much more dynamic, and more as if she knew what she was doing and wouldn't stand any nonsense from the incompetent or dithery. Her election felt like a deliverance. Later, disillusion set in. By 1981 it seemed that she had failed to reverse the nation's economic decline and even worsened it, while her policies were causing unemployment and social unrest of which one manifestation was the Brixton riots. What made this more galling was that she was rejecting all criticism of her performance, ruthlessly sacking anyone in her government who disagreed with her. Of course later, when things seemed to be improving a bit, my attitude and that of many others changed, particularly with all the euphoria over the Falklands. At the first election in which I was old enough to vote, in 1983, I cast mine for Maggie. I continued to support the Conservatives up to 2001 (after which I either didn't vote at all, as in 2005, out of disillusionment with all the parties, or ticked the box for UKIP, until 2017), because they seemed the lesser of the evils. But concerning Thatcher, after '83 I could never feel that unrestrained, exuberant, perhaps youthfully naïve adoration I had previously had for the Iron Lady. It appeared to me that with her head swollen by that massive, and from the point of view of democracy highly dangerous, majority she had become too powerful and autocratic.

And I continued to be uneasy about high unemployment and the consequences for amenity groups, along with society as a whole, of ruthless cost-cutting and creeping privatisation. Once again things had turned sour. I was not particularly upset by Thatcher's fall from power in 1990 and indeed it came as something of a relief; she'd been there too long and become a stifling, intrusive, hectoring presence. How, now that she's gone, should I react to her death? What is to be the final verdict, as I see it, on her career? The film *The Iron Lady* succeeds, intentionally or otherwise, in making you feel sorry for her through focusing unduly on the dementia she suffered from in old age and the contrast, seen through the memories that come back to her in her moments of lucidity, with what she once was (it thus fails to be entirely satisfactory as a dramatic portrayal of her life, being ruined, as is *The Darkest Hour*, by one fundamental flaw). Is sympathy for her, other than that which anyone might feel for a sad, lonely, semi-senile old lady, warranted?

Well, one can only give a balanced picture, which historians, social commentators and moral philosophers are in any case obliged to do. I have no time either for those who viciously revile Thatcher or for those who insist on treating her with a fawning adulation which is nauseating and which I suspect she herself privately found tiresome and annoying, whether it came from toadying ministers or grassroots party supporters. But in her case objectivity is difficult for a lot of people to achieve. She aroused strong emotions, both negative and positive, with the result that uncertainty over how to respond to her, in both life and death, produced inner conflict. At the bash following a funeral which I attended shortly after she passed away a curate referred with relish to the *Guardian*'s suggested epitaph for the late Maggie – "The Iron Lady: Rust In Peace." She then clapped her hand over her mouth, looking aghast, as if realising she had said something not entirely Christian.

The rise of a monetarist economic policy in the West in the later twentieth century was the work of various politicians and thinkers of whom Thatcher was only one. She did not provide the intellectual impetus for it, because she did not have much of an intellect. She rather supplied, in Britain, the political will to put the monetarist philosophy into practice. That philosophy, as opposed to the principle of firm leadership, was not something specifically supported or even, one suspects, understood by the majority of the population. Most people were indifferent to the campaign, with its slogans such as "Tell Sid" (that anyone can now invest in British Telecom), to get everyone to become shareholders – in other words, capitalist businesspeople. The average person does not mind what economic system they live under as long as they can be sure of a square meal and a roof over their head. How *necessary* what happened in Britain under Thatcher was, whatever the attitude of the general public, is very much a matter of opinion. No doubt there were broad social, political and economic forces at work which would sooner or later have brought about a shift to a more monetarist world, though this might not have happened in quite the same way, in each country, that it did. But in history exactly *what* happens, when, and how, is the product of a complex interaction of different factors. Much has been made of the Callaghan government's losing the vote of no confidence by a very narrow margin, and the consideration that it might not have lost at all if one elderly and ill Tory MP had not been fetched out of bed and carried into the lobby of the Commons on crutches to do his duty. Callaghan would have had to face the country before long anyway since he had no overall majority and the Lib-Lab pact had collapsed. However, it is generally believed that the 1979 general election could have swung either way, and one must also take into account the vagaries of the first-past-the-post system. There was already beginning to be a feeling within the Labour government that the power of the unions, who were continually striking in support of inflationary pay rises – and it was this which lost Callaghan the election if any one issue did – needed to be curbed. But the realisation may have come too late.

What of course clinched the matter was the behaviour of Labour *after* the election, when they were in opposition. Parties do tend to fall apart in opposition, but any doubts about their ability to govern which a significant section of the electorate may have entertained as a result of the Winter Of Discontent were reinforced by the subsequent fratricidal strife between different factions within the Labour movement – a house divided against itself cannot stand – and an association with "Loony Left" policies that are still regarded dubiously even today. There seemed, if not to everyone, to be "no alternative" to Margaret Thatcher because although she governed harshly and in a way damaging in many respects to society, that was preferable to a party who could not govern at all. It seems hard for rational people to deny that what Thatcher did could have been achieved at much less cost in terms of deprivation, unrest and social atomisation. But the general decline in the calibre of British political leadership meant that no-one was available who had the right combination of strength of purpose with intellect and compassion to be a preferable alternative.

What exactly, then, did Thatcher achieve and was it overall for the country's benefit, or not? Well, we shall never know without access to a parallel universe where the course of events was different, and there remains the uneasy suspicion that all the traumatic upheavals she brought about were in the end unnecessary, but on the grounds mentioned above, i.e. that in the circumstances she was the lesser evil, she did more good than harm. By how wide a margin is another matter. Not, I think, a very wide one actually. Thatcher was preferable essentially from the point of view of style of government, which is a different business from ideology. From a practical perspective the unions needed to be curbed – where industrial disputes did not affect it the state of the economy had ceased to be such an issue – but that is precisely what the word suggests, a practical matter, and nothing necessarily to do with attempting to implement a wholesale policy of privatisation. In domestic affairs, Thatcher's achievement was to extend the privatised economy significantly and to create a society where the profit motive dominated in people's thinking. The second part of this sentence needs to be qualified because it is obvious from the indignant way Tory politicians in the 1980s talked about the breakdown of law and order that they did attach some importance to the moral codes of conduct, the rights and obligations, which should regulate human behaviour. Unfortunately they never managed to resolve the conflict between their support for those things and the effect of their economic policies, which by cutting public services and placing too much power in the hands of the rich – encouraging, if unintentionally, individual self-betterment against communal values – was to cause the poverty and social alienation which breeds crime. Furthermore, as I said above the privatisation policy as such did not necessarily have a mandate from the people, and its consequences have in many ways been disastrous.

Many of Thatcher's actions were described by her opponents as crazy; she was suffering from Mad Cow Disease. It is I think going too far to suggest she was clinically insane, though there may have been other mental conditions which help to explain her personality and behaviour in government. The wholesale destruction of resources does not make sense unless her intention was to recreate them in a different and, she believed, improved form (otherwise, it *would* have been crazy). Thatcher's apparent insensitivity and avarice can only be accounted for by a belief, sincere but myopic, that privatisation really would make for a more efficient and wholesome society. It partly explains why the health and education sectors have not always fared well in the past few decades. It is not true to say that they have never spent any money on either; but what Tories during and since the Thatcher era have really wanted to do is to privatise such vital areas, in accord with the logic of their programme, rather than leave them within the clumsy and overbureaucratic, it was thought, public sector. They have so far failed to do so – it would be pushing public opinion too far – but their not being really committed to upholding them in their present form means their attitude to them has always been one of unease and this has prevented problems from being addressed effectively.

As well as lining the pockets of a relatively small number of people involved in business and commerce, Thatcher achieved at least a reasonable degree of prosperity for most British people. But the potential threat to this prosperity was Labour's inability to govern, in the unlikely event of their being elected in the first place, rather than not everyone being an entrepreneur. The privatisation thing, which was erected by Thatcher and her supporters on the substructure of the conviction of the people – or a large enough percentage of them – that she was a much-needed "strong woman", did spiritual harm to society whose consequences we are now seeing all too clearly and which mean that I am now more forgiving of those who hated, and still hate, Thatcher than I used to be even if I don't endorse their sentiments.

There is little doubt that by 1979 the unions were overmighty and the public sector excessively restrictive. But except from the purely practical perspective we have mentioned, Margaret Thatcher merely replaced one monster with another. I think most would also agree with me that unless their victory in 1979, 1983 or 1987 would have resulted in complete instability – and that is something we can only speculate over – the spiritual damage Thatcherite policies have caused has been in one sense a worse evil than anything Labour might have done, if in power, before Tony Blair took them over and transformed them (into what in itself could be called a Thatcherite party, but it still wasn't quite the same kind of thing). Unless the damage to Britain's prestige would have seriously weakened the NATO alliance against the Soviet Union – and that is a highly questionable suggestion – I myself would have been quite prepared to lose the Falklands war in order to avoid the social fragmentation and erosion of community values, if it had come to such a choice between different considerations. And that is something I am not in the least bit comfortable saying. With most political leaders, the anger and ill-will felt at their more controversial actions fades with time, though some people will always entertain grudges. It's unlikely that a degree of animosity towards Thatcher should persevere on the part of a significant percentage of the population the way it does unless she really had done some genuine harm. They can't all be stupid or wicked.

Thatcherism never quite succeeded in getting Britain back on its feet because no economic philosophy, and no amount of ruthless streamlining and costcutting, can reverse the effects of a nation's relative long-term decline compared to others. If anything, once artificial barriers to competition, of the sort which Thatcher so much disliked, are removed it becomes all too clearly exposed to them. Even she could not fail to recognise the reality of the global economic situation; according to the logic of her own philosophy, if she sold anything off it had to be to the strongest and most efficient economy, America. In geopolitical affairs she undoubtedly did the patriotic thing, standing up for British interests by military action where necessary, even if the battle might have to be fought on and over the status of two small islands in the South Atlantic rather than in a global or continental arena; yet in other areas she reinforced Britain's diminished status, emphasising the contradictions between the different aspects of her programme. And although she, along with US President Ronald Reagan, is seen by some as being among those who by standing firm for Western "democratic" values (both in geopolitical and, through liberal policies towards the market, economic matters) helped bring down the Soviet Bloc and end the Cold War, Britain's role in that process was very much as a junior partner, as it always had been in the post-war world – though John F Kennedy no doubt appreciated Harold Macmillan's fatherly advice over the Cuba crisis, his aides later confirmed that the United Kingdom's role in the affair was essentially peripheral. More recently, the continued erosion of Britain's manufacturing base has led to most of the commodities her citizens require both for basic sustenance and for maintaining the quality of life being supplied by China and other East Asian nations.

Returning to domestic issues, the policy of an unrestrained free market is of course no less flawed than socialism, since it is likewise the product of fallible human beings. One system will not necessarily be any better than the other if there is poor education and training, as I think we are now discovering. If companies have too much power to hire and fire it will actually damage the economy by taking people out of the labour market, and fiddling the statistics by claiming they are in work when actually participating in useless training schemes, as has too often been done in the past, will of course only disguise the true extent of that damage. Nor is one's status (being on welfare or not being on welfare) or behaviour (being thrifty with one's cash, or not) in the economic sphere the only criteria by which moral uprightness can be judged and entitlement to privileges assessed with the aim of encouraging social responsibility. It may not be someone's fault if they are on benefit, and while undoubtedly we should be thrifty where we need to be, there will be plenty of opportunities, which won't necessarily have anything to do with economics, in our private and public lives to show our moral fibre, by our response to this or that testing situation where a difficult decision has to be made or we must resist the temptation to do something unethical. In any case, to suggest it's all to do with how we acquire and manage money assumes that we are all natural capitalists when in fact, because everyone is different, some of us may not be and therefore will not be able to provide for themselves when the support of the state is taken away.

We cannot confuse liberty for the private company with liberty for the individual, who whatever their political sympathies may not be business-minded. The two are not the same thing. One reason why so many Britons have emigrated to France in recent years is that they find the high price tags which have been slapped on everything oppressive and, if anything, an obstacle to their happiness and self-fulfilment. The Thatcherite society is certainly not the same thing as the ideal society. And finally, as we are aware from recent and bitter experience, if the financial sector is not sufficiently regulated it can itself be the cause of economic recession and decline.

Some of these problems are systemic, inherent in the assumptions behind the monetarist doctrine Thatcher so enthusiastically espoused. Others, however, could have been avoided, and if they were to be remedied now would make the system more acceptable. Thatcher's fault was that she failed to see where her policies might ultimately lead. But to be fair to her, she would not have condoned that outcome. What she started she did not necessarily intend to finish. None of it would have happened without her, but that does not mean it is fair to blame her for it. Her achievements, like those of Bismarck, were abused by her successors, and in her last years, though of course her mind and certainly her ability to comment on and participate in events had been affected to some extent by dementia, she was probably disgusted by much of what they did or allowed others to do. I don't know how far she would have approved of casualisation in the employment sector, for example, but it was under John Major, who as Prime Minister swung very much to the right, that it really gained headway. It may not, in the end, prove to be Thatcher herself who did the most damage. Privatisation, indeed greed, have become even more fundamental a force in the Britain of the 1990s, 2000s and 2010s, under people, both politicians and businessmen/women, who are in many ways more Thatcherite than Thatcher. And this has happened regardless of the party affiliations of those concerned. In addition her successors have often lacked strength of purpose and decisiveness, for what she created has become so powerfully entrenched that it can survive whatever the calibre of the present national leader relative to hers, or have abandoned ethical considerations in order to placate the media (from an obsession with "image") or interest groups.

We all suffer because of this, materially, socially or, though we may not realise it or care much anyway, morally. We are all Thatcher's children, but it is important to stress that we do not necessarily appreciate it. We are still living essentially under a Thatcherite system; the relative drift back towards state involvement in the economy, a sensible way of dealing with the 2008 recession and one which prevented it from being much worse, under Gordon Brown was only designed to be a temporary expedient and came to an end when the Tories returned to power. Yet the Thatcherism we live under today is as bastardised a version of that doctrine as private armies of retainers were of the feudal system in the fifteenth century. Thatcher for all her faults genuinely wished to do good, whereas the total deregulation of the banking system in the West clearly does not.

What of the lady herself? Thatcher was undoubtedly a remarkable woman and a "great" leader, despite her faults. But she was crucial to British political history in more ways than one. It's frequently been said that it isn't the most intelligent people, these days, who get to the top in business and politics. Certainly Thatcher was the first of three Prime Ministers who were undoubtedly clever in some respects, but lacked *intellect* – the other two being Major and Blair. Instead of denigrating her we ought instead to be asking where the way human society, politics and culture, in the West and perhaps globally, has developed is leading us, what it means and how we should respond to it.

To understand what exactly Thatcher was let us consider two other key figures in twentieth-century British history: Winston Churchill and Bernard Montgomery. Montgomery was self-important and could be petty, spiteful and thoroughly nasty. People like that are often shabby and except in a negative way inconsequential. But Monty also had charisma and the ability, in military affairs, to balance the opposed qualities of boldness and caution, these things elevating him above the second-rate. Churchill possessed the same gifts despite being equally arrogant, as well as often strikingly disingenuous, gaffe-prone and sometimes not that clever (though this is diverging from the point a little, it's also interesting that while he sometimes seems to demonstrate a shallowness of intellect he did have a marvellous command of language and a certain wit, both of which are normally absent in the intellectually shallow). He was clearly more than just an upper-class buffoon with all the prejudices of his kind. It was these characteristics, in combination perhaps with others that normally would have been harmful in their impact, which made these two men what they were and ensured that between them they were able to win the Second World War on the British side.

Their example shows that human beings are creatures of infinite variety, even if some varieties are rare. Margaret Thatcher had many qualities which one sees in people far less able or successful than she. We can recognise her type. It is narrow-minded, intellectually limited and thoughtlessly domineering. It generally does more harm than good (as opposed to more good than harm or an equal measure of the two). Yet Thatcher differed from other people in this category by having something which, as with Churchill and Montgomery, is difficult to define and which raised her above the commonplace and insignificant. It is best described as strength of character coupled with a certain skill at arousing admiration and loyalty among potential supporters. It gives you stature, something which consists either of this indefinable quality we have been talking about, or of intellect, or of both, though the intellect may not be essential. But certainly intellect and intelligence are not the same thing. Even if the former usually goes with the latter, the converse is not necessarily true. Thatcher was "intelligent" enough to go to Oxford, where it is clear her lack of "intellect" made her appear stupid in the eyes of her peers who consequently looked down on her, wondering if she really ought to be there, as sadly often happens in such cases. This explains her subsequent antipathy to the place, which was reflected in her policies on higher education later on. It is one area where we can, indeed, feel sorry for her, even if her behaviour over the matter seems vindictive. I did encounter her type on a number of occasions at College.

At the same time as being in some ways intellectually challenged Thatcher was a conviction politician rather than led purely by how she would come over on the media and thus be perceived by the public (though she did see the need for image consultants, until she reached a point in her premiership where she ceased to give a damn what people thought of her). That was probably one reason why she was respected more in her old age by former colleagues than, for example, Harold Wilson (even though Wilson's supposed lack of principle has been exaggerated). She was clever in how she exploited the weaknesses of her opponents (the latter being an essential ingredient in her success, without which, it's important to appreciate, she would never have come to power). But as well as being intellectually narrow I think she also lacked emotional intelligence, or, if she possessed it, the ability to express it. Both defects meant she took things in too literal a fashion, sinking the General Belgrano even though, as I understand it, it was sailing away from the exclusion zone which had been imposed around the Falklands; she was concentrating single-mindedly on the question of how far it was a threat to British naval forces, to the detriment of other issues such as military ethics. According to her logic, the whole point of a war (and the code of conduct did not say there shouldn't be one in the first place) was to win it and therefore the "etiquette" had to take second place where the two things clashed; any obstacle to victory must be removed whenever the opportunity arose. After all, you couldn't conduct a debate on how to fight a war, from the ethical viewpoint, if one wasn't going on in the first place, and it was being waged for a purpose. And once a decision was arrived at through this kind of reasoning it could then be enacted, against all opposition, by a strong and commanding personality.

The same intellectual and emotional limitations explain why Thatcher attempted to push her economic programme to its logical conclusion without stopping to ask if she could achieve the same result at less cost. It could be of enormous benefit in getting the job done because it meant she wasn't troubled by the doubts which might assail someone more perceptive and sensitive, but the consequences for society were devastating. Though the unions needed to be dealt with firmly whatever happened, she insisted, as her biographer John Campbell reminds us, on introducing a completely new economic system, with all the upheavals that involved, during a severe recession. The free market philosophy, preferring a minimum of public spending and of restrictions on how banks and businesses operate, works best in periods of prosperity; in periods of downturn it is likely to add to the misery suffered by ordinary people. It's not that it can't be done in the end, if you've the will; it's rather a question of the human price. But Thatcher was a dynamic, go-getting personality whose revolution, she felt, would have run out of steam, losing momentum, if she waited until the recession was over before going ahead with it.

In her determination to implement the policies she was so sure were essential, Thatcher prized (as another logical consequence) loyalty and ideological soundness over other things, promoting to high ministerial rank people who were obnoxiously arrogant, such as Nicholas Ridley, and surrounding herself with henchmen who could be abrasive, like Norman Tebbit, or plain rude and bullying (Bernard Ingham, though his lasting devotion to her is nonetheless genuinely touching). It came at the cost to her that if she didn't at heart personally like them, which might sometimes be the case though not with Tebbit or Ingham at any rate, they could be a bit of a chore.

Such people as Thatcher can often come across as cruel when in fact they're not. Those who in some ways aren't very bright try to get their way by hectoring because they don't know how else to do it, although it may depend upon the precise situation they're faced with. To be honest I often *did* feel sorry for Thatcher because she could never understand why people were so angry at the effect of her policies, and therefore was all the more upset, beneath that Iron Lady surface, by what she saw as their ingratitude. It's only a theory, but I wonder if, as well as being in any case of a particular and relatively rare human type, she could also have been an "Aspie" (Asperger Syndrome sufferer), as I have suggested was Enoch Powell. Enoch caused a lot of trouble, in his case in the field of race relations and by wrecking a party, for the same reason as Thatcher – a difficulty some of the time to see or be moved by the consequences of one's actions, which is perceived as being one aspect of the condition. I said Asperger Syndrome "sufferer", but it would seem from these two cases that the condition does not, in itself, necessarily lead to unhappiness, though one will of course still experience all the trials and tribulations everybody else does, including the frustration of political objectives. As a woman, Thatcher would have been a rare example of it. It would help explain why she sometimes came over as spiteful, as with her attitude to universities (see above). She could not differentiate between justified resentment at unfair treatment of herself or another and the carrying out of a policy simply because it seemed the right thing to do; or realise the impossibility of penalising some injustices without doing collateral damage.

Not actually a wicked woman, Thatcher intended I am sure to genuinely do the country good; it was just that she wanted it done on her own terms. What she ultimately hoped to do was privatise everything, in the sincere belief that it made for a healthier economy. She just did not like large sums of money being in the hands of the public sector. Because the policy was unpopular her intentions could not be admitted to too openly, though they were always suspected, and this gave rise to the conclusion, not entirely incorrect, that "creeping privatisation" was being introduced, in a sneaky and dishonest fashion. The policy was regarded with suspicion, as a charter for wealthy bosses, in relatively poor working-class Labour-voting areas. I think a lot of the resistance to Thatcher's reforms was due to her hectoring and high-handed ways, which caused offence; the disadvantaged did not want prosperity from *her* hands. This may have been the wrong attitude for them to take. At any rate Thatcher did get her way, more or less; and although marginalisation and disparities in wealth have re-emerged as issues in recent years, what is noticeable – as noticeable as the tendency of former "Wets" like Kenneth Clarke and Kenneth Baker to return to the fold – is how many of the deprived areas later benefited from the stimulation of private businesses, no doubt often run by the very people who a few years before were objecting so stridently to Thatcherism. It is not that Thatcher failed to restore prosperity to the nation but rather that she did so in a way which resulted in the exclusion of certain groups, such as the homeless; an exclusion which in some cases (notably the homeless) still goes on today. Also, prosperity is relative and it may be a case of the goalposts being moved; though things are better overall than they were in the 80s some people nonetheless feel they do not have quite the same opportunities or standard of living as others. Apart from this, whether you think Thatcher improved the economy depends on whether you liked her or not.

I was speaking again of Enoch Powell. It's funny how these two people, him and Thatcher, seem to have such a lot in common even though their political careers turned out so differently, one characterised by quixotic failure, the other definitely not (on economic policy Powell was ideologically a forerunner of Thatcher, though this may only be true in the chronological sense; there is no evidence she or her supporters in Britain *consciously*, at any rate, sought to emulate him). Powell and Thatcher were the only leading British politicians in the last fifty years to have any real stature, and now they've gone. Truly the end of an era, in a way which highlights something very depressing, and worrying, about public life today.

Margaret Thatcher, I believe, has now gone to be judged by a higher court than ourselves who isn't given, I think, to undue flattery but will not condemn without reason either. Until we know what his decision has been it might be fitting to let Powell have the last word. He once said that all political lives, "unless they are cut off in midstream at a happy juncture, end in failure," because that was the nature of politics and of human affairs. This is far too pessimistic, not least because figures like Gladstone or Churchill or Lloyd George are remembered more, or as much, for their successes as their mistakes. If the mark of success is to be viewed in such a way posthumously, and it ought to be, they cannot be counted failures. Being ejected from power against one's wishes, as happened to Thatcher (and also Lloyd George), has not been an uncommon experience but nor has it been that of every Prime Minister. But there is nonetheless *some* truth in what Powell said. Thatcher will be remembered more than anyone else for having done harm and good to the same degree, especially as the defects of the Thatcherised state become more and more apparent. Part of what Powell meant, I think, is that in this life at any rate you don't get any thanks just for being the lesser of the evils. Because you don't.

The other thing I want to say here is that in all fairness, when Maggie was Prime Minister and I was unemployed the unemployment was my own fault. When John Major or Tony Blair were Prime Minister and I was unemployed, the unemployment was someone else's fault.

Appendix One: Why Thatcherism Has Had Its Day

Right-wing free-marketism is nothing new. One historic proponent of it was Adam Smith, author of *The Wealth of Nations*, in the eighteenth century. His face appears on the current £20 note (an indication of the homage the contemporary commercial establishment feels it ought to pay to him, and which it feels we ought to pay to it). In the 1970s and 80s monetarism gained new ground as a reaction to the Keynesian and corporatist policies which constituted the prevailing orthodoxy and which were increasingly felt to have failed, producing stagnation, industrial unrest and a restrictive authoritarianism characterised by excessive bureaucracy which stifled initiative. This was especially so in Great Britain which was plagued by strikes and inflation for much of the late 1960s and the 1970s, culminating in the "Winter of Discontent". A further moral and spiritual boost may have been given it by the determination of right-wing politicians like Ronald Reagan and Margaret Thatcher to make a stand against the perceived threat to Western liberties posed by the Communist Bloc, whose policies of state control with all their apparatus of totalitarianism was seen as the antithesis of all that was (a) libertarian and (b) financially wise. The intellectual ground was prepared by such figures as Friedrich Hayek and Milton Friedman. In Britain, Margaret Thatcher created the political circumstances in which monetarism could flourish. The support she gained among her own party had its roots in an almost pathological fear of a return of the kind of situation Britain had so often found itself in in the 1970s – inflation, economic decline, strikes – and which, because this was an era when the public sector was dominant, led to the latter becoming identified with it. The events of that period, which they had no wish to see repeated, left a scar on the minds of patriotic right-wingers who felt the country's standing had been brought low and its self-respect dented.

Thatcher resigned as Prime Minister in 1990, but the society she created survived her fall – which was due largely to personal failings that appeared in the eyes of a significant section of the Conservative Party to jeapordise its chances of re-election – and is still with us today.

For a while it was not clear in which direction John Major, who succeeded Thatcher, would take the Tory Party, but from about 1993 there was a shift to the right. It was about this time that casualisation, the tendency for firms to take on employees on a purely temporary basis and often not convert it into a permanent one, began to bite. (Initially it was encountered mainly in the civil service, but this makes little difference to many of the points I seek to make in this article since the aim during the last twenty years has been for the public sector to imitate the private as much as possible).

The Thatcherisation of society was endorsed and even taken further by Tony Blair's New Labour after it won the General Election of 1997. The trouble was that Labour, realising that Thatcherism was the order of the day, decided it was unlikely ever to regain power unless it embraced it, and adopted a philosophy of "if you can't beat 'em, join 'em", most notably in the excision of Clause Four, by which all industry should ideally be nationalised, from its manifesto. There was a slight shift back towards state intervention during Gordon Brown's premiership, largely as a response to recession, but in essence Labour continued to pursue a monetarist policy until the end. Certainly David Cameron, arch-Thatcherite and indeed arch-businessman, showed no desire to experiment with statism or Keynesianism when he took over in 2010 as head of the Conservative-Liberal Democrat coalition. If anything Cameron, like Thatcher, took the view that to work through the monetarist system was the key to ending the recession. Along with cuts; and so "austerity" was born. The upshot of it all is that even though memories of the "Winter of Discontent" are ceasing to be of psychological importance as time moves on – an increasing number of British people were born after it happened, indeed after Thatcher had been and gone as Prime Minister – we have become more and more wedded to what is effectively still Thatcherism (could one call it neo-Thatcherism?), in that it generally dislikes regulating the private sector; partly out of greed and partly because we now cannot imagine anything else and so don't want to experiment with alternatives to which we aren't accustomed and which we are afraid might not work out.

In order to examine whether the dominance of monetarism in British, and throughout modern Western, society is truly beneficial we need to examine the claims made by its defenders to see if they are valid. Here it may be necessary to repeat points made earlier in the chapter.

(1) A society where the free market rules is a free society.

As previously stressed it is a mistake to confuse liberty for the private company with liberty for the individual. It may simply mean that the ordinary citizen is forced to pay the high prices which the company charges for its product, and in some cases is denied by it the chance of a steady job and thus, through the income one would generate, a good standard of living. In any case, judging by the increasing number of complaints about the "nanny state" interfering in the lives of ordinary citizens through excessive bureaucracy (seen in restrictive health and safety regulations, for example), the open market has completely failed to bring about the freedom its defenders claim it does; the experience of the last few years shows that where society as a whole is concerned, what is wanted is not the lifting of restrictions on private businesses – which can produce exactly the opposite result to that intended – but a more sensible approach by government to the framing of general policy.

As an example of how the free market actually works against the aspirations of the individual, I (and a great many others) have had enormous problems over the last twenty years achieving success as writers, our strenuous efforts being rewarded with a constant stream of rejections. One might say that it was always thus with publishing, but the situation has become worse because of certain factors which were not operating in previous eras. I had one rejection where the publisher's reader said that she liked my writing style but that my proposal "did not fit in with our current schedule." Disturbingly, this shows that the actual literary quality of the book has become something distinct from "marketing", from the consideration of whether or not it ought to be published. It works against individual self-expression (for the individual expresses themselves among other things by their writing, art or other contribution to culture). I suspect that the publishers are concerned only with what will please the majority (and thus net the publishing company the biggest possible profit in the shortest possible time). The majority is of course entitled to its pleasure but other things need to be allowed a look-in as well.

(2) Freedom of enterprise in the economic sphere, by virtue of the culture of self-reliance it creates, is essential for building the moral fibre of society.

This sees affairs purely in terms of economics; not only is this somehow disturbing, it is also impossible to extrapolate from one particular walk of life, however important, to the human world at large.

There will be plenty of opportunities in a person's personal and professional life for their worth to be tested; important matters where a decision must be made. How we handle people who are causing us problems, where we stand on important issues of the day, how we treat people of different race, sex, religion, political affiliation to ourselves. Whether we have a privatised or a nationalised economy doesn't make any difference to that. Human affairs are a matter of politics, in the workplace (whether we are in the public or the private sector), in sex, in cultural activities, and in personal and family relationships; and what counts is how those things are managed. It could be argued that the moral decline evident in the West is due not to the predominance of Keynesian economics – something which has now ceased to be the case – and the welfare state but the decline in traditional foci of authority such as religion, and, in combination with cultural and technological changes, of other socially cementing institutions (with whose values monetarism potentially conflicts as it emphasises individual initiative and profit over common obligations to Mankind as a whole). The decline in social morality and cohesion has if anything worsened strikingly since monetarism became the dominant socio-economic philosophy in the West.

The creation of a privatised economy has not in fact made a lot of difference to the building of a culture of self-reliance according to the monetarist/libertarian philosophy. The only people who have achieved self-reliance are those who have done so well in the private business sphere that they don't need state protection anyway, and don't suffer except as a result of the recessions which monetarism has failed to prevent and if anything has been responsible through running away with itself. Not everyone has the urge to go into business or the aptitude to succeed in it. The businesses which do survive, even where they are not actually run efficiently, are generally the largest and most powerful ones, those best equipped to withstand economic storms, so that the system ends up being not a monetarist free-for-all, in a way that *benefits* all, but rather a new kind of elitist monopoly. At the other end of the scale in some respects there are still too many benefit scroungers, whom the government has failed to deal with. And many who *did* "get on their bike and look for work," in Norman Tebbit's words, in accordance with the Thatcherite philosophy on such matters never found it, because they had already been on the dole for too long in an employer's view, regardless of their abilities or level of commitment. People have been given freedom but not the tools to do anything with it, the long-term unemployed being one very good example. It raises the question of whether monetarism really has created a climate in which "self-reliance" produces rewards.

Human nature is unfortunately flawed. Giving the private employer free rein may simply mean that (s)he has unrestricted opportunity to put their personal prejudices and peccadilloes into practice, among other things sacking people just because they don't like their face (though of course they wouldn't say that this was the reason).

Spiritually the damage is just as serious. Though in some respects the tone of society has improved, in others we have become more selfish, ruthless and single-minded in getting what we want, in achieving wealth, status and a certain image, whether through aggression, manipulation or slick posturing (all tactics which businesses use at some time or other), and less deterred by the possible effects on others. Since it is a crucial way of selling oneself, financially or metaphorically (though the concept is generally one of a commercial transaction), employers are often in effect more concerned with the image of a person than with whether or not they can do a job properly. This leads to inefficiency and paralysis. The preoccupation with image also promotes the celebrity culture which makes it more difficult for ordinary people to get by and also combines disastrously with the relative moral decline evident within society. If someone sells, by attracting high viewing figures or by a product being associated with them, then they will be given a high profile even if their behaviour is offensive and morally corrupting. Because sections of society have become debased enough (partly due to the dilemma of post-modernism) to like them despite or perhaps because of their conduct, television executives etc. are reluctant to sack them, as opposed to suspend them for a short period. This helps to set a bad moral example. The elitism of rich over poor has spread to other areas of society, everything being interconnected. Money buttresses the cult of celebrity because celebrities sell, their glamorous image boosting the ratings. Generally it is harder for the talents of ordinary people who do not have an established track record of fame and success to be recognised. They may be *more* deserving of fame and success than those who achieve it, but are not considered quite so marketable.

Yet another harmful social consequence of Thatcherism, and its effect on one's purse, is that as prices go up charities are forced to be more and more persistent, even aggressive, in their campaigning; apart from the fact that this alienates people and makes them less inclined to give, the charities are angling for money which often isn't there, because the public are having so much trouble trying to make ends meet that they can't afford to be generous. The various causes suffer from the inherent defects of the system with or without an actual recession to make the problem worse.

(3) In a monetarist system healthy competition will be the norm and will benefit society as a whole.

The idea behind the free market is that it will result in greater efficiency and greater consumer choice as firms strive to make the highest quality product, which will prove more popular and thus net the company more profit than its rivals. But companies can still have too much of a monopoly or resort to sneaky techniques in order to increase their gains, to the disadvantage of the consumer. On the subject of monopolies, the strong can still dominate the weak and those economies that are in decline, in a relative or absolute sense, can do little about those that are thriving and thus in a position to inundate them with merchandise which, as long as you can generate profit through its having to be replaced in a short time, doesn't actually need to be of high quality.

(4) A private company will necessarily be run more efficiently than a public one, because entrepreneurs will naturally make the decisions that will result in a good quality product and therefore an advantage over one's competitors.

We dealt with this argument to some extent under the previous heading. In addition, it is not actually the most able people who get to the top in most concerns (I was told this on one "get you back to work" scheme). Then there is the issue, mentioned elsewhere, of poor education and training – a symptom of how successive governments have grievously failed the state school system – which negates any benefit that may be supposed to accrue to society from privatisation. If companies are suffering across the board from poor workmanship/management, then none has any advantage to be lost or gained in relation to another.

A further difficulty is caused by the tendency of companies to contract out certain services, or public bodies and trusts to apportion different services to different firms. This can be used by a company to make things easier for itself and to avoid responsibility when they go wrong. It makes for a confusing situation where accountability is difficult.

(5) Thatcherism assumes that it has the support of all society's members.

It does not. Research by the government in the 1980s reported little interest among the vast majority of the public in initiatives such as the "Tell Sid" campaign to promote share ownership in newly privatised companies. What people are most interested in is fair, sensible and competent government and not ideologies (for Thatcherism is clearly an ideology, a "narrative" if you like, in that it embodies a principle – in this case that the free market should be supreme – which it seeks to apply to the whole of society) which may not always be appropriate and can be disastrous when enforced too rigidly. If you trouble to talk to them you will find they are angry at the high prices they have to pay for commodities even in times of economic hardship and feel the situation has got completely out of control.

(6) Thatcherism assumes that everyone can be a capitalist or be able to provide for themselves through their own thrift.

But it will be difficult for them to do so if the cost of living rises as it is doing at the moment. When people do not have enough money in their pockets they are not going to be able to buy the (possibly expensive) products private companies make, so privatisation will not benefit the vast majority of the public.

Thatcher & Co hoped to make everyone into a capitalist, but failed to realise that in an imperfect world this was not possible. (A), because of the very fact that we are all different (Thatcher herself would have claimed that she was opposing rigid conformity and allowing each person to develop their own individual talents), which means that not everybody has a business mentality and can therefore participate effectively in the kind of world she was trying to create. (B), in that imperfect, and increasingly complex, modern world it is not feasible for an individual person to provide for all their diverse needs by their own efforts rather than the state's. (C), if services are to be provided by private companies, who of course charge for their products, there will inevitably be a price tag on everything. This makes it harder for those not already very wealthy – again, we are not all born to be entrepreneurs – to cope, especially if they have families to support and/or are on benefit or low incomes, and in time of economic recession. Luxuries have to be cut back, which means that one is simply doing what is necessary to survive – buying the essentials – rather than achieving the quality of life which Thatcher promised to give us all and which are a mark of success, of realised ambition. And even then, it is often still difficult to manage. To become the wealthy success story Thatcher wanted everyone to be requires a strong financial base to begin with, and that's just what is being denied to millions of people, unless they have the kind of ruthless ambition that is (a) not common to most of us, in the respect we are talking about, and (b) must, because of the obstacles involved, often require harsh practices, at which a lot of people may baulk, to succeed. Instead, many are caught in a poverty trap, for some a benefit trap, which they cannot escape from. (It may be noted that the very poor cannot save up for long periods for the sake of future prosperity without suffering extreme hardship, and so cannot meet the high standards of thrift and "good housekeeping" Thatcher so approved of). Again on a personal note, I found that whenever I did get a job much of my salary went towards my rent, my Housing Benefit being cancelled because I was deemed no longer to need it; this was not a great incentive to find work.

Disadvantages of the free market

(1) It furthers the atomisation of society by over-stressing individual freedom (and that only in the economic sphere and for the entrepreneur themselves), as against the socially cohesive role of institutions.

(2) It lowers the moral tone of society by stressing the profit motive to the detriment of altruism towards one's fellow beings. In the first instance this may not have been intentional, but the obsession with free enterprise has nevertheless been such as to bring it about.

(3) It assumes that human nature will not be corrupted by the opportunity to make money quickly and on a large scale, that bosses will not abuse their power. In fact companies put a quick profit before efficiency and accountability, are ruthless in making people redundant, and resort to "hire 'em and fire 'em" policies which do not benefit the jobseeker. Thatcherism takes little account of the flaws in human nature.

(4) Commercialisation extends into areas where it is inappropriate, even ludicrous. English Heritage now have a "Customer Services Department", not for those wishing to buy products from its bookshops/souvenir shops, which is what one would expect, but for people contacting them to call for a particular historic building to be preserved in its traditional form, for example. I recently wrote to them protesting about a local authority's allowing of an application to convert an old mill to residential accommodation, and asking if they could help in opposing it, but they wrote back saying they could do nothing and that they thought the council had made the right decision. Do I get compensation, then? Or can I "buy" the building's retention for posterity, perhaps outbidding the person who wants to demolish or convert it? This is so obviously not what happens or is intended to happen that the new commercialised terminology is ridiculous and even offensive. The preservation of historic buildings is a cultural matter for the benefit of society as a whole, not a financial transaction whose consequences apply only to individuals.

(5) The money-making/managerial aspect becomes more important than doing the job properly. There are engineering firms which have more accountants than they have engineers, or none at all, on their Board of Management. This must clearly result in technical inefficiency. Obviously it is important to *have* accountants on the Board, if the company's financial affairs are to be kept in proper order, but surely not to the detriment of a proper understanding of the very activity around which the company is based!

Some people charged with the running of heritage projects such as industrial museums, working mills etc have little specialist understanding of the museum's brief and are simply doing their job because it is a career, or for economic gain. This means that culture may suffer and the vital role of the organisation as preserver of the traditions, and thus the collective self-consciousness, of society be lost.

Thatcherism has had its day; it has outlived its usefulness and become a liability. Unfortunately, both politicians and businesspeople are still too in love with it and reluctant to even consider the possibility of change. The general trend over the past twenty years has been to transfer more and more vital functions to private organisations, not less.

The aim should not be to get rid of capitalism altogether but rather to reform the way it is practised. It is not desirable that companies should have to rely on costly government subsidies rather than stand on their own feet. What is desirable is for them to operate under greater restrictions and for some of the enormous wealth they have been permitted to amass in recent years to be used by the government to help it meet budget deficits rather than put increasing pressure on the public sector and the ordinary citizen. Such taxation need not be a permanent institution but it is essential until such time as we have managed to build a fairer world – something like the mixed economy which operated in this country before Thatcher – where "society" and the free market stand in the correct relationship to each other.

Monetarist thinkers like Hayek believed that the free market would benefit society as a whole because the selfish, profit-oriented motives of the businessman or woman would ensure that in their own interest they would perform a high-quality service which would be what the public wanted, while the mutual desire to outdo one's rivals fostered a dynamism which boosted the economy. We have already pointed out that this does not take into account the effects of poor training, shortage of supply and a nation's long-term economic decline. It is also bound to cause moral damage to society by freezing out altruistic motives, in a way which may be more harmful than economic recession (and in a massive contradiction encourages just the kind of thing – a lack of upright ethics and social responsibility – that the right-wing Tories who supported Margaret Thatcher claimed, and still claim, to loathe). The danger surely is that the selfish motive can take over; Remember the lady from Riga

> "Who went for a ride on a tiger.
> They finished the ride
> With the lady inside
> And a smile on the face of the tiger."

Appendix Two: The Decline Of England

History suggests that all civilisations, and all empires – the Roman, the Aztec and the Inca to name but three – rise and fall, go into decline and eventually collapse, to be subjugated and/or absorbed by other powers. There is no particular reason why Britain, or the West as a whole, should escape this fate. We should bear this in mind whenever we (understandably) complain that things are not as good as they used to be. We ought not to be particularly surprised if that is the case. Not least because the bigger they come, the harder they fall. The first to become powerful and dominant are the first to lose that position. Britain was the first industrial nation, in the modern sense, and had the largest empire, ruling a third of the Earth's surface as well as, she liked with some justification to think, its seas. She was the strongest economy in the world, at least until the United States began to overtake her, and its greatest military power, with the best army and navy. As a consequence her decline in the twentieth and twenty-first centuries, though gradual, has been that much more marked. Even if it is something that could have been expected it is still useful to examine the process, whose causes in fact are complex, in some detail.

The decline can if one likes be dated to as far back as the (relative) agricultural and industrial depression in the years 1873 to 1896, which among other things produced a sense, expressed in Kipling's poem *Recessional,* that the best of the good times might be over, and to the faults in military organisation exposed by the Boer war, but it was by no means an even process. Or Britain would not have retained an empire, not latterly called that, until at least the 1960s nor been able to play such a significant part in the Allied victories in the First and Second World Wars. However those conflicts proved to be crucial stages along the way since they were Pyrrhic in their effect, leaving her, along with the other European powers, economically weak. Britain's part in Hitler's defeat, which has tended to serve the same function as a heroic folk tale, undoubtedly contributed to her image of her own greatness in a way that disguised the fact that this was really her last fling as a first-rank world power. It was something she afterwards felt she had to live up to, when new realities made that impossible. But unfortunate as this might be, it was probably inevitable, and it makes no sense to suggest Britain should not have acted as she did in 1940. Anyone who stood up to the likes of Hitler was obviously doing the world a favour. Even if the war could eventually have been won by America and Russia without Britain's participation, it would have taken longer and probably resulted in the loss of even more lives. Britain was providing valuable support to America, just as she later did in Iraq; and there was far more justification in overthrowing Hitler in 1939-45 than there was in overthrowing Saddam in 2003.

From the late nineteenth century Britain was already beginning to be rivalled as an economic power by Russia, Germany, Japan and America (and as a military power by Germany and Japan). She is now overshadowed by them, though except in America's case the process was not without hiccups, namely the devastation wrought by unsuccessful wars – which by enabling Germany and Japan to start again from scratch actually boosted their economies – and the stagnation caused by Communist economic policies. In addition we are presently in the second stage of the process, one which affects the whole of the West including America; the rise of the tiger economies of Asia and the Far East, particularly India and China. Britain's decline has been accelerated by the exhaustion of her native mineral resources, on which the Industrial Revolution was built; this among other things means she is economically and therefore perhaps politically dependent on those countries which still have a generous supply of the commodities she needs. Coal mines (which would have been worked out at some point anyway, with or without Margaret Thatcher) have mostly been closed. The heavy industries on so much of which Britain's past prosperity and world power depended have been superseded by new sectors in which she has lost out to younger and more vibrant economies who have been better able to gauge and respond to the spirit of the age; she is also at a disadvantage vis a vis nations who are just beginning to fully exploit their own mineral resources – like China. It means she can no longer afford to police the world, except as a participant in wars and peacekeeping operations which may have been initiated by her stronger ally the United States. Or, with a few small (and willing, probably because they are not viable as independent nations anyway) exceptions to maintain overseas colonies (of course the Empire was also faced with a growth in nationalist sentiment and activity, as was bound to happen after a while, among her subject peoples followed by a political reaction against overt colonialism by the international establishment). It is possible to practise a purely economic imperialism, backed up by military force, as America does but only if you are economically *strong*, which Britain isn't compared to the US, and can afford the military hardware with which to do it.

It can be truthfully said that today other cultures economically dominate Britain. She no longer has, for example, a native aerospace industry, entailing that her defence is effectively in the hands of others. She is reliant on foreign wealth and goods for the standard of living she seeks to enjoy. In a globalised economy, as in any other kind of free market system, the strong prosper at the expense of the weak. In many areas it is very hard, now, to find essential commodities which were not manufactured in one country, China, which is not only damaging to others' national pride and prestige but makes them hostages to fortune, so much depending on whether the product is of the right quality and Beijing has sensible economic policies.

So many British companies are run by foreigners, or products supplied by foreign firms whether based here or overseas, that matters which affect the prosperity of the country and the wellbeing of its citizens are determined by decisions taken not in London but in Paris, Berlin, Brussels, Madrid, Washington, Tokyo or Beijing. Within Europe, Britain's loss of independence in the matter is exacerbated by the EU which these days is supposed to form a completely free trade region in all aspects of economic life. Protection at least has the advantage of safeguarding economies which are vulnerable, whether because they are developing or in decline, but it goes so much against how the world at large, eager for the wealth which the free market can in the right circumstances generate, functions today. We have invested so much in that free market system, financially and emotionally, that dismantling it would not only cause economic disruption but hostility and conflict too. There may be some advantage to Britain in the "Brexit" but equally she could be creating for herself a situation in which she is no longer equipped to survive, or at any rate to prosper.

She would still be subject to the implications of what goes on in China, in fact even more so because she was cutting herself off from Brussels. That dependence is galling. It is not just that we have to put up with shoddy goods. When making complaints or other enquiries about a product one is so often referred to someone in India, or another foreign country, via a call centre there. The modern tendency to "outsource", itself partly due to the rise of some nations while others fall, here ties in with the fact of Britain's long-term decline. Speak to ordinary people in Britain about the consequence of this and you will see they find it a source of irritation. It can't be denied that accents are sometimes incomprehensible (admittedly a similar problem is caused by the poor diction of the young people who make up so much of the British workforce, but *that* isn't good either and we shouldn't tolerate it). At the same time the geographic distance between oneself and the person one is speaking to and who is expected to deal with one's problem means that the latter is inevitably remote from the matter in hand and adds to the communication issues. In the past the diminution in status of a powerful nation meant that it came to be dominated by other nations, politically or economically or both, and thus had to have dealings with people whose language it didn't speak (in one sense or another), which was always frustrating as well as causing practical difficulties. We are seeing this, after a fashion, in what I have described above. It was also the case that the subjugated nation came to be dominated in cultural matters, so that the newcomers replaced its language and nomenclature with their own.

This is arguably evidenced by the takeover of Abbey National, a British company, by Santander, a foreign company, which has replaced the English name with its own and apparently saw nothing controversial in doing so. It may not have occurred as a result of actual military conquest but the effect, if not the principle, is much the same. We have no way of knowing how far the process will go, but it is happening and it does result in the disappearance of traditional forms and practices. If it continues, there may be serious implications for what we consider to be our historic identity, as expressed in time-honoured names and figures of speech. We either do not have the clout to stop it or there is a political culture, by now deeply entrenched as to be difficult to defy, which blocks action against it on the grounds that the motive is chauvinistic.

In his *Decline And Fall Of The Roman Empire* Edward Gibbon declares that an empire cannot be overwhelmed and conquered by other powers unless it first falls apart from within. This is undoubtedly true; there have been innumerable cases throughout history of internal instability, political fragmentation, economic decline, social collapse and loss of morale weakening a nation's power to resist external aggression, the instability making it possible for the foreign power to invade in support of one faction or the other or on the pretext of restoring order, or simply invade. In Britain's case there is undoubtedly political fragmentation taking place, as seen in the granting of devolution to Scotland and Wales which may be the precursor to either full independence or internal conflict within the United Kingdom. And there is social atomisation and alienation, fear of a growing yob culture. Current sociopolitical issues, and particularly anger at austerity policies and disparities of wealth, could well result in massive social unrest and a breakdown in law and order. There is cultural degeneration, with increasing vulgarity in everyday speech and a decline in artistic standards as commercial viability and sound bites become more important considerations than actual quality. Television wasn't around in Gibbon's time of course, but cultural decline – seen in Rome's moral permissiveness and corruption, both of which are echoed in Western society today – has long been recognised as a symptom of national decline. So too is a fall in the quality of political leadership, something we have undoubtedly experienced in Britain in recent years. Poor judgement and a deterioration if not of intelligence, then of intellect makes it harder to devise solutions to complex problems and adjust sensibly to new realities, and results in inappropriate and misguided policies on which much-needed money is wasted.

Although I have of course no wish to encourage racism, it can't be denied that the relative, but increasing, loss of racial and cultural homogeneity due to the growth of the non-white ex-Commonwealth population – former subjects of the empire – along with more recent immigration from elsewhere has undoubtedly led to uncertainty about national identity and how it should be defined at a time when social, political and geopolitical upheavals have broken down other certainties from which in the past we drew strength and encouragement. Gibbon hints that this was an issue in the decline of Rome. Nowadays, he would probably be hauled before the Commission for Racial Equality for saying so. Similarly controversial to modern people (though mainly politically correct liberals) is the suggestion made a while ago by the historian David Starkey that the majority of the British population were becoming like the ethnic minorities, taking on their faults, and that this explained all the problems that the country was having. I must say I am concerned the Starkey should not be demonised, sidelined, categorised as a "non-person", as happens when political correctness decides it has been offended. But that does not mean I agree with him. It should perhaps be borne in mind that Starkey is not renowned in any case for liking PC, and also that public figures (like people in general, perhaps) tend to get more crotchety with age, also losing the ability to put their views through a proper filter. It's undoubtedly true that when people emigrate somewhere they bring their faults as well as their virtues with them, and no doubt it is possible for some, at least, in the majority community to pick up those bad habits (though I'm not clear as to which of the latter Starkey had in mind), which is not a good thing of course. It could happen through racial admixture, but the latter is something which it is impossible to prevent even if it might have a profound affect upon identities. There are of course positive aspects to immigration; it can undoubtedly benefit the economy, and a little colourful cultural diversity ought not to go unappreciated. The crux of the matter is that unless it is imposed on it by military force, a majority will only ever take up the culture of a minority willingly (and I don't think fancying a bit of Chicken Tikka Marsala now and then constitutes anything harmful). The generally hostile reaction by the majority to attempts at airbrushing certain past figures from history because of slavery indicates in any case that it is defending its own culture rather than taking on a different one. It is best to say that while there are beneficial aspects to the former, immigration and a relative reduction in racial homogeneity can in an imperfect world have a dysfunctional effect, especially when combined with other factors. There are a whole host of factors, not all to do with race by any means, which explain why cultural cohesion, educational standards and administrative efficiency are breaking down in modern Britain.

But the former subject peoples of the Empire, given British citizenship (as Rome's had been given Roman citizenship), and with it the right to reside in the "mother country", have grown in number to the extent of challenging traditional perceptions of things. As well as arguably leading to fears over national identity and thus social tension the immigration has added to overcrowding (in a country which has always had too large a population for its size) and along with natural increase of the indigenous

British put pressure on public services, a major failure of which will lead to rioting and collapse of law and order. The dilemma is that at the same time it is economically *necessary*, because of the need to fill poorly-paid, dirty jobs which British people, and particularly the young with their increased wealth and comfort since the last war, feel are beneath them.

Some of the factors we have mentioned prevail on mainland Europe too, in particular the need to encourage, or at least permit, immigration to make up for shortage of labour. But in Britain's case population pressures are made worse by the ratio of people to space available. It could be that we are seeing a general crisis of the developed world through overcrowding and other things, but the explosion if it happens will happen first in Britain because of the unique problems she faces. With the decline in the quality of her public services, resulting for example in roads and pavements which have not been properly maintained for many years and look like what you would find in a much poorer country, or Lebanon during the civil war, along with her other issues she will be the first modern developed Western country to regress to being, in effect, a Third World one. The problem stems from the cost and administrative/logistical difficulties of trying to meet the diverse practical and other needs of such a large population. Paradoxically, when budgets are cut as a result it makes the issue more difficult to resolve as the necessary financial resources are not there.

Generally Britain is becoming increasingly expensive to run. A large part of that, and something which all developed countries are facing, is the need to cater for an ageing population. The longer we live, the more care we require because of the physical and/or mental infirmities that usually come with growing old. Our situation is in some ways comparable to what it was in the years before the First World War when the Asquith government wanted to spend money on social reforms but could not at the same time pay for the new warships which were a vital part of the nation's defence against potential aggressors. The funds could be raised by a tax on the rich which was eventually implemented, despite a constitutional crisis when the House of Lords, representing the landed interest, threw out the measure. The problem today is that we may not be able to properly care for a much larger number of older people, many with dementia or serious physical illness/disabilities, and at the same time keep in being an expensive nuclear deterrent, especially when the needs of every other sector are taken into account as well. This means Britain may not in the future be able to protect itself from hostile powers who mean more genuine harm than I think the Kaiser ever did. We have already had to cut back our conventional arsenal severely.

On the subject of foreign affairs we have often been accused by our Left, or by those who as they see it are simply trying to be realistic, of "punching above our weight". I do not think we are doing that if our motive in having nuclear weapons is simply to protect ourselves in a hostile and uncertain world.

Nor is there anything wrong in our participating in wars that are just, or being involved along with other parties in diplomacy, in brokering peace deals between countries or warring factions within them. The elitism of the G7 summit on global economic and other issues, which included Britain, who was trying to hang on to her status as a world power (if now a second-rank one), along with the US and other Western nations but excluded emerging former Third World countries like Brazil and India was remedied when it became the G20. So the charge that we are "punching above our weight" has never really washed with me. What undoubtedly is true, however, is that our loss of first-rank status in world politics means that in foreign policy we have to align ourselves with partners who are in many ways unsuitable. To be allied with the EU involves being drawn closer and closer into its political and economic orbit, which we do not want. A closer relationship with the Commonwealth, though it is what I would prefer, means being associated with some countries that have appalling human rights records. And to consolidate the "special relationship" which to some extent exists between Britain and the USA, though it depends on who happens to be in power in Washington, also has its dangers. Even powers with a certain common ethnic, cultural and linguistic heritage are still very different from one another. Britain is not Germany or Scandinavia, and she is not the US, or *vice versa*. America will always have her own agenda and priorities, which may or may not coincide with other people's (whoever the latter are). And she is powerful enough in the end to do what she wants; in the "special relationship" Britain has always been the tail and not the dog. This doesn't matter as long as America's behaviour is defensible. Where it is misguided and aggressive, as it was under George W Bush and may yet prove to be under Donald Trump, Britain must either cut herself off, further losing influence, or be disastrously associated with questionable military inventions and gung-ho attitudes, even when she is not directly guilty of them herself. Where our uneasiness with the EU is concerned part of the reason for same, inevitably, is that we have too strong a past. The Empire, together with our generally being successful at defending our sovereignty through military superiority, gave us a power and independence of which we were proud and which awareness of lingers on in our communal self-consciousness. We do not like to pool it in institutions like the European Union.

Britain's degenerating, in the sense that poverty is increasing and public services deteriorating, to Third World status before other European nations can be said to be partly due to her having had a larger colonial empire than they. To some extent from a guilt complex she felt some obligation to her subject peoples even after they had achieved independence, and so they were allowed to come and live here if they felt that by doing so they would enjoy more prosperity and freedom of opportunity. All that immigration combined with the tendency of the ethnic groups in question to have large families has undoubtedly contributed, over a period of time, to the population growth that puts so much pressure on resources. The Empire is often said to have rebounded on those who created it, which in many ways is true. The crucial factor, however, may more than anything else have been the failure to halt the migration once it had reached the level it needed to make good the manpower losses suffered during the war. (This is not to denigrate people for merely wanting to improve their prospects by living in a relatively prosperous Western nation, rather than a poverty-stricken Afro-Caribbean one, or to keep families together. I should also say that although we don't want to encourage a racial stereotype of the white Anglo-Saxon as being dour and boring compared to the colourful West Indian or African, I don't think I'd like it if we went back to being an all-white nation in the sense we were before *Empire Windrush*; things would somehow seem rather dull.)

But for the sake of historical argument if nothing else, it could be argued that immigration whatever its benefits has been *a* factor in Britain's decline, even if it had to combine with others to play its part. The same qualified importance in the matter can be accorded the philosophy of political correctness, which it was particularly sought to implement in Britain, once the doctrine began to spread from America where it first originated, because Britain having had the largest colonial empire was thought most of all to need lessons in how to treat people as free equals, and because fear and horror of racism led political correctionists to emphasise the chauvinistic element in the complex British national character. PC may have made it relatively more difficult to halt immigration, by identifying such a policy as racist. Of course, actual governments, as opposed to vociferous and to some extent influential PC liberals, dither over the issue rather than dutifully adhere to a common PC line. But if they do dither, it may be because they do not want to seem too right-wing, as much as because they can see that the immigration has its advantages, to the nation as a whole, as well as its disadvantages. More recently the effect, perhaps unintended but no less harmful for that, of PC may have been to encourage immigrants and ethnic minorities to emphasise their own distinctive culture rather than to integrate fully, thereby increasing the potential for social conflict. This is mainly a problem with the more recent influx, but then political correctness as we currently experience it, through what it does and what it insists others don't do, is a relatively recent phenomenon. PC has certainly been disastrous in other vital areas; the reluctance to push children to do well through good old-fashioned discipline, which was seen by liberals as judgemental and liable to cause stress to the pupil, goes some way I believe towards explaining inefficiency in industry. The general fall in educational standards, which both explains the poorer calibre of many school and university leavers (though it may only be relative, and makes no difference to their worth as human beings) and represents an adjustment in line with same, is a problem affecting the whole of society.

How Britain can find its true place in the modern world I confess I don't know. The problem is still that highlighted by Dean Acheson, US Secretary of State, when he commented in the middle years of the twentieth century that she had lost an empire but not yet found herself a role. Some things however are clear. She may have counted for less geopolitically since the Second World War but culturally her achievement has been important, and seen in a profusion of good music (both popular and classical, although it is always the Beatles who one thinks of first) and television programmes. Nor, despite fears prevalent since the 1960s of the "brain drain" to other countries, has Britain been as backward in science and technology as has often been suggested. She can still produce figures of the stature of Stephen Hawking and Tim Berners-Lee, creator of the World Wide Web. Greatness does not depend solely on economic, military and political power; perhaps it doesn't depend on them at all.

Recent British history is of importance as a study of how a superpower declines and the issues it faces in adjusting to a new, in some ways reduced role in the world, accepting the new realities without losing its dignity, prosperity and liberties; the mistakes that are made along the way. In particular the consequences of a large population continually expanding (not only because of immigration) within a small geographical area and putting pressure on resources, in combination with other factors, should serve as a lesson and a warning to other countries. If Britain is to be the first Western nation to suffer in the general collapse of modern civilisation which sometimes seems likely she may also be the first to emerge from it and forge a new world, just as her being the first to industrialise meant she was the first to decline. All things being equal.

4

Cavalcade of Albion

1

Where exactly does one start a general political history of Britain? (I call it that, though to simplify matters I have left out, by and large, the histories of Wales and Scotland before they were amalgamated with England, even though I am aware that "England" and "Britain" are not the same thing.) Traditionally people tend to kick off with the Norman Conquest – historians do, at any rate – which I have always objected to because it gives the impression the Anglo-Saxons somehow had no political organisation worth speaking of. This was not the case, but there is a justification for beginning wih the Normans in that they so totally replaced the previous administrative and political structure with their own, whether or not they were right to do so. (By the way, the polity which was replaced in 1066 was strictly speaking an Anglo-Danish rather than an Anglo-Saxon one as the Danes, who ruled the land in the early eleventh century, had exterminated the "Saxon" nobility, a fact recorded in the *Anglo-Saxon Chronicle*).

In the past the Normans have been portrayed as saving England from tyrannical and incompetent rule, as represented by King Harold. But it is unfair to judge the Anglo-Saxons by the standards of Harold, or of Edward the Confessor. Better to say that the Normans, seeing their opportunity, struck when the Saxon state was going through a bad patch, a period of weakness. Harold was not an outstanding ruler, at any rate by comparison with some of his predecessors; Edward was a fairly common Christian type, deeply and admirably pious but less able and effective in a practical sense, failing to detect the growth of Norman influence within the country and check it. Had William the Conqueror been up against Alfred the Great or Athelstan it is doubtful whether he'd have stood as much chance of success.

The Norman kings are often considered to have been more autocratic than their Saxon predecessors. This may have been because William I was uneasily aware his claim to the throne was tenuous (his conquest of England was achieved partly through military victory and partly through exploiting family connections, along with the existing Norman community in England, in what comes over as a rather sneaky inside job). It is claimed by some that Edward the Confessor promised the throne to William, but Harold destroyed all the evidence of this. That may be so, but the very absence of the evidence means the claim cannot be substantiated. At any rate William was motivated in large measure by greed, and confessed as much on his deathbed. But whatever the legitimacy of their actions in 1066, the Normans altogether nervously suspected that they might have bitten off more than they could chew. England was the biggest prize this land-grabbing bunch of Viking pirates – roughly speaking what they were, though they supposedly became civilised through settling in France – had so far managed to secure, a realm much greater and more prosperous than their other territories, and I think they were a little scared by what they had taken on. They needed therefore to enforce their rule vigorously, with an administrative efficiency which helps perpetuate the myth that the Saxons were disorganised by comparison, but, in order to keep their resentful English subjects happy, no more cruelly than was necessary. In any case, it is reckoned that by the end of the twelfth century the Normans had become indistinguishable ethnically from the "Saxons" (English), suffering (if that is the right word) the fate of many ruling elites throughout history. This process may have been assisted by the fact that many of them had fair skin and fair/red hair and thus were not physically dissimilar to the Saxons – or Vikings – from whom the English were in part descended.

The Norman Conquest did have the effect of burying any remaining differences between Anglo-Saxons and Danes/Vikings (the Normans no longer really saw themselves as the latter) by the imposition on the land of a whole new dynasty with a different sense of ethnic and cultural identity from either and which was determined to tightly control the valuable possession it had succeeded in acquiring, which meant enforcing order on squabbling factions. So it did undoubtedly confer some advantages. It did not end the ongoing resentment, which has continued almost up to the present day, of the Welsh and Scots towards the English, since the Normans had been absorbed into the latter people.

Mediaeval kings were not necessarily despots. John tried to be, but got his fingers burnt. The idea was that there was a contract between monarch and people, even if the "people" was usually defined as the *political* nation, those whose intelligence and status were felt to entitle them to a share in discussions on how the realm was to be governed – and thus the baronage. Though largely self-seeking – if that is not too cynical a view of things – the latter found it prudent, while safeguarding their own interests, to maintain the loyalty of the common people, generally keeping the latter happy, by protecting them against overmighty rulers; this was essentially the thinking behind Magna Carta. The importance of the "Great Charter" was exaggerated during the seventeenth century and later as part of the Whig interpretation of history – it certainly did not eliminate injustice and oppression from the system, or there would have been no Peasants' Revolt – but it made it more likely that a monarch would think twice before seeking to enforce his will against the wishes of the baronage, or the baronage and the (actual) people combined. Some tried and succeeded (Henry III), some tried and failed (Richard II). Of course, where the mass of the population did not feel particularly oppressed, and their lot was no more miserable than was usually the case in the Middle Ages, they generally took little interest in what might have been essentially a struggle between the king and the leading nobles, the former having put the latter's noses out of joint. When it erupted into war they suffered its consequences, which could be disruptive for ordinary folk, but its causes excited them not.

Before the advent of parties and "democracy", political affairs were essentially a question of the king's ability to handle powerful magnates with skill and tact. Instability could result if he failed to do so. Perhaps because of *1066 And All That* we tend still to see mediaeval history in terms of "good" kings, who dealt with their baronage prudently (e.g. Edward III, whose creation of the Knighthood of the Garter helped unite them with the monarchy and with each other in a common concern, the proper governance of the nation, which was also a friendly club) and "bad" kings who did not while also being greedy, tyrannical and unjust (e.g. John). Undoubtedly such a distinction is possible, although the terms "good" and "bad" are morally far too simplistic. Some "bad" kings were not as bad as has been made out. Edward II's favouritism towards Piers Gaveston and others led to serious civil conflict, but it is worth noting that when this was not happening things went reasonably smoothly; government was efficient and not oppressive in the way it was carried out. There is a comparison with Charles I. Edward was unlucky in that he had to deal with a serious famine at one point, but to be unlucky is not in itself a sin. Besides, you can't have superlative rulers all the time and it is not surprising if, between two great kings such as Edward I and Edward III, there is an intervening period in which the monarch is less able by comparison. (Not that being "great" is the same thing as being morally admirable. Edward I's comment on the vanquished Scots, "A man does well when he rids himself of s**t", was reprehensible).

Richard III vies with John for the "distinction" of having been the ultimate "bad" king, not because of his government – he was an able and not, as a rule, especially bloodthirsty monarch who never quite got the opportunity to prove himself in the role – but because it was believed he murdered the Princes in the Tower, the deposed Edward V and his brother the Duke of York, and thus was thought capable of doing just about anything. Once it began to be suspected they had been done away with (after all, how did one explain their mysterious and total disappearance) a very substantial nail was hammered into his coffin, though there were other factors, such as the divisive effect of his usurpation which alienated important people, explaining his loss of support and therefore of power.

The Princes were a focus around which his enemies, such as the dowager queen Elizabeth Woodville, a scheming and dangerous woman, could rally. Removing such threats has been an aspect of factional struggle and power politics all through history. The evidence is not sufficient to stand up in a modern court of law and probably would not have been in a contemporary one, but I believe that Richard did kill the princes; after all they were in his care, he had the opportunity to do it which Henry Tudor (a Welshman and an outsider with fewer of the necessary connections) did not, although Henry might not morally have baulked at it. He (Richard) denied having anything to do with their disappearance, but if someone else was able to get into the Tower and kill them it does not say much for his efficiency. Henry undoubtedly had as much of a motive as Richard, since the princes stood in the way of his own ambitions to be king; while they lived the Tudor dynasty would not have been legitimate. However, to target the person who had the motive but less of the opportunity rather than the one who undoubtedly had both seems illogical, and may be explained by excessive sympathy for Richard due to belief that since he was unfairly demonised due to his spinal deformity (which he was), as if being physically deformed means you must also be morally so, he could not have killed the princes, an argument whose logic is flawed. He may have committed the murders on impulse, the motive (though it is not really a motive so much as a fault) which perhaps also explains his seizing power in the first place, though in both cases there would have to be a background of arguments why and why not the action in question should have been taken.

Attempting to solve historical mysteries can be absorbing. With this one there are things which do not make sense if, indeed, Richard did kill his nephews; but if that were not so it would not be a mystery. Edward of Warwick, son of the Duke of Clarence, had as good a claim to the throne as the princes, but he survived Richard's reign, during which he was kept in a royal nursery in Yorkshire with Edward IV's daughters. It seems unlikely Elizabeth Woodville would have released the girls into Richard's care if she had thought he had killed her sons, while one of them, Elizabeth of York, pledged loyalty to him, telling him in a letter that she was his "in heart and soul". It is possible that Henry Tudor murdered the princes *after* he seized the throne (which may be what Richard's advocates are saying), when he certainly had more of a chance; however this must take into account the two years in which there is no evidence whatsoever for their continued existence. If, as some have suggested, they had died of the plague (their bodies not afterwards being buried in the public fashion usual with royalty because of the dangers of infection) one would have thought Richard should have said so. as it would have let him off the hook. But it would have been so convenient for them if they had that the explanation would not be believed. And it would have looked no less damaging for him if they simply seemed to vanish; which in fact they did. Henry VII never actually accused Richard of killing them, despite the tendency for Tudor spin to blacken his posthumous reputation and so bolster the new dynasty's own moral legitimacy. Was that because of his own guilt? But he would have tried to blame it on Richard whether he, Henry, was guilty or not, and so the only explanation must be that he genuinely did not know what had happened to them (which obviously exonerates him) and he was afraid of looking foolish if whatever reason he had suggested for their no longer being around turned out not to be the case. If they had turned up alive and well he would have been finished anyway, and it seems implausible that he would have taken the throne without making sure that all the other contenders had been eliminated one way or another. Unless it was that he saw his chance, which might not come again, in 1485 as opposition mounted to Richard and made a calculation by which he took it and afterwards would deal with things as they came. He did in fact have to contend with pretenders to the throne who claimed to be one or other of the missing princes, and they caused him enough trouble. And if Henry was *not* guilty Richard would have been the most likely suspect.

It is quite possible, and Henry VII may have been aware of the possibility, that the princes were killed against Richard's orders by his supporter the Duke of Buckingham. Richard did not reveal this because either it would suggest he could not control his own, or people would suspect Buckingham was merely a scapegoat. The jury is still sitting, and personally all I can do is suggest what I believe to be the most likely answer, i.e. that Richard definitely was the culprit, especially as Elizabeth Woodville's disappearance into a nunnery would have ensured her silence if she really did think he had done away with her sons. Until somehow we do find out the truth we can only go by the scenario for which the most plausible justification, in all its elements, can be constructed. Whatever happened, though, Richard was not a monster. Rather, he was at worst a tragic figure whose understandable fears for his own safety led him to commit a terrible act which was wrong despite the reasons for it, and in addition harmed his chances more than anything. He may also have genuinely believed that his regime offered a better chance of stability and of governing the realm in an ordered and efficient manner than a royal minority with the wrong sort of people wielding effective power. That he was a competent administrator, as king and in the responsibilities he exercised when Duke of Gloucester, makes it likely he was right. Not that it did him any good. Of course in political matters, where so much must depend on devious manoeuvring around interest groups and thus on the careful weighing of pros and cons, acting on impulse is never a good idea. It's like suddenly abandoning all caution and jumping out of a window without knowing how many storeys up you are.

As well as notably "good" or "bad" kings there were those who while not outstanding were nonetheless able to maintain order and preserve their position, despite hiccups, if they had enough support: Henry III (who ruled for fifty-six years), Henry IV and Edward IV come to mind. The second and third of these suffered from being usurpers who were not born and trained to be king, explaining to some extent why they made mistakes (from which they learned, in Edward's case) and alienated people. All the same they were able to hang on to power, though Edward in fact lost the throne for a brief period in 1470-71.

Then there is Stephen, who was perhaps not a wicked man but not bright and hamfisted in the way he pursued his supposed right to be king; Richard I who was never there; kings who were competent but unpopular, like William Rufus and the miserly Henry VII; and Henry VI who was of that Christian type which is pious but ineffective (and in this case, mentally ill as well).

The emergence of parliament in the late thirteenth century stemmed from a realisation, following wars between the baronage and two monarchs, that there needed to be some forum for airing and settling differences between the king and his subjects. However, this meant it was essentially a mouthpiece for the aristocrats who controlled the selection of MPs, or the king working through his agents. It could make things difficult for the monarch by refusing to vote the funds he needed for his foreign wars − Edward III in particular ran into trouble − but ultimately it lacked the power, by itself, to enforce its will where agreement could not be reached. Besides, a prudent monarch would seek, working through MPs or nobles who enjoyed his patronage, to get his way by skilled parliamentary management, a knack which the Crown lost under Charles I in the seventeenth century with disastrous consequences.

The rules of the game were changed by the decline of the feudal system, and by the Wars of the Roses. In the latter, though the dispute had been between rival claimants to the throne much of the fighting was done on behalf of one or other of the contenders by nobles with large private retinues, in what is referred to by historians as "bastard feudalism". They did a lot of damage, on top of the general lawlessness which seems to have plagued the land during this period and is described in the Paston Letters. Exhausted by these tribulations, the country proved willing to accept the strong royal system of government, backed by an expanded and efficiently run bureaucracy, which was set up by the Tudors. At the same time the aristocracy ceased to live in fortified castles and furthered their interests by seeking court patronage rather than attempting armed rebellion (with unsuccessful exceptions, e.g. Essex in 1601).

The growth of the royal bureaucracy, fuelled by the administrative upheavals consequent upon such things as the dissolution of the monasteries, which involved considerable transfer of land and wealth to the Crown and its supplicants, both buttressed the monarchy's new power and was generated by it. It provided opportunities for advancement and along with the importance of patronage, the latter being something not only the nobility could benefit from, was what made the Tudor period such a time of unlovely money-grubbing and jockeying for personal advantage, as portrayed in the Matthew Shardlake novels of C J Sansom. The politics of Henry VIII's reign in particular were a hotbed of intrigue and faction in which people sought to push their claims to office, as well as the religious policies they favoured; a game where the stakes were high and sharp practices often employed. Though well aware how the system worked and of the dirty business that went on (he once admitted "They can always get two or three knaves to testify against you"), Henry was often lazy and failed to promote his own interests, leaving a vacuum which those ambitious for themselves and their cause were dangerously tempted to fill. Dangerously because it could mean imprisonment or execution should the mercurial monarch decide to assert himself and not like what he found was going on. (Concerning Henry's tyrannical behaviour and his abominable treatment of his wives it is hard not to conclude that he was motivated by a complex about his masculinity. As well as failing, before 1537, to produce a son he spoke, surprisingly, in a high-pitched reedy voice which some might have considered effete.) Ultimately it was the King or Queen who was boss and in fact the emergence of a new form of royal absolutism was quite possible. But in the end this did not happen. That is, the power of the monarchy increased, and this was part of a general European trend in the early modern era, but it did not increase to quite the same extent as on the continent. It grew enough, though, for there to be the possibility of conflict with a parliament whose position had also been enhanced; under Charles I the two rival, in many ways, powers became locked on a collision course.

During the reign of Elizabeth I, who although keen for everyone to know she was in charge, and dangerous to cross because of her efficient spy system and network of loyal servants such as Burghley, was more a dissembler than a tyrant parliament was able to become a little more assertive. And the mini-industrial revolution of the early modern period had resulted in a gentry − making up most of the membership of the House of Commons − whose increased wealth, status and economic importance entitled them, they felt, to a greater share in political power (a factor which was to recur in British and European politics in the eighteenth and nineteenth centuries, and also explains many of the tensions prevalent in modern China). Or at least to have their grievances properly addressed. They understandably resented it when Charles I, in order to raise more money for his wars and to meet his budget deficit, imposed Ship Tax and began to enforce archaic laws still on the statute book but which no-one had really bothered about for some time. They saw this as a threat to their liberty and prosperity. The cause of the trouble was, to some extent, the same as it had often been in the Middle Ages − the king needing more cash for his overseas engagements, along with other things, than his subjects were happy to give. There was also the problem of evil-disposed counsellors, who were giving a basically good and wise ruler bad advice (the parliamentarians didn't want to seem more confrontational than was necessary, certainly not at this stage to overthrow the monarchy, and so it was desirable if possible to put the blame on these people, just as their effective counterparts in an earlier era had done). In the unfolding drama the role played by Piers Gaveston under Edward II in the early fourteenth century was now being ascribed to Strafford and Archbishop Laud. The conflict which, in England, could be said to have finally brought about the end of the Middle Ages in a political respect arose through mediaeval causes.

There was an additional factor in the equation which proved an especially potent one. In an age when its power over society and government has been effectively destroyed, though it may still command the allegiance of individuals, it is difficult to appreciate just how much of a part religion once played in events; how far it determined the course of British history and thus helped create that national selfconsciousness which is felt by patriotic Britons today even where they are apathetic or hostile towards religious belief itself (failure to appreciate the irony of this is perhaps assisted to some extent by an actual lack of proper historical knowledge). It resulted in a major assertion of national independence when Henry VIII, in accordance with his view of the position and prerogatives of a monarch, translated a personal wish – i.e. to divorce Catherine of Aragon and marry Anne Boleyn, through whom he hoped to have better luck at fathering a son – into an act of official policy and broke with Rome, establishing the Church of England. And it was to have similarly far-reaching consequences in the following century. It doesn't necessarily require a particular person whose motives may be individualistic, even idiosyncratic, as its instrument. It can have the cataclysmic effect which it does because loyalty to God, if you are at all serious about your faith, must come before all other matters, however important (a principle adopted, *in extremis*, by today's al-Qaeda and Islamic State terrorists). It can therefore upset social and political conventions which were previously unassailable – sacrosanct, in a manner of speaking – in a way which would not otherwise happen. Before the sixteenth century there was no conflict between it and them because with the exception of the heretic movements that arose from time to time there existed one single, Catholic church, and the thinking during the mediaeval period, as well as afterwards to some degree, was that there was no distinction between the religious and secular polities – there is a clear parallel with certain forms (still practised today) of Islam – because the King or Queen was appointed to rule by God, and it was therefore a sin to attempt to depose them.

The Reformation changed all that. Undoubtedly there had been a lot wrong with the Church of late, and once the corruption and abuses were highlighted it was possible to believe that the version of Christianity which had been practised in recent years was not the true one, and that radical changes were needed. Plus if the circumstances are right ideas have a habit of catching on. In time Protestantism grew, and what had been done for personal (to Henry VIII) political reasons was reinforced by something more ideological. The idea that there could be different kinds of Christianity, some legitimate and others heretical, was not new but now the split was a lot more fundamental. Since salvation or damnation depended on belief in God through Jesus Christ, to adhere to the incorrect way of expressing that faith, or supporting someone who did – even if they were the king – risked the latter. Fear of Hell proved stronger in the end than respect for the existing sociopolitical structure.

Ship Money, etc., which created a conflict between Court and Country, between loyalty to the monarchy and loyalty to one's constituents, who might be adversely affected by royal policies, was the crucial factor in bringing about the Civil War of the 1640s. By contrast it has been questioned how much of a part religion played, within England at any rate. Certainly it has always been possible for there to be wars of which it was not a cause. But I can't accept that its role was negligible, especially given events later in the century; that the conflict was purely a political and economic one. It might in the end have happened without religion. But the latter was still important enough to make opposition to the Crown, with all the implied consequences, psychologically easier. Far more serious in the eyes of some than Ship Money would have been the Arminian theological beliefs of Charles I and Laud, which verged on Catholicism or appeared to. In the end it was a combination of both grievances which sparked off the war and led to the execution of the King and the establishment of the English Republic. The trigger was Charles I's demands for money, which an alienated Parliament withheld, to pay for his war against the Scots, who had been incensed by his ham-fisted imposition on them of the Anglican Prayer Book. If this is borne in mind, religion acquires a far greater significance in the matter. And considering the pivotal role of the Scots in events, on several occasions, we ought really to be talking about the British rather than the English Civil War. As it was, Charles was forced by his Scottish entanglement to recall Parliament, which he had dissolved in 1629 in exasperation at its intransigence (as he saw it); he now expected it to be his willing tool, on pain of having its liberties curtailed, but its hostility to the imposition of new tax burdens meant that it had other ideas. One can see the whole conflict as a dispute between the elements of the political nation, the monarch and parliament, which did not affect or interest the majority of the population until 1642, and this is borne out by the relative quiescence of the country during Charles I's personal rule. But it was politically serious enough to result in an upheaval that was disruptive and devastating in its impact.

The Republic went through several different phases in an attempt to make itself work, establishing a set pattern which was followed by the French and to some extent the Russian Revolution. It changed from what was supposed to be a civilian affair to a military dictatorship ruled over by Cromwell and the Major-Generals. But Charles I's ineptitude in antagonising important and influential sections of his people, to the point where they felt they had no option but to take up arms, and pursue the war to the point of victory since defeat would have led to their execution for treason, had made necessary something extremely radical, and previously untried, which was without precedent in western Europe and of which there was no practical experience which might have proved valuable. Consequently, it failed. The "revolutionaries" had not been adequately prepared for the power now being thrust upon them, because up to a late stage they had still preferred to think in terms of preserving the traditional national institutions such as the monarchy and House of Lords (Charles' treachery when dealing with them, and in particular his behind-their-back negotiations with the Scots who he sought to bring into the war on his side, was what ultimately convinced them they had passed the point of no return). Things might have been different if Cromwell had accepted Parliament's offer of the crown, but he did not. The Republic, or Commonwealth as it was later renamed, governed fairly well but did not long survive the passing of the one strong personality who was holding it together. It fell apart following Cromwell's death and the ineffectual rule of his son and successor as Lord Protector, Richard. The great Parliamentary leaders Pym and Hampden, who might have made a difference to the course of events, had both died some years before. There was no option but to restore the monarchy.

The episode meant that Britain had got over her revolutions early, and helped to make possible three hundred and fifty years of relatively peaceful political development. During that span of time no-one has succeeded in changing the government of the United Kingdom (as it was from the Act of Union with Scotland in 1707) through violence (though that, or anarchy, could still happen if certain social and cultural tensions get out of hand), allowing the British Constitution to evolve gradually without anyone needing to establish a dictatorship to get their way. In the first instance the personality of Charles II proved crucial. Though not by any standard a great king, he was in some ways a good one. By 1660, both sides had learned their lesson. No-one wished to repeat a venture which had ended in failure and caused considerable disruption, along with loss of life, as well as divided families and opened up deep wounds within English society. King and Parliament met each other half way. Parliament was less keen to mount challenges to royal authority, or the King to push it too far, and any serious disputes which did arise were eventually settled without the need for rebellion. Though it is not true that Charles did not seek to get his way regardless of Parliament's wishes, he was rather more subtle about it than his father, employing deviousness – as in the secret Treaty of Dover with Louis XIV, and his deathbed conversion to Catholicism – rather than open confrontation. And he only did what he could get away with. His affable, easy-going personality, in sharp contrast to the remote shyness of his father which if anything made abrupt and autocratic behaviour more likely, was an asset, even if it extended to his leading a "loose" private life.

There had to be a proper balance of potentially competing forces. Nevertheless, it could be said that in 1660 the Crown was laughing. It still had to be careful, and Charles II could never have been a tyrant of the sort Henry VIII effectively was, but it retained its power to dissolve parliament at will, for example, and in accordance with the whole logic of Restoration no-one was likely to overthrow it (in fact the immediate post-Restoration House of Commons was dubbed the "Cavalier Parliament" because of its Royalist character). Yet by 1700 the situation had been fundamentally transformed, bringing about what might be regarded as the final end, in Britain at any rate, of the mediaeval monarchy (just as the intellectual changes gathering pace during this period led to the waning of the Middle Ages in a more general sense and throughout Europe). The balance of power was upset by a figure who possessed rather less political sagacity than Charles. The latter was succeeded by his brother, James II, already known to be a Roman Catholic. James did not want to impose Catholicism on England against its people's wishes, but he was very good at causing people to think he did. In his eagerness to redress the discrimination, seen in the Test and Corporation Acts, which Catholics had suffered during the previous reign he appointed rather too many of them to important posts, sometimes dismissing the existing Protestant incumbent. It was a late seventeenth-century form of "positive discrimination", applied heavy-handedly and when considered along with James' holding military maneouvres on Hounslow Heath (in other words, close to the capital) and other places, while increasing the size of the standing army (at that time seen as a potential prop to tyranny), appearing to amount to something highly sinister. In the late seventeenth century (during its middle years everything was subsumed within the Crown/Parliament conflict, which was in large measure a political one even if Arminianism may have been a contributory factor to it, and its attendant upheavals) the scares over rumoured Catholic plots to overthrow the Protestant establishment were without foundation. The heightened persecution in which they resulted was to create a defensive mentality among Catholics, as part of which they tended to ignore institutionalised Catholicism's own faults, and this feeling was to last into modern times. But in 1688 the fears of Protestants were understandable, and the birth of an heir to James who would presumably be brought up a Catholic exacerbated them by appearing to make a Catholic ascendancy more likely. Then of course there was the effect of Louis XIV's unnecessary and ham-fisted revocation of the Edict of Nantes, which had granted full civil rights to French Protestants and whose negation caused English ones to fear for their own liberties. It was the act of a man with strength of will and enormous prestige but who, like James, was not clever. And what Louis could do James might also do too, at least that was what people thought.

At this stage we are reminded of the role of personalities in history (it is doubtful if anyone could have forced constitutional reform on Henry VIII, no matter what the factors pressing them to do so, had he decided to stand his ground). It is fortunate that when opposition to him began to mount James panicked and fled to France, thus avoiding another nasty conflict. Parliament seized its opportunity and declared that he had abdicated, which it could be argued was the case – his throwing the Great Seal of England into the Thames, though in essence a petulant gesture of spite, would have appeared to have an air of finality about it. Certainly he was the last monarch who could, if he had chosen, have acted as an absolute ruler, however unwise it might have been to do so, and later ones simply cannot be compared to him in the powers and privileges they possessed, in what they were able and not able to do.

In order that its problems with James should not be repeated, parliament over the subsequent period passed laws, such as that it had itself to be permanent and re-elected every three – later seven, and now five – years, which effectively restricted the power of the monarch to make policy, though s/he could still appoint and dismiss ministers. It was assumed that parliament would debate financial issues as a matter of course, but it could not be called merely because the monarch wanted money and dissolved by them once they had got it. It is obvious that these laws were designed to limit the freedom of action of a ruler who might, as James had done, convert to Catholicism at a relatively late stage in life (and thus perhaps be already on the throne), or the implications of a Popish dynasty if the heir shared their parent's faith; anyone who already was a Catholic would be barred from succeeding in the first place under the new order of things. Among other considerations this would avoid the bother of having to depose them and the constitutional wrangling deposition might lead to; not everyone had been convinced of the rightness of cutting out James II in 1688 (had *he* been deposed, rather than chosen to abdicate?).

The aim, following the experience of the political nation under Charles I and James II, was as much to curb royal power in general as to safeguard the national religion, although the latter had been one of the issues over which conflict between Crown and Parliament had arisen. But the religious aspect was certainly there, operating in conjunction with renewed fears of absolutism because of James I's actions, and it seems ironic given that within a relatively short period, historically speaking, religion was to cease to be as explosive a factor in political affairs as it had been in the two hundred years or so following the Reformation, with of course exceptions such as the Gordon Riots. Catholics continued to labour under severe disabilities until 1829, and are still prevented from succeeding to the throne today (though how much longer this ruling will survive in the modern, "inclusive", secularised world, where the religious choices of monarchs may not be seen as mattering and the monarchy itself is much reduced in power, is uncertain). But, perhaps because of the influence of science, Christianity came to be practised in a more rational way (in fact over the next three centuries it came on most people's part to be jettisoned altogether as a serious commitment, for better or for worse). On a personal level it was seen as a matter of choice which Christian denomination you belonged to and there was generally less inclination to make a fuss over the matter. This became extended to the political sphere; you did not become the ruler of a country, by whatever means (and this included invading and conquering it militarily) in order to change its religion to match your own, by making it corporately Catholic or Protestant. In the Jacobite rebellion of 1745-6, whose aim was to restore them to the British throne, the Stuarts may have been backed, and hosted, by France, a Catholic country, and been themselves papists but the rising's primary motive was political. Religious considerations still mattered; a country which was emotionally and spiritually strongly Protestant would have had an additional reason for resisting the Jacobites. But for whatever reason, there began in 1689 a process which was to end in the monarch becoming little more than a figurehead. Although the issue did not entirely go away, never again were there to be major constitutional crises over evil counsellors or foreign entanglements, because the king or queen's wishes simply did not matter as much as they had before.

The early Hanoverian monarchs – especially George I who was hampered by a language barrier, not being able to speak English fluently – found close involvement in British political affairs tiresome, largely because their freedom of manouevre was more restricted, and steered clear of them to some extent, being at least as interested in the fortunes of their native Hanover. Where they did concern themselves with things British it was more from a rigid (and admirable) Germanic sense of duty, which required that there should be a Protestant succession to the throne of one of the most important nations in Europe, than as the assertion of authority over a personal fiefdom. The attitude of William of Orange, who had been invited in (at any rate his invasion was not opposed) by the political establishment to replace James II in 1688 as William III, had been similar; connected with it was William's struggle against the power of Catholic France under Louis XIV, in which he needed an ally, and England did not take issue with this motive since she saw France as an economic rival and a threat to her liberty. But as a result of feeling distanced from or alienated by purely native concerns foreign-born monarchs tended to leave discussion and if necessary resolution of important matters to the Cabinet, composed of members of the government who were invariably MPs. They thus lost valuable ground.

George III, though by his own lights a good man, who does not deserve to be remembered chiefly for having gone mad, lacked the cleverness to be able to pull off a restoration of royal supremacy in what was by then a much altered situation and eventually gave up the attempt. The upshot of it was that by the beginning of the nineteenth century, Britain had changed from a monarchy (it was and is still a *constitutional* one, but then in a sense it always had been except when a King John or a Henry VIII, the latter dominating by the force of his personality and his skill or that of his clients in managing the system, was on the throne) to an oligarchy of aristocratic landowners, grown powerful and prosperous on the agricultural improvements which preceded the Industrial Revolution and the expansion of trade as Britain's foreign empire burgeoned. Through established convention the right of the monarch to dismiss ministries ceased to be exercised, the last one to use it being William IV in 1834. Queen Victoria wisely refrained from ever taking such a step despite her strong predilections for or against certain Prime Ministers; the row over her choice of Ladies of the Bedchamber, which seemed to indicate a political bias, taught her to be careful.

The royal prerogative, by which the sovereign could refuse to sign a parliamentary bill when it was put before them, had fallen into disuse since the days of Queen Anne. Anne's death also marked the end of the Stuart era (the throne had reverted to the family when William III died childless; since she was a Protestant, as well as a suitable candidate in other ways, there were no obstacles to her succession). It is regarded as Elizabeth I's principal failing that by not marrying and producing an heir she made necessary the importation of this disastrous dynasty, who seem less canny than fits the traditional picture of

Scots. But Elizabeth's personality and temperament were such that one suspects she could not have been the effective ruler she was had she not been her own boss in all affairs, including marriage. And she would not have had any patience with a husband who was weak and pliable, there only to father her children. It is also possible she had an aversion to coition following molestation when a teenager at the hands of Thomas Seymour (now there is a genuine case of "historic" sex abuse), although the rumour remains unconfirmed. She nonetheless used sex appeal to get her way, and by procrastination successfully resisted the pressure to marry from her councillors; but then Elizabeth was an arch-dissimulator, having had to learn the art in early womanhood when she was under suspicion of treason and heresy, with the consequent threat of execution, and generally a victim of the dynastic and religious politics of the time, frozen out by a neglectful father and then imprisoned by a Catholic sister hostile to her suspected Protestantism. It was a way of surviving, and ingrained in her a habit which she was not to lose, partly because it came in so useful to her later on.

But to return to the Stuarts, it is questionable whether they were all that disastrous. Their problem was that they did not produce any *outstanding* monarchs, as the Tudors did. Otherwise, things weren't so bad most of the time. James I obviously had more experience of Scottish than of English politics. While rough Scots bonhomie might be all right as far as it went it did not necessarily provide a solution to England's governmental problems and religious conflicts, and if it didn't it would be resented if anything. But it was only under James's son that things went pear-shaped. The Catholic discontent that led to the Gunpowder Plot, which would certainly have been disastrous had it succeeded, was a symptom of the difficulty of ignoring ideologically prejudiced elements who were also powerful; you could only go so far towards emancipating papists in the early modern era, as Elizabeth had found (characteristically, she took pains to appear a religious moderate while always siding with Protestant opinion in the end).

Charles II's pragmatism helped to ensure the peaceful conduct of affairs in the years following the Civil War. Anne was a sound enough ruler, within the more limited context in which restrictions on the power of the monarchy forced her to operate. And it is possible to feel some sympathy for Charles I, narrow-minded and foolish though he was. As Sharpe's study of his personal rule makes clear his day-to-day government, in which he did not generally interfere, was competent; it was over purely political rather than administrative issues that he caused problems. His dangerous obstinacy may have been due to a medical condition, in those days undiagnosed (I am not sure what it would now be called), in childhood which affected his early intellectual development; "Baby Charles" could not walk or talk properly until he was five. He comes over in the end not as a wicked man but rather a sad one who was merely doing what he believed to be right, and paying the consequences. One can certainly conceive of Cromwell, who was himself a man of conviction and conscience, feeling respect for Charles on account of this, as in the famous painting of him gazing down reflectively at the late King's corpse, even if there is no evidence that he actually did so.

We may ask why the principal factor which led to the collapse of the Republic in 1660 and the restoration of the monarchy, namely the inability to find anything workable to replace the latter, did not also lead to the collapse of the 1689 settlement, if that settlement was effectively a repudiation of monarchism in its traditional form. There are several possible answers to this question. Firstly, although he did not really command its respect Charles II's preference for accommodation rather than confrontation with parliament meant that it had come to see itself as being in a partnership with the monarchy, working with the king for the proper government of the nation and the common good, rather than as necessarily subservient to him. Secondly, impatience with royal absolutism (or what was perceived as such) and royal promotion of unpopular religious doctrines, which had proved themselves threats on two occasions in recent decades, overcame in the minds of the political nation the factors that worked against a fundamental break with the past, a casting aside of systems one was familiar with, that were tried and tested. Thirdly, perhaps, the new scientific wisdom that was beginning to percolate throughout those orders of society who were at least educated meant that it seemed irrational to be too dependent on a hereditary monarchy. Fourthly, because that monarch still retained some residual power the parliamentarians could tell themselves that they were *not* abolishing it, were *not* overturning the past. And in due course the monarchy was to evolve a new role for itself as a crucial focus for patriotism and national identity and thus a defuser of serious internal conflict, a unifying factor. It was easier for the institution to do this because James II's impulsive decision to flee to France, rather than standing his ground, in 1688 meant that it was less associated with violence.

*

Much of the structure of British government and politics in the modern era took shape in the eighteenth century. In 1782 the post of Secretary of State was abolished. It had originated in the sixteenth century, the holder being a glorified clerk dealing with the monarch's correspondence but who later evolved into something a little more important politically. It finished up as something roughly equivalent to the modern Foreign Secretaryship, which replaced it, except that at times when foreign affairs were particularly important, and the holder of the office was a certain kind of strong personality, the Secretary could effectively be Prime Minister in all but name, the most obvious example being William Pitt the Elder during the Seven Years' War. Now this was no longer possible; the trend was towards fully specialised departments whose holders were not necessarily in a position to be powers behind the throne, although their influence might still be crucial.

The Prime Minister, as the name suggests, is the monarch's chief minister. Some, such as Robert Harley (Lord High Treasurer), exercised the powers the post conveyed before it was actually created, just as William Pitt (as Secretary of State) did so afterwards. As suggested, the importance of the position in more than a ceremonial and/or administrative sense could depend until the late eighteenth century on the personality of the incumbent; Walpole, generally regarded as being the first "Prime Minister", undoubtedly exercised real power from his appointment in 1721. In theory the Prime Minister was, and still is, the First Lord of the Treasury, as the Lord High Treasurership had been renamed, although his particular role in the area of finance is now titular only. The premiership is of course recognised as an official, salaried post though oddly this did not happen until the 1900s. Ultimately it inherited the place in the scheme of things which had been occupied by the Lord High Treasurer, Secretary of State or, until the seventeenth century, the Lord Chancellor; the latter office, dating back to the Middle Ages, was initially primarily legal in its functions but came to acquire a political dimension, the holder being a source of advice to the monarch on important matters. The Lord Chancellorship survives as a law-making agency and as a cabinet post. In the seventeenth and eighteenth centuries the Cabinet replaced the monarch's Privy Council as the source of executive power, tending to sit without the King or Queen being present, though the Council continues to meet occasionally from tradition. This development was made possible by the early Hanoverian monarchs preferring to leave government to ministers and MPs rather than intervene directly in British affairs. The longer royal powers went without being used the more they decayed; because the more accustomed parliamentary politicians were to operating without the monarch's close supervision the more unacceptable such supervision became. As the Crown withdrew into the background, relatively speaking, the centre of political affairs and focus of interest in them shifted to the various factions in parliament. Elections, in which people were perceived as standing in the Whig or Tory interest even if they did not have a formally constituted party organisation behind them, were important in determining the political colour of a ministry or at least the balance of power within it.

Well before the time of Walpole it had become obligatory for the chief (by name or otherwise) minister to sit in one or other of the two Houses of Parliament even if he might be a royal appointee. Ultimately, it could be said that political power rested in the Upper House, where of course the higher aristocracy sat (many holding a Commons seat until they succeeded to their inheritance) and which had been abolished during the Commonwealth but restored in 1660, until the Parliament Act of 1911 because it could throw out legislation which the Commons had passed should the measure not appeal to it. In the end serious problems could be avoided by persuading the monarch to create more peers from the governing party, where there was a clash. Before Reform became an issue in the nineteenth century, however, the interests of

Lords and Commons were the same, essentially involving the preservation of the nation's prosperity (and their own) and the upholding of the existing social structure. The Commons grew in importance with the rise first of the gentry and then of the ordinary citizen (who was initially that even if they later became, through success in business, part of a new ruling elite or system of elites). And in time it became practically impossible for a Prime Minister to be a peer due to the greater responsibilities of government, which meant that the amount of important legislation being considered, on a relatively quickfire basis, by the Commons as initial law-making body increased. They would have to renounce their title, as Lord Home did in 1963.

By a conjunction of different factors − personalities, religion, accident, politics and economic prosperity (which reduced discontent) − Britain made a peaceful transition from an absolute (though most of the time it had not really been that) monarchy to a parliamentary oligarchy, in a way which has always fascinated this writer. While on the continent the power of the monarchy increased, across the channel it declined. The Jacobites in 1745, who were essentially seeking to restore the Stuart family to the throne although given past animosity between the two "nations" and the feeling north of the border that Scotland had not done well out of the Act of Union their rising was inevitably to some extent an Anglo-Scottish conflict, put forward their own programme to address the social injustice prevalent to a greater or lesser degree in Georgian England as part of their propaganda efforts; but this was the last time things could be seen in terms of dynastic rivalry. Social revolutionaries, whether foreign or home-grown, viewed the institution of monarchy as a manifestation of unjust privilege and a parasitic drain on financial resources (and were more likely to do so as its actual political power, and thus practical *raison d'etre*, decreased). But they never identified the particular "ruling" family with the regime they were seeking to bring down, the way they might have done in the past. For some time after the late seventeenth century the average person probably continued to think that the monarch possessed more or less the same degree of power as they had in previous eras; however the erosion of that power seems of a piece with the end of prophecies that they would lose their throne or be replaced by a supposedly dead predecessor who in fact survived, as if their character and policies would make a difference (or there would be no point in the prophecy), and of the belief that they had some kind of supernatural power to cure disease. A political sea change, the realisation that to uphold a near-absolute monarchy was no longer a good thing, combined with the intellectual transformation consequent on the scientific revolution of the early modern period, though it might take some time for the latter to filter down through the whole of society, superstition (though not tending to involve kings and queens) persisting in backward rural areas even into the twentieth century. Although in a Europe-wide context the process was not even − continental monarchies retained a considerable measure of real power into the nineteenth and early twentieth century, and people were being burnt at the stake in Peter the Great's Russia long after the practise had ceased in Britain – in the British case at least the conjunction of one fundamental shift with another, and the point at which this happened, means a case can be made out for there being no real "early modern period", a transition phase between the mediaeval and the modern. One gave way more directly than is supposed to the other, the date at which this occurred, if one can identify a date at all, being 1688-9. Certainly, given the changes which took place then and subsequently the Stuarts, had they been victorious in 1745, would have been very unwise to attempt to exercise the kind of power they had enjoyed before the Glorious Revolution.

In order to preserve what remaining influence it had, it became even more important for the Crown to manage parliament (something George III was not good at). Because its power resided increasingly in the ability to appoint or dismiss ministries and their heads, as opposed to other prerogatives which had tended to lapse, the emphasis, for those who were engaged in politics at a high level yet excluded from actual office, shifted to gaining the favour of the heir to the throne, whose circle became an alternative power base. But this could mean a long wait, apart from relatively brief periods when the monarch was incapacitated by illness (as in George III's first madness). In time, even the Crown's residual power ossified, though today it is regarded as still important because in the British psyche it fulfils a certain vital need. Like all peoples at some point we feel the attraction of ritual and ceremony, and in a country which tends to have a low opinion of its political leaders there is a reluctance to dignify the latter by making them the object of it. In the first instance, it was kept on because it acted as a focus for national identity, rooted in tradition, and because republicanism seemed a foreign, alien, un-British sort of quantity. But as far as the political action, and interest in it as that which is truly significant, is concerned the emphasis shifts from 1689 onwards to the aristocratic politicians who dominated the two houses of parliament, made up the government and formulated policy; the peers, plus the higher gentry (the latter being the group who had been instrumental in the parliamentary opposition to Charles I which had triggered the civil war). The revolutionary idealism of the war and Commonwealth period, which, filtering down to the lower classes as disruption to the usual order of things let the genie out of the bottle, had at one point resulted in politicised soldiers and working-class people had petered out by the Restoration, defeated by failure to agree on the form the future polity would take and to create revolutionary institutions which would last. Because of this and because of the decline in the monarchy's power the "court and country" division – "court" meaning the Crown, its minsters and clients, and "country" the (narrow) electorate whose interests the MPs they returned to Westminster had to take into account – which had led to the war became subsumed within one between the aristocracy and wealthier gentry and the rest of the population, leaving aside the subtler class distinctions which exist in most sociopolitical structures and complicate the picture. Actual social antagonism, between rulers and the urban/rural working class plus those middle class people who were excluded from the franchise and thus from any share in power, seems to have been muted throughout the first half of the eighteenth century. This was because economic conditions during the period were such as to mitigate the hardship which is a factor in producing unrest, even if it was the privileged who benefited most. The "ordinary people" had less of a quarrel with the aristocracy or with the Crown, which stood as the symbol of the system, and therefore accepted the latter, as they always had where its basic features were concerned (severe taxation and unjust laws might be a different matter, depending on who they affected most). This contributed to the eighteenth century being generally a time of remarkable political stability, in that the essential sociopolitical structure was preserved or changed peacefully regardless of the fluctuating fortunes of governments and of individual politicians.

All the same their greed, encouraged by the nation's rising prosperity (something which stemmed besides other factors from financial reforms, designed to assist the funding of William III's wars against France, in the 1690s), made the aristocracy by and large a coarse, corrupt and unlovely lot, concerned mainly with defending their wealth and privileged status. They lacked the moral nobility, stemming from sincere political and religious convictions, of their forebears in the Civil War period. But the religious revival of the later eighteenth and early nineteenth centuries, though it might not have pleased atheists, undoubtedly lifted the tone of political life (and of society as a whole) to some extent. And continuing socioeconomic change meant that in time they were joined in power by a certain number of "commoners", since social demarcation lines have never been entirely rigid.

Nonetheless, what happened in 1688-9 was not the creation of a democracy, despite the extent to which Whigs/Liberals lauded it at the time and subsequently, but a shift of power from one interest group (the monarch) to another (the aristocracy and gentry). It was not an extension of political liberty to the whole nation. There has been enough hype over the business for the whole thing to be downplayed, even dismissed as a nonsense, by some – the not so "Glorious" Revolution – perhaps explaining why its 300th anniversary in 1989 was a muted affair. For Catholics, who see it as having been an attack on them which was unwarranted because the threat posed by James II had been exaggerated, the lack of true democracy in the matter helps to justify rubbishing it. However, the "hype" is not entirely that. The "Glorious Revolution" can be celebrated because it was bloodless and because it was a rebellion, in effect, against a bad (though not in the sense that he was evilly disposed) king, and therefore for the overall good. Even those, in 1688, who thought James II was being over-demonised may have decided his "deposition" was for the best. And the move away from a (potentially) absolute monarchy, whose actions might damage ordinary people as well as the "nobs", obviously counts as political progress.

But it was not democracy. And it was a frequent and justified complaint from John Wilkes onwards that the franchise was too restricted. Partly it was the influence of the Enlightenment which was at work, but there was another operating too. The country was able to go full steam ahead (in a manner of speaking) with the Industrial Revolution now that dynastic conflicts were out of the way. To their anger the new middle class of entrepreneurs and skilled artisans which grew up as it gathered pace, increasing both in numbers and in prosperity, were largely denied votes and, almost by the same token, the right to stand for parliament. It was a way of preserving the supremacy of the existing order, whose abhorrence of change seemed justified by the excesses of the French Revolution, the latter setting back the cause of reform considerably. Like Bismarck, Pitt the Younger saw progress and prosperity in terms of administrative rather than political reform. But in the long run the issue wouldn't go away and eventually the social unrest discontent was causing led, through fear of something even worse than the nation's rulers having to share power a little, to the First Reform Act of 1832. The politicians never conceded more ground than was necessary at any one time to avoid bloody revolution. By their harsh new Poor Law and the transportation of the Tolpuddle Martyrs for wanting to form a trade union Earl Grey's ministry showed that they were not social liberals. But roughly speaking governments kept pace with gradual socioeconomic developments, widening the franchise periodically, though they never moved fast enough for the likes of the Chartists, whose mass agitation in 1848, inspired by events in Europe, brought the country closer to revolution than it had been since the civil war. The Conservative party was to generally oppose extension of the franchise but pragmatically adjust to it whenever it was enacted by the Whigs/Liberals as in 1832 and 1884, attempting to attract the new voters' support. "Tory Democracy" as espoused by, among others, Richard Cross, key minister in the governments of Disraeli and Salisbury, was something of a sham in that in practice it was more concerned with alleviating the physical condition of the masses than with granting them a say in politics. It performed much the same role as Bismarck's social welfare system in Germany. But the process of democratisation was to continue, with further reform bills in 1867 and 1884 giving the vote to the lower-middle class and working class and women finally being enfranchised in 1918.

Once the need for a widening of the franchise had been acknowledged, and the change been carried out, the priority for the leaders of the various political factions was to adapt to the new situation, managing the altered status quo and concentrating on maintaining order and prosperity (through reform of existing institutions, whether the aim was greater democracy or administrative efficiency) within the framework created by it. The factions had each to try to win over the new electorate. They were not quite parties in the modern sense, but were gradually evolving into them. Of course there had always been distinct interest groups in parliament, as with any organisation, but the beginnings of the party system can be traced back to the emergence of the Whigs and Tories in the later seventeenth century. These were relatively loose groupings whose membership could be interchangeable, and which lacked a formal administrative structure – they were tendencies rather than organisations – but they were nonetheless vitally important. Through the exercise of influence, especially in an age before the introduction of the secret ballot and when social deference was still strong, they could win general elections, affecting the composition of parliament and thus, if not at first the character of a ministry (though it might be a Whig-Tory coalition), determine to a certain extent what that government or the monarch was able to get away with. They came together, as parties do whether in embryonic or more crystallised form, over issues, the most important of which was at that time the succession to the throne. Opposition, for nationalistic or religious reasons, to Roman Catholicism was not always taken beyond a certain point. The Whigs, who got their way in 1688, would have been prepared to overthrow the rightful monarch if they seemed to be acting autocratically and to be taking the country down a path not congenial to the majority of the political nation. The Tories were not at that stage the party of the Church of England and thought deposition a dangerously radical, indeed heretical step, despite being uneasy about James II; the preservation of what they saw as the principle of legitimacy was more important than the precise way in which one worshipped Christ. Thus many of them were Jacobites, even if they did not go so far as to support the risings of 1715 and 1745. They *became* the party of the Church because, since they had failed to uphold the legitimacy principle but required a platform and a *raison d'etre*, logic demanded it of them.

The Tories eventually became the Conservative Party and the Whigs, in 1859, the Liberal Party. The Conservatives, on the whole, still preferred to maintain existing institutions in all their sanctity, while the Liberals were more prepared to make changes to them, and in particular end the exclusive rights enjoyed by the Anglican Church in religious matters; although, while there has historically tended to be, in two-party "democratic" political systems, a conservative and a progressive (whether Liberal or socialist) party the division between tradition on one side and change on the other has not always been clear-cut. On the Tory side, the man most responsible for adapting the party to the new age and bringing about its transformation to the Conservatives, in which process the Tamworth Manifesto of 1834 was a crucial milestone, was Sir Robert Peel, one of the three towering figures of nineteenth-century British political history. Peel was wise and humane enough to know when it was necessary to adjust to new circumstances and not try to ignore them. He was attacked by Disraeli for inconstancy, and the charge was justified, but where he changed his mind, over Catholic Emancipation and the repeal of the Corn Laws, it was in the right way; that is, he *should* have changed his mind. There were some things which could no longer be morally excused and/or which imposed unfair restrictions on the ability of ordinary people to cope with adverse economic circumstances.

The political situation, initially because the system was still young, was far from entirely stable. Parties could split, as Peel split the Conservative Party over the Corn Laws within a relatively short time of its foundation. Other major upheavals occurred in 1886, when the Liberals became bitterly divided over Gladstone's Irish Home Rule policy and the Liberal Unionists, as they called themselves, broke away to drift gradually towards the Tories (as the Conservatives have continued colloquially to be known), and during the years 1915-1922 when the formation of a coalition between the Liberals and Conservatives, the former having come under fire for their indifferent wartime performance, split both parties between those who were in favour of the arrangement and those who were not. However, although a party might lose power as a result of this fragmentation, it regained it eventually (the defection of the Liberal Unionists did not prevent their parent body from holding office again in 1892-5 and, altogether more successfully, 1906-15) and the wounds either healed or it was replaced in the scheme of things by a new party inheriting its political niche, as when Labour largely pushed out the Liberals in the early-mid twentieth century. The leader of the largest party, or the dominant one in a grouping of parties, became Prime Minister if victorious at a general election.

Fragmentation characterised most of the period from 1846 to 1859, with politics a matter of shifting alliances between Whigs, Tories and Peelites (those Conservatives still loyal to Peel). But in time, the two-party system reasserted itself, and this trend coincided with the continuing rise to prominence of two men who more than anyone else were to make the system work and so impart true stability to it: Benjamin Disraeli, (Conservative) Prime Minister May-December 1868 and 1874-80, and William Gladstone, (Liberal) Prime Minister 1868-74, 1880-85, 1886 (briefly) and 1892-4.

Both had been active, and well-known, within their respective parties for some time prior to their attaining the highest office. Gladstone began his political career as a Tory but later, in one of a number of cataclysmic changes in outlook and convictions which took place in the mind of this intensely introspective and morally self-doubting individual during the course of his lifetime, switched to Liberalism, though in terms of the pace of events the process was in fact a fairly gradual one. Nothing if not a man of God, yet desiring a career in politics more than one in the church – a puzzling contradiction, albeit reflective of what was after all a strange and complex personality – he reconciled these conflicting pulls by seeing political activity, and the actions of one politician in particular (himself), as potentially an expression of the divine will. Giving people the vote, to be exercised freely without any intimidatory pressure to cast it one way or another – hence Gladstone's introduction of the secret ballot in 1872, despite his not having much personal enthusiasm for the measure – was a means of allowing them to make the choices by which they would do, or not do, what was right by God, as part of the working out of His plans. Our conduct while on earth was a test of our moral worthiness. Disraeli's motives were more prosaic; capturing the electorate for the Conservative Party was a way of ensuring its, and his, political success. But, however much the two men may have been at cross purposes, the removal by his death of the dead hand (in that he was against any extension of the franchise) of Lord Palmerston, Prime Minister 1855-8 and 1859-65, gave them their chance by paving the way for the Second Reform Act of 1867.

The rivalry between Gladstone and Disraeli dominated British politics in the mid- to late nineteenth century period. Gladstone was the reformer, Disraeli the upholder of traditional institutions and practices though nonetheless prepared to countenance social reforms where it suited his political purposes. Which of the two was more successful? It's been said that Gladstone's mistakes endured, Disraeli's didn't. One might acidly observe, however, that Disraeli didn't do enough for there to be as much scope for making mistakes. Gladstone was responsible for a host of reforming measures such as the 1870 Education Act and the secret ballot, the latter of course still on the statute book today and a fundamental component of the democratic system. Disraeli produced rather less of this kind of legislation, preferring to keep things as they were unless it was politically expedient to do otherwise, and not seeing change as a moral obligation. And although Gladstone's myopic obsession with Ireland inflicted lasting damage on the Liberal party – though it was not the reason for that party's eventual eclipse – Disraeli's indolence resulted in a poor performance by and ultimate defeat for the Conservatives in the 1880 election. While although Disraeli in 1867 had shrewdly seen that reform, over which he outbid Gladstone by offering the more attractive package in terms of votes awarded, thus potentially harnessing the enfranchised to the Tory cause, his gamble didn't really pay off in the long run, in terms of electoral success. Having reached the Dizzy heights, he didn't stay there for long, not as Prime Minister. He was premier for a few months in 1868, replacing Lord Derby as Conservative leader, then lost an election in what seems a startling display of ingratitude by the voters, comparable to the Liberals' near rejection by them in 1910 (both cases illustrate that (a) political issues are complex and (b) people do not always behave, politically as in other walks of life, in the ways one might predict). He was then out of power until 1874. He moved to the House of Lords as the Earl of Beaconsfield in 1876, only two years into his second administration, though this did not initially affect his grasp of matters. In 1880 as we know the Tories lost power again, partly because Disraeli was lazy and failed to run an election campaign that was either energetic or convincing. But by now he was an old man and past his best. In the last year of his life he was unable to restrain the troublesome Fourth Party, led by Lord Randolph Churchill, looking upon them with a sort of amused indulgence. After he died in 1881 Gladstone enjoyed a further fourteen years of political prominence, albeit suffering latterly from a waning of his intellectual powers. Though both he and Disraeli had been politically important, and very much in the public eye, for twenty years or so before either became Prime Minister, Gladstone's career lasted far longer. The two most certainly did not alternate as Prime Minister throughout the whole period, as popular imagination probably has it. Their rivalry began, and was noticed, at a relatively early stage.

Which of them was more morally commendable? One is inclined to think Gladstone, on account of his constant struggling with his conscience over religion – was he himself living up to the Almighty's expectations? – and over what was or was not the right course to take on important political issues (it amounted in his view to the same thing). Contrary to what one reviewer states on the back cover of the first volume, Richard Shannon's biography of the man is not all that sympathetic towards its subject. Shannon appears to argue at one point that his convincing himself he had a Christian mission in politics, as an alternative to entering the priesthood, was a way of justifying what was partly a pursuit of power. Perhaps, in a complicated psyche, this was to some degree the case. No-one however deeply spiritual is entirely without ambition. But it could not have been the whole story. Gladstone had too much *stature*, and deliberated too much upon the ethicality of a policy, to have been concerned solely with his own advancement. He was a genuinely religious person who took his Christianity, and the moral precepts which were intended to govern behaviour in the Victorian age, seriously, always trying to put them into practice, and was thus an embarrassment and an irritant to his often hypocritical contemporaries. (*In extremis,* you have to remember that this is the man who as a young student at Oxford strived hard to restrain himself from "self-abuse"). Anti-Semitism, which he is considered by many to be guilty of, apart he genuinely agonised about whether or not to attend Disraeli's funeral (though in the end he didn't), because he genuinely believed that the man's frivolity and lack of moral commitment to a cause had lowered the tone of politics when it ought to be a serious, and Godly, business. Nonetheless he was magnanimous enough to concede in political conversation that Disraeli was in his own way a genius, and I think sincere in his insistence that he did not deliberately intend to set himself up as a rival to the man. As Shannon also relates, when it was put to him on one occasion in his later life that he had spent far too much time obsessed with the question of Irish Home Rule and damaged the Liberal Party in the process, he at least looked as if he thought it might be a fair comment. The lack of conscience, and tendency towards backbiting and sordid chicanery, in mainstream politics increasingly disgusted Gladstone and he was somewhat disillusioned by the time of his eventual retirement. Where he disagreed with the Establishment there was a limit to how far he could oppose its policies and change its ingrained ways of thinking. He could resist imperialism in a negative sense, by inaction (refusing to send troops to reinforce Gordon at Khartoum, or at least procrastinating over the matter) but he was unable to prevent Egypt from becoming a British protectorate, if not colony, during his second administration.

Disraeli was by contrast an ardent imperialist (partly, it was another way of ingratiating himself with the Establishment of which we have been speaking) and also, undoubtedly, bothered about moral dilemmas in politics somewhat less, even if it is unfair to regard him as no more than an unprincipled self-seeker (such people never have that stature which defines the truly great, as it is safe to say both Disraeli and Gladstone were). On the other hand, Gladstone's unbending determination to do what he considered to be right whatever the cost could lead him to be cavalier and abrupt, as well as austere and humourless, in his dealings with people. There operated such a fixation on his part on being Christian that, paradoxically, he ended up behaving in what could be regarded as an *unchristian* fashion. His very agonising over issues of conscience exhausted his moral resources at times; he blew a fuse, avoiding unbearable stress by self-deception and by getting his way through a high-handed authoritarianism.

To balance this, Disraeli could be sincerely generous towards those who had helped further his career, and thus in this respect might be regarded as virtuous, but as an emotional corollary was not inclined to forgive wrongs easily − if his likes were strong, so were his dislikes − and also tended to discard people in a rather mercenary fashion once he had no further use for them. He *was* a little too foppish and theatrical at times; his calling Gladstone "a sophisticated rhetorician imbued with the exuberance of his own verbosity" is one of the most outstanding examples of hypocrisy in political rhetoric ever known!

Altogether though, Gladstone does come over as generally more moral than his rival. Disraeli would have been the more entertaining table companion; Gladstone a better prospect if you wanted to debate theology. At least Gladstone's ultimate motivation *was* moral, and perhaps his faults were failures of character rather than of virtue. That someone can be interesting, and entertaining, and colourful, and outgoing does not necessarily mean they are also morally admirable. The feeling is inescapable that Gladstone did more for ordinary people, while Disraeli, though ready to manipulate them for political gain (as he did others where possible − in the case of royalty, he advised that flattery should be laid on "like a trowel"), rather looked down on them. He showed little interest in the details of the social legislation, such as the Artisans' Dwelling Act, passed by his 1874-80 ministry, seeing it essentially as a chore which was unfortunately necessary if the Party was to achieve the support of the lower classes and thus be helped to stay in power (though he warmed to it once it seemed, misleadingly as the 1880 election showed, to be producing such results). He let the minister charged with implementing it, the able Richard Cross, get on with the job without offering much in the way of encouragement and assistance; and treated Cross generally very badly over this and other matters. Once when his Home Secretary had displeased him he declared, "This comes of giving office to a middle-class man". One ought to feel sympathy towards Disraeli on account of anti-Semitism, which he did experience personally or institutionally. But perhaps those who have suffered from such things ought to feel more compassion regarding the deprivations, however caused, of others.

Disraeli was, let's be frank about it, a frightful snob and a social climber. His reasons for being the latter are perhaps understandable. He came from an Italian immigrant family and ethnically was of a race frequently the target of prejudice and exclusion. What people in those circumstances — outsiders — often do if they want to get on in their adopted country is to identify themselves with its ruling establishment. This meant joining the Tory Party and seeking the friendship and patronage of the aristocracy which made up a large portion of its membership. Accordingly, when Peel appeared in the view of that class to have damaged its interests by the repeal of the Corn Laws, he had to be attacked. It was a crucial stage in Disraeli's self-advancement, winning him both prominence and the approval of his peers. He had found the solution to the dilemma which confronts many members of distrusted and marginalised groups — women, ethnic minorities — whereby you need to be pushy to get on but that kind of behaviour runs the risk of alienating people; give them ("them" meaning at least an influential governing minority) what they want. This and Disraeli's theatricality made it look as if he did not really believe in anything except furthering his own prospects; everything else was affected. As argued above this is unlikely to be true, even if his situation and background are nonetheless crucial factors. His devotion to Conservatism as a philosophy was sincere. It was not so much that he lacked convictions (i.e. that the Conservative Party was the one best suited to govern the country), but rather that he was ruthless (as, in a less skilful way, was Gladstone) in putting them into practice, even though the vagaries or sheer ungratefulness of the electorate might frustrate his intentions.

Someone with his personality would have been a showman anyway (it is curious that he disliked having his photograph taken, so that he is not so well represented in this medium as other politicians of the period). He was also more practical than Gladstone in that he appreciated there was a limit to how far you could harness the rank and file of a party to a cause against its wishes or those of a significant section of it. (Though that does not mean the cause should be abandoned; whereas what would have been his low opinion of Gladstone's Irish policy in the 1880s and 90s can in my view be justified, on account of his (Gladstone's) ignoring, in typical fashion, the feelings of Ulster I regard Disraeli's vehement opposition to repeal of the Corn Laws as entirely wrong). And if, although he showed appreciation to individuals who had helped advance his prospects, he believed that fine moral feelings did not generally motivate politicians (however regrettable it might be, and especially to such as Gladstone, if that was the case), and that therefore it would be wiser to concentrate on attaining, and retaining, power so that what one considered to be the right policies could be implemented this could be seen as a philosophy, a conviction, even if some did not view it as admirable. Too much fretting over ethical issues was tiresome and counterproductive, and it was not only Disraeli who thought so. Many would suggest that most politicians have thought so, and in all periods of history! Disraeli was ruthlessly practical in some ways and romantic and flamboyant in others. The latter tendency could up to a point be symbiotic with the former by giving Disraeli an appeal which helped win elections, as he no doubt appreciated. Many people nonetheless saw him as lazy and airy-fairy, concerned with words more than deeds (it was part of his political philosophy, and another point of antagonism to Gladstone, that unnecessary administrative and legislative activity should be avoided, apart from anything being potentially harmful). So it did not always work. But nor did Gladstone's exasperating high-mindedness. Even if one is to be regarded as more *ethical* than the other, I always find myself inevitably led to the conclusion that in terms of their handling of political relationships, which was obviously crucial to the fortunes of parties and of affairs in general, Gladstone and Disraeli are in every respect quits; it seems to reinforce the symmetry between the two which was so essential in making the political system of the time work.

Out of Disraeli and Peel the latter was the more humane personality in terms of attitudes towards the general population. But the element of primarily political calculation in Disraeli's actions raises the question of how much actual animosity there was in his feelings towards him. He, Disraeli, admired Cobden, who as the principal moving force behind the Anti-Corn Law League, which by repealing the Corn Laws boosted the industrial sector as against the agricultural and thus attacked the interests of the landed aristocracy, was surely just as much his enemy politically if not more so. To a certain extent Disraeli regarded politics as a game which should be enjoyed, and in which undue reverence for one's opponents took away much of the fun.

Perhaps who was the more successful or ethical out of Gladstone and Disraeli depends on one's view of politics; whether it is a moral battleground or rather a ruthless business where, out of pragmatism, attaining and keeping power has to be considered as an end in itself – for the good of the system as much as anything else, for moral crusades can be dangerous – rather than a means to one. But their rivalry created, and maintained, a healthy interest in politics on the part of the public which endured for approximately one hundred years until a decline in both the moral and the intellectual calibre of our leaders resulted in a popular apathy which has become extremely harmful and worrying. People followed Gladstone for moral reasons and because they saw him as their defender; or they were amused by Disraeli's mischievous put-downs of his stern and unbending opponent, who was earnest to a point that could be tiresome and, though this is not really a fair way of putting it, pompous ("Why is Gladstone like a telescope? Because Disraeli draws him out, looks through him and shuts him up", ran the popular joke). It probably did more than anything else to establish the two-party system on a sure footing, despite Gladstone outlasting Disraeli in politics for more than a decade. By this criteria Disraeli was not, as has been alleged, a failure whereas Gladstone was a success; it takes two to tango. The phenomenon of which we are speaking was evident long before Disraeli climbed to the top of the "greasy pole" and he and Gladstone began to succeed each other as Prime Minister, which they did for a surprisingly short period of their joint careers. After Disraeli's death Gladstone was left in some ways high and dry, the sole Triton among the minnows (to paraphrase a remark later made about Lloyd George). It was like a double act which had collapsed in the absence of one of the partners. Certainly, although his 1880-85 ministry was an important one, passing among other measures the Third Reform Act, there are good reasons for concluding that he could have done without the subsequent and final nine years of his political life, whose chief hallmark is the splitting of his party over Home Rule. If parties are the mainstay of the democratic parliamentary system then parties, to be effective in this role, must be united. But as noted the Liberals survived, and this was to a great extent down to Gladstone's continuing prestige as the Grand Old Man − by no means entirely destroyed by the fall of Khartoum, which caused him to be seen for a time as the Murderer Of Gordon instead − the only thing, at times, which held together the disparate elements (moderates, old-style Whigs, Radicals and Nonconformists) that made up the party.

2

After Gladstone's retirement public interest in the political system was maintained by the emergence, or continuing prominence, of politicians who also excited strong feelings for or against them, besides being markedly populist in their approach to issues; namely, Joseph Chamberlain and David Lloyd George. Both − and especially Chamberlain, a figure whom I must confess I have never fully understood − come across as a strange mixture of self-seeker and conviction politician. Both, in different ways, could use sharp practice. They were enemies during the period when their careers coincided, but perhaps, as with Disraeli and Gladstone, achieved more between them than either could have done on his own.

Chamberlain was the founder of a political dynasty about which there ought by now, one feels, to have been a TV drama with Joseph, the patriarch, portrayed as a sort of Blake Carrington or J R Ewing. It would be a tragedy, as much as anything else; there was Austen, a far more decent man than his father, who "always played the game and always lost it", and Neville whose misfortune it was to become so closely identified with a foreign policy ultimately seen as misguided, indeed nearly disastrous from the point of view of the nation's survival. Joseph and Austen are to my mind iconic figures, not least because of the way they dressed (the son clearly seeking to emulate the father); though this is unflattering, and not entirely deserved especially in Austen's case, it is hard to believe they were not in their attire a conscious or unconscious inspiration for Bertie Wooster and/or the *Batman* villain the

165

Penguin, with his monocle and sartorial flamboyance. They seem in more than one respect to symbolise the way in which a certain age has been perceived, both by itself and subsequent eras, the types that flourished during it; though Austen was not really a buffoon, and Joseph − not a nice man, in another parallel with Lloyd George who could be equally cutting about his political opponents − was once described as having "the manners of a cad". As well as "the tongue of a bargee"; his social origins were relatively humble compared to those of most other politicians of his generation, and it showed when the verbal bluntness certain "classes" exhibit, not offensive in itself, was combined with an abrasive personality. He was not quite a true gentleman. It is one reason why Chamberlain − along with Norman Tebbitt, who he resembles in these respects − never became Prime Minister and in fact probably could not have done. The monocle, orchid in buttonhole etc were an attempt to appear "refined"; Chamberlain being, like Disraeli, a social climber. His espousal of radical policies was to some extent a lower middle-class parvenu's way of getting back at an Establishment which he felt to be exclusive. And which, in the form of the Conservative Party, never really accepted him. The mistrust was partly because of his background, partly because it suspected correctly that he remained a radical at heart, using the Tories for his own ends, and partly because he seemed a dangerous, disruptive personality. On the first and third counts (as well as on others) there is a parallel with Enoch Powell.

Chamberlain cut a dapper, handsome and until his stroke astonishingly well-preserved figure. But he was not a nice man. It has not been proved that he hired "henchmen" to harass his enemies and that it was they who were responsible for Lloyd George's near-lynching at Birmingham where he was speaking against the Boer War. But it somehow seems consistent with his character. His behaviour during his friend and political ally Sir Charles Dilke's divorce case was on several occasions odd, and difficult to explain unless he was making sure the affair resulted in the destruction of someone who was also a potential political rival. In an earlier incarnation he had been a Sunday School teacher. He abandoned faith in God after losing two wives in succession to fatal illnesses. That was perhaps understandable, but his subsequent behaviour is an example of how in certain personalities the jettisoning of religion with its stress on virtue and charity, as well as its downside, can have a morally corrupting effect.

Chamberlain had a political machine behind him and with the eyeglass and orchid was an instantly recognisable figure, even before the advent of television. As a national politician he started out from a substantial power base in Birmingham, his adopted city, where as Lord Mayor he was responsible for slum clearances and improvements in public health which established his lasting reputation as a social reformer, on a national as well as a local scale. He continued to press for radical measures in this field and so became regarded as a tribune of the people. However he had always been equally concerned with preserving the integrity of the British Empire, because the creation of an imperial Free Trade area, with tariffs imposed on goods coming into it from outside, could help to pay for the social reforms he wanted. It was for this reason that he broke with the Liberal Party in 1886 over Irish Home Rule, fearing that if Ireland were granted independence the rest of the Empire would follow and his grand scheme be frustrated, and eventually joined the Conservative among whom, as Colonial Secretary and successful prosecutor of the Boer War, he established his credentials as a defender and prophet of imperialism. This did not affect his popularity with the nation as a whole because, then as now, and as the Conservative victory in the Khaki Election of 1900 demonstrates, the masses were as approving of national success in war (in the absence of an obvious reason why the war might do more harm than good, such as could be discerned with Iraq in 2003) as they were measures designed to make their lives happier and more prosperous. They did not have a coherent, intellectual imperialist philosophy, but applauded the preservation, or enlargement, of Empire and the defeat of those who would threaten it because it was a form of patriotism. On his political colleagues, most of whom never entirely trusted him, the effect of Chamberlain's career was rather different and by no means appreciated. The way his brilliant mind worked led him to split himself after a fashion between two parties; to preserve the Empire, so that it could be transformed into his grand Free Trade area, meant allying with the Tories, who were altogether more imperialist than the Liberals, yet the social reforms protectionism would under his scheme have funded were more likely to be countenanced by the latter. And his brilliance was wayward, being combined with a tendency, when he judged the moment was right, to push for what he wanted regardless of the consequences. His resignation from the government in 1903 to campaign for Tariff Reform split the Conservatives between supporters and opponents of the policy and led to their massive defeat in the 1906 election, as people feared it might adopt an economic policy which amounted, or was thought to amount, to a tax on food. Since he was unlikely to rejoin the Liberals, Chamberlain's action had probably finished his career before a stroke condemned him to be largely an impotent observer of the political scene.

He is one of three figures in particular during the past two hundred years to have had a significant impact on the course of British politics without ever becoming Prime Minister or Leader of the Opposition (four, if we extend the parameters a little way back in time to include Charles James Fox), by the following they commanded among the public, sections of the political establishment, or both. Of the other two, the one who comes to mind first and foremost is of course Powell; then there is Tony Benn. There are similarities between the careers of Chamberlain and Powell, besides those already mentioned plus having a West Midlands power base; for one thing, Powell had cooked his political goose by advising his supporters in marginal seats in the Birmingham/Wolverhampton region to vote Labour in 1974, in protest against Heath's taking Britain into the Common Market, before he sidelined himself by decamping to Northern Ireland, just as Chamberlain had thrown away *his* chances prior to the 1906 stroke though he continued to be in the public eye and his stature meant that he was not resented by the nation at large for his behaviour in 1903 and subsequent support for a "food tax". There are also sharp differences; Powell comes over as honourable, if not always sound, in his motives whereas Chamberlain is too scheming, and too vituperative, to give that impression, and although the former, in his usual superb English, wrote a book about the latter it is suspected that he ended up not feeling very well disposed towards his subject. But all three of the men in question had a tendency to wreck parties, if only because, in Powell's case and I guess Benn's too, they felt conviction should come first. Their actions may not always have been good for the health of the British body politic. Arguably Chamberlain succeeded in damaging only the Tories. But whether the Labour government of 1974-9 was a major improvement on Heath's, in terms of managing the economy and avoiding industrial unrest, is highly debatable. And much of the country's problems at that time were the fault of Benn, once he emerged as the spokesman and rallying-point for Labour's left wing, for his insistence on sticking to that position, and undermining Labour leaders who were at least attempting to be moderate, made the party unelectable and condemned the country to eleven years − in fact more, since we are still suffering the consequences of the doctrine − of Thatcherism as the only alternative to what seemed factionalism and instability. I find it hard to feel much sympathy for him. One can have some for Powell − though there are elements for whom it is understandably not easy − and perhaps also Chamberlain despite the reprehensible aspects of his character. The two (Powell and Chamberlain) were both highly intelligent men who one in some ways regrets never gave the country the full benefit of their talents as Prime Minister.

It is also possible to have sympathy towards Lloyd George, despite his sometimes caustic tongue and his dubious private life. The Liberals, among whom he was a rising star, returned to power under Sir Henry Campbell-Bannerman, one of the unsung heroes of British political history, a dull but worthy character who succeeded in holding together a government consisting of diverse and often troublesome personalities, much as Attlee was to do in 1945-51. Asquith, who followed him, may not have been quite so successful at that task but the party was able to bring in vitally important social legislation − old age pensions, national insurance, labour exchanges − and again, it is surprising the nation did not reward it for its efforts by giving it greater majorities in the two elections of 1910 (it could not be blamed for the opposition of a reactionary House of Lords, who were hardly more likely to give the people what they wanted). However a combination of the First World War and the rise of Labour destroyed the Liberals as an instrument of government, except for when they became partners in a coalition. Criticism over the conduct of the war led to the formation of one in 1915, and the following year to the replacement of Asquith as Prime Minister, in which post he had remained, by Lloyd George. Not only did some Liberals see Lloyd George's accession as an act of disloyalty, but after the war the party was divided between his supporters, who wanted the coalition to continue, and those of Asquith, who didn't. It might eventually have recovered were it not that it had been seriously weakened at a time when Labour was emerging as a major electoral force. The latter would ultimately have proved the decisive factor in any case. When the coalition collapsed, the Conservatives having tired of it, it was followed by a short-lived Tory government and then a short-lived Labour one, before the Tories returned to power with a majority which lasted until 1929; but the Liberals never again held office in their own right.

Lloyd George was split between parties, but in a different way from Chamberlain. Historically he was caught between a Liberal Party which was still very much the principal opposition to the Conservatives and a Labour movement not, until the early and mid-1920s, powerful enough to form a government. It is not too difficult to guess what certain prominent figures in the history of British politics would be if they were active in it now, or we suppose their careers to have spanned a more recent period of history. One imagines Lloyd George starting out as a young left-wing Labour MP something on the lines of Ken Livingstone (or Gladstone as one of the more sanctimonious and annoying politically correct liberals). Had he been born marginally later than he was, Lloyd George would have been a socialist or switched to Labour when he was still young enough to make the change. Neither of these contingencies was realised.

At this point, it might be useful to stop and ask who should be considered the greatest British Prime Minister. Here one question begs, or ought to beg, another; great by what criteria? To cast one's vote for Attlee, as a group of left-wing London academics recently did, implies that firmness and dynamism in wartime, such as Churchill displayed, are not at least equally important as social reform, which would be quite wrong; it should be emphasised that Hitler was no bleeding heart social worker. (Generally, Tories in the past have been better at defending the nation's position in the world at large and protecting it or its dependencies from external aggression. Labour or the Liberals are more progressive on social affairs (roughly speaking, this is mirrored across the Atlantic by the performance of Republican and Democrat US administrations; compare Carter and Reagan for example). The problem is not that Tories are *necessarily* cruel and greedy, rather that for most of their history they have been too emotionally and psychologically wedded to the concept that people should pay for whatever service they receive; anything else potentially goes against the principle of thrift, encouraging idleness and moral laxity. Their intentions may still be basically good. Their detractors have often derided them as oafish because their approach is essentially reactionary therefore implying a lack of imagination and thus, by much the same token, stupidity. But having a *conviction* that established institutions and ways of life should be preserved is not the same thing as being stupid. It's just that in politics, at any rate, it is not seen as necessary or desirable to change too much. (Some Labour people are motivated by an unthinking, savage aggression against what seems to them elitist and oppressive and thus are impelled by emotion rather than intelligence, even if their grievances may sometimes be justified.) And you can be radical in a right-wing direction, as Margaret Thatcher was.)

It could be argued the honour we were talking about ought to go to Lloyd George as he was both a dynamic war leader and a successful social reformer (the old age pensions etc); Churchill did achieve things in the latter area during his Liberal phase, but on a smaller scale. True, the war was to run once Lloyd George achieved the premiership for as long as it had already. But we should remember that it was the first *modern* war, which the combatants were still learning how to fight, and at a time before tanks and aircraft were sufficiently advanced to tip the balance one way or another. And it might have gone on for even longer if Asquith had remained in power, since (like Attlee and unlike Churchill) he was a good committee chairman rather than an inspiring warlord.

However, to emphasise the difficulty of giving a verdict in questions such as this, the Kaiser was not Hitler, i.e. a genocidalist bent on world domination in so far as that aim was feasible, making Churchill's achievement more important even if it could not have been accomplished without Russian and American assistance, which intervention may have been inevitable, along with the resulting Nazi defeat, whether or not Britain had successfully resisted in 1940-41. And the social reforming and war leadership occupy successive rather than simultaneous phases of Lloyd George's career. Many of his greatest achievements took place when he was President of the Board of Trade or Chancellor of the Exchequer (it was when he was serving in the latter post that, stepping outside his normal function and in the capacity of a mediator, he ended a major rail strike). He was not so much a reasonably successful Prime Minister as an all-round statesman with abilities above the average (and who by rousing oratory established that rapport with the masses which is essential for the healthy popular engagement with politics we have talked about). During the war, before and after he became premier, Lloyd George had little time to spare for social policy. The war also, through the degree of control over affairs which the government had to assume, made him too powerful, especially with the coalition being extended into peacetime to carry out its "clearing-up" operation. And with power comes corruption; we all know about the sale of honours and the lasting damage it did to Lloyd George's reputation. Perhaps it was a case of someone from a relatively humble background finding it hard to resist the temptation to enrich himself, as well as to revel in acquired status, when the opportunity came along (there is a parallel with Harold Wilson). But it helped to bring about Lloyd George's downfall at the young, by the standard of political lifespans at that time, age of fifty-nine, the reputation it created for untrustworthiness being one of the factors which kept him from returning to power. In the post-war Coalition, although Lloyd George the man enjoyed enough prestige, having "won the war", to be in no way a figurehead he was in other respects shackled by dependence on the Tory Party who did not wish him to continue with his radical reforming agenda, especially when conservatives were alarmed by the forces of change which had been released by the war – Communist revolution in Russia and militant socialism, seen in the labour disputes in Clydeside and elsewhere, at home. Eventually they grew tired of his faults and deposed him. It was tragic, whatever the extent to which, from the point of view of Lloyd George's personal conduct and career, it was deserved.

Equally tragic is the story of Ramsay MacDonald – and, at this time, of the Labour Party. MacDonald deserves sympathy for the way he was treated over his illegitimacy and his pacifism (the former was used as a stick to beat him with for the latter). He overcame this adversity to emerge as Prime Minister in the first Labour government, but, lacking a proper majority, that government lasted less than a year (the one measure it did have time to bring in, Wheatley's Housing Act, was to its credit). When they did come to power with one, in 1929, Labour soon found events overtaken by the growing financial crisis, which led to their replacement after just two years by a National Government.

In the circumstances, and given its inbuilt Conservative majority, the latter was more concerned with retrenchment than with bold socially reforming measures. For agreeing to lead it MacDonald was denounced as a traitor, and became the object of lasting bitterness. The truth, as is so often the case, is to be found somewhere between extremes. He was neither wholly admirable in his conduct during these years, or as black as detractors such as Emmanuel Shinwell (who called him a "treacherous bastard" in an interview many years later) painted him. Yes, he had a streak of vanity, and it is hard to entirely refute the charge made against him that he had grown too fond of associating with the Establishment (on which count comparison is invited with Lloyd George and Wilson). It is also questionable whether there was any point in his action given that he soon became a figurehead in an administration which was clearly Conservative-dominated despite its name; he ended up in the same position as Lloyd George after the war yet without the same personal power and authority. But it is not correct to see him as a traitor even though, in addition to his being attracted by the company of the rich and powerful, he was disenchanted by now with Labour and its bitter factional disputes and talked of smashing it and replacing it with a new alignment of parties. The important thing to remember is that King George V had asked him to take on the job of National Prime Minister and that MacDonald treated it as a request from a friend. One of the most moving features of political affairs in these years is the warm relationship which had grown up between the monarch and this illegitimate son of a fisherwoman ("You have found me an ordinary man, haven't you?"). There was another consideration to be borne in mind. Labour had undertaken to seek power through the constitutional route rather than violent revolution. And by extension, as Britain was a constitutional *monarchy*, in which the King or Queen were theoretically in charge and could at least give advice, was it right to ignore George's wishes? To do so could be seen, in its implications, as a revolutionary, meaning seditious, step. Whether the King was wise to intervene in affairs in the way he effectively did is another matter, but MacDonald's response can be defended. It highlights the wider issue of what a non-Blairite Labour Party can and should try to do when in power, indeed the whole dilemma faced by the chief socialist party in Britain and probably elsewhere. A set of hard left-wing (more so than Attlee's government was) policies cannot be imposed on the country by force, but if it is put to the electorate it will be rejected and the party condemned to the wilderness, as the history of the 1980s shows. Yet if it does not pursue that Leftist agenda, its only course of action, unless circumstances are exceptional, is one that is liberal or social democratic rather than socialist − a softer, pale pink form of Conservatism. This partly explains why MacDonald and subsequent Labour leaders have not been as radical in office as the left-wingers would prefer.

Regarding the events of 1931 one might have replied to those Labour people who accused MacDonald of betraying the cause that if there had been a greater Labour presence in the National Government, instead of just him, Philip Snowden and J H Thomas, the party would have been better able to influence its policies only Bevan, etc., refused to have anything to do with it. However it may have been just as well (and was I suspect to MacDonald's relief) that they did. If, say, membership of the government had been divided more equally between Tories and Socialists and, as would probably have been the case, they had fallen out over how to tackle the recession it would have been paralysed.

3

Three things in particular characterise British politics in the 1920s and 30s. One is the absence from leadership for most of the time of the two towering figures on the political scene in the first half of the twentieth century, Churchill and Lloyd George, who one is inclined to think would have made a difference regarding the most serious problems the country had to face in this period, namely economic depression and, on the international scene, the rise of Fascist dictators with aggressive foreign policies. The second is the dominance in the thirties of the "National" Government, despite economic conditions gradually improving during the course of the decade. (Things couldn't have been too bad if technical achievements such as the great liners *Queen Mary* and *Queen Elizabeth*, and record-breaking steam locomotives like the *Mallard*, were possible; there also took place a massive expansion of the road network, with its associated infrastructure, together with, during the interwar period in general, an increase in numbers of motor vehicles of all kinds. Towns and cities grew considerably, as the sprawling masses of 1930s semi-detached housing making up much of their suburbs testify. Many familiar features of modern life made their appearance in these years, such as popular tourist guides, reflecting a burgeoning travel industry, and paperback books.)

The government's ascendancy was ensured by the self-exclusion of Labour plus the fact that the recession did continue, though less serious in its effects outside certain areas, until 1939. The third, and perhaps most significant, factor in political affairs was that between the wars (and especially in the 30s) Britain was governed by late-middle-aged and elderly men. MacDonald lingered on as Prime Minister, admittedly past his best and in fact semi-senile, until 1935 in which year he attained his sixty-ninth birthday. Stanley Baldwin (Prime Minister 1923-4, 1924-9, and 1935-7 as well as the leading figure in the National Government from its inception) was seventy when he finally retired. Neville Chamberlain became premier, succeeding Baldwin, at sixty-eight and was seventy-one on his resignation in 1940.

These were figures who, inevitably, were to some extent set in their ways and lacking in imagination and foresight. People who saw retrenchment and ruthless austerity measures as the correct way to solve the economic crisis (in the absence of the resources enjoyed by a dictatorship or the caste of mind found there). People who were wary of taking risks. People who saw dynamic personalities like Lloyd George (the past leader) and Churchill (the future leader) as perplexing and not entirely safe, even if of roughly a similar age group to themselves. Of course it hadn't been unknown in previous eras for Prime Ministers to hold office into their seventies or even eighties, and it wasn't to be entirely unknown afterwards (the tendency seems to have died out from the 1950s/60s). But it is hard to dismiss the thought that the presence on the scene of younger men, if they had not been killed in the First World War, would have made a difference. There might have been more flexible and inspired economic policies which achieved their objectives without causing so much deprivation and misery. Rearmament (which would have been a major stimulus to the economy and helped to solve the problems of unemployment and recession) might have started earlier. As it was, those younger men who did occupy positions of some significance or at least seemed to have been on the up, like Anthony Eden or Oswald Mosley, became disenchanted with their superiors' approach and resigned. To be fair to Mosley, had he not left the second Labour government in protest at the failure to take his economic proposals on board he would probably never have started the British Union of Fascists and we would not now be reviling him as a racist would-be dictator (obnoxiously arrogant and anti-Semitic, in one way or another, though he was).

But perhaps, to some extent, a "safe pair of hands" *was* the only way out of the depression/recession (it was certainly the policy followed, and recommended to the electorate, much later by David Cameron and George Osborne). Always taking into account the vagaries of the first-past-the-post system, that the National Government was returned at the 1935 general election (and that Cameron was returned in 2015) suggests many people shared such a view. In the field of foreign policy, it is simplistic to see events in the mid-late 1930s as a case of nasty Stanley Baldwin and Neville Chamberlain sidelining Winston Churchill when he bravely tried to warn of the dangers of appeasing Hitler and by gross foolishness, weakness or both risking a Nazi conquest of Britain (this is the picture presented to us, in the interests of drama, in the 1981 TV series *Winston Churchill: The Wilderness Years*). Baldwin was a genuine Christian, who disliked Lloyd George from a sincere detestation of his sexual morals, and wisely sought the abdication of Edward VIII for similar reasons (as part of a general concern at the King's character and lack of mature judgement, which he thought boded ill for the country, Edward's Nazi sympathies once they became apparent lending support to Baldwin's judgement). Where he acted shabbily, deceitfully, it was because he was not clever enough to get his way through cajolery. His portrayal as a creepy and ingratiating self-seeker in the TV series *The Life And Times Of David Lloyd George* (Baldwin was one of those instrumental in engineering the latter's deposition in 1922) is entirely inaccurate and in fact extremely offensive. And remarks quoted by his biographers Barnes and Middlemass (in a massive tome which is excellent on this period of their subject's career but in which, overall, it is hard to see the wood for the trees) show that he suspected war was inevitable sooner or later and that when it came, Churchill would be the man to lead the nation. But not Stanley Baldwin, who knew himself to be unequal to such a task. Meanwhile, it was perhaps better if Churchill were kept from attaining power too soon. He might have pushed the nation into war before it was really ready. As it happened, Churchill became Prime Minister at exactly the right moment, with Hitler launching a massive invasion of western Europe and well and truly bringing about an end to the Phoney War. Of course the Norwegian debacle, which ironically was primarily the fault of Churchill as First Lord of the Admiralty, worked to his advantage in precipitating Chamberlain's fall. But Churchill thrived best in a crisis and the period of relative inaction, apart from on the naval front, which there had been up until then would not have suited him; it is likely he would have grown impatient and done something which would have harmed the prospects of victory and for which he would ultimately have been remembered. Finally, Churchill's personal relations with Baldwin and Chamberlain were always friendly. In fact Churchill cried at Chamberlain's funeral, where he acted as a pallbearer; something which does not suggest a lasting animosity.

Neville Chamberlain was more inclined to believe appeasement would prevent war in the long run, and remove the need for Churchill. My personal feeling is that although Chamberlain was wrong in thinking Hitler, who undoubtedly hoodwinked him, would be satisfied with what he had gained at Munich and make no further territorial demands in Europe, and afterwards was reluctant to admit to his mistake he was right to realise that Britain could probably not fight and win a war against Germany in 1938 and that therefore there was no option but to appease (it was a case of a Birmingham businessman making a decision based on a cost-benefit analysis). This remains true even if the amount of time Chamberlain bought us would have been limited by the difficulty of carrying out large-scale rearmament in the short term if you were trying to show, albeit for purely pragmatic reasons, that you were committed to peace (had it been possible to do so after Munich and before the invasion of Czechoslovakia in 1939, Chamberlain would not have attracted so much denigration at the time or subsequently). And if no-one could have foreseen that once war did break out it would be nine months before hostilities opened in the West, giving Britain longer in which to build up her armed forces (for one thing, Hitler hoped that the other great "Aryan nation" would see sense and make peace with him, and was giving it the opportunity to do that; if so it was a major tactical error). Hitler in a sense blinked in 1938, in what was either a loss of nerve or, more probably, a miscalculation; he is said later to have remarked that he regretted not going to war then because if he had, he would have won. And it would obviously not have benefited the millions the Nazis sought to oppress, exploit or exterminate if he had. Britain's inability to defeat Germany militarily could not be admitted to openly because it would have been a sign of weakness and thus damaging to the pride both of the nation and its leader, while on a purely personal level Chamberlain's sensitivity meant he was subsequently reluctant to admit to misjudging Hitler. It is also the case that he had an arrogance which included his not seeing the need to explain his motives, feeling they ought to be self-evident.

Of course such prudence as Chamberlain displayed, at a cost, in 1938 ought not to have been necessary in the first place. There was a collective failure, in which Chamberlain shared, to handle Germany properly during the 1930s. Having treated her too harshly after the First World War, by the terms of the Treaty of Versailles, Britain later, out of a kind of guilt complex, was too lenient when under Hitler she began demanding too much, or at any rate taking back what morally she had a certain right to (the Rhineland) but without going through the proper legal and diplomatic channels which would have served to reassure others that her general intentions were not aggressive. At best British policy was confused. Rearmament at an earlier stage, if it had not deterred Hitler, would at least have ensured he got away with less. But it could have been seen as a confrontational or at least militaristic (by definition) act, likely to provoke war, and it should be remembered that the horrors of the previous conflict still lingered in many people's minds; it was understandable if they did not wish to repeat them. At times there was also some uncertainty, equally understandable, whether the principal threat to the liberty of the western world came from Hitler or Stalin. In the end Britain was able to mount a successful defence against Hitler in 1940 by muddling through − a policy (or perhaps it is rather a tendency) which is peculiarly British and can certainly reap rewards even if it is not, nonetheless, to be recommended.

Chamberlain was undoubtedly an uninspiring war leader; but there, as observed, the timing of events worked out for the best in the end. Ultimately it may be said that the bad press he has so often had is not altogether deserved. He had a nice side and a less nice side which caused him to be harsh and arrogant towards those who disagreed with him (it was in part due to school bullying, which often has that kind of effect). But just as it would be unfair to judge Enoch Powell entirely by his views on immigration, so it would be unfair to judge Chamberlain entirely by his foreign policy. He was an effective, and apart from a proposal to disenfranchise certain categories of people reasonably humane Minister of Health and Chancellor of the Exchequer, within the constraints imposed by recession. As Chancellor he was an impressive performer on prototype television, in what comes over strikingly like a modern party political broadcast.

Of his half-brother Austen it may be said that though far from being a fool, he lacked, perhaps because he was too decent a sort, the combination of ruthlessness and skill at political manipulation to be a successful leader of the Conservative Party and would probably have been a disaster as Prime Minister. Nor was he the kind of personality to inspire; *Austen Chamberlain: Gentleman In Politics* by David Dutton is a rather dull book, but then it is about a dull man (one encounters the same problem with biographies of Attlee). He was competent in his various ministerial posts; of course anything he as Foreign Secretary achieved through the well-meaning Locarno treaty of 1925 was destroyed by Hitler's reoccupation of the Rhineland, in fact by the whole of Nazi foreign policy – another example of the tragedy which seemed to dog the political Chamberlains throughout their careers.

4

From the late 1930s party politics began to be transcended in the person of Winston Leonard Spencer Churchill, as he became increasingly the focus of concern over the vital issues of national security and the government's foreign policy; and then by the war, during which for most of the time Churchill was of course Prime Minister. He remains a complex, in some ways enigmatic figure: notoriously vain, but far from being a mediocrity as vain people often are; not intellectually profound in relative terms, yet possessed of a certain wit and a wonderful command of the English language; not above being nasty about people ("Mr Attlee is a modest little man with a lot to be modest about") yet capable of magnanimity and not really bearing grudges; utterly dedicated to defeating the Nazis and prepared if necessary to drop incendiary bombs on the Black Forest or pastoralise Germany, yet bearing no ill-will towards the German people as a whole – one more example of an ambivalence which made his critics think there was something two-faced about him. He was intelligent in some ways, perhaps not in others (meaning he was less likely to be plagued by self-doubt and thus possibly the ideal person to win a war; "nice" people certainly aren't). He loved the thrill of battle but never sought it for its own sake. To put that the other way round, though a serious matter war could also be seen as an exciting game – otherwise, Churchill probably could not have prosecuted it with any enthusiasm and therefore won it.

He was, either at different stages or the same stage of his career, a liberal social reformer and a right-wing sabre-rattler. It may be it was easier for him to be the former because although the product of a "posh" family with aristocratic connections he was not in his younger days particularly wealthy, in contrast to what is frequently supposed about "posh" people, and so to some extent could see life through the eyes of those who found it hard to make ends meet (he also experienced financial hardship during his "wilderness years" in the 1930s, though by then past his liberal, with a small or large "l", phase). At any rate he proved to be competent and humane in posts such as President of the Board of Trade. Paradoxically, it was in warfare that he made his most serious mistakes (Gallipoli, Narvik, Dieppe), largely through over-enthusiasm. Though obviously not a coward he was better at the defensive aspect of war, where his capacity to inspire and embody a national mood of resistance to invasion proved his strong point, than the offensive because there he had too much of a penchant for grand but ill-conceived and ultimately disastrous schemes. By the time the war was taken back to the enemy in earnest Britain was very much the junior partner in a tripartite alliance between herself, the Americans and the Russians, while also having to take some account of the opinions of the Free French, and this greatly reduced Churchill's ability to cause damage, notwithstanding of course that Stalin and Eisenhower were capable of making mistakes too.

In some ways the war was won, as indicated above, by muddling through. The precise nature of Churchill's achievement is sometimes difficult to pin down. But undoubtedly in 1940 he provided the vital *psychological* boost that was needed, inspiring and encapsulating the national will to resist; the only other candidate for the premiership, Halifax, would probably have made peace with the Germans. (In practical terms, the winning of the war was accomplished on the British side by Bernard Montgomery.)

Altogether, both during the war and previously in the Wilderness Years when everything seemed hopeless, and despite his being a flawed and egocentric personality, Churchill's example is a wonderful incentive to those faced with what seem crushing odds to believe in oneself and never give in. He won the Greatest Briton award a few years back because he could be seen as both a defender of the nation against foreign aggression and, by the same token, a guarantor of its liberties; Hitler would probably have destroyed the latter altogether. Hence, he was a prudent, bipartisan, noncontroversial choice out of a list on which some had placed Enoch Powell. Powell deserved the award in some ways because of his patriotism, his commitment to excellence in speaking and writing his native language, his defence of Britain's traditional institutions and identity, the liberties of its parliament, his regard for its history, and his willingness to speak out in what he considered the country's interests regardless of the political cost to himself; but granting the honour to him would have resulted in considerable offence and anger on the part of an important enough section of society, and been very damaging to national unity and community relations.

Whatever Churchill's assets or liabilities as warlord he was not considered the right person to lead the country in the aftermath of the war. It is understandable that he should have felt hurt by his rejection at the election which followed it; and equally understandable that the people should have rejected him. Some disliked him. The picture of a nation standing right behind a revered leader who was seen as a focus for resistance to the enemy can be exaggerated; there was a certain ill-feeling at being expected to make sacrifices while Churchill was relatively safely ensconced in Downing Street. But what most were saying was, "You were the right man to win the war, Winnie, God bless you; but sorry, we don't think you're the right man to win the peace." There was nothing personal. Rather, it was perceived that the degree of reconstruction required after five years of fighting a war more total, in its involvement of the civilian population, than that of 1914-18 would require a proportionately thorough transformation of society (though the Great War of course, because of the work done by women in munitions factories, which had to be rewarded, had led to the introduction of female suffrage). Churchill, whose concern with social reform was not what it had been, at least that was how things were perceived, wasn't the one to provide it, certainly not in a form which would have satisfied the majority of people. (He did of course return as Prime Minister in 1951-55, although the relative success of his government was due more to having an able ministerial team than to his own powers, which were beginning to fail).

And so we had the third, and undoubtedly to date the most successful, Labour government, which those disparaging towards the party might regard as the only one which ever did any good, assuming they were inclined to be even that generous. This would not be entirely fair. But Labour in 1945 came in at the right time, with their finger on the pulse of the nation. Their achievement of nationalising the major industries along with the rail network did not become permanent, being dismantled by Margaret Thatcher. Nothing lasts in politics, or indeed in other areas much of the time, anyway. But the nationalisation caught the mood of the day, fulfilled a certain need, just as Labour themselves did. The wartime spirit of co-operation had created a communal feeling which made the supposed taking of important sectors into the ownership of the people acceptable, even appropriate. Then of course there was the NHS, something of which the country can be justly proud and which is still with us today despite attempts to nibble at its edges (how many people within the business sector or the Conservative party would actually privatise it wholesale if they could is a matter of conjecture). Attlee's government is rightly regarded as superlative, in so far as anything is, and significantly has been held up as an example and contrast to later Labour governments and oppositions who are thought to be performing badly. (In a strip in "The Spitting Image Comic Book" of 1988, medium Doris Stokes, who had recently died, is in Heaven helping some of the people there communicate with the living on

Earth. Attlee, flanked by Messrs Morrison, Bevan, Bevin etc., comes forward. "Doris, we're the Labour government of 1945. Can you tell the Labour opposition of 1988 to get their finger out?" "Why don't you tell them yourself, love," suggests Doris. "You're standing right next to them.")

Of course things did not always run smoothly, and eventually Labour lost power because people had become fed up with post-war austerity and thought the Tories would do a better job of lifting them out of it. They (the Tories) benefited from the subsequent (and according to economics bound to happen at some point) return of prosperity, and the end of rationing etc., and in fact were on a high until a downturn in 1962, which was followed by the damaging Profumo scandal; in all they were to hold office for thirteen years. Churchill was succeeded by Eden, who is another tragic figure in the history of British politics, an example of how the heir apparent, after spending years being groomed for the top job, the king having occupied the throne for too long, makes a mess of it and is out within a relatively short time. There is a comparison with the case of Tony Blair and Gordon Brown, though Brown's failure was for reasons other than an un-British hysteria − possibly the result of illness − of the kind which led Eden to embark on the Suez venture, which either should not have been attempted in the first place or was very badly planned (one can imagine Churchill doing it and "screwing up"), on the principle that Nasser, arrogant and anti-British though he may have been, was somehow the same thing as Hitler.

Then came Harold Macmillan (whose shaky signature, asked for and obtained through the post, I possess). I confess to finding him something of an enigma, as I sense do others. No-one knows the real reason for his sudden departure from Eton, though it is rumoured to have been a flirtation with homosexuality. The steps he took to ensure that "Rab" Butler did not succeed him − which also probably ensured that the Conservatives would lose the 1964 election, as they did − also seem inexplicable. I have not so far located a biography of him which is entirely satisfactory. There remains the haunting sense of secrets never divulged because they were personally or politically too embarrassing, although he came close to it at times in his old age when however well you retain your faculties, control is bound to falter on occasions. It was an awkward and disagreeable moment when, being interviewed by Ludovic Kennedy on his role as a Foreign Office minister during the Second World War, he appeared to be letting slip some startling revelations about the repatriation (perhaps seen as politically necessary) of Cossacks to certain execution in Stalin's Russia. Of his political career it is possible to say that he was a "One Nation" Tory with a social conscience from his days as a young MP in the 1920s, an effective Housing Minister and Chancellor of the Exchequer, and an effective Prime Minister from 1957 until the last year or so of his premiership, which ended in October 1963. At least, whether you agree with this estimate depends on whether you are a Keynesian or a monetarist. My personal feeling is that we should be grateful for the prosperity we enjoyed during those years (even though I myself hadn't been born then!). With Keynesianism, you get periods when the economy is buoyant and everyone (more or less) happy, followed by slumps when everyone, with the exception as always of the wealthiest and thus most able to weather the storm, feels the pinch. With monetarism, until the system overheats through failure to sufficiently regulate the financial and banking sectors (with, again, the richest sections of society being best fitted to cope with the crisis), you get continued prosperity for most but continued deprivation, whether or not it is only relative, for a significant element (those vulnerable through being unemployed or on a low income), especially in the absence of price control. It is a matter of opinion which is the greater evil.

I remember Macmillan as a distinguished-looking white-haired old man, a much treasured survivor from a bygone age, who seemed in the 1980s, when he was in his nineties, to experience a strange revival of his political career, as if the past and present had met and merged. His mind remained in many ways incredibly fresh and alert and even if he might make the same speech twice his elevation to the House of Lords was a cunning way of gaining a new platform from which to attack the Thatcherite economic policies that had begun to get his goat. Comparing the success he had had in past capacities at finding accommodation for the needy in his former constituency of Stockton with the Thatcher government's restrictions on council housing, which had led to widespread homelessness there, he commented that it was a rather sad end to one's life. His intention was blatantly obvious, but all the same the speech should not, in retrospect, be dismissed as mawkish and a shameful piece of emotional blackmail (though it was both), especially given the horrible social consequences, still seen today, of a policy applied in a singularly harsh and short-sighted fashion. How cruel of the wicked Auntie Maggie to do such a thing to an old man! He still knew how to stick the boot in.

During the 1950s the Conservative party drifted, as Labour did, towards the consensus politics which characterised affairs for the next twenty years or so. Their essential feature was a commitment by both parties to the mixed economy, a basically Keynesian financial policy, negotiation rather than confrontation with the trade unions and willingness to solve economic problems through state spending as opposed to encouraging private investment. This approach became known as "Butskellism" after Butler, Chancellor of the Exchequer 1951-55, and Hugh Gaitskell, Shadow Chancellor during the same period, whose economic philosophies were essentially the same. Consensus politics had its origin in the Second World War, when state control and co-operation between the different sectors of the economy – which after all achieved the desired result, as well as fostering sentiments of national unity and community spirit – had of necessity been the order of the day. As Churchill's control of events weakened (though he was less socially reactionary a figure than is often thought, another measure of his complexity) it became easier for the Conservatives to adopt it; since the alternative would have been something too left-wing and seemingly extreme, Labour had no option but to follow suit. Consensus meant that there was less ideological difference than there had been previously, or would be later, between the two main parties and the reasons why one or the other was voted in or out, was seen to have failed or viewed as an inviting prospect, became more complex. It could sometimes produce governments with very narrow majorities, as in 1964, or even minority ones as twice in 1974 when the resulting situation threatened political stability. But generally parties stayed in power for the full constitutionally legal term of five years − slightly longer if they had increased their majority at a second general election, as Wilson did in 1966 − by whose expiry they had begun to make serious mistakes, and enough of the public grown sufficiently bored with them to want a different line-up.

Another important post-war development, evident from the 1960s, is it is claimed a decline in the calibre of political leadership, both morally and intellectually, leading to the substitution of "image" for sound policy, the latter trend being something which has got markedly worse in recent years (and coincided with the increasing role of the media in forming public opinion). The political leaders after Macmillan, who in retrospect tended to be seen as the last of the giants, are often psychologically interesting, as all human beings are, but one finds it hard to regard them for the most part as great personalities (Margaret Thatcher was in a category all her own). The decline is seen by John Campbell in his book on Lloyd George, *The Goat In The Wilderness*, where he contrasts the tone of politics in his subject's time with later decades, as bound up with the character and career of Harold Wilson, who succeeded Hugh Gaitskell − like Austen Chamberlain, perhaps too decent a man (despite in his own case a surprisingly steamy private life) to have ultimately been a good Prime Minister − as Labour leader in January 1963. Campbell claims Wilson saw the mere holding of office as more important than doing anything worthwhile when in it. It is undoubtedly true that he relished coining phrases and delivering quips ("The white-hot heat of the technological revolution...I can't say if there's going to be a general election or not, I haven't been told"), and attempted to glamourise his premiership by inviting film stars, etc., to Downing Street. He liked it seemed to show off, while in matters of policy having a tendency for waiting on events which could prove disastrous.

The blame for all the damage Wilson was able to do rests, in more ways than one, with Harold Macmillan. One imagines, as I am sure some have done, the "Two Harolds" as a comedy duo, with the younger of the pair, Wilson, mischievously mocking the old-fashioned ways of his senior (who admittedly was not of a generation which easily understood the modern world, savvy though he may have been in purely political terms throughout his life). But he (Wilson) owed a lot to Macmillan. The latter was a consummate showman, an ability which, as we have seen, he did not lose with age even if Margaret Thatcher wasn't impressed. He was a master of the newsworthy gesture and the memorable catchphrase; it is clear who Wilson learnt his trade from. It is ironic that the man often referred to as "The Last Edwardian", a symbol of a much more civilised, decent and refined era, should have been responsible – quite unintentionally – for the birth of the vulgar new one.

Macmillan had probably helped to make the rise of Wilson possible by freezing out Butler. The one-year premiership of the patrician Sir Alec Douglas-Home comes across as a strange interlude between the world of Macmillan and that of Wilson, almost the Indian Summer of a vanished age, even if Home did have to resign his peerage to get the job. He was one of the very few *thoroughly* decent men to have occupied the position of Prime Minister, but like Macmillan was out of touch with the younger generation, and also lacked ingenuity. His reply to Wilson's jibe about "the fourteenth Earl of Home", "Isn't Mr Wilson the fourteenth Mr Wilson?" was a feeble riposte which completely falls flat, not least because it misses the not entirely inappropriate point Wilson was trying to make.

But the narrow majority of 1964 suggests that many people thought Home *was* decent and Wilson, by contrast, not entirely savoury. Wilson *did* debase public life, by the kind of aura he gave off. He somehow *looked* like a crook, with a shifty, uneasy air that was compounded by a habit of not always looking people in the eye. There was clearly some deep insecurity at work – of a kind which may be found even in men who are happily married, with children – that among other things made him relish excessively the simple thrill of being Prime Minister, of having power. It was a kind of drug to him. Even if he may not have been guilty of actual criminal behaviour he loved the romance of associating with powerful, possibly dodgy characters (many of whom, like Lord Kagan, unfortunately turned out to *be* dodgy). It was a sign of an immature streak, apart from anything else, and it did him no favours. He once allowed himself to be photographed wearing dark glasses, and with his hands thrust into his pockets, in a way which he ought to have realised made him look, no pun intended, shady. Like some pimp or gangster. And although he may have been sincere in what he professed to believe he always seemed *in*sincere, as if his statements were intended to obscure inconvenient truths and give a false sense of security; to stall. It is ironic, for someone so concerned with image, that image should have done his reputation such damage in the long run. And it's undoubtedly true that Wilson was indolent in dealing with the growth in the power of the Labour Left (the real black mark against him) and so bequeathed an impossible situation to his successor James Callaghan. He was therefore partly responsible for the rise of Margaret Thatcher with all its attendant consequences, good and bad. This is generally acknowledged to be the case by historians and political commentators, and so far all attempts to rehabilitate Wilson in the eyes of posterity have failed.

I would argue, however, that at least a partial rehabilitation is possible. In some respects, things could have been worse. Wilson's cabinets contained arguably more people of intelligence and talent than Heath's and it was perhaps for that reason that they were difficult to control. And besides, this is the Labour Party we're talking about. Wilson's preference for stalling in the short run, of being all things to all men, and for waiting upon events was probably the best approach bearing in mind how fractious Labour has tended to be throughout most of its history. The creation of the "permissive" society through a series of liberal measures, whose immediate architect was Roy Jenkins although Wilson presided over the process, was a major achievement; though there are still people who regard it as ushering in an age of immorality and decadence, it was very necessary because the old mores were either no longer appropriate to the modern world or impossible to police. Wilson recognised this, and probably also saw the value of the legislation from an electoral point of view, through its appeal to a certain constituency, without personally having a great deal of enthusiasm for it.

He had a steadier hand than Heath (whose volatility comes across as rather un-English); this was what counted in a crisis, as many people saw. Even in his second premiership, by which time he was past his best, the magic was still there, initially at any rate; he had the miners back to work within a few days. The 1975 popular referendum on Britain's membership of the Common Market was a shrewd device for preventing Labour from tearing itself apart over the issue and rendering itself ineffective as a party of government. The spate of financial crises suggests that economically the performance of Wilson's governments left much to be desired. But it must be remembered that Wilson, and Heath, and Callaghan, were Prime Minister during a period when Britain was undergoing a further stage in the decline of its economic power, a transition to a new and less exalted status, its problems being exacerbated by events on the world stage such as the 1973 oil crisis and its impact. The extent of the decline, considering the latter as an ongoing if gradual process, had been masked by the inevitable post-war period of prosperity; British popular culture in the 1950s in many ways resembles that of the 1930s, and suggests an attempt to recapture the halcyon days before the war, a denial of the fundamental changes the latter had inaugurated even if they were taking place nonetheless, in sociological as well as geopolitical matters. The vibrant patriotism of boys' papers such as the *Eagle*, and later *Valiant* and *Lion,* was one manifestation of this. It continued even after the reality of Britain's situation was all too painfully exposed by developments in the world at large.

In the troubled and turbulent times which followed this era there was uncertainty about which economic policy, monetarism or Keynesianism combined with government intervention, was the best guarantor of prosperity. Flawed human nature meant that mistakes were often made, and the course of events was influenced as always by personalities. The situation endured until the rigorous, and in the long run, adoption of monetarist policies inaugurated a whole new ball game, one we are still playing. The reason why Harold Wilson and Edward Heath have been described as a double act (the greatest since Gladstone and Disraeli), maintaining popular interest in politics through, apart from anything else, the ability of Mike Yarwood to impersonate both of them, was that they were trying to do the same job – that of tweaking Britain so that it could adapt to changed global circumstances, at a time when the implications of its weakened position in the world, masked and delayed in their effect by the post-war recovery, had suddenly become manifest – and not entirely succeeding. But Wilson's style of government, whatever its defects, was more effective than Heath's confrontational approach.

It is untrue to say that Wilson did not really believe in anything, apart from his own aggrandisement. He did want to restore the nation's prosperity through finding a new role for it in the world of the mid-late twentieth century, and he did want to increase opportunities for ordinary people to better themselves (he saw the creation of the Open University as his greatest achievement in this field). Sadly, neither goal has been fully realised by his successors. But that is not his fault.

My father once said that Wilson was "a nasty piece of work"; my grandfather called him "Flash Harry", probably after the dubious (if likeable) character, played by George Cole, who appeared in the St Trinian's films. I think the key to understanding him lies in appreciating his deep insecurity and vulnerability. This was what made him come over as shifty, through his sly, rather guarded look and other mannerisms, and more disreputable than he really was, having a lasting effect on his reputation. And because so many things were going wrong with the economy, due to the consequences of Britain's long-term decline suddenly being realised, it heightened the impression that he was more interested in the trappings of power than in running the country properly. It is tragic given that he was probably no more dishonest, slippery and self-seeking than many other leading politicians. The tendency to erect a defensive shield around himself, preferring the company of a few trusted advisers, became more marked when things went wrong, which they did after 1966-7, and he felt himself under attack as a result. It could manifest itself in nasty ways: he once hit a reporter, something for which he would nowadays face criminal charges if the assaultee chose to bring them. If he was ineffective in 1974-6 in dealing with the long-term problem of the Left and their increasing power, it was because the heady days of that first, five-and-a-half-year (1964-70) administration had worn him out. Plus he may already, by the time he finally left office, have been starting to suffer from the mental decline which characterised his last years, and which began earlier than is often realised. It explains his appalling lack of judgement over the controversial resignation honours list. If Wilson's behaviour had been such as to harm the nation's moral welfare, age took a cruel revenge for that. He underwent a long but remorseless journey into dementia, for a time at least partially retaining his "marbles" but always a derided, where not forgotten, figure, abandoned by most of his former colleagues. His ego made it hard for him to admit that his faults were due to insecurity and oversensitivity, and it was as if all his mental energies went into maintaining the protective shield against such a confession, none being available to resist the onset of the dementia. This arouses pity as much as anything else, but because it was essentially a dishonest mindset it precluded use of that moral energy which can be of immense value in empowering us mentally and physically even as we grow older.

Though he did not intend it to happen Wilson must undoubtedly bear principal blame for the lowering of the tone of politics, its degradation into an exercise in sound-bites, in terms of having started the process. But there is not an unbroken line of succession from him to Tony Blair. The moral and intellectual decay of public life was not a continuous process. Edward Heath, with whom Wilson alternated in power in what, again, has been likened to a comedy double act (to highlight comparisons with the entertainment industry) – Heath rather portentous and humourless, and Wilson pricking his balloon like a mischievous schoolboy – was a genuinely decent man who remains psychologically hard to analyse. It has often been speculated, largely because he remained all his life a bachelor, that he was a repressed homosexual. It is known that he suffered from an underactive thyroid, though not, according to his doctors, when he was Prime Minister. But some psychomedical condition, or complex of psychomedical conditions, must one feels explain why he was short-tempered, impatient of points of view other than his own, sensitive to criticism, and liable in the end to go for a particular course of action, which might not previously have been considered among the available options, on impulse. It all seemed like a childish fit of pique (he was undoubtedly immature). Powell saw his calling of a general election in early 1974 on the issue of "Who runs the country", having got into trouble with the miners, as "fraudulent". It was really a case of Heath having become annoyed with the unions for wrecking his plans for a proper economic consensus by demanding too much. He wanted to do good for people (seeing the Tory party as an instrument towards this end rather than an end in itself, as Peel had done) whether they liked it or not, and was puzzled and angry when they didn't co-operate, failing to act in what were surely their own best interests. It was odd for a liberal, One Nation Tory to be at such loggerheads with trade unions, whose purpose was to campaign for a decent wage and standard of living for their members – the conflict was certainly a bitter one on the unions' side – though we have to remember that at this time, besides Heath's confrontational approach, the unions were determined on being militant in any case.

Though I don't think he had Asperger Syndrome, Heath also suffered from an autism-like inability to appreciate how his lack of grace and warmth, evident towards colleagues and opponents alike, might offend. In the end he was in power for just three-and-a-half years, his premiership in some ways an interlude in the saga of the Wilson/Callaghan Labour governments and their succession by the iconoclastic Margaret Thatcher.

James Callaghan had similar "stalling" tendencies to Wilson, which led to him being called "specious" by one newspaper columnist at the time of his becoming Chancellor of the Exchequer in 1964, but these can be attributed to the situation regarding the different factions within the Labour Party in which Wilson had landed him; nor did they prevent him having in the public perception a certain solidity and decency (which was perfectly genuine, though at the same time pumped up for electoral purposes).

It is not the case that politicians have always bowed to the media's wishes, or succeeded in looking cool on it. Heath's sensitivity led to his barring reporters from Downing Street, an unwise policy as it made it harder to explain his actions as well as look as if he had something to hide. He was in any case never as accomplished a performer as others, often seeming awkward and ill-at-ease (and I suppose we might mention here such things as his execrable delivery of French). John Major's grey personality, so frequently caricatured, was not an asset where image was concerned and Gordon Brown came over as bad-tempered, a sort of second Heath. It was not always possible to manufacture people for the cameras (in the sense that they looked good in front of them, whether or not their opinions were their own) as was achieved with Margaret Thatcher, Tony Blair and David Cameron. And we cannot say that a politician's being media-compatible or otherwise is the sole determinant of events; although Heath lost three elections out of four (winning that of 1970 unexpectedly), it should be remembered that he failed to win the two in 1974 by very narrow margins. Roughly half the country felt "Ted was right" even if the other did not. There was a widespread perception of him as a moral man whose taking Britain into the Common Market was at least well-intentioned. Certainly one can feel sad that he was ejected from the Conservative leadership and thus, as became apparent in time, lost any chance of regaining high office, at fifty-eight (almost the same age as Lloyd George and also by now a younger one, which makes it even more tragic). He was undoubtedly capable of magnanimity; less Christian, for a person who claimed to subscribe to that religion (and ended his days living in the Cathedral Close at Salisbury), were his ongoing grudges against Powell, whom he ought to have respected as a sincere conviction politician whatever else might be said about the man, and Thatcher. As with Tony Blair, how far what may have been a medical condition excuses character defects is perhaps best left to the Almighty to decide. Heath was certainly a rare type in that he was (I believe) asexual, and since most human relationships *are* sexual, in that you relate differently to the opposite gender than you do to your own, he was handicapped in coming over as awkward and unfriendly to all but a narrow circle of intimates. At the same time a mercurial temperament, arising from psychological flaws, was interpreted as inconstancy, particularly by diehard Thatcherites who disliked "U-turns" in economic policy.

But neither Heath, nor Wilson, nor Callaghan (and certainly not Thatcher) could be described as a mediocrity as Major, Blair and Brown were in relation to them and certainly to Disraeli, Gladstone, Lloyd George and Churchill. If the decline did not start with Macmillan and Wilson, at least not quite, it certainly did after Thatcher.

Another thing which is indisputable is that during the 1970s and 80s consensus politics broke down. It broke down because nothing and no-one is ever perfect; more specifically, because at the same time that certain events were happening in the wider world, such as the oil crisis and its worsening of inflation, combined with the implications of Britain's relative economic decline compared to younger nations, the unions had got too greedy, wishing to increase and certainly not to countenance any reduction in their share of the affluence which had succeeded the austerity of the immediate post-war period and been boosted by the growth of the consumer society. Expectations had risen too high. So the unions resented the refusal to raise wages in line with the inflation, which governments were trying to remedy by what would later be called "austerity" measures, and struck. The situation was aggravated by political and administrative error. A failure to manage the problems mentioned was perceived as a fault of the system itself, though how far that perception was accurate is a moot point. Generally, while the country was experiencing the post-war boom of the 50s and early 60s it was difficult for radical socialist elements to make much headway but when the prosperity began to be eroded it had the effect of emboldening them, making them think they had a case – capitalism wasn't working – and that people would in due course come to support them in large numbers.

Both the Conservatives and elements within the Labour Party started looking for new ways of running things, one left- and the other right-wing, if monetarism is a "right-wing" policy, but both in different ways radical. Depressing as it was, at the time, to be apparently stuck in a situation of instability and poor leadership (in that Callaghan was unable to restrain the unions), if one takes into account that there were moves away from Keynesianism on the part of Labour ministers as well as the Tory Party, that Callaghan led a minority government (though that was not by itself a decisive factor, except in so far as it caused him to make a miscalculation), and that the behaviour of organised labour was bringing matters to a head there seems a certain inevitability about the subsequent course of events. It probably was inevitable that the mere passage of time, the tendency after a while for a significant number of people somewhere or other to get tired of the existing order, would have caused the Tories eventually to adopt and implement the doctrines of monetarism and privatisation. It was a philosophy which, if applied more flexibly than it has been, need not perhaps have awful consequences. But a significant section of Labour didn't like it and in reaction became more left-wing, more assertive, and more determined to seize control of the Party, recruiting young militants to their cause. Though the switch to monetarism would have happened anyway, the more Labour leaned towards the Left the more in the long run the Tories leaned to the Right in reaction to that.

In the end it was the unions who brought Margaret Thatcher to power rather than the general economic situation, which had begun to improve. The effect of wage rises, brought about by industrial action, on inflation, which was incompatible with good monetarist policy, meant they would have needed to be tackled head on, and their power drastically curbed at some point, although it ultimately fell to Thatcher to do that job; it is highly unlikely Labour whether under Callaghan or Michael Foot could have achieved it. When moderates within the unions, and within the Labour Party, lost control over the former it sealed their fate. In early 1979 there took place that series of strikes by various sectors for higher pay that resulted in what became known as the Winter Of Discontent, everyone it seemed jumping on the bandwagon in their desperation not to be outdone by everyone else, and in a way which, if repeated, would certainly have compromised any long-term economic recovery through the working days lost. It seems incredible that such a professional politician as Jim Callaghan clearly was should have presided over something like this, and therefore quite understandable if perfectly sensible and decent people should believe, as some of them do, that he was in the pay of Conservative Central Office (his "speciousness" would have fostered such a conviction). They might cite in their defence his failure to hold a general election in the autumn of 1978, when he could well have won.

I do not think the conspiracy theorists are right. For one thing, the country had by the time in question had minority government for several years and Callaghan wished to avoid a possible continuation of the uncertainty, instability, and restrictions on the government's freedom of manouevre that went with it. He could not be sure what the result of the election would be and preferred to hang on until sometime the following year, in case it made a difference. The opinion polls did not show Labour with a large enough lead. It was a mistake on his part, but an understandable one. At the same time the fact of minority government meant he was constrained in his dealings with the Left, now more powerful because of the state of affairs he had inherited from Wilson, because he did not want to do anything which by aggravating disunity would weaken Labour's position even further. Yet unless he did something about them the Party's chances of winning future elections were diminished, since a significant section of the public was opposed to the ideas of Tony Benn and his allies, for whom they came to see the Party as a potential Trojan horse. Catch-22. Callaghan perhaps could not have altogether predicted the Winter Of Discontent (which would have become identified in the public mind, and probably with some justification, though the Tory press would obviously have been keen to labour the point, with left-wing militancy). But as events unfolded, and seemed to slip out of control, he appears to have become convinced, as remarks quoted in Kenneth O Morgan's excellent biography of him show, that Labour had lost the ability to clear up the mess things had become and that a Thatcher victory might well be inevitable. This may have consciously or subconsciously affected his performance in the 1979 general election, although he was probably not ruling out a Labour victory, which if by a large enough majority would have given him greater authority in dealing with the Left. Unfortunately for him a significant number of voters preferred not to take the risk.

It is still felt the election could have swung either way; but in the end the Tories won. Subsequently Labour's leftward march plus the factional strife it led to, which disunity was exacerbated by the tendency of any party to lose it somewhat now there is no longer the need to hold a government together, handed everything to them on a plate. Benn's influence grew under the leadership of the honourable but naïve and ineffectual Michael Foot, and to some extent that of Foot's more able successor Neil Kinnock. He is to me something of an enigma, in that he consistently and vociferously protested against the evils of Thatcherism yet in effect did everything possible to keep the Tories in power – as surely he must have known it would? It is no wonder that I have often found myself doubting whether he was taking the whole thing seriously; whether he was in truth treating politics as something of a joke. For saying as much after his death I was criticised by a fellow user of Facebook who suggested I had been taken in by the usual demonising Tory propaganda; this person had evidently forgotten the semantic distinction between saying something is the case and saying you're not sure if it is. The theory is at any rate given credence by Benn's suggestion at the time of the 1984 miner's strike that miners should join together with homosexuals to seek political change as both were persecuted groups. I got some stick, too, for pointing out (some years before) the bizarreness of this, but the issue was not whether gay people had the right to engage in political activity if they wanted, which of course they did have. If Benn had known what he was doing he would have realised that your average burly Yorkshire miner would never have welcomed the proposed alliance, since the Labour movement has not itself always been renowned for political correctness. A cartoon in *Private Eye* summed it up adequately. Is it that Benn genuinely was sincere, but also that while intelligent in some ways he was remarkably *un*intelligent in others? Perhaps we'll never know, in this world anyhow.

5

For those members of the general public, and there were many of them, who supported her consistently over the years but weren't among the hardcore fans, Margaret Thatcher was like a marriage in which love had died, except for in 1983 when she prudently called an election while still on a Falklands roll. They disliked her dictatorial behaviour and the damage her swingeing cuts were doing to traditional institutions and the welfare state. But they feared Labour even more, their aversion to it increasing the more left-wing it became, and this feeling persisted even after it had begun under Kinnock to first curb militant activity and then, with the help of its "spin doctor" Peter Mandelson, to set about making itself generally more respectable. There was no alternative. Thatcher's ultimate fall was possible because Labour's rehabilitation had made sufficient progress for it to be concluded the system could survive without her, though of course it was preferable for Conservative government to continue; her megalomania, which was becoming markedly worse, thus rendered her more of a liability than an asset. In the meantime, she was free to implement her policies without serious opposition once she had crushed the "wets" in her party and gained such a huge majority that she felt able to proceed with the privatisation programme whether or not she could claim with justification – though of course she did claim – that there was a popular mandate for it.

There wasn't; most people did not understand the difference between one economic philosophy and another, merely saw Thatcher as a strong leader who above all was not the Labour Party with, among other things, its policy of unilateral nuclear disarmament that seemed to jeapordise the nation's whole security, in contrast to which all other considerations had to be deemed less important, by comparison anyhow. Among the intelligentsia, including those in the pre-Foot Labour Party, there had begun to grow before Thatcher came to power the feeling that a move away from a corporatist and Keynesian economic system and towards a monetarist one might be a better way of avoiding stagnation and inflation (or a combination of the two); but the unions, who by forcing up wages would have a negative effect upon the money supply, had first to be dealt with, and the task fell to Thatcher because Labour did not have the will for it. It was accomplished, following a period during which Employment Secretary James Prior was thought to be adopting a too "softly-softly" approach, through a series of harsh laws against secondary picketing etc. which in combination with other factors have left the unions a shadow of their former selves, unable for example to resist the policy of casualisation encouraged by the Major government, with damaging consequences for some jobseekers' careers, in the 1990s. This dominance of monetarist economics, with the minimum of interference in the private sector (that is, the free market), has its origin in a lasting neurosis about the damage inflicted on the nation's pride and prosperity in the 1960s and 70s and the identification of Keynesianism as the cause.

Thatcher was in office for eleven years in all, from May 1979 to November 1990. She won three general elections the second of which, as noted, massively increased her parliamentary majority. After that milestone she became too confident, too drunk on her enormous power, and ever more disagreeably arrogant, caring progressively less what others thought of her or her policies, which eventually led to her downfall once Labour were no longer, relatively speaking, the threat to the common good which they had been and she was not quite so indispensable. Another thing which happened around this time to lower the tone of British public life, as in some ways it did, was the satirical television series *Spitting Image*, which used puppets of prominent politicians and other celebrities. To some degree unfairly its scatological approach helped to induce a perception of and cynicism towards politics as a shabby business – so, for over twenty years by then, had *Private Eye*, but in this format the humour was much more visible and to a far larger number of people – and therefore contributed to a growing atomisation of society. The late Sir Robin Day, presenter of political programmes on the BBC, had a rather selective sense of humour, possessing his own rather dry one – as well as, despite being capable of losing his temper on occasions, an old-school courtesy which is too often lacking in the media nowadays – but he may have been justified to some extent in his criticisms of the show. There was little to be done about it, however, because political satire is essential in a free society – it doesn't achieve much in practical terms, anyway – and because *Spitting Image* after its first relatively unsuccessful series was very, very funny.

Thatcher's own personality had a negative effect upon society, as touched on above. The author remembers the 1980s as a time when people in authority – or out of it, for that matter – were often rude and hectoring in their dealings with you. Though Thatcher was not an evil person her manner was objectionable and, because she was the most important and most visible public figure, infected others. Despite growing popular disenchantment with politics, political personalities are nonetheless important, in a negative or positive way, in setting examples and establishing trends. Britain in the 1980s became a shabbier place because of (a) Thatcher's way of managing people and (b) the extent to which she was commercialising everything. Onto the latter the political correctness of the 1990s and after grafted a structure of "customer service" and user-friendliness which has done away – though perhaps not universally – with the *overt* rudeness but substituted something which often is no less damaging in its sociopolitical consequences, merely dressed up in subtle forms which cannot so obviously be taken issue with and thus avoiding unpleasant confrontation.

But to return to the eighties, there is no doubt that Thatcher succeeded in changing her country thoroughly, for better or for worse. As observed we are all her children, whether we like it or not; citizens of an essentially privatised society, with all the implications of that. Her personal political fortunes, and those of her party, can be said to have declined after 1983, due to a gradual Labour recovery; following such an election result (of which that of 1997 is another example) things can only get better for the losing party and worse for the winning one, however long the process takes. Tory victories in working-class, traditionally Labour-voting constituencies in '83 seemed to suggest a social gulf was being bridged, and it was therefore tragic that so many of those gains were subsequently lost. But it some respects it was to cease, in the long run, to matter which party was in power.

The consensus of the 1950s to 70s changed, from Heath's replacement by

Thatcher as Tory leader and then the radicalisation of the Labour Party, to a state of polarisation in which the two main parties were ideologically vastly different from one another. Whichever was acceptable to the electorate, even if only as the lesser of the evils, achieved power and the one that wasn't could be kept out of it for years, even the greater part of two decades, so long as it was reluctant to change. The two-party system survived after a fashion, and of course it had been cemented since the mid-nineteenth century by the development of formal structures for canvassing support and distributing publicity, but was it really functional without an electable opposition?

Some of course might prefer the kind of politics which characterised the 80s to the instability of previous decades. But this was not the view of the Liberal/SDP (Social Democratic Party) Alliance, which presented itself as a moderate alternative to both Labour and the Tories. It made things interesting for a time by winning by-elections, showing there was not inconsiderable public sympathy for its views, and did impart to the system an appearance of being more genuinely democratic. Unfortunately it fell victim to the tendency of the public to use it, as they later used UKIP, and have sometimes used the main opposition party, as a "protest vote" between general elections, reverting to their traditional allegiances at the latter. The popular mind does not seem to easily accommodate three main parties in its consciousness, preferring the simpler division between the principal conservative one and the principal progressive one that you usually get and finding it hard to understand what the third party stands for. The Alliance, from 1987 the Liberal Democrats, failed to break the mould; at worst, it had an important but often negative effect by splitting the anti-government vote and making it easier for the latter to repeatedly be returned. The "Lib Dems" can be useful as a coalition partner, as the Liberals were to the National government in the 1930s and to Churchill's wartime administration, but this has not necessarily been to their own electoral advantage. At any rate, when the Alliance, as that, was unable to break out of the straitjacket described the creation by David Owen and Rosemary Barnes of a separate SDP, which did not accept union with the Liberals, seemed gloriously pointless, a case of a split hair on a pinprick. It would inevitably appear as the attempt of a delusionary and megalomaniac (Owen) to create his own private little empire. It may have been a little more than that, but it could never have got anywhere. Owen and Barnes (the latter's loyalty to the former is touching) may have believed in what they were doing but there are times when the question of principle does not apply, and pragmatism is the better part of (moral) valour. The SDP was finished, anyway. Many of its former members later drifted towards New Labour, which was after all a social democratic rather than socialist Labour party; I am not clear as to what happened to them when under Jeremy Corbyn it swung back towards the Left in the mid-2010s. Concerning Rosemary Barnes, one of those "nice people" who set out to reform politics because they were tired of the polarisation of the main parties and the mudslinging between same and saw themselves as representing the ordinary person caught in the middle, only to be burnt by the harsh realities of politics (a profession they were not suited to), it may be said that she was well-meaning but disingenuous, with a brash manner that tended to put people off and led to her being treated badly by some.

The Conservatives held power for eighteen years from 1979, Labour taking that long to make itself fully respectable again. Regardless of ideology, since politics, including elections, is as much about personalities as ideologies, for a party to be in power for a decade or more, having gained for one reason or other a particularly big majority at the outset or (as in 1983) a second general election (though Cameron's in 2015 was not large – the laws governing these matters are never entirely inflexible) – had by its nature a knock-on effect on political affairs. After ten to fifteen years the government had become so exhausted of energy and ideas, and generally lost its touch, and the nation got so tired of it, that the backlash resulted in the opposition party holding power for a roughly similar period. Eighteen years of the Tories (1979-97) were followed by thirteen of Labour (1997-2010). For much of the time and by a similar token the same person was Prime Minister (Margaret Thatcher 1979-90, John Major 1990-97, Tony Blair 1997-2007). It assisted the development of a presidential (that is, like the American Presidency in terms of the power exercised, and the almost monarchical aura surrounding the incumbent) style of premiership. David Cameron (2010-16) headed a coalition government for five years, but until the cataclysm of Brexit he seemed set to continue the trend we have been describing, as did his party, the Tories, especially once they achieved power in their own right in 2015. In opposition, each party went through a succession of leaders of gradually improving quality until it eventually found the one who could lead it back to power; for Foot, Kinnock, John Smith and Tony Blair read William Hague, Ian Duncan-Smith, Michael Howard and David Cameron. A pattern, a depressing kind of cycle, had become established which in many ways was not healthy. Even the date of the general election became standardised, being almost invariably on the first Thursday in May, although there are reasons for that. Most likely to induce cynicism was the tendency of governments to cut short the length of their electoral term from five to four years when things were going well, in case something happened to muck them up in the meantime (Thatcher in 1983 and 1987, Blair in 2001 and 2005), but go for the full five when they weren't in case something happened to make them better (Major in 1992, when it may not have been for his benefit, and in 1997 when it certainly wasn't, Brown in 2010 and Cameron in 2015). In Cameron's case the gamble paid off, though the circumstances weren't quite the same; in the others it didn't. Often when a party has to go the full term it's a sign that its chances are scuppered anyway, although it should be remembered that the much-reviled Gordon Brown was nearly returned in 2010, the outcome of the election being a hung parliament rather than an outright Labour defeat.

In terms of stature and of having the will to transform conviction into actual achievement Margaret Thatcher was undoubtedly the last, to date, truly great figure in British politics, with the reservation that more so than any other such personality the harm she did came close to equalling the good (it is why no statues of or memorials to her can be put up in any public place). She was certainly a hard act to follow. It was inevitable that after the departure of such a dominating figure the Tory party would be unsure in which direction to go and also, perhaps, that her replacement (John Major) should have been someone considerably less towering and less successful; rather like Peter Davison following Tom Baker as Doctor Who. Michael Heseltine (another tragic lost leader, if in many ways unsuitable for the job) would have been more glamorous but was not trusted by a sufficiently large section of the party, which he had to some extent split by his decision to stand against Thatcher, precipitating her resignation when she failed to win a large enough majority in the first leadership election. Douglas Hurd, the third candidate in the second ballot, who would have ruffled too many feathers by his arrogance and abruptness, was taking part purely so that it would not look like a straightforward but divisive Heseltine-Major contest, and this showed in the awkwardness of his manner during the campaign. In the end Major won because he was considered a steady pair of hands (Heseltine could get genuinely rattled when being barracked).

Initially his appointment as Prime Minister was welcomed by many outside the party; he seemed a nicer, more moderate personality than Thatcher, and being a working-class (lower middle-class, anyway) Tory leader and Prime Minister he appeared ideally suited for building bridges. A working-class Tory leader was something I had always wanted (as long as he wasn't Norman Tebbitt, who I liked in many ways but would have upset too many people). But Major's premiership perhaps serves as an object lesson in being careful what you wish for. Not because having a working-class Tory leader is bad, but because once they attain the top job you may find them deficient in some respects as an individual. Incidentally Major remains for the moment the only serving Prime Minister with whom I have had any physical contact. I was attending a meeting (more social than political, though of course politics were discussed) at the House of Commons of the Tory Reform Group (essentially, the left wing of the party), to which I was then loosely attached, in the summer of 1991 when Major suddenly appeared − no doubt bridge-building − and was immediately surrounded by an enthusiastic crowd, including myself. I managed to shake his hand. A TRG official attempted to introduce me to him but we had already lost his attention. It was probably because he had so many others competing for it rather than offhandedness, although with Major it was often hard to tell.

Perhaps partly because of his background, and certainly because of some more personal insecurity, of a kind which when he was a young man led him to have an affair with an older woman, Major while lacking firmness when it was required – leading many to see him as weak – was sensitive to criticism, and therefore all the more inclined to hold on to power despite the frustration caused others by his defects as leader. He did have some of the characteristics often found in a weak man, even if "weak" may be too strong a word by which to describe him. These include a certain authoritarianism (he is reputed to have once said with relish that when he was Prime Minister he could do what he liked). He was not such a nice person as he appeared. It is incontestable that he was badly treated; but unfortunately the image of him as a decent man who was also vulnerable, constantly having to put up with the sniping of his colleagues, has engendered a protective feeling towards him which tends to obscure the less pleasant and also dangerous aspects of his personality.

He was initially uncertain which way the party should turn, ideologically, in the aftermath of Thatcher but eventually, around the time of its 1993 conference, decided to move to the right, starting a trend by which governments both Tory and Labour have become in certain ways more Thatcherite than the Iron Lady herself. The Tories had already begun to promote casualisation, by which those seeking work (and thus to improve their prospects) could be hired and fired at an employer's discretion, delivering a setback to their plans for self-betterment. It smacked of a lad from working-class Brixton managing to climb to the top and then pulling up the ladder, and was very odd behaviour for a Prime Minister who claimed to value equality of opportunity. He supported the bestowing of honours on "ordinary people" and the creation of more universities, some of which had previously been polytechnics, yet in the name of what was thought to be efficiency (replacing highly-paid permanent employees with low-paid temporary ones and thus cutting costs) he allowed the public sector to behave in a way which was socially damaging, breaking the organic link between employer and employed, even if he did not foresee its negative consequences. His "egalitarian" policies may have reflected a continuing, to some extent, post-Thatcher schizophrenia although they had as much to do with a complex over his social origins as anything else. Then there were well-meaning individual measures such as the National Curriculum and the Citizens' Charter which in the long run failed to fully achieve their aims due to an inability or unwillingness to tackle certain structural flaws in British society and politics, including some would say the harmful effects of political correctness. It was the same with the Blair government, though there the failure was made more grating by Blair's management style and tendency towards hype and spin.

Authoritarianism may not in itself be a fatal flaw as long as it is combined with a willingness to listen to advice, something not necessarily incompatible with it. In Major's case I'm not sure it was, or he would listen to the advice but not act on it. He was negligent about things: the two letters I wrote to him, in succession, as a loyal Conservative (which I then more or less still was) protesting about the harm the government's employment policies were doing went unanswered; the Conservative Political Centre, the party thinktank, once arranged a meeting with him at Downing Street but turned up to find that he had evidently forgotten about it and wasn't there, the group being greeted by a policeman who said he'd never heard of them; then there was the neglect of a horse which had been a personal gift from the President of one of the newly independent Central Asian nations. It is not surprising that some people found Major's lack of dynamism extremely irritating, and that the SDLP politician John Hume is said to have shaken him by the shoulders from impatience at the slow progress of the Northern Ireland peace talks (Tony Blair was able to move things along much faster there).

Major lacked charisma, which may not on its own have been disastrous except that there went with it a lack of imagination and intellect, of acumen, which while not by any means leaving him a complete fool made it difficult to hold together a party bitterly divided over the re-emerging issue of Europe, of whether there should be any further reduction of the sovereignty Britain had to some extent sacrificed when she joined the Common Market (now the European Union) and how much. (Plus the party was suffering from its post-Thatcher identity crisis, for the first half of the Major period anyway.) He simply did not have the perhaps indefinable quality which would have enabled him to assert his authority over the different factions within the government or the party as a whole. He could appear on occasions to be acting decisively, but his withdrawing of the whip from Conservative Euro-rebels merely came over as autocratic as well as being a major (no pun intended) miscalculation when the government's majority had been so drastically reduced in the 1992 election. That election was clearly a Pyrrhic victory, which by limiting the government's freedom of manoeuvre made Major's task even more difficult, diminishing his authority (whereas with the kind of majorities she commanded Margaret Thatcher could pick her cabinets from whoever she liked, thereby making sure her ministers always agreed with her). It was a common view in the party at this time, though not too openly expressed, that it would have been better for us to have lost the election; Neil Kinnock would have got in, made a mess of things (at least that was what we thought), and we would have returned to power around 1997 with a much more dynamic and effective leader, whoever they might have been. It certainly doesn't seem fair, looking back, on Kinnock, who came within just a few votes of victory, or on the Labour activist who killed himself because of the unbelievable bad luck which seemed to have narrowly prevented his party's finally regaining power after so many depressing years in the wilderness.

Major was not ideally what the party needed, and was clinging to office partly from wounded ego, but there was not necessarily an alternative to him as Conservative leader. In 1995 he resigned, forcing a leadership election in which he would be one of the candidates, with the exhortation to "put up or shut up". He won. John Redwood was considered a little *too* Thatcherite – at this stage divisions in the party between left and right were still an issue – as well as too lacking in warmth and emotion, or the ability to project them (fatal from an image point of view). Kenneth Clarke would have been far more popular with the public, and was proving a good Chancellor of the Exchequer, but apart from a tendency to gaffes was too left wing, in Conservative terms, and too much of a Europhile. One consequence of the overall (if still relative) decline in the quality of our politicians has been that it is harder to find someone with just the right qualities to be really successful as a party leader or Prime Minister once all the relevant factors – such as where one stands on a particularly divisive issue – are taken into account. Michael Heseltine by now was out of the running, not wishing to be for Major what he had been for Thatcher, in which capacity he had caused enough trouble. Heseltine was of greatest service in the long run as an able departmental minister rather than a party leader. As Environment Secretary his regeneration of depressed areas in both London and the provinces brought him popularity among those who otherwise tended to revile Tories, and he also ensured that the Council Tax was a relative success in a way its predecessor the Poll Tax was not (although there is no reason why the Poll Tax should not have been acceptable if it really was designed around the all-important issue of ability to pay, and was better marketed including not giving the task of implementing it to a particularly obnoxious and arrogant minister who described public complaints about it as "squealing").

I referred above to a tendency among Conservatives to see the 1992 election not as a remarkable achievement one could be proud of, despite the reduced majority, but as an unmitigated disaster for the party, the subsequent five years achieving little and being quite frankly pointless from its point of view. This is not quite true however. The economy, often seen as the most important issue of all, was actually doing well under Clarke (the recession of the early part of the decade, for which of course the Tories being the party in power got the blame, had now passed). But the Tories still lost in 1997, because they were seen as doing badly on other issues which in fact were considered equally important, such as the NHS – a sign of the increasing multipolarity of affairs – and because they had simply been in power for too long. People did not think they could stand much more of the deadening personality of John Major. Furthermore, and perhaps most decisively, Labour now had a dynamic, and young, new leader in the shape of Tony Blair and had also finally purged its programme of all those elements which had previously disinclined people to vote for it. Firmness and dynamism mattered as much as having the right policies; Labour were now playing the same game as the Tories, but doing it better. Another thing which contributed to the massive Tory defeat was a fatalistic sense among party leaders and activists that it was inevitable; their thoughts were not dissimilar to James Callaghan's in 1979. They may even subconsciously have been relieved. But there was a feeling, tacit at least, among a substantial section of the electorate that the Tories had won the argument, whatever else you might say about them. As for John Major himself, some re-evaluation of his premiership, which was not by any means a total disaster, would not be inappropriate, this being the whole message of *John Major: An Unsuccessful Prime Minister?*, edited by Kevin Hickson and Ben Williams (2017). His undoubted faults could lead him to be treated with unnecessary discourtesy; Peter Oborne, in his foreword to Hickson and Williams' book, notes a disgraceful incident involving, unsurprisingly, Alistair Campbell. Major is it must be said a somewhat forgotten figure these days, despite his recent attacks on Brexit which brought him back into the public eye to some extent, but also the nearest thing the country has or is likely to have in the foreseeable future to an elder statesman, although the revelation in 2002 of an extra-marital affair inflicted serious damage on his reputation and tended to confirm a negative opinion of him. He is a cultured man, and also very British in a way which shows that "Britishness" is not confined to those upper strata of society who in the past have been most closely identified with that quality; in the aftermath of the 1997 election defeat he went to watch a cricket match rather than indulge in recriminations and mudslinging. That was somehow extremely "British", and also civilised.

One legacy of the Major years, though the problem had begun under Margaret Thatcher, has proved particularly damaging. There had always been dissatisfaction among many people in Scotland with the Union. The Scots in 1707 had no particular reason to love the English, who had too often treated them with contempt as well as generally besting them on the battlefield; amalgamation of the two countries was dictated to a great extent by economic necessity on Scotland's part. She simply could not compete, as a separate unit, with her stronger and wealthier neighbour. Her relative lack of resources had been the reason why English kings in the mediaeval and first part of the early modern era had never tried to annex her, the Anglo-Scottish wars of the period being essentially tribal conflicts over territory. In many ways it would have been better if the proud Scots nation, who have never liked playing second fiddle to the English, had had a firm basis for independence in the post-mediaeval world (where economic circumstances were different, and comparative wealth mattered more among nations). Whether they do so now is a moot point; but things happened during the 1980s and 1990s to instill in them a desire for some measure, at least, of devolution. Disenchantment with the policies of the Thatcher and Major Conservative governments was not uncommon either north or south of the border. But Scotland's past history as an independent nation, and then a society with a strong sense of national identity and self-consciousness even if politically a part of the United Kingdom, gave her as she saw it a basis for breaking free of their yoke. The Tories had often been seen as the lesser of the evils but, apart from this ceasing to be so much the case with Labour's return to respectability, if one were looking at things from an overall British perspective, it seemed possible an independent, or semi-independent,

Scottish government might be able to contrive some different way of running things efficiently.

The Scots' desire for devolution may have been due to a feeling that their separate, to some extent, nationhood gave them an opt-out clause where Thatcherism was concerned, but after Thatcher's departure John Major had the opportunity to remedy that through policies that were more astute, more compassionate, or both; whatever one saw the problem as. Admittedly (and this was a crucial factor) he was distracted by the internecine warfare in his party over Europe, but he nonetheless bears the responsibility, along with his predecessor, for the breakdown of the Union in its traditional form. The pressure for devolution was eventually met by Tony Blair with the creation of a Scottish parliament (as well as one for Wales) in 1999. The constitutional implications have been problematical, for while preferring devolution to what preceded it not enough Scots are willing to go for full independence, which carries with it certain economic risks (and if things went wrong London would not be happy to pick up the pieces). Therefore, since taking away the right to do so would amount to a final severance of the tie, Scottish (and Welsh) MPs must still be allowed to sit at Westminster and vote on issues affecting the whole of the United Kingdom, while the reverse is not permitted except in certain vital areas. There is a pragmatic reason for it, in addition to political calculation; the latter consideration in any case only applies when there is a Labour government in power which seeks Scottish support on major issues as a reward for granting devolution in the first place (at the moment, there isn't). But the acceptance of something which in moral terms is clearly wrong contributes to the debasement of political life. The trouble with the "West Lothian" arrangement is that it is ethically abhorrent but practically necessary.

These days Scots resent the West Lothian question being raised because they fear the issue is being expedited and don't want to be forced into complete independence when they suspect it wouldn't work; not because they feel an impelling need to spite the English. Their motive is to protect their own interests, as with their insistence in the seventeenth century on the introduction of Presbyterianism in England as a means of safeguarding their own religious settlement. Devolution was initially responsible for a jingoistic surge in anti-English feeling among them, but once things had calmed down a lot of the sting was taken out of that animosity, as it sunk in that they had more or less got what they wanted. There may also have been a slightly embarrassed awareness that things were getting too nasty. This was later combined with a certain humility as Scottish people realised their economic position was not so strong that they could afford to put up barriers; the "New Scots", immigrants many of whom, like the author J K Rowling, were actually of English descent, were needed to keep the nation going. The same factor explained continuing reservations about full independence, which meant that although the Scottish Nationalist Party, who had policies on other issues too, might succeed in becoming the government they did not, in the referendum of 2014, get their wish regarding the matter over which they had come into being in the first place.

Though she nonetheless desired it as an assertion of identity Wales seemed less motivated by anger at perceived English oppression, at least openly, in seeking devolution than Scotland. She abandoned her attempts to militarily resist domination by the English at an earlier stage than the Scots did, not having the size or resources to keep it up for as long. The last fling was Owain Glyndwr (Owen Glendower's) revolt in the 1400s. She let herself be integrated administratively with England in the sixteenth century, knowing she would not be able to resist the strong Tudor state (but also being more inclined to accept it because the Tudors were themselves Welsh by ancestry). Afterwards she concentrated more on preserving her native language and culture than in achieving political independence. Of course she still seeks to do so today, although the language aspect despite the proliferation of road signs, etc. in both Welsh and English is in practical terms less important, since most people in Wales do not speak Welsh and hardly anyone speaks Welsh *only*. But the anti-English feeling which could be detected in the 1980s, and which resulted in English migrants being badly treated, is no longer evident, for the same reason that similar attitudes are no longer evident in Scotland.

What happened in these years regarding Northern Ireland might be considered more acceptable than the "West Lothian" factor from an ethical point of view – with a query remaining concerning the freeing of convicted IRA terrorists, though the measure is not one which can easily be reversed. The issue of Ireland had embittered British politics since the Middle Ages. It was never happy for any part of itself to be ruled by England, whether officially or *de facto*. Discontent simmered and from time to time erupted. There was violence and prejudice on both sides. Undoubtedly those things have often characterised Irish affairs, and in such a way that people who, after the main part of the country, the "South", quite rightly gained its independence in 1923 saw the unwisdom of including in a united Eire a North which was culturally and socioeconomically different from the rest of the island of Ireland and would only have caused trouble were intimidated from speaking out. One explanation for the anti-Irish feeling which may have exacerbated the conflict at times is that the Irish seem volatile in a way which other peoples of Northern Europe are not. You might expect it from Latins or Arabs etc but not from other nations in the region (from whose ancestry that of the Irish is not really much different, a mixture to a greater or lesser degree of Celtic, Germanic and Scandinavian elements). One would have thought that the Scots and Welsh would have as much reason to hate the English, yet they did not go around killing them, or each other, over the matter. The Irish as a consequence appeared particularly perverse. Though the perception was understandable perhaps, there was clearly a degree of Anglo-

Saxon racial chauvinism in it. On the other hand, though it ought when attempting to engage with them to be recognised that the Irish *are* different it is nonetheless questionable how far one should go in making allowances; to what extent is one being taken for a ride by those who claim a distinct "Irish" ethnicity in order to gain some political or other advantage? (I used to think that the problem with the Irish was that they were jovial in an aggressive and actually rather nasty way, treating others with contempt because they did not know how to have fun; any such attitude on their part, or the fear of it on others', has to be met by recognition that the passionate "Celt" and the stolid "Saxon" are up to a point stereotypes.)

Here I might add that without any prejudice or ill-feeling being involved I have always been uneasy about Irish people claiming British citizenship, voting in our elections, appearing on our quiz shows etc., merely because, due to nineteenth-century immigration, they happen to have relatives here. It seems to compromise the principle of nationality, a principle which to me is a stabilising factor and thus essential. It is particularly galling when some people take the opportunity to attack our Christianity, where we *are* Christian (having had an awful time at the hands, literally or otherwise, of Catholic priests) and our politics, in a visceral and often wrong-headed fashion. I draw a distinction of course between this and the ordinary Irish person who simply takes advantage of the law to do what quite naturally appeals to them. There's not much one can do about it and to forbid it would seem like being a bad neighbour, especially given the ill-feeling which Brexit has caused. We ought also to be fairly forgiving; if Irish people desire a platform for their views and a showcase for their talents it is understandable they should seek it through a country relatively more powerful and prosperous than their own where the opportunity is available to do so.

In absolute terms the Irish cannot be better or worse than any other member of the human family. However there does seem to be a vicious, aggressive streak in their gene pool, one which as with all genes is not inherited by every member of the race. I have been subjected personally to unbelievable venom merely for saying that I am a unionist, that is one who believes that Ulster should remain part of the UK. That John Redmond, Irish Nationalist leader in the 1910s, was attacked for condemning *both* the misguidedness of the Easter Rising and the brutality of the British reaction to it, in other words being even-handed, does not look good. And militant Irish Republicanism had a childish, spiteful quality to it; Ross McWhirter was murdered essentially because he had offered a reward for the capture of IRA terrorists and they resented that. The lawlessness in Ireland in the mediaeval period, with no central authority and politics a matter of wars between rival chieftains, both established the Irish reputation for being ungovernable and made it easier for the English to take over. Altogether the Irish (both kinds, Northern and Southern) are difficult for the British to understand; it is as if something about that beautiful land has the capacity to produce both great good (Celtic spirituality and art, representing the positive side of religion) and great evil, and where the latter is concerned can affect Unionists as much as Republicans, although it should be borne in mind whenever the former appear to have been in the past the more intransigent and unreasonable that they were in a siege situation, in that they faced aggressive pressure from the IRA and others to be absorbed against their will into a united Ireland whereas the Catholic/Republican minority could present itself as the victims. The Unionists seem to have felt that any concession to the Nationalists on civil rights, which would raise their profile and empower them, would undermine their (the Unionists') own position, perhaps because emboldening people encouraged them in their political aims and led them to behave in a triumphalist and provocative pro-Republican fashion. There may have been some validity in these concerns. But the problem might not have existed had there been full civil rights for the minority in Ulster right from when the two Irelands split in 1921-3. That there was not was one of the monumental blunders which have so characterised Anglo-Irish relations.

The pattern of those relations during the twentieth century seems to have been one of Irish hot-headedness (e.g. the Easter Rising, an ill-conceived affair which was bound to end in failure, plus the behaviour of certain people just before the Bloody Sunday incident (e.g. Martin McGuinness, who in those days was young and foolish, was strutting about with a rifle over his shoulder – later the person who had been an irresponsible firebrand was the Minister of something or other!)) followed by a heavy-handed British response. The Irish hotheadedness makes the British soldier's job harder and he becomes impatient as a result; he doesn't see why the Irish have to make things more difficult by the way they carry on. Because someone is emotionally restrained, less overtly passionate about things, does not mean they cannot be *violent*, or cruel. The pattern seems to have involved something (the Easter Rising or Bloody Sunday) serving as a catalyst which caused things to harden and made peaceful relations that much harder to establish. What caused the civil rights issue to explode in the late 1960s were socioeconomic changes; rising prosperity throughout the Western world meant that the Nationalist (that is, desiring amalgamation with the Republic of Ireland), and traditionally Catholic population had more to lose by being discriminated against in the housing and jobs market. It only made them more determined in their Republicanism, whether or not they actively supported the terrorism carried out in its name. Since Ulster – like the Falkland Islands – is geographically far from London, though not as far as Port Stanley, and since it had not been causing serious trouble until then, British politicians had tended to put it on the back burner and perhaps did not wake up to what was going on soon enough, although Jim Callaghan as Labour Home Secretary in the late 1960s did a good job of preventing things from getting worse. The Tories were less successful at inspiring a binding together of the communities, though they desired it as much as anyone else. And then came Bloody Sunday which was the real turning point, in a negative sense of course. It is easy to see how it ignited the whole situation and left a lasting legacy of bitterness. If British soldiers really fired, or were ordered to fire, on protestors after they had turned their backs and fled then ideally those responsible should be punished for it. However if the spirit regarding Ulster affairs is to be one of forgiveness and reconciliation, which means even-handedness, then if we were to seek actively to bring them to justice we would at the same time have to rearrest the IRA members released as part of the Good Friday Agreement, which many people in the Nationalist community would object to, even if, for whatever reason, I find it hard to understand such an attitude. Anyhow, for several decades the British and the Republicans became locked in a struggle the logic of commitment to which, by extension, meant that what some called "dirty tricks", e.g. informing and the Royal Ulster Constabulary's "shoot to kill" policy, were used in order to gain an advantage.

The IRA and their supporters fought for the absorption of Ulster into the Republic because they thought they would be free from discrimination by Loyalists/Protestants. They would get a better deal from their own kind. A country which was predominantly nationalist/Catholic would obviously not allow them to be discriminated against. This thinking was understandable even if the means used to put it into practice was not. The civil rights and the United Ireland issues had been allowed to become fatally, at least it was fatal for thirty years or so, entwined due to the government's failure to resolve the former. It was their separation which in the end made it possible to end the Troubles and bring peace. The will to do this was easier to summon up because of sheer fatigue at the conflict and the divisions and the violence. The key, after appreciating that the two issues needed to be divorced from one another, was to trade the ending of the IRA's "armed struggle", and (effectively) that of any sustained political campaign for Ulster to be part of Eire, for power-sharing as a means of resolving the civil rights problem. To those who might object to it this seemed, once minds were brought to focus on the question, a lesser evil both morally and from the point of view of political pragmatism than a united Ireland – which it was. The Unionists had previously objected to power-sharing because in their view it gave too much influence to the Nationalists; though if the former had been kinder to the latter in the first place, there might have been less pressure for it. In the new conciliatory climate great care was taken not to make it look as if the Nationalists and the Irish (that is, Dublin) government were in cahoots to use the initiative to bring about Irish "unity"; the impression that they were had been the principal reason for the collapse of the Sunningdale agreement in 1974. It was less likely that such things would be repeated once the Republic had given up its constitutional claim to the Six Counties, another essential prerequisite for progress.

The release of convicted terrorists (Loyalist as well as IRA, since there had to be reciprocity if the aim was peace and reconciliation) will always be a sore point for many. Sinn Fein would have pressed for it anyway, but politically there was a particular reason why they did so. They realised that through sheer exhaustion they had lost the battle for a united Ireland, and with the South withdrawing its claim to Ulster they had to be able to show their supporters that they had got something out of the talks, especially if they might also have to decommission their weapons. Of course when the final peace agreements were signed they claimed that basically they had won, but all politicians do that sort of thing, and it was a logical consequence of the need to appease their clientele. Essentially, agreeing to their demands on the issue of the prisoners was seen by the British government as a political necessity, however unpalatable. Some claim the IRA were on the brink of being militarily defeated, and that had the British and the Unionists pressed their advantage peace could have been achieved without making concessions of the kind one might baulk at. I have no way of establishing whether this is true or not, although there is certainly the factor of psychological fatigue over the unceasing strife. But both sides were tired of the conflict, and prepared to countenance whatever would end it by keeping most people reasonably happy.

Ultimately power-sharing between the Unionist and Nationalist communities was seen as the only way to guarantee civil rights and so end the violence. To some extent it would amount to the same thing anyway. But if it is at all possible to separate the two issues, then what I would most like to say to the people of Ulster is this. Even if power sharing, at a governmental level, collapses civil rights should not. The lack of them was what caused all the trouble in the first place.

It is sometimes asked who eventually won the effective civil war which had been taking place in Ulster. It is potentially inflammatory to ask such a question in the sensitive context of Northern Irish politics, so maybe one ought not to. We could however make the following points. Crucially the IRA did not get the united Ireland they wanted. The Unionists had to make concessions, but they could have made them long before and without any harm to their interests.

Did the IRA bomb their way to the negotiating table? Apart from the relevant points already made, this might be true in that weariness at the whole bitter conflict created a mood in which concessions were possible, but in another respect it is not. It might apply with the violence in Ulster itself, which would eventually have been sufficient to produce the result in question, but not to the IRA's bombing campaign on mainland Britain. If the British could misunderstand the Irish character then the converse also applied. The aim of the bombing campaign was to make British voters so sick and tired of the whole Northern Ireland entanglement that they would force the government to withdraw from Ulster. This would never have happened, for several reasons: (a) There were plenty of other issues which were of importance to the electorate. (b) The British public would have resented concessions being forced from them by violence, especially where it had claimed the lives of loved ones. It would have been the same as in the Blitz: "We can take it". Overall the idea that the bombings could influence the result of a general election, or that scores of angry protesters would converge on Downing Street demanding a united Ireland, was absurd. The victims of the bombings died for nothing. It is stretching credibility to suggest the IRA could have mounted a bombing campaign which was sustained and intense enough to meet the desired objective, not least because of the proficiency of the security services − though of course they were not infallible − in preventing it. It is true that at one point the British public did indeed get sick of the whole Ulster business and felt Britain should disengage from it. But apart from the fact that this makes no difference to the first two points I set out, there is a third which can be made. If the British public did indeed think their country should get out of Northern Ireland it was not in the kind of spirit that the IRA had anticipated. What they wanted was for Ulster to either become independent, assuming that to be feasible, or be absorbed into a united Ireland so that if that didn't work out, and it probably wouldn't, then at least the problem would no longer be Britain's. The sentiment was, "If the Irish want to kill each other, as it seems they do, let them; we wish them joy of it." Had Dublin appealed to Britain to take Ulster back, it would have been "You wanted your united Ireland, now you've got it. Goodbye." Forcing Ulster into a single Ireland would have resulted both in even worse violence in the north and a loyalist terror campaign in the south; something too many Irish people failed to appreciate. The alternatives would have been for Ulster to have become an independent state, which would not have been viable, or for the Unionists to have left Ulster en masse and settled in Britain in which case, besides adding to population pressures, they would probably have gone to Glasgow and exacerbated sectarian differences already apparent there between Protestants and Catholics, perhaps creating a mini-Belfast or Derry. In the latter case we would have ended up in a scenario where Britain was being damaged as a result of the whole Northern Ireland business and the Irish were saying "You're paying the penalty for all the trouble you've caused *us*, serve you right." Britain would effectively have been humiliated, and she could not afford to have that happen because no nation, whether it is seen as the oppressor or the oppressed, can. For one thing it is not really a basis for friendly international relations, conducted in a spirit of equanimity and brotherhood. At any rate London would not have countenanced it and the British public would not have wanted it any more than they liked being bombed by the IRA. It was a legacy of colonialism, if you like; but Britain had a responsibility to Ulster, and ought not to have suffered because of it, either through unionist intransigence or the IRA.

The bombings seemed to be the ultimate expression of what was regarded, rightly or wrongly, as Irish viciousness. Although John Major to his credit did make some progress on resolving the Ulster issue the initiative might well have folded in the end over the question of releasing imprisoned IRA terrorists. It was something no Conservative government, I believe, could ever have brought itself to do. The party reveres the British state, its integrity, its traditions and way of life, and values the safety of its citizens; and the IRA's activities on the mainland seemed very much an assault on all it held dear. Certainly, one does sense something abhorrent (we touched on it above) about the spirit in which they acted. It is correct in one sense to say that the IRA were freedom fighters, as some people insist, since their motives were partly to relieve the undoubted hardship, in effect oppression, suffered by Republicans in Northern Ireland and they were frustrated (like many) at lack of progress in the matter. But I cannot bring myself to describe them as such in any complimentary way; I don't think very many British people could. It's hard to put your finger on it. The most one can do is observe the time-honoured, and certainly not invalid, maxim of understanding someone's motives while condemning their methods, and leave it at that.

Were they political prisoners or criminals? Perhaps a strange combination of both. If their campaign was carried out in the wrong sort of spirit then they were criminals, whatever else they might be. Some regard the hunger strikers and the "dirty protestors", whose motive was to gain recognition of their "political" status, as brave people, and maybe they were brave in their own way, but if there is something distasteful about IRA terrorism the fact that the dirty protestors refused to perform the (admittedly degrading) ritual of "slopping out", so that they were living in their own excrement, somehow serves to emphasise it. There is a kind of bravery which is not bravery at all, or is at least as much an extreme case of cutting off one's nose – more than one's nose – to spite something or other. Bobby Sands is regarded as a hero by Republicans, yet he attempted to justify the murder of Lord Mountbatten. And the hunger strikers knew what they were doing. Margaret Thatcher is accused of having been insensitive over the matter. She perhaps ought to have said that it was a pity anyone should have to die, whoever they were and whatever they had done (which it is), though I don't know what difference this would have made, but that does not mean her stance was wrong. And she was insensitive about many things.

It is perhaps a little easier to cope with the IRA, for those who find its activities particularly distressing, if one reflects that they had Marxist leanings. It at least explains, where it does not excuse. What may come over as their vicious irrationality seems less startling if we consider this tendency, which seems of a piece with it. Communism by the late twentieth century was divided between those who practised it as a necessary narrative without seriously believing in it any more (the leadership of the Soviet Union) and those who did believe in it but in a fanatical way which was blind to its glaring faults and only led to further intolerance when these were pointed out. One former IRA commander wanted a Communist state throughout the whole, politically united twenty-six counties of Ireland. This would have been a double disaster, not only exacerbating a fierce secular and political conflict in the most explosive way possible but imposing on the whole country a system which was oppressive and inefficient. It should also be borne in mind that the IRA's espousal of a left-wing policy in socioeconomic affairs was partly in order to appeal more to the disadvantaged working-class Catholic elements from whom they drew their support. Their struggle was essentially a nationalist one. Nor were they really "Catholic", their motives being political rather than religious, except when they had had an attack of remorse over their actions and sought confession from a priest.

To be fair, not all former IRA terrorists, in the aftermath of the Troubles and their various manifestations, have quite the same attitude to what they did. The daughter of a British politician once bravely confronted, as part of the making of a TV documentary, a member of the team who had carried out the bombing which killed her father. He appeared thoughtful about the matter and said that although he did not believe his actions were wrong expressed regret – which I believe was perfectly sincere – that people had had to die. This was in strong contrast to the attitude of one of his colleagues who agreed to meet with a relative of a bombing victim as part of an initiative, also televised, by Archbishop Desmond Tutu aimed at furthering the cause of reconciliation (in all matters where a serious wrong was thought to have been committed, not just ones involving Ireland). His attitude was nonchalant and his apology perfunctory, which suggested he had gone on the programme purely in order to be like that. And tends to confirm what a lot of people think about the IRA.

I once while waiting for a bus fell into conversation about the Troubles with an Irish gentleman who was obviously educated and had intellect. It seemed like an intelligent, balanced and rational discussion of a sensitive issue until it turned to the Brighton bombing of 1984, and he said "We nearly got lucky there." We? I said nothing, and do not know what reaction if any he expected me to show, but it seemed a sinister note had entered the proceedings. He had suddenly revealed his true colours, in a way that was alarming and not entirely savoury and suggests what may often be lurking beneath the surface in Ireland. He also said, regarding the bombing and what would have happened had it succeeded in its objective of killing Prime Minister Margaret Thatcher, "You only have to get lucky once." He seemed to think that it would have achieved a resolution of the Ulster situation in favour of the Nationalists. I am unsure about that, and not just because I would be unlikely in any case to sympathise with his views. They would not have got lucky; they would have got very unlucky. I don't quite buy the idea that Reagan and Thatcher by being vital bulwarks against Communism brought about the collapse of the Soviet Union (though undoubtedly the latter blinked first) and saved the free world, but given the state of the Labour Party and the unworkability/unpopularity of many of its policies Thatcher was a necessary evil, a rock against instability, inefficiency and dysfunction. I sense she would have been perceived as such outside the UK. Had the IRA succeeded in killing her, the British nation or most of it would have rallied round the government, the forces of authority and of law and order, in a massive retaliation against Irish nationalism. We would probably have seen the reintroduction of internment. The Republicans would only have been creating more trouble for themselves. Possibly not only Britain but other countries as well would have got involved. It is true that Libya's Colonel Gaddafi sponsored the IRA, as did elements among the Irish population in the United States (NORAID), and also that in the 1990s US President Clinton, not preoccupied as his predecessors had been by the Cold War, and aware that helping to achieve an acceptable settlement would reinforce his popularity among Irish American voters, became closely involved in the peace process. But otherwise the Northern Irish question has never had an international dimension. Ireland is a relatively small country, and Ulster a smaller area still; there would have been anger at the disruption to global stability because of the region's problems, its passions and hatreds. The shock of Thatcher's murder would have acted as a spur to the international community, and the US (led by her friend Ronald Reagan) in particular, to get involved and sort the situation out, which was possibly what my friend from Eire meant. But the immediate "settlement" would have been harshly imposed, and he was estimating that things would have been resolved in the way he wanted. Nothing would have made any difference to the Unionists' refusal to accept any change in Ulster's constitutional relationship with the UK, and their determination to uphold the Union by violence if necessary. Republicans, northern or southern, would not have had an easy time of it; so much so that they would not really have been able to enjoy their United Ireland. In the past it has been the fault of the Irish that their passion at an injustice clouds their judgement so that they sometimes do not know what is good for them (here it must be noted that hard-headed politicians in Dublin were always aware of the difficulties of absorbing Ulster into the Republic, and only appeared to support such a policy for electoral reasons).

What of Ulster today? Generally the peace agreement has held up well but there are danger signs, including social problems of the sort which in the past have found an outlet in political discontent. However this reflects the fact that northern Ireland (along with the Republic) is beginning to suffer from the same problems as everywhere else in the West, i.e. marginalisation, poverty, crime, and the clash between changing times and traditional mindsets, the latter influenced in Ulster's case by traditional Presbyterianism and seen in their extreme form in the killing of a lesbian journalist. And though it seems inappropriate to say so it was almost a relief a few years ago to find violence taking place in the province over immigration instead of the traditional sectarian divide (a decline in the attractiveness of religion makes it more difficult to use it as a label over which to fight). If the Troubles do return it will not be in the same form as before, but rather as part of a general, crazy outburst against everything someone or other finds not to their liking. The Brexit has undoubtedly added to the problem, exacerbating it by the uncertainty and thus unease it has created; difficulties were always liable to be encountered in the relationship between Ulster and what Unionists regard as the mother country if they diverged over an issue of such fundamental constitutional importance. It is the same with Scotland, with the qualification that in the Scottish case the potential for violence is probably much less. It may not actually be as great in Ulster as one is inclined to fear; protests by young people there against the murder of the abovementioned journalist show that they are not prepared to accept intolerance and political violence, and this presumably applies to differences over the province's status as much as anything else.

<h1 style="text-align:center">6</h1>

Nobody expected the Tory defeat in 1997 to be quite as overwhelming as it was. Its scale was partly due to tactical voting by Liberal Democrats who felt they wanted the Tories out at any cost. But it was not really wise to give New Labour, as its spin doctors called it, such a huge majority, for they were no more perfect than Thatcherite Conservatism had been − in so far as they did not amount to the same thing, and there is nothing cheap about such a remark − and in their own way did as much damage to the country. When they got in my feeling, although I had voted Conservative, was that Tony Blair, who still seemed an unknown quantity, should be given a chance, and if I liked what I saw in 2001 or 2002 I might conceivably vote for him then. As with John Major in 1990 I was to be shatteringly disappointed.

To be honest there was always something fundamentally insincere about New Labour, and it followed inevitably from the changes that had been made to the party. That it still called itself "Labour" suggested it was particularly oriented towards the working classes, as Old Labour had been. Of course the name had always been suspect because it implied the middle classes never worked, which actually they did. Not that "Labour Party" members, the less vengeful and class-obsessed anyway, were necessarily indifferent to their needs and interests, recognising for example that their standard of living could go down if they were affected by economic recession or the loss of a breadwinner, and the ultimate aim was for *everyone* to benefit from the creation of what was thought would be a more just society where wealth was distributed more fairly. But the latter point reminds us that previously Labour had been, or had seen itself as, a *socialist* party, i.e. one which as a major plank in its platform believed the most vital industries should be nationalised − that is, run by the government, which meant in theory that they belonged to the people, if the former were seen as the latter's servants, rather than private companies. The terms "Labour" and "socialist" came to be more or less synonymous in the eyes both of the party itself and its opponents.

Once Clause Four in Labour's manifesto, which called for nationalisation, had been dropped and other changes made to its traditional programme there was nothing much that was socialist, that I could see, about the party, and in fact the term no longer seemed to be used much. The whole reformist trend, which began under Kinnock and gathered pace under Blair, was of course always resented by many on the left wing, prominent dissidents including Dennis Skinner, miner's leader Arthur Scargill and Eric Heffer. The name "Labour" was retained to keep them happy and preserve party unity. Some left, notably Scargill; others stayed and, because they could at last sense a real change in the party's fortunes, would grumble but never seriously rock the boat, before or after 1997, so glad were they to be out of the wilderness. But for political reasons, the falsehood that Tony Blair's party was a "Labour" party (though it was not quite clear what the term meant anyway if "socialist" was no longer fashionable) had to be maintained. (And it was perhaps even more false now that the traditional working class, who formed the greater part of "Labour's" constituency, had largely ceased to exist because the heavy industries from which they made their living, notably coal, had been replaced by a service economy, a process that also to some extent reduced the gap in prosperity and living standards between the north of England (previously seen as core Labour territory) and the south.) It had really become, in so far as it was all that different from the Tories in terms of policy, a social democratic party, but the name could not be changed to reflect this because of the uproar that would have been provoked from the Left despite the matter being purely symbolic. The tragedy was that Labour could only get itself back into power by ceasing to be Labour, and in its eagerness to return to office this was something it had blinded itself to. It was a product of the dilemma, referred to above, that except at certain times socialist parties operating within a Western parliamentary context can only make progress by either pursuing policies which are not acceptable to the electorate – who in Britain had given their verdict at four general elections – or by adopting those of the main conservative party and pretending they are nonetheless something different from it.

New Labour was to some extent a coalition, if one where "Blairism" was very much the dominant partner. Though in essence more like the former SDP or the Liberal Democrats, both of whom were attracted to it as a result, than Old Labour it felt for pragmatic reasons as much as anything else that it needed, within limits, to appease the remaining Old Labour MPs and activists within the party and appeal to the traditional heartlands of its support. Where the effect of this was significant, it could also be dysfunctional. Money was diverted from the south of England to supposedly poorer and more deserving regions in the north. This had a lasting legacy which even the likes of David Cameron failed for some reason to address. Today the borough of Spelthorne, in which I live, is unable to pay both for social services and for maintaining its roads and pavements, which look like becoming unusable in a short time. I would have thought that was every bit as serious a problem.

The dichotomy between what "Labour" called itself and any actual meaning the term might have did not matter much provided it governed the country wisely and fairly. But Blair offended both old-style socialists, even if they didn't go so far as to resign from the party, and traditionalist conservatives (with a small or large "c"). The tendency towards privatisation and commercialisation (they amount to essentially the same thing) begun by Thatcher has continued up to the present day, through a period which encompasses the New Labour years, and in fact become more marked, with an increasing number of services being performed by private companies in the view that this makes for greater efficiency than if the state does the job, as well as removing the financial burden on the latter. Labour simply could not reverse Margaret Thatcher's achievement and decided they had to embrace it in order to survive. In so doing they perpetuated all the ills which arose from Thatcherism, as well as its benefits. For one thing the credit crunch that led to the recession of 2007-8 and after, and was caused by banks being insufficiently regulated and encouraging customers to take out loans at a rate which overheated the system, occurred under New Labour. It was not so much socialism as capitalism behaving badly.

Labour was forced by pragmatism to adapt to what have become the two dominant ideologies in society and politics in the modern Western world: monetarist, that is free market, economics, the system which in effect we are still living under (to view things in their full historical context), and, in sociopolitical affairs, that policy which is called, usually derogatorily, political correctness. In accord with the end of the Cold War and the world collapse of Communism, indeed socialism, as an economic doctrine, the political Left transferred its attention to other areas. To some degree it would be correct to say that "Liberalism", as it had developed in the West from the eighteenth and nineteenth centuries, and as exemplified by figures like Gladstone, merged with the remains of Hard Left socialism to create political correctness; for many, whatever their views (some may even be Tories), to be politically correct is what "liberalism" now means. Within Labour this meant an evolution from a working-class socialist party to a middle-class liberal politically correct party. Some thought it was not entirely comfortable with the change. But undoubtedly political correctness, which contains much that is dangerously misguided as well as much that is good, continued to entrench itself under New Labour, who did nothing to curb its more obnoxious features.

The apparent unassailability of what had become the dominant "narratives", along with the historic difficulty for the Labour Party of pursuing a radical approach without becoming too Leftist for the electorate's liking, brought about in effect a return to consensus only it was in favour of upholding the free market rather than state involvement and Keynesianism, which "Butskellism" had not been. It meant that it was sometimes difficult for New Labour, including Gordon Brown when he became Prime Minister and naturally (not just out of animosity) sought to distinguish the character of his premiership from that of his predecessor's, to find exciting new policies with which they could be identified. This helped foster a certain cynicism. The main perceivable difference between the two main parties was that Labour were perhaps more inclined to embrace political correctness than the Tories, at least until David Cameron adopted the same "if you can't beat 'em…" philosophy towards it, most notably by legalising gay marriage, which was done both from conviction on his part that it was just and as a way of capturing the liberal vote. But of course the very success of PC in achieving power and influence meant they could not in any case easily challenge it, should they want to.

Again, the convergence of the two parties in terms of ideology was due to the ascendancy of political correctness (more likely to be obeyed by North Europeans, such as the British, than by more rebellious Latins however much the former might complain about it) on the one hand and free market economics on the other. The Establishment, whether Labour or Conservative in its affiliations, was unwilling to take on either and indeed reluctant to admit to the power they now commanded in the first place. Neither philosophy was always subscribed to at heart by the general public, who simply sought to be at least reasonably prosperous and, hopefully, believed all members of society should have a decent chance in life, without necessarily seeing a particular (and sometimes questionable) set of policies as the means of achieving the latter aim. But their dominance was maintained by powerful interest groups in the business sector on the one hand (today's City tycoons are certainly not Keynesians) and the arts, media, education, local government, in addition to influential pressure groups and quangos, on the other. Neither main party was prepared to take on these people – keeping interest groups happy has always been seen as a crucial part of political management – and there was still a pathological fear that a return to corporatism and consensus would mean strikes, inflation and stagnation. And so no-one could offer any radical approach, that distinguished one party significantly from the other, to the government of the nation and the resolution of the issues facing it. There were instead a host of policies, such as elected mayors for the regions, affecting particular areas which did not necessarily enthuse the public nor make a difference to the most pressing problems. Hence the perception, leading to political apathy, that there was nothing to choose between Labour and the Tories. There was a new consensus (in effect) but it was even more marked than the one destroyed by Margaret Thatcher, and in a negative way, being disillusioning when combined with a feeling that politicians were even more untrustworthy, and even more concerned only with looking and sounding impressive when under the media spotlight, than they had been in the days of Wilson.

In the new consensus personalities (groomed to look "sexy" before the public and media) perhaps mattered more than ideologies, until it all began to seem a bit too false. And *policy* mattered more than ideology did, in the people's opinion anyway. By 1997 single (though important) issues, rather than the basic political and economic system a party supported, could decide the outcome of an election. The effective agreement to endorse a continuation of Thatcherism in one form or another was more on the Establishment's part than the people's but the latter certainly did not want a return to rampant inflation and strikes (and of course they were keen to take advantage of economic prosperity where they could, though that is not really the point we're concerned with). Now that Labour were sound on the economy you could vote the Tories in, or throw them out, on the basis of some other issue, health for example. This as we have seen is more or less what happened.

Regarding Tony Blair himself, there was some uncertainty about what he believed, indeed about whether he believed anything, apart from the need to accept and work with the prevailing sociopolitical and economic trends (from genuinely reforming and benign intentions, though that was not how cynics saw it). Many of his more solid achievements were inherited from Major. And those policies he *did* implement off his own bat he was often uncertain about (although in the case of the Iraq War he showed a remarkable ability to bury his misgivings) in private, pursuing them for essentially political reasons. He had for example strong reservations about Scottish and Welsh devolution, a policy he had inherited from John Smith in such a way that it was effectively forced on him.

Overall, what really mattered was how well the country was governed. The general consensus of opinion, apparently backed up by the evidence, suggests that on the economy Labour did get it right, until the credit crunch happened (they also performed better, I think, on the NHS than the Tories did, a crucial difference). But apart from the fact that Blair was essentially riding on the success of Kenneth Clarke, economics is to some extent a construct, and a good balance sheet may disguise the fact that while some, perhaps the majority, are doing well others are not. Inner-city areas no longer looked as run-down as they had in the 70s and 80s but there was still too large a gap between the well-off and less well-off, still a problem with homelessness and drugs and delinquency, still social atomisation and alienation. All these are issues you are likely to get with Thatcherism if you are not careful; the policy was still doing the harm it had been attacked for in the 80s, if not in quite the same way, yet now with the acquiescence of the party which had originally condemned it so vociferously. There was concern about falling standards of education despite the latter being one of the areas Blair said he wanted to give priority to ("Education, education, education"). And about the transport infrastructure; during this period many of the nation's roads were allowed to get into appalling condition, necessitating the current programme of major repairs. Labour failed to do anything about the difficulties faced by many of the long-term unemployed in making themselves appear reliable, following years out of work, in the eyes of prospective employers. At least half of those on often badly-run training schemes failed to get anything out of them, and the true scale of the problem was disguised by the tendency to classify those on a scheme as "working", which they were not. In effect the government was doctoring the figures, which raises the question: if it could do that, what *else* was it doctoring?

Blair certainly had an odd sense of priorities. While failing to address a range of issues of considerably greater importance, he put a lot of effort into the banning of fox hunting – definitely a politically correct cause, although one with which many people would sympathise. He also proclaimed spiritedly the need to take on the "tyranny of the suit and tie", as if it was a matter of grave social concern. This was a form of political correctness – the philosophy covers a multitude of sins – because formal attire could be seen as an attempt to intimidate or to snobbishly suggest you were superior to those who weren't wearing it. (Perhaps his keenness to overthrow Saddam Hussein was due to Saddam having appeared on TV in suit and tie, and on another occasion in hunting tweeds, instead of military gear in a bid to improve his image.)

And Blair, like Wilson, lowered the tone of public life. He did it by the unequal distribution of voting rights between England and Scotland, even if there were reasons for same. He did it by taking money for his party's funds which had essentially been made, by the businessman Richard Desmond, from the sale of pornography (arguably, if we are to avoid unhealthy sexual repression pornography has its place in society, but it should stay there; even Mrs Thatcher would not have taken the philosophy that "business is business" so far). He carried to even greater lengths than anyone else the trend for political leaders to behave according to how they should come over on the media, tailoring everything they said and did for its consumption and making speeches which had been prepared for them by professional "spin doctors". His own "creators" were Peter Mandelson and Alistair Campbell.

In the public's eyes his greatest offence, of course, was committing Britain to participation alongside America in the 2003 war with Iraq, despite a lack of convincing evidence that Saddam Hussein had weapons of mass destruction. Evil tyrant though he undoubtedly was, the removal of Saddam's strong hand explains why more people are being killed in Iraq now than under his regime, through religious conflict and persecution which he, being interested simply in power politics and maintaining his personal rule, had always kept in check. The civilian government set up after the war has been seriously destabilised by Islamic militants, many of them coming in from Iran. It constitutes a further stage in the escalation of the developing global conflict between radical Islam and the West. Anger at the war on the part of Islamic fundamentalists was almost certainly responsible for the terrorist atrocities in London in July 2005, though the government in its investigation into the matter was notably reluctant to explore the possible connection.

The grotesque farcicality of Blair putting himself forward as a peace envoy to the Middle East, a capacity in which he achieved remarkably little, doesn't really need commenting upon. A particular example of his being totally unsuited to such a role was his assigning of Lord Levy (acting for the British government) to the post in the belief that it would redress a certain pro-Palestinian bias in popular and public affairs. He appears not to have considered that the appointment of a Jew would be perceived as just another example of the opposite tendency; even if such a view of it was unsubstantiated, he was being extremely injudicious. It would surely have been better to have someone who was neither Arab nor Jew and thus less likely to provoke accusations of partiality from either side. There would I am sure have been no shortage of people happy to take on the task and perhaps do something to halt or at least mitigate a terrible conflict which has plagued the part of the world in question for far too long.

Blair changed the law of this country so as to make it easier for it to sell arms to Israel – arms which in all probability, the Middle East situation being what it is, would be used at some point to kill Palestinian civilians. There was no need for him to have so assiduously done what would only serve to attract hostility to Britain on the part of people like al-Qaeda when Israel could in the end have got the bulk of what she needed from the Americans (as usual). And returning to the Iraq war, if the justification for it was that we were liberating oppressed minorities or dissidents we would by the same token have had to invade a score of other countries as well.

Blair had a very strange and somewhat alarming sense of logic. It could have been called convoluted but it would be more accurate to say that it was purely and simply absurd. When questioned by a reporter about the public's fears regarding the war, and their perception that it was wrong, the defence he put forward was staggering. His argument was that their opposition to the war showed their concern about the issue, which he was addressing by prosecuting the war! The implication of this, if we may conduct a little philosophical exercise here, would be that (a) the opposite of something is in fact its essence, and (b) people essentially wish for something other than what they indicate by their behaviour. What an actual professor of philosophy would say about this I have no idea.

On another occasion, tackled on the possible consequences of the conflict, Blair adopted an incredulous tone and said that if he thought they would be harmful "I, I wouldn't do it {i.e. involve Britain in the war}, would I???!!" Such a reaction to one's policies being questioned is inappropriate where there are legitimate grounds for doubt (even if this applies both ways). Of course those who actually supported the war weren't necessarily stupid. But given the arguments against it, plus Blair's whole attitude to issues and the way he defended his views on them, his response does rather sound like someone indignantly denying that monkeys playing with matches in a gunpowder barrel could be dangerous.

Blair at one point wanted international law to be changed to make it easier for war to be declared on regimes such as Saddam's; to embark on adventures about which many people might have serious misgivings. The disastrous results that would follow if the world community was committed to attacking every country that had or was thought to have a nasty government can be imagined. Not only did Blair continually assert that two plus two equalled five, but he was seeming also to assert that it *obviously* made five, and no-one but a fool could possibly think otherwise. The earnest solemnity with which he tried to defend his Iraq policy when it became apparent serious opposition to it was mounting merely introduced an element of bathos. There was a certain change of image, but it didn't amount to much. Initially on Iraq his approach came over something like, "It is quite right to say that two plus two equals five, *AND THE RIGHT HONOURABLE GENTLEMAN KNOWS IT IS!!!!*" It soon became clear, however, that such had failed to win the public over. So what Mr Blair then did was this. He stood before us with his hands clasped before him and addressed us in a grave, subdued, dignified tone of voice. "I know some people will talk about common sense...that we must choose the lesser of the evils, that we should not go from the frying pan {though unless you were a Kurd or one of his domestic political opponents, Saddam wasn't really that} into the fire.

"But I know...that two plus two *does* make five...that two wrongs *do* make a right...and that my policy that this country...should take the step of committing its troops to an invasion by air, land and sea of the fire *is* the correct policy...and that history will prove me right. Thankyou."

And if that didn't make sense to us, it did to Mr Blair.

What explains all this, psychologically? There have been some enigmatic figures in the history of British politics, but Blair, while not having the same stature as the others (possessing the ability to sense a sea change in affairs, radiating an aura of glamour, and grouping the right forces behind you by the force of your will do not, singly or together, necessarily amount to greatness), is the most enigmatic of them all. It is hard to say exactly what he is, and I get the impression this puzzled view of him is not uncommon. It has been said that he is a rare type, a vulnerable extrovert, and this sets one asking questions without necessarily supplying the answers, since it is usually introverted people who come over as vulnerable, and hard to see why extroverts should be so.

Does Blair suffer from a form of autism, of Asperger Syndrome? Having been diagnosed with the condition myself I now find I have acquired the tendency to be constantly detecting it, or thinking I have detected it, in others. This can be unhelpful, excessively Freudian. But something similar to autism could well explain why Blair is unable to see why certain policies, certain attitudes, certain political positions – a Middle East policy so biased in favour of Israel, the taking of money for political purposes from the proceeds of porn, the totally unacceptable involvement of a public relations adviser, Alistair Campbell, in actual policy-making – are wrong and give offence. The cause might be some condition which has the same effect, or the autism be combined with other things whose nature we can only guess at. But whatever it is, it does offer an answer to the question why Blair, an enthusiastically professed Christian, was able to act much of the time in what in many respects was a strikingly unchristian manner. It is possible his Christianity was perfectly sincere. But if the mind is like the body, in that it is an electrochemical complex with which, in an imperfect world, things can go wrong, then it is quite possible for Christians to be affected by medical conditions of a mental nature just as other people are. (Blair's apparent disassociation of Christianity from political morality may also have been a case of pragmatism in a society where an aggressively secular element has become highly influential. It was perhaps the reason why, when a reporter once asked him whether certain of his policies didn't rather go against Christian ethics, Alistair Campbell (an atheist) stepped forward to intervene with the words "We don't do God questions." Apart from anything else, on this occasion at least Campbell was not allowing Blair to speak for himself).

There was also, somehow, something very immature about Blair, as if he was playing with the British constitution and global politics like they were a set of child's toy building bricks. Which of course they weren't.

Perhaps the key, or part of the key, to understanding Tony Blair is to appreciate that he was in large measure manufactured, by Messrs Mandelson and Campbell. Of course, they had been given a job to do and since Blair was their employer, they did it. Someone had to be Prime Minister, and that person required advice on public relations. No doubt they exulted in the power they felt this gave them, which was only human. But it must have been to some extent a two-way process, which meant Mandelson and Campbell could not have gone against Blair's wishes on policy matters in the end (how far Campbell agreed with him about the actual wisdom of the Iraq war, for example, is a matter of conjecture). However, underneath a slick media-savvy exterior lay the real Tony Blair, who for some reason we don't understand was deeply insecure. It showed in the nervous, self-conscious grin (different to his usual one) he sometimes displayed when in the company of other world leaders at a summit. This was reminiscent of the mannerisms employed by the comedian Hugh Laurie, with whom there is a certain facial resemblance.

The most obvious manifestation of Blair's inner vulnerability was his need to identify himself with US President George Bush, the world's most powerful man, over the Iraq question. Bush certainly responded to his advances, and this chemistry helped to cement the London-Washington alliance. There remains the strong suspicion that Bush, who was never as stupid as he liked to appear in order to look cute and increase his appeal to voters, was taking Blair for a ride.

Insecurity also made Blair a control freak. He was intolerant of opposition and determined to freeze it out. The reduction in the numbers of hereditary peers in the House of Lords and their replacement by nominees − "Tony's cronies" − was sought not just because it was thought fair or sensible but because it was a way of consolidating the Prime Minister's power.

Whether Blair's "autism" was a product of his insecurity or combined with it to negative effect we cannot say. But it (the insecurity) was definitely there and explains an unwillingness to admit one may be wrong (while the autism would account for a difficulty in *understanding* alternative viewpoints). It resulted in the evolution of psychological devices whereby Blair was able to convince himself, perhaps by autosuggestion, of the rightness of something most rational people would have rejected. It wasn't lying, as some claimed, in the usual sense of the term but more a form of self-delusion. Although there was a certain justification, whatever the perceived obnoxiousness of the injustice, for granting Scotland and Wales devolution while retaining their MPs' right to legislate on matters affecting England because to do otherwise would be effectively to force Scotland into independence when she was not suited for it, and the Ulster peace process might not have worked unless imprisoned IRA murderers had been released (though that may not reflect well on Irish people), there is no doubt that it (the self-delusion) made it easier for Blair to countenance what others might have drawn back from.

When Blair came out with a totally ludicrous explanation why he wanted to do such-and-such there was perhaps no point in attempting to analyse it, if you understood as far as one could what made the man tick, beyond establishing that it *was* ludicrous. He simply could not admit he was mistaken and searched frantically for whatever supporting argument came to mind, even if it made no sense whatsoever. Another psychological device which he employed as a defence mechanism was to take the moral high ground. Once during the 1997 election campaign he was asked a question he did not know how to answer. He began to splutter, clearly caught out. "Well, strictly speaking, I suppose, I-I-I-I..." His face then froze with anger as he asked the interviewer, "Well what sort of a question is that?" He was covering himself by taking the line that the question should not have been asked in the first place, so that he was excused from replying to it. This is quite a clever tactic in a way; not only is one exonerated from giving an answer, but one is *morally* exonerated from doing so, so that the evasion of criticism becomes sanctified. I'm not convinced, however, that it fools everyone.

For Tony Blair, the Labour Party was a means to an end, the implementation of the policies he saw as being for the common good, as with Peel and the Tories in the 1830s and 40s; less trouble was caused with respect to party unity and governmental stability because Labour's aims coincided with his own, or at least it was prepared to put up with a lot rather than be cast back into the wilderness. By extension, plus autosuggestion, whatever furthered Blair's aims was permissible. It was a psychological condition translated into a political philosophy and by extension a system of government. With a poor grasp of policy, along with his messianic outlook, Blair was better at handling particular issues with which he had a personal concern. This paid dividends when he was right but proved calamitous when he was wrong.

Generally, he met a vital need in that the Tory Party was unelectable for most of the period from 1997 to 2007. He was pretty good on the NHS and, with the reservation that certain groups remained continually excluded from prosperity and advancement, the economy. Efficiency in financial matters was ensured by allowing a competent Chancellor of the Exchequer, Brown, who remained in the post for ten years, to do more or less what he liked. The latter included transferring responsibility for setting interest rates to the Bank of England, a policy which worked although it appeared to demonstrate an undemocratic aspect to New Labour; there is something disturbing (and very Blairite) about the matter not being under the control of an elected government (assuming that is the same thing as its being owned by the people); in other words not being under "democratic" scrutiny. It was fixing that counted, not democracy.

Some might not regard this as a plus but Blair, partly because of his comparative youth, was the first British PM to be "modern", often dressing casually and using contemporary jargon (such as "core values"), the parlance of the private business in a commercialised as well as politically correct world. He introduced this whole ethos into the British political and parliamentary environment. In private life his conduct was impeccable; he has always been touchingly faithful to his wife, who he married across a certain class barrier. Rupert Murdoch's absurd claim that Blair had an affair with Wendi Deng was a figment of a twisted, festering and suspicious mind. However Blair probably helped to discredit the idea of Christianity in politics, for he was a man who would spend hours praying and still come away convinced that two and two made five.

Blair was not a wicked man, but he was delusional. He was not a stupid man, but his intelligence was of a strange, perverse kind. The falsity of New Labour's position, in that it was New to the point of not being Labour at all but would not say so, would not have bothered someone with such a pathological capacity to distort the truth, and who was therefore an ideal person to lead it (the motives of his followers being simply pragmatic). But what made the praise of loyal Blairites in the party, and his more sycophantic admirers generally, who would describe him as the greatest and most successful Prime Minister of modern times, so nauseating was a combination of two things. Firstly, there were the issues he was ignoring and the harm he was doing to the country in so many ways. Secondly, Blair was being kept in power, as Margaret Thatcher had been, by the weakness of the Opposition. The situation the Conservative Party was in from 1997 to 2010 roughly parallels that of Labour from 1980 (when Foot took over its leadership from Callaghan, although the trouble had started before then) to 1997. It went through a succession of leaders who were either duds or, in the case of Michael Howard, worthy but still not what was required for victory, before hitting the jackpot with David Cameron. William Hague, a not untalented individual who through misplaced enthusiasm tragically found himself in a job he wasn't suited for, was somehow unable to get enough people, particularly among the general public, to take him seriously. He did the right thing in the eyes of fellow Tories by taking an attractive young wife, Ffion Jenkins – here proving himself the diametric opposite of Ted Heath – but she was a modern woman who wanted her own career, her own life, and consequently was not particularly visible within the Party and likely to be an asset to it. Ian Duncan-Smith was possibly the worst party leader ever, in his lack of acumen and ability to inspire; it was unfortunate that he told the faithful when having problems with them to beware of the "Quiet Man" (i.e. himself), only for the Quiet Man to turn out, in this case, precisely what he was so often assumed to be – ineffectual. IDS may have been a good soldier, but he was a dreadful politician.

In policy terms what the Tories should of course have done, from 1997 if not from 1990, was to be less Thatcherite in the social and economic sphere, with sensible restrictions on the power of the private sector and no quarter given to policies like casualisation, but right-wing on such issues as Europe, immigration and the preservation of traditional institutions, as would certainly have been a sound strategy in terms of maintaining the party's core support and would not *necessarily* have reflected xenophobia or racial prejudice. Their failure to do this explains the shape of British politics during the past two decades. It would have been a winning combination. In moving to the left in areas where to do so might be appreciated the Tories would be compensating for Labour having stolen their clothes by moving to the right (if being right-wing nowadays includes favouring a monetarist/Thatcherite economic policy, which it does). Unfortunately, there were and are major obstacles to such a rebranding because the Tories who would be tough on immigration, for example, are not the ones who would be liberal in social and economic policy. It's the same problem with UKIP, a large part of whose membership is composed of ex-Thatcherites of the "hang 'em and flog 'em" sort, who left the Conservative Party because on Europe at any rate it wasn't right-wing enough for them. Then as now, voting Tory (or UKIP) would mean getting the right-wing policies one wanted, but not the left-wing ones. With Jeremy Corbyn's Labour it would have been the reverse.

Britain's entanglement in the folly of the Iraq war led to Tony Blair stepping down as Prime Minister in 2007, though he would not admit it to be the cause. He was uncomfortable about being in the public eye with so much anger and opprobrium focused on him, besides the pressure from those who felt it was high time Gordon Brown, who after all had been more or less promised the crown some years before, took over. New Labour staggered on for three years, but by now people were becoming tired of it, and Brown lacked the sensitivity and the cuddly image that might have endeared him to voters. At the same time there was suspicion that a Tory Party led by David Cameron, a "posh" ex-public school pupil who in addition could be seen ideologically as Margaret Thatcher Mk II, would be out of touch with the nation as a whole and therefore not qualified to solve its pressing social problems, however slick a performer he might be on television. The nation was unattracted by Brown but not sufficiently enamoured of Cameron for the election to produce any result other than a hung parliament. It was possibly a symptom of the growing feeling that there was no longer anything to choose between the two main parties ("Whichever way you vote, the government will get in."). It is true that in 1974 Powell had derided the election of February that year as a contest between "a man with a pipe" (Wilson) and "a man with a boat" (Heath, a keen yachtsman). But Powell, the proto-Thatcherite, disliked consensus politics anyway. The nation as a whole had been happy with it as long as politicians were interesting personalities and there was still some faith in the political system as a whole. Neither Butskellism nor having to vote for a man with a pipe or a man with a boat produced political apathy.

The proliferation of issues which the Thatcherite-PC state, if one may call it that, had failed to address (or which, in the case of the Iraq war, arose from the mindset of its leader) led to a certain rise in single-issue parties, e.g. Respect (formerly the Stop The War Coalition), the BNP, the Green Party. In one election the constituency of Kidderminster was won by a candidate whose platform was opposition to the closure of a local hospital. Unfortunately, this tendency had the counter-productive consequences of further splitting the vote; and so the government got in. (Another problem with single-issue parties is that one is never quite sure what other policies and beliefs they have – for they would need to have them – and what agenda their principal area of concern can serve to distract attention from, serving as a smokescreen whether or not it is intended to. Recently some Green councillors attempted to deny church representatives on the local authority's education committee the right to vote at its meetings, presumably from a belief that the church in the modern world is not representative. It was mean because the church has always been interested/involved in educational matters, recognising their importance, and church schools have usually been highly rated. This suggests that the Greens' agenda, besides being environmentalist, is secularising and has much in common with that left-wing philosophy which tends to despise religion. But they may have other policies, too, which are unjust or at least controversial.)

Anyhow, something had changed for the worse in British politics. One effect, not in itself harmful, was the first coalition government since 1945, the partners being the Tories and the Liberal Democrats. This government actually performed reasonably well, however much the Tories might complain that the need to be sensitive to Lib Dem opinion, the not being master in one's own right, prevented them from doing their job properly. One Conservative activist in my area has said that he would have been quite happy for the coalition to have lasted longer than it did. It is not quite clear exactly why it broke down. The reason for the Lib Dems being all but destroyed at the 2015 election is said to have been that they were regarded as tainted by their association with the Tories, but the same public who are supposed to have felt that way returned the latter with a majority large enough to govern in their own right. And perhaps do even more damage. The Lib Dems did not deserve a hammering of the sort they got because they probably prevented the Tories from carrying out measures which would have impacted severely upon the more vulnerable members of society. It may seem totalitarian to criticise the general public but it will have become apparent by now that voters are often irrational, inconsistent and unfair!

Cameron had achieved his victory by convincing enough of the electorate that for the country to fully recover from the recession caused by the credit crunch it needed to be entrusted to a safe pair of hands. That certainly did not mean the Labour Party, which had been led very ineffectually for the last three years by Ed Miliband (his brother David would have been a better investment). This factor proved sufficient to reverse, for the time being, any trend towards seeing the main parties as symmetric in every respect, and thus avoid its electoral implications. Something else now happened to cement that.

Labour had tried the Blairite, social democratic model, the only alternative to which was to go back to old-style socialism including the reinstatement of Clause Four. It seemed to them to be discredited by the Iraq war and Blair's style of government (though the problem had really been one of personalities; at any rate the public saw things more in those terms than as a matter of competing ideologies). They had been demoralised by the backlash against them at the 2015 election, after thirteen years of power, and the deadening effect of Miliband's leadership. And at the same time there was a growing anger within left-wing politics at the still wide, and widening, gulf between the prosperous and the less prosperous – in some cases, unemployed and/or homeless – members of society. Rather than take on the business sector, with whom as a successful businessman himself he identified, and being cast in the Thatcherite mould, David Cameron was adopting, in the shape of "austerity" cuts to the welfare budget, a monetarist rather than a Keynesian solution to the problems stemming from the recession, despite the fact that it was the financial sector, in the shape of the banks, who had caused the trouble in the first place. The wrath of the Left became directed towards the Blairism which they saw as simply a perpetuation of the Tory policies they reviled, and which they were no longer prepared to tolerate (according to their book it was no different from the essentially social democratic "pale pink Toryism" of the Wilson years, and indeed the two did ideologically amount to much the same thing, packaged to look dynamic and exciting). In the end Labour moderates failed to prevent the election as leader of stock 1980s hard-Left figure Jeremy Corbyn, who basically sought to commit the party to all the policies which distinguished it, and disqualified it from office, thirty years before. There was a weird feeling of having somehow passed through a time warp. Consensus had broken down again and polarisation returned as a major feature of politics. Within the Labour party ineffective leadership had been replaced by leadership that was ideologically unacceptable.

To some, anyway. Of course, there are many beyond Labour's left wing who understandably feel some sympathy for Jeremy Corbyn's views, when the Conservative party has increasingly become the party of the well-off – through either greed, or a refusal to countenance unwelcome change – as it was under Thatcher and for the same reasons. Some saw Corbyn as more honest than either Cameron or Blair was. But being honest is not the same as being right. And if Corbyn believed he was riding on a certain revulsion against the status quo, which was not confined to a small minority, then he could afford to be honest because his views and those of people who, without necessarily wanting to vote Labour, sympathised with him coincided to some extent. Whether he would be quite so frank once he got into power and the negative consequences of hard-Left policies became apparent was another matter. We have had moderate, meaning here centrist/right-wing, Labour governments, right-wing Conservative governments, and Heathite Conservative governments. But the form of government Britain has never had, under the democratic parliamentary system, is a truly left-wing Labour one; Attlee's was not that so much as a body of people with a brief to implement a particular set of policies in a particular situation. Accordingly one might have thought Corbyn and Co. should be given a chance. But although it might be interesting to see what happened (the belief of one acquaintance of mine was that the system could cope with it), that does not mean we would necessarily enjoy the experience.

A member of the Labour Party has accurately described Corbyn to me as a good campaigner but not so good a leader. Rather than adopt a hands-on approach he was someone who simply created an environment in which the things he wanted could happen. He did this through having a certain charisma part of which involved portraying himself as actually quite a decent chap, whatever you might think of his policies. Thus he was able to preserve his authority within the party while in practical terms working through ideologically compatible fellow travellers (his henchmen/women, one might crudely put it). It is a familiar story and for that reason highly disturbing. Exact comparisons between Corbyn and Hitler would be dubious, but the methods are often the same. Extremists of Left and Right fall into two main categories. There are those from disadvantaged working-class backgrounds who want to change the system in order to improve their lot, blaming their problems on an entrenched hegemony of the rich and privileged, or immigrants taking one's job, or both. Then there are middle-class activists who, having had plenty of advantages, should have prospered but did not owing to their own lack of application and blame the system for the consequences of their own inadequacies, seeking to bring it down. Corbyn falls into the second category – as did Hitler, a principal difference between the two being that Corbyn identified with marginalised minorities, rather than the nation as a whole, as fellow "victims", the inverted commas applying more in his case than theirs. Like Hitler he was a sociopath and control freak, but clever enough to be highly dangerous, knowing how to exploit deeply-rooted grievances for his own ends. A Corbyn premiership would have been nothing short of utterly disastrous for the country. Generally his way of operating, controversial enough as it was, was not really suited to that post.

There was one way in which a new alignment in British politics, that might or might not prove beneficial, could be brought about. Could the remains of the Liberal Democrats unite with Labour moderates unhappy at Jeremy Corbyn to form a new centre-left party? (There would be considerable opposition to losing the name "Liberal", because it was historic and a link to the days of Gladstone, Lloyd George etc., so it might have been better to call the new party the Social Liberals rather than merely revive the old SDP). David Cameron and George Osborne, who were nothing if not politically shrewd, anticipated this in their attempts to capture the same ground by appearing to backtrack on austerity (and to in other ways shift leftwards, see below).

But in doing those things, in showing that he understood how the average person, or the disadvantaged members of society, felt Cameron always seemed insincere, as if he was acting from political calculation and not genuine compassion. It was all to do with slick presentation, though not arising from an inner vulnerability as was the case with Blair, who was also more sincere in some ways, the real problem being what he was sincere about (comparisons between the two men can be misleading even if one clearly learnt a lot from the other just as, in an earlier era, Wilson learnt a lot from Macmillan). Cameron might have been the lesser of the evils, as Thatcher was. But to those wanting a less unjust and more egalitarian Britain he didn't read as trustworthy.

Though coming from a rather narrow social class he was in psychological terms a normal human being, with none of the curious hang-ups and insecurities of a Blair (or for that matter a Harold Wilson, Edward Heath or John Major). He was highly intelligent and with the strength of character to stamp his will on his party. But there were limits to his courage and moral fibre. He was unwilling to take on either vested financial interests or the politically correct lobby. His right wing saw him as pandering to the latter, doing with PC what Blair did with Thatcherism; hence his legalisation of gay marriage (which some gays actually opposed while the general public, although feeling there was no particular reason not to allow it, were not wildly enthused by the issue). Cameron was also criticised by outgoing Archbishop of Canterbury Rowan Williams for not having done enough to protect the Christian religion from those who vilified it (including the sort who would seek to ban carol services, nativity plays etc. in the belief, often mistaken, that they offend people of other faiths, in what looks like becoming the most alarming threat ever to one of the fundamental freedoms, that of worship, in any western society). Corbyn of course sought to uphold political correctness, but in the old left-wing way (in so far as the former isn't the latter in a different guise). Another fault of Cameron's was that he was a dour Scot (which as with Brown put off enough voters to prevent the achievement of an overall majority in 2010), yet in an interesting combination of contradictory characteristics sometimes without the sound practical judgement which is often seen as going with that kind of personality; this factor was ultimately to have devastating consequences for himself, his party and his country.

The 2015 election at least showed, by the higher voter turnout, that it is possible to overcome public apathy towards politics if issues arise which people are sufficiently concerned about. Whether, outside a relatively small element, they are keen to have any involvement in it other than voting is a different matter. If not, it is part of a general, though particularly strong among the young, disenchantment with institutions. Whether anything can be done about this tendency is unclear. It is due to two factors. One is the emergence of the internet as a kind of rival community to those engaged in collective, corporate activity. The other is a belief that the tone of affairs has been progressively lowered in recent decades. Not being anywhere near as insecure and vulnerable as Tony Blair, David Cameron was not the creature of spin doctors to the same extent, but was no less aware of the need to present the right image before the media, no less suspiciously smooth and polished. Meanwhile the activities of a George Galloway might be amusing to satirists and grist to the media's mill, but they probably alienate a lot of decent and sensible people from political life. When foolish behaviour by MPs seems almost the norm it actually loses its satirical value and becomes merely degrading, as well as downright alarming. Generally political discourse has too often degenerated into childish bickering, with constant accusations of lying etc. The intellectual level of the House of Commons has undoubtedly gone down and we realise just how much has changed in the last thirty years when we reflect that Enoch Powell (whatever your view of him!), Roy Jenkins and Robert Rhodes James once sat there. The art of the gentlemanly or witty insult, as practised by Winston Churchill among others, has been lost.

This has a knock-on effect as it deters people who *are* intelligent and decent from becoming MPs and then ministers, and thus raising the tone of things from what it too often is. Not that politics is entirely devoid of such qualities as intelligence or decency. With the former the problem is too often that it is of the wrong kind, being directed largely towards personal or group advancement, or that there is an *intellectual* stupidity, intelligence and intellect not being the same thing. How much damage is done depends on the position one occupies; there may have been no alternative to Tony Blair as leader of the Labour Party and Prime Minister, but in many ways he would have been far better as an ordinary minister rather than premier, the latter job calling for a quite different kind of skill. (As far as politicians with *moral* stature are concerned, examples I could mention from the last fifteen years would be the late Mo Mowlam and Robin Cook, and Claire Short, all of whom were prepared to at least risk their careers by disagreeing with Tony Blair over Iraq and other issues. Their departure helped to set the final seal on New Labour's spiritual bankruptcy).

The fact that political life can be stressful and also, if you are lucky enough to become a VIP, cuts you off from the world within a security cocoon, an existence not everyone would relish, means that politics becomes less attractive a career to those who are not so keen on achieving power (as opposed to exercising it wisely and morally) that they don't mind the inconvenience. This doesn't mean all politicians are self-seeking. David Cameron may not have been entirely so; he is of a certain upper-class, Old Etonian tradition that perhaps still sees politics as a duty as well as a leisured gentleman's form of recreation. A public school prefect, if that is how one sees him, may in some ways be the best person to run the country. The problem is that his mindset, which is influenced too much by his background and by a continuing collective aversion to consensus politics as a result of the latter's meltdown in the 1970s (which has been transmitted to those who were still at school at the time in question), prevents him from making the changes which are necessary if we are to have a truly just and fair society. I was in many ways pleased when the Conservatives returned to power in 2010, having felt that the odium and ridicule they were subjected to at the time of their 1997 defeat was excessive. But the pleasure has not been unalloyed.

The prominent British politicians of the 1960s, 70s and to some extent 80s do not seem such towering figures as Walpole, the Pitts, Peel, Gladstone, Disraeli, Lloyd George and Churchill, perhaps because the further back in time something is the more it acquires a certain mystique. But they nonetheless come over, if only because political figures were far more in the media spotlight by their day, as a remarkable cast of characters, some admirable, some dubious, some grotesque, but all stamped fairly vividly on the public mind and caricaturable most of them by such as the impressionist Mike Yarwood: Heath, Wilson, Callaghan, Foot, Healey, Benn, Powell, Thatcher, Barbara Castle, Shirley Williams (now the only real survivor of that era), Cyril Smith and Jeremy Thorpe on the Liberal side (notwithstanding the disturbing revelations about their private lives). Somehow one does not react to more recent politicians in the same way. Satire is always healthy, and fun, but when John Major and Tony Blair were caricatured it tended to emphasise what was wrong with them as much as anything else, which wasn't necessarily the case with their predecessors even if you still violently disagreed with the latter's character and policies. There are few whose voices and manner offer amusing opportunities for impressionists (with the exception of Blair and Boris Johnson). Mostly one seems to be confronted by nonentities or reprobates of the kind who appall rather than arouse grudging affection. There are none who are of any *consequence*, unless in a purely mechanical sense.

Apart from Boris Johnson. Boris as suggested above is caricaturable, with his bumbling upper-crust manner which is part artificial and part genuine. And he is an enigmatic, complex character, prone to gaffes yet genuinely able and intelligent. No doubt it's true, as one probing interviewer charged, that he's not a nice man. But the same could be said of Lloyd George (I won't explore the similarities in terms of private life) and Joseph and Neville Chamberlain. Or Harold Wilson, who as noted once hit a reporter and these days would be in serious trouble for it if enough people, or a CCTV camera, had witnessed the incident. Boris imparts something to British politics you might have been forgiven for thinking it had lost, however you might feel about him. That can make him seem dangerously attractive.

David Cameron was in some respects a good Prime Minister. He kept better control of his party and his cabinet than John Major, for example, did. But he was out of touch. He failed to understand that for many people the question of whether Britain should remain in the European Union was a complex one. He assumed, perhaps because of his business mentality, that they would take what could be seen as economically the safer, "better the devil you know" course and vote Remain, not wishing to risk damaging the nation's and their own prosperity.

In the past he had stalled on whether or not there should be a referendum on the issue. But eventually he decided in favour of one, his motive being essentially political. He intended to shut up the United Kingdom Independence Party, who were a potential threat to the Tories' prospects even if they only succeeded, at some time in the future, in reducing a Conservative government's majority or splitting the vote enough to create a significant number of marginal seats, and also to heal continuing divisions within the Tory party itself over Europe. His strategy was to secure opt-outs for Britain from further European integration and then hold the referendum in the anticipation that the majority at least would vote Remain, since the EU no longer seemed so frightening a prospect. No harm would be done from either the Tories' or (what Cameron thought ought to be) the nation's point of view. The Eurosceptics, if still unappeased, would see no point in opposing Britain's membership of the Union if the people had given a conclusive verdict in favour of it, and UKIP's chances would have been wrecked by the same token although they would probably still have remained in being. Cameron was confident he would get what he wanted. He might have held the referendum but insisted on a certain majority in favour of Brexit (which would have been larger than the number who voted for it on the day) before the measure was carried, but he did not even choose to take this option (adopted in the 1979 Scottish and Welsh referendums on devolution), which was certainly open to him even though such a device is questionable if the aim should be absolute democracy (it could be argued that politicians who set such conditions only do so where they are confident the vote will not go the way they don't want). (Referenda are a controversial device anyway, but there is one very good argument in their favour. Very often the majority does not get the policies it wants because the government which is elected at a general election does not deliver on all of them, or wins on the basis of one policy which most agree with leaving a whole host of other areas in which there is disaffection. However, if you isolate an issue from all others by making it the subject of a referendum there is a chance of remedying this.)

Unfortunately, such was the lack of trust people now had in politicians that not everyone believed Cameron's claims that he had secured a decent deal for Britain from Brussels. Some insisted the opt-outs did not amount to much (there are plenty of grounds for thinking they were right), and some others were inclined to believe them. Meanwhile the obligations, financial and legal, which Britain would still have towards the EU would continue to be irksome. Brussels had become identified with unrepresentative bureaucracy and corruption. It was preventing Britain reaching possibly lucrative trade deals with the world outside Europe. Many people were confused as to what exactly would or would not happen if Britain left the Union. Perhaps most important of all, there was a degree of public ignorance on the vital issue of immigration, over which there was great concern for valid (and sometimes not so valid) cultural and economic reasons. "Immigration" became identified with the EU (because of the rights its "citizens" had to live and work in any member state) whereas in fact most migrants were fleeing poverty and war in Africa, Asia or the Middle East. EU citizens living and working in Britain wasn't quite the same thing, and as it was unlikely we could decently kick those people out there wasn't much point in voting Leave because of "immigration", as I myself had come to realise by polling day. Except that if immigration was exerting pressure on the resources of a small and overcrowded country, *any* reduction in the numbers of people going there, whatever their motives and however long they intended to stay, could be seen as a good thing, and there were a few more countries which had not yet joined the EU but might do so in the foreseeable future. (Neither EU nor other immigrants were demons and the desire for a better life or to broaden one's horizons was understandable, but that made little difference to the issue.)

Irrespective of the motives behind the referendum and the complaints that it was unnecessary, therefore proving by its result (if you voted Remain) more trouble than it was worth, when it *was* held it revealed the extent of public concern on the European issue (suggesting that it should have been held, if democracy was a consideration). But perhaps certain matters ought to have been more thoroughly explored during the run-up to it, and it should have been done as a statesmanlike act rather than for the sake of party management. In the end it happened to be the Brexiteers who won, though this surprised many people, myself included, who had been expecting instead a narrow Remain majority. But the whole point about the affair is that there were good and bad reasons for staying in Europe and good and bad reasons for getting out. It meant that many had genuine difficulty making their minds up (my mother changed hers four times), confusion over the issues apart. What else explains why there was such a close result, even if it was not the only factor? It was not true that all Remain people were pinko PC liberals, or that all Brexit people were bigoted reactionaries and dinosaurs, usually of a certain age or above. I know of people sociologically similar to myself − white, middle-aged, Christian, living in the Surrey stockbroker belt, not too happy about political correctness – who were Remainers. And there were youngsters who were Brexiteers, even if constituting a minority among their age group. The fact that areas where there were universities tended to vote Remain did not mean that all intelligent people did so while stupid people were pro-Brexit, rather that certain walks of life are characterised by certain attitudes, in this case liberal and supranational; they are not necessarily more sensible, as if intelligence and ideological outlook are the same thing, which they are not.

The bitterness and divisions between old and young which Brexit has caused are unnecessary and rather silly (though they could be worse). A friend of mine who is a political scientist and knows what he is talking about, and who is also a Remainer so he is not guilty of bias, tells me that very often the young people who voted for Britain to stay in the EU in the 1975 referendum were later the middle-aged people who voted Brexit in 2016. Opinions and outlook change with age, and always have done even if not universally. At the same time one might also put it gently to the young that they might not have been so keen to Remain if Brussels had started doing too many things they didn't like, which given the nature of power might not have been unlikely as its own continued to grow. And perhaps it only had itself to blame for its troubles with the British. UKIP were not, whatever their opponents might say, composed entirely of Fascist loonies. I strongly suspect that many of them were uneasy about severing the tie with Brussels completely and would have been happy to stay with the EU had it reformed itself by cutting financial waste, tackling corruption and relaxing its control of constitutional as opposed to economic matters. Its failure to do so alienated many who might otherwise have voted Remain. David Cameron was doing the right thing in seeking an exemption for Britain from further European integration, but when dealing with him Angela Merkel, German Chancellor and key factor in the equation (who I in many ways admire and who undoubtedly tried to help Cameron, becoming a kind of mother figure to him), sometimes had the kind of patronising expression one adopts when faced with a difficult child or teenager. Brussels should see the whole thing as a valuable lesson to be learned rather than a demonstration of British perversity.

Instead of being vituperative towards those who voted the other way in the referendum, we ought to consider what actually was at stake in it. For some people the important consideration was that Britain be free to make her own laws, rather than subject to ones originating from an extranational authority, which she seemed to have little control over despite the European Parliament, and therefore a cause of concern when they were restrictive or unjust. Others were prepared to put up with these abuses for the sake of safeguarding economic prosperity. What you felt to be the deciding factor in the end depended on how your brain was wired, and brains have never all been wired the same on any issue. It just happened to be the case that what was politically a good idea (because it could be seen as promoting greater liberty) might not be one from the economic point of view, and *vice versa*.

It is often argued, bitterly, that the votes of a racist element in the referendum must have been instrumental given the close result. This is quite possible, and should give decent Brexiteers cause for discomfort. It is very likely that UKIP absorbed a lot of former supporters of the British National Party. The latter had been crippled by faction fighting and by the decision of a judge to rule that black people should be allowed to join it, which they would have done *en masse* in order to wreck it (the judge must have known they would, so s/he rather than upholding the principle that even organisations like this have a right to function without hindrance under the democratic system was pursuing a policy of partiality by other means). Those who had voted BNP because of fears about immigration now turned to UKIP as the next best thing. Fears about immigration need not have a racist motive, although it seems UKIP nonetheless had a problem with racism which it did not fully address. In any event the European Union was identified with an "open doors" policy which was seen as imposing pressure on resources as well as perhaps diluting national identity. It became conflated in the minds of a certain section of the public, not all extremists by any means, with a politically correct view which saw any opposition to immigration as motivated by bigotry and therefore let it go ahead regardless of the consequences; and thus, by extension, with political correctness in general which they wanted to have a go at. Brexit can be seen as payback for all the PC; just as the 2011 riots can be seen as payback for thirty years of Thatcherism, although they were less successful at creating a serious disturbance in the order of things.

But even if it could be proven that racism ultimately explained the Brexiteers' triumph, we cannot deny people the vote because we fear they may be casting it in the wrong spirit. To carry out a psychological test (would the results be accurate?) on everybody before an election/referendum to establish whether they were racist, and if they were to prevent them voting in it, would be questionable itself, raising serious issues of personal liberty. And if we had the right to do this we would have to exercise such authoritarian control more generally as well, since there are probably all sorts of cases where a person's "opinion", expressed in their voting behaviour, is rather a prejudice or misconception.

Undoubtedly the attitude of many Remainers, during the referendum and after, has been disgraceful to say the least. I have little doubt that UKIP and Nigel Farage would have been just as vociferous in their complaints if they had lost. Whether they would have been be quite so *nasty* − they weren't during the actual campaign, anyway, though their claims about immigration may have been wildly offbeam − I don't know. But then since Thatcher it has been the tactic of the Right to try to appear reasonable and to only be reflecting the will of the majority; let the Left, whether defined by its historic form, by politically correct liberalism, or both, rant and metaphorically foam at the mouth, so discrediting itself. And the Left is usually very obliging in the matter. As soon as it suggests that anyone who questions any aspect of political correctness, or the wisdom of permitting immigration beyond a certain extent, is racist (and it ought to be apparent to that person that they are), or that democracy is fine until people vote for something they (the Left) don't like they hand it to their opponents on a plate. The Right can then present themselves convincingly as the voice of reason, representatives of the silent majority, etc.

The Brexit was something which seemed like a good idea at the time, but left many people reeling in horror at what they had done. Including myself, to some extent. I must admit that by the time I came to cast my "Leave" vote I had lost a lot of my enthusiasm for doing so. However, the thing to do now is to make the best of what might be considered, by at least half the population or almost, a bad job. Before the Coronavirus pandemic overtook other issues there was substantial support, from repentant Brexiteers as well as Remainers, for a second referendum. While this should not be entirely ruled out, if we can reach sensible agreements with Brussels, the Latin American trading bloc Mercosur, the Chinese, the Indians, etc. there may not be any need for it. The logic of economics, of capitalism, one might say self-interest, will dictate that in the end the markets settle down and everyone recognises the wisdom of not wrecking, out of spite, one of the largest economies in the world. And even if the Brexit does result in an upsurge in xenophobia and racism, this is unlikely to be reflected in her foreign and economic policy; that just isn't feasible on today's interconnected planet. We couldn't be entirely isolationist, anyway. Besides, young people (who are the future) are these days passionately anti-racist and simply wouldn't let it happen. They may even bring about, in due course, that second referendum and, with the full agreement of Brussels, secure Britain's readmission to the EU, presumably on the basis of the opt-outs whatever the latter do or don't amount to.

It is understandable if the wider world, including former Commonwealth countries, feels its priority is to establish and consolidate their trade links with the EU. But there is certainly a case for our consolidating ours with them and using it as a basis for future prosperity. Greater involvement with the world at large, which a withdrawal from the EU would make essential, ought also to counter any xenophobia the Brexit does encourage. That is how one should look at it.

Notwithstanding arch-Leaver Boris Johnson's victory in an election which was fought partly at least on the issue of Brexit, a case can be argued for holding another referendum if the result in the first was a narrow one and there is reason to believe enough of those who voted Leave have since changed their minds. And if Brexit in the meantime has been tried, and tried sincerely, and failed we could then vote Remain (or rather Return) with a clear conscience. However, at a literary lunch recently I met a Franco-German writer and journalist who told me she did not know anyone who was in favour of the EU either in France or in Germany. If she was anti-EU herself she may have exaggerated the extent to which her views were shared by others; however it has always seemed rash to me to assume, one's own opinions apart, that it is only the British who are being party poopers and there is not a significant element among the population of mainland Europe who like them are seriously disenchanted with the corruption and authoritarianism of Brussels. What those who desire Britain, or indeed any other country, to remain in the EU ought to consider is that they may be trying to flog a horse which, if by no means dead, is far from well. If Brexit *does* work there would be no point in going back on the referendum result anyway.

Meanwhile the problem is that for Brussels to accept it might encourage other member states to break away too. It would undermine the whole basis of the EU, partly by suggesting that Brexit was in fact workable. The EU cannot afford to let this happen, explaining the rough ride we were subjected to in all the negotiations with Brussels over what form Brexit should take.

Until Johnson's 2019 election victory, at any rate, one outcome that seemed on the cards was a "soft" Brexit, arguably the best solution and one which a part of this writer would be relieved at. Another, which in effect happened at one point, was that MPs decided they should determine the matter and rejected any sort of Brexit. As will be touched on again below the implications of this are, and were, ugly. If you are to have a popular referendum at all, for parliament to override it would send out a worrying message that politicians did not care what the people thought. There is a difference between being constitutional and being democratic. That would be so whatever the result of the referendum had been and which way an individual or interest group had voted, despite the feelings of Remainers. Finally, a policy of muddling through and of stringing things out (if that is what Teresa May, who was a politician whatever else she might be, was trying to do) might result in the nation deciding the whole thing was, indeed, more trouble than it was worth and either voting Remain at that second referendum or not objecting if anybody decided that Brexit was for one reason or other impractical and could not go ahead. It would, if nothing else, be a very British approach.

The Brexit certainly produced significant political fallout back home in London. From being in a strong position following his election victory in 2015, after which he no longer needed to depend on the Liberal Democrats, and thus imparting some stability to affairs David Cameron threw everything away, destroying the unity of the Conservative Party by reopening wounds over Europe which had healed to some extent since the Major years and plunging British politics into a state of uncertainty and upheaval which went on for some time and may well resume after Coronavirus. He had resolved to have a referendum before the election, but had failed to anticipate what the result of the former might be. Brexit was something which might work out if all things were equal, but there was sufficient doubt about that for Cameron to be regarded by many of his colleagues as having made a catastrophic mistake. He would have survived had there not been a divergence between what the people, or the majority of them, wanted and what the political establishment necessarily did (something which has bedeviled attempts to resolve the Brexit crisis ever since). In what hopes was an expression of the upper-class code of honour rather than something simply unavoidable, he decided to resign, taking one for the team. Then, in what would have been had his political career ended there a strange and bathetic anticlimax to it, Boris Johnson withdrew from the race for the leadership of the Conservative Party and thus also Number Ten. He might have carried on if Michael Gove had continued to back him, but it seems that when Gove did not he lost his nerve. Unless some murky conspiracy was afoot (always a possibility in politics), one sensed this complex personality was not, at heart, quite convinced he was actually suited to the job of running the country. It seemed sad, though also a relief. Was Boris a brilliant light which ought to be allowed to shine because otherwise the world would be that much darker, or an undisciplined dynamo who might cause no end of trouble? Both, but perhaps too much of the latter (as Mayor of London he was much too keen on privatising, digitalising and developing everything; among other things he ruined Waterloo Station and the curtilage of Battersea Power Station).

Anyway, the premiership went to Teresa May. In many ways it is a sad story, as tragic as David Cameron's self-destruction. At the time, May seemed a good idea; she stepped in when nearly everyone around her had been disqualified by squabbling and backbiting over Brexit, or chickened out as in Johnson's case. It may be that she saw her chance, though I believe she also acted from a sense of Christian duty, thinking she could do some good. She was dour and rather uninteresting, but what the country needed just then was an effective Prime Minister; the job description did not have to include the requirement that they be exciting. Within a year, however, she was to prove something of a disappointment from the point of view of effectiveness, too.

As we have already touched upon, politics has become so debased and degraded that many intelligent people wish to have nothing to do with it. Given that their skills are all the more necessary in a complex world in which the task of government is more difficult, yet has so much riding on it, the situation is paradoxical, and in a most harmful fashion. The field is left wide open for those who are partisan ideologues, careerists or are benign but, although clever in some ways, have no intellectual depth (so they aren't put off by the nature of the game, feeling it to be absurd and unworthy of them). Teresa May (like Margaret Thatcher, although comparisons with the latter are perhaps unfortunate, an Oxbridge product) falls into the third category. In an overall sense the type is not bright, one aspect of this being that while not necessarily wicked they lack emotional intelligence, meaning that they themselves are impervious to stress until it reaches a certain level. May was a sincere Christian, and I think a genuinely nice lady when the stress was not hardening her, who unfortunately was out of her depth. As Prime Minister she lacked the charisma and the acumen which was needed to steer her party, and her country, in the right direction. Her trying to be Maggie (perhaps influenced by the fact that she was only the second woman to become British Prime Minister) and failing, because she was not really like that, came over badly, making her seem harsh and strident. Of course she had been dealt a very poor hand, having to cope with the consequences of the EU referendum and generally to clear up the mess left by her colleagues. And as is the way of the world, when she got things wrong she was vilified, often by those less nice than herself. At any rate, there is no doubt Brexit overshadowed her premiership.

Her calling the election of 2017 has been regarded as a characteristic mistake. But to be fair, she did seem at the time to be in a strong position. I'm not sure the outcome could entirely have been predicted, although without doubt the extent of Tory support was overestimated. At any rate though something was happening, unnoticed by a great many people, which was to deal British political affairs a massive shock.

We were basically still living under a Thatcherite economic system, thirty or so years of which had effectively been the cause of the 2011 riots in London. This system was resulting, as it had before, in marginalisation and a widening gap between rich and poor. Its current incarnation was called "austerity". Even though politicians and businesspeople no longer talked as if the country was in recession, it seemed that swingeing cuts and price rises were still necessary. And the rich were not sharing the burden (it might have made an important difference if they had, but fatigue at the situation would still have led to a violent reaction against Tory policies sooner or later). Young voters, while not necessarily aware of the historical roots of the matter, had finally decided they had had enough, and put the removal of the problem, even if it meant voting for Jeremy Corbyn (where they had reservations about him) before their notorious apathy. Their feelings were shared by a significant number of older people. The rest of the population, including the Tory establishment, failed to realise the extent to which this had happened; had they done, they might have voted in large enough numbers to prevent a hung parliament and the status quo nearly being overturned in a way which itself might have been disastrous (the whole business was highly disorientating, as if Michael Foot had won, or almost won, the 1983 election). It is an awesome thought that had Labour actually received enough votes for Corbyn to form a government it would have meant the final end of Thatcherism, or its disappearance for the immediate future anyway. To those who found the doctrine in all its forms oppressive, the thought was comforting; the citadel was not impregnable after all. The resurgence of the Hard Left was symbolised by the *Morning Star* (originally a Communist organ) now being constantly on display in newsagents' etc. alongside the mainstream papers, instead of touted in the streets by the odd party worker. The impression was reinforced that certain people were scenting victory, and they continued to do so despite the damage inflicted on Corbyn's cause by the anti-Semitism row (among Jewish voters in particular, obviously) and general concerns about his leadership. It is somewhat alarming. (On the subject of why a substantial section of the Labour Party is anti-Semitic, if we concede that that is the case – and Corbyn has certainly created by his attitude an environment in which the prejudice can flourish – the reasons for it are twofold. Firstly, it is because the Palestinians can be viewed in the same light as other oppressed people who the Left have sought to defend in the past, like the blacks. Secondly, socialists have a distrust of corporate influence and Jews are well represented in business, perhaps using this, in a combination with their tendency to stick up for one another, to get their way over matters such as Israel. If anti-Semitism is *potentially* (it may be suppressed) prevalent in the Gentile world at large, then these grievances, the first valid and the second maybe more controversial, can serve as an excuse for it in the mind. In the Tory party it is relatively rarer, apart from the traditional casual bigotry of the landed gentry, for three reasons. (1) Jews are prominent in business and the party unlike traditional Labour is business-orientated. (2) Jews were victims of Hitler, and Hitler is the sort of person British patriots like to see themselves as taking a stand against, even if this sentiment might be retrospective in the case in question because many people in the Establishment would have preferred to make deals with the Nazis, until it became clear this was not possible. (3) There may still be a certain Christian (Church of England) influence on the party, and Christianity arose out of Judaism). Anyhow…

Teresa May clung to power with the help of Ulster's Democratic Unionist Party, not easy people to deal with over the problematic, and especially in a Brexit context, issue of Northern Ireland's status. Meanwhile there seemed no more able alternative to her as leader. Boris Johnson, who appeared to be a kind of political yo-yo, became Foreign Secretary when she succeeded to the premiership, his appointment dictated by the political need to give him and his supporters some representation in government. However his subsequent manoeuvering against May only served to make him look even more scheming and untrustworthy in the public eye and there remained serious doubts about his suitability to be Prime Minister.

As a party, the Tories flirted nervously with liberal policies and "One Nation" Conservatism while not psychologically being fully committed to, and thus able effectively to implement, them. (If we accept that the country is simply getting too overcrowded to meet everyone's needs cheaply, the uneasy and not entirely unfounded suspicion creeps in that austerity, while discredited beyond hope of salvation because it was identified with elitism and exclusion, will continue to be necessary, resulting in a very problematic, and potentially explosive, situation indeed. To find an answer will require qualities none of the leading figures in any party seem to possess). Labour had gone back to the 1980s; so-called "Loony Left" policies might now be more popular, but that didn't mean they would not prove catastrophic if implemented, and the divisions within the party over Trident and other matters seemed uncomfortably to echo those of the past. They might neutralise it as an effective instrument of government once it was in power. The belief that left-wing policies after the Corbyn pattern could be the saviour of society was made possible by the lack of interest on the part of young people in history and the lack of an organic connection between them and it. They were less aware of how left-wing socialism, on either the Communist or the democratic model, had historically failed to solve society's problems and create prosperity.

UKIP now seemed out of the running. Not only could they be said to have achieved their purpose, but they achieved it rather too well; the total collapse there had been in their support must surely reflect, to some extent, a feeling of embarrassment at having voted Brexit and unease at its negative consequences. There remained the possibility of a new Centre Party formed from the Liberal Democrats along with dissident Labour right-wingers, and such a suggestion is lent credibility by the unexpected Lib Dem gains in the election. But this new party would have to break the mould of politics far more successfully than the Alliance did in the 1980s if it was to be in a position to re-establish consensus and build a better Britain. It remained to be seen what impact the new Independent group would have in the House of Commons. But undoubtedly there had taken place a return to the polarisation of the 1980s, with the Tories still the party of the rich and the business sector, still afraid of letting go of Mrs Thatcher's apron-strings, and faced by a Labour Party which had again become dominated by the Left. Over everything hung the shadow of Brexit, which fiasco continued to drag on, both Leavers and Remainers being justified in feeling frustrated and let down by the whole business, but a certain sense beginning to grow that Brexit would never happen. It had suffered from the following things. Firstly, the narrow result in favour of it (although majorities should be respected, the claim that "the people" voted to leave the EU has to be made with some circumspection), which was a recipe for trouble and undermined its basis to some extent. Secondly the wishes of Parliament, which has not in the past shown a marked tendency to abide by public opinion between general elections, diverge from those of the "people" on the matter (a major obstacle). Thirdly, the hard Brexiteers in the Conservative Party, for example Boris Johnson and Jacob Rees-Mogg, had possibly overplayed their hand by being so obstructive in parliament towards Teresa May's attempts to reach a deal with Brussels. They might well as a result have lost their chance, since their attitude had allowed time for reservations to grow. It was still not quite clear what the result would be of a second referendum, but to disallow a narrow result in favour of Remaining while insisting that a narrow one in favour of Leaving was binding can only be viewed as hypocritical, however disgraceful the behaviour of some in the Remain camp. Fourthly, there was the particularly problematic issue of the "Irish backstop", not something other countries contemplating leaving the EU have to deal with and another reason why some might feel the whole thing is too much trouble.

One particularly nasty aspect of the affair has been the unpleasant language used by the Remain camp, most notably, in the last couple of years, the posting of offensive anti-Brexit stickers in public, plus the tone of *European* magazine, a distasteful organ which published an article entitled "Sack The Brexit Voters", apparently not realising that if it was the economic consequences of Brexit which were the reason why it ought not to happen, along with a possible encouragement of insularity and xenophobia, dismissing at least half the population from their jobs would hardly help matters. These things constitute a form of violence yet, distressingly, some seem to think that the only "violence" in the matter has been committed by Brexiteers, simply by their advocating a policy to which the Remainers are opposed and which might have negative implications. This is hardly fair given that during the referendum and for some time afterwards it was Remain who were using the most aggressive language, though the other side, who can be just as bad, caught up in good time. And I ask those who insist that the posters of the offending material are merely taking advantage of the right to legitimate protest, as if there is no distinction between an action in itself and the way it is done, do they want children to see this public obscenity, if that isn't too strong a description of it, and imitate it, so being degraded? Altogether the uncompromising vehemence of Remainers over the whole Brexit issue highlights the difficulty of bringing them "on board" in any attempt to implement the measure and make it work, since it can't be guaranteed they won't try to sabotage things somehow, and as long as the right could claim that they were doing so the business could not be resolved peacefully.

Of course it's not that their anger wasn't understandable. It was possible that Brexit would work out eventually but many people did not want to take the risk; what they could not countenance was economic hardship in the short term, at least, on top of that which they had been enduring for the past decade or so under austerity. Here, it should be noted that Brexit appeared to have been sold us on the basis that we could without too much difficulty switch from membership of the EU to a closer trading relationship with India, China, the Commonwealth etc. If this was the case why was there so much debate over whether in the last resort we should go for a "no-deal" Brexit?

The EU were not helping by their own intransigence. If their attitude was noble and proper rather than controlling, and they simply wanted to preserve their own integrity and present a positive image of themselves, both of which might seem to be affected by a British exit, why did they not just say "OK, leave if you want to, but believe me you'll be sorry" (they did, but in the wrong sort of way), rather than try to bully us into staying (and we cannot remain in the EU on that basis). If any country is destined to force the issue of reform within the EU by leaving it, then perhaps that country is not Britain, for various reasons Ulster being one of them, but a failure of Brexit may encourage it to behave even more high-handedly towards any of its member states the majority (by whatever degree) of whose citizens are not happy with the way things are and want out.

Returning to the situation within Britain itself, Brexit had a damaging impact upon the fortunes of both main parties and so exacerbated a worrying trend. Labour and the Tories were being criticised for failing to deliver either the measure itself or a repudiation of it. In Labour's case Jeremy Corbyn, aware that the country was still divided roughly equally between Brexiteers and Remainers, at least that was assumed to be the case, and deciding that sitting on the fence might be the most prudent policy refused to call for another referendum. Along with the continuing identification of the Tories with privilege and greed the unpleasantness within their ranks over Brexit and constant sniping at Teresa May reversed any success David Cameron might have had in the 2000s and 2010s in detoxifying the Nasty Party. The analogy between the current political situation and that in the 1980s is in one crucial respect not exact. Margaret Thatcher retained sufficient support among the electorate to be re-elected on successive occasions, in preference to Labour, and with large majorities. Now, it was not just that people's patience with spartan Thatcherite "good housekeeping" had become exhausted. Neither party recommended itself sufficiently to enough people to guarantee stability; we might well be looking at a future of hung parliaments and minority governments or ones with slender majorities. It did not augur well.

Meanwhile the merry-go-round continued, and only served to emphasise how divided the nation was over Brexit, where it was not completely turned-off by weariness over the issue. Caught between Remainers who did not want a Brexit at all and Brexiteers who thought the deal she offered was too soft, a worn-out Teresa May finally resigned in May 2019; the wolves gathered to fight over the spoils, with no less than thirteen candidates vying to succeed her initially. Boris Johnson had at one time seemed to be out of the running for PM, having resigned once too often, but was now back in it, if only because he served as the focus for those who wanted Brexit, a hard one if necessary, and were impatient at the way the matter was dragging on.

Voter apathy leading to low turn-outs probably influenced the result of the May Euro-elections, but what they did show was a surge of support for Nigel Farage's new Brexit Party, a replacement for UKIP, on the one hand and for the Liberal Democrats on the other. The Lib Dems did well because (a) they had more or less specifically said, from even before the 2015-16 cataclysm, that they would ignore any pro-Leave result of a referendum, and thus appealed to those who did not want Brexit, full stop, or sought some kind of closure, and (b) many simply didn't like the way the two main parties were behaving (the time-honoured protest vote again). In the past the Lib Dem vote had collapsed at general elections, but this time things might just be different (or so it seemed). Previously, despite disillusionment with both Labour and the Tories, one of the two still retained enough support to command a sort of allegiance from the majority, being seen as the lesser of evils. What might now change that established pattern was things seeming to have reached a new low. There was a fear that as Prime Minister (which he now became) Boris Johnson would in the long run inaugurate a new kind of ugly and enervating class war, Corbyn's middle-class origins notwithstanding. A "Loony Lefty" versus...versus Boris Johnson. Promoting the Lib Dems appeared to offer a way out of that. But it still appeared inappropriate that a party with "Democrat" in its name should disregard the wishes of (the majority of) the people. Furthermore, they had disgraced themselves by condoning the use of bad language, referred to above, in anti-Brexit campaigning. Apart from its contributing to lowering the tone of public life, one couldn't help wondering what Gladstone would have thought of it.

Concerning Brexit itself, the whole business had unfortunately become so protracted, and so acrimonious, with politicians seeming unable to resolve the matter either amicably (in so far as that is easy with controversial issues where much is at stake) or at all, that the majority of the population, including many who were passionately pro-Remain and did not accept the result of the referendum, were now wearily apathetic about it. This was a dangerous thing if Brexit was likely to have disastrous consequences. With Boris Johnson set on steamrolling the measure through the diehard Remainers and Brexiteers continued to thrash it out while the rest simply wanted to get it over with, one way or another. And for better or worse.

Brexit led to a constitutional crisis which was at least as serious as that over the House of Lords in the late 1900s and early 1910s. The majority of the people voted for it (though it was not a majority who voted at all; but then that sometimes has been the case with general elections, whose results we don't disallow accordingly). But parliament was effectively obstructing the measure either because it disagreed with it (in the case of Remainers) or did not think it went far enough (in the case of Brexiteers). Boris Johnson prorogued it out of frustration but the Supreme Court declared this unlawful. One can legitimately object to their decision on the grounds that in law, including constitutional law, precedents can be set and there is an especially strong case for doing that where a measure has the support of the majority of voters in what is supposed to be a democratic society. Nor do the Scottish courts have a right to determine what happens in the country as a whole. Perhaps the Supreme Court had in mind doubts as to whether Brexit was *still* supported by the majority (something which needs to be established for sure). Otherwise, and irrespective of how one voted or ought to have voted in the referendum, their verdict and the fact that it was enforced emphasises something the truth of which has often eluded us this past couple of hundred years. It is not that Britain is a democracy but rather that parliament passed certain laws. By those laws the franchise was extended; but that, as we have seen, may leave us with little more than an elected dictatorship.

With seeming absurdity, in November 2019 Boris Johnson called a general election for two weeks before Christmas; the first to be held at such a time of year for just over a century (which no doubt appealed to Johnson's sense of history, him being a patriot who was very much conscious of his party's past). He obviously hoped that anti-Brexit MPs (and perhaps those whose support of it was too uncompromising) would lose their seats and that his majority would be large enough for him not to have to depend on the support of the DUP. As with all such matters this was a gamble. Unless you are in the position of, say, Margaret Thatcher in 1983 electoral politics is uncertain; you cannot be sure that the mathematics will work out the way you want. Generally Johnson saw the election as a way of securing public endorsement of Brexit. But with most people apathetic regarding the issue, rather than partisan, was that a wise approach? If things did *not* turn out the way he wanted, the result could be disastrous. It might be that enough voters would decide that Labour were unelectable with Jeremy Corbyn, whose faults had only become more evident with time, as leader to avoid the catastrophe of his becoming Prime Minister. He liked to make a noise but was apprehensive about taking on the premiership at the age of seventy (hence his bottling out over the matter of an election previously), so there would be some doubt should he obtain office as to who was actually in charge. But another possible scenario, especially if the public were jaded and fatalistic about the whole business, was that the election made little difference and we were trapped in the same situation of stalemate as before.

Boris Johnson has attracted much opprobrium for his determination to push through Brexit despite its possible (to its opponents, more than possible) harmful implications, which to his detractors indicates a lack both of judgement and of humanity. It seems to give the lie to claims that he is a "One Nation" Tory in the mould of Heath, Macmillan and Ian Macleod (and therefore compassionate and inclusive). The crucial factor is the preoccupation of both Johnson and the political establishment, including the government in its administrative capacity, with Brexit. We have had virtually no opportunity to see how Johnson performs on other issues and so to give what may be a more rounded assessment of his worth as Prime Minister, in both a moral and a practical sense. It makes it harder to view him objectively. That is his tragedy, just as appeasement was Neville Chamberlain's and immigration Enoch Powell's. I am sure there is a Latin, or maybe a Greek, quote in there somewhere.

Of course only time will tell. And at the December election there occurred another startling and unexpected sea-change in British politics, of a kind which was partly attributable to Brexit and the catalytic, if not cataclysmic, effect that issue has tended to have on things. Because of austerity and marginalisation the Conservatives were far from popular, the nation was deeply divided over Brexit, and at the previous election disenchantment with the monetarist state (for that was what it was) had almost resulted in the hard-Left Jeremy Corbyn becoming Prime Minister. But since 2017 concern over Labour's perceived anti-Semitism had continued to grow and the issue become even more toxic. Young people in Britain today are passionately anti-racist, and in their minds the business became tied in with revulsion at racism in general. They decided that Corbyn was now a greater evil than Brexit; after all, Johnson's Leave cabinet included an Asian Chancellor of the Exchequer and Home Secretary, whereas racial prejudice was racial prejudice. They might not have been happy to admit that they voted for Boris Johnson, but vote for him they did, afraid that there would otherwise be a repeat, and more, of what had happened in 2017 with Labour actually achieving power and seeing the longer-established and powerful Conservative Party, led by a younger but more accomplished politician, as the best means of avoiding this. Voting Liberal Democrat might merely have let one of the two main parties – possibly the wrong one – in. For older voters Brexit was the principal factor, along with the other reasons for not supporting Corbyn. Seeing that Johnson was determined on implementing the measure, and tiring of the way the issue was dragging on (something we have mentioned before), they decided to let him get it out of the way so he could turn his attention to those other issues we alluded to (i.e. public services, social care, law and order). They felt he should be given a chance (just as Margaret Thatcher, John Major, Tony Blair and Teresa May had been given a chance). A combination of these things ensured that Johnson's gamble paid off, whether or not he himself fully appreciated all the factors which had led to his astonishing and counter-intuitive victory (arguably no-one did until that Exit poll on the eve of the election predicting his overwhelming majority, which caused people to think about what the reasons for it might be). And Nigel Farage and the Brexit Party stepped aside to let it happen. Whatever the explanation, or explanations, it resolved the constitutional crisis and also ensured that with a larger pool of Tory MPs to draw support from, Johnson was less likely to be caught between Remainers and hard Brexiteers. Nor was he dependent on the DUP either.

By the late 2010s the British political scene had become a hybrid of the situation prevailing in the "consensus" era of the 1960s and 70s, or at least its dysfunctional phase, and that in the 1980s. There was polarisation between a Thatcherite Conservative Party and a left-wing Labour Party, yet minority governments/hung parliaments were either an actuality or at least a distinct possibility. It was the worst of both worlds. Now the complexity of issues and the passion with which they were viewed had the effect of completing the return to the 1980s. As for the future, much depended on whether Labour again insisted on holding on to an unproductive Far Left policy or embarked on a gradual return to the social democratic model, perhaps appreciating that the problem with Blairism, if the latter and social democracy amount to the same thing, was Blair rather than the doctrine in itself. Meanwhile, the Conservatives finally had the large majority they had been seeking since their 1997 defeat, but whether they had recovered their popularity was still an open question. It was probably, as in the 80s, a matter of greater and lesser evils. Certainly Boris Johnson, although like any politician he practised the art of tactical manouevre, knew what he wanted and was determined to achieve it, which is one thing you can say about him, at least. And he would see the election result as a mandate for him to do whatever he liked, not only on Brexit but on all other matters. Were many of those who voted Conservative influenced by a belief, perhaps naïve, that he really was a One Nation Tory? At any rate the marginalised are quailing. The shape of the future will be determined not only by success, or otherwise, in making Brexit work (and many Brexiteers are far too confident on that issue for my liking) but whether or not Johnson really can address the divisions and inequalities within British society in a sensible and compassionate way. At any rate, one suspects he will not have an easy time of it.

With the replacement of Corbyn as party leader, by Keir Starmer Labour appears to have exchanged the hard Left for the soft Left, which is how Starmer's views are described. This is certainly a step in the right direction. Certainly Starmer is a far more likeable and reassuring figure than his predecessor. He comes over as a working-class hero (who although a "Sir" does not use the title, which to traditionalists like me is rather a pity) but without the suggestion of militancy. He therefore may well seem preferable to the country in the long run over Boris Johnson, who because of his personality and 80-seat majority arouses fears that he will simply do what he likes (at the moment he seems to want to concrete over large areas of the country, seeing a stimulation of the building industry by relaxing planning controls as the proper alternative to austerity and the only way of getting the economy back on its feet after the disruption caused by Coronavirus). Johnson is not a fool. His performance over Coronavirus has been as good as anyone might expect given that Covid-19 is a new disease whose precise medical and social impact cannot easily be predicted. I think he is better in a crisis than at other times; ironically he is again being prevented, at the moment, from utilising his full talents by the predominance of one issue – the virus – over all others. But he comes across as sly. He's probably using Coronavirus as an excuse for doing the things he wants or at least preparing the ground for them (helped by the unwisdom in the present situation of organising mass protests). And how can you trust a man who is so obviously milking the "dumb blond" image he tends to project in order to appear cute and appealing, even though it must be apparent that he is doing so?

Though his comments were unfortunately under-reported Keir Starmer criticised the extremist and irresponsible behaviour of the Black Lives Matter movement (for undoubtedly in many ways its behaviour was that) . This would suggest, if he is of the "soft Left", that he is both a liberal concerned with equality and a sensible man – just the right combination, one would have thought, which is needed, as well as being what Boris Johnson, in important respects, is not. But I still have fears for the future. Apart from the damage Johnson may do in the next four or five years with his substantial majority, there are general – not necessarily to do with one man, Keir Starmer – reservations which one is justified in entertaining about the soft Left. "Hard left", a return to which has been tried and failed, would if it had the opportunity return us socioeconomically to the 1980s, with a restoration of trade union power, unilateral nuclear disarmament, wholesale renationalisation etc. "Soft left", being a manifestation of the shift in emphasis which occurred after the end of the Cold War, accepts the Thatcherite revolution, pushing for social egalitarianism as far as is possible within that context; managing a Thatcherite society, as it sees it, more humanely than the Tories. Unfortunately, because that is not always easy to do it often appears more interested in the minority groups it has tended to champion as one of its particular concerns, channelling a lot of its energies into that area, rather than in dealing with general marginalisation affecting a wider section of the population. The Tories have continued to support Thatcherism while embracing greater inclusivity – they now have black MPs, having realised that there is no alternative to, and a greater political advantage in, integrating the ethnic minority population into their system (after all, prosperous businesspeople might be of any race). As politicians did on this issue in the 1970s, the party is following a bipartisan approach; prevent any further immigration if possible (though Boris Johnson felt he had to honour a promise to admit three million Hong Kong Chinese, something likely to be profound in its effects both culturally and socioeconomically, when they started having difficulties with Beijing) but do one's best for people already here irrespective of race. However this still leaves the potentially damaging and exclusive consequences of Thatcherism in general. But – and this is a problem where getting the party to change, perhaps becoming more humane, is concerned – it ought to be pointed out to left-wing critics of the party that if its being *particularly* concerned to promote Thatcherism were to cease this would still leave the other key aspect of its manifesto, its concern to defend traditional ways of life against immigration and the EU, which has also been attacked by progressive elements; if both were to be ditched there would be nothing left for the party to coalesce around, a dangerous thing if the parliamentary and political system depends on there being at least two main parties, Labour and Conservative, with an appreciable difference between their manifestoes.

But what should most concern us is this. With the Liberal Democrats again being squeezed out, the Centre has become the left, as I overheard someone perceptively comment in a local pub the other day. True, it is soft left. But with the Tories still determined to protect the nation's history and traditional identity, harnessing amenable ethnic minority people to that cause, it means the political nation will in the future be increasingly divided on the sensitive issues of race and political correctness.

5

The Bigger Picture

To try to write even a potted general history of the world is an ambitious, one might even say presumptuous, undertaking, in part because you won't be able to fit in as much as you or others might like. All the same there is nothing wrong in giving one's own interpretation of the past and, having studied history at school and University, I felt I should repay the efforts of my tutors and lecturers by keeping my hand in, as I said at the beginning of this book.

What happens in the world, and thus in history if the latter is the recording and analysis of significant events, is due to a combination of, an interplay (often complex) between different factors: fundamental truths about the nature of things; the variable of human free will; and the extent of individual or group knowledge of a given situation, which will affect the decisions taken by those individuals or groups. (No role in the system can be assigned to "accident", though I might use the term as a figure of speech, since the latter implies that something can happen or be the case purely by chance, without an underlying reason, which defies logic.) The question of what explains events in history is a philosophical as much as a historical one, in so far as there is any difference between the two disciplines at this point where they coincide.

The development, or decline, of societies − civilisations − has been influenced in the past by environmental factors, meaning climate change and natural disasters such as earthquakes, volcanoes and famines, and by the particular mental and physical characteristics of an individual or an ethnic group/nation (the latter being usually a genetic mixture to some extent of different races, certain combinations producing certain characteristics; here we may note that a single tribe which may or may not be ethnically "pure", in so far as anyone is, has sometimes been described as a "nation"). These could be regarded as fundamental truths about the nature of things; they may change, so that it is *different* truths which are exercising an influence, but they are fundamental nonetheless. Now it may be that certain events were inevitable, given the way a particular culture or person thought, but their timing, the *manner* in which they took place and their precise consequences are due to the interplay of which we have been speaking.

We would prefer to think that the harmful things, such as World War Two, could have been avoided. Here, we are again faced with a philosophical question; how far can we help our flawed nature? If the variable element in the equation − perhaps the only one, since inanimate objects do not have free choice and God does not change his mind − is free will, then people can choose to act wickedly. Most would take the view that at some point or other along the line Hitler could and should have chosen to alter the course of his career, at least ensuring that the Nazi dictatorship was a benevolent one if that was possible, and making no territorial demands in Europe beyond what reasonable people could view as fair. But what of those who failed to curb his expansionist foreign policy, and so prevent the war, partly because they were short-sighted as to the nature of the threat he represented and partly because they were still affected by the memory of 1914–18 and didn't want to risk the further European conflagration which might break out if he made a fight of it? Should we regard this failure as a venial sin, or as criminal irresponsibility? It is a question the answering of which is not part of this book's brief. Whatever the answer *is*, it seems fair to conclude that there would not have been a war without Hitler, also that Hitler ought not to have done what he did. His career raises the whole question of just how important individuals are in history. No one person can influence the course of events simply because they wish to. I am prepared to accept that their role can be crucial. Though Hitler would have been unable to achieve so much, with catastrophic results, without those whose blunders made it possible no-one else would have dared to try because they did not possess that combination of (misguided) willpower, madness (debatedly) and cool cunning. But given time someone would probably have discovered gravity if Newton had never been born.

What does seem to be the case is that there are primary nexus points (whether due to human error/perversity or not) and secondary nexus points in history, if one thinks of it as like a railway system or other transport network. The Iran/USA antagonism of the late 1970s and 1980s, and the Iraq War of 2003 were secondary nexus points, for reasons which will be explained later. These are branch lines, routes which are important as feeders to the main ones. How important exactly may vary (the same is true for the primary nexus points, and it may be difficult at times to draw a line between the primary and the secondary). The invention of printing was a secondary nexus point – a means to an end rather than an end in itself – but only in relative terms, and in its overall effect it was of more significance than the two prior examples even though it happened at an earlier stage in history, because of the boost it gave to reforming/radical movements in various spheres. At any rate the major historical developments are preceded by ones which are crucial stages on the journey, rather than the main leg of it, but no *less* crucial for that. The Industrial Revolution, very definitely a primary nexus point and more important altogether than any of the others, which began in Britain in the eighteenth century and is still going on today had to be preceded by a mini-Industrial Revolution in the sixteenth century, which saw among other things the appearance of an iron industry in places like the Weald, along with the mercantilist revolution in economic affairs (and some advances in technology would have to have been necessary for ships to make intercontinental journeys as they began to do in the fifteenth century). There also had to be, and was, an agricultural revolution which made it possible to feed the workforce of the future factories; of secondary nexus points this was ultimately the most important. Besides the industrialisation of the past 250 years, other primary nexus points have been the Age of Exploration, the Renaissance, the Reformation and the Enlightenment. Each influenced the one which came after or occurred simultaneously with it to some extent.

There is really only one basic, general trend in history and that is for human societies to become more complex, populous and technologically advanced (even the cultures of tribal peoples, which are more sophisticated than in the past has often been allowed for, have changed over time, the difference really lying in the extent of the change and the manner in which it has occurred). This is not quite the same thing as happens with general biological evolution as that is not necessarily a matter of increasing complexity but rather of species adapting to changed circumstances in whatever way guarantees their survival. Sometimes to evolve a simpler form may be the best option; Man of course removes any need for this by simply altering his environment to suit himself. Historically the process of industrialisation has happened in leaps and bounds, mirroring biological evolution in that respect at least. In the intervals between these leaps and bounds it takes place at a fairly gradual rate. It has by no means been always smooth and uniform; there have been periods of stagnation. And even today some parts of the world have been barely touched by it. At first, the developments that began in the mid-eighteenth century principally affected the West (that is, Europe and those countries which were inhabited/ruled by people of (generally North) European descent). But the nations of East Asia began to catch up from the late nineteenth century onwards. More recently India and Latin America have joined the club. Elsewhere, except in the oil-rich states of the Gulf, things are relatively backward. But people in the poorer parts of the world crave the high standard of living which Western technology brings and where it is not possible to attain it for economic reasons, the problem often being that all the wealth has been siphoned off by a few privileged individuals, they seek to share in it through migration, whether legal or illegal. And those tribal peoples who seem not to want to enjoy its "benefits" have nonetheless been profoundly affected by it, often in adverse ways; the destruction or pollution of their natural habitats explains why, except in comparatively minor respects like learning to ride bicycles or acquiring attractive trinkets such as a wristwatch, they desire nothing to do with the business.

1

The invention of fire was the first step in Man's taming of his environment. Then societies discovered agriculture and so were able to change from a hunter-gatherer way of life, often nomadic as tribes followed the herds of mammoth or whatever animal was their principal source of food and skins, to a farming one. Abandoning (for the most part) a wholly or partly nomadic way of life they settled first in small villages and then in cities (the latter would probably not have been big enough to qualify for that description by today's standards). They kept livestock, domesticated dogs and horses to help in hunting which was still carried out in some cases for food, and would be a form of recreation once a more leisured way of life became possible. Industry developed gradually, in stages, from its beginnings in crude flint-knapping to the use of iron tools and weapons; the discovery that metals could be smelted beginning the process which was to end, if it can yet be said to have ended, in space exploration and computers and digitalisation. At some point the wheel was invented.

The process of invention and technological development has taken place over thousands of years and before the really big "leap" in the eighteenth century was a piecemeal, not an even or consistent, one; if it had been consistent, we would now be in interstellar space if such a thing is possible. There were long periods of stagnation. Much of the impetus came from practical, for example military, needs (though why should it not have done, if the aim was to improve the quality of life or simply to survive) rather than a desire to satisfy curiosity about the universe and how it functioned. Probably both factors were important, together or singly, at one time or another. Sometimes change in one sphere, because of the way it sets the intelligentsia thinking by transforming the order of things and so requiring an adjustment of one's worldview, is necessary for there to be change in another, as with the Industrial Revolution inspiring movements for political reform. And sometimes the change requires, as suggested, a combination of factors, not just those mentioned but also economic, cultural and political ones, in a way that only happens periodically. This became more so with the increasing complexity of societies; in the earliest times, as we will see in a moment, simple curiosity may have been sufficient. One of the contributory factors was probably a particularly gifted individual, who until a relatively late stage in history did not necessarily require formal qualifications in science or engineering, although it is difficult to identify the precise or approximate point at which such an ingredient became essential.

The above applies more, or less, to human knowledge as a whole. There, where the exceptional individuals are concerned the Big Four, as one might regard them (they were big because of the general level to which science had advanced by the time the first of them began his work, as well as their own particular talents), are I suppose Newton, Darwin, Einstein and Freud. Newton and Einstein provided the physics, Einstein building on what Newton had achieved rather than entirely superseding it as some claim. Newton demonstrated the all-important role of gravity in physics; Einstein's achievement was to bring light more into the picture, by showing how gravity bent its rays so as to influence our perceptions of the universe and thus the actions we perform and their timing. In addition there were other figures whose discoveries were crucial and who rank as secondary but still vital nexus points; for example Einstein relied heavily on the work of James Clerk Maxwell. Darwin did the biology, or at least explained how living organisms came to have the forms which they did; Freud the workings of the human mind. Some would add Marx, if the list is essentially intended to be of those who were influential in shaping the modern world, its issues and conflicts as well as its understanding of the universe. If the latter were the criteria this would be fine, but if we are talking of those who made the biggest contribution towards interpreting the universe, I would not include Marx at all. The people who are most likely to are the Marxists. He was influential in the field of economics and political science, and as with any other great thinker not all of what he said was wrong – he was correct to highlight the undoubted flaws in capitalism and its potentially selfish nature – but otherwise, far from identifying any aspect of objective truth, he merely advanced a particular philosophy, founded a particular political (it had to be to take control of the economy) movement which by the end of the twentieth century had been discredited (having caused a great deal of trouble), even if some continue to believe in it nonetheless (the quasi-Marxism of anticapitalist and antiglobalisation protestors). Whereas no-one can deny the essential truth of Newtonian physics and Darwinian natural selection, or I believe Freudian psychoanalysis, even if all four figures may have got things wrong and their discoveries are not the whole story.

Some things would have been discovered independently by different people in different parts of the world and probably, though not necessarily, at roughly the same time. This was true of the most basic discoveries, which wouldn't have required a great deal of intelligence, a coincidence of assorted factors or a particular society or region having an advantage in the matter over others. Even the simplest cultures could have arrived at them if we think of cultures as varying in intelligence and sophistication, although such a view is dubious. Anyhow; one day someone somewhere was idly rubbing two sticks together and realised they were starting to smoke. He (or she; it was the sort of thing a woman could have done just as easily as a man, if we are really to suppose the former less clever than the latter) wondered what would happen if they continued rubbing, and so the secret of fire was revealed. It was perhaps the key discovery since so much else in industry and technology ultimately stemmed from it, from the earliest attempts at smelting through to the creation of artificial materials and the launching of rockets into space.

The knowledge that stones and flints could be made into tools or weapons most likely came about in a similarly "idle" way; someone (male or female, though a woman might not be allowed to personally make use of the discovery if it was not her tribe's custom that she should be a warrior) was banging two together and realised that the sharp edge thus created was handy in carving things, flesh included. Altogether, it was becoming established that the natural world could contain forces, hidden or (at first) imperfectly understood, which were malleable under certain conditions (how could they be created) and therefore capable of being harnessed to Man's purposes. Sometimes luck played a part. Discoveries could be made by accident, stumbled upon, as when something was accidentally dropped into a fire (there was always one person at least who saw the possibilities the accident revealed). But there was a "basic" stage and an "applied" stage which, due to the increasing complexity of the process as more is learned, we have now been in for hundreds if not thousands of years. Man already had the ability to reason, which helped, though it might take a certain type of individual to reason in the right *way*. The discovery how to make vessels out of clay was undoubtedly a more complex business than that of fire because it required a further extension of reasoning, or a combination of the basic and the complex, and thus the involvement of one of those especially gifted and perceptive individuals, needed at all stages of technical development, who natural selection sooner or later produces. At some point someone probably tried putting clays in fire (which of course had already been discovered) to see what would happen. Nothing much did. But later someone idly chucking handfuls of clay into water, and so softening it, would have wondered what would happen if you *then* heated the resulting material, because you had effectively created a new kind of substance which might respond differently to fire from the original one, compared to which it was qualitatively not the same thing, or from wood. Already an alteration had been caused to the nature of the clay so would another change in conditions produce a further transformation? And so pottery was invented. By degrees industry became that more sophisticated activity whereby a range of artificial (that is, using natural materials treated in a certain way) substances could be created.

People already mined for flints. Needing more of them (and perhaps motivated by a desire simply to explore what lay beneath the surface, so far as this was possible with contemporary technology, though practical considerations may have been uppermost), they went down deeper and discovered mineral ores. The same, or different, people now wondered what the result would be if you exposed *these* to fire. They thought, "I know that it bakes clay hard. What will happen if I put *this* in it?"

It was a case of experimentation plus trial and error. A step-by-step affair in which one advance, not necessarily intentionally, led to another, each being built upon to make the next possible. Gradually things were fine-tuned until the desired result was achieved; a pottery vessel of just the right hardness, a timber trimmed to just the right dimensions. A mean, a levelling-off, was arrived at. Technology, of increasing sophistication, became a craft, indeed an art; and a profession, with the knowledge gained being taught, passed on, to those with the right skills to use it.

The realisation that by degrees one could create what had not been possible before, revealing what had not previously been apparent – and which had advantages – led to what is called science, though obviously it was basic compared to that of the modern era. It was helpful but not always necessary for there to be a close relationship between it and industry as there is today when precision and quick results are desirable if not essential (and trial and error less acceptable, though they may nonetheless still be required to some extent). Until the twentieth century, engineers could be their own scientists, or not have to rely directly on the latter. Actual professional qualifications were not seen as vital; all you needed was the right combination of enterprise, dedication and ingenuity. How far it is possible still for there to be such people in the field of science is debatable, but some would regard the passing of the talented amateur as a great pity; the business seems less romantic, more cold and clinical and standardised.

As we've hinted it was possible for both basic and complex scientific/industrial techniques to be invented independently in different geographical regions, though how often this happened, as opposed to the process being discovered in one place and then becoming universal in the "developed", by contemporary standards, world before anyone else might have had the idea is difficult to say. But ideas did spread, though they might not always be taken up. The principal conduit was travelling merchants; others were explorers, soldiers returning from war, invading armies, religious or diplomatic missions. It is probable that transmission of technology from one culture to another sometimes took place by hearsay, or through information that was incomplete leaving its recipients to fill in the gaps according to their own way of thinking (this may have been the case with the European windmill, as we will see).

Leaving aside questions as to whether one race or culture can be more clever than another, at least in certain respects, it is thought that until recently the *general* level of human intelligence did not increase or decrease over time. Why then was technological progress not more consistent; why was air travel not invented in the Middle Ages, for example? Why were Leonardo da Vinci's ideas for submarines and helicopters not practically realised until some four hundred years later? There is perhaps a limit to how much the human brain can achieve at any one time. The principal industrial revolution of c1750 to the present day was clearly preceded by a series of mini-industrial revolutions at intervals, but there were lengthy periods between them when things were static. Only when the big take-off occurred in the eighteenth century did the process become truly ongoing and even then two hundred years, if the latter is considered a long time on a historical scale, separated the first large all-metal structure from the first space station. Besides, along with great reforming cultural movements like the Renaissance the "Industrial Revolution" required a combination of factors, such as occurred relatively rarely in history, to get under way though once it had done it acquired a self-perpetuating momentum. It may have been the same with earlier technical advances, though without the self-perpetuating momentum (at least to the same degree). Thirdly, from prehistory up to the end of the early modern period much invention was motivated purely by the sheer need to survive, biologically and also militarily, in a harsh world and once the most immediate and pressing requirements were met things fizzled out. Clever and enterprising people might still come up with ideas for this and that but apart from a very few no-one, including most of the political and social establishment whose patronage was essential for the projects to flourish, was interested. From the eighteenth century the potential of new technology when applied on a mass scale to create wealth supplied more of an impetus to progress, and later a point was reached when change was taking place at such a pace that there was excitement to see what could be done next. Technology became popular because of the potential it had to raise living standards, for both the rich and (relatively) the less rich, to the level people felt they were entitled to enjoy in the modern world. Older considerations remained of importance in the equation. Humanity is always seeking to improve its lot as much as possible, and in other ways than merely making money; creating new defences against poverty, injury, famine and illness, even if economic or political factors mean not everyone gets to benefit from them. And the need for the aeroplane was accepted once its paramount importance in war and thus role in national survival was realised.

There could still be opposition at each stage of the process on grounds of (understandable) self-interest (e.g. canal owners versus railway pioneers, who they thought would do them out of a living, in the early nineteenth century), or from "dinosaurs" who while content to reap the rewards from recent advances did not think there should be any more, because they just didn't see the need for or were even afraid of them. This was of course a retrograde and narrow-minded approach, until valid fears began to be expressed that the internet might be doing as much, perhaps more, harm than good.

It is correct to say technology can create power structures or reinforce existing ones; that it can have social and political consequences. I don't wish to go into a detailed discussion of the issue here, except to say that possession of a new technology was only significant, once it had first happened, if you had it and a domestic or foreign enemy did not, or *vice versa*, because then there was a distinct advantage. Otherwise, what occurred was no different from when my hypothetical first leaders picked up their stones and asserted their control (see below), in what might also have been an act of personal aggression or might not. Similarly, the invention of the spinning wheel is seen as a masculine device for the suppression of women, or their confinement to gender-specific roles, because it was they who usually operated it. But this was merely a continuation of a custom, albeit originating in a male-dominated politics, which had already endured for hundreds of years at least and by which society was stratified and tasks allocated on a gender basis. My point being that without wishing to insult them or to downplay gender as an issue, whether contemporaneously or in the study of history, those who seek to interpret things in its terms may not be achieving much and in fact leaving themselves open to satire.

It is clear however that technology has an effect on culture; on sociopolitical forms, on modes of thinking and speech. That effect becomes more profound the more advanced, and pervasive, the technology is, although the nature and extent of the interaction varies between societies; Saudi Arabia is technologically an extremely advanced country, though in large measure due to oil extracted by Western companies, but is governed by a monarchy which retains real power and together with harsh criminal laws and restrictions on women may seem to constitute something extremely backward (though the system nonetheless works after a fashion). But it is very different in the West. There, technology seems something which is rational, and also dynamic and progressive; perhaps blunt and to the point. Hereditary rule is by contrast irrational, since accidents of genetics cannot be relied upon to produce good rulers. Even if the First World War had not happened it is somehow hard to see the European monarchies continuing to exist as anything other than figureheads very far into the twentieth century. And ways of dress and speech which seem flowery, or reflective of a patriarchal (or for that matter matriarchal) authoritarianism are perceived as anachronistic, absurd and even pompous. Imagine Mr Quelch, Billy Bunter's long-suffering form master, exclaiming "Bunter, you obtuse boy, how many times have I told you, do not take your I-Pod into the classroom!" and you'll see what I mean. For similar reasons, it is unlikely (and this one feels is rather a pity) that there will ever be a time when, as in *Star Wars* or *Dune*, advanced space travel takes place against a background of archaic political arrangements with Emperors and Counts ruling, or vying to rule, the galaxy. Unless maybe a non-Western culture becomes dominant, and even that may not produce the kind of society portrayed here; we should note that the position of the Saudi royal family has recently come under question, while Nepal abolished its monarchy in 2008. At the same time the code of honour of the Jedi knights is strongly reminiscent of their forebears in the Middle Ages, who prided themselves on their chivalry. Perhaps the converse of the scenario shown in *Star Wars*, etc., is seen in those fantasy worlds where a mediaeval community is capable of advanced technology while retaining its basic social and political structure. It is ruled by powerful kings or queens but may for example have helicopters, called "ornithopters", which are piloted by the monarch's "flightsmen". Something has got seriously out of synch. Even where the technology seems more in keeping with what was possible at the time the inventions portrayed in the science fiction genre of "steampunk" are unrealistic. Though it could perhaps be/have been built, in technical terms a steam-powered aircraft or robot, say, would be no more than a curiosity as it would require a different power source, and a more sophisticated mechanism, to really function efficiently. A Victorian might have the means to *attempt* to build it, though no more, but in a mediaeval context it would not only be an anachronism but an improbable one.

By the end of the Stone Age codes of behaviour had been developed to ensure law and order and protect life, limb and privacy, and economics to regulate possession of property, of vital commodities, so that people did not seek to obtain what they desired through violence (the safeguards of course have never been effective, or observed, all the time). This applied both to essentials and to luxuries (although initially there was no leisure industry as such). Originally a simple barter system, often involving payment in kind, proved sufficient (even in sophisticated modern societies it can still be used where helpful, by mutual agreement of the parties involved in the transaction). But as society became more complex it generally ceased to be practical and was replaced by money payments.

In the earliest societies the most important activity from a practical point of view, hunting for food, was performed on a communal basis, by those men old enough to participate in it. There were also individuals who were skilled at particular tasks and who other individuals, or the tribe as a whole, went to if they needed to replace an arrowhead that had become blunted, for example; specialisation probably began at an early stage. Skills were handed down from father to son, or mother to daughter. As a hunter-gatherer lifestyle was succeeded by a settled, agricultural one (with hunting continuing to be necessary in some societies down to the present day) a process of diversification was encouraged. There were the hunters, or warriors, and there were the farmers. Once metals were discovered there were blacksmiths, coppersmiths etc. As industry expanded, it was impossible for vital tasks to be performed by just one individual and larger workforces, not necessarily composed entirely of family members, came into being, although sole traders might nonetheless remain in business where this was practical and indeed have undergone something of a revival in recent years.

The emergence of a wage economy predated the Industrial Revolution by a millennium and more. Barter having ceased to be practical in a situation where needs had become more diverse, it made sense to pay people for the work they did towards maintaining society in the form to which it had become accustomed and meeting its needs of survival, security, wellbeing. It was a moral obligation; those who contributed to keeping things running smoothly, or at all, deserved some kind of reward. If you had not made that contribution you did not deserve it, beyond the minimum needed to keep body and soul together. Monetary rewards were also an incentive to work hard. It was a cementing principle that reinforced social responsibility and integration. And society as well as the individual profited from it (workers being the people who made up most of the community, after all), because people with enough wealth to become consumers, to use the modern term, benefited the economy through their purchasing power, besides which if they enjoyed an at least reasonable standard of living, something good in itself, they would be content and not cause trouble, preserving social harmony and order. The world being grossly imperfect, this did not in the long run prevent poverty or injustice or discontent any more than economics *per se* has ever prevented all theft (in the sense of physical robbery).

The system inevitably gave power to the employer, who was the person dispensing the wages, over the employee. And as with all organisations, commercial or otherwise, there needed to be a single person in charge, a recognised head of the concern, for things to be run efficiently. There were, in the mediaeval and early modern period, collectives (as well as trade guilds, which acted more in the interests of the tradesmen than the people they employed), and perhaps it was easier for such concerns to exist in a time before capitalism became set in its modern form, but they were not the norm. Marxists, and others, speak of "capital" and "capitalism" as if they only emerged in the eighteenth and nineteenth centuries, but in the sense of private enterprise capitalism had been around for hundreds, if not a few thousand, years before then. It was not necessarily tied up with the traditional social/power structure, as monarchs and aristocrats did not dabble in finance, which they considered beneath them, although of course they needed to balance their books through competent accounting by their Treasurer, and might have to resort to moneylenders – later, to banks – if extravagance, too much expenditure on war and the economic impact of plague had depleted funds. But it reinforced emerging class distinctions nonetheless; it seemed logical that those of lower social status, who in accordance with that could be servants but not masters, received less pay than the person employing them. Status and wealth are closely intertwined. As in all socioeconomic systems, there had ideally to be some kind of surplus once basic needs were provided for in one's daily budget, but this did not amount to much. To be frank most of it was probably spent on beer (some would say things have changed little since!). But within reason, we should not despise people who live that way provided they are happy with their lot. And since expectations were lower in those days, and the socioeconomic structure accepted (so that there was no serious rioting except at times of exceptional dearth), most did not try to change the system by, for example, founding trade unions to campaign for higher pay.

Capitalism had already undergone considerable change in the several centuries preceding the Industrial Revolution, with the emergence of new economic systems such as mercantilism and the growth of international banking houses (trade guilds or their equivalents – at any rate, organisations which in effect were set up to promote the interests of private sector employers – could also be international, a case in point being the Hanseatic League). There had been a global (in that it covered the *known* planet, at any rate) economy ever since peoples first began to trade with each other, and economic troubles in one part of the world could have an effect on prosperity elsewhere. It was not of course politically united, as this would imply a single political *nation*, covering the whole of that known world, and this was ruled out due to both practical and patriotic considerations, as it still is today. But national governments had become economies in that they needed as part of their responsibilities to see they had enough money to meet vital concerns, and this from time to time required taxation. The spirit behind it might be altruistic or, arguably, it might not. The aim might be to raise money for the king's wars, success in which reinforced his prestige, along with his rights over territory. But this could be seen as an extension of the whole contemporary principle that people should be governed by monarchical rulers whose will ultimately was paramount and whose wishes should be deferred to. It did not necessarily make the regime popular, especially when the wars went badly.

If economics was a means of regulating people's behaviour in order to maintain social order (in a more general sense than through the creation and preservation of a class system, though it was to have that effect), then from the logic of this stems everything we are subjected to in its name – panic buying and its consequences, plus those of demand exceeding supply or vice versa, and governments/employers deciding that we are in a "recession" and that cuts must be made in all sorts of services to get the balance of payments right, et al. As society became complex so did the economics, especially as expectations rose (with the gradual growth, among other things, of a leisure industry, though initially only for the rich). The (perfectly natural) aim, on the part of buyer as well as seller, was to better oneself by adding to one's wealth as much as possible, even if the benefits from economic activity might be delayed. The seventeenth and early eighteenth centuries saw an expansion in credit and emergence of the concept of investment, with the great stock exchanges being founded. With the Industrial Revolution, what happened was that the massive growth of industry in its large-scale, labour-intensive form meant that what one might call the employer-worker (as opposed to master-and-servant, a term which although accurate is associated with an age when businesses might consist of a foreman, who was also the proprietor, and a couple of apprentices) relationship became much more important and noticeable. In an age of mass production using heavy machinery the small cottage industry employing a few people, possibly just one, lost out, though it has survived to the present day by catering for specialised markets. The expansion of "capital" and growth in the power of the boss, as we would nowadays call him, spread to connected industries (those engaged in outwork for example) using smaller premises, or even those which weren't so closely linked to others, not least because everyone was producing for that increased population which had been made possible by the agricultural revolution and fed the industrial one.

Often when different factors combine to boost fundamental change in the social, economic or political sphere there is a runaway effect which carries all before it. This was of course most evident in the country where the Industrial Revolution first began. Following its logic, cheap housing sprang up on a massive scale in the urban centres of the English north and midlands to accommodate the former agricultural labourers who flocked to the towns and cities to toil in workshops and factories (at the same time the countryside from which they had previously derived their living was being sold off for development as industry was able to make a greater contribution to the national economy, displacing agriculture to some extent, though obviously this process could not go beyond a certain stage; and then there was Enclosure). Things acquired a rapid momentum which left behind considerations of health, safety, sanitation. And the entrepreneurial classes, naturally seeking to benefit from the opportunities industrial growth created for their self-betterment, tended to maximise profits by keeping wages down. This is not to say, of course, that nothing could or should have been done to improve the lot of the industrial workers. But to understand the seemingly hysterical opposition of governments to any concession which might give encouragement to the "lower orders", in the matter of their relations with employers or the state, and perhaps lead them to demand more, we need to appreciate that the French Revolution, which began as a relatively moderate business, degenerated within the space of several years into violence, bloodshed and regicide. The reactionary attitude of Pitt and his colleagues is not altogether surprising. No doubt the Napoleonic Wars were used as a further excuse to shelve the issue of reform, whether to the electoral or the socioeconomic system. Though probably it was not appreciated at the time that Napoleon was a rather different phenomenon from the Revolution, though he arose from it and was inspired by the spirit of change it fostered; a misguided, often brutal, but not necessarily malign despot who sought a general reform of things according to his own megalomaniac lights rather than someone determined to overthrow the entire sociopolitical system in accordance with a particular ideology and in a spirit of hatred. In so far as this *was* appreciated, it made little difference as it suited the establishment for Bonaparte and the Terror to be identified with each other. Eventually, the passage of time plus the sheer necessity of some form of change led politicians to pass such measures as the Reform Act of 1832 and the Ten Hours Bill, however reluctantly in some cases.

As far as their workers were concerned anyway the "mill owners", to use a generic term, were a new kind of aristocracy. In Britain their relationship with the still powerful landed variety was an uneasy one, but improved to some extent after the 1832 Act, which gave them the vote, and the repeal of the Corn Laws satisfied many of their demands. A more sociologically complex ruling class emerged, though it was one where the old established aristocracy retained much influence, and continued to have tenants (it could be argued that the feudal system survived into the nineteenth century and after, except that of course the tenants did not have to assist their landlords in fighting for the king while the partnership between aristocracy and monarchy was mainly social after the latter lost the greater part of its political power). The nobility continued to look down on those who derived their wealth from industry and engineering as it seemed a dirty, ignoble trade. Their contempt for the self-made man was not justified even according to their own lights, because by now great industrial dynasties had been founded, it still being frequently the case that you went into the family business once old enough to work. But when agricultural depression, which meant that that sector was not as profitable as it had been and the rents from it correspondingly lower, or, later, the impact of social changes after the First and Second World Wars forced them to become involved in business in order to preserve their lifestyle they tended to choose the financial rather than the industrial sector. Either way it has probably done little for their popularity with those of a left-wing disposition, as it is easier to see them as part of an integrated, and oppressive, business class rather than as merely quaint survivors of a bygone age.

Political organisation had probably begun when Man was still little more than an animal, with someone brandishing a stone as a weapon and so making himself leader of his tribe. He needed helpers and so government, which inevitably became a sort of elite, evolved. From this also developed classes, as societies became more complex and stratified (originally we were all working-class); the difference between them was to be reinforced by disparities in wealth. And as societies grew more complex so did the mechanisms for regulating them. In time economic developments or political factors required changes to the established way of doing things, and peoples with a similar way of thinking would devise roughly the same system to replace it.

Simultaneous with all this was the appearance of art, literature (entirely oral in the beginning, then written), primitive music, and the emergence of religion. And the changes in work patterns that came with new ways of life, already described, meant people now had a little more leisure time to spend on cultural activities; plus a more complex society caused people to think in complex terms, the relatively crude art of the Stone Age giving way to something more refined and sophisticated. The process continued until, in our own time, it could be said to have been reversed: the social complexity, with so many diverse needs to meet and on a rapid-fire basis, has meant an emphasis on a high-powered economy, there being consequently less room in employers' mindsets for culture as opposed to image (which sells, and so generates the wealth that supposedly filters down in the end to all people) and, in theory, business efficiency. I am talking of course about that tendency which is referred to as "dumbing down".

The super-civilisations (I use the prefix "super" to indicate that they were especially advanced for the time and especially powerful, not that other societies, including barbarian ones, weren't "civilised") of antiquity developed where there were sufficient natural resources to support them (it was natural disasters, which they would have been less able to survive without the equipment of a modern industrial society, which often finished them off, along with other factors). They required a large population, together with other assets, mentioned below in the context of Rome, which as well as contributing to their own security and prosperity enabled them to dominate neighbouring communities militarily, politically and economically. They fell because of environmental factors, conquest by rival powers and perhaps the local depletion over a long enough period of vital minerals. Plus there is little doubt that moral degeneration plays a part in the collapse of civilisations, because it saps the intellectual and spiritual energy without which they cannot flourish and cannot defend themselves against increasingly powerful enemies. Rome was not the only great empire to fall partly for this reason. Egypt must have been more than the hotbed of immorality it is depicted as in the Old Testament, but there may be a connection between its sensuality as represented by the figure of Cleopatra and the fact that by her time it was little more than a province of the Roman Empire (though the former, if seen as a decline, could of course have been a symptom of the latter, a product of the demoralisation that comes from being brought low, rather than the other way round). Certainly, Cleopatra is portrayed in Shakespeare as symbolic of dangerously seductive influences which lure her lover Mark Anthony away from Rome with its more austere, noble and disciplined values. There may be more than a grain of historical truth in this. It does seem that Cleopatra was a very sexual person with kinky tastes; though such things may not necessarily go hand-in-hand with wickedness, it is often the case that they do. And Anthony left his wife and children for her, something she should have seen as wrong. Shakespeare depicts Anthony as a tragic figure, because he could not resist the spell she cast over him, with fatal consequences; but the fact is that the historically real Anthony and Cleopatra do not come over as very nice people. They were fellow travellers living in what religious puritans not without justification (in this case) would call sin. Octavius Caesar, a cold fish compared to Anthony who if flawed at least had passionate human emotions, but a better politician and leader carefully exploited Anthony's behaviour to further his own bid for power, making much of his rival's shirking of one's responsibilities to Rome and to family by spending so much time away with Cleo in Egypt.

There had been religion since Man first began to conceptualise his thoughts. People's ability to do so, when combined with the natural urge of all living things to go on surviving, made them wonder whether there was a world beyond the grave, and aspire to get there. Where entry to paradise depended on the will of deities, offerings (including human sacrifices) were made to them to win their favour. I suppose it was easier to believe in religion, to anthropomorphise things and see them in terms of a creative intelligence or intelligences (though this raises the question of *why* we do so in the first place) and their activities, before science, in the form in which it developed from the seventeenth century, appeared to suggest the universe was governed by mindless laws and at least cast doubt in the minds of ordinary people that a supreme sentience had anything to do with the matter. It *is* true to some extent that education makes you less likely to believe in religion, in that if science does have that effect, which has often been the case in the past, then the more you are taught about science the potentially less inclined you are to be religious. There is in fact a longer pedigree to atheism than one might suspect (which has no bearing on whether or not it is valid). The ancient Greeks, some of them anyway, were atheists, because they questioned received wisdom, in itself a healthy thing to do. And probably essential for scientific enquiry; because as far as we know the Greeks were the first scientists, which may explain their scepticism if science has a corrosive effect on religious belief.

We cannot easily get into the heads of people at this time in history, but it is possible that religious doctrines in antiquity were not intended to be literally true; they were consciously fabricated as a necessary way of expressing one's awe at the grandeur of the natural world and hope that there might be some existence after death, which business the gods being all-powerful would have control over so that it was important your conduct pleased them. This was clearly not true of the Judaeo-Christian God, who to his devotees was very much real and don't you forget it. But even if it genuinely is a revelation from God religion can't be entirely separated from its historical and social context, since once it enters into the human world it is inevitably subject, up to a point, to that world's customs. In time it became more sophisticated in its forms, just as society did.

Impelled most probably by population pressures, the human race branched out in all directions from its original home in Africa. At the same time the different ethnic groups diverged, because they were inhabiting different geographical regions and the environment had an effect on mental and physical characteristics, through the genes, as well as cultural forms. The first humans were in all probability black, because natural selection favoured dark skin as better able to withstand the burning African sun. Conversely in northern Europe where the climate was so much colder people tended to have pale skin and hair, often accompanied by blue eyes.

The characteristics first appeared when the Indo-European peoples migrated into Europe from Asia. This occurred thousands rather than millions of years ago and it is a sobering, indeed chilling thought that the genetic variations which, by emphasising our diversity, define us occurred so recently on the historic (taking the word to mean the human past whether or not recorded in writing or other media), and certainly the geological, timescale. It somehow has the effect of making us seem fragile, vulnerable; and therefore transitory, inevitably calling to mind the damage our misuse of the planet which supports us does to our own chances of survival.

I imagine the gene pool became muddied, with racial admixture taking place to a greater or lesser extent, from quite an early stage. It might happen through invasion, assimilation, mergers between two tribes, adoption of a child from one tribe into another. The process is still going on. It is arguably better if it happens slowly because then it is easier to adjust to. But eventually the new pattern of things becomes established and cannot be altered, unless very gradually, without meeting resistance.

In the beginning the tribal divisions corresponded to ethnic distinctions, in which physical characteristics correlated with mental and therefore cultural ones, but in the end it came to be accepted that a shared way of life and sense of identity, something which did not depend entirely on genes, was the most important thing. Tribes developed into nations, though not in the sense of their territories having actual defined boundaries except where these could be conveniently represented by natural features such as seas, rivers or mountain ranges (there were no truly *artificial* borders until the modern era, and of course even if it was agreed that one should have them there could still be disagreement as to where they should be drawn). A particular geographical area could be conceived of as inhabited by a more or less culturally homogenous population, and that proved sufficient for the purpose of establishing necessary terms of reference. The names given to "nations" by themselves, or each other, were essentially expressions of identification with something rather than official designations. For a long time they probably thought of themselves essentially as "peoples", even if they possessed the defining characteristics of nationhood such as a common culture, language (a crucial cementing factor here since it makes communication and thus full participation in the culture possible) and sense of identity. And national designations remained fairly fluid into at least the high Middle Ages (was Charlemagne a German or a Frenchman?). Until, arguably, the Roman Empire there was never at any time an attempt to create a single world state embracing all peoples; not only was allegiance to a particular tribe/nation too great, but it would simply not have been practically possible (both these obstacles still pertain today). Rome, of course, could only have succeeded in conquering, if it had been within its resources, the whole of the *known* world (it had a pretty good go, as did Alexander the Great). There were many societies who would not have been aware of each others' existence. Any folk memory of a time when people were all living together in the same part of Africa (and had all been black because of environmental conditions there) had long been lost.

The nations/peoples came into conflict with each other just as the tribes had done. Sometimes there was a genuine dispute over territory, sometimes members of one tribe/nation had wronged another by raiding it and stealing women or crops. The tribe which lost the battle might be displaced or wiped out, or the two sides continue to exist in a state of perpetual feud. But as societies became more sophisticated so did the reasons why they went to war. There also arose what later eras came to call imperialism. Like most trends in history it can be explained by a variety of factors. But it was, and still is, a form of protection, even if it can also be practised simply for the sake of power as with a Hitler or a Putin. In a violent and uncertain world where you could not always be sure of others' intentions, that they would be peaceful towards you, and there was a degree of competition for economic resources (with more land needed to accommodate populations who were expanding because of agricultural improvements which made it possible to feed a greater number) the more territory, and thus wealth (from the products of agriculture or industry) you had the stronger you were. Buffer zones might be created between yourself and an enemy. And if you could attain lordship over other peoples you could control their behaviour and prevent them being a threat. They were also a captive market for your produce. Generally speaking territory conveyed power, and wealth status though you would of course be resented by those you had achieved dominance over. Another factor which was coming to be important was patriotism, a form of group loyalty which focused on the increase of a people's power and influence as an ideal. Of course a culture had to be *able* to be imperialistic, and this was possible where natural resources were such as to provide industry with the means of making military equipment, weapons and armour, on a large scale. Having the right mindset and skills, along with further contributory factors such as geographical location and size of population, was essential if they were to be exploited. In Rome's case the mixture of ingredients was about right.

And so boundary disputes were allowed to develop into annexation, in what was ostensibly a strategy for self-defence. Those who could do this sort of thing, to its utmost practical extent, did; the Romans, of course, were particularly good at it. Those who couldn't, if not protected by geographical isolation, succumbed. As it was Rome succeeded in dominating all of Europe, with the exception of most of Germany and of Scandinavia, plus parts of the Middle East and North Africa. No other empire before the British was so successful, or so long-lasting. The Romans were culturally rather barren, in terms of having original ideas of their own – they borrowed a lot from Greece including their religion – but made up for it by an efficient administration and military organisation, without which of course their expansion would not have been possible. They also had the sense to see that there was value in bringing subject peoples on board, in showing there were benefits to be gained from being a Roman citizen, e.g. certain legal immunities, aqueducts, better roads. Ruling elites at least were keen to lap up the "creature comforts", finding a kind of prestige in aping Roman ways. This made it easier for Rome to convince herself she was indeed doing the peoples she conquered a favour, and so appease her conscience over the whole business.

Of ancient civilisations Greece and Rome, along with Egypt (whose achievement of building the pyramids is admired, while the practice of mummifying the dead has created an iconic image made much use of in horror films, for example) are the two best known today, partly for ethnocentric reasons. Babylon, Assyria, and the civilisations of ancient Asia, America and sub-Saharan Africa are of course equally worthy of study. If they receive less attention it is because they do not have a direct link to modern Western civilisation, which has become the globally dominant one; they seem to be sidings rather than stations on the main line. The "barbarian" societies of both northern and southern Europe inherited the achievements, the legacy, of the Greeks and Romans, though politically they were divided into separate nations or kingdoms plus the dubiously named Holy Roman Empire. In language, science, philosophy, culture, politics and the study of history they supplied the prototypes, the archetypes, the building blocks anyway for so much that was done in the West, and through the latter's influence the world at large, later on. A politician who held or sought a position of supreme power was described as a Caesar, and the rival who metaphorically or otherwise stabbed him in the back (or the front), thinking he was getting too big for his boots, compared to Brutus. Roman affairs demonstrated the truth that political systems were not static; Rome changed from being a republic to a dictatorship, under Julius Caesar, and then finally to an imperial monarchy. Greece, or at any rate the city state of Athens, was actually a democracy, at a time when most other polities in the world were not and several thousand years before they were. This tends to reinforce the view that the passing of the classical civilisations marked a general regression, a retreat from progress; but human sociopolitical evolution does not follow a neatly "progressive" path, and the fact is that until fairly recently in world history democracy has been the exception rather than the rule (leaving out the question of how far it is a misnomer anyway). The exceptions were small states such as Venice which came about in particular circumstances where everyone had to act corporately to make things work, in such a way that autocratic kingship or dictatorship would have been inappropriate. In the Venetian example, refugees from the "barbarian" invasions of Italy (who because they *were* refugees, would have pulled together in mutual support) fled to the marshy areas around a lagoon whose location gave them the opportunity to turn their community into a maritime power, capable of acquiring territories overseas (or inland for that matter) in a way which seems astonishing, through collegiate activity. Protected by its strategic situation, its navy, and its diplomatic skills the Venetian Republic lasted the better part of a thousand years. Of course the Venetians had not anticipated encountering someone like Napoleon, who basically sought to bend the world to his will and had an unshakeable conviction that he could succeed in such an aim where all others had failed. Hitler would have caused them the same problems. Though at least Napoleon was motivated by a misguided form of philanthropism, wanting to do humanity good, as he saw it, whether it liked it or not and concluding that the Venetians had become decadent and autocratic, no longer fitting in with his conception of what was liberal and progressive. Hitler, however he might have viewed himself, did not have that excuse.

But on the subject of sociopolitical and cultural change no historical community has ever been entirely static. In religion Ancient Egypt went through a shift from polytheism to monotheism under the pharaoh Akhenaton. There were also upheavals in the power structure, sometimes due to demographic change which altered the ethnic composition of society, sometimes to political factors, sometimes to both. A native ruling dynasty might be succeeded by one of foreign origin; the Ptolemys, of whom Cleopatra was a member, were Greek, and at least one dynasty are said to have been black, which is perfectly possible although the definition of "black" can be flexible and especially if one is keen to showcase "black" achievements in reaction to white supremacist attitudes. Certainly the (Arab-descended) modern Egyptians are not ethnically the same as the ancient ones, which gives some idea of how total demographic change can be, given time.

Whatever the truth in matters of race, the achievements of all past societies are worthy of some kind of study. We must be careful of course to disentangle where possible their mythologies, or those of the civilisations which succeeded them, from reality. When a written record of past events, perhaps based on a previous oral tradition, was first made there may have been a certain degree of embellishment (that said, there is no reason why Homer's account of the Trojan war, for example, could not be substantially true, including the wooden horse, once it is shorn of any supernatural elements). And what seemed huge and impressive to the people of those times, in proportion to what they expected, might not seem so impressive to us, who are accustomed because of our more advanced technology to building on a large scale. Although we already have a rough idea of how big they were, if we were to travel back in time and actually set eyes on the lost buildings and statues of the ancient world they might seem to us disappointingly small. From the perspective of the present, the past tends sometimes to be inflated. "In afterlife, images grow bigger".

Rome as a great power, an empire, lasted roughly for five hundred years; half a millennium. Inevitably others have sought to equal this. They have not really succeeded, Britain perhaps coming closest. The reason why empires in modern history – the British, French, German, etc. – have not endured, or will not endure, as long as Rome's is because in recent centuries the pace of change, the speed at which history moves, has been greater, and the empires more quickly overtaken by the factors which lead to their decline. Technological and thus political and economic progress, a race in which some win and some lose out, has been more rapid. This applies whether the imperialism is military/political, economic or both.

The Romans' policy of inclusiveness perhaps proved their eventual undoing, especially when they had to play host to large "barbarian" populations displaced by the westward march of the Huns and Vandals. The definition of citizenship became so broad and was applied to so many people that there began to be confusion as to what "Roman" actually meant other than a legal title. The Western Empire failed to resist "barbarian" invaders because there was no clear national identity to serve as a focus for that resistance. This of course does not mean that any degree of immigration or racial admixture is wrong, merely that in an imperfect world those things can be destabilising if they happen on a certain scale.

2

Despite the impression given by cinema, the fall of the Roman Empire was a gradual, piecemeal process spread over a hundred years or so and not compressed into a few as it necessarily had to be for the purposes of a film. It did not happen because the Empire overreached itself; a halt had already been called to its outward expansion and in recognition of its government being a difficult and complex task it had been split into two halves, a Western and an Eastern. The Eastern survived for another millennium or so as the Byzantine Empire, though its fall to Islam in 1453 was largely symbolic as it had effectively collapsed from within some time before. The Western Empire's disintegration was due to a number of causes of which dilution of national identity was one, internal dissension another, while Christianity with its renunciation of old gods may have assisted the process by further challenging the traditional conception of what it was to be "Roman" (its purpose was of course salvation in the afterlife more than preserving a particular Earthly political arrangement).

But perhaps in the end Rome and the Romans were simply swallowed up by the new world which was coming into being as a result of population movements. Of the people inhabiting the peninsula of Italy today some are descended from the "original" Romans – who may themselves have been invaders – some, judging by their fair hair and skin, the Germanic Goths, and some from a darker type, more like Arabs or the traditional image of a Latin, whose origin I can't place. (Some of the Romans were themselves fair; I don't know where this would have come from). There was also a substantial North African element. Western Europe in the early Middle Ages was something of a cultural melting pot. What made assimilation easier was that ethnic identities seem to have been more fluid, more easily adjustable, at this time than at many others, as seems proven by what happened in Britain after the Roman legions withdrew. Following the departure of Rome as an occupying military force (some Roman colonists would have stayed behind, intermarrying with the local population) it was settled in large numbers by tribes from Germany, Denmark, and later Scandinavia proper (excepting Swedes, who seem for geographic reasons to have rather turned east, into what's now Russia, Poland, Ukraine etc., so that there are probably more naturally blond(e) people in those countries today than in the west). As opposed to the quite separate migration of the Goths (who originated in the same part of the world, though where exactly isn't clear) and other northern peoples into Roman territory, which started a little earlier and was due to the westward movement of an aggressive military force, the Angles, Saxons, Jutes, Friesians, Danes and Norse were impelled, along with the Swedish colonisers of the east, by population pressures, a massive demographic explosion being under way in the part of the world they inhabited.

Concerning the first wave of this migration, that involving the Saxons (Germans); Friesians (Dutch, although they wouldn't have called themselves that then); Angles (who gave their name to England despite not being the most numerous of the immigrants); and Jutes (whose precise origin, like that of the Angles, is unclear; they seem to have settled only in particular areas, such as Hampshire or Kent), there is some uncertainty over the exact nature of what happened. Can it with accuracy be called an invasion, or series of invasions? The historical resentment of the Welsh and Scots at the supposed depredations of the Saxons (*Sassenachs*, a derogatory term at one time used by the Scots for the English despite the latter being ancestrally more mixed than it would imply) would suggest so. The Welsh, or the ethnic groups speaking a Brythonic Celtic tongue who later assumed a common Welsh national identity, were supposedly driven out from mainland Britain by the invaders into the region they now inhabit. It may be, though, that time has caused the historical memory to play tricks, become distorted, which can happen with even the most important events over a period of a thousand years. According to current theories the ancient Britons (strictly, Romano-Celts) were left suffering a kind of identity crisis when the Romans, on whom they had modelled their lifestyle, left and resolved it by happily adopting the customs and language of the Germanic "invaders". They were even prepared to let the Saxons impose their own kings upon the country, as seems to have happened. Whatever the truth of the matter we are not looking at genocide or mass displacement of an existing population, as happened with the Native Americans in the eighteenth and nineteenth centuries. The British can be proud that nothing like that has ever happened in their history during the last two thousand years.

The Saxons had not so much stormed ashore massacring everyone as plonked themselves down on the Britons' doorstep and taken their acceptance for granted, which was a form of arrogance; but the Britons did not mind. For another thing, there was a serious population shortage in the land at the time (the Saxons, to arbitrarily apply the name to all the newcomers, would in many cases have been occupying empty territory), and a new infusion was needed to make up this loss and boost the economy. In some cases the Germans (though they might not have thought of themselves as that) were invited in to help repel northern pirates (Vikings?) who were raiding the eastern coast, and afterwards decided to stay, forcibly taking land against the wishes of their hosts. We just don't know the overall story, though military battles were undoubtedly fought, at Mount Badon for example, in resistance to the colonisation. I suspect that in some parts of the country it was an invasion, and as such resented by the locals, while elsewhere it was peaceful. In so far as integration was happily achieved, the migration was solicited, or at least accepted, for economic reasons, and the indigenes even adopted the new arrivals' ways there might seem to be a valuable lesson here for those currently unhappy about immigration into the United Kingdom, whatever its source. Well, maybe. But the country is much more densely populated than in Romano-British times and there are practical issues to do with how many people it can altogether accommodate. And in an atomised and uncertain world with, these days, less of the solace to be got from religion, say, established national and ethnic identities are more important as sources of psychological comfort to fall back on.

But in the fifth and sixth centuries integration *was* achieved, to such an extent that the English came to refer to themselves as "Anglo-Saxons" even though the Germanic element in their ancestry was rather less than popularly supposed as the survival of British place names and of Celtic physical traits (most obviously dark hair, sometimes a broader facial bone structure) within the population, both on a large scale, makes clear. The reason why we have in the past tended to think of the English as a Germanic people is because it became fashionable with the Saxon, Angle and Jutish invasions to be a German, to adopt a Germanic culture and language into which words of French, Celtic or Latin origin were absorbed; there are many which one would think Anglo-Saxon in their derivation but in fact are not, though the reverse can also be the case. But although the Angles, Saxons, Jutes, Celts, Vikings, Romans etc. would originally have counted as separate ethnic groups according to modern standards and terminology, since they were differentiated from each other by both physical appearance and culture, today they survive essentially as genetic characteristics, mutated and hybridised to some extent but often still discernible. (The extent to which individual families are Germanic/Scandinavian or Romano-British by descent is debatable, as admixture means that the percentage of northern or southern European genes within them will have varied over time). From a fairly early stage people stopped referring to themselves as Saxon, or whatever, in a *political* sense as opposed to that of a figure of speech, and if they were to do so today they would be considered crazy.

The reconversion of Britain to Christianity by Columbia and Augustine would have helped create a common culture. The Vikings proved difficult to absorb because unlike the Saxons they conquered by force; they seem to have concluded their colonisation would be opposed but since as they saw it they had no choice in the matter anyway, having been forced from their homelands by sheer population pressure, didn't bother asking. The warriors paved the way for the settlers. But in time they too became part of a tribe called "English", more or less forgetting, like everyone else, their narrower ethnic origins, and simultaneously becoming Christianised. They had nowhere else to go, so it was accepted that they were here to stay. They settled mainly above a line cutting diagonally across the country from the Norfolk-Suffolk coast to the Mersey, which is why there are more fair-haired people there than in the South. Whether, genetically, the British are more Germanic/Scandinavian than Romano-Celtic (excluding for simplicity's sake Jews, Asians, Afro-Caribbeans etc.) is difficult to say and research has produced wildly differing (as well as bizarre) and therefore unhelpful results. One survey concluded that the dominant element was contributed by the Neolithic tribes who were here even before the Celts − unlikely considering all the successive migrations, sometimes on a large scale, that have taken place over the last two thousand years. And another that most people were descended from the Friesians − also unlikely as there were even less of them than there were the Angles. What is the actual truth? But perhaps, these days, it doesn't really matter.

I said that there has been one constant, if not entirely uninterrupted, trend in history, namely the development of society into more complex forms due to technological advance. It has certainly not been towards greater political unity; that, except when brought about by military conquest, is a relatively recent thing, confined to Europe and dented, though how badly we can't say at present, by the Brexit business. A certain homogeneity is achieved where a society (in the sense of a collection of nations bound by a basically similar culture, like the modern West) lives under a common economic system, and this will lead to a degree of political unification, but it will not necessarily mean actual rule in all areas from a single point (i.e. Brussels), and there was not this uniformity before the apparent (and by no means universal) triumph of monetarism in the late twentieth century. That the political, whether in terms of simple control or of administrative and constitutional unity, integration of different nations is not a constant, ongoing trend in history is proven by the fall of the Roman Empire and its disintegration into a host of different tribes/peoples. These may have amalgamated to some extent, but whether or not this occurred the new ethnic groupings which emerged each acquired, in time, their own national selfconsciousness. But the immediate result of Rome's fall was what became popularly known as the Dark Ages, a supposed lapse into barbarism, chaos and conflict. Certainly it had given Europe, at least, a unity (if imposed rather than grown out of the will of the peoples) she was never to experience again. But as the known world increased in size it was doubtful whether the Empire could practically be repeated anyway. Limits to its territorial extent had already been set; it might have trading links with India and China but could never have conquered them. But how disastrous exactly for Europe was the end of the Roman era?

Undoubtedly there were advantages in Rome's hegemony, which were lost when it ended. Its cosmopolitanism, along with its road network and the economic links between different parts of the Empire, enabled a spread of ideas, certainly assisting the rise of Christianity through the evangelical travels of St Paul. But whether its fall resulted in a continent-wide descent into savagery and chaos is more questionable. It is not true to say "they made a desert and called it Rome"; the Romans did have philosophers, and men of letters such as Cicero (politically, a good man crushed by the system) who excelled at both the written and the spoken word. And although they modelled a lot of their culture on that of Greece, at least it shows they did have one. But the "barbarians" who followed them, both those who were instrumental in their downfall and those like the Saxons and Vikings who they had little or no contact with, were not necessarily *un*cultured brutes. In part this was because they had themselves become part-Romanised (Theodoric the Goth being an example), respecting and seeking to preserve Roman culture, literature and customs. But we should perhaps think of *different* societies rather than morally and culturally inferior ones, especially since the latter is a dubious concept which apart from being offensive can lead to racism (it amounts in fact to the same thing). What constitutes "civilisation" anyway? If it is proper moral conduct, then we should reflect that there were virtuous barbarians and decadent Romans (as some Roman writers indeed stressed). Romans could themselves be perpetrators of barbarous cruelty at home and abroad. One problem is that "civilisation" is associated with a certain image, one of grand buildings, well-organised armies (if warfare is "civilised"), and culture (philosophy, art, poetry) in the modern or Graeco-Roman sense, which involves that those societies which don't have such things are composed of uncouth, violent, beast-like thugs who get what they want by bashing someone over the head. It could be argued that any society which is ordered, with a set of rules and regulations, as were all societies from the beginning (and more or less by the definition of "society"), is a "civilisation". Societies do not reach the same stage of scientific and technological development (if those things are equivalent with civilisation in the moral − and most important − sense, something which could be disputed) at the same time. But the absence of anywhere in Northern Europe from an encyclopedia I once browsed through of civilisations gives the unfortunate impression that its inhabitants were dull-witted clods. There is probably an element of inferiority complex in what I say, but it is true nonetheless. And apparent cultural chauvinism can have dangerous consequences; as I have suggested elsewhere it was this sense of inferiority, taken to extremes, which led the Nazis to be, shall we say, assertive regarding the merits of North European − Aryan − culture compared to others.

Perhaps the Celts, Saxons, Vikings etc. simply had different skills. They were good at metalwork (producing *objets d'art* (jewellery, etc.) which are in their own way very attractive, woodwork (the Anglo-Saxons had the forests of the Weald to play with), and stonework, using it to make buildings, and especially churches which are the best surviving examples). It is not patronising to say that this workmanship, which can seem rough-hewn compared to that of the Normans or Romans, is delightful in its homely simplicity. The contrast simply means that the North European mind was different from the Latin or Gallic. And we must remember that Anglo-Saxon England had a literature, e.g. *Boewulf* and the writings of the Venerable Bede. Learning, in the provision of which monasteries were important, was encouraged by monarchs such as Alfred the Great. In terms of government England was more or less a unitary state by the Norman Conquest. In fact King Athelstan, who is politically in some ways more significant than Alfred notwithstanding the latter's defeats of the Danes, which confined them largely to the north of the country but were otherwise inconsequential, was at least able to attempt uniting it with Scotland as one realm of Britain, though that enterprise proved too ambitious. It was also law-abiding; it was said that in Alfred's time a woman could walk all the way from Wessex to Northumbria on her own without being molested. The claim was probably exaggerated but there must be a reason why it was made at all. If some parts of the north were difficult to govern in later centuries (witness Elizabeth I's difficulties with the Northern Earls), this was because of lingering resentment at the Norman Conquest on the part of sections of the population, plus Catholic allegiances, which proved to be strong in the region, acting as a focus for discontent after the Reformation. It should be noted that France was not quite unified until the fifteenth and sixteenth centuries, when Burgundy ceased to act as an independent state in its dealings with other powers, and Italy and Germany (though it is Germans we have been talking about, sort of) until c1870. Altogether, if Anglo-Saxon England was a settled and ordered state, and had literature, then it was a civilisation, and had been for some time before the Normans conquered it and brought it under their own supposedly more efficient and enlightened rule.

The Romans unified a large part of the known world under them. They had an efficient military organisation. They had straight roads (part of the efficient military organisation). They built grand buildings. They had central heating and aqueducts. But with the latter exceptions it can be questioned whether they were much more technologically advanced than some other societies of their time (the central heating and the aqueducts and the grand buildings and the military organisation, plus the extent of the empire they were able to create, tend to give the impression that they were). They had watermills, which with their arrangements of shafting and gearing, admittedly crude by comparison with the technology of the Industrial Revolution, were among the first, if not *the* first, complex machines. But like a lot of things these were borrowed from the Greeks, who in turn had got them from somewhere in the Middle/Near East region; though this I suppose begs the question whether "civilisation" was something inherited by one culture from another rather than present in all cultures from the beginning. By the usual definition of the term, though I do not accept it, civilisation began with the societies of ancient Mesopotamia, who it is thought invented writing and the wheel. It does seem to be the case that, resources and skills (the latter to some extent genetically derived) not being distributed evenly, certain cultures are significant in terms of important historical developments while others essentially inherit their achievements. Harping too much on this can lead to a derogatory belief, little better than outright racism, that some cultures can only become civilised through *imitation.* By this token Rome, "Anglo-Saxons" and today's surviving tribal societies might all be looked down on as backward if not inferior. I think it is better to say that each culture adds something important of its own to the chemical combination. Undoubtedly the peoples of northern (and southern) Europe built on the scientific and artistic achievements of Greece and Rome and it is a matter of conjecture, at least, whether their civilisation would have been so splendid without that influence. But north Europeans, while sometimes lacking in imagination, had a certain skill with practical things which made possible the Industrial Revolution once combined with other elements to trigger off the process. At worst, from the point of view of their own cultural prestige, they were dwarves standing on the shoulders of giants – and therefore able to see further. At best they created something which through the hegemony (part of a wider Western one) of Britain and the USA made them the dominant force in the world. Arguably they still retain this position, if the basic power structure in America is seen as WASP (White Anglo-Saxon Protestant) in nature. Of course WASP is often just a figure of speech, having more to do with shared culture than with precise genetics/ancestry; the hegemony is currently facing serious challenges; and though there is normally a *dominant* race or culture, because that's the way the world is, there is no such thing as a *superior* one.

At any rate we should be grateful that the development of technology, whether or not it is a requirement for being "civilised", does not happen at a constant pace. The Romans were undoubtedly more progressive than the Anglo-Saxons in terms of personal hygiene (the latter rarely if ever washed). It is not entirely true that the Anglo-Saxons neglected Roman architectural and engineering achievements; in one case an aqueduct remained in use in England for several hundred years after the Romans pulled out, although this may simply have been a matter of letting what was already in existence continue to serve its purpose. But generally it was not the case that they studied hypocausts etc. and were put in a "technological" frame of mind whereby they sought to develop what they found on settling in Britain into something even more sophisticated. That they didn't, and often let Roman buildings fall into disrepair without even taking them over and adapting them for their own use, has unfortunately reinforced their reputation as cultural yobs. But if they had − or if the Romans themselves had taken things further in this way − we might well have all blown ourselves up by now!

Given that some cultures may be better at particular activities than others, without anyone being "inferior", and maybe combined with other things it is quite likely that the supplanting of one culture by another could lead to cultural decline in some respects, if never in all. (Here it should be stressed that "culture" is not necessarily the same thing as "race", on which subject people may be particularly sensitive regarding the matters under discussion; a culture is a society of people who may originally have been ethnically disparate but follow a common way of life.) The Anglo-Saxons not having central heating is an example of this. And the quality of art in the West undoubtedly declined after the fall of the Roman Empire. In the sculpture of the Graeco-Roman world (less so in its painting) one finds astonishingly realistic, and expressive, depictions of the human face and form; we see those faces in the street of any city today. It is something absent in the Middle Ages and not recaptured until the Renaissance, when it makes a comeback in both media (although to my mind the Roman sculptures are superior to anything the modern world has produced).

But assuming that the Romans were "civilised" and their immediate successors were not, by 1100 if not before it could be said that a new European civilisation had emerged to replace their empire. It was not a single administratively unified body in the way the latter had been; it consisted of an assortment of by now distinct national groups (plus some who were still essentially tribal in nature) inhabiting vaguely defined, though coherent enough in the public mind to supply terms of reference, territories. These groups governed themselves, or perhaps it would be more correct to say that they were governed by their own rulers, since there was no such thing as democracy in the contemporary Western world. (There had not been, by and large, since Ancient Greece, and even there the majority of ordinary citizens were excluded from the franchise. "Progress" does not mean a sustained and steady advance towards political liberty any more than it does towards political *unity*.) But Charlemagne, the first Holy Roman Emperor (crowned 800), had created a kind of successor to the western Roman Empire, though only symbolically since it did not by any means rule over the whole of western Europe, as opposed to a large chunk of Germany (then a region rather than an officially recognised state) and the Low Countries, within which its control was often loose. The achievement of the Romans had not been replicated (in the sixth century the eastern Emperor Justinian had tried to reunify the two halves of the former Empire but was only partially, and temporarily, successful). But if Charlemagne's was not an empire in the Roman sense, and sometimes only questionably one in others, it did provide a degree of stability, and the symbolism was important. It was debatable how far the Empire was holy — and since Charlemagne and most of the people he ruled over were of Germanic descent or culture, it was stretching credibility too far to call it Roman, though its ethnic composition was not the point anyway. Because the identification of particular peoples with particular territories, which became "nations" if not in the modern sense, was still incomplete and because the Empire fragmented for a time following Charlemagne's death, when it was divided between his sons, the Frankish or "French" western parts of it split off from the rest, which became increasingly Germanic in character. But it did reinforce the impression of Europe as a coherent entity, and the Emperor did have the power to take on the Pope over such matters as the appointment of senior figures in the Church, in what was to prove a long-running political and theological dispute as to when the temporal authority, which was supposed to have been appointed by God, should take precedence over the spiritual. However he didn't always win.

Tribal disputes over territory, whether or not one regards "tribe" as being synonymous with nationality, in the modern West anyhow, have always been a feature of human behaviour, though in western Europe they more or less ceased to be a source of violence during the twentieth century as a reaction to the increasingly destructive effects of warfare in the industrial age. The process by which tribes became nations (or kingdoms, which they generally were apart from the odd republic) after the fall of Rome and the fundamental change this brought about to the map of Europe was a long, fraught and haphazard one which lasted a millennium and a half and has only ceased to be a cause of war in the last hundred years or so. As well as be considered important on account of their strategic significance should war break out, and thus vital to one's legitimate interests which included security, territories could be fought or haggled over between powers who each thought they had a historic right to them or could change hands due to dynastic marriages, the resulting family connection enabling ruler A to claim territory B as part of his domain or so he supposed. It produced the seeming absurdity of Hapsburg Spain ruling the Netherlands, separated from it by enough of a distance to be vastly different in climate, geography and culture, for several centuries. The Holy Roman Emperor might also be the Archduke of Austria and king of Spain as with Charles V or, latterly (and confusingly), the "Austrian Emperor" as with Francis II. Although the German states always made it clear that they were not subject territories of the Hapsburg family, that family did in practice acquire a monopoly of Holy Roman Emperors from the fifteenth century even if they still had to be elected (it had been the case with other families in the Middle Ages, until in 1078 the states decided that no-one would become Emperor simply because he was the son of the German King, a principle which was observed for several hundred years at least). To clarify, the Habsburgs ruled both their own lands in Austria and elsewhere and, less tightly and autocratically, the wider Empire; each set of territories had its own, separate administration at Vienna. At one point Joseph II was Holy Roman Emperor and his wife, Maria Theresa, the Hapsburg Empress. It all emphasised the fluid and confusing nature of European geopolitical arrangements, a continuing legacy of population movements plus the fall of the Western Roman Empire in the fifth century, before they were rationalised to a considerable extent by Napoleon in the 1800s (his abolition of the Empire left the Hapsburgs as rulers of Austria alone). And as evidenced by the wars of the Spanish, Polish and Austrian successions dynasticism remained a cause (rather than a pretext, which is not quite the same thing) of armed conflict into at least the eighteenth century, when monarchs on mainland Europe had more power than was to be the case later.

The Holy Roman Empire has never been a household name among those with no more than a basic knowledge of history, due to its odd and confusing nomenclature and the ambiguity of its position. It did attempt from time to time, and with varying success, to assert its control over Italy, historic centre of the former Roman Empire, and thus be more like what it claimed it was. Intervening in Italy was not too difficult because that region was until the mid-late nineteenth century a patchwork of different states, some based territorially on little more than a single city although they could nonetheless become very powerful, e.g. Venice. This and other states tended to conclude treaties with France, the Empire, England etc. in their own right as would any sovereign country. The Pope in Rome, besides being the spiritual counterpart in the West to Charlemagne and his successors, had also acquired temporal power in the region around the capital and this further hindered the political unity of Italy and its attempts to become anything more than a "geographical expression", as Metternich described it. (Being a temporal ruler meant of course that the Pope had to use military force or political chicanery and double-dealing to pursue what he saw as his interests, and in later centuries this had the effect of tarnishing Christianity's image. It was and is strongly suspected that he used the threat of excommunication as a political weapon, to make rival potentates cede him territory, rather than a spiritual one; at any rate his enemies tended to be unimpressed by it. Theologically the practice can be questioned unless one accepts the doctrine of papal infallibility. The latter is a dangerous notion since it can be misused by a flawed human being who merely seeks an excuse for their actions, or is simply in error, the consequences either way being potentially disastrous. God might not agree with the injunction, and the excommunicated therefore not necessarily be in spiritual peril.)

In Germany the most powerful of the states, Prussia, emerged in the eighteenth century as a serious rival to both the Empire (of which it had never been a part) and Austria, the other principal contender for regional hegemony, thanks to Frederick the Great. And although it may not have been what Frederick intended it was Prussia which later proved instrumental in building a unified German nation, something the Empire never was although it is correct to say that it ruled over a common "German" cultural polity, with other peoples and language groups sometimes tacked on, and indeed saw things in that light. True, there were Kings of Germany from the Middle Ages, and Emperors were usually elected from among their number by the other German potentates after the French portions of the Empire split off, but the German states were no more one country because they were governed, in theory or in practice, by the same person than were England and Scotland before the 1707 Act of Union. The Nazis did regard the Empire as having been the first Reich, i.e. unified German polity, but it was not strictly speaking that. Perhaps the point is that Germans had seen it as such during its heyday; by 1500 it was being referred to as "the Holy Roman Empire of the German nation" rather than the "Roman Empire". Initially the Emperor had seen himself, however presumptuously, as the inheritor of the Caesars, and for the good of the Western world, and in accordance with this all his territories mattered equally to him. Later he became to some extent the focus for German nationalism. The last Emperor not to see himself in this light was Charles V, more of a Spaniard, who found the task of ruling his widespread territories too arduous, especially when he was fighting a losing battle against the spread of Protestantism in Germany, and eventually retired to a monastery. By the eighteenth century the empire was being referred to as the German rather than the Holy Roman Empire, the non-German territories – such as Burgundy, long absorbed into a unitary France, Italy, the Netherlands and the Swiss Cantons – having mostly been shed, or shed themselves. The alliance with the universal Catholic Church had been shaky long before it was shattered by the Reformation, the electors having declared in 1338 that the Emperor was entitled both to call himself "King of the Romans" and to rule as German king without reference to the Pope.

Like other rulers the Emperor had to play a geopolitical game of chess if he was to maintain and/or increase his power, and eventually lost to more skilled players. His role in Europe was never the same after the Reformation with its profound political consequences at a time when politics and religion were inextricably wedded; because he might be a Protestant. There were to be no more coronations in Rome. Nor did the Empire ever recover from the dislocating effects of the Thirty Years' War. Nonetheless its final disappearance was regretted. But Napoleon had changed the map of Europe too far for it to be restored – and increasingly Prussia, to all intents and purposes a sovereign state, came to be seen as the agency of a unified Germany rather than a resurrected Holy Roman Empire. By the eighteenth century the Empire had been surpassed as an arbiter of Europe by strong unitary powers such as Britain and France, the latter proving in the end its nemesis. The early nineteenth was a period in which the German states apart from Prussia and Austria were militarily weak compared to France and Russia (rising powers between which Germans feared they might be trapped), and so patriots felt that nothing existed to give full and proper expression to their aspirations. And although Germany was always to be (she is now) a federal entity, with separate state legislatures – after unification in 1871 some states even retained their own monarchs, the most notable being mad King Ludwig of Bavaria, though these were subordinate to the Emperor in Berlin – she was much more so in the days of the "Holy Roman" Empire, with no capital city, as opposed to royal court (not necessarily the same thing) and far greater powers over finance, administration and justice being reserved to the elector princes and free towns. Nationalists in Prussia and other regions of what was culturally and geographically, at least, a "Germany" felt that both patriotic aspirations and political and military security demanded something more.

But in the Middle Ages, the Empire's existence did help in initially giving post-Roman Europe a sense of order and continuity. And the fact that the Emperor was crowned by the Pope, which remained the case until the sixteenth century, represented the link between the political and spiritual dimensions of the new polity. Emerging nationalism during the Middle Ages in countries like England and France, which saw themselves as powers acting in their own right and in their own interests, and in England's case had never been subject to the Empire's jurisdiction, worked against the Emperor being a sovereign ruler over all the West. But the by now triumphant religion of Christianity, along with the development of the feudal system in which land was held from the local lord in return for an obligation to fight for him in the king's wars (or a civil war), served to forge cultural and sociopolitical unity and common identity. Religion was used to bolster the social and political structure, which it was honestly believed God had ordained, the consequence being that in the thinking of the time religious unity and political unity/stability were not separated and if the former were lacking the situation constituted a threat to the whole existing order. There was an element of power politics in this, of course, but such is to be expected. The identification of religion and political organisation with one another explains why Charlemagne forced the German Saxons, who were still holding on to the old pagan ways, to convert, massacring thousands of them when they proved obdurate. This is the only thing I have against him; apart from its generally controversial nature, "Blythman" is in origin a Saxon name, and if the Saxons who came to England and the Germanic people who gave their name to the part of their country called Saxony are the same, which according to the British Museum is the case (email to author), he could be said to have slaughtered my relatives. One gets the impression that the Saxons, whether in Germany or Britain, were an unruly lot who wouldn't always play ball, which meant that the Normans had to be both harsh and judicious in dealing with them, but did they not have a right to follow their own beliefs and customs? (I speak as a Christian.) One can condone Charlemagne's actions only by regarding them as inevitable given the mindset of the time. He incidentally was a Frank, a member of the Germanic people who gave their name to France, ironically considering the animosity which was to arise between the latter and Germany in later centuries, until they got tired of fighting each other and for better or worse set up the EU.

By extension the contemporary association between religious uniformity and political order was a reason why the Byzantine and Holy Roman Empires did not unite, recreating to some extent Rome's achievement and without necessarily having to embark on military conquest; the obstacle being, of course, the doctrinal split between the western (Roman Catholic, with its headquarters in Rome) and the Eastern (Orthodox) church, which endures to the present day though without causing as much bitterness as it probably did initially.

The new European polity (in so far as it was a *single* polity) was more or less safe from external aggression. The chief threats in this respect had been the Vikings and the Muslims. The Vikings were by now tamed, although they will never be rid of the reputation they have acquired for unwarranted brutality. If you are looking for something to call the roads on a new housing estate and find inspiration in the peoples who have contributed to the making of the British nation, you can have a Norman Road and a Saxon Road but call anywhere Viking Road and people will think it is inhabited by marauding berserkers. The Muslims (in many ways less brutal), had been on the march since not long after the foundation of their religion in 622. Like Christians of the time they saw no distinction between the religious and the secular and viewed themselves as a single sociopolitical community (holding on to this principle, as many Muslims still do, after Christianity had effectively abandoned it, even if it did not prove practical in the end to create a single Muslim nation). This civilisation sought power for the sake of its own protection and because it believed itself to be more enlightened than the Christians even if it wasn't necessarily going to force people to change their religion. Islam undoubtedly wanted to militarily conquer Europe, and the face of the world would have looked very different if it had succeeded. But it did not succeed, though it got as far as central France before being defeated, at Poitiers, by Charles Martel, King of the Franks (who were again proving instrumental in the creation and consolidation of Europe), in 732. This was the closest a non-European power has ever got to occupying and subjugating the continent; whether the attempt could ever be repeated, and succeed, is an interesting question but one whose discussion can be postponed until later.

A common Christian culture did not prevent the peoples of Europe from warring against each other because of disagreements over territory or competing dynastic claims (the belief of English kings that they were entitled to rule France also, because of family connections going back to the Norman Conquest, led of course to the Hundred Years War). Religion was a culturally unifying factor (even after the Reformation, though not to the same extent), but not a politically unifying one, at least not between nations rather than within them. Sometimes the family connections were exploited to lay claim to a particular region, sometimes it was the whole country which was coveted. Often the issue was simply one of needing to give testosterone-fuelled young aristocrats something to do. But it is without question that post-Roman Europe had by this time become a "civilisation", if there is any distinction between "civilised" and "uncivilised" societies. It has been claimed by those with a guilt complex or seeking to get their own back for past differences that the West was culturally inferior to Islam, its chief rival at this time. Rubbish. Admittedly it had benefited from inheriting the achievements of Greece and Rome, which it did partly because of the Muslims who made sure that records no-one else seemed interested in preserving were not lost. *Someone* had to develop "civilisation" in the Graeco-Roman sense first; but it is a fact of history that societies can borrow from, and also catch up with, one another. They can advance, or decay while others seem to flourish culturally and in other respects, the process being one of rise and fall, fall and rise. But to get to the point, the high Middle Ages saw the foundation of the great Western universities and also the building of the great cathedrals, a feat which displayed considerable engineering skill. There was a flourishing of monasteries, which with their libraries and *scriptoria* became centres of learning. Technologically, this period of Western history saw the invention of the vertical windmill, which is significant.

Here a personal interest in a rather esoteric, in some people's view, subject has in fact proved very illuminating. Watermills and later windmills were the first complex machines. Watermills (which the Saxons were happy to use), are thought to have been inherited by the Greeks, and thus the Romans, from a Near Eastern people. Such things as wind-driven prayer wheels were known in antiquity but the first true windmills were built by Muslims in Persia (now Iran) in the ninth century AD/CE. However they did not catch on outside the region. They had arms or "sails", which the wind blew round to operate the machinery, mounted in a horizontal plane on a vertical axis. In the twelfth century, when windmills first became common in Europe, someone there, whose name is sadly unrecorded, had the idea of turning the machinery of the watermill, where the power source, the water, was at the bottom and the gearing and millstones above it, on its head. In the windmill the power source (the wind) was at the top and the gearing and millstones below. It seems unlikely the West got the idea from the Muslims, through the Crusaders (who I don't think went as far east as Persia), since the windmills it built from the twelfth right through to the late nineteenth century were of an entirely different design, with the sails mounted in a roughly vertical plane on a horizontal axis. A few horizontal windmills were built in the West but much later. By contrast, from the late twelfth century the vertical windmill became common in Europe wherever the geography (flat ground with few windbreaks, although the upper slopes of low hills would also do) was suitable. That said, it is of course quite possible that it was only the *form* of the device which was different; that rumours of wind-powered mills in Persia reached the crusaders in Palestine and by that route arrived in western Europe where they inspired engineers to build such devices by "turning upside down" the watermills which already existed in that part of the world to serve as a pattern, or a crusader chanced to meet a Persian merchant who told him of the windmills but happened not to say exactly how they functioned and was not pressed on the matter.

The West may have successfully adapted the technological achievements of other cultures, where it was aware of them, or it may have had the same ideas independently; but in the long run it was much better than, say, China in *applying* the technology, using it on a grand scale (this may have been because the Chinese had a different sense of time and thus of the pace of history). Rockets and paper were invented long before anyone in the West thought of them, but the fact remains that the Westerners mass-produced these items and the Chinese didn't, not until much later.

Climate change played its part in the West's technological progress and cultural flowering during the mediaeval period (warmer weather increased agricultural yields thus creating both the prosperity which funded building projects etc. and the workforce with which to carry them out), but then it has been instrumental in the history of other societies too. No, the West and Islam can be considered of equal calibre as civilisations. They defeated each other in war, maintaining a balance of power, although geography rendered the south-eastern quarter of Europe particularly vulnerable to the advance of the Ottoman Turks who eventually succeeded in conquering it (in this region they were eventually to come up against Russia, with the latter's emergence as a new player on the international scene, having previously been on the periphery except as a trading partner, thanks to eighteenth-century rulers such as Peter and Catherine the Great). Altogether the farthest they were able to get in the West, after Poitiers, was the gates of Vienna, from which they were repulsed in 1683.

By the eighth century Islam had taken over North Africa and in fact ruled Spain — the only country in western Europe to be more than briefly under its dominance — for a few hundred years, being expelled from its last foothold there around the time Columbus was setting out for the New World, in what might seem to be symbolic of the global triumph of Western power. In a sense the West-Islam conflict was not a religious war because the Muslims did not seek to proselytise, socially advantageous as it nonetheless was for those who did convert; rather people did not want to be dominated by an alien culture, which culture derived to some extent from religion as the West appreciated. This was understandable even if Islamic rulers were often, it has to be admitted, less harsh than Western ones towards subject peoples. It could be argued that Islam has declined culturally, in some areas morally, since but so in many ways has the West.

On the subject of civilisations at this time mention ought to be made of the Aztecs and Incas. They seem a curious affair, a product of the failure of technological progress to take place at a uniform rate everywhere, in that they were like the Romans translated to a later time and different geographical context. They established considerable empires whose subject peoples were expected to be grateful for the technological and other benefits thus made available to them (though it may be that they were). They had an efficient army and road network, aqueducts, and writing (in the Inca case by proxy, with different coloured beads (*quipu*) representing different things, which proved sufficient to run an effective civil service). But they were less advanced than certain cultures which had arisen elsewhere in the world and which were now expanding overseas. They did not know the wheel or the horse, two things that rendered an army even more efficient, because more mobile, and allowed the Spanish conquistadors to overwhelm them.

Then there are the Mongols. They seem odd candidates for the description "civilised", partly because they appeared to belong to the oldest kind of society, the nomadic (though they had tamed the horse and in fact relied on it for the swift mobility which, along with their general skill at handling the animal, was the key to their success). They had an urge to conquer and became settled through the need to keep hold of the conquests. The process required ordered government. The Mongols undoubtedly made a contribution (in genetic terms among others, for their features are evident today in many inhabitants of that vast part of the Eurasian land mass which is now Russia, including people who otherwise look Caucasian and even Aryan) to the development of the societies they conquered. But in another respect they did not conform to the standards of behaviour which are regarded as defining "civilised" and in fact in the popular mind have become — their most famous leader, Genghis Khan, in particular — the epitome of what is barbarous and cruel. Their victories were won at the cost of mass slaughter and subsequent brutality in ensuring the continuing obedience of the conquered. Genghis once mounted the pulpit of a church with a Bible in his hand and delivered a mock sermon in which he intellectually rebuffed Christian denunciation of his conduct and pointed out shortcomings in his detractors' own (Christianity seems to be particularly subject to attempts at deconstructing it by people who resent it on ethical or doctrinal grounds, whether or not they are right). This proved he was far from unintelligent, whatever else he might have been. But did a man who had killed thousands, possibly millions, of Chinese peasants, and who sewed up a Muslim caliph and his family in a carpet before causing a herd of horses to stampede over them really possess much moral authority? (Another Mongol warlord, Timurlaine, used one defeated enemy as a physical footstool and forced his wife to work as a naked waitress).

We may presume, although we will never know for certain, that such atrocities would have happened in the West if the Mongols had conquered it as they did the East. They got as far as Poland, about which one shivers to think, though they didn't stay. But they got no further. The general view is that the West was ill-equipped in terms of military tactics, and because of its national rivalries and divisions, to have successfully resisted them if they had pressed on to the North Sea and English Channel. There may be a cultural inferiority complex at work again, but I can't believe it wouldn't have rallied and united to defeat them in the end, especially once rumours of their atrocities, which in many cases would have been true, began to spread. It's another thing we can't be sure of, because the Mongols never came. Why not? Opinions seem to differ, in a perplexing example of how historical truth can be difficult to arrive at. Some say they overextended their lines of supply and communication (it is indeed hard to believe that even they would not have been overstretched if they had seriously attempted to take the West wholesale). Some say they failed to attack the West in force because they considered it to be not worth having (which is insulting, although perhaps one should be grateful). Some say they were hamstrung by the power struggle which broke out back home following the death of the Khan Ogedei. I suspect it was a combination of all three. It is one of the great "might have beens" of history. Certainly this was one occasion when the West was menaced militarily by a power from outside it, something that was not possible after the Industrial Revolution. It might be unhistorical to attribute major past events to divine intervention, but it does often seem as if some transcendent Providence was preserving the West in its established form – by what happened in 732 and 1683 and what failed to happen with the Mongols – having decreed that it should play the pivotal role in world history which it did. This might or might not be the explanation, but the effect was the same.

Leaving aside necessary circumspection as to how the term should be used, it's worthwhile asking in what sense the Jews have constituted a civilisation regardless of association with a particular territory where they form the majority of the population (which of course is the case in the political nation of Israel) or a ruling elite. If neither of these contingencies is a requirement of "civilisation" then yes they do, in a way which comes over as rather sweet. Israel was a major power in the Middle East, feared and respected, for a relatively brief period under David and Solomon before she became fragmented into two kingdoms. Then followed the Diaspora, the Babylonian and Roman occupations leading to the Jews being dispersed across the developed world (returning to their ancestral homeland at one point and then being expelled again). They left either because they were deported or because they simply found the situation they were faced with intolerable. Israel was reconstructed as a political entity in 1948, but is home to rather less than half the world Jewish population, most of which is happy to go on living in the "host" countries (as it has done for the best part of two millennia). Partly because past persecution has bred solidarity, Jews have close ties with one another, creating to some extent a distinct community within a community. And they are undoubtedly an intelligent race as their artistic, cultural and scientific achievements show. Initially, the significant feature of their society was their devotion to their religion, which as well as encouraging literacy (often absent among the common people, at any rate, in the West throughout the mediaeval and early modern periods) and learning among them proved globally significant because out of Judaism developed Christianity, still arguably the leading world faith although not growing as fast as Islam. In C S Lewis' words, "It was given to the Jews to show Mankind how to behave towards God". Judaism had a literature and mythologies (and produced historians like Josephus), but in secular terms its achievement, let us be frank, was less spectacular than that of Greece and Rome and Jews had something of an inferiority complex vis-à-vis those societies during the classical period. In its heyday Israel was not renowned for building great cities and highways on the Roman scale; nor on extending her military and political power beyond the Middle East, though she was never really interested in doing that sort of thing anyway. (One exception to unimpressive, if that is how we should regard it, architecture must have been – significantly – the Temple in Jerusalem, sadly destroyed in the Masada revolt of AD 70, and never rebuilt even when the conditions for that were more favourable, which has always seemed to me surprising.) It is worth noting that to Christians, and presumably devout Jews, the religious contribution was the most crucial one possible.

Undoubtedly, the later cultural accomplishments of the Jews had a lot to do with the Diaspora and the Gentile societies whose achievements they could benefit from, plus the tendency of hardship and persecution, aggravated by a feeling of loss at separation from one's homeland, to produce original thought. No doubt genetic factors (which may determine the *way* in which someone responds to a particular situation, and particular opportunities) played a part too. I'm certainly not saying they weren't clever enough to have been able to do it otherwise, rather I'm talking about what makes possible the *expression* of talent. Some of that is internal, some external; had the external factors not been present it is difficult to say what difference it would have made.

In some ways the Jews were not really achieving their true potential before the Diaspora. We do not know how Israel would have developed without it, just as we do not know what course world history as a whole would have taken without the Jewish contribution. But without in any way belittling them, in a response to those who might be tempted to suggest that the Jewish race are cleverer than all others and that world civilisation would not have been possible without them, a dangerous thing because it breeds resentment and thus anti-Semitism, it could be argued that although during the mediaeval period they were often educated and literate where ordinary Gentiles were not, they could not have achieved what they later did without the Gentiles, because they were using the facilities the latter had created. (The fact that Israel is a democracy while her Arab neighbours mostly are not must owe something to European influences as a result of the Diaspora.) It was a partnership, even if anti-Semites did not see things that way. The Jews possessed the ability to take the culture of a land where they had settled and fuse with it, adding to it the talents that it brought out in them. The boost they got from full engagement with the Gentile world, plus their never having established a civilisation that was splendid in the same way that classical Greece and Rome (to whom Western society was conscious that it owed so much) were, led to the Nazi myth that they were bloodsucking leeches who could only prosper by preying parasite-like on other races. That it *is* a myth is obvious to any sensible person. They did not so much drain Western society of its cultural vitality as enhance it, which they are still doing. The scale of the Jewish achievement has sometimes been masked by the tendency of Jews at one time to adopt Gentile names because they felt it helped the process of assimilation.

Outside their own community, Jews in the mediaeval and early modern periods performed a valuable role as doctors (as well as in the less noble profession of moneylending, though that was hardly their fault if prejudice barred them from so many other jobs). But though they might produce scholars of note such as Moses Maimonides they were only able to make their maximum contribution when they became fully integrated and emancipated from the late eighteenth and early nineteenth centuries, as part of the spread of liberal ideas throughout the West with the Enlightenment. This new involvement with the "mainstream" culture was to have profound and interesting effects on them. On one level we are naturally biased towards our own ethnic kind; on another we are aware of our obligations to the rest of humanity, have a sense of belonging to a broader family and are altruistic towards it (at least that is how things should be). Jews did not all respond to emancipation in the same way, of course, but when the barriers to it were lifted many of them, wishing to benefit the wider community but not having a stake in its established order, since they had been barred from the Gentile world for so long, found an outlet for their aspirations and good intentions in reforming or radical political movements such as Communism (for which far-Right elements reviled them). This was combined with a certain tendency, once they began to assimilate, to dilute or even lose one's Jewish identity. Some Jews, aware that Gentiles resented their success and were afraid of being outshone by them, became almost embarrassed, even contemptuous, of their Jewishness. For others it continued to mean something. It is true to say that the Jews have retained their distinctness while other races, cultures or nations have been absorbed into new ones and disappeared, though any assertion that this will be the case in the future needs to be qualified in that many people are becoming more defensive of their traditional identities in the face of cultural and demographic changes which appear to threaten same. Jews are themselves, of course, a mixture of different races, though they succeeded remarkably in giving those elements a common identity, one which was to be strengthened by suffering. (Here one may note the parallels between the Jewish experience and that of blacks, which have caused many of the latter to identify with the former. Black people too had their "diaspora", largely due to slavery, and the "Back to Africa" movement might be seen as analogous to Zionism, that is the desire to return to Israel and make it a national home for the Jews). What is undeniable is that assimilation proved, both at the time it began and subsequently, a double-edged sword from the Jewish point of view (nor of course could it be reversed). It made them seem less incestuous and remote and therefore may have decreased the likelihood they would be persecuted; but at the same time their entry into general communal life attracted the hostility of those who were inclined to be anti-Semitic in any case.

The question is a complex one when someone can be Jewish by race, religion or both; but it should be stressed that although, generally speaking, Jews are a separate ethnic group according to physical characteristics, culture or both Judaism is not strictly speaking a nationality, unless one sees Jewish people as having dual loyalties which one is entitled to do (have dual loyalties, that is), and which I suppose might be the case with some people. Jews count as full citizens of the countries in which their forebears settled, and are generally patriotic. Nor I think are the majority of them racially conceited except in the sense that anyone, to a greater or lesser degree, is so by nature.

China, of course, was a great civilisation throughout the whole of the period we have been talking about since early on in this chapter – that is, what in the West are called the "Classical" and "Mediaeval" eras. She was once thought to have been the *first* civilisation, although that honour is now believed to belong to the Mesopotamian cultures of Sumer, Akkad and Babylon. Her history before the modern age is of course every bit as worthy of study as Europe's; the same for that of civilisations in other parts of Asia and in Africa, or for that matter tribal peoples. If I haven't, so far, focused on all these societies as much as some would feel I should it is largely for reasons of space. China had a civilisation while not being as *technologically* advanced, latterly, as the West, and also relatively unknown to it despite commercial contacts via the Silk Road and the information brought back by explorers like Marco Polo. Though it took hundreds of years to change this state of affairs was not, of course, to last forever. Meanwhile there were rebellions, civil wars and changes of dynasty, just as there were in Europe; proof that at heart, people were just the same everywhere.

3

The mediaeval world was not set in stone. It changed considerably over the millennium, from c400 AD to c1500, to which Western historians have given the name "Middle Ages", going through three distinct phases. Towards the end of the period, in the fifteenth century, the feudal system, which had never quite recovered from the economic consequences of the Black Death in the 1300s, disappeared and was replaced by one of court patronage. Monarchs and aristocrats no longer lived in castles but in stately homes. Instead of knights and retainers they buttressed their power through a rigorous, and highly efficient, bureaucracy. Though such things were not of course unknown previously, and would not be unknown later on in history, the patronage system, as operated by the monarchs themselves or by those seeking advancement, could lead to intrigue, which might be of a murderous kind. In the popular mind the extreme example of this is the activities of the rulers of the city-states of Italy (aristocrats who, thanks to the anarchy of warring peoples, some flooding in from elsewhere, that Italy descended into with the fall of the Roman Empire, and the conditions arising from it had effectively become their own monarchies). And particularly the Borgias, who seem to represent the ultimate debasement of public life. This nepotistic family wielded secular power over Rome and its associated territories, and at one time the religious power as well in the person of Pope Alexander VI, a porn merchant who practised incest and generally did more than anyone else in history to degrade the office. They sought to extend their influence throughout Italy as a whole and were quite prepared to murder, torture and unjustly imprison to get their way.

About one of them, at least, we can be more forgiving than was the popular tendency before the present time. Lucrezia, Alexander VI's daughter(!), has too often been regarded as just as wicked and perverse as her father, and brother Cesare, when in fact there is no basis for such a view. In the 1960s there was a strip in *Valiant* comic in which an antiquarian buys a portrait of Lucrezia who, another character tells us, was involved in the black arts, i.e. witchcraft, "along with all her other crimes" whatever they are supposed to be. Through the portrait Lucrezia's evil spirit becomes active, purely for malicious reasons creating a doppelganger of its purchaser (his stolen reflection) who commits a murder for which he is arrested and tried. After proving his innocence by demonstrating that he was somewhere else at the time, he destroys the portrait by consigning it to a furnace with the words "Burn, witch, burn!". In the strip Lucrezia's hair is dark, when in fact she was a blonde. Presumably dark hair is more in line with conveying the idea that a woman (or man) is mysteriously and sinisterly evil. This is itself an absurd stereotype, but if we are not comfortable with it we can go for the alternative; i.e., where we do not fete blondes unduly we see them as cold-hearted, scheming gold-diggers. (Or as dumb dupes, mere puppets in the nefarious designs of people more intelligent than they.)

There is no evidence whatsoever that Lucrezia practised black magic. Generally, if she had been as bad as certain other members of her family there would have been too much evidence of that for Sarah Bradford to credibly write a sympathetic biography of her, even if there is a tendency in any case for women authors and historians to defend other women who have been accused of heinous crimes and moral iniquity by a male-dominated world. Essentially the criticism which can be levelled against her is that (a) she committed adultery and (b) she did not vigorously oppose the bloodthirsty activities of her family. The two things seem to add up in people's minds to make her a monster. But as Sarah Bradford is in effect arguing, you have to view her in the context of her time and its brutal political realities. Nor is she particularly repellent as a person.

If she did commit adultery it was because the dynastic alliances through marriage, for geopolitical gain, which most states sought in those days meant she might be wed to someone she did not necessarily love and so would seek affection and sexual satisfaction elsewhere. Here her situation was no different from that of other women of royal (or in this case quasi-royal) status in the mediaeval and early modern world. The same might apply both ways; look at all those English/British kings who had mistresses. And if she was a pawn in these things (a woman below the status of actual queen could not be anything else) it was because she did not have much choice (and she knew that). How far she could practically have rebelled against it is not clear and the same goes for the brutality and bloody power-grabbing of the other Borgias. Whether she would have been in danger from her own flesh and blood if she had, in some way, chosen not to be a part of it all is hard to say. She might, and perhaps inevitably, have been swayed by family loyalty in failing to speak out or act against the system. But although she was unable to influence Borgia policy to any significant extent, she does not appear to have been the *instigator* of gratuitous cruelty. Indeed she took what opportunities she could to prevent it. When left temporarily in charge of the affairs of the Duchy of Ferrara, because her husband the Duke was away on important business, she ensured it was governed fairly, overturning unjust legal decisions, freeing those imprisoned unfairly and passing laws against persecution of Jews. Otherwise, her behaviour might not seem very heroic. But at worst she was an intelligent and in many ways decent woman trapped within a ruthless system; not a monstress. As for the belief that she committed incest with her father the Pope, the charge remains unproven. In general, her case is an indicator of how easy it is for historians to be misled by popular prejudices and misconceptions, and how the actual truth can turn out to be almost disorientatingly different.

The importance of the Renaissance and Reformation in European, which at this stage, as you will have gathered, is what we mean by Western, history was that they established permanently in the consciousness of what we would call in modern terms "opinion formers" the idea that things could change, be questioned. The change might take the shape of rediscovering the forms of the past, as in the Renaissance, though its end product was nonetheless a cultural flowering, or it might be something completely new in its inspiration. But the movements in question started a gradual trend of enquiry which continued through the Enlightenment of the eighteenth century to bring into existence the world we know today. The Renaissance happened for a number of reasons, of which the most important was probably the decline of the feudal system, and other social and economic changes, as a result of the Black Death, which made commerce (no longer so closely controlled by the nobility) more important in national life. Merchants acted as contacts between different cultures, and there continued especially in periods of peace to be trading links between the West and Islam (on the principle of "business is business"). The Muslims had preserved many classical texts which the West had lost; at the same time, when the Byzantine Empire, the inheritor through the Romans of the ancient Greek civilisation, finally fell to Islam in 1453 many of its scholars fled West, bringing their obvious classical knowledge with them. Thus Western culture was able to reconnect to its past, synthesising classical scholarship and philosophy with mediaeval, in a way that enriched it and stimulated it. Then there was the invention of printing, which helped to spread ideas, in England and Germany from c1450, and the decline in the prestige and effectiveness of the traditional Catholic Church. The latter factor led to the Humanist philosophy which was not, unlike "humanism" as perceived and practised in the modern world, necessarily a complete rejection of religion; rather, it stressed that although Man had to meet the standards of behaviour and spirituality set by God in order to achieve salvation he could do so by his own efforts, with less dependence on the intervention in the process of the established church as the infallible agent of His will. Early modern humanists, most of them anyway, were not atheists as such. After all, their thinking was important in the creation of the intellectual background for the Reformation, a religious movement. Although salvation for Martin Luther depended on justification through faith, on earning God's Grace through that devotion rather than on any good works a person might choose to perform, Protestantism was individualistic in that it wanted individuals to be able to read the Bible and partake directly of the Sacrament, since they could not make any kind of "choice", and thus show their worth, in religious matters unless they understood what was going on.

Apart from the general disruption it caused, how significant the Reformation was in an overall sense, as opposed to just the field of religion, may be debated but it was crucial in several respects. On the understanding that Catholics are not necessarily lazy, we might say that the Protestant work ethic contributed to the Industrial Revolution. The Reformation also showed how a movement aimed at changing the way things were done could take off if publicised and promoted sufficiently, using the technique of printing perfected in England and Germany during the previous century (as the Renaissance had). The need for people to be fully conversant with the Bible rather than receive the Word solely through a priest encouraged general learning and literacy. Though one might, I suppose, have instituted a massive educational programme in Latin for the population at large, but conducting church services in English, and translating Scripture into that language, was a manifestation of rejection of the predominance of the Catholic Church which (because of its Roman origins) had always used Latin. Because temperamentally some nations were more inclined to Protestantism than Catholicism, the Reformation was vital in emphasising and promoting national culture and identity. It happened not only in northern Europe but the Romance-speaking countries too, though the latter did not give up their Catholic allegiances. So the Reformation gave a boost to political and cultural nationalism; certainly you can't understand English history and culture since the sixteenth century without it and the same applies to a greater or lesser extent with other countries.

Undoubtedly by the early sixteenth century the Catholic Church had become corrupt and intellectually stagnant. Everyone except perhaps the Church itself, in the sense of its ministers and high officials, must have realised the extent to which this had happened but lacked the will and the courage to change the status quo. As at other times in history it took a charismatic and determined personality, in this case Martin Luther, to start things off. Luther was seeking to reform Catholicism rather than destroy it, but as with Mikhail Gorbachev in a later era things ran away with him. His combative personality made him seem more of a threat to the existing order than he intended to be and provoked resistance from the established authorities. Often, if influential people joined his movement it was from aristocratic opposition to the control the Church had over land, plus its general power, as much as religion. On mainland Europe, as in England/Britain, it succeeded in separating the spiritual from the secular power but, unlike in England/Britain (in the later part of the early modern period, anyway) the monarchy remained politically strong and even tightened its hold. Intellectually, the fact of Luther's boldly challenging the Church's traditional practices and dogma, or appearing to, inspired a re-evaluation of them on the part of others giving rise to theological ferment and to the different strands of Protestantism – Reformed, Lutheran and Calvinist – which were often in bitter conflict. It let the genie, or perhaps the demon, out of the bottle. Although Luther and Renaissance humanists differed crucially in their theology, it had been encouraged by the general atmosphere of questioning which the Renaissance gave rise to, the two movements blending into one another in important respects.

As indicated, reform benefited from factors which had nothing to do with political or religious conscience. The whole thing became tied up with politics alright, but how much it was to do with conscience rather than the personal wishes, which might not be the same quantity, of an individual was debatable. Nowhere was this more evident than in the English case. King Henry VIII wanted to divorce Catherine of Aragon, who had failed to bear him the son he so much wanted, but the Pope would not let him, so he declared the English Church independent of Rome. It was a political rather than an ideological split – Henry remained a good Catholic (which Luther, too, considered himself to be) until his death – but it obviously paved the way for the English Protestant Reformation in an institutional and psychological sense (in terms of power politics Protestants and Catholics were in a state of periodically shifting balance, the influence of either faction at court waxing and waning). Henry's personal wishes respecting his private life provided the opening for a movement which would have affected Britain, as it did everywhere else, in due course anyway, but perhaps taken longer to do so. The religious changes got bound up with English nationalism, the rejection of foreign influences being seen as a patriotic as well as religiously correct thing to do. In fact throughout Europe the Reformation became conflated with territorial and dynastic rivalries, exacerbating the latter and often leading to war. In an attempt to defuse the situation it was eventually agreed that the religion of a ruler should determine that of their subjects, which suggests that either religion didn't matter that much in the business except as a source of labels or, if people were prepared to countenance such an arrangement, that they didn't believe souls were at stake; it was considered sufficient to be a Christian and the doctrinal differences between one branch of the faith and another were viewed as at best unfathomable, and therefore irrelevant, and at worst incomprehensible (plus divisive) hogwash. As a way of avoiding conflict the arrangement did not in the end really work; while the masses could not get their heads round the issues anyway the educated elements, from the wealthier tradespeople to leading aristocrats, could and their attitude was crucial especially where they actually played a part in the political process.

Those for whom the matter was genuinely one of conscience could be placed in an agonising situation. Archbishop Thomas Cranmer is not always well regarded within the liberal Anglo-Catholic wing of the Church of England, because he is seen as having "sold out" when Henry VIII split from Rome, willingly implementing all the doctrinal changes (because he saw which way the wind was blowing) whereas Thomas More did not and paid for it with his head. Perhaps the criticism is just, but it needs to be qualified with understanding and compassion. Cranmer had doubts about the rightness of what he was doing, which preyed on his mind. In his portrait he looks utterly miserable, in a similar way to William Pitt the Younger. With the latter the reason is the cares of office, for Pitt took his job very seriously, along with (possibly) the trauma of repressed homosexuality although the latter need not automatically explain why he died a bachelor. With Cranmer it was duty combined with a troubled conscience. Later he fell into the hands of Mary Tudor; being burnt at the stake, he recanted Protestantism, and then recanted the recantation, which tends to bolster the charge of inconstancy, though it would seem he ultimately did the right thing (if not, theologically at any rate, from a Catholic's point of view). And not everyone finds it easy to stand by their principles when faced with a particularly horrible form of death. Allegedly, Cranmer's last words as the flames rose higher were "I am done on that side, turn me round". If this is true, it suggests that he was glad those agonies of conscience, an Earthly business which would not trouble him in the next world, were over. Life had thrown all it could at him and he had won through. He had nothing more to worry about. It's also said that he at one point thrust his hand into them saying it deserved to be burnt because it had signed so many things that were wrong.

What ordinary people did actually think of the matter perhaps depends on the definition, sociologically, of ordinary. In 1553 Henry VIII's Catholic daughter, Mary Tudor, ascended the throne of England and reconverted it, by burning recalcitrant Protestants at the stake if necessary. Since burning is a particularly nasty way to die she has therefore been demonised as Bloody Mary. The reality is precisely what is so disturbing to those, whether believers or not, who are troubled by the excesses which can be perpetrated in the name of religion. Her portraits, the work of a man who knew his job and was good at capturing the personality of his subjects, do not depict an evil woman but a sincere one who acted from a genuine belief that she was right and also had her own problems. One shows a solemnity which makes clear the seriousness with which she viewed her job, and her mission, as well as an underlying inner torment which actually causes me to feel a twinge of sympathy for her, uncomfortable as it is to admit it. In another, where she appears with her husband Philip II of Spain in what is meant to be a scene of domestic bliss, there is a genuinely loving expression on the Queen's face which is deeply moving (though Philip was either taking her for a ride or simply found he could not give his undivided attention to both kingdoms, and in the end returned to his homeland leaving her pregnant or so she thought. Even today it is difficult for a woman in her forties to conceive without complications, and after five years on the throne Mary died childless; there was to be no Catholic heir, and in what − as with the defeat of the Spanish Armada − seems an expression of the divine will Britain returned to Protestantism under the more judicious (and Protestant) Elizabeth I. Mary's crime was to be devout but relatively unintelligent and by that token narrow-minded, failing to see the stupidity of the mass burnings; her more sagacious sister trimmed her sails to the wind and only burnt Catholics when it was necessary to appease Protestant opinion (political necessity, as she saw it, prevented her from being as religiously neutral as she would have preferred). Elizabeth is said to have actually burnt more Catholics than Mary did Protestants, but then she had a longer reign in which to do it.

But we were speaking of sociology. Among the thousands who died during Mary's "reign of terror" were William Allin, a miller at Frittenden in Kent, and his wife Katherine. He read the Scriptures to the poor, which in contemporary Catholic practice you weren't supposed to do, and as a result he and Katherine were burnt at Maidstone on June 18th 1557 (*The Martyrs Of Kent,* J H Wood, 1885, p11). Allin was a member of what might be called the merchant classes; he may or may not have worked his mill himself, though the latter was common practice, a "grinder" perhaps being employed to do the job. But obviously his intellect had been sufficiently nurtured to understand the doctrinal differences between Catholic and Protestant, which suggests that socioeconomic change had by now allowed educational opportunities to penetrate downwards to some extent. The theology wasn't, probably couldn't have been, understood by those below Allin on the social scale, especially in remote rural areas where the Church, Protestant or Catholic, had a sparse presence anyway, and where, when the crucifixion was mentioned to him, one man said "I think I saw something like that of which you speak at Corpus Christi play, where there was a man on a tree and blood ran down."

As for the extremism spawned by the Reformation, it was evident on both sides of the divide, in reactionary Catholicism and intolerant Protestant Puritanism. The latter is an example of what happens when a latent desire for change suddenly bursts forth and where there is disagreement over exactly *how* things should change, something evident in politics as well as religion as we'll see in due course. But the Reformation could also, by the need for a response to it, be a force for moderation, though it is not usually perceived as such. To their credit many people in the Catholic Church acknowledged that things had been allowed to slide and that the Protestants did have a certain point; the Society of Jesuits, whose reputation for cruel discipline and paedophilia is far from entirely fair, was formed in order to defend and explain Catholic ideas in a rational and non-aggressive way. Without taking sides, this was preferable to the fire-and-brimstone approach of some in the Protestant camp such as John Knox.

As noted, what happened in England under Henry VIII was not an ideological swing to Protestantism on the part of the monarchy or the nation as a whole, but rather a *political* upheaval which saw the country break away from Rome where the control of religious affairs was concerned in accordance with the king's desire for independence in such matters. Subsequently, what happened depended on the personal convictions of whoever was in charge. During the minority of Edward VI change gathered pace under Protector Somerset, a more genuinely committed Protestant. It was reversed under Mary Tudor. (Edward died at the age of sixteen in what seems in more than one respect a tragic turn of events. Certainly it is another great "might have been" of history: how would he, and affairs in general, have turned out if he had lived the rest of his natural (by the standards of that time) lifespan? Perhaps as strong-willed as his father yet less tyrannical, and less extreme in religion than his sister.) Though Elizabeth I could not be quite as moderate as she wished, because people had become tired of constant alternation between different forms of worship the religious settlement of her reign was something of a compromise; one which has endured more or less to the present day. England was to be firmly Protestant but with ornamentation and ritual preserved to a greater extent. The people as a whole were able to accept this, though there remained a substantial minority of Catholics who continued to be disenchanted and also an extreme Protestant element − the Puritans − who would have gone further than the settlement permitted. The Puritans were of course influential in the American colonies, where many of them fled because they disliked the situation at home, and they underwent a resurgence in England during the political and religious ferment of the mid-seventeenth century. Charles I and Laud's Arminianism excited their wrath and they became influential in the anti-monarchic, Republican movement. Cromwell felt he could not ignore them and banned a wide range of festivities, including Christmas, in accordance with their wishes (they thought such things ostentatious and vain, and therefore unGodly) and against what I suspect were his own. According to the tendency of the pendulum to swing, this kind of thing explains the licentiousness of the Restoration period, which was a reaction to it and which persisted into the eighteenth century before itself being followed by the moral and spiritual revival which John Wesley and the Methodists, and the evangelism of the Victorian period, represented. Christian puritanism has survived in some areas, e.g. the Bible Belt of the American South, as a form of belief and of conduct, not widespread or organised enough to merit a capital "P" but still capable of giving the Church as a whole an undeserved bad reputation by associating it with excessive strictness in certain matters (especially sex).

By 1700 the Protestant-Catholic conflict had more or less exhausted itself as a cause of war, civil or international, though there remained the issue of disabilities suffered by religious minorities (e.g. Catholics in England/Britain and Protestants in France) and tensions could occasionally flare up into violence as in the Gordon Riots of 1780 in London, and it was later to exacerbate the Irish issue where, again, the religion got tangled up with the politics. A dislike of Protestantism/Catholicism would have provided an *additional* reason for not wanting to be under the rule of France, or Germany, or Austria, or whoever but not the main one.

Overall we may see the Reformation as a necessary, in the sense of inevitable, expression of the tendency for change to occur, as part of the order of things, in religion as in other matters, and by no means in a constant ongoing process. The fact that the Catholic Church had existed more or less for 1500 years seemed to give it a legitimacy which it was clearly perverse to question; but it doesn't really work like that with societies and institutions, as we will see again later on.

Another crucial development of the period from the mid-fifteenth century to the beginning of the seventeenth was European exploration of the globe beyond the relatively limited contact Westerners had had with India and China, for example. America had of course already been discovered by the "Native Americans", emigrating from what is now Russia. Later the Vikings landed in Newfoundland and Greenland. The significance of 1492 and all that is that it inaugurated an age in which improving communications enabled the West to dominate the world (if never entirely successfully), rather than simply preserve its territorial integrity and way of life against external aggressors. It was not proved to be morally superior because it had done so; rather, it had different skills and a different mindset from those it dominated, both wanting to expand its power and influence worldwide and being good at doing so. The voyages of discovery inevitably altered the outlook of early modern Westerners to some extent by establishing that they were part of a wider geographical world (which was not flat, held up by giant tortoises/Atlas, etcetera), even if they too often showed little interest in and respect for conquered cultures, imposing, often in brutal fashion, their own Eurocentric way of looking at things on the indigenes. There was undoubtedly a lot of courage involved, plus simple curiosity, but the chief incentives were political, religious or economic. Different people, some "good" and some "bad", might have different reasons for taking part in the business, or the same person could harbour a mixture of altruistic and less altruistic motives. Sometimes it was greed for Inca gold, or for whatever riches might exist in lands still to be discovered; though it is understandable if the chance of self-betterment led many of the poorer sections of society to sign up as sailors or soldiers in the armies of Pizarro and Cortes. Sometimes it was a desire to spread the Gospel, which was to be a special incentive for Spain, a Catholic country practising what it regarded as the only true faith; the Church sought compensation for losing northern Europe to Protestantism, as was starting to happen. Conversion in this case was often forced and bloody and the stain on Christianity's reputation has persisted to the present day. The annexation and colonisation of the New World was not necessarily intended to result in the destruction or displacement of indigenous peoples, but this undoubtedly happened on a large scale because of the diseases the white man brought with him. The colonists might remain a small ruling elite or they might in time become the majority of the population.

Initially the business of exploring and then colonising was dominated by the Spanish and Portuguese, who had begun it. They were followed from the later sixteenth century by the British, French and Dutch (the latter at this time emerging as a highly creative and industrious people). The Spanish took central and most of southern America, the Portuguese Brazil (as they named it) and parts of Africa and the East Indies, sharing the latter region with the Dutch. In the eighteenth century France was expelled from North America by the British but left behind a substantial French-speaking population in Canada. As a result of wars they fought against each other in the Caribbean both Britain and France acquired colonies there, some taken from Spain whose global power was on the wane. Territories were frequently exchanged at peace conferences. And Britain of course gained India. There was competition for the lucrative resources of the potential colonies, besides which empire meant prestige. The Franco-British struggle for world supremacy was an example of how traditional rivalries within Europe could be translated to an international stage (so that whatever happened in 1914, the Seven Years' War of 1756-63 was in reality the first world war); though it had more to do with being generally on top and with besting the old enemy, whose success was resented, than territory since Britain had long ceased to make any territorial claims on mainland France, the nature of the game having changed. If the two countries did engage in battle on the soil of continental Europe, as during the War of the Spanish Succession, it was because Britain followed a policy of trying to prevent any one power from being too dominant there; the more of the European coastline, including the Channel ports, which that power controlled the better placed it would be to invade the British mainland, if it ever decided to do so, or threaten British trade. The latter consideration, even if there was no actual possibility of military aggression, was increasingly important to a maritime and thus colonising nation whose wealth derived to a great extent from the sea over which, from the mid-seventeenth century, she had been gradually establishing command.

Prior to this period, England/Britain had been successful (after 1066) in defending herself from foreign invasion – though it could be argued that the French intervention on the side of King John in his wars with his barons, and William of Orange's landing in 1688, amounted to that – due in no small measure to her navy but she had not the weight when it came to land warfare, despite Henry VIII's pretensions that he ruled a major continental power. The only exception was the Hundred Years War in pursuit of the English king's supposed claim to the French throne, where the English were able to occupy a considerable portion of France, but the achievement did not last. In an important respect the conflict was unnecessary. It arose because Edward III wanted to enjoy the lands he held of the French king, but felt humiliated by having to be a feudal vassal, despite or because of the undisputed power he possessed in his own realms. He decided to solve the problem by making himself king of France. It was a matter of pride and also perhaps part of his strategy of keeping his aristocracy happy by uniting them in a common military enterprise. But he was not suffering in any material sense, at least, through having to pay homage for the French territories. The nature of his motivation meant that from time to time he was prepared to abandon the campaign and sign a truce, when fatigued by the fighting; the conflict was not an unbroken series of battles lasting literally for a hundred years. It was restarted by Henry V as a way of bestowing legitimacy on the Lancastrian dynasty, seen with some justification as usurpers, through success in foreign wars. Ironically it contributed to the failure of that dynasty, by being a dangerous distraction from potential political troubles at home, though whether the War of the Roses, or the ultimate collapse of the French venture during the course of the fifteenth century, would have happened if England had been ruled by an abler monarch than Henry VI is at least a matter for speculation.

Britain could take part in offensive operations on land as part of an alliance, e.g. the Crusades. Which ultimately failed to achieve their aim, though that was not her fault, or not hers alone. We have talked of possible military threats to the West from powers outside it. The Crusades were an early example of *Western* imperialism, if one leaves out the expansion of the Roman Empire during its heyday. Though a Christian colony, called Outremer (meaning "across the sea") was founded in Palestine the object was not the political subjugation (to who exactly; there were various Western powers involved in the business) and annexation of the Muslim world, but rather the safeguarding of the Holy Places of Christendom, plus the need to find a channel for military ardour. Insufficient support was given to the Crusader States, apart from any logistical difficulties of keeping them provisioned, and they eventually collapsed, Jerusalem being retaken by the Muslims along with the other conquered territories. This is not surprising given the character of the Crusades, which were prone to degenerate into an undisciplined (and violently unchristian) squabble over the spoils. Although a mutual regard did develop between the leaders of the two sides, who saw each other as brave warriors whatever else they might be, the whole bloody free-for-all, in which Muslims were often gratuitously massacred along with Jews, leaves the Muslim leader Saladin, who among other things held off from attacking a church during one campaign while a Christian wedding was taking place there, looking more honourable than the Christians. Not the only respect in which mainstream Islam, during the centuries in which it and the West were in military conflict, comes off better in moral terms; but that is another story.

Awareness of her relative military weakness, away from the sea, was what led Britain in the early modern period to put so much of her energy into acquiring colonial possessions outside Europe, establishing domination over non-western peoples who unlike the French did not have the resources to resist her, and then safeguarding those acquisitions from rivals. As other countries came to challenge her in this field, and she needed to defend the economic position she had attained through her industrial development and commercial expansion, the need for a strong army, conveyed around the world by her already existing and efficient navy, which might be needed to take on her enemies in North America (or for that matter mainland Europe), she ceased to be a purely maritime military power.

In some cases the age of exploration led through colonisation (not just "colonialism", which in itself means merely the domination in whatever way of one nation by another) to the foundation of new nations, some of which became major players on the world stage if abundant raw materials and the willingness/ability to make use of them, thus creating a great military and industrial power, permitted it. The most important in the long run was the United States of America. Her nature explains the course of her own internal development as well as the role she was eventually to play in global politics. Because the settlement of large territories could not always be a planned, rather than piecemeal, affair, because those territories attracted anyone with a sufficient religious, political or economic motive − basically, escape from persecution, censorship or poverty − to start afresh in pastures new, and because settlement whoever by had to be encouraged to some extent by the existing colonial elite if the nation was to be built up and made economically viable, the result was a society exhibiting a wide range of contrasts. Diverse ethnically, culturally and politically, it was to produce for example both the "hippy" lifestyle of some Californians and the strict Christian puritanism of the Amish and Mennonites. The picture was, and is, complicated further by the survival of some of the indigenous population and by the slaves imported from Africa, the unwilling immigrants. The most fundamental distinction (though it was never absolute; distinctions aren't) was between the progressive, liberal, industrial North and the economically relatively backward, agricultural and conservative South, and it was one that eventually led to war, in 1861. Slavery, as opposed to working for a (high or low) wage, was seen by the North as no longer efficient in economic terms, whatever the moral arguments against it. People who were motivated by the latter would naturally seek to rubbish it on the former grounds, something which is worth the historian bearing in mind if they are seeking to establish how effective it was in practical respects. But the issue of the culture clash between the two halves of "America" (we are of course talking only about one sub-continent) had to be resolved if the United States was to be a truly united, and therefore powerful, and prosperous nation. Slavery was merely the pretext for the conflict and the logic of a war which started over it meant that slavery had to be abolished. The black population did not gain that much by the measure; the Jim Crow laws and general lack, in effect, of civil rights from which they continued to suffer shows that the whole thing was not designed for their benefit. Blacks in America and Britain have always had an ambivalent attitude to those countries; one that is grateful for the advantages they have gained from living there and feeling a kind of patriotism, yet always conscious, and resentful, of the disabilities their race has historically been subjected to. When Michelle Obama on the election of her husband as President of the USA said that for the first time she could actually be proud of her country, it was disturbing and provoked some complaint but one could nevertheless understand it.

After the end of the war in 1865 the priority was reconstruction, the overriding principle that of national unity. No-one wanted a return to disruptive conflict and all concentrated on completing the conquest of the West and the building up of the economy (the conservative and backward South having been defeated by the dynamic and progressive North), which in the later nineteenth century was rapidly expanding towards the point where it would become the biggest on earth. This commitment imparted a stability to American politics which has endured ever since, the main feature of the party system being a straightforward divide between Republicans and Democrats (an additional factor here is the importance of the role and personality of the President relative to that of party). American history in the twentieth century is the history of particular issues, such as America's world role, the continuing impact of mass immigration, the status of US blacks and the civil rights movement. And important as those issues may be, one does not encounter anything like the splitting of the Liberal Party over Irish Home Rule in 1886 or the realignment of parties after the First World War with the decline of the Liberals and the rise of Labour, both of these being features of the British experience. There have until the present time been no serious disagreements over the basic structure of government. Such would imply the possibility of political instability and it is feared that that instability, which might encourage major social unrest, would jeapordise the whole of the achievement which Americans are so proud of, when its preservation is vital not just for the sake of the US' own integrity but, because of its geopolitical and global economic importance, that of the world at large. The system is only now coming under serious threat – as I see it, it is – with the re-emergence of sharp divisions over race and the constitutional issues raised by the blocking of Obamacare.

Large-scale immigration, from wherever there were people who wanted to build better lives for themselves, had negative as well as positive consequences. Naturally seeking their own kind (though there was in due course to develop among them a genuine American patriotism which exerted an at least equally powerful pull), the immigrants formed large ethnic residential blocs each with its own political machine, as embodied in the "boss" system, and criminal organisations (the line between the two sometimes becoming blurred), and representing an electoral force which US Presidents found it prudent to court arguably to the detriment of what was objective and healthy. The most obvious example of the latter has been the staunchly pro-Israel element among Jewish voters, which has tended to work against the formulation of a truly bi-partisan policy on the Arab-Israeli issue. In the case of the Irish community a continuing loyalty to the "folks back home" led some to support the IRA with money and guns, not necessarily with the approval of the US government or the majority of Irish American citizens.

America's perceived aggression and paranoia, much complained about in the twentieth and twenty-first centuries, are like her patchwork nature a product of the circumstances of her birth. For three hundred years settlers had to defend themselves against other settlers, who also wanted as big a slice of land as possible, and hostile natives. It was necessary for everyone to have a gun once they were old enough to be presumed capable of using it safely. This defensiveness became engrained in the American psyche. And America was even more aggressive and paranoid later on because she had so much to defend. You know that the more power and wealth you acquire, the more it is resented by others. By extension from this America has to side, as any country would side in fact, with those nations who are likely to support her, who admire her culture and want to emulate it, even where their leaders are oppressive and corrupt.

4

During the period in which she first marked out her colonial empires, impacting profoundly on the lives of indigenous populations, Europe was herself going through cataclysmic changes, as we have seen. With the Renaissance the Middle Ages gave way to the "early modern" period. New financial policies and socio-economic changes paved the way for the Industrial Revolution, though the latter was not to kick off until the mid-eighteenth century. The switch to new ways of funding government following the end of the feudal system (in which, for example, the peasants had to pay to have their corn ground at the lord of the manor's mill, and weren't allowed to use any other) and the growth of royal bureaucracy meant that monarchical government was tightening its control, in a process which continued into the seventeenth and eighteenth centuries and even beyond to some extent. Paradoxically, at the same time the importance of patronage, which needed someone to dispense it, as the mediaeval power structure was eroded with the decline of feudalism, and an increase in the complexity of government business beyond the ability of the king or queen to supervise it in detail led to the emergence of a phenomenon the Middle Ages had not really known. This was the powerful chief minister who was as important in determining what happened as the monarch, depending on the latter's personality and how much free rein was permitted. Among the earliest examples may be counted Wolsey and (Thomas) Cromwell in England; in the seventeenth century there were Richelieu and Mazarin in France and Olivares in Spain. The ultimate development of the trend was represented by Bismarck in Prussia/Germany. But these statesmen were not necessarily kings in all but name; the hereditary ruler could still overrule or dismiss them if they chose and the example of Louis XIV in France shows that tighter bureaucratic control potentially benefited the monarch rather than their senior employee, provided they chose to assert themselves.

The institution of monarchy – which before the Enlightenment was supposed to have been ordained by God – also benefited from the continuing lack, according to contemporary mindsets, of an alternative to it. The trend for the power of the King or Queen to increase, as in France where it was most evident, was not universal. It did not happen in England due to the foolishness of the much less shrewd Charles I in putting the parliamentary gentry of England, which was more assertive than that of other countries because of its greater socioeconomic importance, in a position where it felt it had no option but to rebel to the point of overthrowing the institution of monarchy, through his absolutist policies and disregard for certain rights. So the English got over their revolutions, and in Cromwell their military dictatorships, earlier than everyone else, by a series of events during which some strikingly left-wing views were expressed, by the Levellers and others, of a kind which in other countries were not to receive serious consideration for at least another hundred years.

But cultural changes were under way which would gradually erode the old order throughout Europe as a whole. Precisely why the scientific and industrial revolutions of the seventeenth and eighteenth centuries happened when they did is a subject which on its own calls for in-depth analysis. But they may be assumed to be the product of various factors some of which came together at roughly the same time. Undoubtedly, the continuing effect of the Renaissance partly explains the astronomical discoveries of Galileo, which came on top of Copernicus'. These discoveries were crucial in bringing about cataclysmic changes in Western thought. If the traditional view of the universe, in which the sun had mistakenly been believed to circle the Earth instead of the other way round, was wrong then what else might be? There followed the groundbreaking work of Boyle, Hooke and Newton on gravity and other aspects of physics. Now both science and industry had been around, even if only in rudimentary forms, since the beginnings of humankind. They existed symbiotically since to some extent one was not possible without the other. The tools used in scientific research had to be manufactured, and it would not have been possible to discover that minerals could be used to make them, or weapons, without a degree of experimentation and of trial and error. Science in a more formal sense was of course known to the ancient Greeks, though they may merely have been codifying, if necessarily, what had long been obvious to anybody with any common sense (even the most stupid and uneducated of barbarians knew that if a body immersed in a receptacle full of water displaced the water it was because the two could not occupy the same point in space and time, so something had to give; it was just that no-one until Archimedes expressed this understanding as a formal theory). There was science in the Middle Ages; it was not seen as disproving supposed certainties in the field of religion because in trying to understand, however imperfectly, the workings of the natural universe its practitioners were drawing attention to the skill of God, the Creator, and thus honouring him (though as Galileo later found out, there was a limit to how far it could be reconciled with the theological beliefs of the Church establishment). It had not, however, advanced much beyond the discoveries of the Greeks, who were hailed as virtuous pagans whose authority in these matters must be respected — and preferably not questioned. Beyond that essential footing it was imperfect and often prone to explore cul-de-sacs, as we now know them to have been, such as the attempt to turn base metals into gold.

The new science seemed to take things further than they had ever been before. The truths it discovered about the universe were more *fundamental*. We were beginning to understand not just what things did, but why they did it. There is a third, highest level of understanding, that of why anything exists in the first place, and since no-one has yet answered that question satisfactorily in conventional scientific terms, maybe never will, there remains the possibility of a creative intelligence as the ultimate explanation for everything. But science as it began to develop from the seventeenth century seemed especially far-reaching in its revelations and implications; as well as more dynamic, its progress more sustained and consistent, because a take-off point had been reached beyond which it could not be arrested. This plus the fact that the development was relatively sudden and rapid, coming after centuries of stagnation, meant there was bound to be a profound psychological impact.

Industry and the new science gradually came together, their union being most apparent in the developments in chemistry during the nineteenth century. In the long run "applied" science was to boost the industrial revolution which was already well under way by the time this fusion really took effect. That revolution had required an agricultural revolution before it could get going, and this occurred in the first half of the eighteenth century with the improvement of farming techniques in Britain by Coke of Norfolk among others. But one could arguably date it back to certain trends during the sixteenth century, or to the invention of the first steam engine by Thomas

Savery in 1698. Thomas Newcomen further developed the latter in the early years of the following century, using it to pump water out of mines. We are back to the question of main and secondary nexus points. The West may have been better at applying technology on a mass scale than other cultures, but even on its own territory that process could take time. Often the initial effect of change is to improve and give a boost to existing ways of doing things. Many people continued to use windmills or watermills to grind corn, especially in rural areas, till well into the nineteenth century and even in a few cases the early-mid twentieth. This was made possible because they were being built bigger and more powerful, with a greater number of millstones and various technical refinements which made them more efficient such as, and especially after c1830, increased use of iron components. The appearance of steam power on a mass scale did not occur for some considerable time; the first large steam flour mill at a port city (London) was not built until 1782. The overall effects of change in any area may take a while to be felt. Nevertheless the Industrial Revolution did begin around 1750-60 in Britain where relief, rich mineral resources, and prior improvements in agricultural techniques and in financial organisation combined to make it possible, and spread gradually to what we now call the "developed" and "developing" worlds, which roughly speaking amount to most of the planet.

The process was as we have observed simultaneous with advances in scientific knowledge, which formed a part of it. It is still going on and is both horizontal and vertical. The successive stages have been (1) the application of steam power, generated using available reserves of coal and water, to industry on such a scale as to make mass production of commodities and therefore the consumer society possible, and as a corollary to this the development of railways and steamships which allow products to be distributed more widely; (2) the invention of the internal combustion engine, enabling cars and aircraft to be built and operated, plus the growth of oil, chemical and electrical industries; (3) electronics, plastics and the jet engine, the latter revolutionising lifestyles and the conduct of business by facilitating rapid international travel; (4) computers and information technology in general, with lasers, fibre optics and robotics; and (5) bioengineering, including genetic engineering, and cybernetics – arguably the final stage as it represents the union of the natural world out of which Man originally evolved with the artificial, and in so doing involves the greatest dangers and most difficult dilemmas. The process has proved irreversible because of the rise in living standards people know it can bring about and do not want to sacrifice.

The impact of this scientific and industrial revolution during the two centuries from Galileo (taking him as an arbitrary starting-point) on Western Man's world-view was profound. It wasn't that people stopped believing in religion, say (though some did). It was possible, and is possible today, to

301

believe the laws of gravity, thermodynamics etcetera were ordained by God or are in some way a part of Him. The discoveries of Darwin concerning evolution and natural history in the nineteenth century were far more damaging to religious belief because they seemed to more flatly contradict what was in the Bible, though there are nonetheless ways of resolving the contradiction. But religious people continued to believe in God, etc., throughout the intervening period and beyond, quite happily accepting the theories of Newton and his peers as compatible with Scripture. It took a bit longer for them to accept Darwin but most did in the end, despite the apparent belief of some modern atheists that they didn't. With Darwin the divorce seems to have been mostly on one side, apart from a relatively small element of Christian fundamentalists (the latter term meaning those who take the Bible literally). The majority of Christians came to accept the theory of evolution as quite compatible with their faith, and the process began at a relatively early stage; let us not forget that when he died in 1882, Darwin was buried in Westminster Abbey.

But from the seventeenth century, due to the general climate of questioning received wisdom that science was creating, religion became divorced from superstition, by which I mean a tendency to believe in something out of ignorance or gullibility. It was practised in a more considered *way*. There were reasoned arguments you could put forward in support of it (as well as against it), but there was apparently no such justification for belief in black magic and sorcery. The witchcraft craze of the mid-late seventeenth century began to seem a silly affair; once it was realised there was no intellectual excuse for it it was easier to perceive that its motive had been hysteria combined with financial gain (payment for services rendered by "witchfinders" like Matthew Hopkins) or a desire for revenge against someone or other. Although prosecutions for witchcraft were to continue, albeit with increasingly less frequency, into the next century, it seems in historical retrospect like the last fling of rampant superstition. It owed a lot to the unsettled conditions created by the civil war and Interregnum, in which old beliefs could resurface with a vengeance as well as new ones flourish, and to the fact that the scientific revolution, though it could be said to have started as far back as Copernicus in the fifteenth century, had not yet got under full swing (for a comprehensive exploration of this whole subject see Keith Thomas' excellent work *Religion And The Decline Of Magic*; there were sociological factors involved both in witch-hunting crazes and the eventual decline in witch-beliefs). But in time witchcraft came to be seen as a delusion which the deluded might be allowed to practise if they really wanted to rather than a real threat to the spiritual health of society, and the statutes against it were gradually repealed, the last in 1736.

It's also worth remembering that Christians by the latter part of the seventeenth century had more or less given up, thankfully, the practice of burning religious heretics or "witches" alive, which was never as common as popular imagination has it in any case; their punishment was to be execution by the relatively more humane method of hanging. Matthew Hopkins never actually burnt anyone, and the scenes in the (otherwise rather good) Vincent Price film of young women being tied to tar barrels and ignited never took place, with perhaps a few exceptions (isolated cases of burning at the stake, or wherever, persisted into the next century and even after; there are always, of course, religious fanatics, just as there are non-religious ones). The film-makers merely thought they would be more likely to excite an audience's emotions than if the women had been middle-aged or elderly. But the (altruistic, if still erroneous) idea that the sinner had to be burnt because the fires were symbolic of the purification of their tainted souls, or that regardless of where they were going when they died their sin was like a physical plague which must be destroyed to prevent it contaminating others, had been replaced by considerations which might not have occurred with a different mindset. Only the sinner's own repentance, along with the final judgement of God, could save them anyway and so the burning made no difference. Symbols were only symbols after all, however important. And sin could only be communicated from one person to another if the latter was wicked or foolish; it was at any rate not a physical thing, though it could have physical consequences, and died with the person who committed it. This shift in thinking may have been due to a new "scientific" approach to matters or it may rather demonstrate that religious thought is itself not static and changes over time (which it does). But there *was* a change, whatever the reasons for it.

After about 1700 religion ceased to be a major cause of war in the West. This was due largely to fatigue at the strife between Catholic and Protestant during the previous two centuries, which had been very destructive and divisive in its consequences, especially the Thirty Years' War of 1618-48. Even if that latter conflict had ceased by its end to be religious rather than geopolitical in motivation, which is itself indicative of a sea change. The general expansion of commerce perhaps meant that economic considerations would become as important, if not more so, than religion in international politics. And of course there was also the advent of the age of "Reason". But that did not mean religion ceased to be a factor of political importance. The Enlightenment, like the Industrial Revolution, happened in stages. For example Catholics and Protestant nonconformists in Britain continued to be denied key civil rights until the nineteenth century. This was because although judicial burning was no longer considered desirable (apart from anything else, because of the pain involved it was seen as uncivilised and barbaric, inconsistent with the modern and supposedly better world that science had inaugurated) the idea persisted in influential quarters that "dangerous" beliefs, which *could* be spread even if not in the same way as a physical disease, must be prevented from being expressed and carry a penalty if they were. Also that religious uniformity and orthodoxy was inseparable from the preservation, for the sake of order and stability, of the traditional political structure, hence the Church of England, which was now the established one, had for everyone's sake to be defended from the influence of "heretics" and that meant not giving them a high profile and platform from which they could expound their views by appointing them to public offices or teaching posts. This was certainly the thinking of a Gladstone, though in his case it underwent modifications with time. Nevertheless as the march of "Reason" continued into his era, these restrictions were removed by such measures as Catholic Emancipation (1829). Religion had come to be seen as a personal thing. To some extent this had already been recognised by the seventeenth century; although a Dissenter might be barred from certain occupations or (at one time) imprisoned for preaching in public it was accepted he could not be forced to change his denomination by torture or the threat of death. He had a right to his beliefs even if he must still suffer their consequences. It was not for the state to decide what his convictions should be even if it could punish him for having them. (Still less, therefore, was it acceptable to invade other countries to force their populations to become Catholic or Protestant). It wasn't, in the first instance, that the doctrines of Heaven and Hell, and the supposed relation of which of the two you ended up in when you died to what you had believed in this life, ceased to matter but rather that people had to be allowed to go to the devil (or to God, whichever the case might be) in their own way. In a further sea change, it was decided that by extension this applied to society at large. It was appreciated that Catholics and Protestant Nonconformists had likewise realised the wrongness, and foolishness, of compulsion in religious matters (and thus were not a *political* threat to the state). In general society, it became impossible to compel people to attend church services or refrain from working on a Sunday. Freedom included the right to not have a God at all, or be casual in your attitude towards him, although that right might be conceded gradually and atheists in public life, where they were much more exposed to the hostility of Christians (or nominal Christians − there was a lot of hypocrisy involved) were treated very badly.

Meanwhile, as society became more complex in its needs due to the effects of industrialisation it proved impossible for the Church to perform many of the functions of local government, such as poor relief, as it had done in the past. This diminished its public profile and thus its influence. There took place a separation between the religious and the secular; this in itself ought not to have alarmed religious people since in one sense the distinction could never exist, if everything was the work of God, but in the area of actual belief it often extended to rejecting religion altogether. Certainly, although many still felt religion to be spiritually essential, a necessary prerequisite for "salvation", a butcher was also essential because you had to get through this life first and while you were in it needed to eat, and yet there was no logical reason why a priest should assume their function or for that matter any other secular role, including that of politician. (The practice of churchmen serving in government had died out in Britain during the sixteenth century, because their attention was diverted from purely political or administrative matters by the religious ferment of the Reformation; it lasted longer in France than in England but was to die out there too in due course along with the *ancient regime* monarchy itself, because of the factors we have been discussing.)

The radical revision of contemporary world views which stemmed from new scientific discoveries led to the Enlightenment of the eighteenth century, which itself had a lasting effect on Western, and thus to some extent everyone else's, history by questioning traditional norms and sociopolitical structures, and more thoroughly than the Renaissance, however profound the latter's consequences were, had. The Enlightenment opposed the monopoly of power enjoyed by monarchs and aristocrats and also the influence of the Church, especially the Catholic Church where Catholicism was the official state religion, upon political and social life. It demanded greater freedom of expression and opportunity, including participation in the political process, for the rising middle class (from whose ranks the scientific pioneers had largely come), and also independence for ethnic and national groups where this was the only way for them to free themselves from systems of government that were seen as alien and oppressive. Though they might play a major part in inspiring the American Revolution, if the latter is considered as a purely political affair, Enlightenment thinkers did not necessarily seek to extend the benefits of inclusivity to those below them on the social scale, i.e. the working class. Britain needed the Enlightenment relatively less, from the point of view of these middle-class reformers, than the European monarchies of the *Ancien Regime*, or Russia where roughly speaking kings and queens still held absolute power (in practice most decisions affecting the government of the realm, and certainly day-to-day administration, were down to the monarch's ministers but he or she had to approve what was decided in the last resort and could have a significant influence on events when they chose to assert their will). Partly through the new climate of change and partly through the interplay of events and personalities Britain ended up with a far more constitutional monarchy, in which the Crown could do little more than appoint ministers, a prerogative which itself was to eventually lapse in anything but a formal respect. The various checks and balances were designed not to ensure democracy but to limit the power of the monarch as against that of the aristocracy – whose wealth derived mainly from the land and who therefore benefited from the agricultural revolution of the early eighteenth century. But no-one was bothered about that. Monarchy had been replaced by oligarchy (which might be said to have inherited and used for its own benefit the bureaucratic structures earlier devised by monarchs to strengthen their control) rather than universal suffrage and popular rule. (Today we have universal suffrage but still, nonetheless, oligarchic government, or so many people would claim, the oligarchy including big business and the remnants of the aristocracy.) In any event Britain could not escape what were to be the principal consequences of the scientific and industrial revolutions, not least because she was where they had originally started and where the industrialisation was proceeding most rapidly.

As emphasised, the techniques and approach required by the new science gave a new boost to the tendency to inquire and to question accepted forms, which communicated itself to other walks of life and became more marked as industrialisation and scientific progress continued. Research and experimentation involved a logical process of analysis and conclusion, while the adoption of large scale mechanisation in industry produced a mindset characterised, as far as it could be in flawed human beings, by an emphasis on the rational ordering of things (mirroring how a machine, which obviously had to be designed in a rational way to work properly, functioned). Though there was and is such a thing as the soulless industrialist concerned only with results, this did not mean that people all became robot-like automatons, but it did perhaps make it less likely that they would believe in something purely because it was customary to do so.

The Industrial Revolution required change in a practical as well as an intellectual sense. It had vastly accelerated the process by which a large middle and upper working class, deriving its income from commerce and industry, grew up. It made the middle, and in time the working, classes feel important and they started to agitate for the vote. They were the muscle or the brains – the driving force – behind the most profound and significant development of the times, the creators of the nation's new wealth, and inevitably demanded that this be recognised in a new political status, involving full participation in the electoral process and thus the chance to not only gain control over their own lives but also express themselves by making their mark on wider affairs.

And the fact that they were so heavily concentrated in cities, with the movement of workers from the countryside as industry became more important in the economy, made them more of a political force and meant that the consequences could be serious if they felt marginalised, their aspirations unmet. Their numbers were swollen by the increase in population which the agricultural revolution that preceded the industrial one had made possible. And the middle-class manufacturers and artisans, who needed to be educated if they were to do their jobs properly, had come under the influence of the Enlightenment philosophers and their intellectual successors.

For reasons given, Great Britain was the first country to experience this issue and also the one to deal with it most successfully. In time it came to the surface all over Europe, but Britain was able to contain it better. Historical circumstances had formed in her a mindset which centred on the idea of peaceful constitutional change, of compromise rather than confrontation. Though the process was not a smooth one and there were times when things could have gone disastrously wrong, she managed to avoid the horrors of the French Revolution.

The explosion did not necessarily require industrialisation, the consequences of same not being sufficiently appreciated by those in power, to happen. The influence of the Enlightenment was enough. By 1789 France had not industrialised to anything like the same extent that Britain had. The former country, bigger than her neighbour and much less urbanised, remained outside the cities a mass peasant society which had not undergone even an agricultural revolution and thus experienced a rise in living standards. Besides being highly vulnerable to recessions, poor harvests, and the rhythms of nature, and generally having to endure a state of poverty, the bulk of the population were looked down on by the ruling aristocratic/monarchic regime and felt themselves to be oppressed by harsh, and antiquated, laws. The Catholic Church was still powerful, perhaps more so than any in Protestant Britain or the German states, and tended to support the existing social and political order. The relatively small middle class was largely excluded from government.

The French Revolution was initially a matter of middle-class activists influenced by the Enlightenment. They perhaps acted to some extent out of altruism for the peasants, but certainly sought to increase their own power against the dominance of aristocrats and the Church and reform or replace the *Ancien Regime* to suit the times. In the turmoil created by the fall of the Bastille influence over what was going on filtered down to the working class, though they did not manage to seize full control of the movement; their discontent and lack of education made them unthinkingly vicious, the brutal shock troops of the Revolution, but also meant they wouldn't at this time have known what to do with power had they achieved it.

Paradoxically, it was when things had got better, with the economic situation improving and the most obnoxious laws repealed, that the Revolution first broke out; the same was to happen two hundred years later with Gorbachev and the Soviet Union, though minus so much of the violence. People were on a high, their appetite for change and for the power to bring it about whetted, and became impatient. Once the unrest began to affect law and order the pent-up hatred of the workers burst forth and the middle-class leaders of the Revolution had to give them what they wanted to keep them under control, while being affected themselves by the runaway craze for change. It was not right, but it serves as a warning to established political regimes not to leave abuses unreformed for too long.

There took place the execution of King Louis XVI, and of Marie Antoinette whose only crime was to be at worst a rather stupid woman (whose "let them eat cake" remark about the starving populace of Paris was probably misrepresented in the feverish climate which prevailed); her charming naivety, though it got her into trouble – historically she was in the wrong place at the wrong time – marks her out as a dumb blonde, at the risk of seeming offensively stereotypical, but certainly not a wicked one. Her apology just before her guillotining for accidentally stepping on the executioner's toe is both sweet and extremely moving. In a recent survey of the French people the majority of them concluded that the execution was wrong.

Subsequently there occurred a complete reform of social and political institutions, including the abolition of titles, the adoption of a new calendar and the legal prohibition of religion; a thorough break with the past. The French Revolution followed a pattern which can be observed, to a greater or lesser degree, in the English and Russian ones. All three suffered from being sudden reversals of the usual scheme of things, though the Soviets proved better at overcoming this obstacle, their achievement consequently lasting longer. The logic of commitment to change, plus fear of counter-revolutionary elements who would obviously seek to take back control (the more so because they regarded what had happened as an unnatural interruption of time-honoured procedures, besides their own status and privileges having been lost), meant everyone must follow the new line, the new orthodoxy, on pain of imprisonment and execution (the English Revolution proving, on the whole, less brutal in this respect than the other two). If all are agreed things should remain as they are, there is less scope for conflict; it is harder to agree on how to change them, especially if the change is a sudden (if inevitable, should oppression and suffering continue) and radical one. Disagreement over the exact way the new sociopolitical order was to develop led to violent purges of those not considered ideologically sound – the Revolution "devouring its children" – and a veering between one form of government, one way of doing the job (always, in theory at any rate, remaining true to the Revolution's basic values) and another. The English Revolution of 1649-60 and the French of 1789-1815 ended in military dictatorships; the dictator model was adopted for a time at least during the life of the Soviet Union although in all three examples it was the dictator themselves who took the initiative, either by a sudden seizure of power when it was judged the moment was right or, in Stalin's case, scheming and cunning manipulation. Cromwell and Napoleon were acting because uncertainty or disagreement about how exactly to proceed, resulting in frequent changes of government or its personnel, was paralysing the conduct of affairs.

In the end all three Revolutions collapsed because they had run out of options, though in Russia the process took much longer and the movement had by the end largely ceased to believe in its own principles (as in fact did the English, General Monk inviting back the King because he could see no alternative). The English and the French had tried to do too much too fast. In the English case, the weaknesses in the system meant that it did not long survive the death of the man who was holding it all together (and was succeeded by his (less competent) nephew; already one of the principal characteristics of inefficient dictatorships, nepotism, had become established). But what has been said above about revolutions applies to a good many radical reforming movements, including religious as well as political ones, which manage to get themselves into power. It may apply especially, at least equally, to religious ones since the nature of religion if believed in fanatically enough can all too easily lead to extremism. I'm thinking of course of Iran and Afghanistan under the Taliban. But the atheist Directory of Paris wasn't much better.

The ideas of the Enlightenment, along with political blunders which discredited the existing system, led to the emergence of non-monarchical rulers in a way which had not been seen for at least two thousand years. They had been known in classical times; Pericles of Athens, perhaps the most famous example, was a senior public official and not a king. Later, they were very much the exception (Venice, Switzerland, the Netherlands etc.) to the rule, and even with a substantial elective element in the system the Dutch *Stadholder* could acquire a quasi-monarchical status. It was the Enlightenment (and not the English Revolution, which at the time and after was regarded by foreigners as a curious and alarming aberration) which really made it possible for the principle to be adopted on a permanent, or semi-permanent, basis in a major power such as France or the United States. If transition from a monarchical to a non-monarchical system of government is seen as an evolutionary progression, then history is not always an even process of "evolution", any more than is biological change. And Holland and Belgium eventually settled for monarchy after they split from one another, having previously formed the United Provinces, in the early nineteenth century; monarchs could survive if they were prepared to rule constitutionally and able to disassociate themselves from unpopular policies. In the long run this was not to happen in France.

Beforehand, there had been monarchies which were elective, such as the Holy Roman Empire, in whose case the practice emerged out of ancient Germanic custom and in later centuries had value as a way of discouraging the Emperor from thinking of himself as an absolute ruler not responsible to popular, or at least aristocratic, opinion. It was not seen as effective or desirable in the militaristic, autocratic, Prussian-dominated German Empire which was created in 1871. In any case the principle had gone into abeyance to some extent towards the end or at least was not inclusive, with Emperors tending to be drawn from a single family (the Hapsburgs).

5

Historically wars have been fought for all kinds of reasons (or combinations of reasons): religion, territory (acquiring or defending it), dynastic disputes, economics, ideology, national independence, race. Of these dynastic ambition had by 1800 ceased to be the most important, though it could still be used as a pretext (Bismarck was particularly good at that sort of thing). The marriage of royals of different nationalities could be diplomatically useful, but was not a recipe for peace; one of the saddest aspects of the slide into World War One was that it happened despite the German and British royal families being related through the Kaiser, who was Queen Victoria's grandson and George V's cousin. Partly the problem was the behaviour of the Kaiser himself (who did not actually get on with his English mother). In any case, with the exception of Russia where the Tsar was in effect an absolute ruler (and where the possession of such power ultimately proved disastrous), the principal European monarchies had by the end if not the start of the Great War become essentially figureheads, the prisoners of the army, one might say (especially in Germany's case) the military-industrial complex, and the aristocratic ruling class. Those sectors might feel a need to preserve the monarchy as a focus for national identity, a narrative, but did not wish it to have any real control over them. The Kaiser's bombast and bluster obscured how little influence he actually had, and was consequential only in a negative way, serving to identify German foreign policy in the eyes of other countries with his own arrogant and irresponsible behaviour.

By then, though he could assert himself on occasions, Emperor Franz Josef of Austria-Hungary was too old to prevent the ultimate breakup of the Habsburg Empire, which the war accelerated. It is fortunate that he did not live to see it. Autocratic and devious, he was not particularly likeable but it is impossible not to feel sympathy for him on account of the quite remarkable run of tragedies he experienced during his lifetime. He lost wars with France (in 1859, over Italy) and Prussia (1866). His brother was stood against a wall and shot by Mexican revolutionaries in 1867. His heir, the Crown Prince Rudolf, committed suicide in 1889. His wife, the Empress Elizabeth, was murdered by an Italian anarchist in 1898. Then of course came the assassination of his nephew and replacement heir, Franz Ferdinand, in 1914. That event precipitated the war which brought about the Empire's end. But Franz Josef believed in it, seeing it as his duty to uphold it and attending to that task with diligence over sixty-eight years despite the many catastrophes. He died, aged eighty-six, complaining that he was behind with his work. Somehow, it commands admiration and sets an example for a world where this kind of integrity and dedication seem to have gone out of fashion. His tragedy was that he himself may have brought about the final destruction of all he cherished. By the time of his death he was more a figurehead, a treasured national institution, than an effective hands-on ruler. But he had a tremendous symbolic and psychological influence. Though the Hapsburg state might not have lightly relinquished its rule over its subject peoples in any case, moves towards federalising the Empire, at least, were inhibited because it was known he would be so much against it. It is not too much of an exaggeration to suggest that he was ultimately responsible for the First World War.

His great-nephew Karl, who succeeded him, had too weak a personality to have a dynamic impact on the situation, and change the Hapsburgs' fortunes for the better. It is unlikely though that by this stage a man both younger and strong in character would have made much difference. Karl might have gained support by pulling out of the war but it is unlikely he could have done anything without the agreement of the much more powerful partner in the Dual Alliance, Germany – and she would have been unlikely to agree, even though as an ally Austria was not as much use to her as she would have preferred. He did actually make peace moves, but without success as we of course know.

In any case, the "rational" modern age saw no merit in giving hereditary monarchies real power. Their value was essentially symbolic, and so it was totally destroyed by military defeat, with which they were identified (the average, probably not particularly politically aware, citizen did not appreciate the gulf between their apparent and their actual power). Had they won it might have been another matter, but they did not win, the exception being of course Britain, though George V's prestige and the fact that he had accepted constitutionalism, as Victoria and Edward VII had done, and so kept his hands clean, meant he would probably have survived in any case.

Monarchy was acceptable as long as it was (a) part of the contemporary mindset and (b) could be relied upon to provide good leaders, or at least was no less effective in that respect than any other way of doing things. But the monarchies' intellectual decline, due to inbreeding, helped to diminish their real power. They would eventually have been relegated to a symbolic role anyway, in the industrial age, but the rise of a particular trend coincided with the diminishing influence of those who were most likely to resist it. By the mid-nineteenth century the British monarchy was very definitely a constitutional one. In 1870 defeat in war, accomplishing what it was to bring about in Germany and Austria-Hungary in 1918, finished off monarchy as a system of government in France, though the Bonapartists continued to enjoy a certain degree of support nonetheless. The other European sovereigns progressively lost their executive role though some retained the right to dismiss governments well into the twentieth century, being consequently politically important enough to figure as pawns in the schemes of Hitler. The extent to which they lost influence varied and their residual powers, within the area in which these operated, could be considerable, sometimes with horrendous results. King Leopold of Belgium was able to exercise a very personal, and brutal, control of his country's colonisation of the Congo, in a way reminiscent of a tyrannical mediaeval absolute ruler; he would not have got away with cutting off the hands of his European subjects, unlike his predecessors hundreds of years before.

Religion had ceased to be a major cause of war for reasons discussed. The most important factors in (European) geopolitical affairs were nationalism and ideology, the two sometimes being combined. As well as democracy (though not for everyone) the Enlightenment in its political expression sought independence for nations (that was, distinct groups of people with their own customs and sense of identity, whether or not they had linguistic affinities with the country they were trying to separate themselves from). This was in contrast to progressive opinion today which sees it as desirable for nations to pool their sovereignty within supranational institutions like the European Union. The American Revolution did not need that much to be a sociopolitical one as far as the internal affairs of the colonies were concerned, since the manner in which a relatively young society formed of colonists had come about meant the franchise was less confined to a narrow privileged elite, though that is not to say social classes didn't exist. It was not like in an older society where traditional sociopolitical distinctions were beginning to grate, and where people were not still engaged in the task of nation-building to the extent of being distracted to some degree from other things. The Revolution was undoubtedly a nationalist one, sparked off by clumsy treatment of the colonists on the part of George III of Britain and his ministers, who failed to realise that a significant number of them, partly because of geographical distance from London, had evolved a different kind of national consciousness, the latter entailing that they felt their own representative institutions should have a bigger say in how they were governed. Up to the Declaration of Independence in 1776 most Americans were not thinking in terms of complete secession from Britain. The problem was that the British had in the past tended to neglect the colonists, seeing them as an undisciplined bunch of misfits (a mistake which was to prove Britain's undoing in the War of Independence, along with the time taken for reinforcements to cross the Atlantic, a disadvantage the colonists did not suffer from). Then suddenly they acquired an importance as a source of revenue to pay for the Seven Years War, and the resulting imposition of taxes drove up the stakes, proving as unpopular in America as Ship Money and the revival of old laws as a means of raising funds had under Charles I in the previous century.

One might say that Britain and the Americans were at cross purposes, due to a misconception on the former's part. The colonists were trying to get the best deal for themselves within the British Empire, Britain to coerce people who ought to be grateful to be part of it and in her view weren't. By her high-handed attitude over the whole affair she alienated many who might otherwise have stayed loyal (though a surprising percentage still did). The Americans saw their separate national consciousness as a basis for rejecting laws which they found oppressive, much like Scottish devolutionists in the late twentieth century. The revolution, like others, became a war when the mother country tried to prevent them striking out on their own, and the decision to go for independence was a logical consequence of what was happening. The term "revolution" implies the concept of completely changing a system of government (either imposed from abroad or home-grown) and denotes a phenomenon which had not been seen before the English example of it; the rebellions which occurred during the Middle Ages and early modern period confined themselves to seeking better treatment from the monarch and the expulsion from office of wicked ministers rather than an overthrow of the monarchy as an institution.

If the motivation behind the American Revolution was nationalist, the French was ideological in character. Can the same be said of the war which followed it and lasted, if one counts Napoleon and his consequences, for twenty-two years? It was ideological in that the revolutionaries sought to extend the supposed benefits of the new order they had created within France to the territories they conquered. But first and foremost they were attempting to protect their achievement from the hostile powers surrounding them, who were alarmed by what had happened, feared it spreading and might try to overturn it. If the French had for this reason to make war on, and perhaps invade, their neighbours they might as well impose on them what they were trying to defend within their own borders. And try to spread revolutionary doctrines, through a fanatical sort of altruism and because if the policy was successful France's enemies would see things her way, pull out of the conflict and make peace. (Though the "reactionary" powers would have feared the Revolution spreading whether the French actively encouraged that process or not.) Wars were fought either to defend ideologies, promote them, or both (I am not convinced the ideology would have been sufficient on its own, without the "nothing to lose" factor, to justify all the effort however appealing the prospect of victory might have been). Certainly the old enmities, the old reasons for waging war, died hard in that there was also in operation, alongside revolutionary fervour, the appeal of getting back at traditional enemies (such as Britain, in the French case). The French Revolutionary Wars were the first ideological ones, although the American War of Independence could be viewed as ideologically motivated if national self-determination is an ideology. But it would be rash to conclude that there was not an element of nationalism in all such conflicts. Nationalism and ideology can become fused if the variety of the latter which has become dominant within a country is seen as the best form of government possible – either for the country itself or, as may or may not be the case, everyone else too – and in fact as an expression of national identity, so that it becomes patriotic as much as anything else to believe in it. This was the case in Soviet Russia, particularly during the Second World War, and Communist-controlled East Germany. And you like to defend, even promote, your own homeland whatever kind of regime is running it.

On the whole, the French Revolution became more a nationalist than an ideological conflict under Napoleon. He believed that France, personified in himself as its ruler, was a rising nation chosen by Providence to civilise and unify the Western world under its hegemony. At the same time, although he dismantled the apparatus of the Terror he held on to many of the more sensible reforms, to do with law and administration, initiated by the successive revolutionary regimes which had preceded him, while adding a few of his own. The result – the *Code Napoleon* – hereafter formed a vital pillar of French government and the territories he conquered also benefited from it to some extent. In Napoleon's mind ideology (although the latter was by now seen simply in terms of sound government) and nationalism did indeed amount to the same thing. A nationalistic war might aim either to simply secure, or preserve, the independence of a territory or to allow it to take over others, the latter from one or more out of several motives namely misguided benevolence, self-protection, mere desire for power. Certainly in Napoleon's case it was not just the last of these which was at work.

He was a dictator but he was not cruel, evil if you like, in the way that Hitler, Stalin, Pol Pot, Idi Amin and Saddam were (nor was Cromwell). He remains a special case. You can be angry with him but it is more difficult to hate him. He sincerely believed that he was continuing the process of beneficial reform which the French Revolution had initiated (as well as squaring up to the old enemy, Britain). And indeed many of his measures were constructive. He unintentionally launched Germany on the path to eventual unification (involving her military defeat of France) by rationalising the map of Europe, doing away with the Holy Roman Empire and with many of the chaotic multitude of different German states that had hitherto existed. He both fuelled German nationalism by the cavalier way his officials and soldiers treated the conquered Germans, once his attitude coarsened and his achievement turned sour, and rendered it practically easier for it to achieve its objectives by his administrative reforms. He also paved the way for the independence of Spain and Portugal's Central and South American colonies through the disruption of colonial rule caused by his invasion of the home countries.

Napoleon Bonaparte was not so much a wicked man but one possibly suffering from megalomania, who attempted to dominate and reform Europe in a way that was well-meaning but misconceived and in many respects destructive. In the end countries generally preferred to govern themselves rather than be governed, in however enlightened a fashion, by others, and of course they resisted. The famous painting showing Napoleon's face made up of skulls and corpses sums up the contemporary perception of him as a man whose lust for "La Gloire" caused death and suffering on a mass scale, which indeed it had. Power corrupted him and made him prone to nepotism apart from anything else. Reforming though he was, he became in the end rather a rival monarch (in fact a self-declared Emperor) to the legitimate, established ones, placing his relatives on the thrones of Europe, rather than an agent of sociopolitical revolution. Under him, in the eyes of the ruling regimes of Britain, Russia, Austria and Prussia, "nationalism" had mutated into a threat to the whole European status quo, one which had to be and eventually was defeated, the great powers subsequently seeking to preserve the traditional monarchical/aristocratic system and through repression where necessary. But Napoleon had helped to light a fire which could not in the end be extinguished, though it might in places be beaten back until other factors served to fuel it. There was a lot of youthful idealism involved, the political energies of young people in those days being directed towards the cause of independence for national groups rather than creating and sustaining institutions like the EU, as they later were.

Nationalism had already triumphed, or was to triumph within a few years, in the Americas (Canada remaining within the British Empire until peacefully securing independence by first the measures of 1867 and then the Statute of Westminster in 1932), though its brief did not encompass the surviving indigenous peoples of the two subcontinents. It triumphed in Greece, where the Ottoman Turks were expelled. It triumphed in Italy in the 1850s and 60s under Cavour and Garibaldi; here, as in the German example, the unification of various different states depended on the military defeat of foreign elements (in this case primarily Austria) whose strategic interests in the region would be threatened by the change in the map and who would therefore seek to oppose it. The lead had to be taken by the strongest of the states, in Italy Piedmont and in Germany Prussia. In Prussia the intention of Bismarck, by 1862 Minister-President, was not to bring about German unification, for which he had little sympathy in itself, but rather to take control of a movement the gathering support for which he could not ignore and use it to his native state's advantage. If Prussia effectively assumed its leadership by vanquishing the powers which stood in its way — Denmark, Austria and France — it would become the dominant force in the new Germany, whose capital would be Berlin and whose royal house the Prussian royal house. He certainly succeeded in this aim but with potentially catastrophic consequences, in hands less able than his own. The state of Prussia was eventually abolished in 1945 by the Allied Control Commission in the belief that Prussian militarism had been a crucial factor in causing war. This was undoubtedly true although it applies more to the First World War than the Second, in which Prussian militarism along with other social and political forces which might have been influential had become subsumed within a polity which reflected the will of one man, Adolf Hitler, and of those who served him out of loyalty and/or fear.

Nationalism continued to be a potent force in Ireland, though this was but the latest form of an old quarrel which continued, on and off, almost to the end of the twentieth century when, hopefully, the Good Friday Agreement resolved it (the issue was by then the status of the province of Ulster rather than of the island of Ireland as a whole).

Nationalism was not to triumph in the Austro-Hungarian (Hapsburg) Empire until after the First World War. The uprisings of 1848 were both nationalist revolutions (in Germany and the Habsburg territories) and attempts to secure greater democracy (in Germany and France). In Germany unification failed to happen on this occasion because of the sociopolitical dimension; offered the German throne by the liberals, many of them middle or even working-class, who had assumed positions of power elsewhere in the region King Frederick William of Prussia refused to "stoop to pick up a crown from the gutter, a crown by the grace of butchers and bakers" (it would have been a different matter if Prussia itself, dominated by its Junker aristocracy, had been the driving force behind events). Frederick William's acceptance of the offer was crucial because the symbolic role of monarchy, whatever its effective political power − which could depend on the personality of the monarch themselves − was still important to many people at this time.

The Hapsburgs ruthlessly suppressed the risings in Eastern Europe, with the help of absolutist Russia, although Vienna had to come to terms with the most powerful of the subject national groups, the Hungarians, to the extent of creating the dual monarchy of Austria-Hungary with leading figures in the Hungarian national movement, such as Julius Andrassy (later Foreign Minister), serving in the imperial government. But the Austrian Chancellor Metternich, champion of the forces of conservatism and reaction in post-Napoleonic Europe, fell from power because he was old and not thought to be handling the situation properly, rather than because the Hapsburgs had any great commitment to liberalism.

National revolutions were not necessarily intended to overthrow a certain sociopolitical structure. Those in Latin America which led to the former Spanish and Portuguese colonies gaining their independence did not result in liberty and social equality within the nations that emerged; the old colonial ruling classes held on to power and the history of the region was to be characterised by oppression, poverty, and conflict between the privileged and less privileged elements, leading to an apparently endless cycle of revolutions and military takeovers, until well into the twentieth century.

There was no successful sociopolitical revolution in Europe in the nineteenth century, though Communists took advantage of the conditions created by the Franco-Prussian War and the Siege of Paris to set up a Republic in the French capital, which was eventually overthrown as conservative forces asserted control. In Britain the situation was contained by a policy of repression combined with judicious gradual reform. The process in France was more uneven, the road much bumpier. The overarching image of the 1789 revolution has tended to obscure in the public mind the fact that France experienced less famous revolutions in 1830 (with which the layperson is perhaps now more acquainted because of *Les Misérables*) and 1848. The Bourbon monarchy had been restored in 1814-15, but the legacy of the Revolution still had appeal and could not be ignored while some people, understandably, continued to admire Napoleon's achievement, so that French politics in the nineteenth century was a hotchpotch, and battleground, of conservatives, radicals, monarchists and Bonapartists. Some measure of political reform was achieved under the July

Monarchy, but sadly the "Citizen King" Louis Philippe failed to live up to expectations and was eventually overthrown. There was a setback for democratic government in 1852 when Louis Napoleon, President of the Assembly and nephew of Napoleon I, seized complete control of the state and declared himself Emperor Napoleon III (the Duc de Reichstadt, the first Napoleon's son and heir, had in the meantime died).

There followed the curious episode of the Second Empire. Napoleon III is inevitably overshadowed by "the" Napoleon, with whom non-historians would probably confuse him. It comes initially as something of a surprise to realise that there was another. He was relatively speaking a pale carbon copy of the first – but only relatively. In the beginning, although he appeared just an eccentric adventurer, he had his uncle's daring and ingenuity, as seen in the way in which he seized power. He is a figure not undeserving of sympathy and admiration. Altogether France did not do too badly under his rule; its industrialisation and modernisation progressed quite considerably (although it is a pity that Baron Haussmann had to sweep away most of old Paris, the Paris that witnessed the events of 1789 among other things; I would have liked to have seen it). She was not so successful in military matters or her general interventions in global politics. One thinks of the ridiculous and inevitably doomed Mexican affair of 1867, whose absurdity is matched only by the vindictiveness of the Mexicans in having the Austrian Archduke Maximilian, who Napoleon had installed as their Emperor, executed. Napoleon, who latterly had lost his touch somewhat, was easily outwitted by Bismarck (who had to deal with France before he completed the unification of Germany, since she would have seen it as a threat to her own position in Europe) and ultimately the regime was discredited by its defeat in the Franco-Prussian War of 1870-71. This led to Napoleon's abdication and the end of monarchy as a form of government commanding significant political support. The upshot of all the above was that through an often tortuous process France had by 1900 become more or less a democracy and it has remained so ever since, in peacetime at any rate, though quasi-dictatorial figures like de Gaulle have been needed at times of crisis in a way they might not in Britain.

As a legacy of France's monarchist, or Bonapartist, or revolutionary past various groups remained for a long time influential, as for example prospective or actual partners in coalitions, while never likely to form governments in their own right. The experience of occupation and Vichy during the Second World War simplified French politics by discrediting some of these factions, who were rightly or wrongly suspected of collaboration with the Germans (always a tricky, and highly sensitive, issue). In fact, it along with the political conflicts and instability which had plagued public affairs in the 1930s, and the near-civil war over Algeria in the late 1950s/early 1960s, was part of a traumatic process from which France eventually emerged all the stronger, although there have of course been problems nonetheless. She became less prone to the farcical blunders that had characterised her history in the recent past, and more confident and united, more sure of herself, more successful in some respects than her neighbour and rival Britain. The business required at some point a strong individual to help bring it about and de Gaulle fulfilled that role. The nearest equivalent to him on the British side was Margaret Thatcher; there the effect, though in some ways beneficial, was not quite the same.

De Gaulle picked France up by the scruff of its neck and by being that strong leader did something towards restoring its dignity. The latter had been lost by the political conflicts of the 30s and their demoralising effect upon the nation, which produced the defeatist mentality that led to conquest and occupation by the Nazis in 1940. Britain has been much criticised by the French for evacuating her troops and leaving France to her fate; but the blame is not hers, even if a patriotic French person, however they felt about the depths to which their country had sunk, might understandably not see it that way. Both countries were to blame for the situation in that they should have rearmed earlier and thus had a better chance of repelling Hitler. But once it became apparent how things were going the British should not have been expected to risk losing the bulk of their army and with it any chance of ensuring their own defence against an actual German invasion, or contributing towards Hitler's ultimate defeat should it become possible to go on the offensive. What salvaged France's honour, along with the pugnacious stance of de Gaulle and the Free French even if the former had necessarily to operate from a distance, was the Resistance, by the obvious courage of the resistors and the risks they were taking, risks which stemmed from bravery as much as or more than foolhardiness, in opposing so vile and brutal a regime as the Nazis. One might question its effectiveness, prior to the Allied invasion, in doing much to undermine the occupying forces; in achieving much more than bringing down vicious reprisals upon the ordinary population. Those French (not necessarily collaborators) who opposed it on those grounds had a point, irrespective of what had gone before; they were not just being unpatriotic. But it helps to discredit any notion of French people as being uniformly craven and spineless.

As Chancellor of the united Germany between 1871 and 1890, Bismarck was concerned with the new polity's domestic affairs as well as its protection from foreign aggression. He shrewdly saw that provided people were reasonably comfortable and prosperous they might not be too bothered about how much political freedom they actually had. He thus set about creating a comprehensive social security system which was the envy of other countries in Europe, and the tactic worked. He was also exploiting national character, which inevitably has an influence on what does or does not happen and can result in exceptions to rules. As Germany industrialised, beginning along with Russia and the United States to outpace Britain in economic performance (having the advantage of being able to copy her example, standing on the giant's shoulders), a large proletariat grew up in her major cities; but that proletariat was hard-working and obedient, more so in many ways than its British or French counterparts, and not that concerned by the franchise being weighted heavily in favour of the Prussian aristocracy. Meanwhile Russia, despite the abolition of serfdom (for which Tsar Alexander II got little credit, being assassinated by revolutionaries in 1861), remained too tightly in the grip of Tsarist absolutism and was not going to change in a hurry.

But undoubtedly new political philosophies and movements were coming into being to address the issues created by the continuing march of industrialisation. Liberal democracy was one attempt to do so, but in certain quarters far more radical solutions were being proposed. Liberals sought to widen the franchise and improve living standards, but socialists were far more vigorous in pushing for the extension of these benefits to the urban working class, which suffered (though not uniformly) from low wages as well as poor housing and education. Then there was what some would regard as the extreme form of socialism, Communism (or Marxism after its founder, Karl Marx). Confusingly, Communists in the past have often referred to themselves as Socialists even though they would go much further than the latter in reshaping society for the benefit of its less prosperous and empowered members. Socialists preferred to achieve change gradually through the parliamentary system. Communists/Marxists would use that system whenever it suited them, but the more diehard from Marx himself downwards wanted a political revolution, achieved by force if necessary, which would place the "workers" in power – the dictatorship of the proletariat. (They appear to have supposed that the proletariat was somehow more virtuous than the rest of society just because it was underprivileged and therefore rightly an object of sympathy, and could therefore be trusted to wield power alone). Marxism's rejection of religion, which it saw as the "opium of the people", was one reason why it became an ideology seeing history excessively in terms of material, economic factors. Historically the ruling elite had always sought to exploit the workers in any trade, through taxation and other methods. The Industrial Revolution, in which the factory owners had become the new aristocracy, if sharing power with the old, provided even greater opportunities for them to do so. The next stage in the historical process would be the eventual rebellion of the proletariat against this situation; for it to take control of government was the only way of improving its lot, since the employers would always seek to increase their own profits and thus to keep wages down, and would freeze the workers out of political power to prevent them rectifying this situation. Marxists might respect middle-class liberal do-gooders, patronisingly refer to them as being the latter, or despise them, but however noble their intentions they just didn't go far enough. Much of the Marxist criticism of capitalist "democracy", in Marx's view a sham, was valid but it was far too negative in its assumption that there could be no significant remedy for workers' grievances within the capitalist system. To be fair, it did have an answer to the charge that it would merely make the proletariat into the new oppressors. Their dictatorship would evolve into a classless society in which *everyone* would share equally in the wealth from industry and agriculture. All would be workers so in due course the social distinctions would disappear anyway. Apart from the fact that everyone who is in a job of some kind, even if they're the son or daughter of an Earl, is a "worker", and the assumption that the proletariat would with superhuman nobility extend their power to everybody else rather than use it to settle old scores, it was (sadly) nothing more in the end than an impractical, utopian pipe dream.

Quite why is a philosophical question; in the context of purely historical study, what concerns us is that Marxist takeovers did eventually happen, but in still predominantly agricultural societies (Russia, China, Vietnam) rather than advanced industrial ones as Marx's thinking predicted it would. This itself indicates that Marxism as an intellectual system which can be practically applied is flawed, but the flaw need not have been fatal. There are other, and more valid, reasons for regarding the philosophy as ultimately a failure, and we'll go into them later. But it requires some explanation that the revolution did not happen in Britain or Germany or the USA, perhaps France, rather than where you might least expect it. The answers are more to do with culture and human nature than with economics. Britain and Germany and the US *were*, by 1900, advanced industrial societies and the wealth created by that industrial expansion benefited enough people for the prospect of violent political revolution to lose its appeal, something which worked to the benefit of the ruling elites (as they themselves may or may not have understood). The German tendency of obedience to authority (which implies *existing* authority) has already been mentioned. As for the US, she was not and never has been a classless society with equal opportunities for all, but although poorer Americans no doubt did not like being poor, and altogether disadvantaged, any distress or anger they felt at it was balanced by other factors in a kind of trade-off. Again the cause of this lay with the way the nation had come about. Part of the frontier mentality was inevitably a rugged individualism which served as a source of both national and personal pride. What improvements one *did* succeed in making to one's condition had to be by one's own efforts and not by the kind of corporate communal state model, in which the individual seemed less important, that Marxism seemed to favour. For these obstacles to Marxist victory to be overcome, conditions within a country had to be far more dire, and the suffering far more widespread, than was the case in the examples mentioned. That criteria was met in Russia, despite her being primarily agricultural, because of the inefficiency of the absolutist monarchical system, which here was trying to govern vast realms through a necessarily complex, and unwieldy, bureaucracy that apart from anything else hindered industrial progress. The result was a hideously suffering population (peasants and industrial workers alike), and things were made even worse by the impact on all this of a badly managed war. Communists, who have always been opportunists, sought power in Russia not because it was ideal material according to Marx's Dialectic but because the instability and discontent arising from the above factors created opportunities that weren't present elsewhere. The same applied to some extent in China. In fact dedicated Marxists could take over anywhere there was a sufficient political opening, and no track record of successful capitalist democracy. A culture of respectful obedience to authority (such as existed in China) was another thing which could be taken advantage of. Nowhere did Communism triumph as the result of a mass uprising of the common people, though that perhaps did not matter much ideologically as in Marxist theory the revolution would be led more or less by an elite anyway (except that in Russia that leadership was more middle-class than proletarian, because it was the middle class who had the education).

6

Not only had agricultural improvements made it possible to feed greater numbers and so provided the Industrial Revolution with its labour force, but industrialisation by producing more efficient farming machinery contributed to that very same process. Simultaneously the scientific revolution, bringing better medical knowledge, was curing or alleviating diseases which in the past had often proved fatal. So the population of the West increased, towns and villages growing in size to accommodate it, and society became generally more urbanised. This and the extension of the railway network helped to gradually erode the old rural way of life, through facilitating the spread of ideas and of the urban culture, although traditional dialects and customs and superstitious ideas persisted in remote areas into the twentieth century.

Along with the steamship, the railway also made it easier for the West to consolidate and extend its power over the rest of the globe. Until the eighteenth and nineteenth centuries no power had ever dominated (more or less) the entire world, as opposed to the *known* (to those peoples, whether they were conquerors or conquered, who lived in it, anyway) world. That only became possible due to the age of exploration, something which itself had been brought about by Europeans, in the early modern period. Europe has never been dominated by any other power, though Islam came close at times. Of course, imperialism could only be practised by those with the technological and thus military expertise to do so: Britain, France, Germany, to a lesser extent Italy and Belgium. (And not, with certain exceptions such as Greenland and the Danish Virgin Islands whose strategic value in a political sense was limited, the Scandinavian nations. This seems odd considering the seafaring prowess of the Vikings, which certainly had a profound impact on the peoples they conquered or merged with. Perhaps the period of Scandinavia's influence and power had simply come earlier, and it had been manifested in a different form.) The Dutch and Portuguese managed for the time being to hold on to their remaining "possessions" in Africa and the Far East. Portugal did not give up hers until the mid-1970s, after everyone else had decolonised, though this was latterly due to the absurd insistence of the right-wing dictatorship which ruled the country in hanging onto them. Russia did not seek colonies in what was later called the Third World, despite seeming to threaten India and Turkey, because her vast territories in Eurasia and the subject peoples who inhabited them already constituted a kind of empire.

Apart from a few small territories (Guam, Puerto Rico) whose populations have not particularly objected to being under its rule, the United States did not in a political respect seek to conquer other peoples, as opposed to sending in troops from to time to time to protect commercial interests, since the dichotomy between this and its pride in its own birth as a nation freeing itself from the shackles of alien rule would otherwise be highly embarrassing. It confined itself instead to economic domination, which might not be quite so obvious though it had become so, and was a cause of complaint in liberal quarters, by the late twentieth century. It showed that if anyone was boss over Cuba, it was not Spain, by a war which looks suspiciously as if it might have been deliberately engineered (what exactly caused the *Maine* to explode?). But it never annexed the country, which as we know was later to become a considerable bugbear to it.

Undoubtedly the US would like to bring all the nations of the world into her economic orbit, because she is an expanding capitalist power. Even she cannot *militarily* occupy them all because it would be too logistically difficult and financially expensive. In most cases however military occupation would not be necessary, because countries either want to integrate with the global economic system or are too weak to resist her anyway. But where there are exceptions to this rule she does flex her military muscle, as we have seen. Purely economic factors undoubtedly play a part in her actions, as well as the sense of any political threat, even if the latter may be the deciding one. It is absurd to suggest that they were *solely* responsible for the 2001 invasion of Afghanistan, or even of Iraq in 2003, but both involvements undoubtedly benefited the US defence industry and provided an additional spur.

During the nineteenth century, US colonial energies were directed towards the westward expansion of the nation from the original settlements in New England. This was undoubtedly white imperialism in one form, and its effects on the indigenous population of the new territories, who were slaughtered in large numbers, and ultimately confined to special reservations, losing their traditional way of life, was devastating. In many cases Native Americans drank themselves to death on the white man's alcohol in order to try to cope with their grief and anguish. It is undoubtedly a very sad story and one can have a lot of sympathy for the "redskins" despite the fact that they, too, committed

322

acts of unnecessary cruelty. Where they massacred whole communities of settlers, who after all had occupied without permission what was undoubtedly their land, it was because their society was not so structured as to have the resources to accommodate large numbers of presumably unwilling captives. Exceptions to this rule, who were inducted into the tribe and its ways, may be regarded as a sign of humanity on their part. They could certainly be capable of magnanimity, even towards an enemy who was seeking to drive them from their ancestral homelands and in doing so inflicting on them unparalleled disaster; it is to their credit that they left General Custer's body untouched, that is unscalped, after the Battle of Little Big Horn as a mark of respect towards a brave, if foolhardy (and to his white peers not very nice) enemy. And although it may seem unlikely, because the nature and effects of the upheaval are not quite the same in both cases, any white person in the West who loves the open countryside, and sees it being increasingly eroded by continuing urban expansion, knows how they feel. The rural world has of course never been static, and Man has shaped its appearance by farming and by measures such as the Enclosure Acts in Britain in the eighteenth century. But it is not the same as the town and the more the latter swallows it up, the more the sense of openness is lost, the less one feels one is roaming free, as the Sioux and Cherokee did in America before the white settlers displaced them. It seems to me that old white people in Britain whose spirits have died when they have had to move from country areas where they have lived all their lives to an unfamiliar, indeed alien, urban environment have essentially been going through the same experience as many Native Americans. Of course in America the vast open spaces are largely still there, it's rather the ability to enjoy them in the traditional fashion which for the "Indians" at any rate has been lost. But the curious empathy which I feel for the dispossessed of the "Wild West" is due to the consequence in both cases being the same. What we in the developed world still have in the way of rurality is not necessarily what will survive in the future, the way things are going.

As for why, in America, the tragedy should happen at all the important thing to focus on is that it is unlikely the white settlers went out there simply in order to be nasty, if often they *were* nasty, to the indigenes. It would have been too much hassle bearing in mind the dangers from those possibly hostile natives, and from other settlers, plus the general sweat and toil involved in opening up and developing extensive geographical areas. Though there were acts of sheer bloodthirsty cruelty on both sides, essentially what happened was that two very different and in many ways incompatible cultures came up against each other. The Native Americans wanted simply to stay where they were and live as they had always done, hunting buffalo etcetera; the different mindset of the whites led them to expand into new territories and mould them to suit their own needs, their own way of thinking, which they continued to do on a global scale until the process reached its natural limit. Unfortunately, such was the nature of the two societies and their lifestyles that economically the

Indians had nothing the whites really wanted, unless it was simply a matter of taking their land en masse and by force, and vice versa. There was no basis for mutual trade on a scale and to a pattern which would have rendered it advantageous to the whites to have left the Indians as they were. At any rate this has been the problem with many of the conflicts arising between Western and tribal societies; in the North American case it may simply have been that the whites wanted, perhaps needed according to their own cultural imperatives, the land. The conflict was a product of a complex and vastly imperfect world. In the end the "Indians" lost it not because they were inferior in any way to the whites, sub-human, but because they were different. Despite being intelligent enough to master guns and horses they did not in the end have the same military and organisational skills; or perhaps they just weren't the sort to create a mass industrial society which could have exploited natural mineral resources to build an army capable of repelling the invaders.

It's also worth reflecting that some of the settlers would have been fleeing from persecution, or poverty, in their own lands. In fact, during the nineteenth and early twentieth centuries America was filling up. Mass immigration (replacing slavery as a source of labour) was needed if such a vast country was to be fully developed, and so it did not make sense for the traditional Anglo-Saxon power structure to forbid it even though it might be thought to be threatening its own position by being remarkably generous in opening the doors to Poles, Irish fleeing from the famine of the 1840s, Italians etc. Perhaps it *was* stoking the flames of future conflict, although it is only in recent years, with a further influx from the Hispanic nations of the Americas, that the demographic implications have become fully apparent. Concerning the blacks, the former slaves, a lot of trouble would have been avoided if they had been treated a good deal better than they were.

Meanwhile, returning to the period of which we were talking, the European nations were engaging in a new phase of empire-building in Africa (where most of the struggle for influence took place) and the Far East. France was to acquire colonies in North Africa (her attempts to penetrate into the south of the continent were less successful, being repulsed by Britain, fortunately peacefully), Indochina and the Pacific. The British were dominant in western and southern Africa, though the Belgians took the Congo, with appalling consequences for its inhabitants, and Italy territories such as Libya and Ethiopia. Germany, a latecomer to the game, also secured African colonies although to her chagrin her empire remained small in extent and unimpressive compared to those of her rivals, who nonetheless feared her ambitions.

As for why all this happened, it is partly explained by the age-old need to seek protection through being big and powerful. Having an empire also gave you prestige, another thing people crave, which explains why ordinary folk in Britain cheered the country's victories in colonial wars for patriotic reasons (while harbouring institutionalised racism, not necessarily wicked, towards the conquered), without having a specific belief in imperialism as a political and/or intellectual doctrine. But these weren't the only reasons. Although wrong about so much else, Karl Marx was right in believing overseas colonialism to be the product of an expanding capitalism's need for new markets – and these of course *were* captive ones. Africa and Asia became the arena in which commercial as well as political rivalries between the European powers were played out. Colonial rule was backed up by military force where necessary. Not only could a rival colonising power be kept at bay but industrialisation made the task of subjugating the native population easier because primitive, in a technological sense, peoples could not resist modern weapons. It was also to make war infinitely more devastating when fought within Europe itself and between forces more evenly matched. Poetic justice perhaps...

In order to justify what it was doing the West propounded the theory that it was superior (how else could it have conquered all these places?), and therefore doing the right thing. This might be simply a crude, biological form of racism towards the indigenous peoples, of the kind dressed up to make it look intellectually respectable in the philosophy of eugenics put forward by some thinkers in the late nineteenth and early twentieth centuries, and the writings of Houston Stewart Chamberlain and other forerunners of the Nazis. Or it might be a more cultural one, which arguably, although one might still object to it, was in some respects not really racism at all. According to this view the West was doing its subject peoples a favour by taking on the responsibility for governing them, something they were not yet capable of discharging themselves, and guiding them towards a better way. Cecil Rhodes, founder of Rhodesia and general imperial adventurer, thought the black races were lagging behind the West in terms of technical ability and cultural achievement but at some point might catch it up, after which presumably it would be desirable to regard them as equals. The suggestion that they needed to catch up at all seems intrinsically denigrating, but it should be remembered that the Celts, Vikings and Saxons might be considered to have been, and were, backward in many ways compared to the Romans, yet the Europe that was descended from an amalgamation of those peoples later achieved a great civilisation of its own. And it perhaps needed to build on the cultural achievements of the classical world, whose memory was preserved by Muslim Arabs, to do so. Political correctionists do not consider it offensive when all *that* is pointed out. And in suggesting that the blacks *could* catch up, Rhodes was clearly implying that they were not an inferior race, who would by their fundamental nature be unable to do so. The current attempts to airbrush him from history by removing his statues from educational institutions are unwarranted, and another worrying sign, particularly from the point of view of historical objectivity, of how PC goes too far (though the malcontents did not get their way on that occasion; they have now, in a development which although hailed by some liberals has some very disturbing implications indeed).

No-one is "inferior", but perhaps it is true to say that races, societies and nations go through periods of cultural and intellectual decline (which need not be permanent). Some would say this is now happening to the West. In the past there had actually been great black civilisations in Africa, in Zimbabwe and Ghana for example. At some point they seemed to have gone downhill. It should not be overlooked that in the first instance many of the black slaves taken by European powers during the great age of exploration for work in agriculture or as domestic servants were in fact sold to them by local rulers who were trying to rid themselves of excess population or of people they just didn't like − the origin of the expression "sold down the river". It seems to me that such a sad state of affairs could only be possible in a society suffering from moral decay, a grave deterioration in public standards. When it goes through this declining phase it is easier for other societies to look down on and seek to dominate it, feeling themselves to be "superior", particularly when they happen to be in the ascendant.

As well as economic and political motives, religious ones continued to be important in colonialism, though not always in the same way that they had been in an earlier era. Western Christian missionaries in Africa, and elsewhere, may in some cases have believed that God had commanded them to "civilise" the black man, but generally they were simply taking advantage of the colonisation to spread the Gospel, which God *had* commanded them to do, and may not have had a doctrine of imperialism as such. In each territory they followed the occupying force, its soldiers and civil servants, because they saw an opening. Sometimes the reverse occured; the colonisers followed the missionaries. Whether or not this caused the latter any problems with their consciences, they could not ignore the divine calling nor were they comfortable with taking on the existing sociopolitical establishment over the matter.

They were generally less brutal than the priests who accompanied the conquistadors, and did not go in for forced conversion. Chinua Achebe's novel *Things Fall Apart* seeks to make clear the demolishing effect of their teachings on traditional African society, seeing their evangelism as an essentially negative thing. Though there may be some truth in what he says, the fact that in the long run Christianity has flourished in sub-Saharan Africa (while in many other places it is in decline) suggests it is not viewed as so destructive by many Africans today. In the American West all three imperatives, politics, economics and religion, motivated the colonisation. Of course the situation there was considerably different from in Africa, where the whites did not displace the locals demographically or, in some cases, have much visible presence or impact at all. Unless they wanted to go against the whole sociopolitical structure, which many of us are reluctant to do even in countries not obviously totalitarian, priests had little option but to endorse was happening or at least not try to prevent it. Some at any rate did seek to broker peace between the white and red man and to stand up for the "Indians'" rights. Of course they did try to make converts where they could; but generally the "Indians" preferred their own traditional religious beliefs to Christian teaching, which here could be more easily associated with mass slaughter and dispossession.

If it was true that non-Western cultures were in decline and therefore needed stewarding (apart from the Ottoman Turks, whose empire was propped up as a bulwark against Russian expansion in the Near East), there was one arguable exception to this rule and certainly to the West's success at putting the philosophy into practice. The two greatest powers in the Far East, China and Japan, could not be subdued in the normal fashion, though it may be said that there was nonetheless an element of compulsion. When Commodore Perry of the USA rather arrogantly presented himself on her doorstep and effectively said "trade with us, be a part of our market, or else" Japan seems to have taken the course of not just accepting the situation but seeking in fact to imitate the West, to boost her own technological development with the help of European advisers and modernising her society by remodelling it to run on Western lines, in a startling and to some highly traumatic break with the past. This pragmatism paid off; though she remained an enigma to Westerners she was considered sufficiently a member of the club to be left alone. She was no longer as "backward" as she had been. Things backfired rather shockingly on the West when Japan turned out to be capable of taking her on in military combat and defeating her. The Russo-Japanese war of 1904-5 ended in a Russian defeat (though it is debatable how far Russia was, and is now, a part of the West). Later of course there was the attack on Pearl Harbour and the capture of British colonies in the Far East. Between these two events a change in attitudes towards the West had led to a curious situation where Japan had emulated its technological achievements out of admiration for them but nonetheless despised its culture, and in particular the habit in military defeat of surrendering rather than committing suicide out of shame. She would visit her contempt on Western captives of both sexes in POW camps.

China in the late nineteenth/early twentieth century remained more traditionally Asiatic and resistant to change. Some thought she should make more effort to copy the West; Sun Yat-Sen wondered if, far from being inferior to Chinese as the latter had historically tended to think, foreigners were not in fact superior on account of their mind-boggling scientific and technological accomplishments. But China was not to catch up with the West until much later, explaining why Japan was able to invade and occupy large swathes of her territory, and appallingly mistreat their populations, in 1931 and 1937. Nonetheless, although she had to accept trading missions in Shanghai and other places, the West never managed to subjugate her in the same way that it had done with India or parts of Africa, for example, not even partitioning her among several countries (though France, Britain, Germany, America etc. all had legations to protect their financial interests).

To some extent this was because of the size of the country and the reluctance of the Western powers to overstretch their resources in holding her down. But I think there was also an underlying respect which inhibited the West from doing more than rattling enough sabres to secure her compliance, some of the time, with Western wishes without actually invading and annexing her; a perception of China as an ancient civilisation, of a higher order than African tribal societies, say, which could not quite be pushed around in the same fashion as others. Racists in the late nineteenth and early twentieth century believed in a kind of ethnic hierarchy in which the white races were superior to the yellow, and the yellow to the black; I think Hitler felt that way, maybe explaining why he was prepared to ally himself with Japan. The idea of racial hierarchies is of course nonsense, but here one can sort of understand how it came about. On the Asiatic side there is an admiration of Western culture and technology, both of which have certainly been emulated in the Far East in modern times. The idea of the Western and Far Eastern peoples as natural allies is a pleasing one and not without justification, provided it doesn't lead to the exclusion of anyone else.

Undoubtedly China during the heyday of Western imperialism refused to altogether lie down, as episodes such as the Boxer Rebellion demonstrate. Writers like Arthur Sarsfield Ward (aka Sax Rohmer) saw the literary possibilities in this. China was effectively challenging the West, marking herself out as an enemy of it, and this captured Rohmer's imagination, inspiring him to create the character of Dr Fu Manchu, who I suppose became the archetypal fictional Oriental supervillain. Of course Rohmer, in the interests of drama, did take things further than China, either at the time or more recently, necessarily wanted/wants to do, by having the Devil Doctor seek to actually destroy the West as a world power. But his actions are motivated by a desire to defend China, even if in his view it means toppling the West from its pedestal, rather than race hatred as such. It is noteworthy that in the books at any rate he has a strong streak of nobility and honour, showing respect towards brave opponents and wishing not so much for revenge as to reshape the world into what he believes to be a better form, one where it is run in an orderly fashion (China has the qualities which fit her to be in charge, but the conquered are to be treated well and allowed to retain their traditional cultures and religions) instead of dysfunctionally. Nor is he a racial stereotype, despite the Hammer films and the covers of some recent editions of the books; as an ethnic Manchu (the latter being the last ruling dynasty of China before the monarchy was abolished by the revolution of 1911) rather than one of the majority Han Chinese he could conceivably pass for a European (as opposed to a stereotypical slant-eyed, evil-looking Oriental).

The empires of the modern era have not lasted as long as those of antiquity, because the pace of change has been faster. The British Empire did best; it can be said to have endured roughly three hundred years from when England first began to settle parts of the New World to the point, reached probably sometime in the 1960s, when there was so little of it left that "empire" seemed a pretentious and anachronistic way to describe it. (The loss of the American colonies has been viewed as marking the end of the first British Empire, but Britain retained the territories she had acquired by one means or another before then.) It was also the most territorially extensive, and is therefore the most obvious target for those seeking to knock imperialism. It makes little difference to an empire's lifespan whether it assumes a primarily economic form; it may even hasten its end. Where there are various dynamic economies competing against each other, the probability is that no one of them will retain a position of supremacy for that long.

What purpose did the European empires of the eighteenth to the twentieth centuries achieve? Were they something entirely negative, a mere exercise of power over supposedly "inferior" people, or is too much being made to go through a politically correct filter? The liberal view is that the imperial powers simply bled their subject peoples dry. This may be true economically (apart from railways, note), but it is not quite so true culturally. Whereas the Germans seem to have departed leaving behind little more than the railways and a reputation for brutality, the French did quite a lot in terms of disseminating their language, in ways which were useful and not just an expression of imperialism, and creating educational opportunities in France for colonial subjects. A lot of Britain's ex-colonies have legal and political institutions whose forms are modelled on the British pattern, and retain a certain affection for their former colonial masters (or at least the older people do). India inherited many fine buildings, which are still in use today, from the Raj; and both she and the West Indies play cricket, frequently defeating Britain at that game which you might think is appropriate! If the former colonies really resented the Empire that much they would not have been happy to create the Commonwealth, which if you like is Empire in a far more acceptable form, albeit relatively lacking in political teeth and essentially a friendly, sometimes not so friendly, club more than anything else.

I have to say I still find it inconceivable that one group of people should decide that another was not competent to govern its own affairs and assume control over them accordingly. Though the Empire could be a focus for patriotism, if it had never happened the British people would have developed some other national and cultural "narrative" which did not include it. It is something which you might feel a sort of veneration and nostalgia for now that it has gone but which, for all you and I know, I might have opposed in the eighteenth and nineteenth centuries had I been alive then. With the reservation that the contribution of colonial troops was vital in defeating Hitler in the Second World War, I think you could make a case for saying that ultimately the world would have been a better place without the imperialism (one can envisage some, at least, of its better consequences happening without it); that overall it did more harm than good. Any good which did come out of it was not necessarily intended. And undoubtedly things did sometimes go horribly wrong (the Indian Mutiny, the Amritsar massacre). Presumably, had the British and other empires not existed countries could still have had beneficial contacts; making trade agreements with each other, visiting each others' territory to study and enjoy the local culture, the scenery and wildlife, as happens now. Although it occurs to me that we may be being disingenuous here, by projecting the values of the twenty-first century world onto a previous era.

And to take a *wholly* negative view seems unwarranted (to say this is not the same thing as opining that the empires were more a good than a bad thing). I have said why already. And if, as is acknowledged by a few liberals, racism can be ambivalent (on the part both of the oppressor and the resentful oppressed), then it is surely possible that some Westerners really did believe, however paternally, that they were doing the conquered peoples a favour; that they were acting in a better spirit than others might have done.

There is something about the British in India, taking them as a case in point, which engages the heart and mind in a way difficult to describe. My father sensed it, going by the massive collection of books he had on the "Raj". On the subject of how racist the business really was, Britain by the mid-twentieth century did seem to be thinking in terms of eventually granting the Indians self-government (in fact she appears to have been for some time, on and off), which echoes Rhodes' belief that the blacks would one day be ready for it. You could say that Congress were too impatient and jumped the gun. They don't seem to have trusted the British promises. But their feelings were probably on the lines of "Oh, so now you think we're sufficiently grown up you're saying we can have our freedom". They felt patronised; they did not wish to have their aspirations satisfied according to a timetable dictated by others. You can't really take issue with that, although it was probably wise from a practical point of view to delay things until the war was out of the way, at least. But of all the non-white subject peoples of the Empire the Indians were the most educated, the most politically literate, the most articulate in expressing their wishes and, consequently, the most ardent in campaigning for self-government. Britain did recognise this to some extent; among the exceptions was Churchill, who did his reputation no favours by coming out so strongly against Indian independence. It was different with the black races, who were not regarded in the same light; again there was a kind of racial hierarchy in operation. After a fashion, this was reflected after independence in relations between the British Conservative Party and the ethnic minority communities which were growing up in the mother country; the Tories had a better relationship with the Indians and Pakistanis than with the blacks because the former were so much more business-orientated (thus being able to improve their situation so that it was harder to look down on them). Not that failure to be business-orientated means *inferior*; and things did change for the black community to some extent after

Scarman.

Mahatma Gandhi was of course right to campaign for India's freedom, even if he made offensive remarks about the West (when asked what he thought of Western civilisation he replied that it would be rather a good idea). He was constantly at war with the bad side of his nature; he referred to imported British textiles − the fruit of someone's labour, even if it was doing native Indian workers out of a living − which he burnt as a protest as rubbish, yet also visited cotton-producing districts of Lancashire because he felt under moral obligation to explain his actions to the people there. This after all is the man who spent a night in bed with two naked women, never in the end touching either of them, as a test of his chastity. It's tempting to see a certain amount of exhibitionism and self-promotion in all the fasting, going about in not much more than a loincloth, et al, and perhaps there was. But one can be like that and be sincere at the same time, and it is stretching credibility to suggest Gandhi would have gone through the deprivations and heartsearching despite the mental and physical suffering that was often involved purely so he could boast of his own moral excellence. We went to see the Richard Attenborough film on my eighteenth birthday, and I still think Gandhi is an example to be followed even if you don't agree with certain of his views or find him all that likeable whenever the bad side gains the upper hand. His achievement was to act as a rallying point for resistance to British rule, to focus world attention on the issue, and to serve as a model for non-violent resistance which was followed most notably, and successfully, by Martin Luther King (not, sadly, by very many other people). Otherwise, though, how much he accomplished in practical terms is debatable. He may have accelerated the end of the British Raj, but that process was as much due to Britain's having been exhausted by the Second World War as anything Gandhi did.

There continues to be much controversy regarding the partition of India. It is alleged that Churchill, who had got over his earlier notorious opposition to independence, promised the Muslim leader Jinnah a separate Islamic state − Pakistan − in advance of it, because it would deny Soviet Russia, which had now succeeded Nazi Germany as the main potential threat to Western liberty, a warm water port in the Persian Gulf. He saw that the latter region would be of major economic and geopolitical importance in the future − as indeed it was − and wanted Britain along with other Western powers to have a share in its oil-derived wealth. He could accept realities, however reluctantly, and was already thinking of how his country, if the Empire was to be smaller or disappear entirely, could at least remain relatively prosperous and powerful in a post-imperial world. That was natural enough and cannot be criticised. Churchill's policy was followed by his successor Attlee. The thing is, though, that partition may have been for the best from India's point of view too − it is impossible to be certain, of course − even if not all Indians saw it that way. Trying to contain Muslims, Hindus and Sikhs all within the same state might have created even more bloodshed than actually happened and resulted in partition anyway. (It is worth pointing out, from fairness rather than in order to defend imperialism, that often when the colonial powers did pull out civil strife, on a scale which didn't tend to happen on the streets of London, followed before too long. Even if the British may have made matters worse by a policy of "divide and rule", which would have had the effect of emphasising communal differences and antagonisms.)

Gandhi was horrified and deeply saddened by partition. In line with his philosophy of peaceful co-existence he wanted India to be an example of intercultural harmony. Unfortunately the Mahatma, though impeccable in his spiritual credentials, was politically naïve. He had little understanding or appreciation of *Realpolitik*, which is not a dirty word if the policy saves lives. He is said to have told Viceroy Mountbatten that although reason indicated partition might be the wisest course, we should rather appeal to a higher cause, that of love. He failed to see that love needs reason as its servant (it ought not to be its master), and that it is *because* of love that one might sometimes have to take hard decisions, even if the framers of policy are not always motivated by such altruism in reality. There was nothing wrong in simply being practical. The most important, as well as perhaps surprising, thing is that India has remained consistently a democracy (whatever "democracy" in fact means) since independence when so many other Third World countries have fallen victim to the most brutal kinds of despotism or suffered a bloodthirsty anarchy and instability which is just as bad. It is something which the former colonial masters can be proud of without being patronising and which Gandhi, certainly, ought to have appreciated despite everything.

The last serious colonial dispute was over South Africa, where settlement from the seventeenth century by Dutch, English and others, who in 1910 gained their independence from Britain, had produced the largest white minority of any African country; larger than in Zimbabwe, which had the next biggest and where similar issues arose (which have not been resolved so satisfactorily). It felt itself to have more of a stake in the existing order, and had established a polity which it felt would be threatened by granting full civil rights and political participation to the black majority and the "coloureds". But the system of apartheid which was erected in order to prevent that was morally wrong besides inevitably having a damaging effect – psychologically, physically or both – on the other ethnic groups. To describe it as a dictatorship is not strictly true; but if it was a democracy as far as the whites were concerned, it was a dictatorship for the purposes of the majority because they were excluded from the political process. Nor was it feasible either to have a separate white nation. There was some merit in the idea, if it eased white fears and so gave them no reason to preserve apartheid, but whether or not it could have been economically practical the blacks rejected it. The thought of such a disembodied, and possibly hostile element within the country's borders was not to their liking and besides, they wanted the whites integrated into a single South Africa so that their skills could be of use in building up the country. In the end there was no alternative to a free, multiracial state.

One came about because the white government got tired of the cumulative effect of ostracism and sanctions, perhaps also thinking that they could not hold down the rest of the population forever and risked an eventual bloody revolution, and in the end pragmatically realised there had to be change. It always seems a pity that the regime was not brought down by Gandhi's strategy of non-violent passive resistance, especially as he had had contacts with the country, working there as a lawyer for a number of years. It is unfortunately indisputable that Nelson Mandela, black nationalist leader and South Africa's first post-apartheid President, was at one point in his career a terrorist; his *Umkhonto We Sizwe* carried out car bombings, something which Gandhi with his philosophy of *satyagraha* would not have approved of. Later, the "terrorist" became the respected and respectable head of state, a common enough phenomenon in geopolitics and not necessarily something that would have appeased Gandhi, who didn't think people should use violent means to achieve their ends in the first place. But this is compensated for by the way the dismantling of apartheid was achieved with relatively little bloodshed and resulted in a comparatively stable and prosperous South Africa (although not one without problems arising from the legacy of the past). This was partly due to the de Klerk government, although they did try to hang on to as many white privileges as possible.

But the principal credit must go to Nelson Mandela. No doubt he was not the saint or superman he may have been cracked up to be; when you are in prison for a substantial chunk of your life and not seen by the majority of people it is not surprising if myths grow up around you. But he genuinely was one of the last great leaders of the twentieth century. That greatness, belied by his charmingly modest and self-effacing demeanour, which misleadingly or otherwise suggested a certain naivety, rests on two things. He acted as a continuing focus for black aspirations. And his prestige and influence over his supporters enabled him to curb their extremism sufficiently to ensure that the transition to black majority rule was relatively peaceful. As one of royal blood, conscious of his dignity, he resented the humiliation meted out to him by the whites. Like other members of a particular group who were campaigning against, or seeking just punishment for, repression by another, such as Simon Wiesenthal, Gandhi (whose approach might be said to have been adopted in South Africa after all) and Luther King he faced the test of controlling any hatred and resentment he felt and by and large passed it. He saw that the Truth and Reconciliation Commission, which tried to get whites to confess to injustices of any kind they had perpetrated against blacks, "coloureds" or Asians without actually seeking their legal prosecution, was politically necessary, vital for future harmony between the races, as otherwise the whites' unease at the possibility of recrimination would cause them to leave the country *en masse*. A lot of his policy, of course, was pragmatism of this sort but in that respect he was no different from most other politicians, of whatever race, in situations where the achievement of peace and stability required restraint. Perhaps it was because he was so isolated, in prison, from the rest of the world and for so long, and because he was essentially creating political systems rather than becoming a part of the corruption and stagnation they exhibit once they have been in existence for a time, that he did not share the faults of many other leaders both Western and non-Western, and seems to have a greater stature than they.

There is no doubting the injustice of apartheid. In the 1980s I and many other members of the Conservative Party resisted the imposing of sanctions on South Africa, but it was never a comfortable position to take. I guess black South Africans are entitled to an explanation why we did so. For my own part I was afraid that if they created a state of economic collapse and instability it would make it more likely any political revolution that occurred would be bloody and chaotic in nature. The blacks wanted them despite the fact that they would be hurt economically; but I suppose we, not being like them caught up at the heart of the business, felt we could be more objective. Maybe we were right. The course of events meant we never got the chance to find out. It helped that after the collapse of global Communism in 1989-91 the ANC, seen as Marxist in character by Conservatives, no longer appeared so much a threat. It needs also to be remembered that the apartheid regime was a bulwark against other states in the region which were Marxist or potentially Marxist (Angola being the prime example). Had this not been so, it is quite possible the attitude of Margaret Thatcher and Co. would have been very different. This consideration, too, was no longer a factor after the Fall Of The Wall. And mercifully so, because it released people like myself from an obligation we saw as necessary but emotionally burdensome.

In Zimbabwe, which we mentioned a little while back, the Communist affiliations of Robert Mugabe, who became the country's President in 1980, do not for one reason or another seem to have made any difference, at least not internationally. But although the former Rhodesia undoubtedly became a one-party state under black rule – which was, in fact, one man's rule – that state ceased in time to be even ostensibly Communist and degenerated into simple, and brutal, dictatorship. The regime benefited neither the black nor the white population and excused itself by blaming past white imperialism for everything, an attitude which was simplistic and unhelpful. The whites are too convenient a scapegoat. It is true that the imperial powers caused problems for the future by ignoring tribal lines when drawing up the boundaries of the new states at independence (something which post-colonial governments in Africa did not seem able to reverse peacefully), though in Britain's case it could be argued that their motives were benign if misguided, stemming from a desire to create happy multicultural states in what might be seen as an early and certainly half-baked form of political correctness. It was in Africa that colonialism did the most harm, the experiment, if one views it as such, backfiring particularly horribly. Its result was that politicians were inclined to put the interests of their own tribe before those of the nation as a whole in a way they might not have done if it, the nation, had been more homogeneous. Since a tribe might feel at risk from the other tribes, that they posed a threat to its interests, they could pose as its protector and so give themselves a stepping-stone to power. People with an interest in the social, political and economic system which was created were reluctant to allow it to change, with the result that sub-Saharan Africa became locked into a cycle of stagnation, corruption and dictatorship. It has yet to escape from the second and has only partially escaped from the others (though we should note that the disaster has not been wholesale, as evidenced by Botswana). But whatever the West's responsibility for this outcome, the institutionalised corruption which makes it hard for the ordinary African to attain a decent standard of living, regardless of the effects of Western economic policy on the rest of the world, is not excusable, nor is the tendency to venerate elder statesman figures even where their policies are staggeringly harmful to the welfare of the nation. Mugabe was nothing like Jomo Kenyatta, who only adopted a militant posture towards Kenyan whites when he politically had no other choice (he once had to talk for his life when effectively kidnapped by the Mau Mau, who were seeking to pressurise him into doing things their way). But these are African problems, and require an African solution.

*

For better or for worse, by the late nineteenth century Western nations dominated the world at least economically, whether or not they felt the need to reinforce their hegemony by military action/political annexation (they never did in Latin America, before fear of Communist influence in her "back yard" prompted the US to intervene in the region – sometimes by subterfuge – in ways that were morally questionable and in the case of Cuba disastrous, it could be argued, for herself). The Western ascendancy facilitated the spread around the world of Western ideas, and ensured they would have a lasting impact on global politics. Even where actual political control had been relinquished; for although the West still dominates today, just about, for a long time she has been unable to do it quite so easily as in the heyday of colonialism. And those who were once the bigger players in the game have been relegated to the second division. Europe, as opposed to "the West", which culturally also includes the USA, Canada, Australia and New Zealand, is no longer the geopolitical force it was. It was probably inevitable that this should happen eventually; empires rise, empires fall. But the process by which it did originated in the changes to Europe's map during the second half of the nineteenth century, and the fears and rivalries they generated.

7

War is the locomotive of history (Leon Trotsky, though the saying has also been attributed to Marx), its requirements, and its consequences, speeding up the process of change and the pace of events. It determines the way in which things happen and means they occur a lot sooner than they otherwise might have done. It can bring catastrophe even upon nations who are victorious on the battlefield, and their allies. These things are as fundamental a historical truth as the tendency for individuals and organisations to get into positions of power largely because the alternatives are worse, as much as one's own merits. It was the cost of fighting the Seven Years' War (for her a resounding military success) which led Britain to levy heavy taxes upon her American colonies; their resentment was a fundamental cause of the War of Independence. France later got her own back for her defeats in 1756-63 by backing the rebels, but the financial aid she gave them had a crippling effect on her own economy and the resulting hardship – and heavy taxation – helped bring about the Revolution.

The principal cause of war in Europe was most likely to be nationalism, or the response to it. Colonial rivalry might be translated into military conflict on the European mainland, although this in fact never happened, at least not directly in that colonialism outside Europe was the principal deciding factor. There were still territories on the continent whose status was contested. Particular blame for the First World War could perhaps be laid at the door of Otto von Bismarck because of his unification of Germany and what it led to, on the understanding that it is indirect. In order to protect his achievement against a revanchist France, Bismarck, under pressure from hardliners, annexed the French provinces of Alsace-Lorraine which it was hoped would serve as a buffer zone in the event of war. This was a mistake which only succeeded in making the latter more likely by fuelling the flames of Gallic ire. At the same time Bismarck attempted to construct a defensive alliance against France with Austria-Hungary and Russia (the Three Emperors' League). Russia eventually drifted away, but Austria stayed loyal to what became the Dual Entente. Bismarck's policies had a knock-on effect as it was inevitable that other powers, feeling themselves threatened by the arrangement, would form their own alliances to counter it. France, both fearing further German aggression and hoping some day to recover the lost provinces if war – in which she was unlikely to triumph on her own – did ever break out, joined with Britain in the Entente Cordiale, ending for the foreseeable future any likelihood that she and her traditional enemy would face each other on the battlefield (the last occasion they had come close to doing so was the Fashoda Incident, an African colonial confrontation, in 1898). Apart from being generally alarmed by the Kaiser's attitude Britain was seeking an ally against a Germany whose rising naval power threatened her own, and thus her control of the seas and ability to supply the empire from which she derived so much of her power and wealth. In war the German navy could blockade Channel ports and damage Britain's trade, forcing her to her knees (one reason why British policy had always been to prevent any one power from becoming too dominant on continental Europe). Not that the French navy was likely to be much of an asset, but a land victory against Germany would obviously have a decisive effect on hostilities. In 1907 the Russians came in with the French and British to form the Triple Entente, a rapprochement between Berlin and St Petersburg having failed to occur. London and Paris welcomed them as an additional bulwark against Germany. Russia's own motive was rivalry with Austria in Eastern Europe, which she regarded as her sphere of influence but which was dominated by the Habsburg Empire. She could pose as a friend of the Empire's subject peoples, who were becoming increasingly restless for independence, while having her own designs on them. Nationalism became mixed up with power politics, and in 1914 the combination was to prove an explosive one. As with the French over Alsace-Lorraine, Russia did not necessarily seek to provoke a war but knew she had potentially much to gain, in this case regional supremacy, should one occur anyway.

The nationalism issue had two aspects; the centrifugal forces within the Habsburg Empire, which could potentially tear it apart, and Germany's increasing assertiveness as a power. In terms of the course of events it was the former which played, in the end, the bigger role in causing war. But the latter performed a crucial *psychological* role, explaining to some extent the spirit in which the conflict was prosecuted. There were nations who went to war in order to acquire new territory, which they had been coveting for some time; it belonged to multi-national empires, the Ottoman and the Habsburg, which many would argue had no moral right to exist since they were frustrating the desire of peoples for independence. The inhabitants of the regions in question might have seen themselves as being liberated. Germany's position was different. There was no more territory for her to acquire in Africa or Asia, the rich pickings having already been snapped up by others. She could not obtain any in Europe without doing what was illegal and certainly likely to provoke fierce resistance; it would be a matter of annexing sovereign states, or parts of them, without a morally compelling reason. This was why her geopolitical aims, as officially stated, both before and to some extent during the war were confused and ambiguous. Her large navy was essentially a status symbol, a crucial expression of her new power and a sign that she had arrived, meeting the psychological need to be seen as counting for something. The situation can in some ways be compared to that in the Middle East today, with Iran seeking to acquire nuclear power, ostensibly for civil use alone, and Israel attempting to resist this because she sees it as a threat to her own survival. Iran would certainly like to have weapons of mass destruction, whether or not she intends to illegally turn her civil atomic energy programme into a military one, because she resents the fact that within the region only Israel, a tiny country with a population of just a few million, is allowed to have nuclear weapons. It is in her view an offence, a slight. She would not I think be so stupid as to use the weapons against Israel without extreme provocation, despite her aggressive behaviour in the past. Unfortunately, in the case of early twentieth-century Germany, the Kaiser's conduct made it easier to believe that world domination by force if necessary was being actively sought. As so often in history, what people believed was intended mattered more than the actual reality. Once the war was under way, France and Britain thought they might as well teach Germany a lesson.

Under the alliance system, if one of the members of a grouping should be attacked by a member of another (a simple statement of intent would suffice), its allies would declare war on the aggressor. The whole apparatus stemmed from a desire to play safe and seek protection in an uncertain world, plus mutual fear and incomprehension between rival powers. It was something which could prove disastrous in the hands of lesser men than Bismarck and this perhaps more than anything else explains the First World War. Of course you could have seen what was potentially likely to happen, and I am sure many did. The nations of Europe in these years have been aptly compared to members of a chain gang; if one falls he pulls all the others down with him. Whether their rulers could have somehow avoided the conflagration and if so, how, is a complex and possibly unanswerable question. But any attempt at identifying the probable causes of a general European war, and then dealing with them, would to be successful have involved either certain people giving up their nationalist aspirations or certain others refraining from suppressing them; and this I suspect would not have been forthcoming. What made the war possible in the end was the interconnected nature of things.

The discontent of the Hapsburg Empire's subject races was recognised by the dislikeable but in some ways shrewd and sensible Archduke Franz Ferdinand, heir to the imperial throne, who, realising that something had to change, favoured the reorganisation of the empire on federal lines with more power devolved to the different national groups. Whether they would have accepted this is uncertain but I suspect it would have been rejected as a mere halfway house which didn't go far enough. It is also questionable whether Franz Ferdinand, once Emperor, could have carried the measure against opposition from powerful vested interests. In the end the question was overtaken by the war which broke out as an indirect consequence of his assassination in Sarajevo by a Bosnian nationalist on 28th June 1914, and apart from being the occasion for the conflict he is today remembered chiefly for having a pop group named after him.

Franz Ferdinand's murderer was sponsored by elements within Serbia, which had achieved independence but felt she still had unfinished business to conclude and supported other nationalist movements within the Empire. Following the assassination Austria demanded that she hand over the perpetrators among other things. She felt she was being bullied and refused. Austria declared war on her whereupon Russia, acting in her defence, declared war on Austria. Germany, as Austria's ally, declared war on Russia which meant declaring war on France and Britain as well. The German invasion of France was through Belgium, the aim being to knock the French out of the war before the slow-moving Russians could fully mobilise. The Russians were unlikely to be of immediate help to Britain and France on the Western Front, but having to fight a war both there and in the east would strain Germany's resources and that was what she was trying to avoid. If Russia saw that the contest was going to be a more even one she might pull out. Germany probably banked on Britain staying away − she certainly thought about it − but in the end she didn't. She felt she would be dishonoured if she avoided her obligations under the 1839 Treaty of London, which guaranteed Belgian neutrality, and was also (more pertinently, as I suspect she herself saw it) afraid that Germany, whatever her ultimate intentions, would see the invasion and occupation of Belgium and France as a *fait accompli* and use it as the basis for economic and military domination of western and central Europe.

The assassination at Sarajevo, which probably not many people outside Austria were much bothered about, merely provided the trigger for the eruption of volcanic forces which had been seething beneath the surface for years. All the same the way in which Europe let itself be dragged into war in 1914 calls for some explanation. The Marxist view that it arose inevitably from capitalist competition has an element of truth in it; that was one of the volcanic forces. But although such underlying factors may have made war more likely, they cannot by themselves explain why it actually broke out.

I think European statesmen had to accept the implications of the alliance system as otherwise they would have had to reject the whole contemporary mindset with regard to sovereignty and international relations, which they were unwilling to do and perhaps couldn't have done. The principle applied even though the alliances might in some cases be rather "ententes", a different matter to some extent, and not as legally binding as has been supposed; and irrespective of whether the foreign policy aims of one partner might be very different from, though not necessarily in conflict with, those of another. The time was not yet right for organisations such as the European Union, which are the only alternative to defensive alliances, designed however (un)successfully to deter aggression, as a way of keeping the peace. That the great conflict occurred essentially because of the logic of the alliance system meant that war aims were often vague. But once the war was under way justifications had to be found for it. These were readily available in the case of Russia and Austria-Hungary; the latter was defending its integrity against the former who, not necessarily for altruistic reasons, acted as liberator of its subject peoples. Germany did not have such a rationale, if imperialism can be called rational, but she could claim that her "encirclement" by Britain, Russia and France (though it was entirely her own fault) excused the acquisition of territory, such as Belgium and Luxembourg in the west, as a buffer against them. If the alliance system made the war inevitable once the fuse had been lit, the invasion of Belgium and even by extension the punishment of civilian resistance by death (though that is more controversial) could then be defended as legitimate military objectives.

Most people didn't actually want war for its own sake; not quite. Some were jubilant, some fearful even if they concealed their misgivings for patriotic reasons or from a wish not to court unpopularity. But perhaps the dominant element in public, and up to a point official, thinking during the summer of 1914 was one of "Let's get it over with". This did not mean that the war was necessarily seen as disagreeable. The perception was as follows. People were aware of the underlying tensions within Europe, and the reasons for them, and all attempts to resolve those issues had failed. On the surface they weren't too concerned by that. I think they realised, deep down, how absurd the whole business was but felt there wasn't much to worry about because the war wasn't likely to last very long. It would be brief, but so destructive given the nature of modern weapons that within a short time either the best man (i.e. one's own side) would win or the conflict would have a cathartic, purgative effect and by that token would bring about its own end. It would be "all over by Christmas", or by some point not long after Christmas. Everyone would retire after a while sadder but wiser and resolved to mend their differences with one another. In the meantime the business could be treated as if it was some kind of exciting game. I think only this can explain the "Christmas truce" football match between German and British soldiers on the Western Front in December 1914; a strange, surreal and thoroughly wonderful episode which leaves one crying out "Why couldn't things have gone on like that?".

Unfortunately, people failed to realise the true nature and implications of "modern weapons"; that they were actually in an intermediary stage between old ways of fighting and new, one which proved to be by its nature particularly deadly. And the conflict did not prove to be "the war to end all wars", but rather led within just over twenty years to another. The second was in some ways less terrible than the first, and in others more so. If the first seemed exceptionally awful at the time it happened this was because it *was* the first; there had been no precedent for anything of its kind.

The trouble with the First World War was that as rumours (often exaggerated) of enemy atrocities spread, and the nature of warfare at this point in history caused it to be static but bloody, hearts were hardened. The squalid living conditions troops had to endure, and for which you could in one sense blame the enemy, brutalised them. Literally, the opposing sides on the Western Front took up entrenched positions from which they could not back down without losing face. Why not then continue to fight for King and Country, or for the glorious German Empire, and gain whatever you could out of the business including perhaps, for the victor, new territory and/or economic domination of Europe; going beyond the necessary honouring of treaty obligations. In this climate the chances of peace moves meeting with success were slight.

The current state of technology affected the nature and course of the conflict and the also the way warfare was regarded for some time afterwards. Criticisms of the Allied generals' conduct of affairs are not entirely just. Both sides were fighting the first modern war, or equally it could be argued that warfare was at that time going through a transitory phase; thus it was inevitable to some extent that the military leaders did not know what they were doing. Even where they did it would for the foreseeable future make little difference to the outcome of hostilities nor diminish the horror of apparently senseless slaughter. Machine guns could kill people in large numbers, resulting in a stalemate with the combatants returning to their trenches after each engagement with many lives lost but little or no ground gained, or shells turn dugouts into seas of mud where a soldier might drown. But the tank and the aeroplane were in their relative infancy and although by 1918 the Allies were beginning to learn how to use them in combination with one another and the infantry, they had had not yet been developed to the extent where they could give war the degree of mobility it needed to be in some respects (I stress the reservation) less awful. Had the war continued for another year or two, this might have happened (probably bringing about a speedy victory for the Allies given the considerable lead they enjoyed in tanks). But in the intervening period there would have been still more sickening carnage. As it was, we had to wait until the Second World War (or its dress rehearsal, the Spanish Civil War) for tanks and planes to revolutionise battle. And even then, though they made possible the rapid success of Hitler's *blitzkrieg* they could not prevent war still being a horrendous business, one that could leave people permanently scarred in body and/or mind, especially when the reversal of gains was bitterly resisted. Returning to the world of 1914, the reason why the western powers became bogged down, literally or otherwise, in the trenches of France and Flanders was that there had not been a major war in Europe, not that affected the whole continent, for approximately a hundred years and this was the first time generals had had to manage large modern armies (swollen of course by population increase) on such a geographic scale. Mistakes were made, and the armies stalled. They also, thanks to the railways, got to the front line before their supplies and had to dig themselves in while they waited for the latter to arrive.

Because of the embryonic, to some extent, nature of modern war in 1914-18 the pattern it followed contrasts sharply with that of 1939-45. In the "Great War", as it was still being called until relatively recently, both sides – the Central Powers, Germany and Austria Hungary, and the Allies consisting principally of Britain, France and Russia – were roughly evenly matched, particularly on the Western Front, until the end, despite Russia withdrawing from the conflict at the beginning of 1918 (in what was undoubtedly a practically wise, given the strain it was putting on her, as well as ideologically sound decision), the ruling Communists not wishing to carry on what they saw as a capitalist war. It took four years for the stalemate to be broken. The release of German troops in their thousands from the Eastern Front when the latter collapsed tipped the balance against the Western Allies, but they managed to win nonetheless when the cumulative effect of their own dogged resistance, America's entry into the war, and the Allied blockade of the Channel ports Germany had seized – a crucial factor, by virtue of its crippling economic impact – along with their finally learning to use tanks and aircraft effectively, suddenly became manifest, a certain critical mass being reached. Nonetheless it was a close-run thing until as late as the summer of 1918. What happened was that Germany blinked first, though in the view of military historians such as Ian Passingham this was inevitable; they believe she could not in the long run have withstood the effects of the blockade, as well as the other factors working against her. Those factors included the lack of a reliable ally who was not bound to her purely by the alliance system and restricted by geographical considerations from being much of a help in the West. The Habsburg Empire was by this time a decaying corpse, though such was the unwieldiness of the vast but poorly led and organised Russian Army that it was still able to inflict heavy losses on her. The weakness of the Austro-Hungarians, plus the inability of Germany's other ally Turkey to help on the Western Front for geographical reasons, offset the advantages gained when Russia pulled out of the war following the Bolshevik Revolution.

Things were very different in the second conflict, where Germany triumphed on mainland Europe at an early stage and she and her allies remained in an apparently impregnable position for 2-3 years, after which they were consistently (with one or two reverses) if gradually pushed back by Britain, America and Russia until final defeat in 1945, by when Italy had been out of the war for two years. Meanwhile, the suddenness of the German collapse in 1918, and a failure to sufficiently understand the reasons for it, led to the myth of the "stab in the back", according to which Germany would have won if she'd only held out a bit longer but was betrayed by cowardly liberal politicians (the Jews of course had something to do it, at least that was what the Nazis maintained). Not every soldier in the war prized an end to the conflict over everything else; Germany believed herself to have been on the verge of winning and after victory the pains and deprivations would have been over anyway, with national pride satisfied into the bargain. And a young, vibrant nation like her, a relative newcomer to the game of international politics, felt particularly aggrieved when her aspirations were frustrated by first defeat and then the humiliation of the Treaty of Versailles by which she was forced her to give up significant areas of her territory, along with her overseas colonies, and accept the pollarding of her armed forces. The consequences of this for future European peace were dangerous, but need not have been fatal. In the end, when combined with other factors, they were.

The economic consequences of the war led to social unrest and political instability in parts of Germany, with strikes and right-wing paramilitaries fighting Communists in the aftermath of the Hohenzollern dynasty's fall. Order was eventually restored and a democratic government formed. But for a time there was a Communist one, a soviet, in Bavaria. That such things should happen goes against the traditional image of the northern European nations as sober and sensible; it is an exception to the rule that this part of the world has been characterised in modern history by a political stability and liberty often lacking in the rest of it, southern and eastern Europe included. But then so too is the Nazi era. It shows that truths about racial character, though inevitably they will influence what goes on, are not absolute, and thus demonstrates the complexity of human affairs. It also confirms that Communism will only flourish in conditions of either extreme instability or extreme suffering (to some extent the one causes the other), which will not prevail everywhere. These conditions have not been unknown in, for example, Britain, and the few years following the First World War, when among other things there was a slump in trade, creating unemployment, once it was no longer necessary to manufacture guns and shells, were one period when that country came closer than usual to a Communist revolution. Though it only seems likely to have happened in certain places − for Munich read Glasgow − which serves to make the point. It's worth considering, however, that Britain may have avoided violent changes of political system, etc. − and thus be encouraged to think herself superior to other people − largely because she is an island and thus isolated to some degree from the turbulent cauldron of forces swirling in Europe during times like that in question. And also from invasion, which can have a destabilising effect especially when the battle to expel the occupying force takes place on native soil and triggers insurrection by dissident elements who hope the invaders will help them.

8

The war left Europe deeply traumatised at what modern technology could do, and in the hands of so-called "civilised" Man. Of course there had been no change in the overall level of good or evil in human beings; scientific and technical progress had merely provided new opportunities for the foolish (not yet the wicked, by and large), or merely flawed, to do harm. By this token there was no reason to deny that the trouble could not start up again at some point in the future, though hopefully it would not. Meanwhile, how did the collective mind of society, public and politicians alike, respond to the four years of suffering whose horror, through the appalling casualty figures, deeply affected even those who were not directly involved in it? People still thought it would prove to be "the war to end all wars". Or at any rate hoped that it would, which was a different matter. In an attempt to transform this vision into reality the League of Nations was set up according to the principle of "collective security". It was not meant to be a world government but rather a forum in which countries could discuss issues to do with international security and plan action, in the form of economic sanctions, against powers whose behaviour threatened it.

But there was another aspect of Europe's attempt to cope with the trauma of the war, and it reflected an ambiguity which was itself a product of that shock, the confusion and uncertainty it created, being an alternative way of dealing with a problem to which it was not in truth *known* how to respond. On the one hand people were saying "We've been bad boys, but we've learned our lesson and will make sure it doesn't happen again"; the process had just taken a little longer than expected, that was all. On the other hand they were saying "It was all (or mostly) Germany's fault." By this means they were actually seeking to absolve themselves from blame. It was an unfair and also extremely dangerous, as things turned out, approach to adopt. The idea was that German aggression in invading Belgium had been the principal cause of the disaster, though there might have been others. Yet although Germany might have prosecuted the war with particular brutality, there is no reason to conclude she as opposed to something of which all countries were a part was primarily responsible for it. It was not the Germans but the alliance system, and imperial rivalries, which caused the war. Yet under the Treaty of Versailles Germany had to pay crippling war reparations, as well as suffer the penalties already mentioned. It added to the anger and shock felt at the "stab in the back" and created a discontent which was exploited by Hitler and fuelled his rise to power. The reparations also led to economic crisis and political instability within Germany. I don't buy the argument that the harshness of the Treaty of Brest-Litovsk, which the Kaiser's Germany imposed, to some extent, on Russia after the Bolsheviks withdrew from the war justifies that of Versailles, because the latter was concluded with Germans who would not have been responsible for such arrogance and brutality in foreign policy and who had supported the war essentially for patriotic reasons, as many of their compatriots were to do in 1940.

A fairer Versailles would have seen Germany made to pay reparations for the invasion of France and Belgium and the sufferings of their civilian populations (even if her actions could be seen as excusable within the context of the war, realistically the anger felt because of them needed to be appeased), but without the cost being so shattering. Territorially she would have given up Alsace-Lorraine, at any rate. Her armed forces would not have been emasculated, rather the aim would have been essentially to ensure parity between her and her neighbours. It would have been easy to reach such a settlement with the new, democratic, liberal-controlled Germany. And bad enough from the patriotic German's point of view that their country was being unjustly penalised without getting anything in the way of compensation (for she had had no legitimate claims on anyone else's territory). There was no need to make things worse. One is forced to the conclusion that the harshness of Versailles was in large measure due to democratic western leaders' need to

344

placate a public opinion which was enraged at Germany's conduct and at the same time saw no difference between the liberals and socialists who now ran her and the militaristic autocrats who had preceded them, even though there was one and it was quite considerable. It also believed, because of the way he had behaved, that the Kaiser had more influence than he actually did. In the end Lloyd George rightly resisted the demands of the French (and many British) that he be hung. But the whole business suggests that where public opinion actually does exert an influence on the course of events, the consequences can be disastrous.

The Western powers railed against autocratic Prussian militarism, which they felt had caused the war, yet did everything possible to scupper the Weimar Republic's chances of survival. It was especially important they did not do so as a break in the continuity of history is an occasion to which men must rise, assuming they have the foresight to see the importance of what is happening and the need to respond to it correctly. German democracy was a fragile plant which required careful nurturing, but did not get it. Altogether it was not placed on a firm enough basis to survive the effects of the further economic dislocation which occurred, after a peaceful and stable interlude in the mid-late 1920s, with the Great Depression. Though there had been some significant progress towards democracy, on the eve of the First World War political power in Germany was still very much vested in the Prussian Junker aristocracy. When the war brought about the collapse of the Hohenzollern regime, with which the victorious allies would not deal, she had thrust upon her the kind of democratic system of which she had little experience and therefore could not operate as successfully as the British, whose governmental arrangements had evolved gradually over a period of several centuries and even allowed for the retention of the monarchy, albeit in "constitutional" form. The way she was generally being treated did not help.

Another example of the double standards practised by the Western Powers was their extolling the virtues of the League of Nations and collective security but not (initially) allowing Germany, one of the potentially most important nations on the continent, to join the League. Although now "democratic", she was still being treated as an international pariah. This was rectified when, by now led by the respected Gustav Stresemann – whose unfortunate death at only fifty-one in 1929 may have been a pivotal point – she was finally admitted to the organisation. It was Hitler who took her out again. (Stresemann may have wanted to restore Germany to what he considered her rightful position, one of power, in European affairs but it is unlikely he would have gone so far as the Nazis). And nor was Soviet Russia allowed in, at first. The strain of the war and the disastrous performance of the Tsarist armies, followed by Kerensky's unwise decision not to pull Russia out of the conflict, made possible the Bolshevik (as the Russian Communists were at this point known) revolution of 1917. Russia was taken over by an ideology which seemed threatening, because it was prepared to achieve its aims by violence while also exporting itself, and which the civil war where White Russian, that is anti-Communist, forces were backed by the West against the "Reds" failed to defeat. Even after she committed herself to "socialism in one country" she was regarded with suspicion; apart from the violence, she was a bad influence, for significant elements within Western nations shared her governing ideology, and the wealthier sections of society feared any threat to their position. It might in fact have made little difference if the Russians had been brought on board, since the Soviet Union, like Nazi Germany, did what it wanted to and nothing else. But at the time their exclusion showed a serious lack of judgement on the part of the Western democracies. Freezing out key players on the international scene from the League's deliberations was not a sensible way to achieve unity or consensus.

Another thing which didn't help was America's refusal to get involved. A young nation which has only recently succeeded to a position of world power may be undecided as to what role exactly she wants to play in global affairs. What empire-building America had indulged in outside the continental USA had been of a kind that not only eschewed actual annexation, more or less, but was genuinely motivated, in part, by altruism, a belief that the poorer and less influential countries would benefit from being drawn into the American economic orbit, freed from rule by those who simply wanted power, and encouraged to develop true democracy. She naturally sought to express herself on the world stage, but at the same time to be idealistic (this resulted in a sort of schizophrenia whereby the US resented the British Empire both because it wasn't thought to be motivated by altruistic principles and because it was a rival to America's own ambitions). The world view of Woodrow Wilson, US President from 1913 to 1921, was an extension of this idealism. Wilson was another common Christian type: austere, puritanical, perhaps not entirely likeable, but well-meaning. Apart from the general conduct of global affairs in a civilised and non-aggressive fashion, his Fourteen Points, which were intended to be the basis for the new League of Nations, endorsed the principle of national self-determination, the right of distinct cultures and ethnic groups to make their own political arrangements and express their own sense of identity. American values, which in this case were undoubtedly decent ones, were by multilateral consent to govern the world and so make sure there was no repetition of the bullying power politics which were responsible for the war. But influential isolationist elements in the US thought it wasn't America's business and also that it didn't serve her interests to play a more active role in affairs; she didn't *need* to, facing no threat to her liberty from any geographical neighbour and being prosperous and powerful enough to survive whatever happened in Europe. Congress rejected the Fourteen Points as well as the Versailles treaty and membership of the League. Though American involvement may have turned out to be as much a nuisance as a boon, given more recent history, it was a short-sighted policy which made the task of managing the new world order much harder. We do not know whether, if

Germany had achieved a victory in the West in the First World War before America had fully mobilised, confronting her with a *fait accompli*, she would have accepted that situation or attempted to overturn it, militarily, on her own. She would probably not have been able to do the latter in 1918; it might perhaps have been possible in the second war, though in the end the contribution of Britain and Russia certainly helped facilitate it. But America's period of isolation from 1919 to 1941 provided a "launch window" during which it was easier for Hitler, once he had built up his armed forces to the right level, to achieve his aims.

The post-1918 world was certainly fraught with potential danger. The impact of war brought about what nationalist rebellions in the nineteenth century had failed to accomplish. The Dual Alliance victory on the Eastern Front had only been achieved by the Bolsheviks pulling Russia out of hostilities, not by a glorious German-Austrohungarian triumph. Ultimately the Hapsburg Empire was identified with a defeated Germany, and the monarchy, which served as the symbol holding the whole structure together if anything did, collapsed. Hungary separated from Austria, and as pent-up nationalism burst forth other new states appeared, such as Czechoslovakia and Yugoslavia (both of which by the end of the century had fragmented in turn, but we are jumping the gun). Poland, in the past something of a playground for other countries who carved it up between them, became fully independent and, rightly or wrongly, it was decided she should be given a corridor to the sea, to help ensure her viability by boosting her trade, which meant taking territory from Germany to the latter's anger. These relatively small nations, along with Rumania, Bulgaria and Albania all of which had already been in existence as more or less sovereign entities, were vulnerable to the aggression of one or other of the larger states which for some reason, territorial disputes or mere empire-building (if the two didn't amount to the same thing), might seek to swallow them up. Russia had always had her eye on them, but for the moment was occupied with other things, namely internal power struggles and the ongoing modernisation of the country. Besides, she would have had to be sure that a resurgent Germany would not snap up all the prizes first. It was in fact from that source that the real threat to Eastern European liberties was to come, for the moment, and the blunders of British and French politicians helped to give it its opportunity.

Another consequence of the shattering effects of the Great War was the appearance of totalitarian political systems, and not only in Russia. It is important to recognise that the war was not perceived in the East in quite the same way that it was in the West. In the former, the longer front line meant that troops were more dispersed and so no trench system, with all its attendant horrors, developed. Plus, the association of the war with the nationalist revolutions it led to, with the gaining of political freedom for millions of people, meant that it could be regarded as in some ways if not in others a good thing. But in the west the rise of Hitler and Mussolini was to have devastating consequences in an international sense. There were some westerners (Hitler included) who enjoyed the war and even desired a repeat performance, if their side had lost, though not all were necessarily fascists. The responses of those who saw the war in a thoroughly negative light assisted those who had rather different feelings about it, whose psychological trauma though explained by it was not of quite the same kind as others', and who sought to translate their wishes into policy. (It should also be said that the slaughter on the Eastern Front, despite the absence of trenches, would not have encouraged a rosy view of human nature within the collective consciousness.)

After the war there was a profound feeling, already touched on. within western Europe of shock and disillusion. Industrialisation and technical progress had, it seemed, merely provided people with new and more effective ways of killing each other. Religion was discredited for many because a benevolent God would surely not have allowed such horrors to occur (however understandable the sentiments behind this conclusion, the possibility was overlooked that the carnage, horrible as it was, might have been a modern example of the abuse of human free will rather than non-existence or perversity on the part of a deity). But Mankind was also disillusioned with itself. If we were responsible for our own destiny then it was to our infinite shame that we had let such a bloody and destructive conflict break out despite our supposed civilisation. At the same time the effects of continuing industrialisation and mechanisation, and the expanded bureaucracy needed to cater for the needs of growing populations, seemed dehumanising. The fact that it was impossible to go back to a mediaeval or Stone Age way of life, for that didn't appeal to people either, resulted in our being at the mercy of blind historical forces, such as the process of industrial and technological development, over which we had no control. Man was simply a cog in a vast machine which had run away with him, and this feeling was combined, after the war, with a sense of purposelessness and lack of direction. Old certainties and securities had been destroyed and replaced with nothing. In the long run of course things were to level off and people would fully adapt to industrialisation and even welcome the benefits it brought. But at this point in Western history that process had not, for many, yet begun. And because the West was now dependent on intensive industry, in whatever form, for its standard of living any slump in industrial production would itself produce aimlessness and loss of self-respect, in the form of unemployment. In Germany, all these things were exacerbated in their effect by that nation's particular situation; one of bewilderment at the rapid military collapse at the end of the war and then the crushing indignities of Versailles, combined with having to get used to a new and relatively unfamiliar political system. Within Europe as a whole the attempt to find a new direction and a new purpose produced some strange, and often terrible, results.

Fascism can be regarded as the second of the ideologies which emerged as a way of dealing with the world forged by the Industrial Revolution, though it was essentially a twentieth century creation. The word "fascist" might reasonably be applied, though sometimes it is best viewed as a figure of speech, to any person or system which effectively imposes itself on people regardless of their wishes and ignores or disregards all points of view but its own (we may encounter such things in "democratic" societies). In an ideological sense it basically means a non-democratic system of government which has the characteristics just described but formalised and translated to a national scale. According to this standard Communism, in the way it tends to be practised once in power, could be described as fascist. But there is one important distinction, which is that whereas Communism, at least professedly, has a particular policy aim, namely the abolition of private industry in order to spread profits more equally, Fascism (which like its ideological rival may achieve power by subtle rather than violent means, and always claim to have the best interests of society at heart) is simply a preference for dictatorship because it is believed to be the best form of government. As part of this it identifies itself with what it sees as the interests of the nation and is intensely patriotic, indeed nationalistic. This can be externalised in an aggressive foreign policy, but not necessarily; it may depend on what scope there is for territorial expansion and what resources are at its disposal (Franco's Spain was not expansionist). Where there is the scope, the regime may seek to recover or appropriate territories which it believes rightly belong to it, in order perhaps to avenge unjust treatment by other powers. It is easy to see how Fascism came to have appeal in Weimar Germany. In the Nazis and their supporters the notion of Aryan racial supremacy, already current in some circles before the war though not really a cause of it, and fuelled by the complexes Nazi leaders had about their own personal inadequacies plus envy at the Jew's success in business and science, became conflated with nationalist dislike at the country's apparent victimisation and with the general psychological effect of 1914-18.

In Germany and elsewhere Fascism seemed to provide an antidote to the feelings of atomisation and dislocation prevalent in post-war Europe. To be part of a Nazi paramilitary group, or the rigidly disciplined army of a totalitarian state, with a badge and a uniform gave certain kinds of individual a sense of belonging, of comforting conformity, notwithstanding that the individual might be said to lose their independence and identity to some degree in such an environment. In one of the paradoxes evident in reactions to the war, indicating the confusion they reflected, it was itself an antidote to existentialist angst, a way of responding to the tendency for standardised regimentation that goes with industrialisation and bureaucracy by giving oneself up to it. In conformity one finds freedom. At the same time a closer association with one's own race or nation helped reinforce a sense of identity. Fascism also gained support because it seemed more efficient at dealing with the economic crises which afflicted Europe in the early 1920s, as the war boom became exhausted with the end of hostilities, and later when the unrestrained prosperity of the 1920s turned out to have a payback. Undoubtedly it *was* more efficient, in some respects, than democracy, but at a cost, that of having to experience its darker side. And although state control of the economy, in its extreme (Fascist) form – or for that matter its democratic one – may be necessary and acceptable in times of crisis, once the worst of the trouble has passed, as it had in Europe by the late 30s, and economic conditions have been normalised it is a hindrance and a source of stagnation, except when everything is geared to war production and then it is only the military who benefit, other sectors suffering deprivation. The Nazi state was actually very inefficient in many ways, partly due to the tactic of "divide and rule" adopted by its leaders when assigning governmental posts (where responsibilities may overlap), and this renders the Star Trek episode *Patterns Of Force*, in which a well-meaning Earthman takes over a developing society on an alien planet and runs it administratively on Nazi lines, because the Third Reich is thought to have at least provided stable and ordered government, rather unfortunate. Divide and rule is practised to some extent in democratic political systems by leaders out to preserve their position and implement their policies but it is especially characteristic of dictatorships because for the dictator there is so much more at stake. The government will usually have come to power through force and is composed of people committed to it as an instrument of policy. Since this determines the whole character of the regime its leading figures will use the same methods to overthrow the dictator, possibly resulting in his murder, if they think he does not have the right policies or has decided they are a rival and therefore threatens their own survival by what he might do to neutralise them. He becomes paranoid and suspicious. Divide and rule is the result, and by its nature it leads to rivalry, amounting to hatred, between the key figures of the regime, to whom the paranoia and suspicion are therefore communicated. It can also lead to administrative inefficiency; thankfully, at crucial moments this may have prevented the Nazi war effort between 1939 and 1945 from achieving its desired result.

At first people were prepared to overlook the downside of Fascism (by the time they began to have second thoughts, it was too late). Partly, as noted, its appeal was because democracy did not seem to be solving Europe's economic problems; it might have made a difference if many young and talented minds had not been killed in the war, so that she did not appear to be governed by conservatively-inclined old men who lacked the ability to come up with imaginative ways of dealing with the depression and its effects. Fascism depended of course not on conventional power structures whose effectiveness might have been weakened by, for example, the sociological consequences of war but by a single charismatic individual and his supporters, who could bend everything to their will. It was easier for them to do so in a culture which had less experience of democracy. The Nazis used – as did the Communists in Russia – the new phenomenon of the mass media to promote themselves, advertising their achievements through cinema newsreels, which focused on spectacular technological and engineering projects, surrounding which there would always be a certain glamour, such as autobahns and airships and broadcasting propaganda over the radio.

Fascism did indeed lead to aggressive foreign policies, most obviously in Hitler's case but also in Mussolini's (Abyssinia/Ethiopia, Albania) and Japan's. The League of Nations proved entirely incapable of curbing them through sanctions, which are a notoriously difficult way of punishing the actions of a determined international troublemaker (their cumulative effect over time may be another matter, depending on the resources of the offending power, except when up against the pig-headedness of a Saddam Hussein who is quite prepared for his own people to suffer the sanctions' consequences).

Communism was another (apparent) answer to the problem of postwar angst, not least because it suggested that the war had been a product of imperialism in the first place; it was the capitalists who had screwed everything up, not humanity in general. As we have seen, the Communists seized power in Russia not at the head of a massive popular uprising but by exploiting the mistakes of Kerensky's Provisional Government and the conditions prevailing in the country because of the First World War. A relatively small group of people were able to take over and then gradually consolidate their hold, extending control from the capital to the country as a whole through sheer determination and a policy of ruthless coercion. In the long run (meaning until the stagnation of the post-Khrushchev period destroyed enthusiasm for the system) Communism triumphed in Russia, winning the allegiance of the people, because a certain number from Lenin and Trotsky down were seriously committed to it, because Russia's disastrous experience of capitalism under the Tsar meant the idea of a workable alternative was not established in the public mind, and because in the end that public didn't have any say in the matter (it may not even be correct to say that there was anything like a "public" in the Soviet Union). Since they controlled communications the government could prevent the governed finding out enough about the West to protest at the disparity between its standard of living and theirs. These factors explain why Communism triumphed anywhere, in fact. Where there was no tradition of democracy it made it easier for any totalitarian regime, regardless of ideological colour, to achieve power. Certainly no Communist government was ever able to take over a country where capitalist democracy had succeeded in creating a reasonably prosperous and ordered society. But where there was this lack of such a track record then people *would* give their support to a Red Regime, often enthusiastically, because as far as they were concerned Communism was at least no worse than all they had suffered under the Tsars, or whoever, and might even at times be preferable. In Russia itself, it made it easier to identify the ideology with the expression of patriotism, especially when the war with Nazi Germany broke out in 1941. And when the leadership got things right at home. The backwardness and stagnation of Soviet Russia compared to the West was relative, and to some extent remained so until the collapse of the regime towards the end of the century. From the 1920s the

Soviets embarked on a massive programme of industrial development, which could be viewed as simply seeking to create national prosperity, and was accompanied by slogans on the lines of "Socialism means Industrialisation" as a matter of course, though it could be interpreted as covering the embarrassing fact that Communism had not happened in an advanced Western-type society in accordance with Marxist doctrine. Obviously the programme of agricultural and industrial modernisation brought benefits, even if the brutal way in which the richer peasants, the kulaks, were forced onto collective farms, some losing their lives in the process, was unnecessary. If you were one of those who had suffered and lost loved ones because of the business you resented the regime; if you weren't, you probably thought Stalin was a good thing. It is true that he found Russia working with the wooden plough and left it with the atomic bomb, though it was electric lighting, etc., which the Russian people appreciated having and not necessarily atomic bombs. One has to admire that achievement.

Stalin had originally been a criminal, renegade and terrorist who had attached himself to the Bolsheviks because he had no stake in the existing system; he needed an alternative narrative, the one which Russia eventually in the later twentieth century rejected because it no longer suited its purposes. The logic of it meant he had to present himself as a Bolshevik/Communist and act as such, even though he would have chosen any other means of self-protection, and of attaining power, had it been the only one available. He was a brutal thug but an astute one, more so on the whole than for example Saddam, who manouevred himself into a position of supreme power through cunning and charisma and propaganda (making out that he had been a far closer associate of the honoured Lenin than was actually the case). He was undoubtedly a dictator, the Soviet version of Napoleon or Hitler, though unlike the former in that he was definitely in one sense evil. He had a peasant coarseness one aspect of which was a casual attitude to human life, made more excusable in his own view by such a vast country as Russia having so many people to spare. It was no trouble to sacrifice one more Cossack or kulak. The chilling ease with which he could decide to dispose of anyone, including his close entourage (which was not quite so markedly the case with Hitler), who had displeased him or seemed a potential rival must have made it unspeakably awful to work for him (resigning would of course have been seen as an act of disloyalty), and it got worse when in his old age he grew even more paranoid and suspicious. It's no wonder that after his death the dictatorial model was dispensed with and he himself airbrushed from Soviet history. Time has blurred Russian views of his era to the extent that a popular Stalinist cult was evident in the early years after the collapse of Communism, when many weren't too happy about the way things were going and Vladimir Putin had not yet emerged as the new focus for strong patriotism. The downside of Stalin's rule has been overlooked, including the effect of his purges of the army which was to do away with many good generals and gravely weaken the country's ability to resist the Nazi invasion – an invasion Stalin himself had long suspected would one day come, even if its suddenness took him by surprise (he had serious deficiencies as a war leader).

This may be a political philosophical rather than a historical issue, but of the two competing totalitarian ideologies during the twentieth century, which in its nature and consequences was worse – or were they as bad as each other? The question is a very difficult one to answer. Both Hitler and Stalin (along with Mao in China later on) were prepared to kill in large numbers to get their way. A ruthless intolerance, when it leads to that kind of thing, is not to be applauded even in what is sincerely believed to be a good cause. Not all Communist regimes have been as brutal as Stalin's – on balance Soviet governments from Khrushchev's onwards were not – though they nonetheless treated political dissidents badly and denied people civil liberties which were taken for granted in the West. By the 1980s, however, Communism in Russia had degenerated into a system which was kept in being purely for the benefit of those at the top and not from genuine ideological conviction. In terms of people being tortured or unlawfully killed things seem to have been worse in countries where Communist rule was a more recent phenomenon and dedication to Marxism more genuine.

Some Fascist regimes appear relatively benevolent, such as that of Mussolini (though he did murder political opponents); the worst cases of anti-Semitism on the part of Italian Fascists were probably down to the influence of Hitler, the dominant partner in the Rome-Berlin Axis. I can't really be certain on this whole point because I've never known anyone who was an Italian Fascist in the 1920s and 30s. You might say that Communism – in itself rather than as something used for the personal benefit of an individual or faction – was preferable because it had an ideal, that of creating a more egalitarian society, whereas Fascism was simply about power. But in conditions of instability where democracy wasn't working a Fascist government, whether as a permanent or interim measure, might seem a good idea. Communism had a lot of support in inter-war Europe from people who failed to spot its flaws (such as that outlawing private enterprise was only possible if you took away political liberty). They were in error, but were they wicked? It is difficult to say what they would have done – supposing they were allowed to do it – if they had actually gained power and realised after a while what Communism in practice actually meant; but some would certainly have been disillusioned (and in real life were, once they saw what Stalin was doing in order to achieve his aims). Whether a Fascist is inherently wicked as long as they are a Fascist, in all cases, is hard to say; I once overheard a conversation on a train in which someone said that they had known a member of the British National Party who in actual fact was a really nice guy. Could it be that this was true, in more than just the way Hitler and Goebbels might have seemed charming to those who weren't being exterminated by them? I just have no way of knowing for sure.

Hitler sought to exterminate whole races, but it occurs to me that if the essence of Fascism is dictatorship it need not have a racist character. By virtue of his being a dictator Cromwell could be called a Fascist, even if the conditions which brought him to power were different from those explaining the rise of Hitler, Mussolini or for that matter Stalin. Yet he let the Jews back into England (and was generally more humane than he is often given credit). And Communist regimes sometimes have not treated ethnic minorities very well.

Hitler often appears worse than Stalin because he invaded other countries − so too did Stalin after 1945, but not in the sense of a large-scale military campaign, which would have caused much greater loss of life, nor did the Communists mistreat the inhabitants of those countries in quite the same way that the Nazis did the people of Occupied Europe, though they can be said to have mistreated them nonetheless. It somehow seems unlikely that Mussolini or Franco would have done the same, even if they had had quite the resources possessed by Hitler. Concerning Stalin, it is of course morally no less serious if you slaughter your own people and not someone else's. And given the reforming zeal and virulent anti-capitalism of true Communists, along with the age-old factor of lust for power, it is at least possible to imagine a Communist leader who if they had the means to do so would have attempted a continental or even global takeover with the aim of spreading the faith, before the advent of nuclear weapons and MAD made this unwise. At great human cost in terms of lives.

The only conclusion I find I can come to in the end is that Communism is marginally preferable to Fascism, but only in the sense that *individual* Communists can be misguided, perhaps a little crazy, rather than bad, whereas Fascists don't send out the same signals or not as much. I suspect it may depend on where you are. Westerners as a whole are not morally superior to other people, but it seems to me that Western Communists have often lacked the genuine brutality that was seen in Russia, where it may have been a product of the Eastern European character, and the Far East. This is irrespective of the fact they have never for the most part enjoyed actual, or at any rate sole, power. I think the other left-wing parties in France in the late 1930s were right to join with the Communists in a Popular Front against the Fascist groups, to prevent the latter taking advantage of the country's economic and political troubles the way the Nazis had in Germany. But in terms of its *effects*, once it is adopted on a governmental, national scale, Communism is not *overall* better than Fascism even if the difference between the experiences of people in post-1945 Eastern Europe and those of the Chinese under Mao's Cultural Revolution is taken into account. One thing is clear; if Soviet Russia lasted into the late twentieth century and Nazi Germany did not, it was because (a) she had been militarily the victor in 1945, and (b) her nuclear weapons made it impossible to challenge her except at a terrible price.

9

The end result of flawed British, French and US policy-making in the aftermath of World War One, combined with the appeal for a certain element of Fascism, was the rise to power in Germany of Hitler and the Nazis. It is probable that had the country remained in a state of unrest and political instability they would have seized it by force, justifying their actions as necessary in the public interest. In the end, though, they did not need to.

Hitler was not triumphantly swept to power by the will of the majority of the German nation, as it is important to realise (some people still seem to think he was). Due to the vagaries of the Weimar Republic's electoral system, the Nazis were by January 1933 the largest party in the Reichstag but without having received the largest number of votes in the previous general election; at any rate they did not have a majority over all their opponents combined. There was undoubtedly a popular element at work, which is not surprising considering the discontent over the Treaty of Versailles, etc. Even though some of the worst features of the Treaty had been remedied before Hitler came to power hatred of it was vital in giving the Nazis their initial boost; afterwards, in addition to those grievances which remained, they seemed the only people capable of sorting out the instability, chaos and economic problems in which the country had become mired. But at the same time many Germans considered the Nazis to be a bunch of (dangerous) cranks and misfits who would drag the country into war and associate her with morally abhorrent policies. We are talking, after all, about a population most of whom were sober and sensible (as on the whole the majority in any given society is). But in conditions where there is desperation, frustration, marginalisation, socioeconomic collapse, and Nazis may seem the only guarantor of stability, many sober and sensible people will do what they otherwise would not. It is at least forgiveable. In the end, Hitler did not receive anything like the majority of votes that would have given him the Chancellorship under normal conditions and in a system like that which operates, for example, in Britain. What happened was that the Nazis had received sufficient support for them to count as major players in the negotiations that were going on, in an environment of crisis, between the principal parties in the Reichstag. Hitler became Chancellor largely as the result of a backstairs deal with his political rivals, who mistakenly thought they could control him. The Nazis were initially just one of various elements in a coalition. Along with his own cunning Hitler subsequently used the Enabling Act, which gave him emergency powers in a situation such as that prevailing because of the economic depression and the threat the resulting discontent was posing to law and order, to consolidate his position, eventually establishing a one-party dictatorship with himself at its head. Considerations of national and racial character can play a part in these things, and he benefited in the long run from a Germanic tendency to submit to authority, which by extension included not opposing its foreign policies, regardless of the exact means by which it got into power.

In one respect his regime was not an oppressive despotism, as far as the majority of Germans were concerned. Because of Nazi race theories and the value that was put on being "Aryan" they were not despised by their leaders in the same way that some African dictatorships (from simple wickedness and elitism) have despised the people they ruled over. When we speak of the Allies having liberated (Western) Europe by winning World War Two, does that include Germany? It does not in one sense because most Germans were not mistreated and oppressed in the same way that the Nazis mistreated and oppressed those people in occupied countries who they considered inferior. And a good many of them did support the Third Reich. But they were liberated in another sense for they were undoubtedly debased and brutalised by being forced to participate in the regime's atrocities, or stand back and let them happen, and suffered from the effects of its policies as the tide of war turned against Germany and they were subject to intensive bombing by the RAF and USAAF plus the destruction caused by the Allied ground invasion and military resistance to it. There is evidence of a lack of widespread enthusiasm for the war on the part of the civilian population in the run-up to its breaking out in 1939, and they were even less likely to be enthused as austerity policies in which the economy was put on a war footing to the detriment of other areas began to bite. The soldiers, sailors and airmen did what soldiers, sailors and airmen always do, i.e. fight for their country. They were motivated by patriotism and a desire, perhaps understandable, to make up for the defeat of 1918 and get back at those responsible for the Versailles humiliation. Some people, in addition to having those motives, were diehard Nazis. Of course any individual member of the armed forces who *refused* to fight – or anyone in whatever capacity who opposed the war – would face severe penalties. There never has been a more striking case of a population harnessed, for whatever reason on their part, to the support of such a lunatic set of policies. Their enthusiasm, whether they were military or civilian, would have been kindled for a time by the spectacular victories of 1940, which again can be put down to patriotism (explaining, at least, what might otherwise seem more perverse, as in the case of popular rejoicing in Britain at success in colonial wars) but gradually evaporated as things began to turn sour. In the meantime, an additional justification for the war could be supplied by raising fears of the Red Peril, i.e. Russia, who it might be added had been an enemy in the First World War, before the Bolshevik Revolution. Hitler had whipped up such feelings before hostilities actually broke out, the aim being to justify them. The Nazi-Soviet Pact would therefore have puzzled a good many people, unless they were canny enough to see (as in fact Stalin did) that it was intended as a temporary measure until Hitler felt ready to launch his invasion of Russia. But by then, the Nazi system was so firmly entrenched at home that people either believed whatever excuse the government gave for its actions or were not inclined to risk the consequences of dissent. Those who actively opposed the regime – and if successful would have ended the shame and the deprivations suffered by the German people as a result of their leaders' lunacy – were at best imprisoned and at worst executed, and this I feel serves to make the point. I have gone into the reasons why people are afraid to stand up to totalitarian rulers, and how far they may be forgiven for their inaction, elsewhere; suffice to say that although this should not be said lightly, we cannot condemn people for what we would not find easy to do ourselves were we in their position.

World War Two would not have happened without World War One. It could be regarded as unfinished business; at least that was how Hitler saw it. In spirit it was in any event a nationalist war, fought to gain revenge for 1918-19 and so restore Germany's pride. But in what way exactly was it supposed to achieve the latter objective? It could be argued that except for the controversial matter of East Prussia and the Polish Corridor Hitler had got what he wanted, made his point. He had recovered the Rhineland and rebuilt Germany's armed forces till they were at least on a par with Britain's or France's, and in breach of the Versailles treaty, without the western powers lifting a finger to stop him; reparations had already been considerably scaled down; his homeland of Austria had been absorbed into the Reich, as was his wish; and the Saarland had voted in a plebiscite to be reunited with Germany. What really caused the 1939-45 war was the annexation of territories to the east, namely the bulk of Poland and Czechoslovakia, over which Hitler had no legitimate territorial claims. Though it would have been, and was, a satisfactory revenge for Versailles Hitler invaded France, Belgium, Holland, Denmark, Norway etc. because the opposition of the western powers to his eastern policy, reflected in their guarantees to Poland, meant he would have to anyway; he might as well go the whole hog. Much as he would have liked to teach the British and French, and particularly the French whom he despised as a nation, a lesson revenge was nonetheless a secondary motive for him, though never far behind. He could have achieved his aim of making Germany self-sufficient (in so far as any nation can be) by draining the wealth of the east as part of obtaining *Lebensraum*. This explains why he saw no problem, from his point of view, in certain nations of western and southern Europe remaining neutral in the war, being spared invasion (where geography did not give them a strategic military significance) and forcible absorption into his new order. Either they were ideological allies (by virtue of being Fascist), like Spain and Portugal, their neutrality made them useful as a financial banking house or diplomatic channel (Switzerland), or they were considered fellow Aryans (the Swedes, Finns and Norwegians). As it was Hitler succeeded in occupying and achieving domination, militarily, economically and politically, of central and western Europe in a way the Kaiser might have if it had proved possible and which he, Hitler, certainly delighted in. Neutral countries would inevitably be sucked into Germany's orbit, anyhow, by virtue of its being the strongest European power in all respects.

Elements of Hitler's foreign policy were dictated by the old fear of Germany being encircled, trapped between hostile powers namely France, an old enemy, and possibly Britain, in the west and Russia in the east. The Nazi-Soviet Pact of August 1939 was intended to neutralise the latter as a threat, in the short run anyway, so that Hitler did not have to fight a war on two fronts if the western powers opened hostilities against him while at the same time he was double-crossing and invading Russia, as he intended to do. Though the modus operandi was different it served the same purpose as the Schlieffen Plan, by which Germany in the First World War had hoped to eliminate France from the conflict by a lightning invasion through Belgium before dealing with Russia. (In both cases the plan failed, though in the earlier conflict this was not instrumental in Germany's defeat since the Communist revolution led to Russia's exit from the war.) In fact it has been suggested that the first and second World Wars should be viewed as a single conflict, separated by a twenty-year truce. Certainly, in addition to what has been said above, the features which characterised the Second are strikingly present, in at least embryonic form, in the First: hostility towards ethnic minorities, indeed amounting in some cases to genocide (the massacres of Armenians by Turks); the appearance of potentially devastating new weapons; the phenomenon of "total war", involving the targeting of civilians (as in the Gotha and Zeppelin raids on Britain) and their mobilisation, in a non-military sense, to further the war effort through their roles in industry (the "Home Front"); and an increased role for the state in the direction of the economy, as was considered necessary if all a nation's resources were to be marshalled in the cause of victory. The thesis that the world in the first half of the twentieth century underwent a new "Thirty Years' War" is valid in all but one important respect; it assumes the second conflict followed *inevitably* from the first. Had steps been taken to revise the territorial and military aspects of the Treaty of Versailles before Hitler started doing it by force, he would morally have had much less of a leg to stand on. Had he continued to pursue an aggressive foreign policy with all the likely consequences for Germany, as much as for anyone else, it is a pretty safe bet he would have been overthrown by the Army. Many of the latter still had a sense of honour which recoiled at what he was doing or planning to do, though it was combined among those of an aristocratic or monarchist background, some of whom wanted the Kaiser back, with a snobbish aversion to the son of a middle-class customs official. Other than simple patriotism, what motivated many who served in the German armed forces during the Second World War was anger at Versailles, and once the cause of their resentment was removed the high command would have been much less inclined to participate in dangerous gambles.

Considerable progress had been made by the time Hitler came to power with easing the unfair reparations burden, and in fact it was lifted for an indefinite period at the Lausanne Conference in 1932. But the military imparity still remained, and since Germany had not been sole cause of the Great War was unjustified. The Anglo-German Naval Agreement might have been viewed as a step in the right direction, though it was signed at a time when Hitler still mistakenly believed he could forge an Aryan Alliance between Germany and Britain against France. At the time and in retrospect, for those three countries to have armed forces of roughly equal strength might seem to be creating a situation whereby Germany felt threatened by the other two powers in alliance plus possibly Russia. But what counts are the reasons why a war might break out, and therefore how it can be avoided. The causes of the Second World War were, in the end, simpler than those of the First, which can be frustratingly complex for those seeking to analyse them. Ultimately it boils down to Hitler plus those whose mistakes gave him his start and then, in the 1930s, let him get away with so much. In the end, German democracy did not prove strong enough to withstand the impact of the Great Depression. Despite the apparent settling of the reparations issue the vagaries of the electoral system, lingering resentment over Versailles and the French occupation of the Ruhr in 1923, and the fact that the harsh military-style discipline of the Nazis seemed to a significant number the only way to solve Germany's problems combined with Hitler's own cunning and the folly of his domestic and foreign opponents, who did not take him seriously or at least thought they could control him, to bring him to power and keep him in it. They enabled him to prosper even when some of the factors which explained the Nazis' success had been removed from the equation.

He was able to expand Germany's armed forces to at least their pre-1914 level by simply ignoring Versailles, before anyone got round to dealing with the issue through negotiation. And we are speaking of a madman – in one sense or another – who because of the factors mentioned above was able to enforce his will at home and abroad. He had ambitions which went beyond the overturning of Versailles. He was a loner and sociopath who buried his inadequacies in an identification with the race and nation, if one viewed them as the same thing, which to him (an Austrian by birth) necessarily meant Germany rather than the multi-ethnic Hapsburg Empire. In their actualisation his desires followed a certain logic. He wanted Germany to be self-sufficient economically because in his view it was degrading for her survival, her welfare at least, to be dependent on what might be "lesser races". Such a position is not tenable in the interdependent modern world and indeed has always been somewhat suspect.

To nationalist considerations and the redressing of grievances over Versailles Hitler appended the idea of Aryan racial supremacy and also of *lebensraum*, the belief that Germany needed "living space" in the East (plus the natural resources to be found there) for her expanding population, involving a tie-in with the race aspect because millions of Poles and other "inferior" Slavs would have to be exterminated to make way for the settlers. It was a factor not present in 1914-18, at least not to the same extent. The second war when it broke out rendered the execution of the racial policy possible, in fact inevitable as long as the Nazis persisted in their beliefs, because it meant Hitler had passed the point of no return (though while he had a good go at wiping out the Jews, he was not able to start on the Slavs before military reversals made it impossible). He was afflicted by a kind of fatalism, which among other things meant that when he was finally toppled he more or less brought his country and its people down with him, not fortunately to their complete destruction although it might have seemed so surveying the ruins of the Fatherland in 1945. By his own lights he deserved to fail, having proved unequal to the struggle; though he also claimed that the German people had let him down, which emphasises the appalling nature of the man when one considers that he had led them – forced them, given that his regime was ultimately based like all totalitarian states on terror – into a disastrous war in support of a fantasy, with dreadful consequences for themselves as well as others.

Did he aim to take over the entire world? I think he would have liked to, if it had been feasible. The theory is that he wanted to dominate and neutralise as a threat anywhere where there were Jews and which therefore constituted a legitimate target. The USA (with its particularly large Jewish population) would probably have been too much for him to take on, in the sense of invading and occupying it. And one finds oneself thinking that although America entered the war before the truth of what was happening in the death camps was fully revealed, if Hitler intended in the long run to adopt the Final Solution (as opposed to simply expelling Jews from Europe) – and it was being planned in detail before Pearl Harbour – the pressure from US Jews, on top of other things, would sooner or later have made America's participation in the war inevitable. It would have been an example of how his fatalism proved itself to be his undoing (which it was). We cannot be entirely sure of this. But even if he was not to actually invade the west in a military sense I believe Hitler aimed at a Europe dominated economically and politically by Germany, with the support of other "Aryan" peoples such as the British and Scandinavians, and including Russia west of the Urals. Within German-controlled territory all non-Aryans would either be exterminated or used as slave labour. But those who were Aryans would look to Germany, the most powerful "Aryan" nation in Europe, for leadership and protection. Once the message had sunk in that this was the best way to manage things, or at least that there was nothing in the end which other Europeans could do to overturn it, troops would be withdrawn from any western territories that had been occupied since direct control would no longer be necessary. The British Empire would be allowed to remain (had British defeat in war with Germany raised the question of what was to happen to it; it would also have raised the question of Britain's Jews, whose deportation to Auschwitz would probably have been demanded). Russia east of the Urals would either be ruled by Japan or, if that was not feasible, could look after itself. Even if not quite universally dominant the "Aryans" would be strong enough to protect themselves from domination by others with the dilution of blood, etc., by mixing with other races which such things often entail. (The United States could be seen as an Aryan, or at least Aryan-dominated, nation but it was presumed that for the time being she did not want to be part of Hitler's grand scheme.)

I think if Hitler had been able to obtain his *Lebensraum* in the East (wiping out all Jews there at the same time), and unite all Germans including those of the Sudetenland and Danzig in a (Jew-free) Reich but without having to invade any part of western and southern Europe, he would have gone no further than that, regardless of his desire to exterminate world Jewry. But his aggressive grabbing of territory raised fears that he would strike west next – it seemed that unless someone finally stood up to him nothing was going to stop this extraordinary (and possibly mad) man in his apparent desire to annex country after country, and Germany's humiliation in 1918-19 certainly gave him a motive, it might be thought, for adding Britain and France to the list. There was also a belated feeling that Britain's honour had been compromised enough by appeasement, even if we attribute the policy to justified pragmatism rather than cowardice. If this meant the war would escalate to engulf most of Europe (plus North Africa) Hitler was quite prepared for that, particularly if it meant he could kill Jews in Holland or France, and had no objection to effectively annexing the whole continent. He was glad at the opportunity military victory gave him to do so; it was an extension of the policy of widening your objectives as circumstances allowed. He did not mind if the French were paid back for Versailles.

Despite isolationist tendencies within the US, the new power bloc Hitler would have created if he had been able to enlarge his empire to the maximum possible extent would have existed in an uneasy relationship with an America which, priding itself (albeit hypocritically in important respects) on its love of freedom, would not have been happy to coexist and have to deal on equal, and global, terms with such a regime (Jewish lobbying apart). It is hard to conclude that there would not in time have been some kind of incident which sparked off war. But of course what Hitler calculated was that he would be first to develop weapons of mass destruction. Had he succeeded in that goal he could at least have ensured that America was careful what she did, even if it was impossible to physically conquer her. Or, if it did not prove possible to deter her, or someone else, from developing their own WMD, perhaps secretly, a nuclear standoff would have developed for the foreseeable future as in the Cold War. There is no telling how long things would have gone on that way. Hitler himself, with his belief in a cold, merciless and Godless (despite his spuriously suggesting on occasions that he had divine support) universe where nothing was permanent did not expect his glorious new Reich to last forever, though a thousand years would do. At any rate he would have a pretty good try.

He would have been satisfied with the geopolitical arrangement I have described. It might have been a case of the Cold War breaking out a little earlier than it did, dividing the world into two opposed camps, with perhaps a non-aligned third if enough people wanted to be independent of both Hitler and the Americans and were able to assert that independence. But he knew how far he could go. It is *possible* he might have tried, once he had subdued British-controlled Egypt, to occupy the Middle East in order to have access to its developing oil industry, as well as the resources of south-west Russia. Whether he would have succeeded is a moot point but many think it would have overstretched his military resources. He was not yet in the position that America currently enjoys, that of being a truly global power. America's world hegemony is based on the ability of jet aircraft to cover much greater distances than was possible with petrol-driven ones, plus the speed and efficiency of modern communications which of course include not only radio, these days, but satellites and the internet. Commands can be received and acted upon, and armies resupplied, much more quickly. Of course the US does not find itself participating in conflicts which cover a whole continent, or substantial part of it. In an age of WMD, still potentially a factor in world politics, it is unlikely that such wars could ever break out. But they are not necessary for America's purpose in any case. Her geopolitical power was made possible by her economic and industrial might and technological sophistication, but at the same time the Cold War meant she could pose for a range of countries as the champion of freedom, against the totalitarian and oppressive USSR, in a way Hitler could not once the true nature of the man was revealed, and the fact that the conflict was being conducted by proxy with each side having spheres of influence in different parts of the world meant her reach was indeed global. Plus for those outside the Soviet orbit creating economic prosperity, which everyone naturally wanted to do, was best assured by allying oneself with the world's wealthiest nation, whose ideology and aims were the same as one's own in this respect. It helped further a planetwide extension of American power and to some extent culture. When the other side collapsed without a fight due to its internal weaknesses, America was left in a strong position as arguably the only remaining superpower. And she still acts as she did in the Cold War days, using her technology to defend those spheres of influence against new, albeit very different in nature, threats such as Islamic terrorism. Now if Hitler had been victorious in the Second World War he would have had the opportunity to fully develop the jet engine, and would have become what America has in the modern world. Or something like it; we do not know how the rest of the planet, under American leadership, would have fared, whether it would have in some way have collapsed or been able to survive as an alternative political system.

As America has herself found, power can be expressed, aims achieved and spheres of influence maintained through one's proxies without having to exercise direct control of a country. During the Second World War there were clear-headed, if not necessarily morally admirable, people who probably correctly did not believe that Hitler's purely territorial ambitions extended beyond Europe, apart from the campaign in North Africa whose strategic purpose was to attack the British Empire through Suez (Britain so far having decided not to throw in her lot with the Nazis), because this would simply not be practical. So Indians (a few Congress leaders) and Arabs (the Mufti of Jerusalem), races who Nazi ideology regarded as inferior, were happy to do deals with him if it was to their advantage. Hitler for his part was prepared to treat with such people if pragmatism demanded it, as perhaps one might use a beast of burden. He probably had a similar view of the Italians, who it could be argued were not for the most part Aryans, but were indispensable, if also something of a liability, to his Mediterranean strategy. Some tweaking of the definition of Aryan, especially where there had been a considerable degree of admixture, might be required. Of course the Mufti of Jerusalem had one thing in common with Hitler, and that was a hatred of Jews.

It was not necessarily apparent before 1941-2, when the exterminations began, that Hitler intended if he could to systematically destroy all Jews in the countries he occupied rather than just drive them out through persecution and discrimination. But it was clear he had no time for them and would probably go for one of those options or the other. In the end we declared war on him because of his foreign rather than his domestic policies, which was the correct principle to adopt though it does not make the domestic policies any less repugnant. But if it was his foreign policy aims which were the crux of the matter we had ample notification of those, at any rate as far as Eastern Europe was concerned, since they had been set out in the 1920s in his autobiography *Mein Kampf.* (I confess to having had a copy at one time. It is turgid, rambling and unreadable, and arguably more damage is done to the Nazi cause by publishing it freely than by banning it as some would.)

Looking back, it is easy to identify what should have been done. Originally, Germany was punished far too harshly and when, under Hitler, she began demanding too much, she was not dealt with firmly enough; an example of how Mankind often gets things the wrong way round. Ideally the Treaty of Versailles should not have been so unjust in the first place; the problem was that the Western democracies were defending a status quo that was questionable from the point of view of fairness, involving they could not quite take the moral high ground, and this gave the Nazis valuable ammunition. Once Hitler had come to power in 1933 (if not before), a conference of all the major European powers, including Germany, should have been held at which it was resolved to abolish the remaining controversial clauses of Versailles and allow Germany to possess armed forces roughly equal in strength to Britain and France individually. Her former colonies could have been returned to her if desired (why should she lose them, but Britain keep *her* colonies, assuming colonialism was acceptable in the first place?). She should perhaps also have received back some, at least, of the territories she was forced to cede in 1919.

The abandonment of any claims for additional territory in Europe might or might not have been made a condition of the above at this stage. But removing the more understandable causes of German grievance would have ensured Hitler had less moral authority for an aggressive foreign policy and made it more likely he would have been overthrown, probably by the Army, if he persisted in pursuing one. If he had refused to attend the Conference, and there was evidence of German rearmament, gradual rearming by Britain and France should then have begun, the aim being as far as possible to match Germany. The same if he (or a suitable delegate) had attended the Conference and agreed to its aims but Germany had subsequently been guilty of rearming beyond the levels permitted. (Without rearmament he would not have been able to invade Poland, Czechoslovakia etc.)

Morally, Hitler could be viewed as justified in reclaiming the Rhineland, which was after all his own "back yard", and in annexing Austria if, as was at one point the case, the majority of Austrians desired it (though we should not forget the dirty tricks, including murder, which he used to make sure he got internal support for his action; he didn't like to take chances). What was alarming was that he had done these things without first discussing the issue with the other European powers. There was a disregard for international law which set a bad precedent in any case and was much less acceptable where Germany did not have right on her side. It was the way things happened rather than what happened which counted most of all. Hitler's flouting of the rules would have been a less serious matter if he had not done anything which was unacceptable on moral, let alone legal, grounds. In those moral terms the annexation of the Sudetenland was far more controversial; because it included so much of Czechoslovakia's industry and natural resources it undoubtedly compromised her viability as a state, adversely affecting more people than benefited from it and desired it and contravening national self-determination. Plus, the evidence suggests that although the German-speaking population of Czechoslovakia might have been pleased to be reincorporated into the land of their ancestors, they were not that bothered all told and Hitler was merely stirring up trouble for his own ends, by the same means he had employed in Austria. There should at most have been a proper plebiscite held under direct international supervision, with the threat of military action if the Nazis attempted to take the region by force. At any rate the aim should have been to ensure that if Hitler tried to redraw the European map beyond what a fair revision of Versailles dictated, the Western powers were strong enough militarily to deter him from doing so, if not defeat him in actual combat.

But this never happened. Of British Prime Ministers MacDonald was by 1933 past his best, in fact already on the verge of senility, and Baldwin had little understanding of or empathy with foreigners. Neither of them was interested in a top level meeting with Hitler to thrash it all out. France was preoccupied with its internal problems (entailing that Britain, under Baldwin's successor Neville Chamberlain, had to take the lead in dealing with Hitler in the policy of Appeasement). The US was still keeping out of things. Another problem was that people did not take Hitler seriously. As Andrew Marr highlights in his own review of global history (Macmillan 2012), he told the world exactly what he was going to do in advance, and the world did not believe him. As he had probably calculated, the mere fact that he had done so (surely foolish since it had given his potential enemies forewarning of his plans) served to make him more ridiculed. The double bluff worked, because Hitler knew his opponents' weaknesses, even when they were foreigners whose countries he had never been acquainted with at first hand, and how to exploit them. He knew how to gradually push forward his policies as those weaknesses allowed, aiming higher and higher as it became apparent how much he could get away with. It was something he had learned from Bismarck; the difference between the two being, as has been stressed, that the latter, though not a very nice man as it happens, was not an evil one either.

Hitler found he was able to make progress much faster than he had anticipated, in the end going to war in 1939 rather than 1943 as he had originally planned, because the diplomatic situation plus (to a lesser extent maybe) the state of British and French rearmament − and these were advantages he might have lost later − favoured him so much. Before Munich, where he knew he could get what he wanted without diplomacy he saw no need for it. The crucial issue was rearmament, since his caution meant he was less likely to go to war if there was an equal or greater chance he would be defeated than that he would be victorious. In the former scenario it is quite probable the German Army, who outside the SS remained relatively honourable, would have overthrown him rather than embark on a conflict which might well prove disastrous for the country. But Britain and France did not begin to rearm at an early enough stage. There were several reasons for this. France as already mentioned was paralysed by internal political conflicts. While to some extent, Western politicians were uncertain who was the greater threat, Hitler or Stalin. At first, no-one had had much time to spare for worrying about the Bolsheviks/Communists. Germany's priority was to defeat the western Allies, and vice versa. Once the First World War was over attention was able to turn to Russia. Initial attempts to overthrow the Communists by fomenting civil war failed, and then they seemed for a time to recede as a threat because they were concentrating on tightening their hold, and implementing their policies, at home ("Socialism In One Country"). But later it did seem they were back to encouraging international revolution, backing the Left in the Spanish Civil War (which business was in some respects a dress rehearsal for 1939-45, although Russia's aims during the latter conflict were *initially* to protect herself rather than to spread Communism). And there was of course the existence of the Comintern.

There were elements who considered Hitler to be a vital bulwark against Communism (which he despised because of its international nature, feeling it went against the primacy of the individual nation state, and because he believed it was all got up by Jews), and should be left to do what he wanted. Certainly Communists had active branches in many Western countries, which made it look more as if they were trying to take over the world, even though Russia itself was not at the moment being territorially aggressive in Europe and would think twice about such behaviour as long as Hitler remained a potential adversary. And Stalin's bloody purges during the 30s would not have endeared many foreign observers to him. Of course Hitler's treatment of Jews and political opponents was no better, but it was not considered sufficient in itself to justify a general European war, an attitude which was of course quite correct if nonetheless ruthless. The fear of, or at least wariness towards, Russia made possible the Nazi-Soviet Pact which allowed Hitler to invade Poland, giving him a free hand in Eastern Europe and a vital breathing space in which to build up his forces to the point where he could then repudiate any treaty he had made with Stalin. An alliance between Russia and the western powers was ruled out by Neville Chamberlain and his colleagues because it would antagonise Germany, making her feel as she had felt in the period up to 1914 that she was being encircled and thus rendering war more likely. But the most important factor, on the whole, in the failure to stop the Nazis in their tracks was a very understandable fear of repeating the horrors of 1914-18, which Europe might do if Britain and France started a new arms race with Germany. And still, many people doubted Hitler would go so far as he eventually did.

With hindsight, it may seem that there really should have been an alliance between Britain, France and the Soviet Union, that this was the way to stop Hitler in his tracks, and so it might have proved. It was practically the right policy and also the morally correct one if ethics involves doing what ensures the greatest happiness for the greatest number or at least prevents them from suffering any more than is necessary. Both Hitler and Stalin were brutal dictators who coveted the territories of other countries, and as has already been pointed out Stalin, as an individual, was probably responsible for more killings of innocent people overall. But Hitler was more extrovert in that he was prepared if necessary to conquer the whole of Europe (apart from certain countries whose neutrality he for one reason or another tolerated), should it be the only way to achieve his objectives. Whereas Stalin (probably) would have been content with domination of the east in order to insure himself against future German aggression; this he set out to achieve, successfully, after the war and by infiltration of Communists into important positions, without the destruction, trauma and loss of life that is inevitable with full-scale military action, even if the tanks were always ready to back up the local authorities in suppressing serious dissent. It would have been better to have dealt with Hitler first, sandwiching him between the western powers and the Soviets in the event of war, and then Stalin if necessary.

But this would not have been apparent in 1939. And if Stalin, emboldened by having defeated Hitler, *had* pushed on into western Europe (after all, in 1814 Russian troops taking part in the defeat and overthrow of Napoleon had got as far as Paris) it would have been harder to resist him without the intervention of the United States, which was then isolationist. Conversely, there were fears that Stalin might prove an unreliable ally due to the damage he had done to his own army in the recent purges, when many good generals were shot as ideological traitors on spurious grounds. Nor did Britain and France seem altogether reliable allies to Stalin; even after the invasion of the rump of Czechoslovakia, which proved once and for all that Hitler could not be trusted (in making a deal with him Stalin thought he was essentially buying time; that, or something like it, was also what Chamberlain believed *he* was doing) their rearmament had not reached sufficient levels to inspire confidence in either themselves or potential friends. Equally importantly, Poland felt threatened by the Soviet Union as much as by Hitler which was understandable given Russian carving up of Polish territory, and suppression of Polish liberties, in the past. Britain and France were quite justified in thinking that there was little point in a pact with Stalin to guarantee the security of Poland if the latter felt at risk from the very power it was proposed they make an alliance with. The Poles refused to allow Soviet ground and air forces to cross their territory; it was therefore absurd, even wrong, to ask the British people and parliament to authorise going to war, with all the sacrifices involved, on their behalf, and rendered additionally questionable by the necessity, if Germany was to be attacked by Britain and France from the west while Stalin came in from the east, of violating the neutrality of Holland and Belgium (though in the end it was only Germany which did so). How could these things be excused when the liberties of Britain and France were not themselves necessarily at stake? So Chamberlain only went through the motions; because his efforts to reach an understanding with the Russians were so half-hearted, Hitler ultimately outbid him. He was being excessively cautious (a younger man perhaps would not have been). Or, arguably, he was in fact making the right decision; one will never know. Certainly the armed forces of Britain, Russia and France outweighed Germany's numerically. Although France was politically traumatised and paralysed, militarily she was quite strong; her tanks, for example, were actually of better quality than the Germans'. But the latter nevertheless won the Battle of France the following year, emphasising that perennial truth of martial affairs; within reason a smaller and poorer quality (in some respects) force can triumph over a superior one if it is properly deployed and led with the right combination of skill and boldness. The British were reluctant to open hostilities, until it seemed there was no choice, because of the deficiencies of France, let alone Russia, as a partner in a military alliance, in addition to the other reasons which might apply.

From a combination of various factors – uncertainty about Stalin, the general fear of another great conflict, failure to take Hitler seriously followed by a misplaced trust in his good faith, reluctance to rearm at the right time – Europe stumbled into war in 1938-9. By the time it decided that another war was preferable to Nazi domination of the continent, it was too late to deter

Hitler and so prevent a second terrible conflict under cover of which appalling crimes against humanity, besides the usual carnage which happens in wartime, were committed. To say that the war happened because of the indolence of Baldwin and the weakness of Neville Chamberlain is an oversimplification. It's more true to say that there was a policy of inaction followed by one of muddling through that was both necessary, though it ought not to have been, and quite inadequate. There could have been no war without Hitler, but equally there could not have been one without those who by their lack of foresight and planning made his aggression possible. He is supposed to have regretted that he did not go to war in 1938 over the Sudetenland, because he would have won. We do not know how true this is; certainly Britain was able to repulse the Luftwaffe in 1940, but two years had gone by in the meantime. The British and French leaders were playing safe, as they saw it. A Hitler victory in 1938 would have been no less awful than what was to happen over the next seven years. It should be noted that there is a belief the German Army High Command were planning to overthrow Hitler if Britain and France stood firm over Czechoslovakia and declared war rather than opt for negotiation. But if Chamberlain and Co. knew of these rumours, they probably decided not to risk the consequences if something went wrong.

It could be argued that there was no question of "buying time" in which Britain and France could more successfully resist Hitler, if that is what Chamberlain and his colleagues were trying to do (as has been claimed), because the logic of the appeasement policy meant Britain could not rearm; and it was not foreseen that there would be a "Phoney War". But as there was a risk either way, it could equally be argued that you might as well appease.

One last thing needs to be said on the subject of why there was a Second World War. In the British television series *Foyle's War*, set during that period of history, the eponymous police inspector's sergeant attends for a time the meetings of a right-wing organisation which does not believe Britain should have declared hostilities against Germany. He confesses to being puzzled (as some were in 1914) as to why she thought it necessary to be drawn into a European war at all. In a way, you can see the point of view this fictional character represents. Britain and France had treaty obligations to Poland, as part of an alliance system which still remained in place as a principle of international diplomacy, and had in effect been responsible for the 1914-18 conflict, but why had we gone to war in defence of, to paraphrase Neville Chamberlain's words, "people in faraway countries of whom we know nothing"? It didn't seem that Hitler had any territorial claims against Britain, beyond the military need to invade and conquer an enemy power if it is essential for victory. In the last resort he would have allowed her to retain her Empire provided he was given a free hand in Europe. You can't, in fact, identify any purely *practical* reason why she didn't keep out of it all from the start. The explanation must lie in a combination of things which would not have been crucial in themselves but which together amounted to a certain critical mass. British policy had always been to resist the excessive dominance of one power on the European mainland, and Hitler's behaviour was simply becoming too frightening. Furthermore, Britain had given her word to protect Poland and was afraid that her honour, and thus her standing in international politics, would suffer if she did not keep it. It might affect the willingness of people in the future to deal with her.

And the conquest of western Europe in May-June 1940 meant that the war was no longer a conflict over "people in a faraway country of whom we know nothing". From then on, as far as Britain was concerned, it really was a just one. It wasn't only the Jews and what was happening to them, much as some people think that motive ought to have been sufficient (where it wasn't a factor at all, this was of course deplorable). I don't think we wanted to buy our freedom, and the retention of our world power, from the likes of Hitler. Not just the political persecutions, including the anti-Semitism (racism towards Jews went on throughout the West, of course, but outside Nazi Germany was relatively less serious and often ambivalent), but *also* the habit of invading and occupying countries without their consent and on a big scale made clear Hitler was a bad one, to understate somewhat. He was worse than the Kaiser or Napoleon, however disastrous their consequences had been. It would have been a debasement, a denial of the decency we did in fact value at heart, to let him get away with it, and in our geographical neighbourhood, while being what we were, doing what we wanted to do, effectively on his sufferance. It was something he never fully understood, to his own loss. After he had gobbled up the rump of Czechoslovakia, and Poland, no-one could be sure what else he would try to do and it might not be wise to dismiss fears that he would seek to avenge 1919 by turning his attentions west. In practice, he was only going to do so in so far as it seemed necessary to ensure the success of his Eastern policy. But it was a sense of honour and dignity which ultimately drew Britain into a conflict which resulted in the end of her worldwide empire and indeed of her whole status as a first-rank global power.

Hitler had to follow up his bold initiatives in 1938-9, and Britain and France, among other considerations, to honour their obligations to Poland. But both sides had ended up in a position where, although hostilities had been declared, neither was quite sure of its ability to defeat the other, on land or in the air, and so there ensued the "Phoney War". Once it was ended by the Nazi *blitzkrieg* in the west, the course of the conflict was very different to that of 1914-18, although there are similarities between the two scenarios. Instead of the opposing sides being roughly evenly matched throughout, the mistakes of the Western powers in foreign policy planning before the war had left Germany in a position where she could become the undisputed victor, apart from her failure to overcome Britain, within a year of hostilities commencing. That she did fail to overcome Britain always seems puzzling despite it being clear that Hitler and Luftwaffe chief Goering made serious errors in their deployment of the materiel at their disposal in the air war they needed to win before the German navy could land troops on the enemy's shores. It was a combination of these logistical and tactical failures and Hitler's belief that Britain, who he in many ways respected (as a successful empire-builder and also, in his thinking, the other great "Aryan" nation in Europe), ought to be allowed to come to her senses and make peace with him (he was probably in contact with influential elements in the country who favoured such a policy). To this end he preferred in the long run to try to bomb us into submission rather than invade us, which he did not want to do both for the reasons stated and from fear of overstretching resources which he wanted to commit to the conquest of Russia, as a Slavic power the greater threat according to his ideology. I think if he had really pushed the invasion of England he could have brought it off, although perhaps at the cost of having to forego one or two of his other victories. Strategically, his switching from the bombing of airfields to that of cities was his principal, and decisive, mistake. Bombing the cities merely stiffened civilian determination to prosecute the war without destroying the industrial capacity to do so, as the Allies were to find out later on when the situation was reversed.

Because of Hitler's other commitments there was always a certain half-heartedness about the affair that helped Britain in the end to survive, along with the courage of her own people whether civilian or military. But it seems likely that she would have been forced to sue for peace in the end, accepting in effect satellite status, since there was no way she could invade western Europe and defeat Hitler on the ground, taking the fight to the enemy, on her own. She would have lost with more honour. But what prevented her from losing at all was not Winston Churchill's rousing speeches, and this isn't to knock them for what they were nor to denigrate the whole civilian and military war effort, but General Eisenhower. Given that Hitler intended to declare war on the United States and Russia anyway at some point, believing they would need to be taken on and defeated for him to achieve his goals, Britain's resistance in 1940-41 was of limited geopolitical significance. In practical terms, it essentially meant that having already been free she was more able when the time came to give useful support to her allies, and thus shorten the war to a certain degree. That of course was a good thing. Meanwhile, the failure to overcome the RAF might, one supposes, have been seen as an early defeat for Hitler, which ought to have been psychologically damaging to him and given crucial encouragement to his enemies as El Alamein and Stalingrad later did. But he did not then have the USA and Russia arrayed against him as well, so it mattered less. And the Blitz was intended to appear a pounding of Britain into submission. So also was the Battle of the Atlantic, which it has to be remembered was not won by the Allies until 1943, and if they had lost it, too many ships carrying vital supplies being sunk by Donitz's U-boats, Britain at any rate would have been out of the war. To save his face, Hitler could always claim that his actions made sense from a military point of view, that he had simply switched to a different strategy. German bombing of British cities in fact went on until 1945, although on an comparatively smaller scale (the V1 and V2 attacks were alarming, but failed to change the course of the war).

Prior to D-Day the British Commonwealth did pull off one major success through its own efforts, defeating Germany in eastern North Africa; Alamein being the turning point. The British can justly take pride from being the first in the conflict to really show that Hitler was not invincible. Alternatively some would portray this theatre of war as a relative sideshow, leading to one wondering why Rommel, the Nazis' best general (though not a Nazi himself) was not employed on the Eastern Front where surely he would have been of far greater use, considering how the course of the war turned out. But it would not have been a sideshow if Rommel had succeeded in taking Egypt, as was never impossible. Undoubtedly the North African campaign, at this stage, was to some extent a colonial war on Britain's part, for she was worried that Hitler would overrun Egypt, including Suez, and thus control the route to India, and so it was never likely the Americans, who were suspicious of her imperialism (and in any case were still building up their vast military machine, a process which took a long time as in 1917-18), would play much part in it, before the Operation Torch landings which were directed against Italy. But it would hardly have been any better and would probably have been worse if a regime like Hitler's had been able to wield the kind of global power that Britain still did or America was to later on, notwithstanding the inability for it to actually deploy troops much beyond Europe.

Of course the campaign as a whole was essential to gain control of the Mediterranean, knock Italy – Hitler's main European ally, who was also correctly perceived as the softer target – out of the war and then invade Germany through "the soft underbelly of the Axis beast". Military historians will always debate the point of it in view of Italy's unreliability as a partner and the fact that ultimately the outcome of the war was largely decided in the north. For one thing, Operation Anvil, the invasion of southern France, was not resisted by the Germans for tactical reasons, and so the popular mind tends to be unaware that it ever happened. The value of the Mediterranean campaign lay principally in the overall pressure it put on the Axis and in its tying up of resources Germany might otherwise have used in northern Europe, thus prolonging the war. It was also necessary psychologically for the Allies, and particularly Britain, to show some evidence of victory in one sphere or another. At Alamein, what tipped the balance against the Germans was problems with supply, already starting to become evident though not yet fatal to Axis chances, plus the fact that in Montgomery Rommel had finally come up against an Allied commander who was at least his equal, possessing an ability rare among his countrymen at that time, namely that of combining dynamism with caution, the latter quality being something Rommel arguably lacked. Monty wore down his opponent by skilful attrition, a more considered and effective version of "muddling through". Ironically in view of the awfulness of the regime he served, and with no intention on my part to be unpatriotic, Rommel if not the better commander was in some ways the better human being. Both men had the ability to be a father to the troops under their command and encourage them to give their all, but Monty had a nasty side which was never evident in Rommel and which became worse as success made him conceited and inclined him to think he did not have to keep it under control. He also, it appears, became slightly deranged. It seems unlikely that either would have happened to Rommel.

In 1940-41 Germany had effectively expelled her chief adversary from Europe and with the exception of nations who both sides found it advantageous to keep neutral, such as Switzerland and Sweden, was master of all of it from the Pyrenees to the Norwegian fjords and from the Atlantic to the border with the Soviet Union, the latter now running through luckless Poland which had been partitioned according to the Nazi-Soviet Pact. Stalin agreed to the deal because although he did not trust Hitler, whose ultimate intentions for Russia were almost certainly sinister if *Mein Kampf* was to be believed, he wanted at that stage to avoid military conflict with him, being unsure of the outcome. Britain of course held out until Hitler's folly in both invading Russia (who he had always intended to double-cross) and allowing his ally in East Asia, Japan, to antagonise the US by attacking Pearl Harbour and so drawing her too into the war resulted, in 1941, in the creation of a coalition against him which he could not in the end hope to overcome. It might have been different if he had had better allies but as in the first war Germany did not. Japan was too far away to be of much help and in any case had only brought disaster on the Axis cause by involving America. It always seems peculiar that Hitler did not realise the gross unwisdom of allowing her to do so, fatalism apart (he anticipated he would have to face the US at some point and in fact did declare war on her in due course). Mussolini's Italy was militarily incompetent, save one or two good generals, and pulled out of the war in 1943 when "Il Duce" was overthrown. Strategically, Hitler's actions do not make sense unless he hoped that Japan would tie up America in the Pacific while invading Russia from the East (which in the end never happened, allowing the Soviets to use Siberian troops to great advantage at Stalingrad and after) and also threatening Britain's Asian possessions. He was encouraged in the belief she could do this by her remarkable success in conquering large areas of land and sea, in eastern Asia (almost to the borders of India and the coast of northern Australia) and the western Pacific, within such a short time; not bad for a small island with limited natural resources of her own. It is always hard to get inside the mind of an extraordinary (this is not to praise him in any way) man whose ambitions were so wide-ranging as to seem crazy, but I think Hitler aimed at holding off his enemies long enough to develop superweapons before they did and so decisively defeat them. Or at least get them to stand off, though in effect it is the same thing.

As it was, the gamble failed. America's military and industrial power enabled her to fight a war on two fronts, in the Pacific and in Europe, and Japan, from whom Hitler was expecting too much, would probably not in any case have had the resources to take on her, Britain and Russia simultaneously. Germany had to bear the brunt of the European conflict, in which she was overrun before either the V-weapons or the atomic bomb could serve as a force capable of tilting the balance in her favour (regarding the latter, the Allies got there first, to Japan's cost; Hitler had by then already been defeated). The V-weapons failed to achieve their objective because of the way the conventional war had gone; the infrastructure, in terms of production facilities and fuel supplies, which would have made them truly effective was being destroyed. The same applied to the Messerschmitt-262 jet fighter; it could not be produced in large enough numbers. Hitler had run out of time. The reason why he never developed chemical warfare, as it was feared he would, may have had something to do with his own experience of a poison gas attack in the First World War. But it was probably also the case that with far more mobile armies chemical weapons, which in the first conflict had only affected soldiers on or in the immediate area of the front line, seemed an apocalyptic business; the danger to whole civilian populations raised the stakes too high even for him. The Allies had similar reservations and confined themselves to protective measures (we still have our gas mask). Of course the idea of nuclear weapons, illogical though it may seem, is that the mere threat of using them means you don't have to. At any rate, Hitler never perfected them, and from when the tide began to turn in 1942-3 to the end of the conflict in Europe in May 1945 was a gradual, but inevitable slide down to defeat for Germany, bar one or two temporary successes. This involved a massive cost in lives thrown away for no ultimate gain, plus wasted investment in military resources which failed to achieve their purpose. (Germany could not have held out for so long without the technical brilliance and organisational skills of Albert Speer, and even he was unable in the end to stave off the inevitable.) Though there was never a defeat more necessary, there is something infinitely depressing about it. But the Allies knew that if they relaxed the pressure in the slightest the Axis would recover and regain the advantage. It was why the British and American policy of pushing on gradually towards Berlin, mopping up every single pocket of resistance, rather than going for an all-out march on it was justified, despite Montgomery's opposition; they were dealing with an enemy who, for reasons about to be explained, it was unwise to leave in one's rear and thus risk slowing down progress in any event. Axis troops fought on from simple patriotism, ingrained fanaticism (particularly in the Japanese case) or because hardline Nazi cadres made sure they did; the more they realised they were losing the war the more savage the Nazis became, and the more they tightened their control. There was also the fear that the Allies if victorious would exact a ghastly revenge on Germany for all the suffering she had caused ("Enjoy the war, the peace is going to be terrible"); paradoxically, the more viciously she fought as a result the more such an outcome seemed likely.

But perhaps those much-vaunted superweapons would prove for the Axis the great deliverance. Hitler also believed that the Allies would in due course fall out and Britain and America make their own peace with Germany. What he failed to understand was that despite their reservations about Stalin and about Communism the western powers had come to the conclusion that the Soviet Union was the lesser of the evils. Certainly he had done nothing to persuade them that he was not the greater, and his treacherous attack, even if it was expected, on the country he had made a treaty with only two years before had if anything increased the sympathy felt for Russia in the "Anglo-Saxon" world. Though he had gobbled up parts of Poland in accordance with the Nazi-Soviet Pact, had shown aggression towards Finland and certainly encouraged Communist parties in the West through financial support and advice, becoming involved in the Spanish Civil War of 1936-9 (an ideological struggle, as well as a rehearsal for what was to come) by proxy, he had not unlike Hitler embarked on a wholesale policy of militarily conquering and annexing all his neighbours, even if something like that was to occur later on; he was still following in that respect the policy of "Socialism In One Country". He had not as was feared taken advantage of the pact with Hitler to attack the West and it is debatable how far he had any wish to do so. The Allies may nonetheless have been suspicious of the Soviets and expected that they would replace Nazi Germany as principal enemy after the war but had taken the decision to postpone dealing with them, in whatever way circumstances rendered necessary/possible, until Hitler had been defeated. The latter's belief, which he entertained long before the outbreak of war, that the US and Britain would (eventually) side with him against the Communist threat was an exception to the acumen he otherwise showed in his dealings with foreign powers and his understanding of their psychology, though latterly it owed much to his increasing desperation and delusion as his world collapsed around him.

Germany lost, anyway. The Allies broke out of their original beachhead in Normandy through a combination of sheer attrition, the achievement (already evident) of air superiority, which made up for the inferior calibre of their tanks compared to the German panzers (though being smaller than a Tiger, a Sherman was thereby more manoeuvrable, especially in the little sunken lanes of the *bocage*), and the disruption they had succeeded in causing to enemy fuel supplies. Meanwhile the Russians were advancing steadily in the east.

Hitler was successful when he was concentrating on a single objective, or set of clearly defined objectives, which exploitation of the failings of his opponents could give him the opportunity to achieve if he were only bold enough, and he was. He might not be entirely sure of victory, and this placed him at times in a state of nervous tension, but in the end events did work in his favour; he was on a roll. He was not so good when, as a result of having pushed his luck too far, things began to go wrong, especially when they did so on more than one front so that he felt besieged, under attack from all sides, both literally and psychologically. Then he grew even more stubborn, more adamant in his refusal to listen to criticism in arguments over how best to allocate resources. He got rattled, lost his clear head, and this at least accelerated Germany's military and economic collapse even if, after 1942-3 if not 1941, it was simply inevitable. As a soldier, although brave, he had never risen above the rank of corporal and so lacked the skill at and experience of grand strategy which might have enabled him to win even when the odds were against him, or at least preserved his advantageous position. And the very fact he had been militarily so successful in 1940-41 – despite the caution of his less bold but professionally more qualified generals who did not believe he could pull off such a string of victories – encouraged him subsequently to think he was invincible and did not need anyone else's advice in such affairs. Of course it was not so.

Ideological movements of the left or right that are in one respect or another revolutionary, and which begin with a small group of fellow travellers whose loyalty has to be rewarded, filling governmental posts once the movement attains power is even more a case of "jobs for the boys" than with conventional "democratic" administrations. It means that someone is in an important position more for political reasons than because they are suited for it. Hence Goering was ultimately responsible for the Third Reich's economic affairs without being much of an economist, and head of the Luftwaffe without any experience of the strategic side of running an air force; although a skilled fighter pilot in the First World War he had not held high enough rank. The story of the German war effort is essentially one of professionals being led by amateurs. Militarily the Nazis also suffered from the sheer range of their victories in 1940-41. It meant that when the Europe-wide empire Hitler had created came under serious assault from the Allies he was fighting a war on two if not three fronts, seriously overstretching his resources and finding it impossible to strengthen one front without withdrawing troops from another and thus weakening it. In the end, the Axis lost because they misunderstood and underestimated their opponents, overreached themselves, and did little to merit the support of the populations of the territories they conquered. Also, the different partners in the alliance could not always lend each other effective support. It was Hitler's war; and because he could not see that willpower alone was not sufficient for the job, Hitler's defeat.

What, in the end, was the point of it all? Inappropriately, or so it might well seem, the war benefited Germany in some ways more than it did the victorious powers, by being so destructive in its effects that it enabled her to start again from scratch, to become the economic powerhouse of post-war Europe whereas they were badly damaged by the cost of their triumph. But Hitler's intention had been to win. And it is obviously preferable wars should not break out in the first place, whatever the beneficial consequences that may arise from them for both winners and losers. A necessary war ought not to *be* necessary.

From what should have been Germany's point of view, this one wasn't. By the 1930s there was beginning to develop a feeling in Europe that the country had indeed been badly treated at Versailles, and this led many to be lenient towards Hitler, to the extent of condoning his unauthorised reoccupation of the Rhineland. He could have capitalised on this and indeed he did, but in the wrong way. Had he waited he would have got all the offending clauses of Versailles removed. Instead, he exploited sympathy for Germany's just grievances to go much further than was morally warranted. In fact, had he stopped with the annexation of the Sudetenland − at the very most − rather than gone on to do what he had no right to under any circumstances, he would not have attracted the opprobrium which his subsequent behaviour obviously did. (At least this applies with foreign affairs; preferably he should not have persecuted the Jewish population of Germany either.) As it was, a war had to be fought to reverse unjust actions − the illegal occupation of a host of countries − with millions of lives being destroyed on both sides. The economic success of Germany after the war, which with hiccups has continued down to the present day, would seem to give the lie to any notion that she needed "living space" in the East or to seize the oilfields of the Caucasus for her own sole use. And outside Germany Hitler's Reich was essentially a matter of holding down populations who although they managed by and large to cope with the deprivations of occupation, having no option, had no enthusiasm for the Nazis (beyond a few collaborators − and this is always a difficult and sensitive issue) since they obviously did not see any justification for the latter's action in invading them. Only a few had the courage to actively resist the Germans but that did not mean that the rest liked them. The conquered countries got very little out of it; they were bled dry, the products of their industry and agriculture being siphoned off to Germany and not even benefiting the latter much in the long run. It was simply power backed up by thuggery and by fear.

The benefits gained by Germany herself were short-term, if one disregards the advantages of being able to start again more or less afresh, as she had to do after 1945 due to the almost complete annihilation of her economy and infrastructure. The German people were on a patriotic high during the first half of the war because of Hitler's victories, but their wholesale reversal between 1942 and 1945 meant the sacrifices that had to be made were ultimately unjustified and purposeless. Except for certain military types, most of them ended up thinking they would rather not have gone through the whole experience. Hitler did, in some ways, give the Germans back their self-respect once he came to power, by sorting out the country's economic crisis; there is probably no-one, not even him, about whom *nothing* positive can be said, with the reservation that the bad may outweigh the good when the final balance sheet (as it were) is drawn up. The way he did it, through strict state control and massive public works programmes, is controversial and monetarist economists in particular would pour scorn on it. It works best as a hopefully temporary expedient in times of severe recession/depression; as anything else it is clumsy and restrictive and more likely to work against economic prosperity. It ought not to be considered a substitute for conventional employment, and so it should be expected that those working on the projects will not be paid the same wages as they would receive in normal conditions. I think if one is given the choice such schemes are preferable to the psychological and social consequences of mass unemployment, even if there is a danger they may degenerate into cheap slave labour. But in the case of Nazi Germany, any benefits they may have brought were in the long term subsumed within the deprivations caused to more than just the previously unemployed by an economy geared principally to war.

The crimes of the Nazis were not worse, morally, than what plenty of other people have done throughout thousands of years of human history but the Nazi regime is the most intellectually bankrupt of any that I can think of, because there was so little rational justification for what it did. This obviously applies to its ideas about race (some of which even Hitler thought were silly) as much as anything else about it. The lengths to which Nazis went, out of an obvious inferiority complex, to prove from archaeology the cultural pedigree of the Aryan race were laughable to say the least. A case in point is the suggestion that the word "hieroglyph" is derived from the ancient German "ir", "og" and "liff". It means one cannot take seriously anything else Nazis say on such subjects. I have not personally checked whether the Saxons (Germans, through whom the English could also be claimed to be an Aryan race) carried a banner with a serpent on it at the battle of Hastings, but I wonder what the authority for the assertion is and would not be surprised to find it had none whatsoever.

The only grievance the Nazis had with which any reasonable person can sympathise is Germany's treatment in the immediate post-First World War period. Beyond this there is nothing positive to say. They may have been right to point out that the acts of Allied nations were sometimes morally questionable themselves, but this is a case either of logs and specks, as in the Bible, or people living in glass houses – whether they are Nazis or not, but the principle certainly applies in the former scenario – needing to bear in mind the effects of hypocrisy on one's architectural infrastructure.

It is possible that over time the Nazi state would have evolved into something more benign, though there would have to have been some soul-searching over the Jews (and not only the Jews). If Nazi-dominated Europe had been efficiently and relatively humanely run (neither criteria was met), if after a while, having won the war, the regime no longer needed to grab so much of its subjects' wealth for itself and could give them something back in return, Europe becoming under its rule a prosperous economic unit, it's possible more people would have accepted the situation and indeed given the Nazis wholehearted support. It may be that Hitler genuinely believed this could and would happen if it were given the chance to. Fair enough, except that people like to be in control of their own destiny whatever use they make of the freedom. And how long exactly it would have been before this acceptability was achieved one doesn't like to say.

After Hitler one would have had to deal with the SS, who by the regime's downfall were becoming increasingly more powerful (though one does not like to whitewash him it is possible to argue that by 1945 he had become to some extent their prisoner, as people do become the prisoners of the systems they create). They were in some ways even nastier and crazier than he. He certainly thought so (it was they who were responsible for the lunatic exercises in archaeology mentioned above), though his own beliefs about the Jews were absurd enough. An aghast Himmler (Reichsfuhrer SS) once commented when told of conduct unbecoming by someone or other that he would never have expected such a thing from a blond man. The question is often asked how far Himmler and not Hitler was responsible for the Holocaust. It is true that Hitler had no clear idea what to do with the Jews or other undesirable, un-Aryan elements until Himmler suggested the "Final Solution" and the gas chambers, but he certainly did nothing to discourage him. In fact it was Hitler who created the climate in which the whole thing could become possible in the first place, by leading a political organisation with an avowedly racist programme, which he essentially endorsed, to victory in Germany and then a position of supremacy in Europe. If he became trapped by it all in a way he may not entirely have cared for at heart, that was his own fault. Whom gods destroy…he achieved nothing in the end except to create a situation where people are over-sensitive about matters like race and where bitterness and ill-feeling on account of what Germans did under him have persisted for many years, some people still being poisoned by it in the 2010s. Fascism as a political philosophy was discredited internationally by his association with it, Franco's in Spain being the only, apart from neighbouring Portugal, arguably Fascist regime to survive the war, because it wisely kept out of it (like Portugal), and last into the later twentieth century.

The question remains of to what extent Hitler, and the other leading Nazis, were mad (and thus not, it could be argued, responsible for their actions). The answer seems to be that they were not clinically so, but nonetheless were influenced by conditions and complexes which do not affect "normal" people, or they could not have done what they did. There is quite a large territory between normality and outright insanity in which these factors operate. For simplicity's sake, if nothing else, we will assume that they were sane enough to have perceived the wrongness of their actions and to have behaved otherwise had they chosen to do so. Much depends on the definition of evil. One finds oneself coming to the conclusion that Hitler's, or for that matter Goering's, Himmler's, or Goebbels', was of a different kind from that of the thug who would directly physically assault the object of his hatred, eyes gleaming and mouth twisted in a chilling leer, with the words "Now you're getting what you deserve, Jew." Or for that matter from a more educated and intelligent person who would rather look on, but otherwise acts in the same way. It did take the form of a festering resentment against certain things and a brutal determination to destroy them whatever suffering was caused in the process. Perhaps it was evil of a kind, accompanied by delusion, and we know that a lot of suffering *was* caused in the process. Even if we conclude that Hitler was delusional rather than wicked, it would not make him and his kind any less of a menace.

It will be noted that Hitler, along with quite a few other Nazis and a fairly large percentage of the people who supported the regime, were Catholics or (in Hitler's own case) originally from a Catholic background, later lapsing. Undoubtedly in history there is a "family tree" of religious and political movements, in which characteristics of one can be replicated in others or at least have a bearing on their rise. When a belief system, in which one may have been brought up from childhood, is discredited to some extent, among societies or individuals, its forms may crop up again elsewhere, still having an effect on the way people think and behave. The result may be benign, or it may not. It would be wrong to demonise Catholics and I do not intend to, but in the past it has tended to be a more autocratic religion than, say, liberal Protestantism and many Catholics have been perfectly happy with that, which in itself is fine. Some would say that liberalism is more likely by its nature to lose direction. And those for whom religion in any form had lost its appeal, because of the impact of Darwin, the growth of general scepticism, and the supposed mindlessness and heartlessness of the universe as revealed by the horrors of the Great War, but who still felt the need for some sort of authoritarian guiding force might well be driven to support a dictatorial but effective political party. Of course what we see here is a perversion of something which was not in itself necessarily wicked. Let go of God if you wish, but be careful what you put in His place.

Apart from genocide and the morality of certain types of warfare, issues whose discussion belongs as much to a book on moral philosophy as to one on history (where the former is concerned, the debate is not of course over whether it is *right*), the Second World War raises important questions to do with occupation, or the likelihood of it, and resistance. Where is the line to be drawn between collaboration with the invaders and simply doing what one would in any circumstances, or had no choice but to do? Indeed, to ask whether "collaboration" is ever justified may be to put the same question. And what about the alternatives? The issue is most vividly highlighted in the case of Marshal Petain, a military hero in World War One but leader of Vichy France in World War Two. Petain was always a character more inclined towards compromise than confrontation, as his handling of mutinies in the French army during the first conflict shows. He may also have felt, as did others, that it would go easier for France if the Germans were dealing with a respected national figure such as himself, who could act as a buffer. In short, though not everyone would agree, his actions can (conceivably) be defended. Someone else who I can't help thinking of in this whole context is Herge, the Belgian creator of Tintin, who attracted opprobrium for continuing to produce the cartoon strip in which the character appeared for a Nazi-controlled newspaper throughout the German occupation of his country. In my view his decision was wrong, though it comes over as movingly tragic that this man who wrote stories about an intrepid adventurer facing all manner of lurid perils found his own courage wavering when the crunch came; that he then chose not to fight injustice but to effectively co-operate with it. Would it have been more honourable for him to "run"? Actually, maybe it would. The dilemma was certainly faced by residents of the Channel Islands, the only part of Britain to be occupied during the war, once German invasion became imminent. Some chose to be evacuated while others didn't. It would have been patriotic to stay (there might also have been the thought, "If we leave the place entirely to the Germans, I don't like to think what they might do with it"), but forgiveable to go. If you had stayed, there would not have been much you could have done in the way of resistance, because of fear of punishment or the simple impracticality of resisting (one Jerseyman points out, "We couldn't have taken to the mountains because (a) we didn't have any weapons, and (b) we didn't have any mountains."). But if you went to England you could have helped the war effort there, and by extension everyone else who somewhere in the world was suffering because of the Nazis. One might view it rather cynically as a cover for cowardice, but because it had a rational justification this seems unfair. At worst it highlights the complexity of the issue. To illustrate what I mean, consider General de Gaulle staying behind in 1940 to lead the French resistance, but being captured and executed (had that happened).

For ordinary people there was a sensible code of conduct which enabled one to survive, though how often it was observed varied. If a German soldier greets you in an amiable way, a simple hand motion, combined with a brief smile and nod, neither necessarily unfriendly, rather than to overflow with warmth might be the best response. If you get into conversation with one, discover that you have a common interest in stamps, happen to mention that you have this or that rare album, and he asks, perhaps hesitantly, if he could see it refusing would come over as bolshy and be interpreted if it got out as unco-operativeness and rudeness towards the occupying forces, thus making things more difficult. What to me was undoubtedly wrong was the abuse inflicted on "Jerrybags", those women who formed romantic relationships with German soldiers. The women should have been careful − perhaps they were − not to tell their beaus anything which the latter might have felt it their duty to report. But those relationships happened because both the Germans and the people they ruled over were human. Though such a distinction is always going to be simplistic to some extent, the view in the Channel Islands today seems to be that the ordinary German was more or less a decent person, while his commanding officer very often was not. The most deplorable, and even "deplorable" seems an inadequate term when a life has been taken, case of injustice by the Occupation authorities was the execution of a Jersey woman for resisting the advances of one soldier, something she was entitled to do, while another who had thrown excrement at troops, which might have been thought far more an offence from the Germans' viewpoint, received only a prison sentence. It's this kind of thing which demonstrates to the world the necessity of defeating people like Hitler.

The final comment which I find myself making on the Second World War is that although politically it might be seen as a single (interrupted) conflict with the First, militarily it marked an intermediary stage between modern warfare in its earliest form, as in 1914-18, and the present situation. Because it was more mobile wider areas came under enemy occupation and so suffered the traumatic consequences of same. It was a highly intense conflict because of this mobility and because of new or vastly improved technologies. So there was particular scope for heroism and the creation of legends as people fought back in one way or another against the oppressor, if one sees it as that (it had of course its own stories to tell in the matter). This legend-building can still happen in today's world, it happens in all war, but not on so large a scale if armed conflict must either be a matter of localised, if nasty, engagements or, if it does come to the worst, someone pressing the red button. WMD as we shall see changed everything. One reason World War Two continues to excite so much interest is because we know there will never again be anything like it.

10

The First World War was not really that, being confined largely to continental Europe apart from some of the naval battles plus parts of the Middle East and operations against the German colonies in Africa. The Second was more of a global affair because of the need to defeat Japanese imperialism in the Far East, but there were still vast geographical areas, in Asia, sub-Saharan Africa and the Americas, which saw little fighting. But World War Two is the last case to date where conflicts within Europe could have a significant effect upon the international scene. Hereafter the continent ceased to be such a big player, unless Russia is counted as part of it (this would not have been the case if Hitler had managed to acquire nuclear weapons before anyone else, because of the capacity to destroy, and thus leverage, which they represent). As a result of what happened in just three years, the period from the turn of the tide at Stalingrad and El Alamein to Germany's final defeat, the focus of world politics shifted, as it had been gradually shifting already only the process had now been considerably accelerated. The two "world wars", the second happening as a result of the first, had exhausted Europe economically and thus destroyed her influence to a great extent. They left the Soviet Union and the United States, whose size, large populations and vast natural resources best equipped them to survive the strains of war, as the two dominant global powers – superpowers. Everyone else gravitated into their orbit where not simply refusing to take sides. Certainly no third power, with the possible exception after a time of China, could seriously challenge them, and alter the geopolitical status quo, once both had nuclear weapons as was the case from the late 1940s. Germany was not likely to be a threat as her economy and infrastructure had been totally shattered by the war and there were other reasons, too, why she wasn't going to start another one in a hurry. There was the stigma of having been instrumental (though she did not of course bear sole responsibility) in bringing about two world wars and a Holocaust. Secondly, she had suffered too much from the last war; an aspect of this was that after she had fought her enemies almost to the death there could be no more myths about stabs in the back, no sense that national pride needed to be avenged. Thirdly, she would simply not be allowed to cause any more trouble after all that had happened. Although it was not fair to regard her as more perverse than any other nation on earth, it is natural to be wary of any region of the body where there has several times been an infection, even if it has been cured. Germany remained under the rule of the victorious Allied powers until the Federal Republic was established in 1949. By then it was divided into two, the FR and the German "Democratic" Republic (East Germany), and this of course had the effect of further weakening it, reducing its ability to be aggressive supposing that it wanted to in the first place.

Now that Hitler was out of the way, Stalin established Soviet domination in Eastern Europe by engineering Communist takeovers in all those countries which had just been liberated from the Nazis or had avoided German occupation by supporting them. For those small and vulnerable nations one kind of tyranny was now being replaced by another which was only marginally better. They became Soviet satellite states where democracy was effectively done away with and any moves towards free speech ruthlessly suppressed, with the aid of Russian tanks if required. The only exceptions were Yugoslavia and Rumania, led by respectively Nicolae Ceausescu and Josip Broz (Tito), maverick figures following their own line in foreign policy who Moscow tolerated because they were, after all, Communist (and not democratic, it must be said). In optimum conditions, with a strong economy, plus her massive population, generally huge size and resources, and armed forces of the right quality Russia stood a chance in the absence of a nuclear deterrent of invading and occupying western Europe. But the optimum conditions have never all been present. (One would also have to assume American non-intervention, regardless of whether any conflict which did break out over a Russian push to the English Channel would have involved conventional or nuclear weapons. In 1945 both the Americans/British and the Russians were probably too exhausted by the effort of defeating Germany to take things any further.) Nor is it clear that she has ever seriously thought of doing it, threats apart. The motive behind Stalin's actions in the post-war period was the time-honoured one of self-protection through the creation of spheres of influence, something any country with the ability to do so seeks whatever ideology it is governed by. He also wanted to create a buffer zone against a resurgent Germany (nuclear weapons notwithstanding, old fears persisted), that power having been Russia's enemy in both world wars. Once it became apparent that the West was the greater threat from his point of view, his "empire-building" served a different purpose, beginning with the foundation of the Warsaw Pact.

Part of Stalin's strategy was the incorporation of Germany east of the line to which Russian forces had advanced by the end of the war into a Soviet-led Eastern Bloc. That they had been able to get so far has been called an indictment of Eisenhower, Commander-in-Chief Allied Forces, as military commander; it certainly made possible the appalling and vindictive treatment of the German civilian population by the vengeful Soviets. But had there emerged a less exact balance of power, geopolitically, between Russia and the West it is possible the former would have felt more threatened – perhaps, in the nuclear era, with catastrophic consequences, even if it was only a matter of what the East *thought* the West was going to do.

After recent history West Germany could do nothing other than behave, feeling prohibited from arguing its case too strongly on any issue. It was aptly described by one British newspaper as an economic giant but a political dwarf. It was through being the former that it expressed itself. Fortunately, calls by Stalin and others for its pastoralisation had been resisted, Western leaders appreciating in the end that such would fatally cripple Europe's economic recovery and learning from the lesson of the early 1920s when the effect of reparations had contributed to the post-World War One slump. There was also a certain feeling, after the massive devastation caused her by both the ground war and the Allied bombing, which resulted in appalling poverty and hardship, that Germany had been punished enough. She was to make amends by participating in a general economic rebuilding of Europe, the latter helped of course by cash injections from the USA (the Marshall Plan).

Militarily, West Germany was not in the mood or the position to refuse being firmly integrated into the new North Atlantic Treaty Organisation (NATO) set up in 1949; it wasn't as if there was any other option. She thus became a fundamental part of a new alliance system reflecting new geopolitical alignments. From 1955 NATO, consisting of the United States and the other Western (in a geographical or cultural sense) democracies and set up to counter what was seen as the potential Soviet threat to the free world, was faced by the Warsaw Pact countries (Russia and the East European satellites, the latter having little choice but to be members). As noted this order of things was reinforced by Russia and America's possession of nuclear weapons. (Along with Britain and France. Britain, reluctant to abandon her superpower status, or anything which might at least suggest she still had one, developed her own nuclear bomb in the 1950s although it was unlikely she would ever be able to use it without America's consent. France's independent nuclear deterrent was and is a symptom of a general desire to be one's own master, something also expressed by her withdrawal from NATO in 1966 (while remaining culturally tied to the other Western nations and unlikely to ever side with the Soviets). She was better able to pursue this semi-independent path by not being bound to America in a so-called "Special Relationship".)

The idea was that if one power bloc launched a nuclear attack against the other it would itself be annihilated in retaliation, and therefore wouldn't take the risk. Nor would a conventional war break out, in case it escalated into a nuclear one. This was the doctrine of MAD (Mutual Assured Destruction). The acronym delighted the nuclear disarmament lobby, who thought the whole business a (dangerous and expensive) waste of time. The mere existence of nuclear weapons produced tension and threatened the survival of civilisation as we knew it, if not the actual human race. And for what? Why have a weapon if you were never likely to use it because of the consequences (the situation was tautologous)? Even more, what was the point of having conventional weapons if they were never likely to be deployed because that might itself lead to a nuclear holocaust? Much better to spend the money allocated to the development of both conventional and nuclear arms on social services, say. One can see this point of view, but there are several things wrong with it. Weapons of mass destruction cannot be uninvented, and it is therefore better to have them out in the open. The way the psychology of the matter works is that no-one can be entirely *sure* they would not be used whatever the retaliation they might provoke, and so political leaders play safe by not doing anything which might result in first a conventional and then a nuclear (or, conceivably, just the latter) exchange. It might seem irrational but then human beings are, and in this case the irrationality serves a useful purpose. It does keep the peace, as is demonstrated by the non-occurrence of either a nuclear war, or a conventional one on the scale of World War One or Two, in the Northern Hemisphere during the last seventy-five years. The danger of course is that the weapons may eventually fall into the hands of someone who cannot be deterred, e.g. a religious fanatic who believes he is carrying out Armageddon in accordance with God's will. But they cannot be uninvented. Meanwhile, the best way to reduce the likelihood of a nuclear holocaust, if one does see it as likely, is by *mutual* arms reduction, as occurred under Reagan and Gorbachev, and by attempting to resolve the issues over which people might conceivably use WMD if they thought the stakes were high enough. It would not be wise to scrap the weapons altogether in case their deterrent effect was needed at some stage.

The absurdity of the Cold War, as the East-West divide and the heavily armed peace that resulted from it became known, lay not so much in neither side ever being likely to use the ultimate weapon at its disposal, if you understood the reasons for that, as the dichotomy between the threat each actually presented to the other and the reality. Perhaps it is easier to see this with hindsight. It was quite understandable if Stalin's behaviour in eastern Europe after the war raised fears in the West about Soviet aggression and led to the belief that he coveted Britain, France etcetera, if not America should that become possible, too. It was correct to say that one of the great European empires of the past still survived, in a different form, and was if anything extending its control. But this was essentially the creation of spheres of influence as was later to happen, in not quite the same way, but with both superpowers being involved, in Africa and Asia and Latin America. Russia always had to cope with the cost and administrative effort needed to govern her own vast territories, as well as keep her satellites in order, and economically could not have afforded to both militarily conquer Western Europe and hereafter maintain her domination of it whether directly or indirectly. This became especially true as the Soviet system increasingly stagnated over time. In some cases a whole campaign of invasion and occupation of other countries might actually stimulate a nation's economy, but this was not possible with the inflexible, decaying, too tightly-controlled socialist system where it would merely have produced further collapse. The West for its part would have found an invasion of Eastern Europe and Russia in order to liberate it for democracy economically extremely draining despite its greater prosperity. Waging war through proxies (something which, incidentally, could be viewed as helping lay the foundations of globalisation) was relatively less expensive as well as, since the proxies did not themselves possess atomic weapons, an alternative to risking nuclear Armageddon.

But in its different forms the Cold War was almost, if perhaps not quite, a case − maybe unique in history − of a whole geopolitical system, with all the hassle and expense involved in keeping it in being, arising from an innate human tendency to seek something to be afraid of, writ large. Even the preference for "spheres of influence" rather than outright conflict on a world scale would ultimately have played a limited part in furthering one side's aims against the other's without causing Armageddon. If it had encroached on the other's sphere sufficiently to genuinely threaten its interests, its prosperity and way of life, for example by creating a belt of Communist states who refused to trade with capitalist ones (supposing they wished to take things that far), the stakes would have been raised high enough to risk nuclear war anyway. A lot was about simple face-saving, and that is why America and Russia competed to have the largest nuclear arsenal. It could be dangerous in that it increased the probability of a holocaust occurring by accident, especially in a climate where the sabre-rattling made it *look* as if aggression was intended. I have already mentioned several times the age-old suspicion of other people's intentions, something you can't always be sure of. This fear leads to empire-building in order to be as strong and powerful, and so as safe, as possible. We can't shake off the feeling that if we abandoned all our weapons, conventional or nuclear, and our spheres of influence someone less altruistic than ourselves would take advantage of that to cause trouble, maybe threaten our liberties, even if there were practical difficulties involved for them in doing so. They probably would, though on what scale and in what way, and who "they" might be is hard to say exactly. But it would not have been a case of the Soviets attempting to invade and conquer the West. The important thing to understand is that that is not a good reason to be a Communist. Those left-wing people who were defensive of Russia did not necessarily act from ideological sympathy with her (though of course some did), but rather objected to the tendency of Western leaders to demonise her, as part of the Cold War sparring match, when their own countries and culture were far from perfect.

What produced the Cold War was a combination of the factor mentioned plus a mutual incomprehension and misunderstanding which became set in stone over time, though not unbreakably as it turned out. The nuclear and conventional stand-off which arose between the opposed power blocs was a kind of play-acting which effectively acquired the status of a ritual. Both sides maintained a large conventional arsenal because they felt naked without it; it was a more physically obvious and more public form of defence than a relatively small number of nuclear missiles hidden away at top secret locations. And of course, with any luck if a conventional war *did* break out it could achieve its objective without becoming a nuclear one. The point of threatening the latter was partly to avoid the former, but in the curious psychology of the whole business no-one minded this logical inconsistency. On the Soviet side the ideological conflict with the West was used as a means of keeping the existing regime in power, though more because they felt an instinctive psychological need to justify themselves in the eyes of those they governed than because they feared being overthrown by internal revolution, so tight was their grip. It has been claimed that the West acted from the same motives, but this suggestion is most likely to originate from those left-wingers who dislike the capitalist economic and political system anyway. Though it is valid to some extent – there was a lot of talk about defending our free society (in other words, the Western sociopolitical system as it currently existed) from the Communist enemy – and the West was certainly not without its faults, Westerners would have preferred their own way of life to the Soviet model because it didn't take a lot of common sense to see that it was freer and generated a lot more prosperity, even if sometimes this was only so in relative terms. With ordinary Russians the propaganda didn't work because over time, as information about what the West was really like gradually filtered through, they could see the difference too. It was partly the huge spending on defence which explained the misery of their lot; the Communist economic system could not fund a vast (if cumbersome and inefficient compared to Western forces) military machine and ensure high living standards for the average citizen at the same time.

Altogether, Communism had become simply a way of having an ideological identity, which would serve as a "sales pitch". The fact that the system was not democratic, with an electorate the leaders had to appease in order to stay in office, made it possible for the same personnel to retain power into old age, past the point where mature wisdom has become narrow-minded reaction against change (the same happened in China during the Mao years). Besides which revulsion at the excesses of Stalin, and Khrushchev's folly in taking the world to the brink of nuclear war in the Cuba crisis (he appeared to be prepared to go over it, though he may just have been bluffing in order not to lose face; all the same, I'm glad I missed the whole affair), had led to a more collective, bureaucratic leadership which avoided the dangers inherent in having a single strong man at the top but contributed further to ossification. It was not a system which encouraged involvement of the young, people with fresh ideas and reforming zeal. Basically, in Russia the Marxist system was by now just a means of keeping the existing elite in power. The contrast between this and those genuine Communists who might still be found in many places, and whom Moscow supported as part of the geopolitical power game, is ironic and bathetic, even grotesque. I am prepared to believe there could have been a few people in CND whose motive was to render the West defenceless in the event of war with Russia, so the latter could invade and impose Communism upon it. They received funds from Moscow, which after all had the money, though it was certainly not being spent on improving the ordinary Russian's quality of life. But they were being taken for a ride by people whose motives were no longer really ideological at all.

It is important also to appreciate that Communism became inseparably entangled with what was rather nationalism, despite the attempts by Marxists to draw a distinction between the two in practical terms. Communist countries, like all countries, were inevitably nationalist states whatever else they were, since no-one can entirely escape the pull of identification with a particular territory and polity. They therefore maintained that Communism was better for China, or Russia, or Vietnam, or wherever, as well as being a good thing in itself. National affiliation, divergences in the *way* Communism should it was thought be implemented, and the undesirability of creating national units that were too large to be governed effectively all worked against the political integration of Communist countries. And ethnic/national minorities were persecuted because either they were not considered a true part of the nation, which was a culturally damaging factor as well as entailing that loyalties were suspect, or because they were not as a people, defined by temperament and culture, thought likely to accept the changes Communism brought to established ways of life. Or both.

Technology had again revolutionised the nature of warfare and thus altered the world political situation. A new Hitler, whatever his precise war aims, would have had to take on both the West and the Soviet Union, the task proving impossible even if neither had possessed WMD. As it was the latter (which only Russia, America, France and Britain had) allowed the East-West divide to determine the whole global geopolitical order. No third party could attack both blocs, or for that matter one bloc in support of the other, without massive penalties which it could not afford to incur. At different times Japan had seemed a threat both to Russia and to the West. She never actually intended to invade either, for it would have been beyond her resources, but was rather concerned to assert herself as an imperial power of at least equal status to them in the regions where countries sought colonies (in all the justified outrage at her treatment of captured British soldiers in the Second World War, it is I suppose worth noting that those soldiers had been defending what were essentially colonial possessions, although Britain's imperialism was a far less brutal affair on the whole). She did perhaps covet Australia, and if successful would have given us the rare, in fact more or less unique, spectacle of a predominantly white nation conquered and occupied by a non-white one, though the only thing we can really say with certainty as to what this would have been like is embodied in the word "nasty". As with the Mongols and mediaeval Europe, however, she never got that far. And the manner of her defeat in 1945, the devastation caused by the atomic bombs dropped on Hiroshima and Nagasaki, put her off the idea of war probably forever. Plus, the defeat and subsequent occupation had been at the hands of the West, which set the initial conditions for the new post-war democratic Japan, and was a culture she had in the past admired if ambiguously at times. Consequently Japan became integrated firmly into the Western economic system, participation in which expressed the way her own society had developed. Culturally, now the militarism of a General Tojo (or which he did not do enough to restrain) had been discredited, she was back to a situation, still prevailing today, where she admired and often imitated the West while in many ways being as different from it as was possible to imagine. Additionally there was shame and embarrassment at treatment of Allied POWs, not to mention atrocities committed against the Chinese during the invasions of 1931 and 1937, even if, due to the Oriental culture, this was expressed in terms of "regret" rather than an apology. Most certainly, Japan was not after one brush with the atom bomb likely to risk annihilation by courting another.

China, with her huge size, population etcetera probably had the means to forcibly annex other countries in addition to Tibet, in which she had long had an interest, and the Nationalist enclave of Taiwan, but her industrial resources would first need to be developed properly. That task, whether or not its ultimate aim was world domination, along with the associated political upheavals kept China preoccupied in these years. I'm not convinced an occupation of Britain, the US or indeed most other places would have been on her agenda even if it had been feasible. Mao did sometimes talk as if China was going to rule the world, but *plus ca change*; this was no more than the kind of attitude expressed by her rulers in previous centuries, when their belief was in essence that they did rule the world but such was their natural superiority, which ought to be self-evident, over everyone else that they didn't need to assert their status. It was of course little more than a conceit but it did become true, in a sense, later on and this was – is – by no means to everyone's liking. Meanwhile there was periodic tension with Russia, whose line Mao was not prepared to obsequiously follow, but this resulted only in border scuffles.

Nuclear weapons did not prevent the breaking out of localised wars outside a geographical region encompassing Europe, Russia and the United States, and there were to be many of these. In nature they could be just as terrible as the First and Second World Wars. Sometimes it was a case of the superpowers waging war by proxy, the only way they could safely do it in the nuclear age, as in Korea which was the only occasion Russians and Americans actually engaged each other (mainly as pilots) in direct military combat. Each superpower would back one side or the other (to the extent of sending military advisers or combat personnel, plus hardware and cash) in an attempt to stake out a sphere of influence for itself in what came to be called the Third World. For the USA and Soviet Union it was a logical extension (logical extension explains much about the Cold War) of the Great Game they were playing.

The choice for any given nation of the world was whether to follow the Western sociopolitical and economic model – that is, "democratic" capitalism – the Communist one as supposedly typified by Russia and, from 1949, China, or be "non-aligned". This included former colonies of the European powers; for Europe could no longer afford colonies after the devastation of the Second World War had just about bankrupted her. The Japanese seizure of Hong Kong and Singapore in 1942 could be seen, like the outcome of the 1904-5 Russo-Japanese War, as the writing on the wall in that they demonstrated the West was not invulnerable and could be bested by so-called "inferior" races. Although in Japan's actual case it didn't amount to that much, since she became so drawn into the Western orbit, the lesson was almost certainly a general encouragement in the long run to others. But the other significance of the war for the issue of colonialism was that it made it impossible for the West to permanently recover what it had lost, or to hang on to what it still had. In retrospect the enlargement of the British and French Empires after the First World War by assumption of power over territories in the Middle East (e.g. Palestine, Iraq, Syria) formerly "belonging" to the Ottoman Empire, which had finally collapsed, seems like an Indian summer. It was a combination of the draining effect of the wars on national finances and greater restiveness on the part of the colonised – the only territories which wanted to remain so were very small islands in the Pacific who had not much scope for striking out as independent nations anyway – which clinched matters. Often the leaders of independence movements were people who had been educated in the West and benefited from it; given the wrongness of colonialism, certainly after people have made clear they no longer want it, this cannot be seen as ingratitude even though, somehow, it still seems to come over that way. It's not in the same category as an Islamic terrorist with British or American nationality using the knowledge they have gained in their adopted countries of computers to plan atrocities against their fellow citizens.

Between the 1940s and the 1970s scores of territories in Asia, Africa and the Caribbean achieved their independence, sometimes with bloodshed as the imperial power sought to retain them, as France did in Vietnam and Algeria, sometimes peacefully. These new countries had to decide on their future mode of government. Some went Communist, though they did not necessarily take their orders from Moscow. Others sought close and friendly relations with their former colonial overlords – in a sense being drawn into a position of new subservience to them, since it is those who are most experienced in operating a given economic system, and therefore most prosperous among the nations subscribing to it, who call the shots. Economically, you were either Communist or capitalist (you might be the latter, receiving Western aid and produce, but not democratic). Politically at any rate it was possible to be non-aligned, though that might depend on how powerful you were.

It was certainly possible for China. She could be accurately called a developing nation, and until recently was described as the most powerful one in the "Third World". The latter term was intended to mean the world other than the United States and her European allies, on one side, and the Eastern Bloc on the other. It did not necessarily amount to the same thing as "non-aligned", since those booming capitalist nations of the Far East, the "Asian Tigers" as they later became known, were firmly integrated of their own choosing into the ultimately US-dominated world capitalist system, while those countries anywhere who were receiving aid from Moscow could be said to have aligned with the Soviet Union even though relations with it might not always be smooth (it might of course be supporting rebel groups, who were Marxist, rather than the government itself, which was not). China, too big to militarily occupy as the colonising powers of the late nineteenth and early twentieth century had concluded, was able to pursue its own course. That course was Communist, though Chinese Communism was not quite the same thing in concept or execution as Russian Communism. The Communists triumphed largely because of the lamentable incompetence, as administrators and political tacticians, of their chief rivals, the Kuomintang or Nationalist party of Chiang Kai-Shek. One can't help thinking that Christian politicians like Chiang and, earlier, Sun Yat-Sen, though they might have been going to Heaven (Mao probably was not, bearing in mind the Cultural Revolution) were no match for more practical, and more ruthless, figures who had the cunning to successfully exploit the weaknesses of their opponents. Mao was one such personality (it helped, in his own case, if you were physically a lot taller than nearly everyone around you, as it had helped Henry VIII). He believed that "political power grows out of the barrel of a gun"; this was cynical but probably correct, since even in the West, where democracy had for the most part triumphed by the early twentieth century, there lingers the suspicion that "if voting changed anything they'd abolish it" – which I think means that if it meant doing too many things the politicians considered impractical, or were simply not to their liking, because they had lost the ability to manage the system, they would find some excuse to ditch it for dictatorship. Mao certainly stamped his will on his country in a way which may have done more harm than good. He believed characteristic Chinese traditionalism was holding back the country's progress so he ruthlessly eradicated it in a bonfire of time-honoured social forms, killing anyone who stood in his way. The population loss actually hindered the cause of progress. For China's economic boom to really take off his heavy hand needed to be removed and eventually was, by old age and death; afterwards it took a long time for her to recover from the trauma inflicted during the years of his rule.

Something needs to be said about Europe proper during the Cold War era. The alliance system had caused World War One, and to a certain extent World War Two, and was now discredited as a means of achieving peace within the sub-continent. Hence the move towards pooling sovereignty in a supranational body, the European Economic Community as it was originally known. It was essentially collective security in a different form. Basically it arose from a desire to prevent the two most powerful nations on the mainland of Western Europe, France and Germany, from going to war again, their animosity to one another having been to some extent the cause of the conflicts of 1914-18 and 1939-45. But for the best results, it had to include everyone. What was previously unthinkable because it went so much against contemporary mindsets was now no longer so. The only alternative to the alliance system was now being gradually adopted (within Europe itself, that is; most countries there were part of a wider geopolitical arrangement, that is NATO ranged against the Warsaw Pact).

It had certainly to be an economic union, because once you have seen the benefits of making trade common property you will not jeopardise prosperity by going to war with your partners in it. But it was inevitably, and not without design, going to become something more at some point. Economic union in effect means political union, in proportion to the degree to which the former occurs, on the principle that whoever pays the piper, even if the funds are held communally, calls the tune, and political union is ultimately necessary if there are to be no single powers with the ability to upset things by aggressive behaviour. Hence the European Coal and Steel Community led to the European Economic Community and then the European Union (What kind of union? Note the chilling absence of the word "economic" in the title). Remarks by Jean Monnet and Robert Schumann, well-meaning founders of the ECSC, indicate that economic integration was intended to lead to political sooner or later, though it is not clear whether everyone who was involved in the process saw it in that light. It is unlikely whether Britain would have gone along with it if she had, partly because she was not sure she needed to be involved anyway. True, she was bound to be looking for a new role in the world now that her Empire was fast disintegrating, and the retreat from colonialism at least suggested an orientation towards Europe. (The Suez debacle was a psychological watershed, ramming home the point that things were different now. Suez was an ill-advised attempt to reassert supposed British world prominence rather than an international initiative, in which Britain would have been participated, aimed at ensuring, by economic sanctions if necessary, that Colonel Nasser made the Suez Canal available to other countries as a trade route and on reasonable terms. This approach would have allowed Britain to retreat from Empire with dignity; as it was, though Nasser was always inclined to gloat over her relative decline, and he did, Eden's impulsiveness and botched attempt to turn back the clock allowed him to take the moral high ground. When the ghost of Suez was finally laid, it had necessarily to be on the much smaller scale of the Falkland Islands.)

But at this time Britain's economy still looked strong enough to survive on its own, as arguably it was subsequently. The economic benefits of joining the Community were at least debatable. As for the appeal of the EEC as a means of avoiding future wars in Europe, that was less strong for Britain because she had always felt, as an island and as a maritime nation whose power and prosperity had traditionally derived from overseas trade and colonies, psychologically distanced from her neighbours on the continent. She could conceivably have kept out of both the general European wars, although there were good reasons why in the end she did not. Should she not now be focusing instead on her close ties with the USA? In the end she did join the Community, but it was an unhappy association which culminated in the "Brexit" vote of 2016.

If it was an attempt to guarantee European peace the EEC was a pointless exercise anyway, because everything had become so subsumed within, and dictated by, the East-West alignment of the superpowers. The alliance system was back with a vengeance and potentially even more destructive than before, as it involved possession of nuclear, perhaps chemical and biological, weapons! However, the deterrent effect of the WMD meant there would no longer be wars spanning continents, because sooner or later they would involve a country that had nuclear armaments. Wars *within* continents were a possibility, but that would not include Europe where both Britain and France had nuclear deterrents, meaning one was unlikely to risk going to war with the other; and nobody else did, including Germany, not allowed to possess WMD in any case because of her recent history and who would therefore not contemplate what clearly amounted to suicide. The deciding factor behind the ECSC and EEC was the sheer psychological impact, the horror and grief and guilt and remorse, of two wars in which modern technology had allowed the devastation to be especially extensive and shattering in nature. They felt they simply had to do it. And there is the question of whether the European Union acts as a useful model for supranational organisations, of a formal political nature, in the post-Cold War era (given its current difficulties, the answer could conceivably be "no"). But in the long run, and without us fully realising it, it is nuclear weapons which have kept the peace in Europe and not the EU. (Those stationed on European soil, and the whole US military infrastructure there, plus the fact that it would have been a Soviet invasion of Western Europe, America's principal ally, that triggered any Third World War constituted the region's main geopolitical importance in these years).

The third option where geopolitical arrangements are concerned is a single world government. The League of Nations was not that, nor was the United Nations which replaced it from 1945. The impracticality of such an organisation, plus a continuing desire for national sovereignty to be preserved, ruled it out. Only in Europe, because of the wars which had taken place there, was there any attempt to create anything like a single *regional* power; bodies such as the Organisation for African Unity have not attempted to bring about political integration the way the EU has. On the subject of the UN, it has lasted longer than the League of Nations did and has perhaps proved more useful, although again it is the nuclear factor rather than collective security which has overall kept global peace, at least before 1991. The trouble is that no-one is going to abide by its rulings if they don't actually agree with them and therefore think the consequences of doing so would be negative. Great power influence, the weight a nation's economic and military resources give it in world affairs, determines what really happens on the global stage, as before. The UN's most valuable role, apart from its cultural ones, is as a mediator in disputes, bringing warring sides together and hopefully working out a lasting peace settlement between them; in this way it serves as a convenient way of solving problems without anyone losing face.

From the early 1970s another alternative means of waging war, besides using proxies in struggles over spheres of influence, emerged in terrorism. The terrorists might be acting more or less on their own or they might be state-sponsored. Where the latter, the terrorism was a means for small countries (e.g. Colonel Gaddafi's Libya) to retaliate against what they saw as oppression by larger ones, whose conventional military forces they could not hope to overcome. By means of sabotage, murder, assassination and hostage-taking, terrorists sought to change the political situation in either the world at large or a particular part of it. Blowing up airliners, or hijacking them and threatening to kill the crew and passengers unless some at least of one's demands were met became a favourite tactic in the age of mass air travel. Terrorism had been around in one form or another since early times, but now modern science and technology, which enabled anyone with enough knowhow and resourcefulness to construct a bomb, had given it new opportunities. How far it actually succeeded in its objectives was debatable. Compared to guerrilla warfare, into which it might blend with the distinction between the two becoming hazy, and which was more like conventional military activity, its efficacy can be said to have been limited. It always looked a cowardly way of doing things especially as the target so often had to be innocent civilians, since terrorism was not the same thing as conventional war, where there was perhaps more scope for acting honourably, and military objectives would be too well-protected. By its nature it could do little more than inflict pinpricks, if rather nasty ones. And it might only stiffen the resistance to it of both the public and the governments of other countries (or the host country, if the conflict was internal), in whose eyes its methods – or even its aims – were inevitably discredited. Its principal achievement, although one does not like to give it the credit, was to focus attention on the issues which gave rise to it, but that is not the same thing as solving them. Otherwise, it had a geopolitical significance in that those nations believed to be sponsoring it became pariahs, at least in the eyes of the terrorists' victims.

This could lead to such incidents as the 1986 US bombing of Libya, which was tragic in that it killed a number of civilians instead of Colonel Gaddafi. But usually it was an unequal contest; the guilty state was employing terrorist methods because it was not powerful enough to wage a proper war. So in normal conditions terrorism is unlikely to cause a global conflict in the sense of two or more powers fighting one another militarily across a wide geographical area with the risk of bringing in more countries, especially if one party has nuclear weapons (which so far terrorists have thankfully failed to get their hands on) and the other doesn't. This certainly couldn't have happened in the Cold War era because the principal factor in world politics, determining how the others operated, was the East-West divide, and the states sponsoring terrorism would not have included Russia or her East European allies because it would have been taking too big a risk of serious superpower confrontation if they were found out. Iran, which was larger and more geopolitically important than Libya because of her greater oil reserves, might have been another matter. But if, as some think likely, she carried out the 1988 Lockerbie bombing in revenge for the shooting down (as a result of error, perhaps heavy-handedness, rather than deliberate intent to murder) of one of her airliners by the American warship *Vincennes* a few months previously, she appears for the very reason we have been talking about (plus relative unfamiliarity with the techniques and infrastructure of terrorism) to have employed a proxy, most likely a Palestinian terror group.

Terrorism of course acquired a new political significance in 2001, because of the particular nature of the "9/11" attacks; but we will come to that later.

Perhaps the most important of the host of terrorist organisations to emerge in the 1970s and 80s were the Palestinian ones, because of the issue which gave rise to them and which they had the effect of drawing attention to. In the Cold War period there was one regional conflict which because of its nature might, especially when the superpowers got involved, have transcended the consequences of the East-West duality for world affairs, and catastrophically. It all stemmed from the sufferings of a particular people over thousands of years, and the mindset produced by the cumulative effect of the latter in some of them. Like the Cold War itself it was a product of the 1939-45 holocaust. The Nazi attempt to completely wipe out the Jews of Europe, resulting in the extermination of some six million of them, was seen as the final straw, after so many massacres and persecutions. Those Jews who had not been safe from the horror in the victorious or neutral nations and therefore felt it most keenly, if they had survived but lost relatives or been worked almost to death in labour camps, now wanted a place where they would be protected from any repetition of it. The logical choice was their ancestral homeland in Palestine, which had the advantage of being emotionally appealing. Tough immigration laws, themselves due partly to anti-Semitism, prevented them taking up residence in Britain or the US – which could be viewed as a serious mistake, though naturally Israelis are grateful for it, on those countries' part in view of the consequences to the world of what happened instead. This was accompanied by, and helped to explain, a feeling that the British and Americans had not done enough to help in or before the war, even though they had admittedly been instrumental in defeating Hitler and so preventing an even bigger *Shoah*.

The trouble was, of course, that in the meantime there had grown up in Palestine a substantial Arab population which would feel its status and identity to be threatened by large-scale Jewish settlement. There had already been some in recent years, and it was substantial enough to cause serious rioting, where there had previously been peace between the two races, in 1936; a demonstration that in racial conflicts it is numbers, rather than mere differences, which cause the trouble. Whether if there had been no Holocaust the immigration would still have continued, with the same consequences that it eventually did have, we cannot say. But after the war it became a flood which could not be held back. The Arabs resisted and a period of guerrilla warfare began between the two sides. Britain, which had acquired a mandate over the region – at best, a poisoned chalice – in the Treaty of Versailles after the First World War had the thankless of task of trying to keep order and as often happens in such cases was blamed by each side for not giving it what it wanted. It was a particularly unhappy episode in British imperial history, which ended in both tkragedy and humiliation for the occupying power, who was forced to make an ignominious withdrawal having suffered such things as the blowing up or hanging (or both, though in the right order of course) of her troops by Jewish terrorists (Arab ones proved equally murderous, note). At one point the division of Palestine between Arab and Jewish territories, which might in some ways have been the right solution, was proposed. As with other historical questions there are conflicting accounts of events; some insist that it was the Arabs who wrecked everything by failing to accept partition, others the Jews. I won't go into the rights and wrongs of the matter as I have done so adequately elsewhere. It will suffice to re-emphasise that the Arabs were originally a nomadic people who changed to a settled existence and the logic of this meant that land became all-important in their psyche. It now seemed to have been taken from them. They might in any case have been unhappy at the presence of a large, perhaps growing, Jewish population on their doorstep, fearing that in the future it might make further territorial demands. As it is, we know what happened in 1946-8 and what the consequences, including for the world at large, have been.

The trouble was that as a symbol of Jewish defiance of anti-Semitism, which it was, Israel was sacrosanct both to Israelis themselves and to a significant number of Diaspora Jews, who feared that its destruction would give encouragement to anti-Semites everywhere (and so it would, although this wouldn't necessarily have led to a repeat of the Holocaust, and I suspect there are many people who, if Israel were somehow to be destroyed, would while not being underjoyed nonetheless go on respecting Jews in general as they would anyone else). The West, while hostile to the prospect of her creation, pragmatically decided to regard it as a *fait accompli* once it had happened, as a matter of *Realpolitik*. I think there was little other option. The Arabs, of course, were not so objective. The logic of accepting Israel's existence required that she receive aid where necessary and be helped to defend herself against her enemies, as in the 1973 Yom Kippur War. To the Arabs this looked like conniving at an unjust state of affairs. It led to both Israelis themselves and Israel's chief protector, America – whose Presidents were motivated by awareness of the electoral weight of pro-Israeli Jews in the US, plus, when it became obvious that she had nuclear weapons, a need as the world's policemen to consider what Israel might do if left with her back entirely to the wall – being the target of terrorist attacks. Terrorism became the principal means of striking against Israel after the Arabs had twice, in 1967 and 1973, failed to destroy her militarily. The attacks, carried out by diaspora Palestinians with the support of Arab nations hostile to Israel, such as Libya and Syria, continued throughout the 1970s and 80s. Their culmination was probably the 1988 bombing of Pan Am flight 103 over Lockerbie in Scotland, unless one believes the atrocity was carried out by Libya purely out of revenge for the 1986 US attack on Tripoli (I do not, as you'll see). After Lockerbie, the shock it caused (though not to those who knew it was going to happen in advance, if the rumours that they did are true) and its exposure of serious weaknesses in airport security this kind of hit became much harder to pull off (later, of course, it was realised that a hijacked aircraft could itself be used as a bomb, if you were prepared to kill yourself in the process). Terrorist attacks in general continued, but in new forms and with new players at the game, who in some ways were more deadly, replacing the old.

It is worth saying a little more on the subject of Lockerbie. Until the even more horrific events of 9/11 which, unfortunately in many ways, have diverted attention from it it was the worst ever terrorist atrocity perpetrated against the West. Originally the suspects were Iran and Ahmed Jibril's Syrian-backed PFLP-GC (Popular Front for the Liberation of Palestine (General Command)), which split from the more moderate Popular Front for the Liberation of Palestine in what seems like the beginnings of a fragmentation akin to the fate of the Judean People's Liberation Front in Monty Python's *Life Of Brian*. After Saddam Hussein, with his annexation of Kuwait, became in the eyes of the West a threat to international security, and they needed allies against him attention switched to Libya, two of whose nationals were eventually extradited for trial in Holland. One of the accused was acquitted and the other sentenced to life imprisonment, to be freed a few years later on health grounds. There remains a significant body of opinion which maintains that the wrong country was fingered and that the trial was a stitch-up or at any rate left too many questions unanswered. It is correct.

Libya undoubtedly had a motive for Lockerbie, which suited her all the more for the role of patsy, and it is unlikely Colonel Gaddafi shed any tears on the West's account, though that does not mean she did it. But after the 1986 attacks on Tripoli Gaddafi, out of prudence, was much less inclined to sponsor terrorism. Lockerbie was two-and-a-half years after Tripoli, but only six months after the *Vincennes* incident. In the Iranian case anger would have been a lot fresher, more likely to supply a dynamic, an impetus, for what happened. If the bomb had been of the same type as that then favoured by the PFLP-GC (several examples of which were found when police raided a house in Frankfurt being used by members of the group a couple of months before) it would have exploded 38 minutes into the flight, which it did. (Additionally, I understand that Iran Air Flight 655 was shot down four days before a certain Muslim festival; Lockerbie was four days before Christmas).

Altogether, it makes far more sense to believe the bombing was carried out by the PFLP-GC on behalf of Iran than that it was carried out by Libya. The evidence for Libyan involvement is deeply flawed at best, as an analysis of the 2000-2001 trial makes clear. There is no evidence at all for the perpetrators being the Abu Nidal Group (Abu Nidal allegedly claimed responsibility shortly before he died, but all sorts of people have claimed responsibility for Lockerbie, or pointed the finger at this or that person/group, whether they are deluded conspiracy theorists or terrorists delighting in confusing and taunting their traditional enemies). I think Iran made use of the PFLP-GC's expertise in planning terrorist acts and constructing explosive devices. PFLP members bought the materials used to pack the bomb in Malta, where the group had a cell, as a decoy, and the fact that there had been PFLP activity in Frankfurt might have inclined people to think it had got into the system at the airport there, when in fact it went on at Heathrow through the simple device of taking advantage of chaotic security. The culprit was an Iranian airline official who would have been aware of conditions there and also worked for his country's secret service. Malta being geographically much closer to Libya than Frankfurt or London, it was easy to make a case for Libyans having been involved in the business. They supposedly put the bomb on a connecting flight to Frankfurt. But expecting it to pass through security at *three* airports was surely taking an implausible risk, whatever the situation at each. It should be stressed that the other anti-Western, anti-Israeli, terrorist-supporting nations of the Arab/Muslim world were quite prepared to let the Gaddafi regime, which they did not have much regard for, take the rap. When, at a conference of regional leaders, Gaddafi proposed shooting down the pro-Western King Hussein of Jordan's private plane with a ground-to-air missile even President (Hafez) Assad of Syria rejected the scheme as stupid and childish − in other words, typical of him.

The PFLP-Iran trail was only abandoned when events in the Gulf region necessitated a new geopolitical alignment. Iran and Syria were required to be at least neutral in any war with Saddam; in other words they had to be regarded as (more or less) friendly countries, and actively prosecuting them for state-sponsored terrorism would clearly be inconsistent with that. It was *Realpolitik*, and I am afraid it was justified in view of the outcome had things been otherwise. At the risk of seeming heartless they could have been much worse than the deaths of 270 people at Lockerbie. The exact consequences if rapprochement with Syria and Iran had not occurred are difficult to estimate but according to the logic of the matter, and human behaviour needs to be governed by logic if public affairs are not to be conducted on an arbitrary basis with possibly disastrous results any coalition (by commission or omission) against Saddam would work better if relations were cordial. Besides, if the new Middle Eastern *détente* had broken down conflict might have arisen, or been heightened, between the US and Syria/Iran, and this would have rendered vastly worse a situation where Saddam had to be dealt with as well. The instability, and consequent loss of life, would overall have been far greater than occurred at Lockerbie on 21st December 1988. The politicians involved in the cover-up were not demons; but they were debased, as politicians are by their scheming and chicanery, through having to orchestrate such a whitewashing and the browbeating (on the one hand) and evasion (on the other) which by extension is necessary for it to succeed. It is one reason why I am not a politician. Though the view of the general public, as the years went by, was probably that one needed to "move on", in targeting Libya for Lockerbie there was also a desire, partly political and partly, in a way distorted by the pragmatism to which we have referred, altruistic, to appease the Lockerbie families (especially the American ones some of whom, with respect to them, have in my view been far more vengeful and obsessive than the British) by making it look as if something was being done. It is understandable if they are out for blood, so to speak. But the psychological need to see *someone* punished for the murder of their loved ones blinded a number of them to any suggestion that an innocent man had been framed.

After the fall of Saddam you might have thought the considerations which led to the coverup would cease to apply, but there were several reasons why the establishment chose to try to perpetuate it. The politicians are seeking to preserve the reputation and (apparent) respectability of a system, and not only their own positions while they hold them, and are fearful of the consequences for stability and order should it become discredited (an open admission of deceit and/or serious error proving more likely to have that effect than it being obvious anyway to discerning people that the truth was being suppressed, such is the curious nature of human psychology). Secondly, despite the disaster he had suffered in 1991 it could not be absolutely guaranteed that Saddam would not cause trouble again, and if he did it was best that he was surrounded by powers who would assist the West by either offering her active support or at least not having their own issues with her.

Syria herself was becoming a part of a new world order which the US did not want to upset, partly because it desired the credit for helping bring it about. The fall of the Soviet Union and the opportunities it seemed to present for a better global polity created a spirit of change which permeated all sorts of areas. Also it appeared that some progress had been made on the Arab-Israeli question, with the peace moves initiated by Norway after the Palestinian *intifada* seemed to highlight the necessity for it; in line with the new climate that was developing Hafez Assad had actually on one occasion mentioned Israel, as opposed to "the Zionist entity", by name. Towards the end of Bill Clinton's second term as US President he and Assad met in a bridge-building exercise, although the film clips suggest they did little but smile at one another rather awkwardly. Though the peace process fizzled out in the end, the psychological effect of there being for a time a new mood of optimism and accommodation meant that nobody wanted to return to the situation which had prevailed in the previous two decades and of which they were perhaps becoming tired. And again, there was the emergence (most spectacularly in the original World Trade Centre bombing of 1993) of new forms of terrorism to which the regimes in Damascus and Tehran did not necessarily subscribe. Neither America nor her former enemies in the Middle East wanted to complicate matters by resuming their old quarrels. The cause of obtaining justice for the Lockerbie victims suffered from, among other things, changing circumstances. It might be to further upset the new order for the sake of the old.

Nonetheless, there is every point in still probing, in keeping the issue alive, as this makes it more likely that should it become possible one day to reveal the truth about Lockerbie, or even make new arrests, such will happen. Meanwhile I suppose the West has had rather a raw deal over the whole affair. America did eventually compensate relatives of the passengers on Flight 655, though without issuing an official apology. Libya compensated the Lockerbie families, but was not a guilty party. Iran has never admitted responsibility for the bombing of Pan Am Flight 103. The best course of action, if anyone was going to prosecute her at all, would have been for her to have handed over those at her end who commissioned it while America both offered compensation and apologised for the *Vincennes* affair. But Iran could reasonably have objected to this as lopsided; there is a difference between having to pay compensation and say sorry and being put in prison for life. Captain William C Rogers III, the warship's commander, was arguably guilty, if not of murder, then of manslaughter. It emphasises the complexity of the whole Lockerbie affair, in terms of the latter's moral and legal ramifications. *Private Eye* recently referred disparagingly to one Lockerbie conspiracy theorist as "the self-styled Professor of Lockerbie Studies". Actually, for a university to have one is not so daft an idea as it might seem, given the nature of the whole intricate and problematical business, in all its aspects. It serves as a test case for all kinds of questions.

In recent decades the West has been fortunate enough to remain comparatively stable, prosperous and safe from external aggression. But in a flawed, and also interconnected world Westerners cannot expect to avoid suffering altogether or be assured that when it is caused deliberately the wrongdoing will be punished. It would probably be best for relatives of the dead of Lockerbie to accept that they will probably not get the full justice they seek in *this* life, not least because those who could have been involved in carrying out the atrocity, or covering it up, are dying off. In the meantime, all we can do is get on with living as happily as we can, in defiance of those whose hatred led them to cause suffering to others. And also to work for greater understanding between the West and the Middle East (it is extremely alarming that Iran thought the shooting down of Flight 655 to be *deliberate*, rather than reckless, and specifically timed in order to mar the abovementioned religious festival) in such a way as to generally minimise the likelihood of horrors like Lockerbie, in so far as one can in our darkening world.

Some good, in terms of combating terrorism, did come out of the decision to put a lid on the question of Syria's complicity, through harbouring the PFLP-GC, in Lockerbie. Syria and the US were united by a common alarm at the behaviour of Saddam Hussein and if this was the case, and Syria was relying on US military power to neutralise the threat he seemed to present, then Damascus had to be friendly or at least non-hostile towards America. Part of this package was a certain accommodation with Israel, support of whom was a vital ingredient of American foreign policy. So Syria ceased to sponsor groups like the PFLP-GC, who became less of a threat as a result. They were also, as noted, frozen out to a greater or lesser extent by the new boys. They had been essentially political organisations, designed to bring about political change, in a particular part of the world and it was only by extension, in pursuit of the aim in question, that they operated on an international basis, blowing up Israeli airliners and also attacking US targets because of America's pro-Israel policies. They were not concerned with fomenting worldwide Islamic revolution. Operating from Lebanon, the PFLP-GC continued to supply arms to Palestinian militants because for Ahmed Jibril Israel would always demand to be destroyed whatever happened, but he confined his activities to the region itself since he did not wish to be identified/confused with the newer, and in some ways nastier, Islamic-based groups which internationally were doing what he, Abu Nidal etc. had been doing before on the same level. He and Nidal would have been just a couple of drops in a wider ocean whose waters had been contaminated by elements even they were alarmed by and uncomfortable with. But one thing is clear; were it not for the Palestinian issue Lockerbie and a whole host of other terrorist incidents might never have happened, because the groups who carried them out would not have existed.

The Arab-Israeli conflict matters because for reasons given there is nothing Israel would not do if it was necessary to ensure her own continued existence, whatever the cost to others. The mere fact that she is prepared for Westerners to suffer in her defence is proof of this. To be fair, I am not convinced all Zionist diaspora Jews would support her if it came to a straightforward choice between her survival and that of the rest of the world. Their seeking to ensure that she gets what she wants (which isn't necessarily the same thing as her surviving at all, though she might think so) is probably partly due to an awareness of the dangers to the planet at large of upsetting her. But she is certainly prepared to risk others in what she believes to be her interests. And maybe even risk herself – the Samson option. It is claimed that the world came close to nuclear war between America and the Soviet Union in 1973 because America backed Israel and Russia the Arabs. If this is true, it begs the question. But there was probably a greater danger of Israel using her own nuclear weapons, once they were fully developed, if she felt sufficiently threatened. Since none of her enemies has them and would therefore not take silly risks the situation would be unlikely to arise. If an enemy were to *acquire* WMD, not necessarily with the aim of attacking her, the same would apply. Would she however launch a pre-emptive strike out of paranoia? And are people like Islamic State deterrable anyway? Whatever happens, nobody who is in their right mind wants to take any chances. (It is still possible to commit terrorism against Israel. But the most dangerous of the forms it takes is HAMAS firing rockets into her territory from Lebanon, and a localised nuclear attack to deal with the threat is not yet possible without inflicting too much damage on herself, as well as being one step too far in the eyes of world opinion, which is already concerned at the effects, already seen, of conventional military responses by her.)

As for the Palestinians, one feels they have too often failed to show the right response to the situation. Their own behaviour has been brutal and thuggish (though this doesn't of course apply to a Hanan Ashrawi or Edward Said) and lost them a great deal of sympathy. In particular the murder of Leon Klinghoffer, an old man in a wheelchair, on the *Achille Lauro* simply because he was a Jew sticks in the mind. One of their leaders, referring to the particular horror and sadness of a successful airline bombing, once commented "Trap people on a plane with a bomb, then when it goes off the Palestinian cause dies with them". Their internal squabbles and faction fighting have not helped. Enough of them have been sufficiently corrupt to abandon the cause and work for Mossad or the CIA in return for money. The spirit of T E Lawrence probably bemoans the creation of Israel as an injustice against the Arabs, though of course we can't know for sure. But he must also despair at their own conduct. His comment in the David Lean film that unless they get their act together and stop fighting one another they will always be "a silly people" who the world won't take seriously is certainly true in the case of the Palestinians, and the lesson is one they have yet to learn.

Before we conclude this analysis of the shape the world had assumed by the time the next cataclysmic event, the revolution (as it can accurately be called) in the Eastern Bloc during 1989-91, occurred we need to consider a development which in some respects foreshadowed elements of what was to become the new global order. Whether it was a primary nexus point of history or a secondary, but still crucially important, one is a matter of debate. But in 1979 the corrupt and autocratic Shah of Iran, a US ally, was overthrown in a revolution which, in a strange echo of events in Russia in 1917, was begun by moderates and then taken over by extremists, the latter being Islamic radicals under Ayatollah Khomeini. A strict form of Islam was imposed on the country, those who resisted suffering severe penalties including death. Much like the Soviets the regime faced external opposition but overcame it, its eight-year war with Iraq ending in a stalemate. It despised "decadent" Western culture, regarded non-Muslims as unclean and in foreign policy was fiercely hostile to Israel and America, calling the latter the "Great Satan" and seeing it as the epitome of everything that was bad – greedy, corrupt, immoral – about the West's world dominance. It particularly hated the US because she had backed the Shah, whose behaviour and lifestyle was un-Islamic. Her embassy in Tehran was raided and a number of the staff taken hostage, not to be released until over a year later; an attempt to rescue them ended in disaster. Iran demanded that the Americans hand over the Shah for trial, which they refused to do, not wishing to bow to the demands of what appeared to be, and was, a bunch of brutal fanatics. We have already mentioned the *Vincennes* incident. There wasn't a lot either party in the quarrel could do to seriously damage the other, because Iran's economy depended on her oil trade with the rest of the world, and *vice versa* to some extent. But Iran remained a thorn in America's side for years, and an inspiration for militant Islamic elements even if it could not be proved she was directly and in material terms supporting them.

Although the West at any rate was becoming more and more secularist Iran's defiance of her showed that radical religion could be a serious geopolitical force in the modern world, and it is hard to believe that its example did not serve as an inspiration to the likes of al-Qaeda later on.

11

What about social issues during the two centuries following the all-important Industrial Revolution? Unless one is writing a whole book on the subject a discussion of them must focus on what has happened in the West because it has been there that the most startling changes have taken place. Though "Third World" countries after 1945 faced the decision whether to base their society and economy on the Western or the Communist model, many have never enjoyed anything like the equal opportunities (roughly speaking), the high living standards or the facilities for leisure which are features of life in the West.

Reading this chapter so far, a visitor from Mars might be forgiven for thinking that human history has been made more or less entirely by men. This has not been altogether the case in any culture. Of course, even when performing menial tasks women were making a vital contribution to society, which can be praised without being patronising. And the wives of male rulers could exercise a decisive influence, for good or for evil, from behind the scenes (so women were not as powerless, in effect, before the modern age as it might appear). One might also mention strong *female* rulers such as Elizabeth I of England, Catherine the Great of Russia, Cleopatra, and Boudicca/Boadicea, and those are not the only examples by any means.

They do seem however to be exceptions that prove the rule. By one of the absurd anomalies that characterised Western (not only Western) law and society a woman could have the most important job in the land, that of ruler, while in every other area her sex were confined to domestic or minor industrial roles. In a *general* sense women were subordinate. How far this was, and is, a problem and an injustice is of course culture-dependent. In some societies women have been in a subservient position for centuries and few within the society have questioned this. It might be because they would be in trouble if they did, but can we be sure of that? A significant number of women in strict Islamic states have tried to rebel, adopting the dress and customs of the more liberal West, but is it a foregone conclusion that if codes of behaviour were relaxed their sisters would immediately follow their example? They might simply be different, even if they should be allowed to make their own choices in the matter whatever everyone else does. It may be presumptuous to impose modern Western values on a people, regardless of the benevolent spirit in which we might do so.

The West itself has, since the nineteenth century, been a different matter. The Industrial Revolution and the Enlightenment had the same effect on women workers and their chances of advancement as it did on male ones, although it took longer to manifest itself because many liberal thinkers, though progressive in other ways, stopped short of female enfranchisement. Men had become accustomed to a position of dominance in society, to running it as if it was a cosy male club, and they naturally if wrongly baulked at the threat to their status they thought would follow if women (roughly one half of the population) were empowered by being given the vote. The change would be psychologically uncomfortable and thus difficult to adapt to. And women thought differently from men, so who knew in what unwelcome ways they would reconstruct things if the vote conveyed enough power on them? There was also a failure to understand the female mind in an age when the science of psychology was still in its relative infancy. If a woman seemed more likely to scream and cry when under stress, and was therefore unreliable and not to be trusted in a leadership role, it was because she was coping with the stress by letting her emotions out, as a kind of safety valve. Men tend to bottle theirs up, which is not always the best approach. To some extent the arrogance that too easily comes with power, and would if it was women who were in charge, led men to think they didn't need to understand these things.

But something was gradually happening which could not be resisted without unpleasant consequences. As society became more complex work patterns had to change; it was impossible for only men to do certain vital jobs, and women to be confined to the professions they had traditionally entered (in which they were often home-based and unpaid). The fairer sex were needed more and more as clerks, teachers, doctors, scientists. And like working- and middle-class men a few generations earlier they thought it absurd that when they were so important in the scheme of things they did not have the vote. Because the vote would only be due recognition of that new importance. It was a sign of status as much as was living in a posh house with lots of servants, or owning a car. Without it empowerment would be absurdly incomplete. They desired, and deserved, what seemed the ultimate freedom, the granting of a say in how society was governed through effectively becoming a part of the political process. (There had not yet developed the cynicism which saw the right to vote, for any individual irrespective of gender, as of dubious value given the true nature of politics.)

Undoubtedly the suffragettes were in the right, even if some of them were too extreme in their methods and language. The vote should have been granted to women in Britain a lot sooner than it was, for an increasingly ugly situation, characterised for example by force-feeding of women prisoners, would thereby have been avoided. In a photograph of the incident there is a very nasty expression on the face of one of the policemen trying to hold back a crowd of protesting suffragettes; it is one of extreme impatience, amounting to hatred, at all these women causing trouble. Men were reluctant to give in to female demands and thus seem to be rewarding militancy; the longer a dispute over an important and sensitive issue goes on, the harder it is for both sides to back down or make concessions even when they want to. In the end we don't know what would have happened if the matter had not been resolved by the First World War, in which women proved vital to the war effort through their roles as nurses and munitions factory workers. By taking the line that everyone, including the women, had pulled their weight and so ensured victory, thus deserving some reward, such as the vote, men could save their faces over the matter. I'm sure there was also a growing, if grudging realisation that women were certainly not more stupid (and thus less trustworthy where political and other important matters were concerned) than men, considering the state of the world.

The question has been raised of whether the suffragettes can be regarded as terrorists. It led to an unedifying row in the pages of the BBC *History* magazine in which a male historian seemed overconcerned to establish that they were, the tone of his article leaving him open to the charge of sexism, and a female one responded with justified indignation but in a way which, because she referred to him by his surname and did not use his title or first name, came over as discourteous. In fact whether the suffragettes were terrorists or not depends on your definition of terrorism; it is perhaps a moral and philosophical issue more than a historical one. If the definition includes obstruction, protest, and acts of vandalism such as burning out (empty) houses and letterboxes, which were designed to at least cause serious inconvenience, then yes they were terrorists. But by and large they did not use or attempt to use the far more dangerous methods, including assassination by one means or another, which are more usually associated with the term.

By the end of the twentieth century Western women were allowed to do just about any job, or participate in any cultural activity, which they were physically capable of. A question mark remains over certain military roles, but for biological, and possibly psychological, reasons which are more difficult to argue with. As with race there can still be institutionalised discrimination operating in a subtle way, besides what is known as "sexist behaviour" or "sexual harassment" (groping etcetera). The "Women's Lib(eration)" movement of the 1970s, which later became subsumed within the general rise of political correctness, was designed to combat this. It has not succeeded, and perhaps never will succeed, in entirely eradicating it but there is no doubt the position of women in the West today is markedly different from the state of affairs in Emmeline, Christabel and Sylvia Pankhurst's time.

In the Church of England, equality took a lot longer to achieve because those opposed to the admission of women to the clergy could always produce theological reasons (not, in the end, accepted by all Christians) why it was wrong. The trouble is, and this applies to all cases where social change is resisted, that because political and social evolution happens in leaps and bounds, mirroring biological evolution, existing sociopolitical forms have endured for so long people think they have thereby acquired legitimacy. Nor is the process in any case an even one, regardless of whether the eventual outcome is inevitable. Just as biological evolution does not necessarily produce forms which are larger and more complex, but simply those most suited to a given environment, social history is not a continuous and consistent advance towards full equality in everything, "leaps and bounds" or not. The crucial factor is what happens to be the norm, the way of thinking, at a particular time. To again take Christianity as a case in point, the Church in its early days (probably because it started off as a small body of people, organised on communistic lines, in which everyone had to serve in some important capacity or other) had women in senior positions in its hierarchy. They could be deacons, if not bishops. Is it true to say that subsequently horrid sexist men sidelined the women and established, as they did in other walks of life, a male-dominated social and political structure which endured until moves towards greater gender equality began in the nineteenth century, to eventually achieve success and end several thousand years of oppression?

Not quite. It was merely the case that society had settled into a patriarchal mode which happened to endure for a historically very long time. Women were prepared to accept a subordinate role and were not embittered but powerless feminist activists with a burning desire to change society only cruel male repression prevented them doing so. It *could* be cruel (King John's practice of selling widows was one abuse outlawed in Magna Carta) but only by the standards of the time; in other words, the practice of subordinating women was not cruel *in itself*. As in many other things a sliding scale was in operation. The real problem arises when society begins to change again and some people resist it.

A class system persisted in the West into the twentieth century and beyond, though it varied in rigidity between countries (it was at one time said to be worse in France than in Britain, for example). It mattered less once living standards, a determinant of "class" to some extent, began generally to rise, because fewer people felt they were in a position of suffering actual physical and mental deprivation. Indeed class became to some extent differentiated from affluence, because with greater equality of opportunity it was easier for a working-class person to acquire fame, status and wealth if they had the right skills. Commerce was one area where they might prosper although they usually had to build their business up from nothing, by hard work and sometimes ruthlessness, because they would have been shunned within established sectors of the economy which were dominated by the middle and upper classes. The growing leisure, recreation and entertainment industry enabled a talented working-class boy or girl to achieve success and recognition as a footballer or pop singer, because these were either relatively new areas or ones "posh" people had often, if not always, turned up their noses at. And because, again, a more complex and heavily populated society required the participation of everyone to run opportunities were created for the working class to study at university and so gain access to a whole range of professions – science, medicine, politics being examples – which had previously been denied them. In some ways the obstacles they faced were no longer economic so much as social; certain clubs, and certain *branches* of industry were effectively closed to them because these remained dominated by the public school-educated upper class, who understandably were trying to preserve a certain culture, a certain way of life, a certain identity, one expressed in speech and dress and mannerisms and which would seem diluted by the London or regional accents working-class people tended to have. Indeed there are some situations where a "working-class" accent *wouldn't* seem right, which is why BBC newsreaders still speak in a Home Counties way. The latter is probably best for the purpose; one exception is, and always has been, the mellifluous Welsh of a Huw Edwards.

By the late twentieth century Britain, the US and to a lesser extent (for the moment) France all had large non-white ethnic minorities living within their borders. For the most part this was a legacy of colonialism, slavery or both. In Britain's case there had actually been a not inconsiderable black (let us call it that, although the term has always disguised a degree of variation in actual skin colour) population, mainly located in London, before imperialism really took off in the eighteenth and nineteenth centuries. This immigration was a consequence of Britain's emergence as a global maritime and commercial power in the 1600s and 1700s. Shakespeare's "Dark Lady" is thought to have been of Asian or Afro-Caribbean extraction. The size of this nonwhite element or its existing at all comes as a surprise, the reason being, it is claimed, that it was airbrushed from history. Perhaps, being still relatively small, it was simply absorbed into the mainstream population by intermarriage. Perhaps also political correctness exaggerates its scale to some extent. But there is little doubt that it *did* exist; and it also seems that it was treated with much greater respect than nonwhite peoples were to be shown in later times.

The change in attitudes can be ascribed to the advent of the age of imperialism, and also to slavery, the two being tied in with one another to some degree. Over two hundred years Britain increased the size of its empire considerably, acquiring India and many territories in Africa. She had to justify what she was doing and so the doctrine evolved that whites were a superior race on a civilising mission. By a sort of logical consistency, this inevitably fed into how people of the same or similar ethnicity to the colonised, living in the mother country, were regarded. Whatever the economic arguments for it, and that is a very controversial issue, slavery had the same effect – one which debased the whites as well as the nonwhites – because you could not really view and treat people as equals as long as you deemed it fit to enslave their ethnic fellows and deny them all the rights of free people. Even after the slavery was abolished, "black" and other ethnic minority groups tended to be generally ignored and confined to lowly, menial tasks. This attitude persisted into the twentieth century despite the fact that after the Second World War there was a second, far larger nonwhite influx into the country from the African, Asian and Caribbean colonies. By the 1970s when the process was slowed down considerably due to public concerns these had achieved independence but mostly joined the British Commonwealth, a voluntary association of former colonial territories with which the mother country had, as a philanthropic goodwill gesture, certain legal as well as spiritual ties; these enabled Commonwealth citizens to claim British nationality and with it the right to live and work here. Originally the immigrants had been sensibly invited in to make up for labour shortages as a result of all the people who had been killed in the war. We were happy for them to do the dirty jobs but otherwise took little notice of them until it was realised that due to different demographic patterns they reproduced faster than the native white majority and fears were aroused regarding the social, cultural and psychological impact this might have (it would be naïve to suggest that pure racism did not also play a part). Whether or not those fears were justified, the size of the nonwhite population was ultimately too great for it to be ignored, and by a gradual and bumpy process opportunities for black and Asian people (outside the health and transport sectors, where they were already performing valuable service) increased. This was achieved partly by "positive discrimination", though it wasn't always admitted to; clearly the Labour parliamentary constituency of Hackney North and Stoke Newington chose Diane Abbott to be their MP because they preferred a young black woman to the elderly white male Ernie Roberts (the sitting member). For one reason or another, although there remained discrimination it became increasingly confined to particular areas.

America's situation was by the end of the century roughly similar. Here, though, the black population was much larger and consisted almost entirely of the descendants of former slaves (slavery had been thought essential to provide a labour force without which, initially, the new colonies would not have been viable). The process of equalisation had also been far less violence-free. Not only had a civil war been fought partly over slavery, but discontent because of the restrictions, official or otherwise, that blacks continued to suffer, e.g. segregation and denial of the right to vote, led on occasions to serious social unrest. Whether, in a very different world from today's, the slavery *had* been justified for the economic reasons mentioned is a moot point; but the blacks did have a right to ask that they be allowed to enjoy full civil liberties in a way that was consistent with its abolition. It was right that the slave owners should have been compensated, since by no means all of them were inhumane, but wrong that they should have got the best of the deal. The ex-slave would probably have been better off under a decent owner than he or she was after emancipation. Either they should have been compensated for their enslavement or – more practically, since the cost of compensation might have been prohibitive unless the sum involved was in each case a pittance – they should have been granted the same rights as other citizens with proper anti-discrimination laws to enforce that principle. And generally given a fair chance in life, which is what their descendants in Britain and America want today.

In Britain the nature of the situation, and of the problem, is different today from what it was in, say, 1981 when race riots seemed to threaten law and order and social cohesion. Many of Lord Scarman's recommendations following the unrest concerning the need to economically stimulate run-down black areas, which were perfectly acceptable if his support for "positive discrimination" was not, were sooner or later adopted (indeed there arose the phenomenon of the "buppie", the black upwardly-mobile professional). Somehow the image of the Rastafarian in dreadlocks sitting on a street corner in Brixton breathing out his hatred to the world because of his feelings of marginalisation while smoking pot no longer carries credibility. The *material* deprivation of the black population has blended into a more general resentment, one shared by many young whites, against exclusion of whatever kind, to a greater extent than was the case in 1981. In the 2012 riots, even though much of the trouble took place, and had begun, in black areas a distinct racial element was less obvious. The problem is in many ways a psychological one, arising from lack of career advancement, more than a physical one. It arises from the "good old British compromise" whereby minorities are overpromoted in certain areas such as advertising but nonetheless prevented from attaining positions of real importance and influence in society. As with the middle-class industrialists in early nineteenth century Europe, merely having a better standard of living than before is not enough.

The black and Asian population is generally far more assimilated than it was in the past, but there are exceptions to this integration. It has been commented that the ethnic minorities take little interest in white history, or in cultural events which reflect that history and celebrate the institutions which are rooted in it. They are hostile to that past because it is one in which they were enslaved, excluded and treated with little respect; this attitude is understandable, but has been encouraged unduly by liberal white historians. The only exceptions are when past racism is studied with the intention of morally condemning it and highlighting its effect on the status and interests of the ethnic minority population today. Whites are more likely to take an interest in the minorities' history than the converse. The psychological and social consequences for the nation as a whole are potentially serious as long as racial demography continues to change.

*

No-one likes being in a monotonous and boring job, whether clerical or "blue-collar". But within the West the Industrial Revolution became from the 1920s and 30s somewhat less grim for the average person. There had already been (relative) improvements in living standards, plus the emergence of a leisure industry for working- and lower middle-class people with music halls and affordable holidays to the seaside by train. And with the growth of a new leisure sector based on the mass media of film, radio and television, all of which offered escapist entertainment as well as education, scientific and technological progress seemed more of a friend, bringing pleasure into one's life rather than simply allowing one to earn enough to keep body and soul together. The increasingly "fantastic" nature of comic books from the thirties, with the appearance of characters like Batman, Superman and Wonder Woman, could be viewed as part of the same process, though comics, and the popular press in general, had already been around for some forty years; at any rate they had a similar beneficial effect, whether or not it was intentional. Identifying with such figures was a way of coping with dehumanisation, atomisation and existential angst, a far better one than to join a Fascist paramilitary group in which you were supposedly a "superman" by virtue of your ethnicity or power to intimidate. It became the case that popular fiction could, up to a point, draw out poison by sublimating the urges whose non-fulfilment helped to spread it. And it was easier for this healthy trend to do its work because the adventures of superheroes could be presented in several different media, film and radio and TV as well as the printed page, like those of any fictional personality. For as things levelled out and the average person became wealthier regardless of profession, even though there were still disparities of income and thus in living standards, more people could afford to buy radios and TV sets and go to the cinema.

What we were seeing in these years was the birth of consumerism in its modern form. As the century progressed it was to make industrialisation seem even more of a good thing, through the ability to buy its products, which included relative luxuries (TVs etc) and labour-saving devices such as vacuum cleaners and dishwashers. In material terms the quality of life had improved for millions of people. It could be argued however that some of this was itself dehumanising, in a different way to the factory systems of the eighteenth and nineteenth centuries; the increasing reliance on technology for our entertainment was a process which eventually had serious atomising effects upon society. But the worst of it was yet to come. Nor do I want to get into a discussion of whether violence on TV and in films has a damaging impact on the moral tone of things, although the evidence suggests it is not that significant in this respect *by itself*. Popular entertainment, made more accessible by the new technology, might be thought to "dumb down", to use modern parlance, but educational causes could also benefit.

It could certainly be argued that in improving the quality of material existence technology and consumerism had impoverished society spiritually. When life here on earth is fairly cushy people feel less need to turn to religion, with among other things its promise of a better world after this one as consolation for all our troubles and deprivations. Religious belief had been in gradual decline since the Enlightenment, but the process accelerated considerably during the twentieth century, with churches beginning to close as congregations lost interest and drifted away. Popular culture in the forms it now took became a rival to religion, something seemingly far more interesting and exciting. Another factor in religion's loss of appeal was the sociological changes which gathered pace after the war, the principal ones coming in the 1950s and 60s.

The more important people of whatever gender or class felt as integral components of a now booming post-war economy, with many of the previous restrictions to patterns of work gone, the more they thought they should have what they wanted, and what they wanted was different from what their parents' and grandparents' generations would have been satisfied with. In Britain especially the two world wars had themselves been a major catalyst, particularly the second as this had a more direct effect on life in the country itself, being a mobile conflict which for one thing necessitated defence against aerial attack on the homeland, now a greater threat altogether than in 1914-18. It was a more total war in the demands it made on both civilian workers and armed forces personnel, and because of the need for everyone to pull together social barriers were broken down (if not entirely) with, for instance, women doing many jobs normally reserved for men. The process which had begun in the previous century was now given a further boost. As the new work patterns had resulted in victory it was felt that they were thereby vindicated.

In social matters, women wanted more sexual freedom but also, and by more or less the same token, access to more reliable forms of contraception so that their fun was not spoilt by the fear of unwanted pregnancies – and so they could spend as much time on their careers as on bringing up children. This was not necessarily a selfish thing as it was naturally intended that any children one did have would enjoy the same freedoms when they were old enough. The mood of the time was sensed, and combined with new scientific discoveries and the influence of progressive-minded individuals to radically transform existing mores. The Pill became widely available from the early 1950s. In most countries the right to an abortion was allowed, whether conception had been intended or not; as well as the family planning aspect freedom was hardly freedom if it did not extend to control over one's own body, which one did not have if one was expected to have a baby essentially because somebody else had decided one should.

By 1967, when the abortion laws in Britain were relaxed, there was a feeling among a large enough number of people, many MPs included, that the process of liberation had gone too far, and aspirations had changed too much, for the "permissive society" to be dismantled without seeming totalitarian. To this was added, in the case of homosexuality which Britain legalised in the year in question, an understanding that the old law could not be effectively policed anyhow (and that what had previously been illegal was not something you could actually help, though not everyone shared this view). Clearly it wasn't only heterosexual women (and men, for obviously both desired the pleasure of unprotected sexual intercourse) who were benefiting from the new climate of opinion. As before in history, the questioning of received wisdom in one area had led to its being questioned in another, in a knock-on effect. And there were things which didn't necessarily require laws to be permissible or otherwise, since although arguably they were sins they were not, in legal terms, crimes. By their nature they involved men as well as women. It is believed sexual promiscuity became more common in the 1950s and 60s, partly because of factors mentioned above. Of course there had always been and always would be people who were sexually incontinent (or for one reason or other chaste). But the probability is that by 1970, 1980 at the latest, the majority of single people in the West between the ages of sixteen and thirty were in the category of not being especially promiscuous yet not virgins either. Though the Pill and perhaps abortion would certainly have made a difference, it is quite possible that in fact previous generations were not much less promiscuous, merely made more determined and successful efforts to hide it. But now there was less guilt and embarrassment about the business, even if it still didn't and normally wouldn't take place in public unless "free love" communes counted as that. Very natural desires, not always possible to satisfy exclusively within marriage, had come to the fore because of the general climate of liberation which could be compared to a tide, unstoppable once released, that was sweeping everything before it. Marriage in any case was seen not as a prop of decent society but as an outdated institution which simply imposed on the partners the stuffy conventions of middle-class respectability and was an imprisoning factor because you were always being expected to live up to a certain standard, put on a front, for the supposed sake of social cohesion. A growing number of couples began to live together without their relationship having any official sanction, although marriage remained fairly popular if only, in many cases, as a ritual more than anything else.

The sexual revolution has often been linked in the minds of traditionalists with other changes, which in some cases had been going on since the Industrial Revolution, to add up to something altogether tragic and dysfunctional, perhaps more harmful altogether than the sum of its parts; the destruction of all that was ever positive, wholesome and desirable. Not only was proper behaviour going out the window, it seemed, but changes in work patterns and lifestyle were breaking down the traditional family unit, and improved transport connections causing communities to lose their foci, their heart and soul, as more people were educated in towns rather than at the village school and shopped at supermarkets on their outskirts. But the march of progress, according to which it made little sense not to be where most of the action was, while concentration of diverse products at the same outlet was better for the consumer with more cash in their pocket than before as the postwar boom gathered pace, seemed irresistible. Question marks remain over cohabitation, pornography, homosexuality and premarital sex, in some people's eyes anyway (with cohabitation I will only say that in my view marriage is *preferable*); and divorce undoubtedly can have harmful psychological effects. Otherwise the social changes, though they might sometimes have negative consequences, were not *inevitably* morally and spiritually damaging, with the arguable exception of the decline in religion. They did not lead to the eradication of virtue. It might no longer be possible, in the majority of cases, for all members of the same extended family to live together in the same household, because it was not practical given the pressures and demands of modern life in the West. But unless selfish by nature people still valued their elderly relatives and protested if they suffered in poorly managed care homes. It was perfectly possible for family members to still have meaningful relationships with one another. That they might not go into the same hereditary business as their forebears did not necessarily make any difference to this. And as in due course became apparent, if a child spent too much time absorbed in the new (or relatively so) medium of television, which was now more available to consumers, and consequently failed to develop social skills, this was more the fault of individuals (the child themselves, or their parents) than society as a whole, or the technology. (The potential effects of sex and violence on TV and later videos/DVDs on society, already referred to, are a moot point, but most would concede that the real problem concerns children of a certain age or a relatively few susceptible adults. It is the same with pornographic magazines.) Nor did the majority of young people gloat over the fact that they knew more (in a technical and intellectual sense) than their elders, because of wider educational opportunities and choice including access to universities. They were simply taking advantage of what was on offer where, for a combination of reasons such as with the fifteenth-century Renaissance, people were increasingly ceasing to think and behave as they had formerly done.

Not everyone was particularly militant about the social (including sexual) revolution, and most did not carry it to what in any circumstances would have been unacceptable lengths. But the general preference was for self-expression in all areas, for not being restricted in one's choices by traditional mores and customs. The sense of exhilaration as this desire was met was such that many felt they didn't need religion to be on top of the world, to get a "buzz". In any case Christianity as it had traditionally been taught and practised, with an emphasis on many of the things which were now being discarded as old hat, such as marriage, seemed an outdated, and restrictive, business (this was so even where parents adhered only to the forms of religion, seeing a social value in them, and were no longer so sure about the theology). There was an experimentation with Eastern religions for a time, though as with so much of the rebellious youth culture of the late 1960s this proved to be for most a passing fad and was replaced by a more materialist secularism. Religion in the orthodox Western, that is Christian, sense seemed oppressive, always saying "don't do this, don't do that". The retreat from it was made possible by an intellectual revolution which had begun when scientific discoveries seemed to disprove the truth of the Bible. In fact, there is no reason to think they do, unless one takes Scriptural passages literally, which is not the only option. Nor was it impossible for Christianity to be compatible with pop music or contemporary styles of dress or speech. And it could compromise with the new morality up to a point, though the process of accommodation was to be a long and by no means smooth one. Its problem was that it had not, initially, tried to understand modern society or to make itself appealing to young people. It later remedied the first deficiency, though how successfully this was achieved depended on individual churches. It has still not quite remedied the second, although latterly this has been as much because the young resist getting involved in it in the first place as for some other reason. Unfortunately from its point of view, though, the idea that you were under no particular obligation to believe in God and could live quite happily without Him caught on, and has become so established that it is difficult to dislodge it from its place.

The attitudes and aspirations of young people were crucial in all the above because it was they who would want to change things, to embrace the new order in which they were growing up, rather than stick to established ways as their parents naturally did. The difference in outlook between the generations was what produced the rebellious teenager of the 1950s – and all subsequent periods, for most people become more conservative with age, leading to conflict with their children, even if "conservative" or "radical" amount to different things at different times. Change always seems more exciting, more interesting, more positively good to a younger person and the youth of the 1960s sought to place themselves at the vanguard of it as they became aware of how the world was developing, of how the increasing prosperity of the West highlighted the difference in living standards between it and other parts of the globe and even within its own society. Whereas James Dean wanted largely to hang around with whoever he liked and take the car out whenever he wanted, not wishing to have to defer to his parents' wishes in the matter, his counterpart in the sixties went on protest marches against the Vietnam War or the nuclear arms race. In part it was a fashion, a trend, which lost appeal after a while (it has resurfaced to some extent in recent years), but it amounted nonetheless to the creation of a counterculture; as did Dean's less political, except in a family context, rebelliousness, though his assertion of independence has of course become accepted as an established norm.

1960s political radicalism was of two principal kinds; the vague, woolly philosophy of "flower power" hippies who talked of "love" and of its conquering the world without specifying how this triumph was to be achieved, and a more focused and militant activism based on an existing political creed, Marxism, or variant of it. Both protested against the Vietnam War, or the social injustice and regimentation which still existed in the West, and there was often a confusing, to the faithful as much as anyone else, mixture of the two elements ("Now there's revolution but they don't know what they're fighting", sang Jethro Tull). Neither succeeded in achieving the objective of toppling the established order with all its evils. To overthrow the deeply entrenched vested interests which ran society at home and abroad, or get them to change their policies where they were determined not to do so, would require the use of force, in other words a certain ruthlessness, which the peace and love brigade had professed to have turned their backs on. The peaceniks failed in particular to understand that America could not by now easily disengage from Vietnam, misguided though the war had been in the first place, without losing face; *Realpolitik* dictates that nations must avoid humiliation if they are not to encourage their enemies, those who threaten their interests, by appearing weak. As for the genuine hard Reds, even if they were sincerely committed a lot of their behaviour was posturing or seen as such, as the front cover of a 1968 edition of the British satirical magazine *Private Eye* makes clear with the aid of the usual speech balloons. Revolutionaries posing in front of the statue of Karl Marx in Highgate Cemetery, London, chant "There's no business like show business". Marx asks them to kindly leave the stage. There was a third category of revolutionary, one who was at heart was not really committed at all. Paradoxically, the sixties had created a new surge in left-wing activism but also a culture of hedonism which meant that the radical movement was often regarded as itself a bit of fun, and no more. This kind of "rebel" might only ever go on one protest march and that purely in order to see what such occasions were like. It was something to tell their children and grandchildren.

Most people probably kept out of it. For one thing they were quite happy to live off the benefits of consumer capitalism and saw no need to change things. Freedom to do what one wanted could easily become a selfish, materialist affair, with no necessary connection to a prescriptive ideal that was supposed, at any rate, to benefit society as a whole. The militants did not have enough support to resist the authorities when they acted to deal with student riots such as those in Paris in '68. In the end the business fizzled out, as was inevitable with something that was, to some extent, a craze. Its exhaustion eliminated those for whom it was at best a passing fad, or who could not in the long run sustain their revolutionary ardour, and left only a relatively small number of zealots, now (2020) elderly or in late middle age, who remained loyal to the cause but have been mostly ineffectual.

The early 1970s were a sort of post-orgasmic (if you will pardon the analogy, though it isn't entirely inappropriate) aftermath to the heady days of protest and of shattering conventions for the fun of it. Whereas the music of the sixties had been brash and confident that of the seventies is more thoughtful, subdued, introverted, the product of a realisation that the problems of a troubled world were not going to be easily solved, certainly by putting flowers down gun barrels. The dream had died. In places a certain cynicism crept in. In the sixties those who rebelled against the established conventions of society, including criminals, might be romanticised; in reaction to this the 1971 film *Get Carter* portrayed gangsterism (correctly) as a bleak, violent and sordid business about which there was nothing funny at all. In politics, the revolutionary hard core did not necessarily abandon their radical activities straight away but their anger, though still there, seemed muted (partly because middle age was starting to kick in). And they were not so much in the public eye, so newsworthy, as before. In the end many were seduced by the material benefits of capitalist society, becoming drawn into the system and even lecturing, in a way which whatever its politics fell short of advocating violent protest, at the universities where their sort would earlier have been paragons of left-wing virtue. This tendency became especially marked in the 1980s, as the monetarist approach to economics demonstrated that it could bring rewards if you went along with it. There was nevertheless a certain radical revival in Britain at this time, in opposition to the policies of Margaret Thatcher, but it merely succeeded in creating the phenomenon of the "Loony Left", essentially a continuation of the hard socialist ideologies of the 60s but unsuited to new conditions; it was seen as "fringe politics", eccentric at best, and if anything helped to keep Thatcher in power. There is an element of social protest in many of the dark, moody "tech noir" tunes of this period; as often happens an art form, in this case music, became a vehicle for a left-wing counter culture as one of the outlets by which the latter could express itself in a situation where its enemy (Thatcherism/Conservatism, which it saw as both socially reactionary and a destroyer of economic opportunity) was apparently impregnably entrenched in power. Those haunting, sometimes terrifyingly so, strains seemed to reflect anguish at the social and psychological consequences of Thatcher. And though she was no more "homophobic" than any other heterosexual person at that time the sudden prominence of gay or gender-bending artistes (e.g. Boy George and certain members of Frankie Goes To Hollywood) who were not in the least ashamed or uncomfortable about their sexuality and lifestyle was one aspect of sociopolitical self-expression, protest maybe, in a society where homosexuals though no longer by legal definition criminals continued to be subjected to official or unofficial forms of discrimination.

But eighties music falls into two types; as the decade progressed the more commercialised kind − brash, but repetitive and stale where its sixties counterpart had been catchy and enjoyable − took over more as pop producers became concerned simply to make as much money as possible by being populist, often not really caring about the quality of the song. One can be overcritical of 80s music, but before that decade there was no such thing as *bad* music, with a very few arguable exceptions; even the much derided "bubble-gum" tunes of the late sixties and seventies could be catchy and pleasant to listen to. As a reaction to the decline there arose the "indie" labels which have turned out much good stuff, pieces that are thoughtful and melodious even if, in my view, pop music has never quite managed in recent decades to reattain the heights of its golden age, which lasted approximately from the 50s to the mid-80s. Punk had for a brief time in the late seventies been a medium for protest (e.g. "God Save The Queen" by the Sex Pistols), but its nihilistic character eventually began to repel people and it seemed as much a means of being offensive just for the sake of it. The death of Sid Vicious in early 1979 was the symbolic event that seemed to mark its end, as psychologically significant as the unpleasant events at Woodstock ten years before. Much nicer to embrace New Romantic, then beginning to emerge, which had style, wasn't really offensive and was certainly escapist fun while it lasted (Adam Ant!). You couldn't call it vapid, and yet it seemed to hark back pleasingly to an earlier era where people were less concerned about ideological politics. The seventies were in many ways an intermediary stage between the idealism, admittedly often confused or superficial, of the sixties and the unashamed hedonistic materialism of the eighties. Incidentally, if the examples I have quoted by way of making these points seem Anglocentric, it is because Britain has always been a trendsetter in such matters.

There was one other development during the whole 1945-91 period, besides 60s radical politics, which initially appeared as if it might make a difference to the human situation yet conspicuously failed to do so, at least in the ways people had expected and perhaps hoped. In 1957 the Russian satellite Sputnik 1 became the first man-made object to leave the Earth's atmosphere (whether the early intercontinental ballistic missiles had done so on their test flights is a moot point as it is a matter of scientific debate where exactly space begins). Russia followed this up with a lunar probe and, in 1961, the first astronaut, or cosmonaut. Alexei Leonov took the first spacewalk in 1965. America was by the latter date catching up in the "space race" and in fact it was she who in 1969 stole a march on the Russians by becoming the first (and so far the only) power to land people on the Moon. It seems incredible that the latter feat was accomplished within just twelve years of the race beginning; indeed to think that Man has even walked on the surface of another world, as it effectively was, at all. The incredible nature of the achievement is one reason why some people today doubt it actually happened. If it did, what seems equally strange is that it has never been repeated (though it still could be). Even if they weren't particularly interested in the business all told, the successes in space exploration in the 1950s and 60s inevitably caused people to think of moonbases, space stations, men on Mars, interstellar travel, permanent colonies on other planets. Space stations have been placed in orbit and proved useful in terms of scientific research and docking facilities for the space shuttle. The other images remain within the realms of science fiction.

It was all very disappointing, especially for real space enthusiasts; we felt cheated, as if we'd been psyched up for something that in the end failed to happen. There are several reasons why it didn't. Manned space travel was expensive (as was space exploration in general), because you had to spend that much more on life-support systems for the astronauts. By 1972, when US President Nixon was facing an election, there were already doubts as to its economic feasibility. And so, needing to spice up his campaign and not wishing to take chances, Nixon abandoned for the moment the idea of a

417

manned landing on Mars and went for the safer option of the space shuttle, which captured the imagination in that it was the world's first (partly) reusable spacecraft and had a practical application in terms of what happened back home, but wasn't designed for use much beyond Earth orbit. The oil crisis of 1973 and the subsequent world recessions further put paid to grand large-scale enterprises of the kind most likely to enthuse people as well as most important, arguably, in terms of Man's place in the universe. The emphasis has since then been on less expensive unmanned probes, from which we have learned a lot that is scientifically valuable but much less glamorous. As for the space shuttle, it was useful and aesthetically pleasing, like Concorde (a comparison with which is appropriate for more than one reason), but really little more than a glorified orbital breakdown truck for repairing faulty communications satellites, however vital this work might have been to the companies involved. NASA tried to make it do interesting things, so that the shuttle programme became at one point something of a circus, but their consequent eagerness to get it spaceborne led them to cut corners, with the tragic results seen in the 1986 *Challenger* disaster.

Another problem was that although people marvelled at the Moon landings and applauded the technical ingenuity which went into the business space travel in general did not – sadly perhaps – excite them much in the end. Neil Innes' Bonzo Dog Doo-Dah Band were right; the urban spaceman did not exist. What concerned the ordinary citizen most was that they should have a roof over their head and a decent standard of living. And there was a growing appreciation that space was a cold empty wilderness dotted with unappetising lumps of rock which harboured no life, no interesting alien civilisations for us to meet (and was the prospect of actually encountering them really rather scary?) so far as could be seen. All the action was taking place here on Earth. The Soviets did not need to worry about public opinion, and certainly continued with their own space programme, among other things launching their *Mir* space station in 1986 (their own version of the space shuttle, obviously copied from the American, made one journey but never in a metaphorical sense got off the ground). But whether the reason has been cost or political upheavals Russia has not to this date come anywhere near to a manned lunar or Martian landing. China might be a different matter; it's a case of "watch this space" (ha ha), but then that has tended to be true of China generally.

Some were and are very cynical about the whole thing. Undoubtedly it was motivated in the 50s and 60s by national ego on the part of the chief participants, Russia and America; by political and military considerations. But Ferdinand and Isabella had hard practical reasons for financing Christopher Columbus, once he had convinced them that there might be economic benefits from opening up the New World. And undoubtedly the bravery of the astronauts and the technical skills which went into the space programme, on both sides, deserved praise. There are also minerals on the Moon, and probably other planets as well, which could be of a certain practical and economic value on Earth. If colonisation of outer space did become feasible, and had enough public support, it would relieve serious overcrowding on the home planet; and to meet another intelligent civilisation, from which we might learn a lot (and hopefully *vice versa*) would undoubtedly be a fascinating experience. Finally, (manned) space travel is an extension of the urge to directly explore new horizons, without which we would be intellectually and spiritually stagnant (the apparent sterility of our solar system, and of the only planets we have so far discovered outside it, notwithstanding). Perhaps the Moon landings have such an iconic status, in one way or another, were such a marvellous achievement, that it would be sacrilege to repeat them (as with England's winning the World Cup). At any rate it continues to seem sad that nothing like the 1968 Apollo mission in which the astronauts did not land on the Moon but travelled a certain distance beyond it, and which was therefore in some ways a more significant achievement, is likely in the foreseeable future to be repeated. And that an office block called "Astronaut House" in Feltham, Middlesex, put up in the 60s and no doubt intended, if a trifle pretentiously, to be by its name a symbol of the modern age, as space travel undoubtedly was once it had moved out of the realms of science fiction, has equally symbolically (one can't help thinking) been demolished. And that people are now so cynical about politicians and the blood-stirring great achievements of the past that some believe the Moon landings were faked. I can't myself prove to anyone's 100% satisfaction that they weren't, but the consequences if the deception were found out, the existence of that piece of moonrock in the Science Museum in London, and cosmonaut Valentina Tereshkova's sincere and magnanimous statement that she believed the dedication and courage of the Americans was quite sufficient for them to have pulled off such an achievement, would seem to trounce the conspiracy theorists.

Large-scale, manned exploration of the solar system was something you always felt ought to be happening, somehow, but wasn't. Science fiction as seen on film and TV during the 1960s and 1970s – a golden age of television for both children and adults – both contributed to this feeling and helped assuage it. It was as if the process was taking place in two parallel worlds, one real and the other fictive, and that what was happening in the latter compensated for what was not happening in the former. There was *Star Trek*, *Doctor Who*, the Gerry Anderson shows and *Blake's Seven*, along with the much more realistic, in that it did not feature things whose scientific plausibility had yet to be established, fare such as *Moonbase Three* and the *Doomwatch* episode *Re-entry Forbidden*. The universe was being conquered by proxy. Science fiction continues to be fairly popular, but now it seems to give the public everything they want, and feel they need, where space is concerned; they aren't too bothered about whether it happens in reality. Generally, although further lunar landings and missions to Mars, etc., have not by any means been ruled out they are very much on the back burner; no-one is pushing for them the way the Apollo programme was pushed. Tragically in many ways, we have spurned outer space for cyberspace, technological skills being channelled into the development of computers and the internet (as well as general scientific research of course), often with damaging social consequences that can actually have the effect of *limiting* horizons. For me the overarching feeling is one of regret that a process by which what we were seeing in a plethora of TV sci-fi shows was turning gradually into reality was interrupted, and is still a long way off resuming.

The space programme had practical value in that it stimulated the American economy, and by that token other economies (as part of this, some of the equipment used in astronauts' protective clothing has actually been available commercially). Another consequence of it may turn out to be even more practical, depending on what happens in the future. By the end of the 1980s the Reagan-Gorbachev détente and the start of serious arms reductions, reflecting what appeared to be a genuine commitment to the business on the part of both superpowers, had to a great extent quieted fears about nuclear warfare and its consequences. Other issues, which had already attained a degree of prominence, now came more to the fore in the public mind, or at least that region of it which was politically aware. One was poverty (linked in the Third World to susceptibility to famine) and the increasing disparity in wealth and quality of life between the West and the remainder of the planet; between the prosperous nations of the northern hemisphere and the much less prosperous, apart from Western colonies such as Australia, New Zealand and (if you were white) South Africa, ones of the southern. A big question was whether Western policies in the field of international trade, which naturally were designed to preserve the West's own dominant position in the global economy, were retarding progress in solving the problem. The second issue which emerged as crucial during the period was the effect Western industry was having on the natural environment. If it went unaddressed the consequences might possibly be even worse than nuclear war. Friends of the Earth and Greenpeace had already joined the assortment of pressure groups dealing with social issues such as housing, abuse of women and prison reform which sprang up in the 60s and 70s in the West and which were not necessarily composed exclusively of radical political revolutionaries, despite what the Right often thought, as opposed to people who were genuinely concerned about the problems of a complex, modern, industrial society which was continuing to change at a fast rate. Photographs of the Earth taken from space, in fact the whole space programme, made it clearer than ever before that we lived on a lonely, beautiful, vulnerable planet which until we knew otherwise had to be assumed unique; the only world with any kind of life, let alone intelligent life. Our own activities were now threatening this isolated pocket of it in a cold, dark, frighteningly vast universe.

Many of the pressure and amenity groups, whether local or national in their concerns, which began to appear from the 60s onwards could be said to be cultural in purpose, rather than political in the sense of seeking to recruit support for a good cause among the influential through lobbying, although they might sometimes find it necessary to do that too. A further development of the Big Society, as one British Prime Minister was later to call it, if it can be seen as embracing all human activity that has a valid purpose was the growth of organisations concerned with the preservation of industrial monuments, including such things as traditional water- and windmills, plus the more popular steam railway locomotive and other vintage forms of transport. This was not by any means a new thing, having begun in the later Victorian period, but now it was mushrooming. It reflected a widening of history's brief and also a recognition, already evident in certain schools of art, that what was intended primarily to serve a practical, utilitarian purpose could also be a thing of beauty. It was to some extent hobbyism. It was also part of the expansion of the leisure industry, along with the opening of castles and stately homes to the public; for people would pay to see a working windmill or ride on a steam train again, thus contributing to the upkeep of the concern. The majority of those involved in the movement, and in more than a casual sense, were indeed hobbyists, though they might also have a serious academic interest in the business, and often eccentric. But although it was the ordinary public who were its bread-and-butter the buffs provided the essential workforce for restoring and maintaining the mills etc. in the first place. Sadly, industrial archaeology is no longer taught as a separate subject at universities and societies concerned with the study and enjoyment of it are suffering from declining, because ageing, membership; unless it is merely that the young express their interest through internet chatsites rather than in face-to-face meetings. Bodies dealing with the related subject of local history have also undergone a period of expansion followed by decline.

12

Old men can be stubborn, resistant to openmindedness and change, sometimes belligerent; and especially as they grow older. The Nixon-Brezhnev détente of the early 1970s was succeeded by a more hawkish attitude to international power politics on the Soviet side, as seen in the 1979 invasion of Afghanistan, another example of preserving spheres of influence, and the cancellation of further arms limitation talks. The Americans followed suit, since belligerence tends to be met by belligerence, the other party feeling vulnerable otherwise. The collapse of détente in the middle and later years of the decade was partly due to the departure of its architects, Richard Nixon and Henry Kissinger, from office and a disassociation from their style of government which resulted in their replacement by those less politically adroit. Nixon of course had been discredited by Watergate, and was eventually forced to resign, but one wonders if it was right to throw out the policies with the man, as in effect happened. He was a nasty piece of work, who made offensive remarks about student protestors shot dead by police, but like the very wise former British Foreign Secretary and Prime Minister Alec Douglas Home I don't (while being reluctant for the sake of modesty to claim equal wisdom) share the wholly negative view of him which became common. He did help lead the world further away from nuclear war. Though morally repugnant in certain respects he was in practical terms a good President, who happened to be in charge at a time when America was still going through a period of traumatic social change and soul-searching. One can have a certain sympathy for him; another common view of the man is that over Watergate his only crime was to get caught. Can we really say that he was much more underhand and devious than many other politicians? Partly it was a personal insecurity which led him to use deceit and chicanery to get his way and protect his position. Psychologically, this was I suspect the consequence of a too strict religious upbringing; it serves to highlight the dangers of the latter but also those of reacting to same in the wrong way. Those who reject stifling religion-derived morality often end up kicking over the traces altogether.

The insecurity made Nixon reluctant to admit his own complicity in Watergate even though it was obvious. The impression he gives during the famous Frost interview is of a man struggling to do the decent thing and confess his guilt, but not quite succeeding. He is trying to find a formula for doing so with which he is comfortable, and in the end chooses to say that he was at fault in not properly controlling his subordinates, rather than that he told them to do what they did. How far this satisfies him is not clear. He seems to achieve a kind of peace but is still nervous and selfconscious. He is almost admirable, but not quite. Was it a coded message, a way of saying "Yes, I was guilty" but obliquely? We can't be sure, and so it fails to achieve its aim. The calculated compromise of a half-apology is insufficient both for Nixon's purposes and ours.

The trouble was that Nixon couldn't claim to be acting in the best interests of the free world if he didn't subscribe to its values, which necessarily included honesty and fair dealing in the area of politics. As for Kissinger, he and Nixon had a brief under *Realpolitik* to get America out of Vietnam in a way that saved her face, and this is why the process took so long with setbacks such as the airstrike of December 1972. Kissinger was undoubtedly involved in "dirty tricks" operations such as the overthrow of the democratically (though not by a strict majority of the popular vote, note) elected Communist government of Chile, or turned a blind eye to them. It does leave a nasty taste in the mouth. Perhaps it was an inevitable aspect of the Cold War power game, and the "sphere of influence" thing; the playing out of conflicts by proxy. Kissinger would have been one man fighting against an entire system had he tried to oppose it, and most likely he pragmatically concluded that there was no point in doing so. Whatever the explanation, it seems odd that Respect (the former

Stop The War Coalition) should have attempted to get him tried before an international court for some of the things he did, the charge being one of war crimes, when there should from their point of view be the overarching consideration that he was instrumental in ending the Vietnam War, and it was surely preferable that it *was* ended, irrespective of the way the conflict was dragged out and from motives which might not impress left-wing liberals.

Jimmy Carter's insipid, compared to some, personality and his incompetence as a conductor of foreign policy, which resulted in America's humiliation by Iran over the hostage crisis, associated the Democratic Party with weakness and inability to defend US interests. Like many Christians Carter was decent and compassionate but lacking in a sometimes essential forcefulness and ruthlessness; a better man than he was a President (and thus the reverse of Nixon), in the words of one later commentator. Something more than that was seen as necessary to deal with new Soviet aggression; the consequence was a Republican victory at the 1980 Presidential election under Ronald Reagan, to many an alarming figure: an elderly former cowboy actor, not very bright, and right-wing zealot whose pugnacious language respecting the Soviet "evil empire", as he came to call it, led to fears he might actually be happy to start a nuclear war. And indeed, Pershing and Cruise missile bases were set up in strategically vital Western Europe, causing a lot of fuss at Greenham Common, in response to the new SS20s Russia was wheeling out; by 1984 it looked as if two old men, Reagan and whoever the Soviet leader was, were between them about to totally wreck the aspirations of the young by destroying world civilisation. It is (genuinely) one of the nicest, most warming, things about this era of global history that such a figure as Reagan was actually to be instrumental in ending the nuclear arms race (though not the possession by either side of nuclear arms, in itself) and therefore, so it seemed, guaranteeing peace and saving the world. The fact that Reagan was already beginning to suffer from a kind of dementia, and had a poor grasp of political issues, meant that he deferred to people more competent and more discerning than himself, and could therefore be controlled, while serving as a useful front for the administration because of his communication skills as an actor. There are two kinds of US President, those who will be their own boss once in office and those who are malleable. Fortunately, Reagan fell into the latter category. Unfortunately, Donald Trump falls into the former.

What made a shift in US attitudes possible was a sea change in Moscow. In the end, the Soviet old guard simply died off. Brezhnev passed away in 1982, his successors Andropov and Chernenko in 1984 and 1985 respectively; three leaders in the space of as many years. It had become, apart from anything else, too farcical a system to be sustained. The only option was to permit the accession of a younger man, Mikhail Gorbachev, to the leadership in the hope that he would breathe new life into things. He did, but got more than he bargained for.

A vital aspect of Gorbachev's fresh approach was the establishment of a new nuclear détente. There seemed no harm to the Soviet Union in reducing its nuclear and conventional military infrastructure, and so eliminating a cause of fear and tension in the world, provided the United States made corresponding concessions. Gorbachev had the energy, initiative and boldness to see this and to transform it into actual policy. The US had to respond to his overtures as it would otherwise lose the moral high ground. It could also feel that it had won the Cold War by standing firm and so extracting concessions from its enemies, although for diplomatic reasons the boast could not be too open. The professional thespian Reagan could always be persuaded of the benefits to his image from taking on a new role, that of peacemaker.

The other main feature of Gorbachev's policy was reform at home. It is important to realise that he was not, initially, trying to dismantle the Soviet Union or to end totalitarian Marxism in Russia. As he − and his colleagues − saw it he was reforming the system in order to preserve it. It would become more efficient and so more able to justify itself, in its own eyes and those of outsiders. And so he embarked on *glasnost* (openness) and *perestroika* (restructuring), with the aim of encouraging more open criticism of officials and so give them an incentive to run things better. A frank discussion of systemic problems was essential for solving them. The policy was to be applied throughout the whole Eastern bloc. As it gathered pace it unleashed a pent-up tide of anger and resentment at all the inefficiency and elitism of Communist rule, whose undemocratic nature had resulted in the dominance of local cliques which could not be brought to book when they fouled up by failing to deliver food supplies or other goods on time, as they frequently did because there was no mechanism for keeping them on their toes. Throughout the incredible autumn and winter of 1989-90 there were widespread protests in all the Soviet satellite states, including East Germany, which eventually led to the fall of the ruling Communist regimes there and their replacement by democratic governments. And without too much violence, except in Rumania which had always been a special case. Ceausescu was a far more reprehensible figure than Gustav Husak, Todor Zhivkov, Janos Kadar etc.; drunk on power in a situation where he had turned the state into a family heirloom, and subjecting his people to absurd and draconian policies which were reminiscent of Stalin and Mao at their worst, he had sadly changed from a hero who had resisted the Soviets to a personality who could be demonised and was. The summary execution of him and his wife shocked many in the West, especially since it happened to take place at Christmas, although it is believed by some that the pace of events simply moved too fast for there to be a proper trial. If heads had had time to cool the outcome might have been different.

Why did Gorbachev not send in tanks to crush the uprisings in Hungary, Germany, Bulgaria, Czechoslovakia and Poland, in the manner of his predecessors in 1956 (Hungary) and 1968 (Czechoslovakia) (for he did not)? The answer was that on the Russian side there was a connection between foreign policy considerations and internal ones. A state which practised repression against its satellites might be thought aggressive enough to use nuclear missiles in anger, and this was not compatible with the new détente policy, which mattered to Gorbachev because the more nuclear weapons there were in existence the more dangerous a place the world was, even if the "red button" was unlikely to be pressed except under extreme provocation, and he wanted to be rid of the constant fear of global destruction. Nor would the repression have fitted in with the spirit behind his reforms. The fact that *glasnost* had tended to highlight what was wrong with the system without actually doing anything about those faults meant that if there was at the same time a return to the ruthless suppression of dissent it would lead to the perception that he had achieved nothing. Altogether Gorbachev was following a certain logic, and becoming imprisoned by it.

The foreign policy factors explain why there was not, apart from the fiasco of 1991, any attempt to reverse the Gorbachev reforms by a coup d'etat. To be a nuclear power carries with it a certain responsibility; the internal disruption and instability which might result from a coup attempt could cause the weapons to fall into the hands of extremist hardliners. The Soviets themselves had been as worried as anybody else, at heart, about the effect of a nuclear holocaust, national and ideological pride apart, and now that thanks to Gorbachev they had had the experience of being free from that fear, so it seemed, they didn't fancy a return to the old days. Altogether, the 1991 coup failed because there wasn't enough support for reversing a process which had simply gone too far.

The inevitable result of it all was the dismantling of the Soviet Union itself, just several months after the failed coup, with the Baltic states, the Central Asian republics, Byelorus and the Ukraine all gaining independence. If Gorbachev could not send the tanks into Poland, East Germany, Czechoslovakia etc. then nor could he send them into Kazakhstan, Ukraine, Azerbaijan or Estonia. He resigned, which seemed sad to the wider world considering all the good he had done in its eyes, and democracy and the capitalist system were both established within the new Russia.

Gorbachev had not succeeded in revivifying the Soviet Union. I visited it on a package tour in October 1990 and was struck by the ubiquitous black market touts, a sign that the mainstream economy was not considered to be operating satisfactorily, and by the paucity of goods in the shops (they tended to turn up in bulk, their arrival precipitating a rush in which one girl looked like she was being crushed to death). But Gorbachev's reforms *destroyed* the system, without meaning to do so; he could not resist the consequences of his own policies once they became apparent. There had never before been such a case of a fundamental transformation in world affairs being achieved so peacefully it was almost ludicrous.

The changes in Eastern Europe obviously implied the reunification of Germany. Soviet military power had hitherto prevented this, as perhaps had the focusing by East Germans on the Communist system as a source of national identity and pride, part of a necessary psychological readjustment after the division of the country. But now that the basis for such an allegiance had been destroyed there was no logical reason for resisting reunification. Unless you were afraid that it would make Germany too powerful and risk a repeat of past wars (such a fear may have been present even if it was conceded that German aggression was not the sole reason for them, for there might still seem involved a major alteration in the balance of power). Gorbachev however had the sense to see that West Germany was too firmly integrated into the Western capitalist democratic system, of which all Eastern Europe including the former East Germany would now become part, and which required peace to function properly, to want to wreck things, as well as too traumatised by the consequences of past belligerence. So in October 1990 the two Germanies became one. It seemed "fair do's" to rejoice at this still relatively young country, divided for forty-five years, being granted its legitimate rights of self-assertion, now that it was safe to do so.

The way in which the fall of the Soviet Union occurred requires some explanation. There seems no other example of a great power, one might say an empire still, collapsing entirely through its own cumbersome weight, its own stagnation and inefficiency, and not through foreign conquest. The latter would not have been possible anyway due to the danger of retaliation with nuclear weapons. Gorbachev was presiding over a system so rotten that any attempt to reform it would simply accelerate its end, like an old building that has been allowed to become so derelict that it cannot be restored because as soon as you touch it it collapses. His reforms inevitably aroused high expectations that were not, because of the unwieldiness of the political and administrative structure, going to be met sometime soon, unless you got rid of Communist oligarchic totalitarianism altogether, and when disillusion led to unrest he was trapped by his commitment not to use violence to suppress that discontent, indeed by his whole policy in both the domestic and the foreign sphere. The process ran away with him. Things could not have continued as they were but equally they could not be transformed without wrecking what Gorbachev was actually trying to achieve. It was an impossible task. There is a certain parallel with Bismarck, in that Gorbachev was bringing a new world into existence for the sake of the old, except that Bismarck calculatedly took control of a process that was already happening (knowing that the other German states would look to Prussia to give them what they wanted, national unification, because she alone had the military means to do so, and be subsequently beholden to her). Perhaps Bismarck too became the prisoner of his own policies, but with him there was less discrepancy between what was intended and what actually happened. And Gorbachev was trapped whether or not, as some historians claim, he had secretly become convinced Communism was a dead letter in any case. He wanted the Soviet Union to be endorsed by popular vote following democratic reforms. In this respect he was somewhat naïve. He failed to see that the Soviet state was so bankrupt, in more than just the financial sense, that

426

any chance of achieving such an aim had disappeared. If people no longer had to have such a system imposed on them against their wishes, why should they choose it of their own free will? If you really are serious about democracy, then you run the risk of cherished policies being thrown out by the electorate if they are not to its liking, and implemented only periodically depending on who is in power; in other words not being permanent.

That the Soviet Union did succumb due to its own internal weakness, and to reform acquiring an unstoppable momentum which exposed the flaws in the existing system without rectifying them, is a testimony to the fact that the nuclear deterrent, the principle of MAD, works. Normally a powerful totalitarian state only collapses because of internal revolution or invasion/subjugation by a foreign power. The first was not possible because of the tight political control (it happened in the satellite states but only when Gorbachev, as we've seen, held back from military intervention). The second was not possible since the nuclear stand-off prevented a conventional war which both sides were afraid of starting because it might have become a nuclear one.

Right-wing commentators claimed that by refusing to give up their nuclear arsenals, as well as maintaining strong conventional forces, Ronald Reagan (succeeded as US President from January 1989 by George Bush Senior) and his ally, British Prime Minister Margaret Thatcher, had brought about the ultimate triumph of freedom and the capitalist democracies over which they presided because in time the Soviet system disintegrated as a result of its own defects, without having had the opportunity to conquer and impose its way of thinking on them. This needs to be qualified in that it is doubtful whether the Soviets, sabre-rattling apart, ever seriously intended a military invasion of Western Europe. Whether they would have attempted it if their economy allowed it, and there was no nuclear deterrent, must remain conjectural. But what exactly would their motive in doing it have been, by Gorbachev's time, since Communism as an evangelical ideology was no longer subscribed to by the old guard in Russia except as a way of constructing a political identity?

The key factor was economics and it is in that field that Reagan and Thatcher can be said to have been victorious. What is undoubtedly true is that the "capitalist democratic" system had been shown to be more robust, more dynamic, more successful at creating prosperity than its Communist rival and this was what in the end brought about the latter's downfall. It wasn't that there was no poverty or, to use a term coined later, "marginalisation" in the West, or that she didn't have political prisoners (though these may have been protesting at particular actions by their governments rather than the political system as a whole, or the bulk of the people, significantly, did not feel sufficiently disadvantaged to want to follow them). The bottom line was, she was better on the whole at giving ordinary citizens a higher standard of living than that most East Europeans experienced, while at the same time allowing much more in the way of personal liberty and free speech. It is tempting to downplay

Thatcher's role in the West's victory out of dislike for her and because Britain has often been seen in the post-imperial era as a dwarf trying to act like a giant. But, if military factors were important in Russia's "defeat", she did allow America to station her missiles on British soil (though so did West Germany on hers). She was generally a staunch supporter of the US, which was the most powerful Western nation and therefore the chief bulwark against the Soviets, in a way that France and West Germany weren't quite. In the end the latter two countries would have stayed loyal to NATO, but they always gave the impression of toeing the US-British line reluctantly, and France did its own thing wherever possible. Because it was so important they were friends now the two countries usually acted, or failed to act, together, as a partnership excluding Britain, in geopolitical matters and this remained the case after German unification, with serious consequences for the effectiveness of the European Union as a military force. (Or, previously, West Germany had simply let France tell it what to do. That is not to say it was not capable of acting on its own initiative and for the best. Willy Brandt's *Ostpolitik* was a well-meaning and justified attempt to reduce tension within Cold War Europe by forging friendly links with the East.)

But undoubtedly Thatcher, along with Reagan, appeared to have succeeded in creating a vibrant and successful capitalist economy within her own country; and it was not just a capitalist economy but a free market one, governed by monetarist principles with little or no state control. Of course there were a lot of things wrong with it, and this was not necessarily apparent to foreign observers, distance plus relative unfamiliarity with the true situation distorting perspective. But it is often true that as Christ said, a prophet is better regarded outside their homeland than in it. This was certainly true of Gorbachev who paradoxically, while he was viewed by Westerners as a liberator and a bringer of peace, did not enjoy popularity among Russians after his retirement because he had merely exposed the faults in Soviet society without remedying them.

1989-91 had a knock-on effect around the world and led to the global collapse of Communism as a political force, those states which professed still to practise it becoming gradually indistinguishable from capitalist ones, with the sole exception of Stalinist North Korea whose leaders always have been an odd lot in any case. Left-wing rebels in Third World countries either made peace with the government, their funds now cut off, or their struggle ceased to be specifically Communist. The Marxist regimes which disappeared were replaced by ones which were not only capitalist but politically democratic, in line with the principle that democracy could not function effectively without capitalism and *vice versa*. Not everyone subscribed to the latter view outside the West. I do not know if this is a specifically Chinese kind of model for the development of politico-economic systems, since like many Westerners I find the culture in question a difficult one to understand. But in China under Deng Xiao-Ping (who is considered the last of the "Red Giants") the Communist Party embraced free-market capitalism while retaining its name and its political control. As Deng had intended from the start; 1989, the year which saw the fall of the Berlin Wall and the collapse of Communist governments in Europe like dominoes, also saw the massacre of pro-democracy protestors in Tiananmen Square.

It should not therefore be forgotten that a quarter of the world's population were still living under totalitarianism, and they still do, though the Chinese government is more of an oligarchy than a case of absolute rule by one individual. But there seemed to have taken place the world triumph of capitalism, if not quite of capitalist *democracy*. Most countries, in Europe, Asia, Africa and the Americas, had either embraced it or were subject to it through the economic dominance of the West, the major exception to which had now disappeared. It was a triumph so complete that the American writer and political thinker Francis Fukuyama spoke of it in a famous book as if it might be the "end of history". In spite of popular perceptions he did not say that it definitely was; but this meant he was contradicting himself. The theme of the book seemed to be that because all rivals to the capitalist model had been so successfully discredited, identified with oppression and with a stagnation which had proved their own undoing, it would never be seriously challenged and so history had come to an end if history meant major events such as the collapse of a widely adopted belief system. How likely is this? Fukuyama was talking essentially of *economic* systems, and as we saw there is not necessarily a correlation between the kind of economy a country has and the nature of its government. There was also the question of religion, which was by no means dead as a social and political force, whatever the form it took, as future events were to show. Speaking of religion, Christians at any rate held that history was not so much likely to end, in that everything became crystallised in the same form, as building up to a goal, i.e. the final collapse of the earthly order as a result of all its problems, followed by the Last Judgement and the transformation of this world into the eternal paradise which they called Heaven, or the Kingdom of God. They could not say exactly when this would happen. But certainly the earthly realm had never shown a propensity to stand still.

For now, capitalism did appear to be the dominant economic system, and it was a dominance not just of capitalism but of a particular brand of it – monetarism, which was considered a more efficient way of administering the economy than the more corporatist, regulated, Keynesian model which had been established wisdom in the West for many years after World War Two. Within democratic capitalism some divergence of thinking on economic matters had been permissible, although the advocates of monetarism were claiming that Keynesianism and state control were not in fact democratic and that the people had now been "liberated" from them. (It is important here to appreciate that the people, who little understood the finer points of economic theory anyway, might not have voted monetarist leaders into office because of it; there are many factors influencing a person's choice at a general election). Corporatism in the West had indeed degenerated into a rather stagnant system which held back economic growth, and it was eventually dispensed with not only there but throughout the entire capitalist world, which preferred to follow the example of Reagan and Thatcher. Monetarism appeared to be a better way of managing the economies of complex and also consumer-orientated societies.

Not only had international capitalism triumphed over its enemies, creating a community of nations bound together by adherence to the monetarist philosophy, but it seemed for a time that peace had broken out around the world. This feeling was already evident before 1989, with the Eastern Bloc appearing to be moving towards liberalisation and détente with the West, and some encouraging signs of progress in South Africa. The monetarist victory was itself in many ways an influence for peace, because it served as a unifying factor. By much the same token, since its concern was to maximise profits, which required free trade as well as laissez faire – it was basically a return to the system which had operated in Victorian times, social consequences included – it demanded good relations between nations, war having a disruptive influence on trade and causing protectionist barriers to go up. Large, in terms of size and resources or population, and (potentially) prosperous nations such as China, and past aggressors like Japan and Germany, realised there was more to be gained from attempting economic, rather than military, domination, through working the free market capitalist system so as to do better out of it than others. (In that her rise challenged Western interests and aspirations it was ultimately China rather than, as many including Michael Crichton in his novel *Rising Sun* had predicted, Japan who assumed the role of so-called "Yellow Peril" in this changed world.) Especially when the continued existence of nuclear weapons, awareness of which must have remained present at the back of the mind despite détente, served as a reminder of the potential cost of belligerence.

Up until the time the upheavals actually happened no-one could possibly have foreseen that the world would be so drastically reshaped, with the events in Russia and Eastern Europe, the reunification of Germany and the release of Nelson Mandela presaging the end of apartheid in South Africa. Previously it was anticipated that these things would take many more years to achieve, indeed might never become reality. And although some had reservations about Germany, it all seemed to decent and fair-minded people a jolly good thing. There was cause to be optimistic about humanity's future. We were in an interim period between the bad – though not everyone subscribed to that view – old days and the discovery that the new monetarist order could create its own evils. And economic factors did not necessarily mean there would be political peace within nations, especially where they were not fully integrated into the Western system and where there was a culture of violence and instability. Or between them either, as it in fact

430

turned out, not least because the Middle East continued to be a trouble spot and not just over the Israeli-Palestinian issue. The post-1991 world proved if anything to be far more dangerous and unstable than the pre-1991 one. During the Cold War the subsuming of everything within the East-West duality, the geopolitical domination of the two power blocs and their rivalry, had ensured a kind of order. That stabilising factor was now removed.

As it happened, the cracks became evident almost immediately. There now enters upon the stage the pantomime's Demon King, or so some appeared to be portraying him, in the shape of Saddam Hussein, dictator of Iraq. In August 1990 he annexed Kuwait and its oilfields, and by so doing, in addition to the action being questionable in itself, appeared to threaten Saudi Arabia. Britain and America, still acting as the world's policemen with the former in the junior role out of the two, as well as the Saudis decided they couldn't have this and issued an ultimatum to Saddam (always so called in order to distinguish him from King Hussein of Jordan) to withdraw from Kuwait or they would declare war on him. The prospect loomed of a major conflagration in the Middle East.

I well recall the feeling of dread I, along with many others, experienced in the build-up to hostilities. It is not presumptious to say that one got a whiff of what Cuba must have been like. But that was because political satirists and sensationalists in the media played up the dangers involved, which may have been considerably exaggerated. In the end resolution of the conflict was achieved relatively speedily, within just a couple of months, and easily, the whole business seeming almost absurd given how frightened one had been earlier. Expelled from Kuwait, defeated by the West's superior numbers, better organisation and on the whole higher quality equipment, Saddam more or less gave up the fight and sent his air force to Iran, with whom he was now on friendlier terms, for its own protection. The greatest risk was probably that Israel would be dragged into the war by Saddam's rocket attacks on her, but this was eliminated when his Scud missile convoys were taken out. Saddam did set fire to the Kuwaiti oilfields, but Red Adair put it out. Russia had traditionally supported the Arabs against Israel and the West, but she didn't get involved, being preoccupied with internal political matters and not wishing to have anything to do with an obvious, and indeed dangerous, bad character like Saddam. In any case she was not particularly into war, as opposed to peace, at this time. Certainly the First Gulf War (though it should be called the Second if we count the Iran-Iraq conflict) did not develop into a general global one, as some seemed to be suggesting it would at one stage.

What was the significance of the whole thing? The West, in alliance with the Saudis (in fact as part of a multinational force, although the EEC (as it was then) failed to pull its weight apart from Britain) had defeated an attempt by a Middle Eastern, Arab power at territorial expansion. How far exactly Saddam's regional ambitions extended was hard to say, which is why some in the world at large decided life would be a lot safer without him, although he probably did not intend to annex Britain or America, for example. But Iraq had the fourth largest army in the world and the largest in the Middle East, which made it a lot easier for him to achieve his aims, whatever they were (in essence I think he wanted the power, and thus status, that comes with land and economic resources). That state of affairs had been created by the West, which had armed him, and it was to get a lot of stick from its own liberals as a result. It certainly regretted it, as with Osama Bin Laden and his followers. But in both cases the reasons may have been valid. You cannot always predict the future. Arming Bin Laden and the mujahideen of Afghanistan, who later formed the nucleus of al-Qaeda, in order to expel the Soviets from that country was certainly understandable in the context of the Cold War power game. In Saddam's case, it was Iran which seemed the greater threat given its provocative behaviour, its anti-Western statements and its leaders' virulent hatred of Western culture.

He was not justified in using what the West had given him to wrongly invade and occupy another country. The West had an excuse for a vigorous military response because it needed to defend its friends in the region, who guaranteed its supplies of the oil which despite the tendency of the substance to be a cause of war in the Middle East and the ecological effects of burning fossil fuels it could not attempt to do without, unless risking an equally disastrous collapse of modern industrial society. There was a further pragmatic, *Realpolitik*al justification in that if the West, or anyone else, did not protect its allies they would not be seen by others, whose help might be needed at some time in the future over whatever issue, as trustworthy. And it would have been genuinely unethical, *Realpolitik* aside, to have let down those whose support you had expected in the past. It was simply not practical to get involved in all instances of someone being illegally annexed but the West surely had a right to be concerned where its own interests were in one way or another threatened. Finally, although the West would in the last resort have traded with Saddam, if necessary, in Kuwait's oil there was, as with Hitler, a genuine feeling that this was an overall bad egg, someone who needed to be contained and who the world did not want to have to deal in vital resources with, even if there might seem to be good reasons for leaving the matter be.

After his defeat in 1991 Saddam was never, in truth, as much a threat to geopolitical peace as before it. So the question remains whether Britain and America needed to press on to Baghdad to topple him, as some (including naturally the Kurds and other elements he was persecuting) felt they should have done. Where oppressed minorities were concerned, it was not practical (and might in many cases have been undemocratic) to overthrow the governments in all countries where they were to be found, and if Saddam were removed on their account so, morally, would many other regimes have had to be. President Bush (Senior) was a ruthlessly practical man, as one would have expected from a former head of the CIA. He dealt with the pragmatic and possible, not taking unwise risks, and for that reason was a good President. His perceived wimpiness was actually this kind of ruthless practicality, though it had uncomfortable consequences, leading him to concentrate on Libya as the supposed perpetrator of the Lockerbie atrocity when to many people the finger seemed to point to Palestinians sheltered by Syria, because Syria's non-intervention, at least, was required in the war with Saddam.

Bush decided in the end that Saddam himself should be left where he was. Whether this was the right policy in terms of subsequent world history is impossible to say. It could have gone either way. Had Saddam been overthrown in 1991 there would not have been another Iraq war, for which there was much less justification and whose consequences really were disastrous, in 2003. But that further war need not have happened; it was the act of a President who was either less cautious, less sensible, than his father or was acting in accordance with a rather sinister political calculation, or both.

And it is important to appreciate the principal factor behind Bush Senior's restraint in 1991. It wasn't just that Saddam's ability to do harm had been significantly reduced (he had managed to save his air force but lost much of his other military hardware), meaning there was less point in taking risks anyway. He was popular among many Arabs because of his opposition to Israel. (Pro-Palestinian feeling was one reason why a longstanding friend of the West in the region, Jordan's King Hussein, spoke out against the war in apparent support of Saddam, in a stance that disappointed many but was understandable considering that seventy per cent of Jordan's people were Palestinians.) This was part of a wider desire not to upset Arab and Muslim opinion by doing what might be viewed as Western imperialism. There was concern also at the effect on Saudi Arabian opinion of seeing, among the US forces stationed in the country, women soldiers smoking cigarettes for example. It indicated growing awareness of the issue already beginning to replace the Cold War as the crucial one in world politics.

There was war also in former Yugoslavia. The region had always been, before and after the collapse of the Hapsburg Empire, a hotchpotch of different races and nationalities, with religious divisions (not necessarily in the sense of conflict) between Christian and Muslim superimposed over ethnic tensions involving Croats, Serbs (who did not at this time have full political independence), Bosnians, Kosovans and Slovenes. A fairly peaceful multiracial state of affairs survived removal of the iron hand of Tito, which had ensured order and balance, by eleven years (it was probably the fall of Communism which made the crucial difference rather than the departure from the scene of one man, although in this case the latter probably didn't help). The geographical distribution of the races was such that it was not so easy to divide the region up into different countries according to the Wilsonian principle of national self-determination without one ethnic group fearing that another was going to dominate it (by contrast Czechoslovakia split peacefully into Slovakia and the Czech Republic). The result was that whereas national independence was achieved with little bloodshed elsewhere in Eastern Europe, the Balkans were ravaged during the 1990s and early 2000s by a series of very nasty civil wars in which the sinister policy of "ethnic {and religious} cleansing" was applied. There was armed conflict on the mainland of Europe for the first time since 1945, and as with the "Troubles" in Northern Ireland it went on until people simply got tired of all the fighting. All one can say is that although it is obviously preferable to have full racial integration a policy of encouraged migration followed by partition, rather than being strictly politically correct, might in practical terms be preferable to devastation and genocide. It is not a nice choice to have to make. As well as the conflict being unpleasant in itself, there was a fear that Russia might come in as the traditional protector of the Serbs, as part of sphere-of-influence building (with no Tito to resist her). Only Russia was not in a fit state to contemplate such things just then, as we'll see.

If the Cold War had not prevented relatively small-scale local conflicts from breaking out, whether or not they tied in with the East-West ideological confrontation, they were not less likely to happen now that it was over. As well as in the Balkans there was civil war in parts of Africa, e.g. Rwanda. It might be a continuation of previous wars or a case of feuds which had been simmering below the surface but suppressed under Soviet rule, and now burst forth. There was some trouble in the Central Asian and Caucasian Republics, which had no tradition of democratic government at all (Poland, Czechoslovakia etc. had some, although it had been interrupted by Hitler and Stalin) and where there was less of a mechanism for containing political disagreements peacefully.

Russia herself was a cause for concern in these years; the sudden disrupting change both to democracy and to the capitalist system, partly because it involved taking on new responsibilities to which people were unaccustomed, was psychologically and in practical terms hard to adjust to, and the downsizing of the armed forces following détente added to rising unemployment. As well as the economy suffering, with the structural problems it had exhibited in the Soviet era being carried over into the democratic one, there were all kinds of social issues including alcoholism, prostitution, absenteeism. The state of the country was alarmingly similar in many respects to that of Weimar Germany; she was losing her self-respect and the relative decline in her military strength, and thus her ability to assert herself, angered many staunch patriots. There were fears that a discontented troublemaker, a would-be demagogue, would exploit the situation in order to take power, whether democratically or by force, and be a Soviet Hitler or a new Stalin, either restoring Communism – for there were many who now recalled the "good old days" with affection – or adding a purely nationalist dictatorship to the list of different forms of government Russia had experimented with.

Among the potential consequences of instability, continued economic decline and administrative inefficiency was considered to be the theft of Russia's remaining nuclear weapons. This merged with general concerns about "nuclear proliferation". In the end, it would appear that safeguards were sufficient to prevent terrorists, rogue individuals or local warlords from getting their hands on the nukes, and this has remained the case to the present day. But a legally constituted state manufacturing its own WMD, as was bound to happen eventually according to the law of probabilities, was a different matter. With Cold War geopolitical alignments now a thing of the past there was less chance of Russia and America getting together to block something neither of them would have considered to be in anyone's interests, their own included, because it complicated and risked destabilising international affairs. In their different ways both were too busy attempting to cope with the aftermath of the old system's collapse. Russia seemed to be in decline, if not falling apart, and the West, when it was not busy trying to sort out Saddam Hussein or the conflicts in former Yugoslavia, was unsure exactly what should be considered the main threat to world peace and stability in the new, more fluid and multipolar situation. NATO seemed uncertain what to do, apart from peacekeeping operations (backed up by force) in a particular part of its territory (the Balkans), until the emergence of Islamic terrorism as the number one enemy, or so it seemed, gave it an additional lease of life. It was also morally difficult for the West to keep its own weapons of mass destruction (as protection in an uncertain world) but object to others developing theirs. In the end, it was not a rogue individual or faction, or what could be regarded as a rogue state (Iraq, North Korea, arguably Iran) which got in first out of those others but India and Pakistan. Neither was a "rogue state", but the two were traditional enemies and so there was real fear as to what might happen now. However MAD continued to apply, as it would do unless one takes the racialist view that Indians and Pakistanis are less worthy as people to be trusted with the power to annihilate on a mass scale. (One might include Israel in the equation but she had always been a special case, determined not to let Masada fall again whatever the cost but, equally, prudent and restrained enough not to unleash Armageddon without genuine provocation.)

All the same, as in the Cold War but maybe more so now, the greater the number of nuclear weapons there were in existence the greater the chance of some catastrophe occurring, perhaps by accident. And agreements on the restriction of nuclear arms were much easier to reach when there were only two powers that had them (excepting the British and French nuclear deterrents, which were even more for show). The process will be a lot more difficult with a whole host of countries who possess, or are actively seeking to possess, the weapons, each of them intending to use the bargaining counter that they represent to secure its own ends. As I suggested earlier on, rather than limit nuclear proliferation itself, which is controversial, we should perhaps rather seek to ensure, through diplomacy, that the issues over which the weapons might be used are resolved.

As we have more or less observed, the aggressive nature of our species can and does result in at least localised wars breaking out, whether there is an international Cold War going on or not. By the mid-1990s there was a feeling of frustration among the great and the good, to use a figure of speech, that the expectations of a better world which events of 1989-91 had given rise to had not really been met. It fuelled the desire to live up to that promise. At the same time, with survivors of the Holocaust – the living evidence of it – beginning to die off and the Holocaust itself receding further back in time there was a fear that people would forget how hideous such things were; punishing further atrocities would serve to focus attention on the matter apart from anything else. For example there was pressure for international intervention to end the genocide in Rwanda. The trouble was that this raised questions about sovereignty, even where, as in the Rwandan case, the minority was a very large one and the consequences of attempting "ethnic cleansing" therefore more awful in terms of scale. There were also practical issues of cost and logistics, a danger of military resources becoming overstretched. NATO involvement in the Balkans was controversial enough for some people. Certainly, although western European nations might have felt they had no option but to do something if a nasty war was taking place in their own backyard (not necessarily the same thing as an ideological commitment to intervention), you couldn't get involved everywhere there was an oppressed minority (or majority); and where would you draw the line between intervening and keeping out of things? It resulted in unconvincing attempts to deny that the persecution of the Rwandan Tutsis amounted to genocide; obviously one's heart goes out to them, but so too, in a different way, does it go out to the White House spokeswoman who had to make such a statement before the cameras. Her discomfort and unease are obvious and she ought not to have been placed in such a situation. It would have been better to have used the "g"-word but declared honestly that America could not for various reasons commit herself to military operations. In the end, by inaction or evasion the principle of humanitarian intervention by the international community in such matters was rejected, though Saddam Hussein's treatment of the Kurds was invoked as at least an additional reason for the 2003 invasion of Iraq. It was probably necessary; but of course that was no consolation to the Tutsis.

One shaft of light amid the gloom was the ending of the violence in Northern Ireland, although the geopolitical significance of that conflict had been largely confined to the region in question. But terrorism continued to be an issue, in fact an even more geopolitically significant one, in the new world "order", because the most important of the new terrorist groups that were emerging had a world mission. The global triumph of the liberal, capitalist, secular (in that religion and politics were not mixed), Western way of life was not unqualified, in that a significant counterculture existed to challenge it. I am not talking of "New Age" travellers, or the anti-globalisation movement which arose later on. The disappearance of one of the two parties in the principal global divide would be bound to leave a vacuum that something or other would seek to fill sooner or later, coming into conflict with the remaining superpower, America (to what extent post-Soviet Russia is still one remains debatable, but during the 1990s she was preoccupied as noted with internal problems). That something was radical Islam.

Even among tribal cultures in remote regions of the planet everyone has a world view, an idea of how it would be best for us all to live, notwithstanding that they cannot impose it on others and may not have much contact with them anyway. Usually, though perhaps not necessarily, this ideal pattern of living has some resemblance to our own since we are all a bit culturally egocentric. Radical Muslims were, as they saw it, trying to bring order to the fragmented post-Cold War world. Human affairs had always been messed up anyway, and in the new conditions it seemed there was a chance to put things right. And we are particularly likely to want to change the way others live when we think it is having a bad effect, materially or psychologically, on the way *we* live.

Muslims were not, of course, necessarily radical in the sense of being militant, still less were they all wicked. But it is not necessary to be either for unrest to occur, and a certain percentage are always likely to *become* radicalised. At any rate Islam, both within the West (because it was acquiring large Muslim minorities through immigration) and without it, was to become the fastest-growing religion in the world and this was bound to have cultural and political consequences whatever happened. It was a revolt, not necessarily violent at present, against secularism and it filled a certain gap left by relative decline in the fortunes of Christianity.

The Islamic conquests of the early Middle Ages had left Christians a minority in North Africa, and they had always been one in those Asian countries which were predominantly Muslim. They were now declining in numbers in the West itself (this is to exclude, as I think one should, those people who call themselves "Christian" but have no real religious commitment and often a poor understanding of doctrine). The Church had always had a problem making itself look exciting, especially to younger people, in the modern world. Generally it was going through a crisis in its relations with the latter. The difficulties of justifying Christian doctrine in the face of science and of sceptical humanist philosophy led some clerics to compromise, explaining that things which the average practical person might have some difficulty believing, such as the Virgin Birth, were actually meant to be "figurative" rather than literally true. The Church of England in particular was often accused of being too liberal, watering down the Gospel message in a way that reduced its impact. David Jenkins, the controversial Bishop of Durham, appeared to be denying the literal truth of just about every fundamental aspect of Christian doctrine; there are grounds for thinking he was not actually as radical in what he believed as appeared to be the case, but the language he used made it look as if he was. Some felt he ought to have taken the hint when York Minster was struck and damaged by lightning shortly after his appointment. One vicar declared he did not actually believe in God but went on being a priest until he was eventually sacked. A consequence of all this was that a significant element within society decided Anglican doctrine could mean whatever you wanted it to, could be interpreted however you liked, literally or figuratively. This increased the derision they felt towards it, which was extended to encompass Christianity in general.

The Church was also divided between conservatives and liberals on the issue of ordaining women and homosexuals as priests, and these disagreements could be bitter ones which did not seem very Christian. Altogether it seemed to have lost its way. The particular examples I have quoted of division and of doctrinal vagueness are British ones, but they reflected a widespread perception throughout the Western world that the Church (meaning the institution as a whole) was disunited and ineffective, while unable intellectually to give clear and satisfactory answers to searching existentialist questions. There was therefore a haemorrhage in its support. Within the mainstream West those potential believers who were disillusioned by it became agnostics or atheists. For the main part Muslims thought that if by and large their white Western fellow creatures did not seriously commit to a Christian way of life and belief system then there was no reason why *they* should. They pointed out the disunity and ineffectiveness and argued that their own faith had strengths which made it a better option. In Islamic doctrine the basics seemed clearer and there was less scope for uncertainty over what exactly the faithful were expected to believe, and to do. (Although where women and gays were concerned, the principle was very often that the former should be excluded from important positions within society and the latter ought not to be what they were, on pain of imprisonment or worse!) There is no direct connection between the David Jenkins affair and the rise of al-Qaeda, but the former was nonetheless a symptom of the phenomenon which, on a wider scale, led to the latter.

Muslims did not actively seek converts within predominantly "white" (they themselves or their ancestors tended to inhabit or to have come from non-white nations) societies, preferring to avoid possible hostility and concentrate instead on trying to project positive images of themselves. They did not object to it if some whites did embrace the faith, as sometimes happened. But generally the increase in Muslim numbers came from among Asian and African populations, including those in Western countries. It was largely because communities which were already Muslim were growing in size, having large families for cultural or economic reasons. However, at the same time many of those whose forebears had been Muslim, but who themselves had become influenced by secular and liberal ideas derived from the West, especially likely if their country had been a Western colony, now rediscovered the old religion.

Muslims were uncomfortable with the secular Western way of life. They might have liked it a bit more if the West had been more genuinely Christian and therefore, perhaps, less permissive among other things. The devoted follower of one religion can often respect the devoted follower of another, despite their theological differences. But the West was not more Christian. And she had certainly become more permissive, because the monetarist economic philosophy, which stressed individual self-advancement through maximising profits, could have a hardening effect on ordinary people (contrary to what its well-meaning propounders might intend), one which spread to other areas of life besides business. It promoted a tendency which began with the birth of the "permissive society" in the 1960s and perpetuated it in a bastardised, degraded form, worsening any negative (as opposed to neutral, or positive) consequences it might already have had. For example, within obvious limits set by the law some women would dress indecently, inappropriately, purely because it was what they wanted to do. Either it was part of their self-expression (they claimed) or they were simply trying to shock for its own sake. There were liberal Muslims who might not care much about this sort of thing. But stricter forms of Islam were becoming commoner as a reaction against Western practices, even if those who advocated the former would never have condoned killing Westerners or in other ways causing them harm. And Muslims felt more unhappy with Western permissiveness where they lived shoulder-to-shoulder with it, as in London or Paris or New York, though out of pragmatism or because it was the right thing to do they respected the peculiar customs of the "host" community. They also were not happy about such things as the controversial American/British invasion of Iraq in 2003, which because it was unjustified looked like an imperialist act against an Arab, and therefore mainly Muslim, country, with whom they felt solidarity as co-believers, Islam being a world faith community in which a common religion came before ethnic and national differences, to a greater or lesser degree.

Among a certain element such sentiments flared into hatred. It is not clear how far exactly these extremists would seek in the end to go. The language they use, which helps inflame the situation, suggests they want to conquer the whole world, should that prove possible, and force it to become Muslim, killing those who resist. I think they would like to do that if they could, partly because it would seem to be a way of protecting Muslims against hostile non-Muslims. Their feelings towards the West make it quite likely that they would be happy to force Western women into harems, which those women would find degrading and oppressive. To dismiss such suggestions as racist as the politically correct tend to do is probably unwise. But how much of what the extremists utter is rhetoric, at worst the sort of thing one says when one is angry, because they know at heart it is not attainable? They are disturbed, dangerous, possibly mad in either a clinical or a non-clinical sense. But I suspect they can be pragmatic in their own way and that those living outside the West, at any rate, would be content with the removal of any Western presence from Muslim countries. However that would not be a good thing, even if the West thinks it could adapt to it to some degree, because it would create a very sad kind of global apartheid and because the West still for the moment needs the Middle East's oil reserves.

A certain question mark remains over the Western-domiciled extremists. Like most people they like to have their cake and eat it. They do not want to return to the lands their parents and grandparents came from, which are less prosperous and stable than their adopted homelands and where they cannot call on the Western legal system for help when it suits them to do so. But nor are they happy with the way things are here. Hence we cannot rule out the possibility they will seek in the future to use violent methods to overthrow the governments of Britain, France, etc. and establish Islamic rule, over white fellow citizens as well as Muslims, there, even though most of them fight the *jihad* overseas rather than at "home" because domestic intelligence services and police forces in the West have become more effective at rooting them out. They will become more confident as the number of Western Muslims grows because as it does so will the numbers of potential extremists, in proportion; just as any growing white population will contain more potential paedophiles, for example, or criminals whose motivation is not political or religious.

Extremist Islam was to some extent a way of dealing with the Muslim version of post-modern *ennui*, the desire to find a cause in a fragmented, multipolar world where the old ideologies with their stabilising effect had been discredited. Sometimes it seemed as much this as a quantity which people believed in for its own sake (there's a difference). Though such was to be expected perhaps it had a crazy, irrational, confused character. It often broke its own laws; the militants would smoke, drink alcohol and meet with Western prostitutes, in contradiction of strict Islamic puritanism. It was often the product of poor education and ignorance in Muslim communities around the world, including Western ones, and thus a debased version of Islam; young Muslim militants were foul-mouthed and often incoherent in their televised denunciation of all the West's wickedness. It was also not one movement but a number of different organisations, representing a tendency rather than a single formally constituted body, of which al-Qaeda (The Base) and its leader the renegade Saudi Osama Bin Laden happened to become the most notorious. Its *precise* motivation could vary; the bombings in Bali, Indonesia, had a racist character, one of the perpetrators declaring that he was happy because he had succeeded in striking a blow against the "whites" − this was understandable, though still unjustified, given that whites made up most of the population of the West, the society whose culture and imperialism the militants abhorred. Other extreme Islamists objected not to whites as such but rather anyone who was not a (radical) Muslim, meaning that the racial aspect was less important for them.

But in so far as the militants believed in anything it was that Western society was decadent, immoral and corrupt (a view with which one could have some sympathy) and that Muslims should be insulated from its damaging influence; a principle which the radicals attempted to endorse by military conquest, as in Iraq and Afghanistan. (They were not impressed by efforts to ensure that branches of MacDonalds in the Middle East did not serve food containing ingredients which in Islam were ritually unclean; but then almost by definition, extremists don't invariably listen to reason). Their wrath was concentrated especially on America as the dominant Western nation, one with a particularly vibrant and particularly (in fact, since its very creation) monetarist capitalist economy. The philosophy of individual self-help was inevitable in a nation begun from scratch in often arduous circumstances, but it had led to something which could repel a culture like Islam where the community always acted to help its members in times of trouble. And America, now more or less the world's only superpower, was in a unique position to do whatever it liked, using modern technology and communications to impose its will over all the planet in a way that had not been possible for anyone prior to the twentieth century − America's century, as it is often described. Military intervention in other countries, both during and after the Cold War, had been partly for economic reasons since any dynamic and therefore expanding economy looked to acquire new markets as well as protect old ones, and America wanted foreign countries to have economic systems compatible with hers, as well as ruled by friendly regimes, if trade was to be easy and profitable or take place at all. But perhaps people simply resented her power, as much as anything else.

The militants were not in fact anticapitalist as such, did not draw their inspiration from Communism, but under monetarism the capitalist system had become more greedy and corrupting and this was what they were reacting against, without necessarily having a complex theory of economics and sociology. In the West their discontent was partly on account of having suffered, like other people, from monetarism's social consequences, becoming marginalised; immigrants tend, initially, to settle in relatively poor and underprivileged working-class areas and the sense of alienation is heightened when the gap between rich and not so rich grows. And they would inevitably become a ghetto, cut off from wider society and unable to some extent to share in the benefits membership of it conveyed, because of the tendency for like to attract like and unlike to be, perhaps naturally, wary of it.

Moderate Muslims might secretly be pleased, or at least a part of them would be tempted to feel pleased, by a major terrorist atrocity against America because of the arrogant way she seemed to have been acting, but had the decency to suppress it. They might become radicalised if poorly handled disputes and culture clashes between the West and Islam led them to consider their interests threatened. There was also a suspicion on the part of wider

Western society that Muslim communities, while not necessarily aggressive towards the rest of the population, were turning in on themselves and operating their own system of sharia law; something not good for the cause of future integration.

Impatient with their more pacific co-religionists, the extremists embarked on a campaign of violence which did not spare innocent people, men women and children alike. Previously terrorism had been largely political and ethnic in motive and this was certainly the case with that aimed at Israel and her American protectors. Arab terrorists had not necessarily been devout Muslims. Now the cause became subsumed within a wider religious terrorism which sought not only the end of Israel – the Palestinian issue, because of what was at stake there, having carried over from the old order to the new – but the expulsion of the West from the Muslim world, if not its global destruction as a culture. In the end attacking Israel directly was left to Hamas, an Islamist group though it did not quite have the apocalyptic, even genocidal outlook of a Bin Laden (except perhaps where Israel was concerned), while others undertook the holy struggle against Western and Israeli/Jewish interests worldwide (the existence of Israel was seen as a crime against Arabs, and therefore against Muslims, in which Jews were complicit because many if not all of them were also Zionists). But generally the whole business became tied up with religion in a way it hadn't been before, the old primarily political terrorists being effectively excluded, and this made it more dangerous since a religious terrorist might be especially fanatical, difficult to dissuade from killing if they thought it was the will of God.

What also helped to make the new terrorists a greater threat altogether than the old was that they did not need the protection or money of a rogue state such as Libya or Syria. They might have it nonetheless, Afghanistan and its ruling Taliban (though no longer Libya or Syria) being an example. In terms of citizenship they could be from any country with a sizeable, or even a very small, Muslim population, including previously friendly, from a Western point of view, Islamic states such as Saudi Arabia where there was in fact widespread hatred of the oppressive and elitist monarchical system of government. They might hide amid the growing Muslim communities which most Western countries now had including the USA. They operated and kept in touch using modern communications and in particular the new phenomenon of the global Internet, which was where they obtained much of the information they needed to build their bombs and other weapons, and e-mail. They would have taken advantage of those things anyway. But they helped al-Qaeda and Co. to function as a stateless, international force which was more difficult to pin down than one associated with a particular country or countries. The enemy, as it was with justification increasingly perceived to be, was now a decentralised religious terrorist organisation whose support was not confined to a single geographical area and which, additionally, could not be reasoned with the way others might. The West's old rival, Islam, had come back to haunt it in a different, and nastier and more deadly, form.

The first indication that the new terrorism had arrived was the attack on the World Trade Centre in New York in 1993, which killed a number of people but failed to topple the building as had been its aim. Other atrocities followed, such as the bombings of the USS *Cole* and of US embassies in several African countries. But the really big one was yet to come. It came because a group of particularly clever and cunning terrorists, who planned the operation meticulously, saw how airliners, instead of being hijacked or blown up, could themselves be used as bombs. The Sunday before it happened I was walking on the Sussex Downs. It was a beautiful day which afterwards seemed almost the last normal one before the world changed in an unexpected, shocking and in so many ways particularly unpleasant fashion. The month was September, 2001, and not August, 1914, but comparisons with the First World War have never seemed far-fetched.

It is said that everyone remembers where they were, what they were doing, when they first heard the news of "9/11", as with the first moon landing or the death of John F Kennedy. On that Tuesday I was at work when a colleague shouted out across the shop floor that two aircraft had crashed into the towers of the World Trade Centre, totally destroying them. I confess that at first it did not quite click with me that this must have been a deliberate act. But as the afternoon wore on it gradually became clear that airliners had been hijacked and then flown, with the passengers aboard, into the Twin Towers. It seemed a calculated act of symbolism apart from anything else, and was more horrible thereby. But it also seemed that a third plane had been piloted into the Pentagon while a fourth had crashed, possibly, as we later learned, as a result of the passengers and crew attempting to overpower the hijackers, while on its way to a destination which was unknown but probably the US seat of government on Capitol Hill, Washington.

Not everyone's experiences would have been quite the same. Personally, though, I got little sleep that night. I used to sing cheerfully while at work but from then on never did (a month after the atrocity, I was made redundant due to its effect on the industry in which I worked). I felt subdued, crushed. After all a still predominantly white culture, my own, had been attacked in a particularly horrific and unprecedented manner. Knowing what sort of people had perpetrated the attack, and their feelings towards the West, I felt victimised and vulnerable. I really did, for the first time as an Anglo-Saxon Westerner, get a sense of how the Jews must have felt in the past, and knew there was nothing excessive in such a reaction. I had often thought that political correctness was unfair towards my ethnic group and culture, targeting it as if it was the sole perpetrator of injustice when in fact it was not. But this was something even more disturbing. Another overwhelming feeling was one of disorientation. It was like seeing the sort of thing that normally happens only in cartoons make an unwelcome intrusion into real life. Had anyone previously suggested that Arab terrorists would carry out a bombing using aircraft with live passengers on them it would have been dismissed as sensationalist racism, and probably regarded with scepticism even by those who weren't especially PC. It came as a profound and troubling shock to discover that they actually were capable of doing such a thing, and I expect caused political correctionists quite a lot of problems. Incredulity at the idea (in what was supposedly a deeply racist society) was probably one reason why no-one foresaw 9/11. It does make the whole thing a little easier to cope with if you understand why it happened the way it did, something I didn't in my initial horror and revulsion; military aircraft could not be used as security at the airbase would have been too tight. Not that the deaths of other infidels besides those in the buildings and on the ground would have caused the terrorists or those behind them any remorse. But the crawling horror of it all lingered for years afterwards and I doubt it will ever go away entirely. It helps if you reflect that it wasn't only "white" people who died but then that makes it a bit hard on the others. Generally the trauma of the business had a coarsening effect on Western society; one way of dealing with it was to regard horrific forms of killing as in some way normalised, and this I think explains why crime shows on TV have got darker and more disturbing in recent years. Not the least negative consequence of 9/11, though it was justified to some extent, was the tightening of security measures everywhere and the excuse governments had to be more controlling; Big Brother was finally here, fifty-three years on from Orwell's novel and by courtesy of airborne Islamic terrorists.

9/11 obviously involved the immediate perpetrators of the atrocity perishing themselves. It was another form of suicide bombing, a practice which had been used by Muslim-motivated terrorists since the 1980s (they did exist then, but were not so much in the forefront of events). The bombers were told that if they died in the process of striking a blow against the infidels they would go straight to Heaven, and it worked (meaning that they swallowed this promise, whether or not it really did get them into Paradise, which is doubtful unless perhaps one takes the view that they were deluded rather than wicked). It took the best part of twenty years, however, before anyone used a hijacked passenger plane as the weapon, though 9/11 was some years in the planning because planning was what an operation like that required. The conclusion is hard to avoid that although terrorism is never something one likes to encourage, its motives apart, it had got nastier along with everything else.

How *should* we have reacted to 9/11? I think that while admitting to its past sins the West needs to be prepared to defend itself as a culture and emphasise that it is not really any worse morally than other people; they would have caused an equal amount of trouble had they been the ones on top. We should also have restrained ourselves from unwise actions, from taking it out on people who had nothing to do with the business. For us to go crazy was precisely what the terrorists wanted; we would have been rewarding people who flew others into skyscrapers or forced them to jump to their deaths from the burning buildings. It's a point many in America missed. The terrorists must have calculated that 9/11 would seem worse than any other atrocity previously perpetrated against the West, because due to its scale and nature it would be, and that would produce just the kind of reaction they wanted. Sickeningly, it could be argued that in some ways they got their wish.

Part of the significance of 9/11 was that it proved a terrorist attack could be more than a nasty, even a particularly nasty, pinprick. It might have had even greater geopolitical significance than it did if the Capitol had been devastated as well, for then US government would have collapsed, and an enemy could have taken advantage of the situation to invade if they had had the resources (the terrorists didn't). There was probably no-one else both able and willing to do it, and even if they had been *willing* they might have been deterred by the possibility of nuclear retaliation if those manning the infrastructure for same had kept their wits, but America could not ignore such an exposure of potential vulnerability (the domestic consequences would have been profound, in any case).

Paradoxically 9/11 was a one-off, never likely to be repeated because of the reaction and the security precautions which would now be put in place. But it had achieved its purpose, which was to spark off a *jihad* in which the Islamists would either be victorious in their aims or at least show they were not going to passively accept a global state of affairs they found intolerable. Their psychology was such that they would go on fighting the holy war for a thousand years, or forever, if necessary.

Resulting in the deaths of around 3000 people overall, 9/11 was the worst terrorist atrocity committed so far in terms of numbers killed. Realistically, given the scale of the slaughter, the way it was carried out and the threat it had posed to the very functioning of the state it was inevitable that America should have retaliated militarily, though nonetheless there were some who insisted she should not. It was the only way for her to have managed her psychological trauma and as such was forgiveable. Of course, it is easier to act in such a fashion against a country than against a globally dispersed movement. The supposed mastermind of the whole business, Osama Bin Laden, was being sheltered in Afghanistan by its extreme Islamist government, the Taliban, who were refusing to hand him over; at least that was the official story. When the deadline for surrendering him expired, Britain and America went in. I cannot personally confirm or deny the rumour that the Taliban were about to give in when the invasion began, and didn't really get a chance to comply with Allied wishes, or that 9/11 was actually not the work of Bin Laden and al-Qaeda at all but of a Palestinian (and Islamic) terror group. That is the nature of some of these conspiracy theories. This one does make a certain sense. The Taliban's behaviour might be attributed to the Muslim code of hospitality towards a fellow believer, but surely such an instinct, admirable in itself, should here have been offset by revulsion at Bin Laden's crimes, which had shamed Islam, and reluctance to give the faith a bad name – besides a practical fear of arousing the wrath of the West against them. They must have known what the consequences of their actions would be. And for Palestinian terrorists to have been identified as the guilty parties would have been dangerously inflammatory; many would have blamed Israel for 9/11 since, anti-Semitism apart, it could be argued that it was partly her intransigence, and America's support for her, which had rendered a proper peace settlement with the Arabs, and thus the defusing of an issue which had cost many Western lives, so hard to achieve. Had US forces had to go into Israel itself in order to ensure justice the result would have been particularly explosive. On the other hand, it could be that the Taliban simply saw things in the light of a commitment to the never-ending *jihad* and were quite prepared to invite their regime's almost certain fall if necessary. After all, Afghanistan has in the past proved notoriously difficult for Western invaders to hold down. At any rate, America's actions in the aftermath of 9/11 can be excused. If any regime was going to be toppled it was better that the Taliban, with their general intolerance of anyone not a strict Muslim, their treatment of women and their rejection of progressiveness in matters like education, which amounted to taking an entire society back to the Middle Ages in cultural terms, fell than that a government not as deserving of censure did, even if Hamid Karzai, who could himself be extremely nasty, was merely the lesser of the evils. Bearing this in mind, the requirement to avoid targeting people who might not have actually been responsible for the carnage in New York can be qualified. The Americans would have gone into Afghanistan in any case, to necessarily lance a certain psychological boil, whatever other factors (such as openings for US companies wishing to build pipelines, etc., in the country) might have been involved. And when something as awful as 9/11 happens the more good that can come out of the response to it the better, even where it benefits a different people from those who were the atrocity's principal targets.

The US President, George Bush (junior), declared a "War on Terror", which was in itself not an unreasonable thing to do unless you actually wanted the terrorists to succeed in their aims. Anxious to avoid being targeted traditional enemies of America such as Fidel Castro of Cuba (not that he represented much of a threat by now) and Gaddafi of Libya declared their support for her. Even in Iran there were protests at 9/11, which again may have been a form of pragmatism more than anything else although one would like to think not. Endeavouring to get into America's good books proved to be wise, for Bush now identified several rogue states, constituting an "Axis of Evil", which he saw as threats to the American way of life and to world peace, and therefore had to be neutralised somehow. In fact Iran was among them, which seemed ungrateful and deeply disturbing. Another was Syria, which had sponsored Palestinian terrorism during the Cold War era. The third was Saddam Hussein's Iraq. It was not clear how much this was rhetoric, designed to appease and comfort a traumatised nation, but things did seem to be taking an alarming turn, going beyond whatever 9/11 may have rendered justifiable. In some ways wisely (she did not want trouble with her own Muslim population) China refused to get involved, as did Russia. Britain only did, once it became clear Bush was going too far, because of the messianic delusions of her Prime Minister Tony Blair and his need from psychological insecurity to cosy up to the world's most powerful man. In the end Bush ran out of time, by the end of his Presidency, in which to carry out any plans he might or might not have had to invade, or at any rate bomb, Iran and Syria. He had spent too much of it trying to cope with the disaster he had created in Iraq, which included the political fall-out for the Republican Party.

Just how far was it necessary to go in order to satisfy America's need for someone to vent her grief and rage on? There would have to be an at least superficially plausible reason, in the context of 9/11, with which some connection had to be made, for selecting a given target and, ideally, no risk of causing serious geopolitical problems (arguably not encountered so much in the Afghan business, partly because the terrorists viewed it as part of the *jihad* anyway). In 2003 the latter considerations were ignored, or it was wrongly believed they did not apply. At any rate it was decided the target should be Saddam, whether or not there were to be any others once he had been dealt with.

The rogue states ideally had to have some connection with Islamic terrorism, which was the enemy, unless it was to look like America was simply lashing out at anyone she didn't happen to like. The government of Syria was not harbouring terrorists of the Bin Laden variety, who she found rather alarming. As, in fact, did Iran, which had been moving back towards friendly relations with the West and didn't want to jeopardise that. At most she was to play in subsequent years a sort of double game, encouraging militants in Iraq (at least it was said that she did) but in very cautious fashion so that she could avoid being fingered. Pragmatic in her own peculiar way, she did not wish to deliberately merge the religious militancy and radicalism she had displayed in an earlier period with that of al-Qaeda. She was moving towards a more secular, in that the leading figures were not necessarily priests, form of government, and even developing what looked something like a democratic system although the results of general elections were highly suspect. She liked to taunt the West in the person of the irresponsible and provocative President Ahmadinejad. But she was not altogether the threat she used to be. Iraq on the other hand could much more easily be demonised.

The US had ten years before fought a war with Saddam, who was undoubtedly a brutal and scheming dictator, persecuting his ethnic minorities and prevaricating over allowing United Nations inspectors into Iraq to look for weapons of mass destruction, which he would certainly have liked to get his hands on. The war had been over his illegal occupation of a neighbouring country, and when forced to withdraw from it he set fire to its oil wells out of spite, causing ecological and economic damage. On the other hand his was a secular regime and even though he might conceivably have been foolish enough to sponsor or shelter Islamist terrorists as a way of getting back at the West it is not likely they would have had much to do with him (despite a novel I wrote in which I had him and Bin Laden uneasily team up, largely due to plot requirements), since they regarded him not without justification as a false Muslim who had only played the religious card when it suited him politically to do so. He would have found them hot property and they would probably not have been allowed to plan anti-Western atrocities from a base on Iraqi soil. There was in fact not the slightest evidence that he had any links with them at all but 72% of Americans believed he had; again, they needed someone to take it (it being 9/11) out on. The trauma went deeper than at first appeared the case. Which helped Bush's purposes although the pretext for the invasion had to be the relatively more convincing one that he was trying to develop WMD (which someone like him would probably use to at least *threaten* his enemies).

I was one of those who marched against the Second (Third?) Iraq war. My reasoning, probably shared by a good many other people, was that even Saddam would not be so stupid as to use nuclear weapons in anger against Israel, Britain or the United States. The loss of both Iraqi and American/British lives, and the danger, wisely avoided by Bush's father in 1991, of inflaming Arab/Muslim opinion by appearing imperialistic, which would provoke more acts of terrorism by al-Qaeda and its fellows, was therefore not justified. Looking back, I am much more sympathetic towards the pro-war viewpoint than I then was. Firstly, there was Saddam's gloating on TV over 9/11. This was one manifestation of a disingenuous streak. Although astute in the way he seized and kept hold of power at home, he was not so good at understanding foreign opponents, in contrast to Hitler. He did not anticipate that the West would object to his seizure of Kuwait and was surprised, and angered, when it did. He thought that appearing on TV with the children who were among those he had taken hostage as "human shields", to be used as such when war broke out, would so move the West that it would refrain from attacking him and thus jeopardising these young lives; in fact the tactic didn't work because it was met with disgust as a cynical example of emotional manipulation. This disingenuousness meant you could never be quite sure what he would do, know how seriously to regard his threats. If he had had WMD it was almost certain he would vow to use them to cause chaos if his demands (including being allowed to reannex Kuwait?) weren't met. And I have a feeling that a relatively small but powerful nuclear device, causing much disruption while avoiding a general holocaust, might well have appealed to him as a weapon of choice.

In retrospect, though, I believe we were right to oppose the war the way we did. For we now know that Saddam possessed no WMD − or even the components for them − at all, and that the evidence he did was fabricated. It is unlikely, especially after the Kuwait business had identified him as a big league troublemaker, that he would have succeeded during the twelve years separating 1991 from 2003 in smuggling in the right materials and in enough quantities. As for his post-9/11 taunting, understandable as the reaction to it might be, there comes a point beyond which it is not right to essentially start a war, with all the suffering and disruption it causes, out of revenge.

So why then *did* President Bush (Junior) go to war in 2003? I think it was from a combination of factors, as with many other historical events. Firstly there was Saddam's televised "Look how your beautiful buildings have been destroyed" speech, which again demonstrated that extraordinary (and now fatal) disingenuousness. It is something which seems to be overlooked by those seeking explanations for what happened. We often do not attach enough significance to certain events at the time they occur. I would suggest that the taunt became embedded in the American consciousness, subconsciousness at any rate, and that without it the war might never have been. Already for a number of years Saddam seemed to have been thumbing his nose at the US, remaining firmly in power despite economic sanctions, and now he was being mocking in the aftermath of the most horrifying attack anyone had ever made upon her. Actually, what difference there would have been if he had kept silent or offered support is uncertain; but what he had *not* done was to express sympathy, in contrast to much wiser people in Cuba, Libya and Iran. If he had, it would have been much more difficult to justify the war. In the end his soreness over Kuwait got the better of him. A pretext was still needed to make it look as if revenge *wasn't* a factor, and his behaviour over WMD supplied one. He procrastinated over the weapons inspections, making it look as if he had something to hide, because playing games with the West, teasing it, keeping it guessing as to the true nature of things, had always been a favoured tactic of those elements in the Arab/Muslim world who were hostile to it for political or ideological reasons. When faced with a stronger enemy the thing to do, if you can't fight it and win, is to confuse it. Saddam wanted at least to go through the motions of not letting the West push him around. From the point of view of his survival his tactics backfired; it could be said to some extent that while he had failed to understand the West, at the same time the West had failed to understand him. Enough people thought he really did have WMD, or was on the point of producing them, to help in justifying the war.

In the end, the crucial factor was US domestic political considerations. Bush might have felt vulnerable because he had become President by a narrow majority in an election whose close result was still contested by some. In any event 9/11 proved a Godsend to him. In targeting Saddam he was playing on the anger of the American people in order to boost his own popularity. He was never as stupid as he seemed, and acted dumb because he knew it looked cute and increased his appeal. If not particularly intelligent he was certainly cunning. He cleverly identified and associated himself with a certain constituency which served as his power base; that constituency was the right-wing, "neocon" element in the Republican Party, which often took its inspiration from Fundamentalist Protestant Christianity. It believed America had a divine mission to fight for truth and justice and to civilise the world. It took the Bible literally and thought its policies were God's will; indeed, some believed they were preparing the way for the Apocalypse and Second Coming of Christ, which would be followed by the Last Judgement, the Rapture for those who were "saved", and the advent of God's Kingdom. Even if their actions had disruptive consequences, this would help by hastening things along. The establishment of the state of Israel was foretold in Scripture, as one of the events preceding the End, and it must therefore be protected by removing those who posed a threat to it, such as Saddam. Although there is no evidence of a sinister Jewish plot to cause the war, prominent neocons were or had links with Zionist (that is, believing in a policy of "Israel right or wrong") Jews, a number of whom served in Bush's administration. How far Bush himself shared their beliefs is a moot point but the fact that he was a born-again Christian (whether or not that Christianity was sincere) helped him gain these people's favour. He also courted the sort of Republican who took a "the only good Indian is a dead Indian" attitude to America's enemies and who later supported Donald Trump. Finally, he simply liked the idea of doing what many felt his father should have done in 1991, but which Bush Senior had baulked at. Iraqi oil was at least an additional consideration; as the US was determined on invading Iraq anyway she might as well take the financial pickings to be gained from it.

A surviving element from the old order proved, through the war which its behaviour made possible, to be the means by which the new one became further established. A secular regime was overthrown in a way which created openings for revolutionary movements whose orientation was religious as much as political. Saddam was the last of the good old military dictators (he was so closely associated with the Army that he can be seen that way), some of whom threatened world peace by their actions and could be portrayed as international bogeymen (the moustache, ubiquitous if not universal among such people, seemed to complete the image). The type had gone from Latin America, Chile's Pinochet being one of the last examples of it, as she moved towards democracy although countries in the region had never gone in for territorial aggression beyond their own borders. Indeed America seemed to be making a determined bid to get rid of all international bogeymen who had not, like Gaddafi and the Iranians, made themselves reasonably respectable. In the long run, she didn't quite succeed and in some ways only made things worse.

The removal of a strong-willed and powerful, if wicked, leader often results in instability and could geopolitically be the greater evil. Peace-keeping after the war was a difficult operation, especially when Afghanistan had to be held down as well to prevent the return of the Taliban, and Britain and America eventually pulled out leaving a weak civilian regime continually plagued by terrorist violence as militant elements, many of them from outside the country, moved in to take advantage of the opportunities created for them. The result was killing on a scale greater than that seen in the country under Saddam, who mainly targeted ethnic minorities and political opponents and had not been entirely unpopular with his own people despite having brought down UN sanctions upon them. Many Iraqis probably ended up wanting him back, if that had been possible (the matter was clinched by his execution at the end of 2006, in a way which had the character of a public lynching by his enemies and did not bode well for the new Iraq). The militants' aim as elsewhere was to create an Islamic state, either as part of a single world one or in its own right. Iraq had been a relative sideshow compared to issues such as the rise of radical Islam, and arguably the state of Russia, but now the secondary nexus point had fed into the main one.

It has been argued that with better planning, including the retention of the existing Saddamist police force, the Allied occupiers would have created the right conditions of stability and order. I concede this point, now. But it didn't happen. And since the war, without which all the trouble would never have occurred, was unjustified in the first place, and you can't invade every country that persecutes minorities or, in all fairness, discriminate in the matter – even to say "Well, you're right there but let's deal with one of them at least" seems irresponsible and casual in view of the cost in lives etc. involved – the argument that Bush and Blair were thereby justified in what they did doesn't wash. As it was, the war contributed to making the world a more dangerous and unstable place. Among other things it can be no coincidence that Britain and Spain, the two countries which had supported America over the business, both suffered terrorist bombings within two years of the invasion. For the first time Islamic terrorism, directed against an indigenous population of long standing, had actually taken place on the soil of a Western country. Fortunately no popular pogrom of Muslims followed, but it was clear the multicultural society which the white majority was expected by liberals to accept was now physically dangerous to the former, in that it could harbour people who actively sought to kill them (along with anyone else who got caught up in an atrocity) in order to make a political/religious statement. Saddam had not, as feared, turned out to possess chemical weapons with which to massacre the invading US and British troops, but in other respects the arguments of those who had insisted the war would be a bad thing were vindicated. Official enquiries found no connection between it and the terrorism but this is generally regarded as another example of the disgraceful whitewashing with which demands to reveal the truth have been met.

For the general public suspected otherwise. The Spanish Prime Minister lost an election and reaction to the war helped to cause the resignation of Tony Blair in 2007 when he might otherwise have carried on for a few more years. Even the American public, the keen edge of their anger and anguish in 2001 having been blunted to some extent by time, were beginning to realise now that the war had been a mistake and the thinking and policies which led to it were discredited, coming to an end when the Republicans lost the 2008 US Presidential election. Their legacy would take a lot longer to eradicate. (The effect on George W Bush himself is seen in his failure to attend the inauguration of Donald Trump, a President who seemed to embody much the same aggressively right-wing values as he had, perhaps even more so; either he did not wish to add to his unpopularity among more moderate elements or he was seriously embarrassed, perhaps conscience-stricken, by his past record.)

There are some academics who still believe that support for the war will be vindicated in the end. It is hard to see how this can be, in no small measure because of the time that has now elapsed since the conflict (fourteen years, during much of which there has been chaos and instability in Iraq). This means that any possibility of the evaluation being correct has become subsumed within events. The instability has gone on for so long that if it stops, leading hopefully to a more peaceful and stable state of affairs, it will simply mean that it has stopped, as the civil war in Lebanon did, after fifteen years, in 1990, and as bad things do tend to stop eventually, as unfortunately do good things, even if they are followed somewhere in the world by more bad things. Any causal connection between the 2003 Anglo-American invasion and the establishment of a better order in Iraq, supposing we can be optimistic enough to predict that the latter will happen in the foreseeable future, will have been lost. The problem is that the war could only be said to be justified in the negative sense that it stopped Saddam from developing WMD, and in fact he didn't have the right materials for that. We could only vindicate it if we had access to a parallel universe where it did not happen *and* Saddam went on to use the WMD to establish a regional hegemony for Iraq. Even supposing that he would have been allowed to risk nuclear war with his principal enemies, we do not enjoy that advantage.

In some ways the danger to the West itself from Islamic terrorism seemed to recede during the late 2000s and 2010s. More effective security, whatever its implications for the personal liberties of Muslim and non-Muslim alike, meant it was harder to repeat something like the London bombings of 2005. More often Western-based jihadists would decamp overseas to fight the war in Africa and Asia where conditions were less stable and the ability to wage a proper campaign against terrorism therefore restricted. Those parts of the world saw frequent attacks by new militant groups such as Boko Haram and Islamic State, who if possible were even nastier than al-Qaeda which they were beginning to displace and which may have been fading from the scene anyway (Bin Laden was finally located and killed by the Americans in Pakistan in 2011). They undoubtedly went in for burning people alive and forcing women into sex slavery. Their targets were Christians or people who were not considered strict enough in their Islamicism. And massacres of non-Muslims did continue to happen in the West, mainly in France which had courted trouble by perhaps unwisely banning certain forms of Islamic dress such as the veil, something a more tolerant Britain had so far refrained from; a sign that often the terrorism needed something to spark it off, so that otherwise the terrorists might not be that bothered. Not of course that the atrocities were thereby justified. The problem was that if the French government now relaxed its policies towards Muslims it would look like rewarding extremism, and so there was potential for hearts to be hardened. In the long run, Islamic terrorism in all countries with a Muslim population increased as social marginalisation and alienation did, although it was more likely to be of a crude home-made variety (as the makeshift character of the bomb at Parsons Green tube station, London, suggested though it nonetheless caused shock and injury), and often involve guns, control of which had always been difficult in certain British cities including London, rather than explosives. Or someone would try to run down people in the street. There was also an increasing tendency for the terrorists to be lone individuals, feeling especially cut off from the rest of society, who had no links to any larger group.

Most people took the view that the nation should pull together in the face of the threat, which involved not demonising all Muslims, and this was of course the right attitude to take, but it didn't mean the problem would go away. And many chose to be wary of Muslims, because after all you couldn't tell which of them were the terrorists and which weren't, rather than treat them to actual verbal or physical abuse, the idea of which was uncomfortable; it was a very British response, but it didn't help the cause of full integration.

Globally the situation deteriorated with the "Arab Spring" of the early 2010s, when revolts broke out in Libya, Egypt, Syria and elsewhere against dictatorial and often corrupt secular governments of whom people were now becoming tired. At first the movement, in which protest in one country encouraged protest in another, was warmly greeted in the West which saw it as a re-run of events in Eastern Europe twenty years before. Maybe now there would be a chance to really establish liberal, democratic Western forms of government in the Arab world − something Bush and Blair had been trying to do in Iraq, and which encountered the difficulty that sudden changes to the traditional way of doing things could not be accomplished smoothly. Maybe it was because there was more a culture of political violence in these lands, compared to the former Soviet bloc (excepting Yugoslavia), besides which they were also more backward and stagnant (the effects of rigidly-applied Communism in the Eastern Bloc notwithstanding). But the "Arab Spring" led to instability and bloodshed rather than a peaceful transition to democracy. In Syria the government did not fall, as in Egypt and Libya, the result being instead civil war between supporters and opponents of President Assad. The disruption led to a refugee crisis which threatened to cause serious overcrowding and pressure on resources in the already heavily populated West, where most of the refugees wanted to go because of the freedoms and comparative prosperity enjoyed there. It would certainly have caused mass suffering if the refugees had gone somewhere else, or stayed in their homeland. And then, of course Russia got involved. Meanwhile, guess who was taking advantage of the instability. Terrorism by extremist Muslims, including the murder of Western tourists, had been happening in Africa and Asia since Islamic radicalism began to spread in the 1990s, but now it got even worse. Even if Westerners were safe in their own countries, and that was ceasing to be the case, there was a possibility they might no longer be able to visit certain overseas destinations, broadening their understanding of those places, with the danger that there might emerge a divided world whose parts comprehended each other not.

The unrest resulted in the deposition and murder of Libya's ruler Colonel Gaddafi. As we all know he was a strange man, whose regime is not easy to categorise. It was Muslim, more than Saddam's had been, but not Fundamentalist in character; nor was it democratic. The West's siding with the rebels, after rapprochement had occurred between it and Tripoli, a process encouraged for the sake of economic links, seems ungrateful and requires an explanation. The reason was that the West set great store by and trumpeted its pride in its own democracy, which had not been won without a struggle taking place at some point, and since the Libyan government was a dictatorship opposed by rebels seeking political freedom it had little option but to support the latter against its former (during the previous few years anyway) ally.

After Islamic terrorism the most serious threat − it might even be the greater threat, or an equal one − to world security was or appeared to be Russia. There had earlier been fears that her economic and social problems would lead to dictatorship and the emergence of aggressive nationalism on the Hitler pattern. In the end something like this did happen but not in the way one might have expected. It was assumed the Hitler figure would be General Lebed or Vladimir Zhirinovsky. In the end neither got their chance. Former KGB officer Vladimir Putin restored Russia's prosperity and gained much support at home as a result but the methods he used against his political opponents and the extent of his personal power, which he continued to exercise *de facto* as President following his resignation as Prime Minister, led many in the country and outside it to wonder if it really was a democracy. On the foreign stage, Putin seemed to be flexing Russia's military and political muscles, recovering as he saw it the prestige lost when the Cold War ended and the Soviet Union fell. He was a strong and authoritative leader who had given his country back its self-respect, but now the power he enjoyed was going to his head. It seemed as if he was trying to rebuild the old Soviet "empire" that had collapsed in 1991, as he increased Russian influence in the Ukraine and annexed the until now autonomous Crimea. The excuse given of protecting Russian minorities sounded disturbingly like Hitler's pretext for occupying the Sudetenland. What Putin was certainly doing was orienting Russian foreign policy towards the country's traditional spheres of influence (in principle, doing no more than any other powerful nation might whatever its political system). He was following the same policy as the Tsars and the Soviets. One of the spheres of influence was the Middle East, where Russia had supported Arab governments against the West and Israel during the Soviet period. Hence Putin backed Assad of Syria against Western pressure to depose him and end the civil war (hopefully solving the refugee crisis), and this made it difficult for the West to intervene politically where such intervention might have been justified (in a way the last Iraq war was not) and hopefully productive, for fear of the consequences. Putin's calculation may have been that the refugee crisis would prove useful to him by destabilising it. He certainly saw it as a rival; it was alarmed by his actions and had imposed sanctions on him, harming the economic achievement he had pulled off at home as well as affecting the financial situation globally. How far exactly he intended to go and at what cost was uncertain; maybe he had gone a little mad. But he certainly seemed prepared to risk a confrontation, provocatively sailing his aircraft carriers, on their way to the Mediterranean where they would be based in any military operation to defend the Syrian government from its enemies, down the English Channel instead of around Scotland in order to more visibly make the point to the West. Russia still had a formidable military machine, including WMD, and there were rumours Putin was even prepared to contemplate a small nuclear war, as Saddam might have done, in pursuit of his aims. It all seemed very scary and not what the world really needed just now. Relative success in confining Islamic terrorism to Africa and Asia, plus a belief (whether or not correct) that it was too geographically dispersed a force to be as much of a threat as it seemed, besides its not having the protection of formally constituted states, persuaded Putin that he did not need to unite with the West against it rather than introduce a third and possibly complicating element into the equation of world politics. Altogether, Russia is geopolitically a problem, perhaps always has been. She is simply too big to be easily accommodated anywhere. With the fall of Communism, what is she "in it" for except her own aggrandisement, purely and simply? And she would be too powerful, too dominant or intent on trying to be, within a European Union enlarged to include her. It renders it unwise to split the EU (like the Roman Empire, though perhaps such a comparison is unfortunate at the moment) into western and eastern halves to make it less unwieldy, less clumsily authoritarian, since it is obvious which power would dominate the eastern one.

America seemed almost to be taking a back seat in these years; at least that was the impression given by the less interventionist foreign policy, a reaction against the Bush era, of Barack Obama. Obama was also preoccupied with trying to get his domestic programme, including the health reforms to which were given the name "Obamacare", through a Republican Congress. The constitutional system by which the US President can be of one party and the majority of the Senate and House of Representatives another is in my view ludicrous. It may just be that I'm naturally biased towards the British one. But it seems inconceivable to me that if Hillary Clinton had won the 2016 election for the Democrats the country would have tolerated four, perhaps eight more years of legislative logjam while the party tried to pass its policies into law against Republican obstruction. There would have been a constitutional crisis like that in England between 1906 and 1911 when a Liberal government's progressive measures were consistently thrown out by the House of Lords. The Lords were not elected whereas Congress is, but that wouldn't solve the problem. Though it may not have been specifically intended to produce that result the system which so often leads to the President being Democrat and Congress Republican, or vice versa, arose from a desire for checks and balances which were meant to ensure that no leader became too powerful. Whereas the British constitution was able to evolve over time into something a consensus in favour of which could be created, more or less, America in the late eighteenth century was a new nation asserting its independence against what it saw as royal tyranny. The latter view was not entirely accurate but undoubtedly George III possessed some residual power and was determined to assert it, including in the matter of the colonies, if not add to it. This perceived kingly absolutism was obviously not something the new republic wanted to emulate. America is a relatively young country and still influenced by the circumstances of its birth; it may be that in time she will see you don't need to earn the money for your medical care to be truly independent and self-reliant. But if she does, it won't be because of Donald Trump.

Barack Obama is one of the few genuinely likeable people to have been American President or British Prime Minister during my lifetime. The exception to this is a certain anti-British attitude, born of the resentment of one half of his ancestry against what had been the most obvious colonial power, which meant he did not do enough to defend Britain over pollution from a BP oil production platform in the Gulf of Mexico, something which wasn't entirely her fault. (And although his removal of the bust of Winston Churchill from the Oval Office (Trump put it back) was more understandable, since as a non- or partial WASP Obama could not have been expected to view the Special

Relationship in the same way as most previous Presidents, it did highlight the potentially worrying divisions within US society and politics, of which more below.) Otherwise, I have nothing against Obama personally and think he deserved his re-election in 2012. The main criticism of him is that although he didn't do anything much wrong he didn't do anything much right, either; he seemed wishy-washy and ineffectual. Although it's always ugly to bring race into things, it may be that in the light of America's past his consciousness of his ethnic identity influenced his behaviour while in office. He may have thought, "I'm the black {though strictly speaking, mixed race} guy. If I do this or that and get it wrong, you know what people will say." How far this really is true I don't know but you could argue that the oddities of the political system didn't really give him the chance to do a great deal anyway during his two terms of office. "Yes we can". No you couldn't, actually, but it wasn't for the most part his fault. He did get some kudos from the killing of Osama Bin Laden. But for what he failed to do he deserves sympathy rather than condemnation.

Obama won in 2008 because to some extent the future was on his side. Demographic changes meant the blacks and other ethnic minorities, who had traditionally voted Democrat, were starting to outnumber the whites in many areas. He and his supporters were on a high. On the other hand the Republicans then and in 2012 were ridden with doubt and insecurity. They knew that in future the white population would be a lot smaller, maybe even a minority, and understandably perhaps were disquieted by the implications of that. Yet there was a limit to how far they could try to prevent it – if they did the result might well be civil war – or be seen to be trying to prevent it. They were afraid of upsetting moderate opinion but were also responsible to a certain right-wing constituency which was unhappy about the way things were going. This ambiguity affected their performance and the way they were perceived by the electorate and particularly floating voters. They came over as shifty, ill at ease with themselves. It was the angst of the WASP in a "multicultural" society, and a sign that America was deeply divided. At the same time, it was sad that as a further sign of that division, and in a country where the President himself was of mixed race, which had been hailed as, and was even if hyped, a great achievement many blacks still felt alienated and ghetto-ised and there could be riots over the behaviour of white policemen. There were definitely two Americas, even if the line of demarcation between them was sometimes blurred.

One was (largely) white, Republican, and Trump-supporting, and its outlook was formed, historically, by the nation's early years when there definitely was the dominant WASP polity in which its emotional and cultural allegiances were sunk. The other was non-white, or sympathetic towards non-whites, liberal, Democrat, and with a different national vision if still subscribing to a common American identity in many ways. It reflected the way in which two Britains were emerging on the other side of the Atlantic, even though they might live together more or less happily and profess the same overall "British" identity. Again, the boundary could be blurry. But in the United Kingdom young people, who were urbanised, politically correct in outlook and pro-Europe, and out of sympathy with the past increasingly grew apart from their older, conservative, Brexit-voting fellow citizens who were more inclined to stress the value of tradition and the fact that Britain was still a primarily white society, especially if they lived in rural areas. One striking fact was that Christianity was not a focus for this kind of demarcation, as it had been in the past, because this time the decline in religion was general and affected all age groups even if, by comparison, older people were still more likely to go to church than their children or grandchildren. The situation was not quite the same in America where Christianity remained a far more influential political force even if there was justified suspicion that the Republicans only saw it in that context, angling for votes in certain waters.

The extent to which the white population of the USA has shrunk tends to be exaggerated. It cannot have shrunk that much or Donald Trump would not have been elected President in 2016, despite the dangers of assuming that all blacks etc. are Democratic supporters. In Trump the Republicans finally found a leader who is not afraid to say, or to hint at, what he really thinks, not at all troubled by feelings of angst or propriety. I think all the fuss over him is because what he really wants to do is preserve the WASP, or at least white, ascendancy in the States, in that it remains numerically the majority. He may or may not actually *hate* ethnic minority people; hopefully he makes his most offensive comments mainly in order to reaffirm his loyalty to the constituency which elected him in the first place. Perhaps the best policy from his point of view ought to be to freeze further immigration into the country while respecting the minorities already there. More controversially, he could also try to limit the overall birth rate on the grounds that like immigration it is imposing too much pressure on the resources of that complex, populous modern state we have so often talked about. He might be seen as having a valid case. But there would be suspicion he was doing it for racial reasons, which would at least partly be the truth.

Undoubtedly Trump has been over-demonised. His successful management of the economy works to the benefit of racial integration, because when things are not going well economically people tend to blame ethnic minorities ("They're taking our jobs", or, worse, "They caused it"). Of course if you think someone is racist, if you are against them on a particularly sensitive issue, this will colour (dare I say) your attitude towards them and you will not feel inclined to praise them on any account. But the historian and political analyst have a brief to be objective. That should not blind us to Trump's faults. The economy has been his big success, and since he himself is from a business background this is not surprising; but he fails to see that in politics you also need to be a politician, a profession in which some skill at handling people is required − you can't just say what you think. There are other issues which matter every bit as much; it's not *just* the economy, stupid.

It is doubtful whether Trump has the sensitivity needed to implement in the long run a bipartisan policy in matters of race. But whether in any case he can halt the demographic changes which would threaten the whites' position as the majority ethnic group, without doing things too many people would regard as unacceptable, remains to be seen. His election would have been impossible, of course, without the defection from the Republicans of disgruntled white working-class voters who feel the Democrats neglected them through being overconcerned with ethnic minority interests. Since it was Republicans themselves who rendered Obama less effective by scuppering his legislative programme, this is rather unfair.

Basically, Trump has sought to resolve issues by sticking a size ten boot through all the things he and his supporters believe were damaging America: political correctness, the pusillanimity thought characteristic of Democratic administrations, the weakness and demoralisation of the post-George W Bush Republican Party, isolationism and non-assertiveness in foreign policy. The list also includes green concerns, Trump believing as do many hard free-market capitalists that to turn from the burning of fossil fuels to renewable energy risks harming America's economic prosperity and thus diminishing her greatness. How far all this is a sensible solution can be vigorously debated. But the USA's behaviour under Trump is designed to show, after 9/11 and with such global trends as the rise of China as an economic powerhouse plus the challenge of Islamic Fundamentalism to the dominant (and exemplified by America) Western world view, that she is still here and on top. I detect a faint uneasiness behind it, which is unsurprising when things have happened to produce insecurity. Is Trumpism really sustainable except at the cost of a major world disaster which will engulf America along with everyone else, through the harm to the environment and the wars which result from provocative and aggressive actions? How much 9/11 is proving instrumental in the fall of the American Empire, if that is what is going to happen, is a bone of contention; in itself not that much actually, since America was not destroyed as a sovereign state and military power and in due course recovered economically. It is chiefly significant by virtue of having engineered, as a reaction to it, an underlying assertiveness, resurgent under particular conditions, within American Republicanism which by going too far risks rebounding catastrophically. It is at least a contributory factor in the process, though there are others.

Surprisingly, it seems, Trump has in fact avoided George W Bush-type escapades abroad until now. But it was always likely there should be one under his Presidency; let us hope difficulties over Iran, though at the time of writing the crisis appears to have fizzled out somewhat, do not turn out to be it. At least Trump is not being as bellicose in his attitude towards Russia as he has been towards China, and in fact is extremely friendly towards Vladimir Putin. It is something which seems surprising, but also highly fortunate. It can best be explained by Trump and Putin being so similar in character; personalities who are determined to get what they want and not take any nonsense from those who might stand in their way.

Meanwhile, it would I suppose be easier for the world to better deal with its problems if it possessed some degree of economic and/or political unity. But how essential this requirement really is is a matter of conjecture. It can itself become problematical as centrifugal tendencies may arise in reaction to it and tear the structure apart, as happened with the multi-ethnic empires of the past. It caused some consternation when in June 2016 Britain voted to leave the European Union. The stock market got jittery because it thought this would adversely affect the country's economic performance, and even lead to the collapse of the EU as a whole. One might comment that if it did have the latter effect that would not argue that the institution had been a very robust one, but let this pass for a moment. There undoubtedly would be some disruption from such an outcome, and it would occur at a time when things are troubled and unstable. But provided all things were equal, I suspect Europe and the world at large would find some way of staying reasonably prosperous if they wanted to, which of course they do. There are also fears for legal and political co-operation against terrorism, but if the threat is serious enough this will be achieved.

Because Europe has lost so much of her economic and geopolitical importance, albeit still only relatively, it matters less in a global context what happens to the EU. Besides, there is no comparative organisation, involving a diminution of the national sovereignty of its members, anywhere else in the world nor does there seem to be much of a demand for one. It only exists in Europe because of the events of the latter's history, and in particular wars which were especially devastating because of her technological advancement. And as a single political (rather than an economic) force Europe cannot really assert its will, other than join in general international peacekeeping operations, because it is reluctant to do so. It was right to keep out of the 2003 Gulf War, but nor did it get involved much in the 1991 one which was far more justified (one problem is that after the two world wars of the twentieth century, in which it was heavily involved as an instigator and participant, Germany is still too inhibited from flexing its military muscle). Britain's tendency to back up America against the disapproval of the former's European neighbours is sometimes a good thing.

The international capitalist monetarist hegemony was coming under attack not only from militant Islam. Its globalised nature enabled a foreign company to effectively determine a national government's policies, where they were thought to affect the company's interests, and this was especially resented as capitalism became more and more ruthlessly concerned with maximising profits and cutting costs. A certain element began to protest against it, often violently. They were angry at private companies who had freedom to hire and fire and who charged more and more for their products, making necessary an austerity which limited options and reduced personal prosperity. The majority of the protestors, who were organised on an international basis and with the resources of the internet behind them, were young people who were overworked and underpaid (and had to fund themselves if at university, student grants having been abolished), at a time when the price of everything was going up, though that price rise was affecting all those on low incomes and struggling to make ends meet. They disliked the power of big business, which could afford an opulent lifestyle way beyond most people's means, and additionally could suffer if a company based in China, Japan, America, Germany or France decided to make staff at any of its national branches redundant. In a historical tendency for the same phenomena to recur in different forms, there were parallels with the radical protestors of the 1960s. Apart from being politically correct (the PC and anti-privatisation "narratives" not necessarily going together), opposing the power of the private sector was what counted as left-wing now (and to be right-wing meant defending it, among other things, however far you were prepared to accept political correctness). In fact in their publicity the protestors frequently attacked not just globalisation but capitalism itself. When the Wall fell and the Western way of doing things seemed to be triumphant over the repressive Communist system in which the state controlled the economy, the big mistake of right-wing thinkers and commentators was to confuse "liberal democracy" with the free market, as if the two were one and the same, the political arrangements and the economic ones being inseparably connected. They *are* connected, but the connection is not two-way; it does not automatically mean that if you have one you will have the other in every respect. To those in the contemporary world who are affected by the private sector's determination to increase prices, putting strain on the consumer, and any "hire and fire" policy it may be operating, the consequences of which they cannot escape from, while CEOs and the like are living quite comfortably protected by the favour shown towards big business by government, it is that private sector which is oppressive, which is the obstacle to freedom.

Now that the monetarist version of capitalism, which was the one capitalists favoured and effectively that we were still living under even though the terms "monetarist" and "Thatcherite" were used less, had been shown to have serious defects, often serving merely to highlight the gulf between those who profited from it and those who didn't, there seemed to be taking place a revival of supposedly discredited Communism. At least, a Communist society was presumably what the protestors were intending to put in capitalism's place; it was never quite clear. It is possible they were to some extent confused in their philosophy, as their 60s forebears had been; and judging from the slogans on the stickers they placed on lamp posts and the like, some protest groups actually favoured anarchy.

But certainly these new movements were unlike what many of their counterparts in a previous generation had sought to be; there was a very real hatred towards what they were seeking to bring down, manifested in both verbal and physical violence. In the 2000s and 2010s those decent and sensible people who genuinely wanted to end the injustices within society were hamstrung by being caught between an incestuous and greed-obsessed upper class (defined according to wealth, social status, political power or all three) and a foul-mouthed, aggressive element who would have gone further in trying to change things than was preferable. Hence the protestors remained, for now, a relatively small if newsworthy group who could never have gathered enough support to make a difference. It was a similar problem with the Stop The {Iraq} War Coalition, although there was less, in my personal experience, of the bad language; the business was too dominated by the Old Left, who opposed not just the invasion of Iraq but that of Afghanistan too, and insisted in linking the campaign to all kinds of left-wing issues with which it had nothing to do. One problem with a world that was in many ways multipolar, with the ending of the old duality in which two powerful competing ideologies dominated everything, was in fact the complicating and sometimes confusing survival of elements from that previous era which combined with new issues to render achievement of a better global order more difficult.

Within the world capitalist system itself there was taking place a power transfer that was both economic and also, because wealth conveys influence, potentially political to some extent. Globalisation and monetarism have helped to avoid wars, which some will win and some lose but which prove damaging in certain respects to all, because of the opportunities they seem to provide for creating wealth. They depend on an international economic integration the jeapordising of which by warfare risks destroying prosperity. But this can't negate an unassailable fact of human affairs, one of the inescapable truths of history, namely that the fortunes of some powers wax while others' wane. Those countries which industrialised first began to decline first, especially as their supplies of native raw materials became exhausted. The balance of power, economically and perhaps in other ways, had shifted after the Second World War from Europe to the Soviet Union and USA. Now it was shifting again, to the former "Third World", and especially the strongest nations within the latter, namely India and China. Countries which in many cases (not quite China's) were former colonies of the West were rising to world prominence. For the moment at least the development was a purely economic one. But the West certainly felt it.

Two hundred or so years ago Napoleon predicted that China, the sleeping giant, would one day surprise the world. That has now happened. It took a long time, as is the way with China, but it happened. The Communist Party's policy of divorcing political control from the nature of the economic system has worked. What is astonishing about the global economic scene in what has so far elapsed of the twenty-first century is the way China has come to dominate everything, making many if not most of the commodities which Britain, France etc. previously manufactured themselves on their own territory. The consequences for Westerners are in many ways undesirable. They have meant that everywhere is flooded with cheap Chinese goods of poor quality, which depresses native industries and also makes life more difficult for the consumer because they have to be replaced more quickly, causing difficulties for the less well-off who need to pay particular attention to budget-balancing. China of course is only doing what the West had done before it. The Chinese are not demons; in fact they want the West to remain at least relatively prosperous because that makes it more valuable as a trading partner and helps to bolster their own economic growth. But I feel they lost their soul when they became a mass capitalist power. I preferred the old, traditionalist China, though not because I wanted it to remain economically weak compared to the West, and a lot of the respect I used to have for the country has gone.

Should Europe, no longer the economic powerhouse which the United States comparably speaking still is, band closer together in order to better resist a Chinese hegemony which is not altogether good for her? The trouble is that further European integration may well be opposed. Britain had secured "opt-outs" from it, which would have hindered the process in any event, but some wondered whether these amounted to all that much and ultimately she voted to leave the EU. This will undoubtedly, in itself, hamper Europe's ability to become a single, and possibly stronger, economic unit. And what if Britain's desire to be more independent from her is shared by other European nations? We have tended in the past to assume it is not, that it was only Britain who was being awkward and refusing to join the party out of excessive sentimentality for a past in which one could be one's own boss, but it occurs to me we have no actual proof of this. What if the EU collapses? It has been pointed out that young people, who are the future, are mostly supporters of it. They are not so much influenced by the past – they of course do not share in the living memory of the two world wars, which in any case are fading with time from the collective consciousness – as by the fact that they have grown up with the organisation and with the doctrine that it is a guarantor of racial and international harmony. (I'm not clear what the anti-globalisation protestors think of it; in some ways it potentially goes against all they stand for, yet as the element from which they come is often vehemently anti-racist and anti-nationalist they ought to be in favour of it). Not all of them voted against the "Brexit", just as not all ethnic minority people did. But with people living longer now, the different stages in a person's life are stretched out, so that clashes of culture and outlook between age groups become prolonged and are therefore more dangerous.

Generally the Brexiteers wanted Britain to be free of absurd and restrictive laws originating from Brussels. The problem is that the nature of the overall situation, in politics and other areas, in our time means the efficacy and desirability of a policy, or of its opposite, has become very attenuated. What politically may be the right thing is not so economically and *vice versa*. This is one factor inclining some people to take a pessimistic, even apocalyptic view of humanity's future.

Can we regard the West as being threatened jointly by Islamic militancy and the rise of the "Third World" (including former colonies which might rejoice if the boot were on the other foot?). The nature of monetarism means that it is a better option to seek economic rather than political/military power, even if the latter is within your means, and those who aren't doing so well out of the system would not (virtually by definition) have the resources to defeat you in armed combat; at any rate to try would be a foolish risk to take. But could China (the most likely candidate) invade and militarily occupy the West, an enterprise which would have to include America, if its economic policies were not to her liking and in her view threatened her interests; in other words if she felt she had no choice? Geography alone would not be an obstacle given America's own success in enforcing its will globally. I don't know if China's military strength, at the present time, would permit it but we should remember that her industrial resources are considerable and expanding. (She would not embark on the venture from anything other than economic necessity, having not the religious motivation of hard Islam or, in the present world, any other ideological reason; wars over large areas, involving occupation and perhaps annexation of territory, are expensive and bothersome). But even if she wanted to do it she wouldn't while the West still possesses nuclear weapons; though they have such things themselves, the Chinese are in many ways a sensible people and thus among those least likely to start a nuclear war which might involve their own annihilation. China engages in industrial espionage, and seeks to create spheres of (economic) influence for herself in emerging parts of the world such as Africa, but probably won't threaten to press the red button. However the situation might be different if the West's economic decline meant it was no longer able to afford a nuclear arsenal.

If all things are equal, the East-West divide of the Cold War years will eventually be replaced, following the current period which is one of transition from one geopolitical order to another, by a North-South divide between the still predominantly white, relatively wealthy, and secular or Christian (the latter often only nominally so) nations of the North and the predominantly non-white, very often Muslim and relatively poor nations of the South; the latter might actually become dominant, in a way that resulted in the whites/West being economically depressed and feeling politically ignored. A similar situation would emerge if the whites became minorities in most of the countries where they are still the majority, including the United States, the world's most powerful nation – a very real possibility eventually, given the current nature of demographic change, and also in view of the past ironic. They would then experience a massive loss of influence worldwide, which would inevitably affect their expectations and self-perception and also their power to protect themselves from those wanting payback for historic racialism and imperialism (although hopefully the nasty situation this implies won't happen, which as indicated in chapter one is at least a possibility if, again, all things are equal). Certainly the fate of the whites, whether or not they resist what is happening in the long run, will be one of the two most pressing geopolitical issues in the twenty-first century (the other is the continuing struggle to fight global warming and its consequences for the physical environment while still hanging onto prosperity, comfort and technological advance). If the whites did try to preserve their status by freezing out the ethnic minorities, and the result was the latter emigrating back to their historic homelands rather than civil war, it would of course reinforce the new world division.

Some of it (the new geopolitical partition of the world) has already happened, purely racial factors notwithstanding. The transition is not necessarily smooth and even, the embryonic new order being visible with hindsight, anyhow, through the fading old one as through the walls of a transparent womb. The North-South economic divide, to which the Brandt Report of 1983 drew attention, was to some extent evident before the end of the East-West political one. It remains despite progress over the Third World debt and an increase in economic growth − not necessarily benefiting everyone in the countries concerned, for economics is to some degree an artificial construct − in some areas. And resentment at poverty and marginalisation is felt in particular by Muslims, both in the West and in other parts of the world where suffering results from the globally unequal division of wealth; here it is aggravated by a potential culture clash with other belief systems.

Concerning the political and military consequences, the West will of course try to prevent fully-fledged radical Islamic states emerging out of the instability in the Middle East and North Africa (or at all). But if it happens in enough places, they may only be able to do it in a few cases (if any). They may find themselves overstretched if the problem is sufficiently widespread. They may not be able to prevent, in the worst possible scenario, the creation of a belt of radical Muslim states extending all the way from Morocco to Indonesia (almost to the coast of Australia). It would not be practical for all those countries to form a single Islamic state, but the chances are that some of them at least would be able to work together, form a military alliance. Aggression against the West itself seems unlikely as long as she has weapons of mass destruction, but she would be potentially vulnerable to militant Islam, as she would to China, if she could no longer meet the economic cost of maintaining them (which might well be the case given that she also has to accommodate an ever-growing, and ageing, population). There is also the question of how far religious fanatics are deterrable. But unless they prove not to be or the West does give up its WMD it will not be possible in the modern age to change the existing world order, in the sense of an upheaval comparable to the effects of 1939-45 or 1989-91, by force; unless the explosion of discontent is a blind lashing out at all one dislikes without regard for the consequences.

If a decentralised terrorist movement like Islamic State or al-Qaeda manages to take over a country (because obviously it would like to, given its aims) then it will cease to be decentralised and become a rogue state. Should other countries follow, then our new world order will emerge. If Eastern Europe/Russia could consist of a whole band of states each of which was governed by an oppressive regime against the wishes of its inhabitants, then so could the Middle East, Africa and Asia. There might be an influx of migrants – adding to overcrowding, irrespective of skin colour, culture etc. – to the West from countries like Australia who would inevitably feel threatened by what was happening on their doorstep.

This new and very grim situation would be the next stage in world history. But how far will the tendency towards multipolarity work against it happening? Will the future simply be a confused mess? One factor which prevents things being clear-cut is Latin America. Overcoming a lot of the sociopolitical divisions and the other evils of her past, she has bucked what seemed at one point to be a global trend, outside Europe and the vibrant economies of East Asia, to become far more prosperous and far more politically stable, even if the picture is not entirely rosy. She doesn't have a large Muslim population or any tendency to be drawn for one reason or another into military engagements overseas. Geopolitically though not economically she is and always has been, apart from Cuba in 1962 and America's general and often paranoid fear of Communism in its backyard, unimportant. For these reasons she is not seen as a target/threat by Muslim extremists. She therefore doesn't fit easily into the geopolitical equation I've described. Also, Russia seems to be staking its own claim to world or at least regional predominance, irrespective of what Islamic State might do. Under Putin it does not really enjoy a friendly relationship with the West. And China concentrates on sustaining her economic boom, otherwise staying out of things. She was sometimes spoken of during the Cold War as the third superpower; today she is undoubtedly a superpower in economic terms, and probably has the potential to become one in others, but she still retains a certain Chinese preference for not being involved with the world at large unless absolutely necessary.

But Latin America's prosperity etc. is itself a factor making for stability, extending it to quite a large portion of the world. There has been some social unrest in Brazil, a product of the effects of monetarist policies along with the corruption said to be widespread throughout the region, but these are internal issues and don't at present either have a geopolitical aspect or threaten political order within the sub-continent. And if radical Islam becomes a serious

466

enough threat both Russia and China (the latter having Muslim populations within her borders) will side with the West against it in a case of choosing the lesser of the evils.

If we bear these things in mind our new North-South alignment would indeed seem to be the shape of the future. The division would not of course be quite clear-cut ethnically, religiously or economically. The North would include China plus the Far East and the south, for simplicity's sake, a rising (and largely Hindu, though with a significant Muslim population) India. There is in any case some disagreement over what constitutes "white", with many Latin Americans having black or Indian (that is, Amerindian) ancestry. On the Eurasian land mass the line would be drawn roughly east from Gibraltar through the Mediterranean, above Turkey and across to the Central Asian republics, and then down to Kolkut (Calcutta) or thereabouts.

But apart from inevitably being arbitrary, would it necessarily ensure a stable if far from perfect geopolitical order? For one thing, if Arabs are capable of resisting Messrs Assad, Mubarrak and Gaddafi to the extent of causing instability, even civil war, are they not capable of resisting Taliban or Islamic State-type regimes with the same effect, even if one successfully held down Afghanistan for a number of years and was only dislodged by foreign intervention? The result could be anarchy rather than a state of affairs politically dominated by Islam. The impact on world trade would be considerable. Nor would it necessarily be confined to the "South". China's economic expansion is slowing down, as booms naturally do after a time, and this exacerbates the stresses and discontent created when the boom widens the gap, even in relative terms, between rich and poor. And the fact of economic prosperity will lead to greater demands for democracy and political plurality, for the very same reasons that it did in the West in the nineteenth century; those who play a part in creating wealth feel they deserve some recognition of and reward for that. Meanwhile, in the West itself potential for radicalisation among disaffected young Muslims means that the battle against militant Islam may be fought on two fronts, a factor which whatever its ultimate consequences will serve to complicate the overall situation.

So in 2020 a general collapse of social and political order planetwide was just as likely to happen as a new form of Cold (or Hot?) War. And over everything loomed the consideration of the natural world and whether its resources would be capable in the long run of sustaining a growing global population, either at all or at an acceptable environmental cost. In the 1960s and 70s the main concern of environmentalists had been general pollution: CO_2 from car exhausts, toxic gases from power station chimneys, industrial waste dumped in lakes, seas and rivers, the radioactive detritus from nuclear plants or atom bomb tests. From the 1980s it was atmospheric heating caused by the burning of fossil fuels, which although contributed to by some of the problems mentioned came to overshadow them all. Valuable ground began to be lost at an early stage; monetarist governments did not care to be told, a relatively short time into their ascendancy, to interfere with the way private industry conducted its business. One Conservative Party manifesto contained a chilling reference to "oversensitivity to environmental issues". The Thatcherite and Reaganite revolutions came at the wrong time for the planet. The rapid expansion of China's economy from the 1990s lent a new dimension to the problem. She, India and the remainder of the "Third World" could not industrialise to the same extent as the West (as they wanted to do and as the West had no right to prevent them doing) and thus enjoy the same living standards, through ensuring (potentially) a more equitable global distribution of wealth, without causing so much disruption through the greenhouse effect that the quality of life would deteriorate anyway. Global warming caused/would cause in the future floods and typhoons which by inundating coastal areas (in the West as much as elsewhere) in the first case and wreaking general devastation in the latter would make certain regions uninhabitable and create the phenomenon of the environmental refugee (on top of the millions already fleeing from war and political instability). Overcrowding in inland cities would reach unmanageable proportions. So far no-one had found a way of solving the problem by making renewable energy, which did not pollute the way oil did, or the vast untouched coal reserves remaining in China would, truly efficient and cost-effective. The supply is variable and can't generate enough power to provide for the whole modern industrial infrastructure all the time; storage is important, but what is being stored isn't available. Plus wind farms though environmentally sensitive in one respect aren't so in another; they are a visual eyesore, and consequently unpopular.

Many other measures intended to reduce pollution of one kind or another, such as regulations affecting building design and recycling of rubbish, were either bureaucratically annoying and stifling, or inefficiently administered (certainly in the case of the recycling), or both. Much of what it was insisted had to be done for the sake of the planet's future was seen simply as a nuisance, one less likely to be tolerated if there was the slightest possibility global warming was not human-made after all, as a not inconsiderable body of scientific opinion claimed. Meanwhile, nuclear energy did not pollute – unless of course a reactor was to melt down, and the more nuclear plants were in existence the greater the probability of this happening, and happening more than once. What was really needed was a system where you could switch between different sources of power (oil, gas, coal, solar, wind, nuclear) as required, but this would be both technically and administratively complex, indeed clumsy, with more scope for mistakes. In any event the Chinese were not going to be told to leave their oil- and coalfields, which would be a vital part of their future economic expansion and prosperity, untapped.

Meeting the needs of inflated populations would be rendered even more expensive, and practically difficult, by the consequences of climate change which would be disastrous whether the cause of the problem was emissions from industry or the phenomenon was a natural one insufficiently understood. In the West the situation was aggravated by improved medical technology and quality of life, which meant that people lived, and stayed relatively healthy and active, longer but placed a grave burden on the state once they did begin to suffer, in extreme old age, from dementia or physical illness/infirmity. And so far there seemed no prospect of the colonisation of outer space becoming a safety valve to relieve the overcrowding and other problems at home; assuming anyone wanted to live out there anyway, the process was not taking place fast enough to be our saviour, because the money which would have to be spent on it was needed to deal, however effectively, with Earthly issues of a kind which in any case risked overwhelming us before space exploration began to bring serious rewards.

13

As a Westerner I am always potentially handicapped in understanding other cultures, as perhaps they are in understanding the West, by relative lack of familiarity. It does seem though as if a general nastiness, arising from the interconnected nature of the world's problems combined with frustration at our inability to solve them but always made worse by intolerance and incompetence, is affecting everywhere, even if social propriety and convention prevents it being fully apparent much of the time. Scientific and technological progress does not necessarily make man much wiser, or happier. Often its only effect, besides making possible better ways of killing people, has been to lower the intellectual and spiritual level of society through the more negative consequences of television and social media. The Islamic extremists who plan terrorist atrocities against the West using its own computer technology may be effectively making the point that a society can be technologically advanced but (in their view) morally decadent. But this could apply to the terrorists themselves. They are not necessarily unintelligent, and obviously can master technical things. But they are intolerant in religious and cultural matters to the extent of harbouring hatred towards those they see as enemies, treating prisoners barbarically. They are practising a debased form of Islam characterised by fanaticism and bigotry rather than spearheading a glorious Islamic cultural revival. But it is undoubtedly true that the West, too, is going both forwards and backwards. Many of the following examples are from my own British experience but going by what I can gather from the general grapevine are part of a wider Western phenomenon.

Though change in the modern era has been a more or less continuous process we can identify three principal milestones in the social history of the West since 1945. The first was the birth of the "permissive society" in the 1960s. The second was the triumph of monetarist capitalism in the

1980s. The third was the advent in the 1990s of the social and political philosophy that has become known by the term "political correctness". All three trends had lasting effects and at the same time became entangled with one another and with further developments – the secondary, though still vital, nexus points of social history – such as the increasing role of the media, the obsession with image and advertising, and the cultural effects of the internet and information technology in general, to give Western society the form it has today (as well as explain much of its dysfunctionality). Political correctness and monetarist capitalism became in effect the two dominant "narratives"; in the 90s there took place a kind of fusion between them, for reasons given below. Everything crystallised into a matter of those two belief systems, all other ideologies having become in some way discredited because they seemed aggressive, leading to wars, or intellectually disproven, or had been shown by bitter experience to be ineffective at ensuring economic prosperity while at the same time requiring an unacceptable degree of political control. Religion had either been rejected or divorced from secular political and economic affairs, on a group basis anyway. We had been put off ideology by the events of history, including the religious wars of the early modern period. The result was a society in some ways sterile and spiritually bankrupt, concerned only (if not necessarily in a selfish way) with making life as pleasurable in a *material* sense as possible; this materialism was bolstered by the increasing belief on the part of enough people that physical science was the only reliable way of understanding the universe.

The triumph of political correctness, which evolved from the structuralist philosophy formulated and taught in French and American universities in the 1960s and 70s, was made possible because left-wing socialists, while seeking as always to work themselves into positions of influence – in the arts, education, and local government for example – in order to remake society according to their beliefs, had succeeded in making themselves more respectable. They accepted the triumph of monetarism and abandoned trying to change the *economic* system in a way the majority of society, despite being unhappy in many respects at the way things had gone, did not want. They redirected their energies towards changing social attitudes based on race, class and gender, which had always been a major concern for them. They took over subtly, as they had sought to do in their previous incarnations; the difference now was that the right, not realising what was happening in the flush of its triumph over Communism, failed to act in time to prevent political correctness, which was to develop into something they tended to vehemently dislike, becoming so established that it was difficult to dislodge. It grew exponentially in a process which at first may have been unconscious and uncoordinated. It operated through freezing out those who did not agree with its thinking or methods, once political correctionists realised they had become powerful and numerous enough to do this. It was initially mainly concerned, and still is mainly concerned, with promoting groups that had hitherto been marginalised – women, ethnic minorities, homosexuals – and protecting them from being offended or discriminated against. It later extended its brief to outlawing forms of behaviour, in whatever area, which might be supposed (correctly or not) to unsettle people and thus lead to a situation which might be hard to control (it ended up being essentially a means of managing a complex and multipolar society which in truth rather perplexed it). It operated partly through changing language, inventing new terms, often clumsy and bizarre, to replace ones which it considered in some way inappropriate. There was also an unspoken agreement to stress some things and downplay others. It is widely suspected of operating, particularly in the field of employment, a policy of "positive" discrimination in favour of women and minorities, though the charge is not always easy to prove. Where such a policy was indeed in operation the reason was overcompensation arising from a collective guilt complex at past racism, etc., combined with a belief – hopefully false – that society was so institutionally prejudiced, once left to its own devices, that positively discriminating was the only way to secure advancement for the groups it was sought to benefit.

In many ways great strides have been made in equal opportunities over the last few decades. Where they create serious obstacles to self-fulfilment (other than not being admitted to a certain club) class differences, despite perceptions, are really a matter of wealth rather than birth, accent etc. The reasons why certain "working-class" urban districts are still deprived are more to do with economic factors than social prejudices. With the reservation that the *uppermost* level of business is possibly still dominated by the public school "old-boy network", given the tendency to "pull up the ladder", a greedy parasitic businessman is nowadays as likely to be someone from a working-class or lower middle-class background as not. It all depends on whether you have the skills to make good in business and finance; since not everyone has, a degree of elitism is inevitably preserved. Class is something that is difficult to define anyway, because of uncertainties over what yardstick should be used. And the traditional image associated with the expression "working class" is of someone connected with trades such as coal mining and steel, which have increasingly been superseded in the economy by service industries and IT, whose workforces are socially much more diverse.

Women now do most of the jobs men can, including be Prime Minister or Chancellor, and are on the whole better represented in all those professions, one exception being big business whose top management is still strikingly male-dominated, explaining the sexism and even harassment encountered at that level. It has been claimed that if more of the heads of major companies were female capitalism would be practised in a more compassionate and egalitarian fashion. I am not entirely convinced of this.

Trends in politics, sociology and economics cannot be explained entirely by attitudes to matters such as gender. If we in the West have become too closely wedded to uncompromising, even ruthless monetarism then that is a problem which will affect everyone to some extent, male or female, white or nonwhite. And there are examples of outrageous and indelicate behaviour on the part of women executives.

The situation with regard to ethnic minorities is less clear-cut and the question a little more controversial. Like other traditionally excluded groups, blacks and Asians have found an outlet for their talents in the field of entertainment, where they are far from unappreciated. In Britain one thinks of Lenny Henry or *Goodness Gracious Me*. Then there are fine black actors like Chwietel Ejiofor, Idris Elba, Denzel Washington, Samuel J Jackson. And pop artistes like Jimi Hendrix, Joan Armatrading, Stevie Wonder (if I can't think of more recent examples it's only because of my age). What ethnic minorities really want, of course, is to have the same opportunities at all levels and in all areas of society. How far this aim has been achieved is a matter of debate and appears to vary between countries. In the US, George W Bush's Republican administration contained two blacks, both occupying very senior positions: Condoleeza Rice (National Security Adviser) and Colin Powell (Secretary of State). (Though the definition of "black" is a moot point; Powell's skin is actually paler than mine). And one who was of mixed race actually got to be President. In Britain, by contrast, there seem to be few if any ethnic minority people at the top in any walk of life. In the legal profession, it was pointed out once that there was an over-promotion of blacks and Asians at barrister level; but at the same time none were evident among High Court judges. There seemed to be a sort of system of checks and balances in operation; EMs were being underpromoted at one level to compensate for overpromoting them at another. The aim was to increase their representation, and thus their power and influence, but not by too much; to give them something but assuage white fears at the same time, in a compromise which was unlikely in the long run to satisfy. It had in mind the future and reflected underlying tensions over the situation of whites, and how they should perceive themselves, in a society where they would have ceased to be numerically, and thus presumably politically, dominant.

How much progress towards greater equality was due to political correctness, as opposed to changing times or the practical impossibility of excluding a growing ethnic minority population from the life of the nation is difficult to say. In its basic aims, of course, PC could not be objected to, if they were simply to address just grievances. But many people felt it was going too far, that it *did* overpromote the minorities in the media and official publicity, that it glossed over uncomfortable truths and avoided tricky issues, ignoring valid fears on the part of whites and downplaying instances where it was they who had been the objects of discrimination. It was open to the charge of being hypocritical, of creating its own nonsenses and injustices.

It had been judged compatible with monetarism because a thriving economy needed the participation of all sections of the community, as producers and consumers, and so none could be excluded. Unfortunately, in other ways there was a contradiction between the two ruling ideologies, or at any rate between political correctness and the effects of the "make as big and as fast a profit as possible" mentality into which monetarism had degenerated. Because what sold was sexiness, youth, and "image" – that is, "looking right", and so there was a danger of simply pandering to public preconceptions and prejudices (or those of the companies, who in a free market capitalist system had considerable power). Under political correctness people weren't supposed to be marginalised, not given a job or other career opening, because they were ugly, fat, wore glasses, etcetera. Yet even in a pre-PC era it was easier for someone like the nerdish-looking Buddy Holly to get by as a pop singer. Nowadays, you just wouldn't fit the bill. People judged too much on first impressions, which surely went against the apparent PC code of considering an individual on their own merits. It led to the growth of the "cult of celebrity", by which all that mattered was that you "looked good" in an advertising agency's eyes, appealing to those whose tastes might be simple (no need to waste resources and thus jeopardise profits on engaging with anything more complicated when you didn't have to make lots of money). The prospective star didn't need to have much in the way of actual talent. It undoubtedly assisted the "dumbing-down" of society. It was hard for anyone not already an established star to become famous, to achieve recognition, since all promoters had to do was pick from a narrow pool of people who had the right qualities to appeal to a mass audience.

Something similar seemed to be happening in the field of literature. Many aspiring authors reported failure despite persistent efforts over a number of years to get into print, to interest conventional publishers, agents and booksellers in their writing. They were forced to take the independent route, more or less doing their own marketing, which was a tortuous and backbreaking business without the resources of a proper publishing house/agent behind you. To be fair, this was to some extent not the publishers' fault. It was a case of the "big society" getting out of hand and collapsing under its own weight. Everyone wanted to be the next J K Rowling or Ian Rankin and so publishers got inundated with manuscripts, receiving more than their readers could cope with and being forced to pick just a select few at random from the "slush pile". Some years ago the British government became sufficiently worried that the next Rowling, or Rankin, or Shakespeare, would be overlooked and started a scheme by which non-established authors could have their manuscripts read, for a price (which might have deterred people needing to do careful budget-balancing, especially when of course they still had no guarantee their submissions would be accepted). I don't know what came of it, but things are no better for the majority of self-published authors two decades on. What particularly rankles with talented members of the latter fraternity is that their material gets rejected while rubbish by an author who happens to be a celebrity (but who may be past their best) or simply happens to have that mass appeal is not. There may also be a fear of taking on certain types of novel, which are perhaps different in their approach, in case it doesn't work out and a publisher loses money. Whatever the reasons for it all are, it is one example of how the politically correct, supposedly egalitarian society is actually less pluralistic than that which existed in the past – may be said in fact to be elitist.

In addition to the shortcomings of its partner in the ideological alliance, political correctness, as noted above, caused trouble by its own failings. It led to poor discipline in schools because it was thought wrong to talk down to children (at any rate it was seen as talking down to them) in the sternly paternalistic manner of old, even if that might actually be the right approach. Such was seen as old-fashioned (often the concern of political correctness was to be "modern", because to be modern was to be politically correct, all that came before PC being associated with snobbery, racism, elitism etc.) and also intimidating. PC also made certain subjects taboo because they could be uncomfortable, and adjusted the language to suit. People were referred to as having "passed away" or "passed on" rather than "died". Death was not really talked about, partly because it might have meant discussing such topics as religion and the afterlife, and PC was unhappy with them after all the trouble they had caused (it was kinder to Muslims, who could be seen as the victims of Christian prejudice, than it was to the Church but not on account of their actual beliefs, as opposed to the right to practice those beliefs in peace). To be honest though the mere fact of living longer, and more comfortably than one's ancestors did, also helped to ensure that people were unprepared for death when it struck at their families and friends and therefore found it so much harder to cope with.

Under PC as it has developed over the past few years it is essentially wrong to try to persuade me, even if not particularly aggressively, to do something I hadn't already decided to on my own initiative, even if I don't go so far in response as to take legal action. I cannot attempt to convert you to a different religious or political point of view. That is to invade your personal space, and to cause you offence or distress. It ties in with contemporary apathy towards religion or politics and results in a society which is atomised, disjointed. The tendency to make an official complaint, or to sue, when something happens to someone that they consider insulting or inconvenient is perhaps a manifestation of this, though often the motive is financial gain. It is product both of the environment created by political correctness and of a society where price rises make life difficult, leading some people to try and grab as much as they can by way of compensation, especially when resentment is felt at the widening gap between rich and (relatively) poor. Now the fear of prosecution causes organisations to take elaborate legal precautions against it, which can be very frustrating for those who have to sign the disclaimer forms or, in the writing of fiction, want to break into a particular genre but can't because of copyright restrictions designed to protect those already established in it. Other laws, again designed to forestall any likelihood of being sued but also reflecting a fear of illness, injury or death as quantities now particularly repellent, plus threatening to the ordered and thus controllable state of things, sought to avoid the remotest possibility of anyone suffering physical harm. The excessive concern with health and safety led to complaints about the "nanny state". Both the private and the public sectors were running out of control; complicating attempts to deal with the problem through confusion as to which of them was responsible for it. In a more bipolar age things were a lot simpler, at least.

Political correctness can't have been unaware of the flaws at its heart, but nonetheless disliked any criticism of itself. The criticisers were "judgemental", "negative", "confrontational", "aggressive" and "ranting". Or worse. Because PC acted as a bulwark against racism etc. those deconstructing it and so preventing it fulfilling that function were either seriously misguided, or racist themselves. The accusations of bigotry served to raise the temperature over the issue because they were naturally resented by those who were not guilty of it, as much as by those who were. It prevented frank and sensible discussion of subjects like race or immigration, when it was not irritating whites while at the same time failing to give blacks and Asians what they really wanted. Undoubtedly it could turn the tables by making the groups which had previously been guilty of marginalisation and discrimination into victims of them, through an often erroneous conviction that they were not the ones with the problems or likely to be. This led at one point to serious concern that disadvantaged ethnic minority districts in British towns and cities were receiving all the cash for regeneration projects while equally disadvantaged white youth got nothing (explaining why the far-right British National Party was doing well).

The problem is also encountered in respect of gender, where it ties in with the issue of sex as an activity rather than in the sense of sexual *politics*, although the latter come into it. As with other issues it is hard to say what is due to political correctness and what to the simple fact of social change, although the former, of which feminism, a doctrine descended from the "Women's Lib" movement of the 60s and 70s, is a part has certainly encouraged women to be generally assertive of their rights and aspirations in a way that sometimes has an unpleasant aspect (after all, they are the victims of sexism and exclusion and not men, who are the *perpetrators* of it and don't deserve excessive sympathy).

The social changes which began in the 1950s and 60s included a more open attitude to sex, with the inclusion of explicitly erotic passages in popular and literary fiction, scenes of nudity or intercourse in some films and TV programmes, and the availability of pornographic magazines. The reluctance of previous eras to explore sexuality in this way had been condemned as narrow-minded and a restriction of one's potential for self-expression and -fulfillment. In the 1970s, when the idealism of the previous decade had run out of steam, the explicitness became vulgarly commercialised. In a less repressed age, it was considered that sex would sell, because it was what people wanted to read about. Accordingly there was a profusion of paperback fiction books in which the sex scenes (which did not necessarily contribute anything to the plot) were shall we say far less inhibited. This helped to deal with unhealthy hang-ups, but it also led to a belief that it was far easier to casually jump into bed with someone than in fact was the case, that the mere establishment of friendly relations would within a short time lead inevitably to intercourse, and also gave rise to false (if maybe not *always*) notions of what a woman might be prepared to do for a man. In other cultures it seems to have given Western women an exaggerated reputation for promiscuity. Many illusions were to be cruelly shattered by brute experience. A lot of the trouble was due to Harold Robbins, probably the worst offender, although to be fair his novels were as much a psychological study of powerful men who were simply out to get what they wanted, in sex and other areas, as anything else. You can actually get frustrated flicking through a Robbins waiting for the dirty bits to come along. A complex character, he was undoubtedly using his other literary intentions to excuse his own obsession with sex, but there is a sense in which the latter is a vehicle for the story as a whole, as much as the other way round. (Concerning the alarming proclivities of his characters, reaction to them probably varies between "Tut, what filth", "Rubbish, it's not like that" and "Chance would be a fine thing".)

The sexual frankness of the permissive society was condemned by some as immoral and degrading. In my early teens, being more puritanical than most people at that age, I tended to agree with them. I was appalled at what I saw on a visit to Soho, aged thirteen, in 1978. But it seems to me that something has now happened which is even worse.

Pornography was condemned by feminists as exploitative and degrading to women. During the 1990s and after, however, it became clear that women themselves did not always share this view. Many decided that they didn't like being told by other women what they should be offended by, and started to take a greater interest in the business, though it was not necessarily nude men who were the object of it (nor other women, though it could be an expression of lesbian attraction). In being less reluctant to be photographed nude (sometimes they were pregnant as well) or in provocative and revealing poses they felt they were simply expressing their own sexuality, as they had a right to do. All this was fine in itself. But their behaviour was often lewd, going beyond what could be seen as tasteful. And altogether, this new form of sexual liberation was to degenerate into something downright disturbing.

What had happened was that a kind of "bastard feminism" (some call it "post-feminism") had emerged whereby female empowerment and self-expression were seen in terms of women acting more like *men*, including getting drunk and behaving in a coarse and offensive way. They were sharing in men's faults as well as taking on their roles. Here what might be called "bastard political correctness" kicked in jointly with the "I can do what I like, get what I want" attitude encouraged, intentionally or otherwise, by monetarist economics (which promoted individual desires and ambitions over "society" and its codes). In both cases things were happening that the founders of those doctrines, to be fair to them, had never intended. It was certainly not monetarist, theoretically anyhow, to dictate to me how I should behave and thus try to circumvent my personal freedom.

The impact from the mid-1980s of AIDS, a disease which could be transmitted by casual sex and which was eventually fatal, as well as incurable (it still is, though sufferers live longer), on sexual attitudes and behaviour was considerable. Complete sexual freedom was now a dangerous thing or, if you chose to take the recommended precautions, less exciting than before because you had to fumble to put on a condom and the "protection" did reduce the thrill of the experience to some extent. Sex lost its appeal in a general, that is promiscuous, sense as well as becoming tied up, if I may so put it, with gender politics. It became more about power, dominance over one's partner, and about self-expression (or self-advertising). I wear revealing clothing for its own sake and not necessarily because I want to entice someone into bed. Because of the influence of political correctness and feminism it was the female partner who was empowered and triumphant, although of course you could still get abusive and controlling male ones. There had emerged in some ways a new puritanism (as part of which prostitutes were forced off the streets by public hostility and police clean-up campaigns and took to operating from home or rented premises, advertising themselves as masseurs or escorts, while restrictions were placed on the opening hours of strip clubs and lap-dancing establishments). But it had an unsavoury aspect. Now men began to feel they were the ones who were disadvantaged and discriminated against. Their wives/girlfriends could withhold sex as a weapon and more easily ditch partners they had gone off or had serious differences with. Where a relationship broke down there were greater restrictions on the men seeing the children than on the women, presumably on the principle that *if* the man took the opportunity to abduct the child he would be more likely to succeed because he was physically stronger. I believe this injustice has now been rectified, but it was symptomatic of a worrying phenomenon. Men also,

477

perhaps, had cause to think they were prevented from being men, were being feminised (in what might seem a mirroring of the alleged genetic trend for girls to become physically more like boys, that is bigger and stronger, and boys more like girls). Another contemporary example of language change is the tendency for "blonde" to be increasingly spelt that way, with the feminine "e", regardless of whether one is talking about a fair-haired man or a fair-haired woman, and a brown-haired man can be referred to as a brunette, with an "e", rather than as a brown-haired man. And although I don't know how many men would, like me, seriously object to travelling on a pink bus because pink was not a very masculine colour you can be pretty certain that their complaints would be met by the reply that they were merely upholding "gender stereotypes". Altogether, it was probable that men were being affected to some extent by redefinitions of what traditionally constituted and defined masculinity, how it was expressed; for example they could now marry each other rather than marriage being exclusively a case of men marrying women. Because of the interconnected nature of things any attempt to alter the situation of minorities and the way they are treated risks feeding back somehow into the majority, and this is not necessarily a harmless thing even if it is only *gay* men whose aspirations (if they regard the business in question as a serious one) the revised marriage laws apply to. Probably more dangerous on the whole is the idea, arising from an increase in cases of transsexuality, that any distinction between the sexes in how they should behave or are perceived is "gender stereotyping" and should be discouraged.

And in professional matters too there are areas where the sexism of the past (and to some extent present), a case of men freezing out women, may actually have been reversed. There seem to be far more women involved in publishing, whether as publishers themselves, agents or readers, than before and I am increasingly worried that they may be unduly influenced, when deciding whether to accept or reject a manuscript, by a woman's view of things, for example being uncomfortable with a novel in which a heterosexual male writer quite innocently explores the sexuality of female characters. It is not too far-fetched to suggest that this is happening or that it could happen, and the danger is that it may leave men without a voice. It is quite possible for tables to be turned in an unwelcome fashion, if the pressure for change is so great that it goes too far and there is a failure to appreciate that it is doing so.

Another area where men were becoming disadvantaged was the Church of England, though that was not for unchristian reasons, at least not entirely. More women were being ordained as priests than males and I suspect this is due less to positive discrimination than to the fact that women are in many ways emotionally stronger, better able to cope with a potentially stressful job which is nowadays made worse through the pressures put on the institution by shrinking congregations, financial shortages and often secular hostility. Men do not like the situation and often put it down automatically to a monolithic and merciless politically correct establishment which they can do little to oppose, becoming depressed as a result. They consequently fail to challenge it. They may be guilty of the traditional male tendency to moan at problems without doing anything about them, failing to fight one's corner and therefore suffering; but it emphasises how demoralised they are.

Regarding sex as a recreational pursuit many people got tired of it altogether, partly because of the reasons mentioned, partly because they were entering middle age, and partly because any trend towards sexual licentiousness tends to exhaust its appeal after a while. Since they were no longer much interested in religion, they got their comfort in food instead, leading to an obesity epidemic which placed considerable strain on the British NHS. They were also eating as a distraction from their inward fears for the future and about the way society was developing.

Generally as far as social behaviour was concerned, there was an increased relaxation of conventions, a continuation of a process which had been taking place gradually for the past hundred years or so but accelerated during and after World War Two. Political correctness and a desire not to lecture people on how they should behave may have had something to do with it, but it is also the case with human beings that the pendulum swings, an age of repression being followed by one of liberalisation, both officially and unofficially, although the process may take time to reach its maximum possible extent. There was now much less formality in speech, dress etc. People wore casual clothes, even in church, where previously they might have put on a suit and tie, though exceptions were still made for special and public occasions. Women almost universally dressed in trousers rather than the more feminine skirt, and jogged or competed in athletic events with their midriffs bare (no doubt further upsetting Islamic fundamentalists). To some extent this was due to the odd weather patterns resulting, and especially in a north European climate, from the impact of global warming. The temperature was often higher, or at least muggy, and you felt uncomfortable being too buttoned-up. Alternatively it could suddenly go cold, in which case trousers provided more insulation. I'm not sure what explains the tendency at one point for female beachwear to leave the crotch partially exposed, the effect being both ugly and indecent, but this has now thankfully gone out of fashion.

First-name terms were increasingly used on initial acquaintance and in official business beneath the level of national or local government. (Undoubtedly the modern image-obsessed business sector encouraged this development, regarding formality as something too stiff, old-fashioned and off-putting). Retired Army officers stopped using the titles "Colonel", "Major" etc. For various reasons regional accents became less pronounced, surviving mainly among older people (the northern English ones seem to be an exception). In England they were replaced if anything by the "London" accent, which was becoming more dominant partly because resisting its spread was thought snobbish, although it was not really Cockney but a bastardised form of the same often referred to as "Mockney" (the Home Counties accent, which formerly reigned supreme thanks to the BBC, seems to have reasserted itself of late in reaction to this, and one hears less of the glottal stops which had crept into the speech even of people who in other respects were "well-spoken").

One trend that was certainly not very savoury was the freer use of four-letter words in all contexts regardless of who, including children, might be listening, as if they were a part of normal everyday conversation rather than something which had a place but ought to stay in it. It was most noticeable among the "working class" who had undoubtedly become vulgarised, partly because the supposed leaders of society had not set a good moral example by their own conduct; as an offshoot of that the swearing was partly an expression of anger at the elitism and greed of the wealthier sections of the community. The upper classes had also been debased in their own way; they were concerned mainly with making money and spending it on horses, yachts etc., which is not necessarily the same thing as culture. Indeed they too swore more frequently, though still not to the same extent. If only because a blunter way of speaking is most associated with the working class (who ought not thereby to be demonised), it jarred. Meanwhile bad language was becoming more common in popular music, one example being the hate-filled lyrics of rap which were an expression of rage at social alienation and inequality.

Although many people would still apologise if they accidentally walked in front of you, and stand aside to let you pass when it was polite to do so − in fact, this kind of courtesy seems, pleasingly, to have become more common − in other ways society was becoming vulgar. There was less inclination to put one's hand over one's mouth when yawning. In notices prohibiting people from urinating in public or exhorting them to clear up after their dog if it defecated while being taken for a walk there was no reticence about emphasising the point by a symbolic representation of the bodily functions in question. You often saw posters with a (trick) photograph of the dog squatting − as if to defecate − over a pot of money, representing the fine. Only the other day I was rightly shocked to come across in a local library a book actually entitled *Merde* (the French word for "shit"), about the funny/downside of life in the EU, which featured on its front cover the statue of Belgium's "Janneke Pis" doing what it is most famous for, i.e. urinating. The stream of pee is continued artistically onto the book's spine. Sometimes it was not so much that something was vulgar as that there was a preference for the colloquial which, snobbery apart, seemed absurd and not inconsistent with "dumbing-down". Britain's National Lottery became the "Lotto". I also find myself thinking of a pub in Ashford, Middlesex, called the "Black Dog" and whose sign formerly depicted just that — a mysterious and possibly spectral creature reputed to turn up from time to time and either good or evil in its purpose (it seemed at least semi-intelligent). The current one shows a vaguely Snoopy-like cartoon character (not particularly black) who one suspects has little understanding of or engagement with culturally interesting folk legends, any more than the people who put the sign up.

On a higher level dumbing-down is a consequence of lack of interest in ideas, ideologies, in the belief that they have been discredited. Whatever its exact causes it has become something of a national concern in recent years, and rightly so. It means that whereas in the 1950s and 60s and for a while afterwards, university education being more widely available, children and young people often knew more than their parents, nowadays the converse is more likely to be the case, except in matters such as the technicalities of computing and "social media". If we wanted to be very blunt about it we might say that the young have had their heads stuffed with political correctness, plus knowledge of information technology, but not much else. One thing which needs to be said, though, is that this is not really their fault. If they are indoctrinated with and absorbed into a way of thinking, a system, which whatever its better points is dangerous in what it neglects and in what it is preoccupied with the blame usually lies with elements in the older generation, because they had the opportunity to do it. They were the ones holding the levers of power in education, politics, etc. In this sense the criticisms the young frequently level against the old are valid. But of course we ought to remember that it was only a relative few out of the "old" who started the trouble, and the rest, not all of whom read the *Daily Mail*, continue to disapprove of what has happened.

As controversial as the dumbing-down, for some, was the fact that people were generally more willing to be seen weeping on TV over a bereavement or other catastrophe, in a way which previously would have been viewed as unseemly. It was one manifestation of an apparent wish to jettison any standard of behaviour inherited from the past as outmoded and repressive. As part of that same trend certain social institutions either lost favour, though not with everyone, or were tweaked so that things happened which up to only a short time before would have been considered inappropriate and therefore unthinkable. Many people chose not to get married and instead lived with "partners", of the same or opposite sex, the relationship now being recognised in law. Though again the change was not universal, women kept their maiden names if they did get married and, whether married or single, styled themselves by the feminist "Ms", "Miss" somehow seeming old-fashioned or sexist or both. Homosexuals could now be wed, either in church (depending on the conscience of the priest) or at a register office, which completely overturned the traditional perception of the institution. They were also to be observed a little more frequently kissing and holding hands publicly, both in the flesh and in advertising. Like other minorities they had gone from a situation where they had no status in a law which was completely hostile to them (pre-1967), through a stage in which they were decriminalised but still subject to certain legal and social sanctions, to enjoying full liberty of expression (the 2000s onwards). It was now socially acceptable to be openly gay; nor was it a barrier to occupying important positions (or any other positions for that matter) within the community. Later, bisexuals and transsexuals emerged as groups whose wish to be accepted for what they were demanded to be met. With the transsexuals, it was generally a case of young people becoming sexually aware and then realising they were in a situation of gender uncertainty, also of the political climate changing in such a way that there was less hostility to their adopting a new sexual identity (equally, they may simply have been riding an equal opportunities bandwagon, though in most cases from genuine need rather than trend). Sometimes an older person who had been struggling with the condition, secretly, all their lives now felt emboldened, because of that changed climate, to confront it and make a choice. In history, transexualism goes back to ancient times, but until the twentieth century was expressed differently, by leading a double life; sex change operations involving a combination of surgery, drugs and therapy were available from the 1970s but occurred on a much smaller scale. The recent apparent increase in transsexualism seems rather startling to many; though largely due to cultural factors it seems unlikely to be entirely so and there is a theory that it can be partly explained by genetic mutations, "something in the water" or both, which may have far-reaching implications for society in the future.

In the past, neither the left (meaning that element which challenges established conventions) nor the right (meaning those who seek to preserve them) has been wholly successful or unsuccessful in establishing its beliefs as common policy, any more than it enjoys a monopoly of the truth. What generally emerges, in a functioning liberal democracy, is some kind of rough compromise between the views of both sides; a consensus, however grudging. In Britain in the 1960s Harold Wilson's government created the Permissive Society, as much because they suspected it was inevitable, or saw choice in certain matters as a moral imperative, as because they agreed or disagreed with what people were to be permitted to do. It was opposed by many, if not most, on the Right; by all those who considered it an affront to traditional, and crucial, values and saw it as identifiable with moral decline. And yet no-one has ever seriously tried to repeal the legislation decriminalising homosexuality in principle, for example, however much they might like to, or, apart from hardened feminists, ban all pornography. There is a recognition that it would be too great an interference with liberty, a return to what is now no longer appropriate. (Morally it is appreciated that some tightening of the laws on divorce and abortion is less controversial, but there is no desire on the part of the majority for a wholesale return to the situation pre-1967.) At the same time there are limits to how far permissiveness should be allowed to go. Or at least, there were. Problems, controversy certainly, will be encountered when it is sought to further widen them. For left-wing thinkers and organisations a dilemma presents itself once the "consensus" is achieved; where does one go after that? Do we accept the new status quo or seek to change things further? To some extent it is a case of something non-tangible, a matter of combating attitudes and perceptions which result in continuing *unofficial* discrimination; but what if further legislation is felt to be required? Some consider the "new liberalism", as one might with justification call it, to be a series of steps too far.

It could certainly be called political, but like (sexual) power politics not necessarily in an ideological, certainly not a formal ideological, sense. It was a case of people basically doing what they wanted to do. Sometimes it might be that an old-style (whatever their actual age) feminist believed marriage was an outdated institution designed to repress women; sometimes it was simply seen as a bothersome and unnecessary business, involving having to keep up appearances and thus restricting true self-expression, which had nothing to do with whether or not the parties really loved one another.

How far had culture declined in the twenty-first century West, given the picture of it (not inaccurate I assure you) I have been painting, so to speak? Actually the prospect is not all bad. I don't have a high opinion of modern art, but then I never have had. It's to some degree a matter of personal taste. I have to admit though that whereas much traditional art is idealised with the intention of presenting a favourable image of some monarch or politician, the modern stuff is a lot more honest, if shocking. Perhaps the real problem is that in the post-modern world we have run out of ideas, and the shocking, which exceeds the bounds of taste and propriety, is all we have left, along with the tacky and pedestrian. (This is partly what the frequently encountered term "post-modernism" means; it also refers, in politics, to the lack of ideologies which enthuse in a positive sense rather than simply lead to conflict. That it is so commonly used suggests, illustratively, that people are aware of the problem but don't know what to do about it.) There has undoubtedly been a decline in the quality of popular music since the 1980s, as observed previously, though this has not affected the "indie" (independent) stuff which is to a great extent a deliberate reaction against it. Rap is particularly repetitive and monotonous, though it is also making a political statement in offensive and sexual ways (it can be heard in less harmful versions). There's a lot of good classical material out there, including the old masters who seem more appreciated now than ever. Attending classical music concerts is a very popular pastime, one thing which reflects well on people in a "dumbed-down" age and is an exception to the trend I have been describing.

The situation regarding literature, in spoken and written form, gives a little more cause for concern. I have already touched on this, but there is more to be said. Another problem I have encountered as an independent author in selling books is that reading is no longer such a common pastime, despite the appeal of J K Rowling's *Harry Potter* stories having popularised it for a while. This is because longer working hours, a modern society requiring people to labour much harder to meet all its requirements, mean there is less time to devote to leisure in the evenings given other considerations such as the need to pay some attention to one's spouse/partner and children. It is also because the internet now functions as a rival attraction. The internet is harmful to the cause of literature, and literacy, in another respect too; perhaps because they're things you rattle off rather than sit down and take care over something about emails, which was not a problem in the days when people wrote letters, works against precision in writing, and correct grammar, syntax or punctuation.

Though generally most intelligent people speak the way they have always done, language suffers from uninhibited profanity on one hand and jargon, which might be called "dumbing up", on the other. The jargon, not necessarily political in purpose, is increasingly peculiar and one feels silly and uncomfortable using it, which ideally should not be the case with any vocabulary. If you have sent an email to someone your computer may register an "incident", which seems absurdly dramatic.

Another disturbing development of late has been the preference of many publishers for books that do not exceed two hundred and fifty pages in length. Apparently, people cannot cope with anything bigger. This puts commercial considerations before other equally important ones and turns the book into a standardised neatly-packaged product in a way that risks preventing it from fully exercising its function as literature; it might have even more to say that is of relevance and appeal, and need the space for it. The commercial considerations and the cultural seem to have become divorced. There's also a tie-in with the tendency towards unblocked text in many publications, because blocked is thought to be intimidating, even for adults. There seems something very immature about this, and it gives credence to the belief that for one reason or another modern people lack the intellectual profundity of their forebears (having among other things a limited attention span). They need to be spoonfed. The word for it is "neoteny", that is the persistence of childish modes of thought into adult life (perhaps because of the lifespan as a whole having been extended). The publishers accommodate with it for commercial reasons; dumbing-down is essential to win over a mass market, which one would not do by talking to ordinary people in too intellectual a language. Perhaps you can't blame them. But monetarism is undoubtedly combining with other factors to produce something culturally disastrous.

I know of a lady who admitted that in her spare time she got up to all sorts of different activities but did not "think". There were too many distractions from intellectual activity, or perhaps the pace of life simply did not allow it. How far was it laziness and how far something cultural? Were there just not enough opportunities to train the brain or did something genetic or medical explain the tendency? Whatever its cause, this lack of depth in the way people thought did not assist in solving the problems of a complex society or answering questions as to where the human race as a whole was going, its place in the cosmos. It was partly that they had decided to leave the business to the scientists. Those scientists were seeking a "theory of everything" which would ultimately explain to everyone's satisfaction how the universe worked. They seemed to have got what they wanted with the discovery of the Higgs-Boson particle. But although the latter might explain why things behaved the way they did, it did not explain why they were there in the first place. And did we really know as much as we thought? Neither Higgs-Boson nor other groundbreaking achievements such as the mapping of the human genome could account for the tendency of people to behave in ways that could not have been predicted – or to be irrational and dysfunctional, to the extent of harming themselves and the planet they lived on.

The intelligentsia increasingly looked to science – which it could be argued is a technical rather than an intellectual discipline – rather than philosophy or theology to account for everything, and this along with factors already mentioned had a profound, in the sense of far-reaching, effect on the general population, who despite dumbing-down will nonetheless follow their lead if they seem clever enough or their views accord with one's personal inclinations. There arose a kind of anti-intellectualism, in that while not necessarily being hostile to intellectuals people came to prefer what was easily digestible and chose not to pursue what they did not understand. It did not help us in fathoming the nature of a complex universe. And it has other, equally damaging consequences. It means that we are less inclined to analyse and question our beliefs, simply going by what is emotionally congenial to us. Thus it is easier, for example, for those who are dedicated to political correctness to find themselves in bitter conflict with those who oppose it or at least question its application; it is something which does not bode well for future social harmony. People will simply defend entrenched positions, whether or not there is actual racism (for example) involved although in such a climate it is easier for anger to slip over the border and become hatred.

I mentioned the social effect of the internet. We were becoming more sucked into popular culture and mass communications than ever before but now there was the Net and "social media" as well as TV and radio. They represented a virtual "cyberworld" in comparison to which the real one didn't seem so exciting. The internet has its beneficial aspects, serving as a medium for raising money for charity, or more easily ordering books and classical music CDs plus itself making knowledge available at the touch of a button, thereby promoting culture. It can also be extremely harmful. Constant bombardment with information through computers, mobile phones and texting, on top of TV, has led to many children suffering mental health problems and is very worrying for the future. Then there is "trolling", which shows how the internet often just brings out people's nastier side in a way that might not happen in other circumstances.

The internet has also to some extent become a substitute for community involvement. Young people discuss things, exchange information, and arrange group holidays etc. on the Net rather than join clubs or societies, whose membership is now primarily middle-aged and elderly and which are suffering such a decline in numbers and therefore finances – especially a problem in an increasingly expensive world – that many are likely to fold in the near future. It could be argued that this is simply a shift of social activity into a new form, by way of modern technology. Clearly it does not leave the community entirely atomised. But it is still sad nonetheless. It is a cause, and also a reflection, of a loss of support for institutions, and institutions have their good points.

The two which have suffered most have been politics and the Church. In the case of politics the decline was because people felt excluded. With better communications and transport facilities, with international airline flights and foreign holidays, the world had shrunk and also revealed more of itself. Travel and the global media broadened the mind and enriched the quality of life, culturally and materially, in many ways. But if people were more aware of what was going on at home and abroad, they were equally aware of their powerlessness to do anything about the harmful aspects of it, the poverty and corruption and oppression and political mismanagement. So the effect of having one's eyes opened could be negative as well as beneficial, leaving one with feelings of alienation and breeding cynicism. What good was one's knowledge if one could do nothing with it, given the way the system worked and its resistance to change? In an age of triumphant non-interventionist capitalism it was suspected, probably correctly, that most decisions were taken by big international companies, and not national politicians, anyway.

Even people in the affluent, supposedly liberated West faced obstacles in expressing themselves fully. It was difficult for non-established authors to "break the glass ceiling". Those with an interest in philosophy were unable to make a name for themselves in that field, if they did not have what were considered the right academic qualifications, because of cliqueism within the discipline. Pressure groups were allowed to have their say, but were never listened to, or listened to but ignored all the same. They, along with writers' workshops and the like, and social media, functioned as "bread and circuses", absorbing people's energies so as to prevent them exercising real influence in a way the politicians and Establishment (or Establishments), whose often inferior intellect and morals would be shown up, would not like. The "Big Society" that David Cameron was always calling for already existed, had existed for some time, but its effectiveness was limited, intentionally or otherwise, by the attitudes and the agenda of politicians themselves, including (some would say especially) Tory ones. As always, what prevented positive change was a combination of vested interests and public apathy.

In business, the pace of work has had to increase to meet the diverse demands of modern society and a company's desire to make bigger profits at a faster rate. Most older people have not been able to cope with it, retiring earlier. This means that industry and finance are now dominated by younger employees who lack the wisdom and judgement that comes with a more mature approach, thus being relatively more likely to make mistakes, while not benefiting from the guidance of an older and steadier hand. Add to this the effect of poor standards of education and training in schools, the result of being overconcerned with political correctness and afraid, perhaps by the same token, to enforce discipline, with standards of recruitment being lowered to match rather than leave society with a diminished workforce and therefore less able to function properly. Plus the distractions, for children of school age, of the internet and the absence, due to erosion of traditional moral and religious codes, of the kind of work ethic which previously operated. The result is that jobs aren't always done as well as they should be, which is frustrating for older people who in their day were accustomed to a better standard of service. The young seemed to be talking a different language anyway, not just in a literal sense or in technical matters (where it can make it difficult for a young person to explain to an older one how a new computer software system works) but also in the area of politics. They were happier to accept political correctness, having been brought up under it. Old people got good medical care, on the whole, as they aged but in other ways were sidelined. Though not necessarily considered racist they were known to be less enamoured of PC and thus more likely to say things which were deemed inappropriate. And a vibrant monetarist economy favoured youth over age as it came with an image of dynamism, energy and thus achievement. With their now greater lifespan the middle-aged and elderly faced an extended retirement during which they would retain their mental and physical skills for longer but be restricted in how they could use them. Altogether a gulf was widening between age groups, characterised by distrust and a major communication breakdown. It was socially a far more serious issue in its implications than the rebellious youth of the 1950s and 60s, being long-lasting and deep-rooted in a way that phenomenon was not.

Another consequence of the rise of the "me" generation, that which simply wanted what it wanted and expected to get it, was that young people would only take the jobs that appealed to them, meaning that those which didn't were either not done at all or were filled by cheap (and exploited) immigrant labour which added to overcrowding as well as raising issues to do with cultural identity by the scale on which it was happening and would happen in the future. The other failings of the modern business sector – poor training (including in English) and discipline and organisational inefficiency – meant the immigrants were not necessarily the asset their hard work potentially made them and thus were more likely to be resented by the native population.

Among other negative things about the management of economic affairs were the tendency to produce poor quality products at higher (partly because the natural supply of some materials was beginning to run out) prices (it wasn't only the Chinese who were guilty here) and "user-friendly" spiel which although desirable up to a point could also be cloying and irritating especially when the item you were being sold didn't work properly or its functioning was hard to understand (older people at any rate would have preferred dealing with a miserable so-and-so but getting something that was comprehensible and did work properly to disservice with a smile). Apart from unintelligible instructions companies would chop and change the way they did things in a manner that could be hard for the customer to cope with; software packages which people had mastered fairly easily and were quite happy with gave way to new ones that were confusing and altogether not, from the point of view of familiarisation with them, rationally designed. You still *could* master the new package in the end, perhaps, but why should you have to? The whole principle was wrong. The sensible philosophy of "if it ain't broke, don't fix it" had been abandoned (its rejection explains a lot of the mistakes made and problems encountered in Britain's attempt to modernise during the post-war period). It might appeal to keen young executives, or older ones going with the flow, to be always trying something new but not everyone could keep up with the pace. It was another example of how companies did what *they* wanted to do and not what the customer did, which went against the whole principle of capitalism as set out by Adam Smith (who would have been horrified at the way things had gone). Change was taking place purely for its own sake, in order to keep things dynamic and exciting and interesting. It was a very post-modern issue.

The preference for privatisation, which sought to take more of the burden of running modern society from the state and so theoretically make it easier to bear, led the state to itself act like a private company in some ways, one of which was casualisation (that is, appointment at the employer's will with no legal safeguard against dismissal at any time) and fixed-term contracts in the civil service. It was a cost-cutting "hire 'em and fire 'em" measure designed to secure cheap labour (the employee was not likely to be staying long enough to achieve a higher grade with a bigger salary) without any of the tiresome legal considerations that went with employing someone in the conventional way. The trouble was that if you took several casual posts in succession, other jobs being consistently unavailable, and none of them led to a permanent position (it might not, in each case, be intended that they should) your work record appeared fragmentary and yourself as a consequence unreliable. A casual post was then the only kind people trusted you with, because you weren't going to be around for that long, before you were replaced by another casual, anyway. You would become caught in a trap in which this was the only sort of job you could get. It was impossible to accumulate enough money to enjoy the standard of living to which you felt entitled if you were going to be repeatedly tossed back onto the dole. The situation was particularly hard for those living in rented accommodation, as housing benefit was stopped whenever you got a job (including a permanent one). If you had to pay rent, towards which went a large part of your salary, then even if the job lasted you were not going to have much more money than you would if on unemployment benefit; no incentive for anyone to look for work and so, once it was found, cease to be a burden on the state.

Casualisation and short-term contracts created an employment underclass which in the early twenty-first century was part of a much wider one including all those who were jobless or on low incomes. It exacerbated a situation in which it was much harder to get back into work the longer you had been out of it – and especially as you grew older. Governments failed to do anything about the problem yet complained, as did right-wing political thinkers and newspaper columnists, about the cost to the taxpayer/state of paying dole money. They might tweak the statistics, as Tony Blair's administrations did in Britain, by claiming those on (often useless) training schemes were working, which they were not. Basically, the world in which you were assured of a job for life, and with the same rights against unfair dismissal as any other worker, unless sacked for gross misconduct had come to an end. In some cases this may have been inevitable and of course there had always been redundancies or jobs which by their nature could only be temporary. But now there was much less job stability, job continuity, than before and it had the corrosive effect of further weakening the ties, values and *corps d'esprit* which held society together. Unless they happened to be a glamorous "high flyer" or in favour with the management, the employee was viewed as a disposable product who was not really worth investing in, and so conversely they did not see any need to be loyal to the employer. It is possible that up to a point the managers of modern capitalism, rather than just being heartless, had become trapped in a system that was degrading them morally but which they did not know how to ditch. The effect was the same.

If the problem for the long-term unemployed in getting back to work is that private employers (or public ones forced to behave like private ones) are too inclined to hire and fire, it could be remedied by the state taking them on in one capacity or another, and employing them permanently unless they commit acts of gross misconduct or there is a some other overriding reason for their dismissal (though this will not solve the problem if the public sector is determined to behave like the private!). The trouble is, not only does this go against the whole contemporary preference of the British Conservative Party and its counterparts elsewhere in the West for working through the private sector and extolling the latter's virtues, it is likely (by the same token) to be rejected because it implies that sector is at fault (having failed to provide people with work and so make best use of their skills). What makes things additionally hard for the jobseeker is that when the economy is in recession and unemployment is widespread, joblessness is seen as a manifestation of a common, and regrettable, problem which the government is working hard to solve but which cannot be expected to go away immediately, but if things are prosperous and unemployment is low the attitude tends towards "everyone else is working, why not you?". It is easier to put your circumstances down to laziness than identify the real causes of them, which are structural.

Western society was collapsing under its own weight as the consequences of runaway monetarism and social change combined with those of a swelling, through immigration and natural increase, population. One factor driving rapid housing development was the tendency towards more single households as relationships broke down or people delayed marriage for longer, wishing to savour the independence of being young, free and single. Cities, towns and villages were all spreading, joining up, to create a standardised urban culture in which one part of the West, indeed the whole developed world, looked much the same as any other. Regional identities, expressed in accent and dialect, began to disappear, as did small local family businesses (although the process by which the large out-of-town supermarket had started to displace them had begun some years before). Many rural districts became simply "dormitory areas" for London and other cities. The trend towards working from home (as people had done in the pre-Industrial Revolution cottage industries) and communicating with colleagues, clients and employers by email could not for practical reasons happen on a big enough scale to offset this.

Build a new town or large housing estate and it will eventually require a transport and industrial infrastructure to service it. New settlements grow up around those installations and they in turn require their own rail and bus stations and shopping centres; and so on. If the process continued in this way there would be no countryside left, apart from farmland and much of that was being sold off and built on as the agricultural sector declined. One felt increasingly hemmed in by concrete and other people. Meanwhile it was decided that urban shopping centres which happened to have been in existence for twenty years or more were looking "tired" and therefore needed revamping, even though there was in fact nothing wrong with them. It all netted handsome profits for some company or other. As a result the character of a neighbourhood changed too fast for its long-term residents to get used to, causing them to experience feelings of alienation. It may be added that the quality of new building was often indifferent, in line with much else of industry.

Each new community, once it became a distinct entity, needed to be serviced by hospitals, schools etc. and there were fears the capacity of such institutions to cope was being exceeded. There was also the continuing disappearance of the countryside, which was psychologically harmful. It was already starting to look less like the countryside, because of the proliferation of street furniture and road junctions designed to meet the requirements of the motor car, which was fast and exciting and also a symbol of independence. General urbanisation of course brought with it the pressures and social problems which were only starting to be experienced in the country because the latter was becoming more like the town.

To paint an *entirely* bleak picture of the modern West would be unfair. Political correctness has certainly eliminated, on the surface anyhow, a lot of the nastier features of the old world, if at a cost. And the tendency to run everything as a (monetarist) business, which meant appearing at any rate to like the customer, being polite and friendly towards them to increase the chances they would be happy to buy something from you, does mean that the person on the front desk or the guard on the train checking your tickets is a lot nicer, far less abrupt or rude, than they would have been thirty or more years ago. It seems to me that the friendliness is often genuine, though perhaps it is the privatisation – in an unexpected and for that reason all the more pleasing way – which has brought it out. Certainly those "old school" individuals whose social attitudes and manner of address, formed before the Second World War, were almost Victorian, and who would have had little time for political correctness because it stood in the way of what they considered discipline (though many younger people would not have disagreed with them there) are no longer really in evidence either in paid jobs or in voluntary organisations (whose own approach has had to become like that of a modern private company for them to survive). They were formidable characters who might have resisted the rise of PC had they been able to, but it was coming in at just the time when their age was getting the better of them, necessitating retirement and then the nursing home. Their kind endured into the 1980s at least but was afterwards somehow no longer there. It is partly a good thing, because they were often disagreeably superior in their attitude, and partly, one can't help thinking, a great pity.

It seems to me, from a British perspective, that there is less crime and "anti-social behaviour" than there was even 5-10 years ago, though this is contested. I feel safer going about after dark, or at all. But this security has been bought at a price. The reason there is less crime is because Big Brother is watching you, or has succeeded in making you think he is. You suspect there is a CCTV camera on every corner. Another factor is awareness of the nanny state; the sense that you can be arrested or otherwise brought within the context of the law for all sorts of silly reasons or for appearing vaguely intimidating, confrontational, means you are less likely to commit a genuine offence. The electronic surveillance has been brought in to compensate for the fact that there are fewer "bobbies" on the beat; it is regarded as a substitute for increasing police numbers. It can of course be used to protect the government from opposition while it is pursuing totalitarian or ethically questionable policies. In other words we may have created a situation where in some respects it is the *government* and not the criminals who are the enemy. Nor should we forget cyber-crime, which is a safer way for a villain to steal money than carrying out an armed robbery and being regarded with particular opprobrium on account of anyone who is physically hurt or mentally traumatised in the process, plus altogether a lot less bother. Here, the wrongdoer has a chance of staying ahead of the law for a time at least, getting round safeguards against hacking until they are improved and then devising new ways of countering them; as with all state-of-the-art technology when it is used for military or criminal purposes, it may be said that a race is taking place. (Of course we should not be led to think that crime in the old, or organised sense does not still happen).

And there could still be what was socially unacceptable or ought to be considered so; under political correctness etc., rudeness manifested itself as a kind of surliness rather than open verbal or physical abuse. It was not really any less objectionable.

I referred earlier to the decline in the popularity of institutions. The retreat of the state from organising national life in favour of private companies, who ultimately were in it for their own benefit and not necessarily the community's, helped de-institutionalise society and thus contributed to atomising it. Institutions also suffered from a loss of interest in the ideologies they might have formed around. Where politics was concerned the cause was as much a matter of general disillusionment with the democratic political process which was increasingly perceived as something of a sham. Democracy had in fact always been a kind of messy compromise between the will of the people and that of the politicians plus the groups whose interests they furthered. It some ways it was really a collection of oligarchies – the politicians themselves, often irrespective of party, big business, the media, the remains of the upper class, powerful ideological elements (the PC liberals) – who were constantly vying for control. This maybe didn't matter so much as long as society was run efficiently, and fairly, in the areas people were most bothered about, i.e. public services and the economy. But now politicians were seen as increasingly remote from the ordinary citizen and more concerned with their own advancement than the general good, while a decline in their intellectual calibre had rendered them less able to solve the problems of a complex world, including those affecting public services and the economy. They seemed to lack the gumption to roll back the frontiers of commercialism, through not having anything to put in its place (it was another post-modern dilemma). For a time in the 2000s there was serious concern about public apathy towards politics, which led to a decline in voting and so prevented the system from functioning properly. Interest picked up later over such matters as whether Britain should stay in the European Union, because the issues now coming to the fore were serious enough, in view of what was at stake, for uninvolvement to not be an option; but by the same token political engagement was happening in ways that were bitter, confrontational and divisive. To some extent populist politics re-emerged, and were practised by Donald Trump and Britain's United Kingdom Independence Party. But they took the form of appealing to a certain element, anti-PC, anti-EU and anti-immigration, which was becoming more prominent as what was effectively a backlash against political correctness grew (because it was thought to be a bulwark against racism and extreme nationalism, membership of an international organisation that had real clout, whatever its faults, could be viewed as and was a politically correct policy).

The decline of institutions also affected organised religion, and religion to some extent had to be organised to be effective, rather than nebulous and unfocused. To some extent it was the "me generation" again; their attitude was, "I don't want some Big Daddy in the sky (God) to whom I'm supposed to be responsible telling me what to do, looking over my shoulder and not liking what he sees. I want to be free of that. I'm my own boss." Religion also appeared to have been discredited on intellectual grounds. This had been a common view since the Enlightenment, but the process had been given a push by Darwin and also by Freud. Basically Freud's achievement as a scientist was to start a process which gave people a greater understanding of the complexity of their own minds and the reasons why they did or didn't do such-and-such. It wasn't always helpful; it has spawned a legion of dubious popular "self-help" psychologists, who often do more harm than good. But we did learn a little more about ourselves. Where religion was concerned Freud established the idea – misguided in the view of believers, of course – that faith was a construct born of an innate tendency to anthropomorphise, or feelings of insecurity which led some to postulate a comforting but non-existent divine protector.

Towards the end of the 1990s, with the Millennium approaching, there was, as tends to be the case at such times, much speculation about the future and whether something apocalyptic was about to happen. But contrary to what might have been expected it did not lead to a revival of Christianity in the expectation that the Last Judgement and Second Coming of Christ were imminent. Or a comeback for religion generally, apart from Islam where the increase in believers was (a) happening anyway and (b) partly due to sociology, and the polytheistic, mystical New Age movement which proved to be a passing fad that did not gain much support beyond an eccentric and esoteric minority. Many people had a "pick and choose" attitude towards religion, including Christianity. One faith was as good as another; you could adopt whichever one you liked, out of personal fancy rather than a genuine belief about the universe and humanity's place in it, as well as ignore the aspects of doctrine that didn't appeal to you while sticking to those that did. You could ditch your religion, either for another faith or for atheism/agnosticism, if you decided you weren't too happy with or simply got tired of it. Any other approach was "aggressive" or "judgemental" towards non-believers. To some extent political correctness encouraged this approach, consciously or otherwise. This was a consequence of multiculturalism – it was offensive and also dangerously inflammatory to inform your country's large Muslim population that it was going to Hell unless it converted to Christianity – and of the religious wars of the past (including recent ones like the Lebanon conflict). This was understandable, but it weakened religion as a social and spiritual force by taking away what was special, unique, about your own particular faith and so diminishing its power to strengthen and inspire.

Most people's attitude to Christianity, traditionally the dominant religion in the West and still exercising a certain cultural influence, was apathetic or casual. Many still felt the need at some point to have some sort of engagement with it but not as a lasting, everyday commitment. Baptism and confirmation were the "God jab" which you felt you ought to have at some time but afterwards could be thought to have done its job, close religious involvement not being necessary. After being baptised and confirmed, most young people were never seen in church again. White weddings were still not uncommon, but reflected similar attitudes to that described, being a ritual which had a certain psychological appeal rather than a symbol of genuine Christian belief. It was little different from the "pick and choose" thing. This was despite the increase in breakdown of "relationships", whether or not formalised in marriage, and of the cohesive family unit, leading to single parenthood and what in the case of dysfunctional working-class families was called the "broken home", having been simultaneous with the decline in religion, suggesting the two were connected through loss of the disciplinary, cementing effect of the latter. Generally Christian marriages were more resilient. Obviously many secular ones lasted too, and to be a single parent was a sign of human fallibility rather than of wickedness. But equally obviously the situation was far from ideal.

A substantial minority – which may have been greater than the number of truly committed believers – were actively hostile to Christianity. The "New Atheists", as they were called, were characterised by a virulent dislike of Christian faith which amounted to a sort of intellectual thuggery. In their view material science explained everything and anyone who thought otherwise, who believed in religion, was suffering from a disease of the brain. They were influential (beyond their actual numbers within society) in the arts, media and local politics, which could make life difficult for Christians. Perhaps because of a fear of incurring their hostility popular culture today abounds with references to Christianity and Christians which are disparaging and in fact, on occasions, staggeringly offensive. Their attitude to religion could be regarded as ambiguous, if not hypocritical. When they attack "religion" for all the harm it has done they really mean

Christians. They are reluctant to go for Muslims because the latter would probably react violently; Christians nowadays tend to turn the other cheek, partly because of the flak they will receive if they don't, and the political and social implications of provoking Muslim wrath are greater because Islam is a growing faith and Christianity, within the West, is not. Besides, Muslims tend to come from ethnic groups which traditionally have been a target of racism, so it doesn't do to denigrate their beliefs and way of life, despite unease at Islamic militancy and the strict social codes which arguably repress women within some Muslim communities. The anti-Christianity of the New Atheists can be a form of political correctness, and indeed local councils have frequently come under attack for banning Nativity plays or other Christian activities because they are thought (often wrongly) to be offensive to Muslims. Sometimes these horror stories may be exaggerated, but it is unlikely there could be so much smoke without a certain amount of fire.

The Church is no longer troubled by David Jenkins-type disputes over doctrine, although there remain the thorny issues of gay ordination and gay marriage. Its problem, perhaps, is that it won't put itself about. In the 1980s Christian evangelists were a frequent, if often resented (and much lampooned) presence on the streets – but not now. At least Christian evangelism on the old pattern still happens, but only so often. The Church is afraid of attracting the ire of the New Atheists or of some local authorities and instead organises coffee mornings, etc., as a form of "outreach", which usually only leaves the average punter thinking that it is composed of "nice people". The failure to pitch things high may, possibly, be the reason why it has failed to arrest the continuing decline in its membership. Many churches are struggling financially, and suffering from loss of manpower, as young people refuse to get involved and congregations (who represent a source of funding) die off. What might be described as a significant rise in the average age of Christians makes it easier to see the Church as an old person's thing, a dinosaur, in a tie-in with ageism, the preference for modernism and the general social chasm between age groups. While from the point of view of tactics and strategy the task of anyone seeking to change the world, spiritually redeeming it as they would see things, is made difficult in Britain at any rate by the Church's being divided between the mainstream establishment and the Evangelicals. The former is too reluctant to promote itself and its message while the latter, though they do not for example street preach the way they used to but confine themselves publicly to handing out leaflets, are growing faster than the Anglicans and attracting more young people but their effusive style of worship (often derogatorily described as "happy-clappy") is not for everyone and they often have "unreconstructed" views on matters like homosexuality.

In terms of its image with the public the three things which in particular have damaged Christianity's prospects in recent decades have been: (1) The exposure from the late 1980s of high-profile televangelists as frauds and crooks. By then Billy Graham, the greatest of the evangelists and undoubtedly honest, was past his best; if you were not already a Christian there was little to be got, many felt, out of attending his rallies, and so his impact was lessened. (2) 9/11 and also the US/Tony Blair response to it, which seemed to identify religion, whether Muslim or Christian, with violence and jingoism. (3) The child sex abuse scandals in the Catholic Church. It is not unfair, however, to say that both the public and the "intelligentsia" allowed themselves to be too easily put off by these things; there was no reason to shun religious faith in general because of the faults, however serious, of institutions, and even institutions were necessary to meet at least the practical needs of believers, as well as spread the Gospel if that was what you wanted to do. No-one should play down the awfulness of what misguided or debased religion has been responsible for; but in a Western world traditionally accustomed to comfort and security, and the freedom to "pick 'n' choose", we wanted everything to be perfect and all that had become associated in any way with something unpleasant was rejected despite its beneficial side. In the case of the televangelists, the problem was partly that the triumph of commercialism had given new opportunities to the corrupt and self-seeking, rather than that wishing to share one's faith was necessarily a sign of something dubious.

Pessimism about the future of Christianity is in global terms a bit ethnocentric. It may be declining in the West (Europe more than the USA, although as observed the Christianity of the Republicans has always been hypocritical and politically motivated). But it is almost universal in Latin America and thriving, indeed growing, in Africa (where it may come into greater conflict in the future with rising Islam) and China (a quarter of Mankind, take note). It has also enjoyed a revival, after the repression of the Soviet era, throughout Russia and the former Eastern Bloc, although this may be a case of restrictions on the *expression* of belief disappearing, more than an increase in belief itself (the latter had been not inconsiderable, beneath the surface). The resurgent churches might seem tarnished by their alliance with certain regimes which, although not practising totalitarian Communism, may nonetheless be autocratic, and often nationalistic, in character. But the post-Communist governments wanted to give themselves an ideological identity, plus support base; sometimes (and especially in the case of Russia itself) the only model was the pre-Communist state, which had been a monarchy associated closely with the Orthodox Church. For their part, the churches sought protection from the aggressive secularism which had arisen in Western Europe and of which they had become aware through the very opening up to the wider world which had occurred through *Glasnost* and the Fall of the Wall.

In the West it is not only religion, out of what may be called the "abstract" ways of viewing the universe because they do not deal in things that are *physically* obvious, which has suffered from the new materialism. Philosophy no longer seems to be held in high regard as a pursuit or academic discipline; though there are still societies based around it it receives little public or official attention and is less likely to be studied as a major subject at university. Again the reason is a reliance on material science to explain everything and a distrust of what cannot be analysed in a test tube. We encourage a technical intelligence but not an intellectual one. It is a form of dumbing down, which can affect people who are genuinely clever in many ways, and doesn't help when philosophy and religion involve complex, "deep" concepts requiring the making of connections that nowadays seem to be beyond many of us. Apart from the general cultural damage it is harmful in stultifying *original* thought, and here it merges with factors which can be described as political, though not openly acknowledged and maybe operating subconsciously. Nothing which goes against the dominant ideologies is encouraged in case it doesn't sell or is politically unacceptable, introducing a random number into the equation and causing things to run out of control if it catches on, and if it doesn't catch on unsettling people. The often eccentric, difficult, even maladjusted, but talented maverick who comes up with revolutionary ideas that transform society is sidelined in a world which despite claiming to want every individual to explore and realise their full potential is in fact one of the most uncompromisingly conformist there has ever been. As noted above those trying to change things are handicapped by a combination of vested interests, in which category could be included politically correct liberals as well as big business, and public indifference. There is a widespread reluctance to do anything which doesn't immediately excite interest, isn't part of your normal lifestyle, means revising your view of the world or involves, perhaps by the same token, coming out of your comfort zone. The general philosophy seems one of "Can't be ***ed". On the last occasion I took part in any political activity, I was among those handing out leaflets at Staines bus station advertising the campaign of a pressure group who opposed privatisation in the National Health Service. A colleague offered one to a passer-by, politely asking if he would be interested in getting involved. His response, before he moved on, was a kind of silent snarl. The expression, I thought, could be described as bestial.

Going backwards...

Another branch of knowledge which has been affected by the way people think in the modern age is history. It is too much concerned with the past to have much appeal. That past is exciting when money is made out of it, and as a sort of pageant when a museum holds events where people dress up in old-fashioned costumes or it is re-enacted in popular TV period dramas. But otherwise, how much do we really understand or value it? At one end of the scale, a modernisation of business or residential premises is even more likely these days to involve throwing items of historical value on the rubbish tip through failure to appreciate their importance. And although I don't wish to be critical of the *alma mater* to whom this book is dedicated, it is symbolic that the history department of Southampton University has been relocated off-campus – along with most other non-scientific subjects. I don't think the tendency seen here affects the Arts, as opposed to the Humanities, quite so much, but then they involve *image* and so are much more important to those growing up in today's world. I am somehow uncomfortable about praising a Communist, but the late Eric Hobsbawm was surely right to express concern, towards the end of the twentieth century, that young people were reaching maturity without any organic connection to the past of the culture they belonged to (or any other). This process is now far advanced. It seems that anything which happened more than ten years ago is of no interest. It is a serious matter because without the study of history we are less able to understand how we got to where we are now, or where we are going. We are unable to see the Bigger Picture.

Generally speaking, we reject ideologies and institutions and concentrate simply on attaining a reasonably high standard of material prosperity. It is as if, not only worn out by past struggles but frustrated by the failure to change the dominant narratives of the day and so avoid their more harmful consequences, we have just given up. The rise in Christianity in China and Africa, in contrast to the picture in the West, indicates that not all cultures develop in the same way. It may be that the Christian revival in those places is a product of an arduous existence, compared to life for most people in Europe or the US, for which some kind of consolation is required, or (by a similar token) a reaction against the totalitarianism of the political aspect of Communism (China's leaders are not too pleased about what is happening in their country, though their efforts to stamp it out have so far proved ineffectual). Without those factors, maybe the phenomenon would not be happening. But it certainly seems that in the West right now the majority of people are walking, one might say sleepwalking, in single file; into a future that looks increasingly dark and frightening.

POSTSCRIPT August 2020
A shadow certainly seemed to have fallen over the entire world with the outbreak of COVID-19 (Coronavirus) in early 2020. This disease, irritating because while, in scale and in the developed world, it is nowhere near as serious a threat to life as bubonic plague in the Middle Ages, it is nonetheless extremely disruptive in its effects has in less than a year become a global epidemic. Certain groups – the elderly and those suffering from respiratory illnesses – are especially vulnerable to it and generally it necessitates strict measures, amounting to a "lockdown", to guard against infection. Businesses have closed and social gatherings been severely restricted (the disease being communicable by breathing), the impact on the economy and on everyday life being considerable and to some extent

psychologically stressful.

What the long-term implications of it will be, for humanity in general, is difficult to say. The consequences in terms of loss of life will be far greater in the developing world, where medical facilities are poorer. In the West the importance of community has been reinforced, as people (mostly) pull together to help those affected ("socially isolated"), though such altruistic feelings were not necessarily absent before. It does not seem they have turned to religion, though it is hard to tell because many churches have been forced to close (they and other concerns are now gradually reopening as part of a relaxation of the lockdown, but there are fears that the latter may lead to a "second spike" of the virus). Religious services as such, along with many other kinds of meeting, are in the meantime being held by videolink (Zoom, Skype) but not everyone is comfortable with such media.

Generally, what is clear right now is that the world is very vulnerable; for if some other international crisis were to happen at the same time that Coronavirus is causing disruption and uncertainty, it could be disastrous. We got a whiff of the possible hazards when anger over the treatment of black people in America and Britain, both historically and in the present day, and sparked off by the unlawful killing of a black man by US police, led to mass protests and rioting, which could have resulted in the spread of the virus, in London and other British cities. During the disturbances a statue of a prominent past local dignitary who had been a slave owner was pulled down in Bristol. This prompted university authorities in certain places to remove other memorials – either a statue or, for example, the name of a hall of residence – to people who had been involved in any way with imperialism or the slave trade, even though the areas in which these institutions were situated had not been subject to social unrest. The Archbishop of Canterbury is apparently now saying that some should be removed from Westminster Abbey. All this happened because the protests had drawn attention to the issue; which was in effect to reward the protestors for acting in a dangerous and irresponsible manner and by the same token set a harmful precedent.

The affair can partly be explained by frustration the way Coronavirus was (necessarily) causing other issues to be set aside; this feeling could affect whites too, with many of their liberals seeming to be calling for a positive response to the campaign of the Black Lives Matter movement, and thus condoning or at least encouraging irresponsible behaviour. Up to a point it was a case of "midsummer madness", one could legitimately say mass hysteria, which fizzled out after a while. But we are living in a generally disturbing period. Though mentioning them might risk departing from the brief of this book, which is a study of history not an evangelical tract about the end of the world, there have during this time of Coronavirus been "signs and wonders in the heavens" – comets and a near-miss between the Earth and an asteroid. Of course, what people make of such things is their own choice.

ADDENDA TO THE MAIN TEXT

P260 As part of the flexibility of religion in antiquity, gods could be moved up and down in the pantheon and given whatever attributes one fancied. A citizen of Babylon once observed sardonically that you could train your god to run after you like a pet dog. This obviously was not possible in Judaeo-Christianity, in which God was God, as revealed to Moses and the other patriarchs, and could not be turned into simply a human construct. He was a single deity without counterpart and who possessed a set of unchangeable characteristics, including power over all things, which had to be acknowledged as a necessary part of belief.

P347 Of course Bulgaria and Rumania avoided Nazi aggression by themselves becoming Fascist (at any rate their governments did) and allying themselves with Hitler during the Second World War.

P494-5 In Africa and Asia hostility to Christians was more likely to be expressed in physical violence and persecution than in the West (though it did happen there, being usually the work of lone psychopaths) and the phenomenon became increasingly common in those parts of the world in the early twenty-first century. It was similarly startling and probably had similar causes. Christians were being scapegoated for the general failure of the world to resolve the issues over which it was so concerned and angst-ridden, and because they (usually) turned the other cheek made easy prey.

APPENDIX

RICHARD CROSS, A VICTORIAN WORKHORSE

A dissertation by Guy Blythman

Originally submitted 1986, rewritten 2020

Contents

(1) Early Life and Youth

(2) Political Career 1857-62

(3) Political Career 1868-74

(4) First Period of Office 1874-80

(5) Foreign Affairs 1874-80

(6) Opposition and First Salisbury Government, 1880-86

(7) India, 1886-92

(8) Later Political Career and Final Years, 1892-1914

(9) Conclusion

(1)

Early Life and Youth

Born in 1823, Richard Cross came from a middle-class provincial and professional family with their origins in Preston, Lancashire. Tanners at one point, they later escaped a life in trade by entering the legal profession, Cross' grandfather, John, becoming deputy to the prothonatory (clerk) to the Lancashire County Court. His father, William, was wealthy enough to purchase a suburban estate, called Red Scar, where the family lived. He held office for a time as deputy Lord Lieutenant of the county. His allegiance was Tory, as his grandson's was to be.

His son William Cross died when Richard was only four, leaving his wife with six children. The eldest, Richard's brother William, was made deputy prothonotary at the age of nine, indicating a talented family. Richard and William were educated at Mr Rawson's school at Seaforth, after which Richard attended Rugby under Dr Arnold before going on to Cambridge, where he became President of the Union, rather than Oxford because as a staunch Anglican he feared the influence of Anglo-Catholicism at the latter place. His brother John, who was at Oxford, advised him to purchase three dozen cases each of port and sherry for his first term; one can only speculate as to whether this explain the problems he had with drink in later life.

The family wished Richard to join John in the church on leaving university, but instead he decided to study law, against the objection of his mother and aunts. At that time, the profession was not considered respectable. John supported him, assuring him that it ought not to damage his reputation but urging him later to be even more respectable by becoming a judge (a profession he nearly did take up as we will see below). Cross' time at the Union would certainly have prepared him for the cut-and-thrust of legal, and parliamentary, debate. After obtaining his BA he took the Grand Tour, then in 1849 was called to the Bar at the Inner Temple, having meanwhile served as a special constable against the Chartists and in the same year, 1848, visited revolutionary Paris. In 1852 he married Georgiana Lyon, with whose family his father had been friendly. Though the Lyons had a large interest in Parr's Bank in Warrington, Cross did not at this time have the means to support a family (William Cross junior had inherited the Red Scar estate when their mother died) and he and his wife spent much of their time at Georgiana's family home in Warrington. In 1855 he considered taking an appointment as a judge on the Isle of Man; had he done so the course of his life and perhaps of British political history in the Victorian era would have been very different, but as it was his friend and legal partner Henry Holland advised him to become an MP. He also tried his hand at writing, editing a compilation of the poor law removal acts to serve as a guide for lawyers. But in 1857 he stood for parliament at Preston. In his memoirs he claimed he had been asked to stand in 1852 but refused because he had only been called to the bar three years before and had only recently married.

(2)

Political Career 1857-62

It is thought that Cross only sought the nomination to further his legal career. This was sensed by his contemporaries and he was perceived as something of an outsider. The perception was heightened by his not joining the Carlton Club, in accordance with the wishes of his constituents, while he represented Preston. Mitchell describes him as an "independent conservative", meaning that he was not (in these years anyway) a part of the Tory "set-up". The *Preston Guardian* newspaper called him "the living mystery of Red Scar" and in the election campaign an anonymous clergyman accused him of being an adventurer using Preston for his own purposes – an unkind exaggeration though it may have contained a grain of truth. Cross was not free from opportunism; when the sitting Conservative member suddenly announced his resignation without previously informing the party's election committee he took advantage of the confusion to press his candidacy (which his brother William opposed). In the end he captured one of the two Preston seats (the other was held by a Liberal) with 300 votes.

At this time Cross was not a particularly liberal Tory, opposing household suffrage or any measure which would give workers the right to vote. In 1872 he was to oppose the secret ballot, and in 1873 Henry Fawcett asked for Cross' help in parliament to secure the appointment of a royal commission as a means of opposing the creation of equal electoral districts. He preferred the physical improvement of the lives of the people (also supporting the appointment of working people as factory inspectors), and ensuring they had a fair wage (telling business leaders at a meeting in 1890 that they could not pocket all the profits) to giving them political freedom. Even in the areas where he might be termed progressive he was not always so. In many respects he was very much of his time, with typical Victorian views concerning the position of women. He opposed bills which would allow men to marry the sister of a deceased wife, make fathers of an illegitimate child liable for the bastard, and prevent women from working at the mouths of coal pits. In a speech to the Edinburgh Conservative Association he said it was his goal "to promote, as far as lies in our power, the improvement of the social condition of the people, not simply in their education, or any other matters, but in all matters." He recognised the need to adapt to the industrial age, which meant dealing with the social evils it had created, the poverty and squalor. Parliamentary legislation would be the means to achieve this, but he expressed what was both a pragmatic and a Tory sentiment when he said that it could not be expected to do everything. He wanted to show people the way to self-improvement; though it might sometimes be necessary for the state to take action he did not wish to do for them what they could and should do for themselves. He regarded the duty of government as being "to give the greatest amount of happiness to the largest number that is consistent with the actual rights of the few", which rather sounds as if he wished to preserve a certain amount of elitist privilege. He was undoubtedly humane; in promoting his Artisans' Dwelling Act as Home Secretary and describing the appalling conditions in which many workers had to live, which clearly horrified him (and he took the trouble to go and see them for himself), he urged the House of Commons "Let there be light." He transferred the supervision of lunatics from prisons to asylums as this would be better for the lunatics, as well as more sensible administratively, and though opposing free education for the working classes advocated that subsidies to those who couldn't afford school fees be paid through the local education authority in order to avoid the stigma of the poor law. But there appear to have been perplexing limits to his humanity; in the 1880s he met privately with the journalist Wickham Stead to urge him to cease publishing pamphlets drawing attention to the plight of young girls in brothels, and though he eventually introduced a bill raising the age of consent he apparently did not think it necessary. He also seems to have advocated the traditional Tory policy of retrenchment and financial prudence when at Kirkdale in 1878 he said that spending, including presumably on humanitarian projects, had to be cut to deal with the current trade depression, although the motive was partly to ease the burden on ratepayers. In the 1885 general election he opposed free education for working-class children, which he called an "insidious" proposal, while supporting their compulsory vaccination against disease; it suggests that while wishing to improve their material condition he saw the advancement of the working classes, whether by adding to their knowledge or giving them the vote, as dangerous, although he may simply have been arguing that one should have to pay for vital services as a way of encouraging responsibility and thrift. He certainly believed that owners of public houses should be compensated for any financial loss they suffered as a result of measures to limit or prohibit the sale of alcohol.

It could be said that in to some extent displacing the upper classes and replacing them as the new aristocracy, the middle classes had inherited their paternalism. There does seem to be something snobbish in the refusal of Cross as Home Secretary to allow the withdrawal of the cavalry from Liverpool because of the city's "dangerous population" and supposed "liability to sudden panics". He thought that similar prudence was appropriate in the case of Manchester. While opposed to political advancement for the working classes, Cross as a rising middle-class man (though he may also have been motivated by a genuine sense of fairness) disliked what he considered the undue privileges enjoyed by the aristocracy, such as church pews being reserved for rich owners: "this is a state of things which ought not to exist." One suspects it did not endear him to the aristocracy. It was a common, and some would say hypocritical, attitude of the time, though perhaps it was natural.

In the late 1850s Cross was making a name for himself as a parliamentary figure of significance; he acquired a nickname, "Stormy Petrel", because his appearance in the Commons was thought to signal a major vote. His good attendance record was a sign of his sense of duty. In 1859 he introduced a Municipal Elections Bill which laid down standard rules for the conduct of elections in the boroughs and imposed financial penalties for corruption. He showed he was capable of taking an independent stand by supporting repeal of the paper duty, the only Conservative to do so when Gladstone, Chancellor of the Exchequer, brought in a bill to that effect in 1860. However he rejoined his party in opposition to the measure the following year, when Gladstone tried to carry it as part of a unified budget in order to avoid the Lords' veto; this Cross, a man of principle, thought unconstitutional. He opposed the abolition of church rates but was prepared to compromise, offering an amendment to an abolition bill which would have provided for certain exemptions, including on grounds of conscience. He eventually brought in his own bill as a private member, but the government refused to allow him parliamentary time and he had to withdraw it. He subsequently decided not to reintroduce it as it might have cost the Conservatives seats at the next election.

Cross was out of parliament from 1862 to 1868. In 1859 he secured a position at Parr's Bank, where a vacancy had been created following the death of his father-in-law. He then bought a house called Eccle Riggs, near Broughton-in-Furness. He wanted to retain his parliamentary seat but was pressurised into standing down by the owner of the bank who felt the two jobs were not compatible. Cross left his law practice at the same time. This together with his resignation as an MP did free up a certain amount of time for spending on various civic duties, showing his sense of social responsibility, besides his appointment as a captain in the 9th Lancashire Rifle Volunteers. He was entered in the Commission of the Peace for the county; became a trustee of Boteler's Free Grammar School at Warrington; was active in training colleges at Warrington and Chester and in a school for the daughters of clergy; was chairman of a board of guardians, the highway board, the Quarter Sessions at Lonsdale and a lunatic asylum; presided at petty sessions as a magistrate.

(3)

Political Career 1868-74

By 1868 he had decided that it was time to return to politics. Although in 1866 he had become deputy chairman of the board of directors of the bank, the esteem in which he was held on account of his civic activities gave him an increased say in the matter. He also had the support of the Derby interest, a major political force within the region, in his candidature, and was further helped by the fact that his brother William was chairman of the North West Lancashire Conservative Association. Financial support was provided by Edward Moss, son of the chairman of the Liverpool and Manchester Railway. In the 1868 general election Cross stood for southwest Lancashire, beating Gladstone, on a platform of opposing the disestablishment of the Irish Church. During the campaign he said, "I will never believe for one moment that any instruction can be worthy of the name of education for a single moment unless religious instruction forms a part of it."

Cross regarded himself as an "independent conservative" free from strict party discipline. This was easier in the relative infancy of the modern two-party system and of the new Conservative and Liberal (replacing Tory and Whig) parties, when things were still a little fluid. In the Commons Cross sat apart from the Conservatives below the gangway with Lord Sandon and W H Smith (founder of the bookselling chain). Representing the new middle class interest in the Conservative Party, they also played a role similar to that of the Fourth Party a few years later, providing an active opposition when the Conservative leadership was demoralised by electoral defeat. At one point they actually considered replacing Disraeli, of whom they were not enamoured, as party leader, and in 1870 they refused to support a proposal for him to visit Lancashire to make a statement of Conservative policy. Whether or not he knew about this, Disraeli chose Cross to challenge the government, which he did vigorously, at the opening of the 1872 parliamentary session, a sign that he was regarded, however grudgingly, as one of the rising stars of the party, and his abilities recognised; he could not be ignored. He had by now built a "power base" within the party both locally and nationally, although there was never any indication that he sought to be Prime Minister; though not without ambition, he was content to be a public servant. He was friendly with Lady Derby who used him to spread the word, telling each person confidentially, that relations between Derby and Disraeli were good. He found a political ally in Lord Carnarvon, with whom he discussed ways of forging better understanding between Conservatives in the Lords and Commons. On the local level, his position was so strong in Lancashire, on account of his contributions to civic life there (in 1871 he was appointed a deputy Lord Lieutenant) that in 1874 the Liberals allowed him to be returned unopposed.

(4)

First Period of office, 1874-80

Cross' appointment to the Cabinet as Home Secretary after the Conservatives won the 1874 election was a last-minute decision by Disraeli. On the final list Hicks Beach was crossed out and Cross substituted. Whether Disraeli knew of Cross' earlier plans to replace him (see above) is unclear, though if he had it would not have endeared him to the man; at any rate there is no doubt he treated him very badly. As a middle-class man Cross was subject to the kind of snobbery to which Disraeli, who identified with the aristocracy, was prone. Disraeli usually addressed him as "My Dear Secretary" or "Dear Mr Secretary". In April 1874 he told Lady Bradford, "I was in the House last night till midnight and only left because I was assured there would be no more divisions. There was one however, and Mr Secretary Cross talked, I see, of the Prime Minister's absence on account of the state of his health! What language! This comes of giving high office to a middle-class man." Early in 1875 he snapped at Cross, "have the kindness to send one the correct titles of the bills which you propose introducing this term." Disraeli was often unhelpful when

Cross wished to introduce some reforming measure; in October 1874 he rejected his plans for reform of the government of the City of London, saying "we came in on the principle of not harassing the country." Another example of snobbery towards Cross was the reaction of Lord Malmesbury, on the occasion of the new cabinet going to kiss hands with the Queen, when someone asked him if Cross was married. Malmesbury replied snootily "I haven't an idea, I never saw the man before." Cross got on the wrong side of the Duke of Richmond by intervening in a dispute between Stafford Northcote and Richmond's brother, who was at the Board of Works, and it was some time before matters were patched up. But people like Cross were of course essential to the party if it was to gain middle-class support and thus be electable in the modern age; so they had to be tolerated.

Cross himself was sometimes uneasy in exalted company. He was initially reluctant to join the Queen at Balmoral as minister-in-attendance when requested to do so, pleading pressure of business. Sir Henry Drummond-Wolff once described a visit to the theatre which he made with Cross, W H Smith and others. Cross and Smith were embarrassed by upper-class manners which seemed offensively loud and brash, something which itself irritated Wolff.

The "exciting" people, especially those from aristocratic backgrounds, disliked Cross as a rather dull, pedestrian figure. In 1885 Lord Randolph Churchill refused to join a caretaker Conservative government unless he were excluded. Lord Salisbury wanted Cross to be Chancellor of the Exchequer but on Northcote's objection to this he returned to the Home Office. When a new Conservative administration was again formed in 1886 Churchill said there would be a general mutiny if Cross resumed his former post (having himself stirred up opposition to him) and rudely suggested that he should retire to the Post Office instead. He referred disparagingly to Cross and W H Smith, both prominent representatives of middle-class Conservatism, as "Marshall and Snellgrove" after a famous department store. In 1881 when speaking in a Commons debate on an amendment to a certain bill, of which he realised he had not got a copy, Cross helpfully handed him a note of the required information whereupon Churchill observed, "A pretty thing affairs have come to...when we have amendments passed around on dirty little bits of paper"[1]. In 1887 there were (false) rumours, on which reporters came to Cross (by this time Secretary of State for India) for comment, that he would be leaving office. At this time an element within the party led by Drummond Wolff, a former Fourth Party member, was trying to oust him; Salisbury and Cross removed Wolff from the scene by appointing him ambassador to Persia.

Cross' measures aroused opposition from those who felt they went against the traditional *laissez faire* philosophy and wanted minimum intervention by government in affairs. At one point the parliamentary draughtsman refused to carry out his instructions to draw up the Artisans' Dwelling Act, which he referred to as "Communism and confiscation". A *Punch* cartoon called it "harassing".

As Home Secretary, Cross was responsible for a considerable amount of reforming legislation (*Punch* usually depicted him carrying loads of bills under his arms). The most notable examples are:

(1) He was charged with bringing in a bill to establish uniform opening hours for pubs, lengthening them at the same time. He was personally opposed to the bill and left the task of supervising its passage through parliament to his undersecretary, Henry Selwyn-Ibbetson. There was trouble and Cross had to intervene, himself handling the matter rather ineptly. The bill was passed but Cross felt he had betrayed his principles and wrote in his *Political History* "I have not much to be proud of in this matter." (2) A Factories (health of women) Bill which reduced the hours of labour for women working in cotton mills to 56 hours per week, as well as raising the age at which children could be employed to fourteen.

(3) The Artisans' Dwelling Act of 1875. This allowed city corporations to force the sale to them of slum housing, which could be torn down and the land sold to private developers, who would then build more suitable accommodation. In preparation for drawing up the bill Cross made tours of the north, studying housing projects in Liverpool, Edinburgh and Glasgow.

(4) The Explosives Act 1875. This regulated the manufacture of explosives with the aim of reducing the likelihood of accidents, although a bill had already been drawn up under the direction of the previous Liberal Home Secretary.

(5) The Employers and Workmen's Bill 1875. This protected workers who struck or left employment and made masters and servants equal before the law. Breach of contract would no longer be a criminal but a civil offence. Cross indicated he would introduce a Conspiracy and Protection of Property Bill to more clearly define those acts which would still be treated as criminal, giving as examples any attempt to bring down the government or willfully damage property. Regarding the law of conspiracy he would submit a clause indemnifying unions against prosecution for acts which would not be illegal if committed by an individual. He disappointed them by making no changes to the Criminal Law Amendment Act, which was seen as outlawing picketing. However when Robert Lowe proposed an amendment to the CLAA which would have extended its criminal provisions to include employers and contractors Cross, who could not accept this, put forward his own amendment which effectively repealed the whole Act.

(6) A bill (1876) to amend the act controlling the enclosure of commons. The Liberal George Shaw-Lefevre opposed the bill because it did not establish permanent public rights to all common land; a compromise was reached by which those who enclosed land had to provide recreation areas and allotments for gardens.

(7) An act (1876) to limit the use of animals in scientific experiments. This was not of Cross' own choosing but was forced on him by agitation on the part of the press and influential figures (the Queen threatened to use the royal veto if the bill already before parliament, which it was thought did not go far

enough, was passed). Cross refused to make concessions on the issue to a delegation of medical men, whereupon the meeting grew heated, but he defused the situation to some extent with a joke concerning his power as Secretary of State to license animal experimentation under the Act: "As the Bill stands I think the only person to be pitied is the Secretary of State." He eventually passed a bill providing for licensing and inspection of vivisectionists.

(8) In 1879 Cross passed a Jurisdiction Bill designed to give magistrates wider powers in order to avoid their being forced by statute to impose unjust sentences. He also established a system of public prosecutors.

(9) In 1878 the second Factory Act consolidated the existing laws relating to factories and workshops into a single coherent regulatory system, closing a loophole by which factories employing fewer than fifty people were exempt. Some factory owners asked for special exemption from the acts to allow women and children to seasonally work longer hours in order to pick yarn, Cross allowed this as an experiment but secretly, without putting the amendment before the Commons as he was supposed to. He shortened the period of exemption from the four years which were originally envisaged.

During his time as Home Secretary Cross ordered investigations into the explosion of steam boilers and where negligence was discovered would have had the Solicitor General prosecute their owners for manslaughter, but this was overruled by the Attorney General. Cross also failed to end common employment, the legal principle by which workers were regarded as implicitly taking the risk of being injured along with their fellow employees.

An Offences Against The Person Bill, which provided that those convicted of assaulting a child or a woman could be privately flogged, was abandoned. A bill to reform the Trade Unions was never implemented. Labour leaders refused to serve on the commission Cross appointed to look into the matter, an indication that the working classes were not grateful to him for his improving measures and indeed entertained some suspicion towards him as a Tory (the latter still being in many ways a term of abuse; "Conservative" was not then in as wide a use).

In 1880 Cross put forward a bill to buy up London's water companies and amalgamate them into a single unified service but it was withdrawn after encountering severe opposition. Part of the problem was the surveyor Cross had appointed to look into the matter, Edmund Smith, who made himself unpopular with the politicians.

Cross wanted to reform county government (as eventually happened in 1888), and in particular reduce rates, but was unsuccessful due to obstruction and lack of co-operation from his colleagues and from vested interests. He appealed to the Chancellor of the Exchequer, Stafford Northcote, for financial assistance to the counties but Northcote refused to help unless taxes were raised. In 1876 the responsibility for developing a county government scheme was taken from Cross and given to the president of the local government board, which effectively killed the measure.

As consolation Cross was permitted to turn his attention to prison reform, one aim of which was to reduce the burden on ratepayers. He proposed establishing a commission, which would control local patronage, to run the system. The visiting justices who governed the prisons would continue in an advisory capacity to the Secretary of State. Opposition to reducing their powers led to the government withdrawing the bill. Dennis Mitchell believes that in drawing it up Cross may have been too much influenced by Edmund DuCane, a self-appointed expert on prisons who he had asked to report on the issue and who was an advocate of central control. In 1877 he reintroduced the bill to give greater power to the justices and it passed through parliament later in the year. He demolished G J Goschen, the only major figure to oppose the bill, by forcing him to admit he had not read it.

As a staunch Anglican, Cross consistently opposed a bill to give other denominations the right to hold burial services in Church of England churchyards. The matter was eventually left for the 1880-85 Liberal government to settle. But Cross spent a considerable amount of time on Church matters, attempting to make the institution more efficient, and in 1878 passed an Act creating four new sees, against the apathy of his colleagues (at one stage he threatened to resign if it was not passed).

Following consultation with the Local Government Board Cross reformed and centralised the factory inspectorate, which was organised along district lines but all under the control of a single inspector (responsible to the Home Office). He carried out a major reorganisation of the Metropolitan Police, appointing the capable Howard Vincent to reform the CID division as Director of Criminal Investigation following the conviction of four Scotland Yard detective inspectors for fraud. Vincent is considered to have been the founder of the CID in its modern form.

Cross had a commonsense approach to legislation. He favoured protection for animals and children but would not intervene to protect adults engaged in potentially dangerous activities, such as ballooning, from the consequences of their own mistakes or foolishness, provided no other lives were put at risk, stating in the case of the balloonists "I have to state that the Home Office has not been in the habit of interfering in matters of this kind". He took the legal advice that it was impossible to stop the distribution of pornography, and believed that interest in such material would die away in any case if it was not publicised by prosecution.

Cross had an enormous number of duties at the Home Office (including such matters as deciding whether to prosecute a youth convicted of an unnatural act with a chicken!). He generally took sensible and humane decisions. He relished the considerable power he enjoyed as Home Secretary, both for reasons of self-esteem and because of the opportunity it gave him to do good. Even Lord Salisbury had to apply to him on one occasion for a decision on the salary to be awarded a clerk of the peace, signing the letter in jest "your faithful servant". Cross was quite prepared to use his patronage, which was increased with the passage of the Prison Act. In theory the Prison Board was supposed to take the making of appointments out of the Home Secretary's hands, but he appointed his friend Admiral Hornby chairman of the Board. Cross' predecessor as Secretary of State, Robert Lowe, had ordered that sub-inspectors of factories be appointed by competitive civil service examinations, but Cross instructed that this be rescinded and Home Office appointment restored. In another compromise, Cross appointed the candidates for office who were then examined. He did not abuse patronage. He made Lord Cairns' nephew a sub-inspector of factories as a favour to the uncle, and placed him at Cairns' request in a locality that would be to his liking, but when asked two years later to promote him from the lowest grade of inspector Cross refused (Cairns resigning six months later). In 1874 when Disraeli appointed Henry Selwyn-Ibbotson as Cross' undersecretary the latter felt he should have a more important post with greater opportunities for speaking in the House Of Commons, and threatened resignation if he did not get it. Cross attempted to raise his profile by letting him introduce the Licensing Bill but his performance was uninspiring and he was not allowed to repeat it; he was moved to a new post in the reshuffle caused by the departure of Lord Derby.

Cross knew when to leave capable subordinates a free hand, and in fact preferred them to act on their own initiative. He disliked bureaucracy when it was unnecessary. When Howard Vincent took his plans for reorganising the CID to the Metropolitan Police Commissioner for approval Cross was angry: "I thought I told you to act upon your own judgement not the Chief Commissioners'." But he backed subordinates whenever they needed it, which was why Howard Vincent was such a success at Scotland Yard. He would refuse support for a proposal if he considered it wrong, as when Vincent sought permission to arrest foreign suspects directly rather than go through the Foreign Office. He could be tough, once rebuking a careless assistant factory inspector in the following words: "It is not sufficient for the Assistant Inspector to visit simply when the Sub Inspector thinks there may be a necessity for it; on the contrary the Assistant should ever be on the alert, seeing that each member of the Staff placed under him is working satisfactorily. There is no necessity for you to study economy in the carrying out of such visitations. It is far more important that the Factories and Workshops Act should be thoroughly enforced than that a few pounds should be saved to government." Though sparing with money he would fight any refusal to sanction expenses that he had approved, considering them justified. In the matter of prison reform he wrote to W H Smith at the Treasury asking him to approve the spending of £50-100 "to save him from walking" when carrying out his personal investigations.

He was always careful to take advice, probably being influenced in framing legislation by Home Office Council Godfrey Lushington, whom Cross later appointed an Assistant Undersecretary. The Permanent Undersecretary at the

Home Office was Adolphus Liddell, a competent man. When he died in 1885 Cross chose Lushington to succeed him, but reconsidered this on Salisbury's insistence and appointed Sir Henry Maine instead. Maine then fell ill and had to resign, whereupon Cross appointed Lushington to Salisbury's annoyance.

(5)

Foreign Affairs, 1874-80

Perhaps it was because he had such a track record there that Cross was identified, as both he and others saw it, with the Home Office, from which he did not seem able to escape. Undoubtedly his reputation rests primarily on that burst of productive legislation during his first stint at the post in the 1870s. But besides the area of his chief responsibility Cross is prominent in one other important issue of the time, in the field of foreign policy – that of the Eastern Question, in the late 1870s. Government policy was to prop up the decaying Ottoman Empire as a bulwark against Russian expansion in the Near East, which threatened British imperial interests and the route to India, and this was the line Cross took. In a speech in Manchester in 1876 he defended the cabinet from charges that it was condoning Turkish atrocities, insisting that by treaty Great Britain had no right to interfere between Turkey and her subjects. From being in the peace party he moved gradually to a more anti-Russian position, concerned among other things by the close relationship between Lord and Lady Derby and the Russian ambassador; this jeopardised Cross's friendship with Lady Derby. Nonetheless he came out in support of conditional neutrality, by which Britain would not become involved in Russo-Turkish disputes unless her vital interests were threatened. He effectively committed the government to this policy, which was endorsed by key figures in the Conservative party including Lord Salisbury, who was to replace Derby as Foreign Secretary, by his speech in the House of Commons in May 1877 in which he scored a major victory over the far more impressive and distinguished orator Gladstone, despite the latter's performance being generally regarded at the time and since as one of the best of his life. In the end it was commonsense and the clear ordering of facts which won the day over rhetoric. Cross showed his versatility by the way he had mastered a brief that was not initially his own, and in doing so aroused much admiration. In May the following year, at a speech in Preston, Cross reassured public feeling over the Turkish atrocities by his declaration that the government's policy was not the preservation of the Ottoman Empire as such. It helped create the climate in which a sensible resolution of Near Eastern affairs could be hammered out at the Congress of Berlin. In August Cross played a key part in defeating Hartington's motion of censure in the Commons over the annexation of Cyprus.[2]

Sandon, Northcote and other leading Tory figures appealed to Cross to put pressure on Derby from resigning over the government's policy. Though the party leaders in Lancashire disliked his position on the Eastern Question, fearing the effect on trade of war with Russia, they were also concerned about the political consequences locally, for the Derby interest had traditionally been very powerful in the county. But as they became more united on the issue Derby's influence waned and Cross assisted the process by appointing Admiral Hornby, his agent without whom he would be much less effective, to the Prison Commission. Cross himself was never a creature of the Derby interest and was able to act independently of it. However he continued to appreciate the importance of local affairs in maintaining political support.

Outside the Cabinet, Cross discussed with Sandon and W H Smith ways of generally strengthening Turkey against Russia, the preservation of the Ottoman Empire being vital, militarily and economically, to Britain's strategic interests in the Mediterranean and Asia. In May 1878, at a banquet in Preston to accompany his opening of a Conservative Club there, Cross was praised both for his domestic legislation and his interventions in foreign affairs. The latter were something into which Cross seems to have become drawn without perhaps really seeking it. He was useful on important issues as a fixer and go-between, being seen as a man of common sense and political acumen. He became involved in foreign matters more out of a sense of duty than because he regarded them as a particular province of his. His motives were not liberal ones, but rather the traditional Tory desire to preserve Britain's position in the world, and thus her prosperity (with a particular sensitivity to the mood in Lancashire). He perhaps summarised his philosophy in a speech in Kirkdale in October 1878, endorsing imperialism as something which benefited the colonies as well as the mother country, and emphasising that it needed a strong foreign policy to defend it. As part of that policy the acquisition of Cyprus was essential because of its strategic position in the Mediterranean, and Afghanistan had to be secured in order to protect India. As a rule he did not recommend intervention overseas unless Britain's rights and interests (including as he saw it the preservation of the empire) were directly threatened, in which scenario he could be what Salisbury described as "insatiably pugnacious", as over the matter of Persia (see below), which was in fact the exception to the rule.

When Salisbury and Beaconsfield went to represent Britain at the Congress of Berlin Cross took over the Foreign Secretaryship in addition to his responsibilities as Home Secretary. He enjoyed his brief stint in the job: "I think the work very interesting, and like it very much"[3]. In his new capacity he met the German ambassador to ascertain his views on the situation at the Congress. In Salisbury's absence Cross and the Cabinet (in which he was left the senior figure) decided that the War Office should administer Cyprus, which had been acquired at the Congress (this was strongly opposed by Salisbury, who also vetoed his suggestion that the export of ammunition to Russia should be stopped). Cross was altogether wary of the Russians and as Secretary for India in the 1886 administration was concerned by their expansion in Asia, particularly troop movements on the Persian border which were designed to put pressure on the Shah, who stated his wish to withdraw from negotiations with Britain for building a railway through the country. Along with Queen Victoria, he felt this to be a potential threat to India. He indicated his concern to Dufferin, the Viceroy, telling him he wished to establish a British sphere of influence in southern Persia. Cross consulted the Persian ambassador, Salisbury and the Queen before sending a personal representative to the Shah to discuss the matter. In this case, Cross' intervention was not a success. A British zone of influence was set up, ruled by a son of the Shah, but he proved too independent and was deposed by his father, whereupon the scheme collapsed. Salisbury acted to curtail Cross' influence in Persian affairs by appointing Drummond Wolff, an old opponent of his, as ambassador to the Shah.

Over the issue of Portugal Cross proved a restraining influence, acting to reduce the likelihood of war. In 1888 Portugal laid claim to the territory in Africa which separated her possessions of Angola and Mozambique. This was disputed by Britain, Salisbury fearing that Portugal might seize the territory by force in which case her colony of Goa ought to be occupied in retaliation. Cross and the Indian Viceroy, Lansdowne, feared the consequences of this and prevailed upon Salisbury to drop the matter. It flared up again the following year with Portugal planning to send troops to the area under dispute, via Mozambique. Cross successfully applied pressure in Cabinet for the British attack to be made in Mozambique rather than Goa; he considered this less inflammatory, not wishing India to be drawn into the conflict. In the end Lansdowne secretly arranged to have the steamer which was to transport the troops to Goa delayed, while the pressure on Mozambique led to Portugal dropping its demands.

Cross was to take over the Foreign Office again from January to March 1880 while Salisbury was ill, though confining himself to routine work.

In October 1876 Cross received the freedom of the city of Glasgow. He visited rebuilt areas and factories in Birmingham, where Joseph Chamberlain, then the city's mayor, gave a banquet in his honour. Despite being a Radical Chamberlain, who had himself carried out a major slum clearance in the city, clearly appreciated the improving legislation of this Tory minister.

Local affairs continued to be important to Cross. After Derby's resignation over the government's Eastern policy he tried to persuade him to accept the chairmanship of a commission on misuse of funds by City charities, not wishing to abandon him. But in 1880 Derby supported the Liberal candidate against Cross in the election, unsuccessfully. Derby's ex-agent, Hornby, continued to be loyal to Cross, who in the end won a resounding victory.

(6)

Disraeli saw the electoral value in allowing Cross to introduce reforming measures, without having much enthusiasm for them otherwise. In any case they did the Tories little good, for they lost the 1880 general election, something which perhaps raises the question of how far Cross' achievements were appreciated and by whom, though it demonstrated that if the working classes were not fully enfranchised they could not show gratitude for what one had done for them. This was the principal weakness in Cross and Salisbury's paternalist philosophy. Also, some groups within the working classes continued not to trust Cross and in the 1885 election the miners called a strike in order to influence the result in Preston, despite the fact that he was promising legislation against mine accidents.

In the opposition years of 1880-85 Cross served on a number of commissions, including that which investigated the City of London livery companies. He and two other members of the Commission produced a "minority report" which concluded that the companies' property was entirely their own and should be free from state interference. He had turned to journalism to supplement his income during this period, and wrote an article for the *Nineteenth Century* magazine defending the companies, as a result of which he was made a member of the Clothworkers' Company.

In the caretaker Conservative government which took office in 1885 Cross returned to the Home Office, suggesting again that he had become identified with that post in the minds of his peers. It was where he might be the Conservatives' greatest asset. He saw through parliament the Bill establishing a Secretary of State for Scotland, but found himself as Home Secretary having to frequently intervene in Scottish affairs due to the incompetence of the first holder of that post, Lord Richmond. He asked if the Board of Trade could provide some employment in the region through a harbour-building programme, and pressed for a Crofter's Bill, which Salisbury blocked. Salisbury also refused Cross' suggestion of a nationwide Employers' Liability Act. During the brief Conservative opposition from February to July 1886 Cross tried to get a new mine safety bill passed but the Liberal government quashed it.

Cross' return once more to the Home Office having been effectively blocked by Churchill, whose allies tried to instigate a revolt against it at the Carlton Club, he became Secretary for India when the Conservatives took office again in July, at the same time accepting a peerage and going to the House of Lords as Viscount Cross. He did this for the sake of party unity, and despite having doubts about his suitability for the Indian post. However he offered to take over routine duties at the Home Office when the then incumbent, Sir Matthew White Ridley, fell ill.

(7)

As India Secretary, Cross was as concerned about administrative reform as he had been in England. He put forward a plan to change the rules of the Viceroy's Council to require the Indian spending departments to submit their proposals to the Finance Minister initially, placing the latter more on the level of the Chancellor of the Exchequer in London. He introduced a new procedure for auditing accounts. He obtained the support of Salisbury and the Council to a programme of large-scale railway construction in India; the Indian government proposed a scheme which Cross vetoed because it made no provision for private enterprise, leading to a compromise by which the government were to build the line from Madras to Calcutta and a private company that into Assam. The builders of the Assam line were given the right to search for coal and oil.

Cross passed an Indian factory act giving Indian workers the same protection from long hours as English ones. Perhaps the most important issue he faced, politically, was that over greater representation for Indians in legislative bodies, and it reflected, as did his policies in England, a basically undemocratic and paternalist attitude. He wanted to give more power to the traditional princes and landlords, not the educated middle-class Indians. In 1888 Cross discussed the question of reform with Dufferin and they drew up a plan for a council two-fifths of whose members would be elected. When Cross notified Salisbury of this the latter was furious, castigating him for ever having thought about it. Cross agreed that they should refuse to publish the scheme, though he rejected a proposal to suppress Indian newspapers to protect the ignorant Indian masses from propaganda. Cross felt that debate over the budget, nomination of members and other procedures could be introduced into the councils without legislation. He drew up a bill enlarging the membership of the Council but without allowing the principle of election (rather than nomination) to it. He regarded the Indian Congress as a nuisance, telling Lord Lansdowne, Dufferin's successor, that they and numerous "Globe Trotters" made the Secretary of State's job difficult.

He was aware that there was pressure for reform and in 1889 made an important concession to British-educated Indians, raising the age at which examinations were sat for entry to the Indian civil service to twenty-three. But discontent remained, and Cross continued to refuse introducing an elective system in legislative affairs, noting "the diversity of people and the scarcity of educated men". An amendment to his bill allowed the Viceroy and Secretary of State to set the rules for choosing key personnel. The Indian Councils Act was eventually passed in 1892 and provided for greater representation on the legislative councils of the Viceroy and governors, but not for the educated middle-class Indians. Cross was as staunch a traditional imperialist as any member of the aristocracy; abroad as well as at home there were limits to his "democracy".

Another controversial matter during Cross' Secretaryship was the Indian army. He rejected a bill on the much-discussed reform of that institution without even submitting it to parliament, apparently because he was wary of having it openly discussed. He ignored Commons resolutions calling for an end to the Indian opium trade and to the brothel system in the Army, presumably, in the latter case, on the pragmatic principle that men will be men.

On the vexatious matter of Ireland, Cross was responsible for its affairs as Home Secretary in the 1870s, though for part of the time he was the official representative of Sir Michael Hicks Beach, the Irish Secretary, rather than actively involved in day-to-day administration. He served on the Irish Prisons Commission at one point in the early 1880s, which involved actual visits to the province during which he refused the hospitality of the Lord Lieutenant because he feared it would harm relations with the Irish; his motives were partly noble, partly a concern for his own safety. As Home Secretary he opposed the Irish Viceroy's plans to move the head of the British spy network from Ireland to the Home Office in London, but was overruled.

Though Cross' primary responsibility in the 1886-92 government was India, he was called upon to help with other affairs from time to time, his prestige as a senior political figure and skilled parliamentarian being recognised. The President of the Local Government Board asked him to conduct the Public Health (London) Bill through the Lords because his usual representative was not up to the task. Cross also took charge of a measure to consolidate the housing acts and spoke in favour of bills to regulate coal mines, provide allotments for labourers and limit for safety reasons the amount of steam allowed in a building. He was behind the Glebe Lands Bill which aimed to help Anglican clergy suffering from the depression because the value of their lands had declined. The Bill enabled the sale of the land and investment of the profits in government bonds and railway stock.

As a staunch Christian and Anglican, and supporter of voluntary religious schools, Cross was opposed to the growing trend towards secular education and was happy to co-operate with political opponents on the matter, at the behest of Cardinal Manning, He fought his 1885 election campaign on the issue of the voluntary schools, with Catholic support. Later he was appointed chairman of a royal commission on education, as part of which brief he sought to combat secularism. In 1890 he served on a cabinet committee working on a new education bill. In the long run, of course, it may be doubted whether his anti-secularist stance achieved much, although church schools themselves continue to be an important part of national life.

(8)

Later Political Career and Final Years, 1892-1914

By this time Cross' son, W H Cross, had become involved in politics. In 1888 he won a Lancashire parliamentary seat at a by-election, being elected unopposed. In 1892 he contracted typhoid and died. Cross' depression prevented him from attending the opening of parliament in 1893, but he remained active in that arena and in 1893 introduced a bill for the establishment of public libraries. He again turned his attention to questions on religion, chairing a church committee on rate aid for voluntary schools. After the Conservative return to power in 1895 he became Lord Privy Seal and also represented the Board of Agriculture in the Lords. He asked to serve on a Committee on Indian finance so that Lancashire, whose prosperity was affected by trade with India, felt its views were being adequately represented.

Cross' later life was in some ways embarrassing, though he was nonetheless perceived as an elder statesman figure until forgotten about with the passage of time. There is some evidence that he began to drink heavily; the rumour was mentioned as early as 1887, by Lord Rosebery. By 1896 he had definitely gained a reputation as a drinker, the Queen despite her liking for him being greatly amused when Lady Erroll, a campaigner against alcoholism, presented him with a tract on temperance. Perhaps his turning to drink was a consequence of his having the bulk of his achievements behind him, and not quite knowing which direction to go.

Cross was altogether quite close to the Queen, who was noted for her strong likes and dislikes. She saw him as a dependable figure on whom she could rely, writing to him in 1886 when dissatisfied with the new Liberal Home Secretary's handling of a riot in Trafalgar Square "Oh! If only *you* were there." In the same year she asked Cross to put forward her views on the situation in Bulgaria, which much disturbed her, to Salisbury, and in 1889 she instructed him to take up with the Prime Minister the matter of Conservative Party (political) organisation. In 1890 she commented upon his agility in dancing, and in 1896 he went with her to Nice, albeit in his official capacity as Lord Privy Seal.

In 1900 Lord Salisbury resigned as Foreign Secretary but, remaining Prime Minister and therefore needing an office in the cabinet, became Lord Privy Seal, necessitating Cross' departure. He retired to Eccle Riggs, becoming closely associated in his latter years with the Royal North Lancashire Agricultural Society and regularly attending the Guild Merchants of Preston. He continued to hold one or two posts in national organisations which were largely honorary; being by now in his dotage, he was finally removed from them not long before his death, which occurred at the age of ninety on 9th January 1914.

Conclusion

We should not judge Cross on his final years of decline, rather on his overall contribution, which rests largely but not entirely on his record as Home Secretary in 1874-80. He was of course not free from faults. He could make mistakes; his appointment of Edmund Smith to look into the question of amalgamating the water companies was a misjudgement and helped to wreck the initiative. Though a skilled parliamentarian he was actually a rather poor public speaker and would sometimes invite ridicule by "gaffes". In 1876 when accepting an invitation to speak at a meeting of the Manchester Conservative Club on the Eastern Question he confided "I dislike nothing so much as going to make a speech in cold blood." He was not entirely without vanity. He resented Gladstone's refusal to grant him a pension in 1881 and 1882, commenting on the Prime Minister's tendency to never forget or forgive a political opponent (slightly unfair, this was essentially a reaction to Gladstone's impatience with opposition and high-minded disapproval of anyone who he did not consider to have behaved in the correct fashion). On his final retirement he asked to be created an Earl, and protested when this wish was not granted. It may be however that these examples reflect a justified belief that his position in politics, and his contribution to the life of the nation, both of which he was well aware of, should be recognised and suitably rewarded.

He was willing to cut corners in framing legislation and securing its passage through parliament, and was not above using trickery to get his way; when his commission to review the matter of trade union reform was potentially hamstrung by the refusal of the union leaders to be involved, he met three prominent unionists, the most likely candidates to serve on it, separately, playing each off against the others. And he was inevitably drawn into the manouevring and chicanery which seems an inseparable part of political life.

In legislative and administrative affairs Cross preferred compromise where necessary/possible, and rarely acted without consultation. He was a practical man rather than a hard-and-fast ideologue. A *laissez-faire* approach was tempered with wisdom and compassion. Cross was admittedly a dull figure, in that he lacked the charisma of a Disraeli or the intellectual stature of a Gladstone. His sober commonsense and reluctance to act without taking advice made him less glamorous. Consequently he has never become a household name. But in this writer's view he deserves to be more famous than he is. G M Young (in *Victorian England*): "In history he does not rank as a great man; on the crowded canvas of Victorian politics he is barely an eminent man. Yet it might fairly be questioned whether any measures ever placed on the statute book have done more for the real contentment of the people." He was as competent, and virtuous, as anyone involved in the business of politics can be, and as the influence of the Christian religion can make someone. He was representative of the high ideals of the Victorian period (as well as one or two of its limitations), and therefore stands as an example of moral propriety to politicians today. Through his tireless legislative activity he was one of the agents that drove the era, in making it more humane and progressive (for to see it as uniformly an age of bigotry and oppression is simplistic). He is generally considered to have been Disraeli's most able minister and received poor reward for it from the man himself, at least initially. Disraeli at least let him get on with it; to be frank he used Cross, as he often used people, and it did not even benefit him electorally, which leads into one final point. Cross' achievements as we have seen were not always appreciated. Historically, he was caught between an upper class which rather looked down on him and a working class which did not trust him, being unimpressed by assurances of his good faith, and did not in any case have the means, before the 1884 Reform Act anyhow, to show its gratitude. In status somewhere between the towering giants of the period and the mediocrities who (to be harsh) have less call to be remembered, he himself represents a link, a transition phase, between the age of paternalism and the age of reform.

SOURCES

Principally:

Cross and Tory Democracy: a political biography of Richard Assheton Cross, by Dennis J Mitchell, Garland Publishing New York/London 1991. And unpublished original MS for this work; thanks here to Professor Paul Smith. Also F J Dwyer, "R A Cross and the Eastern Crisis of 1875-78", "Slavonic Review" no 39 June 1961, p440-458; and Robert Rhodes James, *Lord Randolph Churchill,* Barnes and Co. 1960.

My own observations have of course been added.

FOOTNOTES

(1) Rhodes James
(2) Dwyer
(3) Dwyer

INDEX

Bisexuality 482
Bismarck, Otto von 157, 299, 310, 315, 317, 318, 336
Black Death 285, 287, 426
"Black Lives Matter" movement 243, 499
Blair, Tony 19, 43, 120, 121, 179, 186, 209, 210-11, 212-19, 220, 223, 224, 225, 447, 452, 488, 489, 496"Bloody Sunday" 201, 202-3
Boer War 129, 166, 167
Boewulf 270
Boko Haram 453
Boleyn, Ann 145
Bonapartism 311, 316-17
Bonhoeffer, Dietrich 98, 100
Borgias 285-7
Borgia, Cesare 285
Borgia, Lucrezia 285-7
Bosnia 338, 434
Botswana 334-5
Boudicca/Boadicea 403
Bourbons (French royal dynasty) 316
Bower, Tom 27, 28
Boxer Rebellion 328
Boy George (pop singer) 416
Boyle, Robert 299
Bradbury, Malcolm 12
Bradford, Lady 506
Bradford, Sarah 286
Brady, Ian 51
Brandt, Willy 428
Brandt Report 465
Brazil 134, 294, 466
Brexit 43, 131, 201, 208-9, 227-41, 268, 392, 457, 460, 463-4
Brexit Party 238, 241
Brezhnev, Leonid 421, 423
Brighton Bombing 207
Bristol 14, 23
Britain 43-4, 128-37, Ch.4, 274, 276, 305-6, 320, 324-5, 327, 329-32, 332, 336, 338, 339, 341, 342, 343, 347, 358, 359, 360, 368-9, 370-71, 372, 383-4, 388, 389, 392, 393, 395-6, 406-7, 407-8, 431, 435, 440, 447, 451, 453, 457-8, 460, 463-4, 472, 488; see also England
British Commonwealth 22, 40, 134, 231, 237-8, 329
British National Party 221, 230, 353, 475
British Union of Fascists 173
Brixton riots 33, 110
Broadwater Farm riots 23

El Alamein, battle of 370, 371
Elba, Idris 472
Eleanor of Aquitaine 9
Eliot, George 81-2, 89-90
Elizabeth, Empress of Austria/Austria-Hungary 310
Elizabeth I, queen of England 144, 150-1, 270, 291, 292, 403
Elizabeth II, queen of Great Britain 22
Elkins, Michael 60
Empire Windrush 35
Employers and Workmen's Bill 1875 508
Enclosure Acts 257, 323
England 287, 288-9, 294-6
English Civil War 145-6, 148
English Republic 146-7, 155
English Revolution 307-9
Enlightenment 157, 283, 287, 303, 305, 306, 307, 309, 312
Entente Cordiale 336
Environmental issues 420, 459, 465, 467-9
Erroll, Lady 518
Essex, Earl of 143
Estonia 425
Ethiopia 324
European Coal and Steel Community 392
European Court of Human Rights 18
European Union (previously European Economic Community, "Common Market" 36, 40, 42-3, 53, 134, 183, 196, 228, 229, 230, 231, 237, 312, 391-3, 428, 431, 456, 458, 463-4, 460
Explosives Act 1875 508

Factory Act (1878) 509
Falklands War 110, 114, 117-18, 392
Farage, Nigel 230, 239, 241
Fascism 348-51, 353-4, 378 (see also Nazism/Nazis)
Fashoda Incident 336
Fawcett, Henry 503
Feingold, Oliver 79-80
Feminism 475, 476-8, 483; see also Women
Ferdinand, king of Spain 418
Ferguson, Niall 89-90
Ferrara, Duchy of 286-7
Ferry, Bryan 94
Feudal system 285, 298
Finland 357, 374
First World War 32, 340-42

344-5, 347, 348, 349-50, 355-7, 358, 373, 375-6, 382-3, 383, 391, 393, 425-6, 428, 430, 460

Get Carter (film) 415

Ghana 326

Gibbon, Edward 131

Gladstone, William 14, 27, 30, 159-65, 211, 304, 504-5, 512, 518, 519

Glebe Lands Bill 517

Glendower, Owain 200

Globalisation 460-62

"Glorious Revolution" 156

Goa 514

Goebbels, Josef 378

Goering, Hermann 107, 369-70, 375

Gorbachev, Mikhail 423-7, 428

Gordon, General 161

Gordon Riots 149, 293

Goschen, G J 510

Goths 265, 266

Gove, Michael 233

Graham, Billy 496

Greece 260, 262, 263, 264, 269, 271, 272, 278, 282, 283, 287, 301, 309, 315

Greenland 321

Greenpeace 420

Guam 322

Gulf War (1991) 431-3, 460

Gulf War (2003) 214-16, 239, 452, 460

Gunpowder Plot 151

Hague, William 193, 219

Halifax, Lord (Edward Wood) 177

HAMAS 74, 401

Hampden, John 147

Hanoverians (British royal dynasty) 150, 153

Hanseatic League 256

Hapsburgs 273, 274, 309

Harley, Robert 153

Harold, king of England 138

Harry, Prince 93

Hartington, Marquess of 512

Hattersley, Roy 23

Haussmann, Baron 317

Hawking, Stephen 137

Hayek, Friedrich 121, 128

Lausanne Conference 359
Lawrence, T E 402
League of Nations 343-4, 350, 383
Lebanon 70, 401, 494
Lebed, General 454
Lebensraum 359-60
Lenin, Vladimir 351
Leonov, Alexei 417
Leopold, king of Belgium 311
Levellers 299
Levy, Lord 214
Lewis, C S 282
Liberal Party 157, 158, 167, 168-9, 456, 506
Liberal Democrat Party 80, 192, 209, 210, 221-2, 236, 238, 244
Liberalism 319
Liberal Unionists 159
Lib-Lab Pact 111
Libya 324, 394, 395, 396, 397-8, 400, 446, 454
Liebniz, Gottfried 90
Literature 473-4, 484
Little Big Horn, battle of 323
Liverpool 15, 504
Liverpool riots of 1981 33
Livingstone, Ken 79-80, 168
Lloyd George, David 165, 166, 168-71, 173, 345
Locarno Treaty 176
Lockerbie bombing 21, 394, 396-401, 433
London bombings 2005 214
Louis XIV, king of France 147, 148, 299
Louis XVI, king of France 307
Louis Philippe, king of France 317
Lowe, Robert 508, 511
Ludwig, king of Bavaria 276
Luther, Martin 287-9
Luxembourg 339
Lyon, Georgina 502

Macdonald, Ramsay 171-2, 173, 364
Macleod, Ian 42
Macmillan, Harold 21, 114, 179-80, 181-2
Magna Carta 139, 406
Maimonides, Moses 283
Maine (ship) 322
Major, John 18, 115, 120, 121, 154, 186, 194-8, 199, 205

Mosley, Oswald 108, 173
Moss, Edward 505
Mossad (Israeli secret service) 65, 402
Mount Badon, battle of 267
Mountbatten, Lord 206, 331
Mowlam, Mo 225
Mozambique 514
Mozart, Wolfgang Amadeus 45
Mugabe, Robert 334-5
Mukherjee, Tara 39
Mulley, Fred 110
Munich Agreement 365
Municipal Elections Bill 504
Murdoch, Rupert 219
Music 483 (see also Popular Music)
Mussolini, Benito 350, 353, 354

Nabarro, Sir Gerald 22
Napoleon I Bonaparte, French Emperor 264, 274, 276, 308, 313-15, 462
Napoleon III, French Emperor 317
Napoleonic Wars 257
NASA (National Aeronautics And Space Administration) 418
Nasser, Gamal Abdel 179, 392
National Curriculum 195
Native Americans 322-4, 326-7
NATO 383, 384, 391, 428, 435, 436
Nazis/Nazism 77, 90-91, 270, 275, 283, 350, 355-6, 359, 375, 377, 378-9
Nazi-Soviet Pact 356, 357, 366, 372
Neocons 78, 450
Nepal 253
Netanyahu, Binyamin 66
Netherlands 273, 275, 294, 309, 322, 332, 358, 360, 367
Newcomen, Thomas 301
Newton, Isaac 45, 90, 248, 299, 302
New Zealand 335, 420
9/11 51, 443-6, 447, 448, 449, 450, 459
Nixon, Richard 107, 417-18, 421-2, 423
Nonconformism 165, 304
NORAID 208
Normans 138-9, 270, 277
Northcote, Stafford 507, 509, 512
North-South divide 464-7
Norway 357, 399
Nuclear proliferation 435

Rees, Laurence 52
Rees-Mogg, Jacob 236
Reform Act (1832) 157, 257-8
Reform Bill of 1867 157, 160
Reform Bill of 1884 157, 519, 520
Reformation 145, 275-6, 287-93, 305
Reichstadt, Duc de 317
Religion 144-6, 148, 260, 276, 287-93, 301-5, 319, 326-7, 347, 410-11,
413-14, 437-43, 469, 493-6, 500
Renaissance 286-7, 288, 299
Republican Party 169, 297, 423, 447, 450, 456, 457, 458-60
Respect (formerly Stop The War Coalition) 221, 422-3
Revolutions of 1848 157, 315-16
Rhineland 364, 376
Rhodes, Cecil 325-6, 330
Rhodes James, Robert 225 , 520
Rice, Condoleezza 472
Richard I, king of England 142
Richard II, king of England 139
Richard III, king of England 140-2
Richelieu, Cardinal 299, 305
Richmond, Duke of 507
Richmond, Lord 515
Ridley, Matthew White 515
Ridley, Nicholas 118
Riefenstahl, Leni 105
Robbins, Harold 476
Roberts, Ernie 408
Rogers, William C III 400
Rohmer, Sax (Arthur Sarsfield Ward) 328
Roman Empire 132, 133, 259, 261, 262, 264-6, 268-9, 271, 272, 273, 278,
282, 283, 287
Rommel, Erwin 371-2
Rosebery, Lord 518
Ross, Nick 38
Rowling, J K 199, 472, 484
Royal Ulster Constabulary 202
Rudolf, Crown Prince of Austria-Hungary 310
Rumania 347, 382, 500
Russia 104, 130, 276, 279, 305, 310, 313, 316, 319, 320-21, 322, 327,
331, 336, 337, 339, 341-2, 345-6, 347, 351-4, 358, 359, 362, 365, 366,
367, 370, 372, 374, 381, 382-3, 385, 386, 386, 387, 389, 390, 401, 417,
418, 421, 423-7, 428 , 434-5, 437, 447, 453-6, 466, 467, 496
Russian Revolution 308-9

Russo-Japanese War 327
Rwanda 434, 436

Saarland 357
Saladin 295
Salameh, Ali Hassan 65
Salisbury, Lord 157, 507, 510-11, 518
Sandon, Lord 506, 512, 513
Sands, Bobby 206
Sansom, C J 6, 143
satyagraha 333
Sauckel, Fritz 106
Saudi Arabia 253, 431, 433, 442
Savery, Thomas 300-01
Saxons 266-8 , 278
Saxons (Germany) 276-7
Scandinavia 321-2
Scargill, Arthur 44, 210
Scarman, Lord 33, 331, 409
Schindler's List (film) 70
Schlieffen Plan 358
Schoen, Douglas E 17, 35
Scholl, Hans 98
Scholl, Sophie 98
Schumann, Robert 392
Schwammberger, Josef 102
Science, and culture 485
Science, history of 248-9, 299-302
Scotland 43, 131, 138, 139, 140, 146, 149, 198-200, 208, 266, 515
Scottish Nationalist Party 199-200
SDLP (Social Democratic and Labour Party, Northern Ireland) 196
SDP/Liberal Alliance 192-3
Second World War 6-7, 52, 177, 369-81
Second World War, causes of 356-69
Second World War, consequences of 375-6, 381-2
Selwyn-Ibbotson, Henry 508, 511
Serbia 338-9, 434
Serebriakoff, Victor 88-9
Sereny, Gitta 105
Seven Years' War 294, 312, 336
Sewell, Brian 54, 98
Seymour, Thomas 151
Sex 411-13, 476-7, 479
Shakespeare, William 407

Shamir, Yitzhak 66
Shannon, Richard 161
Sharon, Ariel 66
Sharpe, Kevin
Shaw-Lefevre, George 508
Shepherd, Robert 27
Shinwell, Emmanuel 171
Short, Clare 225
Shrapnel, Norman 20
Siege of Paris 317
Singapore 389
Sinn Fein 203-4
Sioux (Native American tribe) 323
Skinner, Dennis 210
Skype 499
Slavery 14-15, 296-7, 408-9
Slovakia 434
Slovenia 434
Smith, Adam 120, 488
Smith, Cyril 226
Smith, Edmund 506
Smith, John 193, 212
Smith, W H 506, 507, 511, 513
Snowden, Philip 172
Social Democratic Party (SDP) 19, 210
Socialism 319
Social issues 403-17, 469-98
Solomon, king of Israel 282
Solomon, Norman 86
Somerset, Protector 6, 292
South Africa 38, 332-4, 420, 430
Space exploration 417-20
Space shuttle 418
Spain 273, 274, 280, 293-4, 314, 316, 322, 324, 324, 357, 378, 451, 452
Spanish Armada 291
Spanish Civil War 365, 374
Spanish Succession, War of the 294
Speer, Albert 105-7, 373
Spitting Image 190-91
SS 378
Stalin, Josef 49, 52, 53, 308, 352-4, 365, 366, 367, 372, 382-3, 385, 387
Stalingrad, battle of 370, 371
Starkey, David 133
Starmer, Keir 243-4

Treaty of Brest-Litovsk 344
Treaty of Dover 147
Treaty of London 339
Treaty of Versailles 342, 344-5, 357, 358-9, 363, 376, 395
Triple Entente 337
Trojan War 264
Trotsky, Leon 336, 351
Trump, Donald 44, 73, 135, 423, 450, 452, 457, 458-60, 493
Truth and Reconciliation Commission 333
Tudors (English royal dynasty) 143, 200
Turkey 279-80, 322, 327, 342
Tutsis 436
Tutu, Desmond 207
2012 riots in Britain 408

Ukraine 425, 455
Umkhonto We Sizwe 333
United Kingdom Independence Party (UKIP) 110, 192, 219, 236 , 493
Ulster Unionist Party 16, 22, 23, 227, 229, 230, 232
United Nations 98, 393, 448
United Provinces 309
United States of America 71, 130, 134, 271, 296-8, 320, 322-4 , 326-7, 327, 335, 342, 346-7, 360-61, 362, 370, 371, 372-3, 381, 383, 385, 396, 399, 401, 402, 408-9, 417, 418, 422, 424, 431, 435, 436, 437, 440, 443-50, 450-1, 452, 456-60, 464-5, 466, 472
USS Cole 443

Vandals 265
Venice 263-4, 274, 309
Vernon, Tom 59
Vichy France 317
Vicious, Sid 417
Victoria, queen of Great Britain 150, 310, 311, 507, 508-9, 514, 518
Vietnam 320, 387, 390
Vietnam War 414, 415, 422-3
Vikings 138, 139, 267, 270, 277, 293, 321-2
Vincennes incident 394, 397, 400
Vincent, Howard 510, 511
Vinci, Leonardo da 251

Wales 43, 131, 138, 139, 200, 266
Walpole, Robert 153
War Crimes Bill 48-49, 93-4
War in former Yugoslavia 433-4

"War on Terror" 446-56
Warsaw Pact 383, 391
Wars of the Roses 143, 295
Warwick, Edward of 141
Washington, Denzel 472
Watergate 107, 421-2
Weimar Republic 104-5, 345, 349, 355
Welby, Justin, Archbishop of Canterbury 499
Wells, Holly 50
Wesley, John 292
"West Lothian" question 43, 199
Wheatley, John 171
Whig interpretation of history 139, 156
Whigs 153, 157, 158, 506
Wiesenthal, Simon 57, 323
Wilhelm II, German Kaiser 170, 310, 336, 338, 345, 357, 358
Wilkes, John 157
William I (Conqueror), king of England 138
William II (Rufus), king of England 142
William III (William of Orange), king of England 150, 294
Williams, Ben 198
Williams, Rowan, Archbishop of Canterbury 224
Williams, Shirley 226
Wilson, Harold 17, 18, 117, 170, 181-5
Wilson, Robert 62-3
Wilson, Woodrow 346
"Winter of Discontent" 112, 188
Witchcraft 302-3
Wolsey, Thomas 299
Women 403-6, 411, 471-2, 476-9
Wonder, Stevie 472
Woodstock 417
Woodville, Elizabeth 140, 141, 142
World Trade Centre bombing (1993) 399, 443

Yallop, David 82
Yarwood, Mike 183
Yom Kippur War 71, 396, 401
Young, G M 519
Yugoslavia 382, 433

Zaroff, Efrem 57
Zhirinovsky, Vladimir 454-6
Zhivkov, Todor 424

Lightning Source UK Ltd.
Milton Keynes UK
UKHW040626141220
375159UK00002B/216